RECENT ECONOMIC CHANGES

RECENT
ECONOMIC CHANGES

IN THE UNITED STATES

REPORT OF THE COMMITTEE ON RECENT ECONOMIC CHANGES,
OF THE
PRESIDENT'S CONFERENCE ON UNEMPLOYMENT

HERBERT HOOVER, CHAIRMAN

INCLUDING THE REPORTS OF A SPECIAL STAFF OF THE
NATIONAL BUREAU OF ECONOMIC RESEARCH, INC.

VOLUME II

FIRST EDITION
THIRD IMPRESSION

McGRAW-HILL BOOK COMPANY, INC.
NEW YORK: 370 SEVENTH AVENUE
LONDON: 6 & 8 BOUVERIE ST., E. C. 4
1929

CHAPTER VI

LABOR

By Leo Wolman

The labor situation both reflects underlying economic conditions and helps to account for them. In this field, as in others, adequate explanation of puzzling phenomena is delayed by the lack of comprehensive and continuous statistical series. Many relationships that unquestionably exist among the various forces of the labor market will remain concealed as long as the data that might throw light upon them are incomplete and in a measure unreliable. The organic character of the American labor market is often suggested, if not proved, by placing in juxtaposition the best available measures of the elements of the labor market. Such a procedure is employed in this chapter, where what appear to be the significant items in the labor situation are examined with regard to their postwar and prewar manifestations.

I. POPULATION AND LABOR SUPPLY

Probably the outstanding feature of the population question in the United States since 1920 has been the marked drop in its rate of natural increase. In the period from July 1, 1920 to July 1, 1925, the average annual increase in population was 1,800,000, whereas in the years following, from July 1, 1925 to July 1, 1928, the average annual increase had fallen to 1,545,000. The factors making for a slackening rate of growth, immigration restriction and a birth rate that appears to be falling more rapidly than the death rate, are apparently not temporary ones. They may, in view of the present trends, be expected to exert a similar influence for many years to come.[1]

Changes in the rate of growth of the total population do not necessarily reflect like changes in the supply of labor. The rising productivity of industry may from time to time produce an increase in the surplus of labor in the face of a stationary population. Within a given population, moreover, a larger or smaller proportion of the people of a country may seek gainful employment in industry, trade, and service. Again, the inhabitants of an undeveloped area may, through the development of industry, become employed for the first time and thus add to the available supply of labor. In the United States, forces such as these are continuously and simultaneously in operation. From 1870 to 1910, the

[1] W. S. Thompson, "Population," *American Journal of Sociology*, July, 1928, p. 3.

percentage of women in the total number of workers of the country advanced from 14 to 20.6 per cent.[2] The industrialization of the South has likewise acted to increase the available labor supply. The northward migration of the negro has represented in part a net addition to the total labor supply of the country and in part a redistribution of it.[3]

All of these items are significant, but since 1920 the striking changes in the American labor market have been associated with the policy of immigration restriction, the growth of industry in the South, and the falling birth and mortality rates of the country.

Immigration.[4]—While the effects of the war on European political and economic conditions may have reduced the postwar emigration of European labor into the United States, the fact remains that war embargoes and restrictive legislation have produced a condition in this country in marked contrast to that existing before the war. The natural restrictions arising out of the war, and the later legislation, combined to change radically both the volume and the character of American immigration.

The first legislation designed to affect the quantity of immigration was the Quota Act, of May 19, 1921. This law limited the number of aliens of any nationality, to be admitted in any fiscal year, to 3 per cent of the number of foreign-born persons of such nationality resident in the United States, as determined by the Census of 1910. The law of 1921 was later made effective to June 30, 1924. A new quota law, known as the "Immigration Act of 1924," became effective July 1, 1924. By its terms, the annual quota of any nationality is reduced to 2 per cent of the number of foreign-born of that nationality in the United States, as determined, not by the census of 1910, but by the census of 1890. The native-born citizen of Canada, Mexico, Newfoundland, Cuba, and the independent countries of South and Central America, is exempt in this as in the earlier law.

TABLE 1.—COMPARISON OF PREWAR IMMIGRATION AND QUOTAS[a]

	Northern and Western Europe	Southern and Eastern Europe and Asia
Average annual immigration, July 1, 1907 to June 30, 1914........	176,983	685,531
Quotas for year ended June 30, 1922...........................	198,082	158,367
Quotas for year ended June 30, 1925...........................	140,999	21,847

[a] Compiled from the annual reports of the Commissioner General of Immigration, United States Department of Labor. The prewar figures include all immigrants from Asia, not merely from the areas to which the quotas apply; the maximum in any one year for Asia outside the quota areas was less than 20,000.

[2] J. A. Hill, forthcoming Census Monograph on *Women in Gainful Occupations*.

[3] J. A. Hill, "Recent Northward Migration of the Negro," *Monthly Labor Review*, March, 1924.

[4] The material for this section was prepared by Harry Jerome, of the National Bureau of Economic Research.

The purpose of these restrictive measures was to reduce the volume of immigration in general and that from southern and eastern Europe in particular. The expectations under the two acts, compared with conditions prevailing before the war, are indicated in Table 1.

Comparisons between the actual flow of immigration in the prewar, war, and postwar periods show that there has been a drastic reduction in the net inflow. In the prewar period, the average recorded annual net immigration was 664,000; in the war and early postwar period, 179,000; and in the quota period, 312,000. At the present time, then, the annual net immigration rate is less than half of that before the war.[5]

TABLE 2.—NET IMMIGRATION, JULY 1, 1907 TO JUNE 30, 1927[a]

Period	Immigrants	Emigrants	Net immigration[b]
Prewar period (July 1, 1907 to June 30, 1914)........	6,709,357	2,063,767	4,645,590
War and early postwar period (July 1, 1914 to June 30, 1921)..	2,407,908	1,154,256	1,253,652
Quota restriction period (July 1, 1921 to June 30, 1927)	2,473,348	600,037	1,873,311
Year ended June 30:			
1908...	782,870	395,073	387,797
1909...	751,786	225,802	525,984
1910...	1,041,570	202,436	839,134
1911...	878,587	295,666	582,921
1912...	838,172	333,262	504,910
1913...	1,197,892	308,190	889,702
1914...	1,218,480	303,338	915,142
1915...	326,700	204,074	122,626
1916...	298,826	129,765	169,061
1917...	295,403	66,277	229,126
1918...	110,618	94,585	16,033
1919...	141,132	123,522	17,610
1920...	430,001	288,315	141,686
1921...	805,228	247,718	557,510
1922...	309,556	198,712	110,844
1923...	522,919	81,450	441,469
1924...	706,896	76,789	630,107
1925...	294,314	92,728	201,586
1926...	304,488	76,992	227,496
1927...	335,175	73,366	261,809

[a] Compiled from the *Annual Reports*, Commissioner General of Immigration, United States Department of Labor, for the years ended June 30, 1908–1927. Citizens of the United States and "nonimmigrant" and "nonemigrant" aliens are excluded from the data in this table.

[b] Net immigration equals immigrants less emigrants.

The reduction, as it was intended, was felt largely by the groups commonly described as the new immigration. Table 3, in which comparisons

[5] The clandestine immigration is estimated to have averaged about 85,000 per year during the six years of quota restriction and is believed now to be diminishing. The bulk of this immigration are probably residents of our neighboring countries.

are made for the same three periods and the immigration is classsified by country of origin, shows that the reduction in European immigration has taken place mainly among the immigrants from southern and eastern Europe. At the same time, net immigration from both Canada and Mexico is in excess of the prewar rate.

TABLE 3.—DECLINE IN NET RECORDED IMMIGRATION INTO THE UNITED STATES, COMPARED WITH PREWAR RATES, BY COUNTRY OF ORIGIN[a]

(In thousands of persons)

Country	War and early postwar period (July 1, 1914–June 30, 1921)			Quota restriction period (July 1, 1921–June 30, 1927)		
	Actual	Deficit	Excess	Actual	Deficit	Excess
All countries[b]...............	1,254	3,392	...	1,873	2,109	...
All Europe[c]..................	555	3,672	...	888	2,735	...
"Old"[d]..................	292	774	...	710	203	...
"New"[d]..................	263	2,898	...	177	2,532	...
Mexico..................	122	.....	16	297	.....	206
Canada and Newfoundland........	433	.....	242	628	.....	465
Asia[c]...................	49	.....	16	13	15	...
Other countries..............	94	.....	5	48	28	...

[a] Compiled from the *Annual Reports* of the United States Commissioner General of Immigration. The "deficit" or "excess" is computed by subtracting the actual net immigration (immigrants less emigrants) from the net immigration which would have taken place if the annual average for the seven years ended June 30, 1914, had been maintained.

[b] The totals were computed from the full figures before reduction to thousands, hence there is an apparent small discrepancy in each column between the totals and the constituents thereof.

[c] Turkey in Asia is included with Europe and excluded from Asia.

[d] The so-called "old" sources of immigration include the countries of northern and western Europe, namely: Belgium, Denmark, France, Germany, the Netherlands, Norway, Sweden, Switzerland, and the United Kingdom. The "new" sources include the countries of eastern and southern Europe now known as Austria, Hungary, Czechoslovakia, Jugoslavia, Bulgaria, Finland, Greece, Italy, Poland, Portugal, Rumania, Russia, Spain, Turkey in Europe, and certain other small European countries designated as "other Europe," also Turkey in Asia. Owing to boundary changes, the prewar and postwar figures for the "old" and "new" sources are not strictly comparable, but these discrepancies are not large enough to affect materially their comparability for present purposes.

In occupation, the immigration of recent years is radically different from what it used to be. The cutting off of immigrants from the south and east of Europe has meant stopping the flow of unskilled labor, which, before the war, was the preponderant element of the immigration into the United States. The group of unskilled workers shows, in the war and early postwar period, a net immigration of only 4,000 and of 191,000 in the quota restriction period, or a decline of 1,544,000 in the war and early postwar period, and of 1,136,000 in the quota restriction period.

These changes in number, origin, and occupation have been accompanied by equally important changes in the demographic constitution of the recent immigrants. The proportion of males has dropped from 60 per cent before the war to 52 in this latest period. The proportion

TABLE 4.—DECLINE IN NET RECORDED IMMIGRATION INTO THE UNITED STATES
COMPARED WITH PREWAR RATES, BY OCCUPATION AND SEX[a]

(In thousands of persons)

Occupation and sex	War and early postwar period (July 1, 1914–June 30, 1921)			Quota restriction period (July 1, 1921–June 30, 1927)		
	Actual net	Deficit[b]	Excess	Actual net	Deficit[b]	Excess
Total net..................	1,254	3,392	....	1,873	2,109	...
No occupation..................	688	814	....	798	490	
All workers[c].....................	565	2,578	....	1,075	1,619	...
Unskilled workers[d]................	4	1,544	....	191	1,136	...
Servants........................	213	450	....	214	354	...
Skilled..........................	288	442	....	417	209	...
Professional.....................	50	11	....	71	.....	18
Other occupations...............	10	131	....	183	.....	62
Both sexes......................	1,254	[b]3,392	....	1,873	[b]2,109	...
Males......................	463	2,317	....	976	1,407	...
Females....................	790	1,075	....	898	701	...

[a] The "deficit" or "excess" is computed by subtracting the actual net immigration (immigrants less emigrants) from the net immigration which would have taken place if the annual average for the seven years ended June 30, 1914, had been maintained. For example, the total net immigration in the seven years ended June 30, 1914, was 4,645,590. Taking six-sevenths of this we have 3,981,934 as the "expected" net immigration for the six years of the restriction period (July 1, 1921 to June 30, 1927). In these six years, the actual net immigration was 1,873,311, leaving a "deficit" of 2,108,623.

[b] For the prewar net immigration, 71,970 emigrants for whom occupation is not known were distributed among the occupations in the same proportions as those for whom occupation was given. Likewise, 29,708 emigrants in 1909 for whom sex is not known were distributed between the sexes in the same proportion as those for whom sex was given.

[c] Computed by subtracting "No occupation" from "Total."

[d] The classification by occupation used by the United States Bureau of Immigration has no group designated as "unskilled." We have taken the sum of "laborers" and "farm laborers" as representative of the unskilled element.

of the married appears to be slightly less now than before, and children and elderly persons seem more numerous in the recent than in the prewar immigration.

It has already been seen that our changing immigration policy and the fall in the birth rate have resulted in a slackening of the natural rate of increase of the American population; and it is clear that these factors will tend, if they have not already done so, to produce a tighter labor situation than one to which we have been accustomed. It has been pointed out in this connection, however, that compensating influences, such as the opening of unworked industrial areas or the progressive fall in mortality rates, may act as mitigating factors. To measure the accretions in population arising out of these last sources is not a feasible task. Over long periods of time, the extent to which industry draws on the population of an area is in some degree a measurable phenomenon. Thus the per cent of factory wage earners in the total population of

North Carolina was 2.1 in 1889, 4.2 in 1904, 5.6 in 1909, and 6.5 in 1925, and the probability is that little of this relative increase in factory employees was made at the expense of other employments. The same type of computation might also be made with regard to the entry of women into gainful work. But except for pointing out the existence of such changes within the population of the country, the elaboration of such measures would add little to our present knowledge.

There remains, then, some slight reference to the magnitude of the fall in mortality rates which has been a striking feature of American vital statistics of the past decades. Dr. A. J. Lotka, of the Metropolitan Life Insurance Co., has computed the figures of the number of lives saved per annum through the lowered death rate in this country by taking the United States population, as constituted in 1925, applying to it, at the several ages of life, the death rates that prevailed in 1900–1902, and then comparing the total number of deaths that would have been produced by these death rates with the actual deaths in 1925. The results of these computations are given in Table 5.

TABLE 5.—ACTUAL DEATHS IN 1925 COMPARED WITH DEATHS INDICATED IF COMPUTED ON 1900–1902 DEATH RATES

	Actual deaths, 1925	Hypothetical deaths, 1925, on basis of 1900–02 death rate	Lives saved per annum
Total, United States...................	1,389,673	1,962,999	573,326
White, total................................	1,172,251	1,655,467	483,216
White, males............................	634,785	887,793	253,008
White, females..........................	537,466	767,674	230,208
Colored, total..............................	217,422	307,532	90,110
Colored, males..........................	112,871	163,735	50,864
Colored, females........................	104,551	143,797	39,246

While it is interesting to compare these figures of current saving of lives with the estimated deficits in immigration, it should be noted that the fall in mortality rates has been accompanied by a drop in the birth rate and that future improvements in mortality may be more difficult than they have been in the past.

II. WAGES, HOURS, AND LABOR COST

Wage rates are, for many purposes, the most useful measure of the changing position of labor. Piece or time rates represent in one number both the price of labor and its potential earning power. Actual earnings whether by the week, month, or year, measure not only the price of labor, but unemployment and the flow of work as well. Even full-time earnings for any unit of time are affected by the productivity of labor and by the volume of employment, but this last factor does not affect full-time earnings nearly as much as it does actual earnings. While it is important to measure employment and unemployment and their effects on earnings, both the incidence and the extent of employment and unemployment are so complex that they can be best studied directly, and not indirectly through their effect on earnings.[6]

The most satisfactory measure of wages, then, is the rate of wages, time or piece. Where the actual rates are not available, the next best measure would be a record of the changes in the time and piece rates. Unfortunately it is impossible to obtain a reliable series of either rates or changes in rates. Statistics of changes in wage rates published by the United States Bureau of Labor Statistics for a part of the postwar period and for an important group of industries cannot be used because of the inadequacy and uncertainty of the sample.[7] We are, therefore, thrown back on full-time earnings. Of the various measures of full-time earnings, hourly earnings are, for the purpose of finding changes in wage rates, the best. It is true that hourly earnings reflect not only changes in the rates of wages but the rise and fall in the productivity of labor as well. But they do not reflect unemployment, except in the minor degree in which rise and fall in unemployment increases or diminishes the flow of work, and hence increases or reduces even hourly earnings. Where, finally, hourly earnings are not available, it becomes necessary to use full-time weekly earnings whose course is affected not only by the factors already enumerated, but also by changes in the nominal or full-time week. Over short periods of time, however, these variations in the length of the nominal week can be measured and their influence partially discounted.[8]

For all studies of wages during the period from 1914 to 1927, nearly all available series are defective in one or another respect. The list of industries included in each series varies from year to year and particularly from 1914 to 1920. The samples for the industries reported are not in each year equally representative. In general, the statistics appear to improve after 1920, both by the inclusion of a greater number of industries and through the gathering of more adequate and more representative samples. The material on wages, here presented, is the result of the examination of a mass of American wage statistics, collected and interpreted by a number of independent agencies. Whatever methods of interpretation are applied to the basic data, the final results

[6] See Henry Clay, "Unemployment and Wage Rates," *Economic Journal*, March, 1928, p. 1.

[7] *Monthly Labor Review*, July, 1928, p. 133. Similar figures are published monthly.

[8] The questions of definition and sampling, and the meaning and reliability of American wage statistics will be considered in detail in a study, by the present author, of the statistics of the American labor market, to be published by the National Bureau of Economic Research in 1929.

show so many signs of agreement in the various series as to inspire considerable confidence in the raw statistical materials.

The Manufacturing Industries.—The most complete series of hourly earnings in the manufacturing industries is that compiled by the National Industrial Conference Board for the period from 1920 to date. The series includes some 23 representative industries and is, with interruptions in 1920 and 1922, published monthly for each industry and for all industries combined.' A figure comparable with the later series is also given for July, 1914, so that it is possible to make comparisons with prewar conditions. For the years between 1914 and 1920 the Board series is incomplete and is, for that reason, not comparable with the series for the later period. Because the 1920 figures are given only for the last seven months, and the 1922 figures only for the last six months, it is impossible to pick with certainty the high month of the boom and the low month of the depression. The trend is such, however, that this gap appears to introduce no substantial error. The hourly rates for all industries combined are shown in the following statement:

July 1914...	$0.25
Average:	
1920...	.61
1921...	.52
1922...	.49
1923...	.54
1924...	.56
1925...	.56
1926...	.56
1927...	.57

Hourly earnings for this group of industries advanced 149 per cent from 1914 to September, 1920; fell 22.3 per cent from September, 1920, the known peak, to July, 1922, the known bottom; rose again more than 20 per cent from July, 1922 to September, 1927; and stood in 1927 at 128 per cent above 1914.

It is impossible to match the Board series with a similar series from any other reliable source of information. By assuming, however, that the week of highest actual per capita earnings was also the week of full-time earnings, it has been possible to compute, from monthly data published by the United States Bureau of Labor Statistics, the average full-time weekly earnings for 12 important and representative manufacturing industries for each year from 1917 to 1927 and for 42 manufacturing industries from 1923 to 1927. The 12 industries employed, according to the census of manufactures of 1925, 2,856,160 wage earners, and the 42 industries 5,832,302, out of a total of 8,384,261 wage earners. The results of these computations are shown in Table 6. In this series, full-time weekly earnings increased 58 per cent from 1917 to 1920; fell 20 per cent from 1920 to 1922; and were, in 1927, 16.8 per cent below 1920.

TABLE 6.—AVERAGE FULL-TIME WEEKLY EARNINGS

Year	Full-time weekly earnings	
	Twelve industries	Forty-two industries
1917.................	$20.65	.....
1918.................	26.37	.....
1919.................	28.78	.....
1920.................	32.57	.....
1921.................	27.62	.....
1922.................	26.04	.....
1923.................	27.58	$27.67
1924.................	27.51	27.48
1925.................	27.45	27.75
1926.................	27.03	27.66
1927.................	27.09	27.74

But changes in full-time weekly earnings are obviously not comparable with changes in hourly earnings, since full-time weekly earnings vary with changes in the length of the work-week. To put both series on a comparable basis, there was derived the weighted average full-time hours per week for the 12 industries. The full-time week, from these computations, was found to be 56 hours in 1917, 53 hours in 1920, 53 hours in 1922, and 51 hours in 1923 and thereafter.[9] Applying these weighted averages of full-time hours per week to the statistics of full-time earnings per week in the 12 industries, hourly earnings in the crucial years are found to be as follows:

1917.. $0.37
1920.. .62
1922.. .49
1923.. .54
1927.. .53

To make the same conversions for the 42 industries would require computing the average full-time hours per week for that group, an extremely laborious task. All of the available data appear to indicate that the prevailing average nominal week since 1923 in all manufacturing industry has fluctuated around 51 hours. Average hourly earnings in the 42 industries, then, were approximately 54 cents in each year since 1923. Comparisons between the hourly earnings reported by the Conference Board and the hourly earnings computed by this method show that, whereas the first fell 22.3 per cent from September, 1920 to July, 1922, the second series fell in the same period 20 per cent; while the Board's hourly earnings increased 16 per cent from 1922 to 1927, the increase in

[9] There are from year to year fractional differences in the full-time hours per week, but they are so slight that they may be disregarded.

the computed hourly earnings was 8 per cent. At the close of the whole period, however, the difference between the two series of between 3 and 4 cents an hour might easily be accounted for by differences in sampling, by minor, but undiscoverable, errors in computing the average full-time hours per week, and by the fact that comparisons of the Bureau's series were between averages for the year and not between high and low months.

Among the many industries that make up the group of manufacturing industries, there have been great divergencies in the rate of increase over prewar levels and in the movement since 1920. Table 7, showing hourly earnings in a few selected industries, throws some light on the behavior of wages in different industries. Increases in wages in the boot and shoe

TABLE 7.—HOURLY EARNINGS IN SELECTED INDUSTRIES

Industry	1913	1920	1921	1922	1923	1924	1925	1926	Per cent increase, latest year over 1913
Boots and shoes......	$0.31	$0.56	.....	$0.50	.....	$0.52	.....	$0.53	71
Clothing, men's......	.26	.....	.....	.73	.....	.76	.....	.75	188
Cotton goods........	.16	.48	.....	.33	.....	.37	.....	.33	106
Hosiery and knit goods..............	.17	.....	.....	.35	.....	.41	.....	.44	159
Iron and steel........	.30	.75	.....	.51	.....	.64	.....	.64	113
Lumber.............	.19	.....	$0.33	.....	$0.36	.....	$0.36	.....	90
Woolen and worsted.	.20	.63	.....	.47	.....	.53	.....	.49	145

industry appear to have lagged throughout the whole period, although the rates recovered from their fall in 1922. Both cotton goods and woolen and worsteds hardly recovered from the low of 1922. Iron and steel on the other hand had a rise of 13 cents an hour. Important industries not included in this table, because no data are available for most of the period, have had substantial increases in their hourly earnings since 1922. Hourly earnings in the automobile industry are reported as 66 cents in 1922 and 72 cents in 1925; and in foundries and machine shops as 56 cents in 1923 and 63 cents in 1927.[10]

The Building Trades.—The building industry in the United States is probably at the present time more than 50 per cent unionized and is, in the large cities, except for the outlying districts, almost completely organized. For this reason, the movement of union rates of wages gives a fair representation of the general movement of wages in the industry. Union rates of wages in the building industry, as in all industry, exaggerate the inelasticity of prevailing wage rates, since many concessions in rates commonly made during periods of depression and slack business

[10] All of the figures in this paragraph are taken from the reports of the United States Bureau of Labor Statistics.

are not adequately reported. In general, it is fair to say that union rates actually paid rise higher in periods of prosperity, and fall lower in periods of depression, than the recorded rates indicate. But there is no statistical evidence for this suspicion.

Union rates of wages in the building industry show an almost uninterrupted rise from 1914 to the present. In the war and early postwar

TABLE 8.—WEIGHTED UNION HOURLY RATES OF WAGES IN THE BUILDING TRADES[a]

Year	Rate	Year	Rate
1914	$0.53	1921	$1.03
1915	.53	1922	.96
1916	.55	1923	1.07
1917	.58	1924	1.15
1918	.65	1925	1.20
1919	.75	1926	1.28
1920	1.02	1927	1.32

[a] United States Bureau of Labor Statistics. The actual rates from 1914 to 1920 are not published by the Bureau, but were computed from the Bureau's index numbers.

period, wages rose, from 1914 to 1921, 94 per cent. They fell from 1921 to 1922 only 7 per cent and rose again from 1922 to 1927 by 38 per cent, leaving the building trades union rates 149 per cent higher in 1927 than they were in 1914. It must be remembered, of course, that the American building industry has had since 1922 an unusual and prolonged wave of prosperity.

As in all American wages, there are wide geographical divergencies in the union rates in the building industry. A compilation of the rates of wages in 1927 of five important occupations in various cities of the country shows that the high rate is sometimes nearly twice the low rate. These differences, moreover, persist over a long period, but the relative position of the cities does not remain unchanged. In all five occupations, for

TABLE 9.—RATES OF WAGES IN FIVE IMPORTANT OCCUPATIONS, 1927

City	Bricklayers	Carpenters	Painters	Plasterers	Plumbers and gas fitters
Atlanta	$1.40	$0.80	$0.85	$1.25	$1.25
Philadelphia	1.63	1.25	1.05	1.75	1.15
St. Louis	1.75	1.50	1.44	1.75	1.50
Los Angeles	1.38	1.00	1.00	1.50	1.13
Seattle	1.45	1.13	1.13	1.38	1.38
New York	1.75	1.50	1.63	1.75	1.50
Chicago	1.63	1.50	1.50	1.63	1.50

example, the rates in Seattle were, in the years 1917, 1918, and 1919, always higher than those of New York City and nearly always higher than the rates of Chicago. Such variations in the rank of these cities have, however, been rare.

Union Rates of Wages.—An index number of union hourly rates of wages for all reporting trades, prepared by the United States Bureau of Labor Statistics,[11] pursues much the same course as that taken by union rates in the building trades. They rise 105 per cent from 1913 to 1921; drop 6 per cent in 1922; increase 35 per cent from 1922 to 1928; and stand, in 1928, 161 per cent above 1913. At the end of the period, also, the rates are probably higher than they are in industry generally, although it must be remembered that the union rates are almost without exception rates of wages for male workers. Changes in the rates for specific occupations, shown in Table 10, exhibit no startling divergencies from the movement of wages in the building industry. But the freight handlers have a much greater drop in 1922 than the others. The striking feature of this tabulation, as indeed of the index number of all union rates, is the slight decline in rates during the severe depression of 1920 to 1922 and the decided upward movement since 1922.

TABLE 10.—CHANGES IN HOURLY RATES OF WAGES IN SPECIFIED OCCUPATIONS

Occupation	Hourly rate, 1928	Per cent change in hourly rate			
		1913–1921	1921–1922	1922–1928	1913–1928
Bakers........................	$0.95	+179	− 4	+ 7	+186
Compositors (book and job)........	1.12	+120	+ 2	+12	+150
Pressmen, cylinder (book and job)..	1.13	+106	− 2	+16	+133
Compositors, day (newspapers).....	1.18	+ 75	+ 1	+17	+107
Chauffeurs......................	.71	+103	− 6	+27	+143
Freight handlers.................	.86	+137	−17	+27	+149

It cannot be said that the index of union rates of wages is a satisfactory measure of the movement of union wages in the United States. It is, in the first place, heavily weighted for the building and printing industries, which together comprise 73 per cent of the total Bureau sample. Both industries are notoriously in large measure sheltered or noncompetitive industries, in which wages are not nearly so sensitive to changing market conditions as they are elsewhere. The large drop in the rate of wages of freight handlers has already been noted. The rates of pattern makers and of iron molders dropped, likewise, 11 and 18 per cent respectively, from 1920 to 1922. It is clear that a more representative sample of union rates would yield a measure showing more frequent and wider fluctuations than the present one.

The Bureau index, also, is by no means a measure of union rates of wages in the category of manufacturing industries. An examination of

[11] United States Bureau of Labor Statistics, *Bulletin* No. 457.

the union membership covered by the Bureau report shows that, except for the printing and publishing industry, practically no representation at all is given to manufacturing industries. The following statement[12] shows a list of trade groups and the total number of union members in each group.

Bakers	19,170
Building trades	539,423
Chauffeurs, teamsters, drivers	81,260
Granite and stone trades	5,796
Laundry workers	3,876
Linemen	3,464
Longshoremen	40,212
Printing and publishing:	
Book and job	57,832
Newspaper	27,586
Street railways: motormen and conductors	57,289
Bus drivers	2,730
Barbers	23,670
Total	862,308

Unskilled and Common Labor.—Wages of this category of labor will vary with the nature of the statistical sample and with the definition of the terms "unskilled" and "common" labor. It is indeed clear from the available data that the category is far from homogeneous and includes classes of labor that work at a great diversity of rates. In general, the designations appear to apply to low-priced, usually manual male labor,

TABLE 11.—WAGES OF UNSKILLED OR COMMON LABOR, 1914–1927

Year	National Industrial Conference Board[a]	New York Federal Reserve Bank[a]	United States Bureau of Labor Statistics[b]
1914	c$0.20	$0.20	$0.34
1915	......	.20	.34
1916	......	.23	.35
1917	......	.27	.39
1918	......	.35	.46
1919	......	.43	.52
1920	.55	.51	.75
1921	.45	.47	.76
1922	.41	.37	.71
1923	.45	.46	.73
1924	.47	.48	.81
1925	.47	.47	.77
1926	.48	.49	.85
1927	.49	.49	.85

a Average for the year.
b May 1 for the years 1914 and 1915, and May 15 for each year since 1916. The actual rates from 1914 to 1920 are not published by the Bureau, but were computed from the Bureau's index numbers.
c July.

[12] United States Bureau of Labor Statistics, *Bulletin* No. 457, p. 1.

and if they are so understood the statistics of wage rates for the class follow a consistent course. Table 11 presents three independent series of the wages of common or unskilled male labor from 1914 to the present. One series, that of the National Industrial Conference Board, represents the average hourly earnings of unskilled labor in more than 20 manufacturing industries throughout the United States. The second is the hourly hiring rate for common labor in the New York Federal Reserve district, compiled by the Federal Reserve Bank of New York; and the third is the average hourly union rate of wages for building laborers throughout the whole of the American building industry, published by the United States Bureau of Labor Statistics. In this case, as in general, the use of annual averages conceals somewhat the range of fluctuation of the rates of wages, but it is often impossible to find more than a single figure for a year. In Table 12, showing the changes in the wage rates of unskilled and common labor, some attempt is made to find the high and low points and to compute the percentage changes from them, but this procedure does not produce striking modifications in the final results.

TABLE 12.—CHANGES IN WAGE RATES OF UNSKILLED AND COMMON LABOR

Period	Changes in rates (per cent)		
	National Industrial Conference Board	New York Federal Reserve Bank	U. S. Bureau of Labor Statistics
1914 to 1920	[a] +175	[b] +165	+124
1920 to 1922	[c] − 27	[d] − 32	− 7
1920 to 1927	[e] − 11	[e] − 4	+ 13
1914 to 1927	[e] +145	[e] +145	+150

[a] July, 1914 to September, 1920. [d] October, 1920 to April, 1922.
[b] Average for 1914 to October, 1920. [e] Average for the year.
[c] September, 1920 to July, 1922.

A new series of hourly entrance rates for adult male common labor, compiled first quarterly and later semiannually by the United States Bureau of Labor Statistics since January 1, 1926,[13] runs from 6 to 8 cents an hour lower than both the Conference Board and Federal Reserve Bank rates, and, of course, considerably below the union rates of building laborers. Not only is the Bureau sample larger than the others, but its geographical diversity tends to reduce the average hiring rate for the country. Even within any single area, the difference between the high and low rate is occasionally as much as 80 cents an hour. If, further, the rates for common labor employed in general contracting are excluded, the Bureau hiring rate for common labor is often reduced by several cents more. From January 1, 1926 to January 1, 1928, this hourly rate

[13] *Monthly Labor Review*, February, May, September, December, 1926; March, October, 1927; Arilp, 1928.

for the whole country has increased from 40 to 43 cents an hour. On January 1, 1928, when the average rate for the United States was 43 cents an hour, the rates in various sections of the country were as shown in the following statement:

New England.. $0.47
Middle Atlantic.. .49
East North Central... .47
West North Central... .41
South Atlantic... .29
East South Central... .27
West South Central... .31
Mountain.. .44
Pacific... .47

With the full employment of labor during the war years, and the restriction of immigration, first by the war and later by legislation, it has been commonly believed that the differentials between the wage rates of skilled and unskilled labor or between high- and low-paid labor have

TABLE 13.—DIFFERENCE IN WAGE RATES OF SKILLED AND UNSKILLED LABOR

Year	Per cent average hourly earnings of male unskilled are of male skilled[a]	Per cent average hourly union rate of building laborers is of bricklayers[b]
1914..............	72.5	47.6
1920..............	79.0	62.4
1921..............	75.1	63.7
1922..............	72.6	61.3
1923..............	73.2	55.1
1924..............	73.8	57.9
1925..............	73.8	52.4
1926..............	73.6	54.4
1927..............	75.2	53.3

[a] Computed from the statistics of the National Industrial Conference Board for 23 manufacturing industries.

[b] Computed from the statistics of the United States Bureau of Labor Statistics.

been, since 1914, appreciably reduced. This belief is only partially supported by the available facts. Inspection of the wage statistics of many individual industries yields much the same conclusions as can be drawn from Table 13. The margins between the wage rates of skilled and unskilled labor narrowed considerably from 1914 to 1920 and then tended to widen, but were left somewhat narrower in 1927 than they were before the war. The slight variations that appear from year to year are probably the accidental results of changing samples and should be considered of little significance.

The Coal Industry.—Wages in the bituminous coal industry have followed a different course during the period under review because of factors peculiar to the soft coal industry. The industry has for a long time been partially unionized. During the war, organization spread very fast and the union extended its control over parts of the non-union area. Those coal fields which remained unorganized possessed great powers of expansion in output which they were able to exploit whenever they received a competitive advantage over their unionized competitors. Such competitive advantage non-union operators usually enjoy in periods of depression, when both working conditions and wages are more elastic in the unorganized than in the organized mines; and also whenever their organized competitors are shut down by strikes. Conditions such as these, which prevail in varying degrees in all industries that are part union and part non-union, have in this industry played the determining rôle in the years since the war. Rigidity in union rates has been accompanied by great elasticity in the non-union rates, with the result that the area of union control has, since 1920, steadily contracted. Although factors such as freight rates and differences in the efficiency of management have, without a doubt, exerted a strong influence on the situation, they have probably acted to reinforce trends created by the wage structure.

In both the union and non-union mines, wages rose steadily from 1914 to 1920. The trend of union rates of wages for tonnage men and for day labor is shown in Table 14.[14] The first class increased from 1914 to 1920 by 77 per cent and the rates for day labor, 162 per cent. Aside from the marked divergence between the rates of increase of tonnage and day labor, the significant item in the table is the fact that the rates

TABLE 14.—TREND OF UNION RATES OF WAGES

Year	Index numbers of tonnage rates for pick miners at Illinois and Indiana basing points (1914 = 100)	Date	Day rates for day labor	
			Actual rate	Index numbers (Apr. 1, 1914 = 100)
1914................	100	April 1, 1914..............	$2.86	100
1915................	100	April 1, 1916..............	3.00	105
1916................	105	April 15, 1917.............	3.60	126
1917................	121	October 6, 1917...........	5.00	175
1918................	138	November 26, 1919.......	5.67	198
1919................	138	April 1, 1920..............	6.00	210
1920................	177	August 16, 1920...........	7.50	262
1921................	177	August 15, 1922...........	7.50	262
1922................	177	April 1, 1923..............	7.50	262
1923................	177			

[14] The data in this table are adapted from Isador Lubin, *Miners' Wages and the Cost of Coal*, pp. 230, 236.

reached at the peak of 1920 remained unchanged through the period from 1920 to 1923.

Non-union rates also rose from before the war until 1920 and probably at a more rapid rate than the union rates, since the prewar base rates were lower in the non-union mines. But for the few years immediately after 1920, the non-union rates reacted swiftly and violently to changing business conditions. They fell, as is here indicated, in the first half of 1921, again in the second half, once more in 1922, and then rose sharply in 1923. From the peak to the low point, in this period, pick-mining rates in West Virginia fell 28 per cent, in Kentucky 27 per cent, while rates for machine cutting were reduced 25 per cent and 34 per cent in West Virginia and Kentucky, respectively. Much the same thing happened to the rates of day labor. While the going rates of union day labor were from $7.25 to $7.50 a day, the non-union rates fell as low as $4.10.[15]

TABLE 15.—PICK-MINING AND MACHINE-CUTTING RATES, IN WEST VIRGINIA AND KENTUCKY[a]

| Year | Index numbers of non-union rates (Jan. 1, 1912 = 100) | | | |
| | Pick mining | | Machine cutting | |
	West Virginia	Kentucky	West Virginia	Kentucky
1920 (first half)	211	215	210	196
1920 (second half)	225	225	214	213
1921 (first half)	219	209	214	193
1921 (second half)	205	170	204	173
1922 (first half)	163	164	160	141
1923	222	212	212	183

[a] The data in this table were computed from the statistics published in the reports of the United States Coal Commission, 1925.

In 1923 the United Mine Workers entered into a new agreement with the operators, the famous Jacksonville agreement, by which terms the rates of wages then prevailing were made effective for five years. As

[15] See Lubin, *op. cit.* p. 211, from which the following table, showing the day rates paid to inside labor in the non-union Winding Gulf District of West Virginia, is taken:

	Sept. 1, 1920	Sept. 1, 1921	Jan. 1, 1922	Aug. 16, 1922
Machine runners	$7.58	$6.08	$4.68	$7.58
Trip riders	6.92	5.55	4.10	6.77
Drivers, one mule	6.72	5.40	4.15	6.65
Track layers	7.37	5.92	4.55	7.37
Timbermen	7.37	5.92	4.10	7.05
Bratticemen	7.37	5.92	4.10	7.05
Unclassified day labor	6.64	5.33	4.10	6.60

TABLE 16.—HOURLY EARNINGS IN THE BITUMINOUS COAL INDUSTRY[a]

Selected occupations	Hourly earnings						
	Union fields			Non-union fields			
	Illinois	Indiana	Ohio	Ala-bama	Penn-syl-vania	Ken-tucky	West Virginia
Pick miners:							
1922	$0.81	$0.78	$0.84	$0.49	$0.70	$0.77	$0.95
1924	.85	1.01	.91	.53	.71	.71	.76
1926	.85	.97	.81	.49	.70	.60	.73
Machine cutters:							
1922	1.41	1.75	1.28	.58	.99	1.09	1.29
1924	1.38	1.61	1.18	.78	1.05	.87	1.06
1926	1.36	1.51	1.11	.83	1.04	.91	1.11
Inside mine:							
Trackmen—							
1922	.94	.94	.94	.47	.75	.71	.78
1924	.94	.94	.93	.46	.81	.61	.62
1926	.94	.93	.92	.45	.74	.57	.61
Motormen—							
1922	1.01	1.01	.94	.43	.93	.69	.78
1924	1.01	1.02	.92	.47	.85	.62	.62
1926	1.01	1.01	.81	.45	.77	.60	.62
Bratticemen—							
1922	.94	.94	.94	.42	.70	.69	.76
1924	.94	.94	.93	.44	.80	.62	.61
1926	.94	.92	.98	.45	.75	.60	.61
Outside mine:							
Blacksmiths—							
1922	.97	.88	.96	.55	.79	.77	.85
1924	.97	.88	.96	.51	.82	.62	.69
1926	.97	.88	.94	.52	.76	.59	.69
Engineers—							
1922	.96	.90	.86	.50	.75	.78	.61
1924	.97	.87	.93	.54	.82	.57	.59
1926	.96	.84	.92	.45	.81	.57	.62
Laborers—							
1922	.86	.85	.85	.33	.57	.53	.58
1924	.86	.85	.86	.28	.63	.47	.48
1926	.86	.83	.85	.29	.56	.44	.48

[a] Figures taken from United States Bureau of Labor Statistics, *Bulletin* No. 454.

these five years passed, the union rates were progressively less observed because operators broke their agreements with the union and opened their mines under non-union conditions, and because an increasing number of union members took work at rates below the union scale. Wages in the industry accordingly fell through 1926. Hourly earnings of tonnage workers throughout the industry were 85 cents in 1922, 78 cents in 1924, and 75 cents in 1926; and the average hourly earnings of inside and outside day workers were, for the same years, 75 cents, 70 cents, and 66 cents, respectively.[16]

Throughout this period, hourly earnings were persistently lower in the non-union than in the union fields. The salient facts of this condition are shown in Table 16. The division between union and non-union area is not so sharp as appears in this table. Pennsylvania, which is partly unionized, is included in the non-union group because it has in the past few years become increasingly non-union and because rates of wages in the state are now more determined by conditions of the competitive market than by the union scales of wages.

It is probable that wages throughout the industry are lower now than they were in 1926. In the late summer of 1928, the union for all practical purposes abandoned the scales of the Jacksonville agreement, authorized the district organizations to make their own agreements with the operators, and is reported to have settled with the union operators of Ohio for rates 33⅓ per cent below the 1923 scale and in Illinois at a reduction of 18.7 per cent.

Anthracite Coal.—The anthracite coal industry is localized in one small area in Pennsylvania and is practically altogether unionized. Wages are fixed almost exclusively by negotiations between the union, the United Mine Workers, and the anthracite operators, and occasionally by the awards of arbitration boards. The movement of wage rates in the industry shows none of the vagaries of the confused and demoralized soft coal industry. Statistics collected independently by two agencies, the United States Bureau of Labor Statistics[17] and the National Industrial Conference Board,[18] come to much the same conclusions. Hourly earnings for all workers in the industry, excluding contract miners' laborers stood in April, 1927, 194 per cent above the hourly rate in June, 1914. While the Bureau figures indicate a greater rise from 1920 to 1924 than do the statistics of the Conference Board, the discrepancies are mainly attributable to the fact that the Bureau pay roll period was the last half of March, 1920, and the Board's October, 1920. Again the lower average hourly earnings for all workers in the Board's report is in part explained by the omission of the hourly earnings of contract miners' laborers, who, in 1924, had average hourly earnings of 97 cents. The hourly earnings of contract miners are reported by the Board as $1.20 in December, 1924, and by the Bureau as $1.43 during the last quarter of the same year.

[16] United States Bureau of Labor Statistics, *Bulletin* No. 454.
[17] *Ibid.*, *Bulletins* No. 279 and No. 416.
[18] *Wages in the United States, 1914–1927*, New York, 1928, Chap. V

TABLE 17.—HOURLY EARNINGS OF ALL WAGE EARNERS IN THE ANTHRACITE COAL INDUSTRY

Period, last half of—	National Industrial Conference Board (less contract miners' laborers)	Year	United States Bureau of Labor Statistics
June, 1914	$0.28	1919	$0.60
October, 1920	.76	1920	.63
March, 1921	.76	1922	.80
June, 1921	.75	1924	.92
October, 1921	.74		
July, 1923	.75		
December, 1923	.83		
December, 1924	.83		
April, 1927	.84		

Full-time Hours of Labor.—Measurement of the length of the full-time or nominal work-week is likely to involve some error because of the confusion between the nominal and actual hours of work. In busy periods the two figures will closely approximate one another, but in slack times they may be far apart. In reporting full-time hours per week there is some evidence that accurate allowance is not always made for short time and for overtime. Comparison between various series of full-time hours per week does not indicate, however, that the errors so introduced are large or that they have any discernable bias during periods of rising and falling business. As the basis for the computation of piece

TABLE 18.—FULL-TIME HOURS PER WEEK

Year	United States Census of Manufactures[a]	National Industrial Conference Board Manufacturing Industries	United States Bureau of Labor Statistics	
			All union[b]	Union building trades
1909	57.3	....	....	....
1914	55.6	[c]55.0	48.9	....
1919	51.2	....	....	....
1920	....	50.0	45.8	....
1921	50.7	49.7	45.9	....
1922	....	50.0	46.1	....
1923	51.1	50.0	46.1	....
1924	....	49.8	45.9	43.9
1925	....	49.9	45.5	44.0
1926	....	49.8	45.4	43.8
1927	....	49.6	45.2	43.7

[a] Computed from the census classified statistics of hours, by assuming from 1919 to 1923 the group over 60 hours to be 60 hours and the group of 44 and under to be 44 hours; for the census years 1909 and 1914, the group over 72 hours is assumed to be 72 and the group 48 and under to be 48 hours. The error so introduced is slight and has the effect of understating the nominal week in the early years.

[b] Computed from index numbers published by the United States Bureau of Labor Statistics, *Bulletin* No. 457, for the years 1914 to 1920.

[c] July, 1914.

and time rates of wages and as a measure of the volume of available leisure for the working population of the country, full-time hours per week is a statistical series of considerable importance and interest.

Changes in the nominal week since the war are presented in Table 18. They show, for manufacturing industries, a reduction in the nominal week of roughly five hours from 1914 to the present and they also show that prevailing hours are now around 50 a week. The union full-time week is nearly four hours less a week than in 1914, and started in that year much below the nominal week in all manufacturing industries. The union nominal week in the building industry appears to be about two hours less than in 1914, and is still falling as a result of the 40-hour movement in that industry. A large part of the building trades was already on a 44-hour basis in 1914, so that the reduction in their nominal week has been slower than for the remainder of industry. The nominal week of the bricklayers was 44.6 hours in 1913 and 43.8 in 1927; of the painters, 45.1 in 1914 and 42.6 in 1927; and of building laborers, 47.2 and 44.8 in the same two years.

The largest reduction in hours seems to have been in the iron and steel industry, where the nominal week was 66 hours in 1913, 63 in 1920, and 54 in 1926. Hours in the men's clothing industry dropped from 52 in 1913 to 44.3 in 1926; and in cotton goods they fell from 57.3 in 1913 to 51.8 in 1920, but rose again to 53.3 in 1926.[19]

Labor Costs.—Statistics of labor cost are not available in any useful quantity. Light on the probable movements of labor cost can best be obtained from an examination of the data on per capita output presented in the following section of this chapter. The matter of labor cost is, however, so closely connected with that of wages and hours that it merits some additional slight discussion at this point. From the peak of business activity in 1920 to the bottom in 1922, there was a substantial reduction in labor cost owing to the increased per capita output of labor and to a reduction in the rate of wages in manufacturing industries that must have been greater than 25 per cent.[20] After 1922, hourly earnings in the manufacturing industries rose until 1927, probably between 10 and 15 per cent. But this rise in earnings was accompanied by an uninterrupted rise in the per capita output of labor, at a rapid rate until 1925 and more slowly in the years 1926 and 1927. Since 1922 it is more than likely that labor cost has continued to fall through further reductions in the rates of wages, but that earnings have been sustained by the increasing per capita output.

[19] *Bulletins*, United States Bureau of Labor Statistics.

[20] Hourly earnings in the manufacturing industries decreased between 20 and 25 per cent from 1920 to 1922; but, since hourly earnings are a function of both the rate of wages and of output, it is clear that, in a period of rising per capita output, rates must necessarily have had a greater reduction. How much, it is impossible to determine.

These conclusions appear, in some degree, to be supported by what may be regarded as an indirect measure of relative labor cost. The percentage that total wages are of value added by manufacture seems, particularly in the period since 1919, to move up and down with changes in the output of labor. The category of "value added by manufacture" is itself composed of so many items that changes in the relation between wages and value added may in part be due to variations in constituents other than wages. For the period since 1919, however, this does not appear to be the case. The two series are presented in the following tabulation.

Census year	Per cent wages of value added by manufacture[a]	Per capita output (1899 = 100)[b]	Census year	Per cent wages of value added by manufacture[a]	Per capita output (1899 = 100)[b]
1899...............	41.6	100.0	1919...............	42.1	104.5
1904...............	41.5	104.0	1921...............	44.8	107.3
1909...............	40.2	109.6	1923...............	42.7	132.5
1914...............	42.0	108.5	1925...............	40.1	145.4
			1927...............	39.3	149.5

[a] *United States Census of Manufactures.*   [b] See next section.

The data in this table are clearly not comparable over long intervals, since so many factors in the situation have changed to an unknown degree. From 1919 on, they appear to run true to form. It is at first surprising that the percentage that wages are of value added by manufacture should have stood so high in 1921. Per capita output did not have its substantial rise until 1922, and it was, probably, not until 1922 and 1923 that industry had fully adjusted itself to more efficient methods of manufacture.

III. THE PRODUCTIVITY OF LABOR[21]

The measures of the per capita output of labor considered in this section are not measures of the specific productivity of labor.[22] They are the results of comparisons between the total physical output of industry and the number of wage earners employed in producing it. They are not indicative of the changing efficiency of labor. Such measures could be derived from comparisons between the output of industry and the number of man-hours worked by labor. But

[21] The material for this section was collected and prepared by Woodlief Thomas, formerly of the Division of Research and Statistics of the Federal Reserve Board.

[22] For an interesting attack on this aspect of the problem, see C. W. Cobb and P. H. Douglas, "A Theory of Production," *American Economic Review*, Supplement, Vol. XVIII, No. 1, March, 1928, p. 139.

statistics of man-hours are not available until very recent times and then only for a limited number of industries. Where both measures are to be had, they show wide discrepancies. Thus railroad traffic volume per worker increased by 56 per cent from 1899 to 1925, but traffic units per man-hour have been estimated to have increased in the same period by 100 per cent.[23]

Changes in the per capita output of labor, as in total output, may clearly be due to a variety of factors.[24] In the long run, the levels of education and skill of the working population of a country, the growth of capital and the use of machinery, the alertness and ingenuity of management, and the state of science may determine both the direction and the rate of change of industrial production. During shorter periods, accidental or abnormal factors, such as apparently operated from 1916 to 1921, like sudden changes in the length of the work-week, marked variations in the efficiency of labor, resulting either from the state of mind of the workers, from the carelessness of management, or from the replacement of experienced by inexperienced workmen, may conceivably not only interrupt the prevailing trend of production, but also change its direction. The segregation and weighing of all of these factors, or even of the most important of them, are not possible in the present state of knowledge. The most that can be done is to appeal to reasonable hypotheses and to informed common knowledge.[25]

[23] United States Bureau of Labor Statistics, *Monthly Labor Review*, March, 1927, p. 1.

[24] See Productivity per Worker, Chap. II, Industry, Part 1, p. 81; Part 2, p. 103; Chap. III, Construction, p. 248; Chap. IV, Transportation, Part 1, p. 285; Chap. VII, Management, pp. 512–514; Chap. VIII, Agriculture, p. 602.

[25] Both of the elements of the formula for deriving per capita output have serious, if irremediable, defects. The measures of the total output of industry are better for the mining and transportation industries than they are for manufacturing and agriculture; and they do not include the highly important construction industry, for which there are no satisfactory statistics of either physical output or employment. They cannot, by their very nature, take into account changes in the character and quality of the products of industry. Since the statistics of the production of raw materials or of commodities in their early stages of fabrication are more numerous than statistics of highly fabricated goods, the measures are too heavily weighted for raw materials and, consequently, underestimate the rise in total output. In general, there is less material for the new and growing industries than for the old established ones, whose rate of growth has probably already slackened before the compensating influence of the growth of the young industries can make itself felt in the measure of total output. And it is, finally, not always certain that the changing importance of industries is adequately allowed for in the weights used for the computation of average changes in total production.

The employment indexes are probably superior for the manufacturing and transportation industries than for the rest. For manufacturing they are much more reliable in the later than in the early years, although one important series, that of the United States Bureau of Labor Statistics, appears to exhibit a downward bias even during the latest years. All of the series, finally, register the amount of work done

Index Numbers of Production.—The most comprehensive index of production now available is an index of manufactures compiled on the basis of data taken from the biennial censuses of manufactures.[26] Current measures of the growth of manufactures are also provided by the annual index of the Harvard Economic Committee and by the monthly index of the Federal Reserve Board. Both of these indexes have been used with the census index as a basis for interpolation for intracensal years and for extrapolation for the years since 1925, the date of the last published census. It is believed that the resultant series, shown in Table 19, is a reasonably accurate measure of annual changes in manufacturing output. The census index is made up of 138 different products series, representing production in 55 industries, with an aggregate value added by manufacture equal to nearly 50 per cent of the value added for all industries. Both directly and indirectly the series represents groups of industries with 90 per cent of the total value added by manufacture. The indexes used for the noncensus years represented about 40 per cent of total production directly and another 40 per cent indirectly.

Making index numbers of agricultural production involves difficulties that cannot always be overcome. Shifts from the production of dairy and other animal products on a small scale to large-scale commercialized operation, the increasing output of commercial fruit and vegetable crops,

---

by the number of people employed and not by the time worked, and this procedure, as it has already been indicated, may involve misleading conclusions.

The commodities that enter into the aggregate production of a country cannot all be recorded in the same unit. The simplest method of reducing all goods to a common denominator is to express them in pecuniary units. Variations in the resultant aggregates, however, would then reflect changes both in physical output and in prices. Correction for price changes, for many well-known reasons, raises as many problems as it solves. Resort must then be had to the device of the index number, which is an average of the measures of relative changes in the items of a heterogeneous series. In place of aggregates of incommensurable units, such as bushels, feet, tons, trucks, and so on, the index number registers the weighted average of all changes in the number of units of output of the commodities under consideration. Even the construction of index numbers involves the difficult problem of discovering the importance of each industry, so that the changes in the output of each product may be properly weighted. In making the index numbers of this section, value added by manufacture or total value of output were used as weights.

For descriptions of the methods of constructing production indexes, see Day and Thomas, *The Growth of Manufactures*, United States Census Bureau, Monograph No. IX, Chapters I and II and Appendix A; Woodlief Thomas, "Construction of an Index Number of Production," *Journal of the American Statistical Association*, September, 1927; Walter W. Stewart, "An Index Number of Production," *American Economic Review*, March, 1921; E. E. Day, W. M. Persons, and E. D. Coyle, "An Index of the Physical Volume of Production," *Review of Economic Statistics*, September, 1920–January, 1921.

[26] Compiled for the Census Bureau by E. E. Day and W. Thomas, continuing the similar index constructed for the quinquennial censuses by Persons and Coyle. See Census Monograph No. IX.

TABLE 19.—INDEX OF PRODUCTION OF MANUFACTURES, 1899–1927[a]

Year	Index (1899 = 100)	Year	Index (1899 = 100)	Year	Index (1899 = 100)	Index (1919 = 100)
1899[b]	100.0	1909[b]	159.2	1919[b]	213.7	100.0
1900	101	1910	162	1920	221.4	103.6
1901	112	1911	155	1921[b]	169.7	79.4
1902	122	1912	179	1922	222.2	104.0
1903	124	1913	185	1923[b]	260.7	122.0
1904[b]	122.2	1914[b]	169.4	1924	244.7	114.5
1905	144	1915	188	1925[b]	274.6	128.5
1906	154	1916	223	1926	284.2	133.0
1907	153	1917	224	1927	278.7	130.4
1908	129	1918	220			

[a] Compiled from index for census years (1899, 1904, 1909, 1914, 1919, 1921, 1923, 1925), computed by Day and Thomas, with interpolations based, 1899–1919, on Day's (Harvard annual) index, and 1919–1925 on the Federal Reserve Board's index, and extrapolations, 1926 and 1927, based on the Federal Reserve Board's index with allowances for slight downward bias noted between 1919 and 1925.

[b] Census years.

the decrease in home gardens in towns and cities, and the volume of farm products consumed by farmers' families are some of the items for which it is not easy to account. The index of agricultural production here used was adapted by Dr. E. Dana Durand, of the Department of Commerce, from indexes compiled by the Department of Agriculture.[27] It is probable that this series understates the growth of agricultural output over long periods of time.

Annual indexes of mining production are more comprehensive than those for any other branch of industry, owing partly to the adequate statistics furnished by the United States Bureau of Mines, partly to the fact that comparatively few products make up a dominant portion of the aggregate output of minerals, and finally to the relative simplicity of the products. The present index of mineral production was constructed by Dr. Durand. It covers 10 products—6 metals and 4 fuels—with an aggregate value in 1919 equivalent to nearly 95 per cent of the total value of all minerals produced in the United States.

Measures of railroad performance can be obtained from the elaborate statistics published by the Interstate Commerce Commission. The index of railroad performance used here is an average of relatives for passenger-miles and freight-ton miles, weighted on the basis of the respective revenues received from these two types of traffic.[28]

[27] The index from 1899 to 1920 was constructed by Mordecai Ezekiel, from statistics of physical production of crops, livestock, and animal products, and that from 1924 to 1926 by Louis H. Bean, from statistics of gross farm income, adjusted for price changes per group.

[28] This index was prepared by Dr. E. Dana Durand, of the Department of Commerce.

Employment.—For the manufacturing industries there are now available a great mass of current data on employment which, together with the material contained in the biennial censuses of manufactures, affords an adequate view of fluctuations in employment. For the period before 1914, the supply of information is not so plentiful, and conclusions regarding the earlier period are, consequently, less certain. The annual index of the number of persons engaged in manufacturing from 1899 to 1927 is shown in Table 20. This index, based on data for the census

TABLE 20.—NUMBER OF PERSONS ENGAGED IN MANUFACTURE, BY YEARS, 1899–1927[a]

(In thousands)

Year	Wage earners	Salaried and other	Total	Index (1899 = 100)
1899[b]	4,713	577	5,290	100.0
1900	4,968	612	5,580	105
1901	5,184	647	5,831	110
1902	5,554	683	6,237	118
1903	5,784	713	6,497	123
1904[b]	5.468	746	6,214	117.5
1905	5,906	820	6,726	127
1906	6,251	894	7,145	135
1907	6,483	967	7,450	141
1908	5,714	1,000	6,714	127
1909[b]	6,615	1,064	7,679	145.1
1910	6,807	1,079	7,886	149
1911	6,855	1,095	7,950	150
1912	7,167	1,109	8,276	156
1913	7,277	1,123	8,400	159
1914[b]	7,036	1,127	8,163	154.3
1915	7,200	1,270	8,470	160
1916	8,550	1,410	9,960	187
1917	9,220	1,550	10,770	204
1918	9,420	1,700	11,120	210
1919[b c]	9,096	1,717	10,813	.....
1919[c]	8,990	1,679	10,669	204.4
1920	9,080	1,620	10,700	205.0
1921[b]	6,938	1,313	8,251	158.2
1922	7,630	1,400	9,030	172.9
1923[b]	8,768	1,499	10,267	196.7
1924	8,120	1,480	9,600	184.0
1925[b]	8,384	1,474	9,858	188.9
1926	8,500	1,475	9,975	191.1
1927	8,260	1,470	9,730	186.4

[a] Census year figures, with interpolations based on annual indexes of employment, compiled 1899–1914 by Professors Cobb and Douglas, 1914–1919 by Woodlief Thomas, and 1919–1925 by Federal Reserve Board, and extrapolations, 1926 and 1927, on basis of Bureau of Labor Statistics index, with allowance for downward bias.

[b] Census years.

[c] One set of figures includes data from establishments with product valued at over $500, and the other from only those establishments with products of over $5,000. Index numbers are computed from comparable figures.

years 1899, 1904, 1909, 1914, 1919, 1921, 1923, and 1925, was constructed for the period 1899 to 1914 by Cobb and Douglas.[29] The index from 1914 to 1919 was prepared by Woodlief Thomas from data collected by the United States Bureau of Labor Statistics and the New York State Department of Labor. From 1919 on, the index of the Federal Reserve Board was used.[30]

The statistics of the number of workers in railroad transportation were taken from the reports of the Interstate Commerce Commission and represent total employees of railroads in the United States. In some years estimates were made on the basis of reports for Class I roads.

In agriculture and in mining, no such long and continuous series of employment data are to be had. Actual counts of the number employed can be obtained only for the census dates and these are less frequent than for manufacturing industry. For agriculture and mining, therefore, the use of the employment data are more valid in long than in short-time comparisons.

Per Capita Output.—Per capita output for each of the four main divisions of industry, and for all combined, is shown in Table 21 for the periods indicated.[31] From 1899 to 1925 the physical volume of production of farms, factories, mines, and railroads in the United States increased by 136 per cent while, population grew by slightly over 50 per cent. Thus production per capita of population is now nearly 60 per cent greater than it was in the final years of the nineteenth century. The volume of output for each worker engaged directly in production has, during the same period, increased by 76 per cent. The increase was not an even one over the whole of the period, since output per worker increased 18 per cent in both the first and second decades, and 27 per cent in the six years from 1919 to 1925.

The greatest rise over the whole period was in the per capita production of minerals, which increased 99 per cent. This rise reflects chiefly the rapid increase in petroleum output. The process of producing petroleum requires a relatively small supply of labor, and the value of output per person is greater than that for any other mineral product. The rapid growth in petroleum production, consequently, has added proportionately more to the total output of minerals than it has to the

[29] *Op. cit.*, p. 147.

[30] For the method of constructing this index, see Federal Reserve *Bulletins*, December, 1923, and May, 1925. Since 1923 the Board's index has been made from practically the same data as that of the Bureau of Labor Statistics and the fluctuations of the two indexes are in substantial agreement.

[31] Production in agriculture and in mining fluctuates widely from year to year, in the former because of the weather and in the latter largely on account of strikes. To level out these wide fluctuations and to make the statistics of all four groups comparable, the statistics are presented in the table in the form of three-year averages.

TABLE 21.—INCREASE IN PRODUCTIVITY OF MAJOR BRANCHES OF INDUSTRY

Period and branch	Number of workers (thousands)		Index for end of period (beginning = 100)			Weight value at beginning (millions of dollars)	Weighted index (end)
	Beginning of period	End of period	Workers	Output[a]	Output[b] per worker		
1898–1900 to 1908–1910:							
Agriculture	10,700	11,400	106.5	113	106	3,500	3,955
Mining	600	1,010	168.5	190	112.5	600	1,140
Manufactures	5,300	7,430	140	150	107	4,830	7,240
Railways	970	1,575	162.5	185	114	1,300	2,405
Total or average	17,570	21,415	122	144	118	10,230	14,740
1908–1910 to 1918–1920:							
Agriculture	11,400	11,300	99	119	120	6,100	7,259
Mining	1,010	1,050	104	145	140	1,240	1,798
Manufactures	7,430	c10,930	147	145.5	99	8,530	12,410
Railways	1,575	2,035	129	162	125.5	2,390	3,872
Total or average	21,415	25,315	118	139	117.5	18,260	25,339
1918–1920 to 1924–1926:							
Agriculture	11,300	10,700	95	114	120	15,700	17,898
Mining	1,050	1,050	100	127	127	3,175	4,032
Manufactures	c10,780	c9,810	92.5	122.5	134.5	24,750	30,320
Railways	2,035	1,860	91.5	100	109	5,040	5,040
Total or average	25,165	23,420	93	118	127	48,665	57,290
1898–1900 to 1924–1926:							
Agriculture[a]	10,700	10,700	100	153	153	3,500	5,355
Mining	600	1,050	175	348	199	600	2,088
Manufactures	5,300	c9,950	189	268	142.5	4,830	12,940
Railways	970	1,860	192	299	156	1,300	3,887
Total or average	17,570	23,560	134.5	236	176	10,230	24,270
Mining, excluding petroleum	576	858	150	244	163	......	....
Petroleum	24	192	800	1,268	158	......	....

[a] Averages for all branches computed by weighting component indexes according to the relative importance of the several branches in 1899, as determined by value of product, given in next to last column of table.

[b] Averages for all branches computed by dividing the average index of increase in output by the actual ratio of total workers at end of each period to total at beginning. The figure exceeds the weighted average of the indexes of output per worker in the several branches, because the largest increases in number of workers occurred in those branches in which average value of output per worker was relatively larger.

[c] The differences in the figures given for number of persons employed in manufactures for 1919 and 1925 are due to changes in the size of establishments covered, and to certain exclusions of industries formerly reported. The 1925 figure, for comparison with 1899, was estimated from the percentages of change from census to census.

number of persons engaged in mineral production, and thus accounts for the rapid increase in the per capita production of minerals.

The general trend of agricultural production during the century has shown practically the same rate of growth as population and has not varied widely from this rate for any long period of time. The number of

CHART 1.—GROWTH IN PRODUCTION PER WORKER, 1899–1925

Index numbers for 1925 with 1899 equaling 100

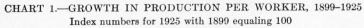

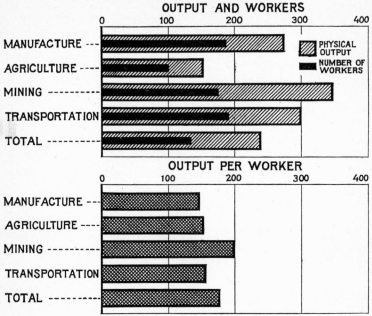

farm workers increased slightly in the first decade of the century, but has subsequently decreased by about the same amount. The productivity of agricultural workers had its smallest growth in the decade from 1899 to 1909 and its largest in the postwar years.

Over the whole period, railroad traffic volume per worker increased 56 per cent, a rise slightly in excess of the increase in agriculture and manufacturing. Both the number of workers and the volume of traffic increased very rapidly during the first decade, while per capita output rose 14 per cent. In the second decade, traffic volume and number employed grew more slowly, but per capita output rose 25 per cent. From 1919 to 1925, there was a decrease in the number of employees and practically no change in traffic volume.

Productivity in Manufactures.—With regard to the postwar period in American economic history, beginning in 1919 and ending in 1925, the most striking changes in the productivity of labor took place in the category of manufacturing industry. In the first decade of the whole period, the increase in the per capita output of labor in both mining and railroads exceeded that of manufactures. The next decade witnessed an actual drop in manufacturing per capita output at the same time that there were notable advances in agriculture, mining, and rail transportation. But in the latest period the rise in manufacturing productivity was far in excess of that in the remaining three groups.

Much light can be thrown on the nature of the course of total and per capita output in manufacturing industries by an examination of the annual statistics given in Table 22.   It is seen here that both production

TABLE 22.—PRODUCTIVITY OF MANUFACTURE, BY YEARS, 1899–1927

(Index numbers, 1899 = 100)

Year	Persons engaged	Volume of production	Output per person
1899[a]..	100	100	100
1900..	105	101	96.2
1901..	110	112	101.8
1902..	118	122	103.4
1903..	123	124	100.7
1904[a]..	117.5	122.2	104.0
1905..	127	144	113.3
1906..	135	154	114.0
1907..	141	153	108.5
1908	127	129	101.5
1909[a]..	145.1	159.2	109.6
1910..	149	162	108.7
1911..	150	155	103.4
1912..	156	179	114.6
1913..	159	185	116.3
1914[a]..	156.2	169.4	108.5
1915..	160	188	117.5
1916..	187	223	119.2
1917..	204	224	109.8
1918..	210	220	104.7
1919[a]..	204.4	213.7	104.5
1920..	205.0	221.4	107.9
1921[a]..	158.2	169.7	107.3
1922..	172.9	222.2	128.5
1923[a]..	196.7	260.7	132.5
1924..	184.0	244.7	133.0
1925[a]..	188.9	274.6	145.4
1926..	191.1	284.2	148.7
1927..	186.4	278.7	149.5

[a] Census years.

and employment dropped in years of industrial recession—1904, 1908, 1911, and 1914—and reached new maximum levels in years of unusual activity—1903, 1906, 1907, 1909, 1913, and 1915.   In 1915 both production and employment began to expand rapidly.   Production reached its maximum in 1917, but remained at a high level until 1920.   After 1916, however, employment began to increase more rapidly than production, and per capita output began to fall.   From the peak of per capita output reached in 1916, productivity receded through 1917 and 1918, and reached its low in 1919, when per capita output was smaller than in any year of ordinary industrial activity since 1903.   All of the rise since

1904 was lost in two years, 1918 and 1919. During 1920 and 1921 productivity rose, but only slightly.

CHART 2.—THE GROWTH OF MANUFACTURES, 1899–1927

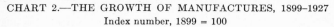
Index number, 1899 = 100

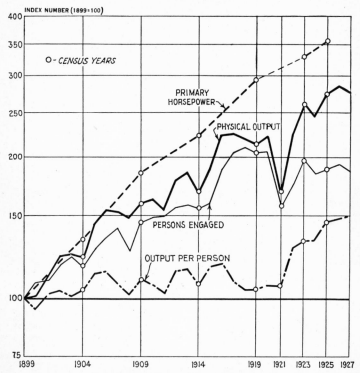

The startling and unexpected change came in 1922. Total manufacturing output was then as large as in 1920, but employment was much smaller than in any year since 1915. Output per person then increased by 20 per cent. Not only was this the largest increase that had ever occurred in any single year, but it also brought the productivity of manufacturing to a level higher than any reached in the years preceding. In 1923 the rate of increase of productivity slackened and there was a rise of 3 per cent. In 1924, a year of recession, both total output and employment were reduced and there was no change in productivity. But 1925 was again an exceptional year, showing an increase in per capita output of 9 per cent. Thus the total increases in the four years since 1921 amounted to more than 35 per cent. Changes in 1926 and 1927 were slight.[32]

[32] In view of the probable error in the estimates for 1926 and 1927, since there are no census figures for any year after 1925, the changes recorded for these two years are too small to be significant.

A satisfactory interpretation of the unusual increases in productivity in 1922 and in 1925 should, of course, take into account the fact that they represented, in part at least, the recovery from a condition of abnormally low per capita output, and that the drop in productivity in 1917, 1918, and 1919, in a measure interrupted an upward trend. The figures indicate, however, that had the rate of increase of the period 1899 to 1916 continued, output per worker in 1922 would have been below the level actually achieved in that year. In 1916, the peak year in the period beginning 1899, per capita output was 19 per cent greater than in 1899. This rise took place over an interval of 17 years. From 1916 to 1925, a period of nine years, productivity increased 22 per cent. The increase, likewise, for the 16-year period from 1909 to 1925, was 33 per cent, as compared with 10 per cent from 1899 to 1909. The average annual rate of increase for the later period is twice the annual increment during the first decade. Again, by regarding 1922 as a year of recovery, and by comparing the increase in output in 1922 over the year preceding with increases in other years of recovery, it is found that the year 1922 stands by itself. Thus, after depression years there were increases in productivity of 9 per cent in 1905, 8 per cent in 1909, 11 per cent in 1912, and 9 per cent in 1915; whereas the rise in 1922 was 20 per cent.

Productivity by Industries.—Much that is obscure in accounting for the variations in total and per capita output may be clarified by inspection of the course of production in some of the branches of the general category of manufacturing industry. It has already been seen how breaking up the mineral group into its parts revealed the important rôle played in the growth of mining as a whole by the development of the petroleum industry. Similar data for the analysis of manufactures are presented in Table 23.

This table gives indexes of production, persons engaged, horse power installed, and output per person, for census years by major groups of manufacturing industry. The group indexes are not computed from the total figures reported by the census for these groups, but for selected industries in each group. The industries selected are those for which statistics of physical volume of product are available. About 50 per cent of all industries, measured either by number of persons engaged or by value added by manufacture, are included in the index, but among the several groups this proportion varies from 20 per cent for paper and printing to practically 100 per cent for tobacco products.[33] In a few cases the index is not typical of the entire group, but the data on physical volume of production, persons engaged, and horse power cover the same industries and are, consequently, comparable with one another. In general, the indexes for the tobacco, textile, vehicles, nonferrous metals,

---

[33] These percentages for each group, together with other information regarding the representativeness of the index, are given in Day and Thomas, *op. cit.*, Appendix A.

TABLE 23.—PRODUCTIVITY OF MANUFACTURE, BY INDUSTRIAL GROUPS IN CENSUS YEARS, 1899–1925

	Index numbers: Base, 1919								Per cent of increase, 1899–1925
	1925	1923	1921	1919	1914	1909	1904	1899	
All industries:									
Physical volume of production	128.5	122.0	79.4	100.0	79.3	74.5	57.2	46.8	174.6
Number of persons engaged	92.4	96.2	77.3	100.0	76.4	71.0	57.5	48.9	89.0
Primary horse power	121.8	112.8	.....	100.0	76.0	63.3	45.7	34.2	256.1
Output per person engaged	139.1	126.8	102.7	100.0	103.8	104.9	99.5	95.7	45.3
INDUSTRIAL GROUPS									
Iron and steel:									
Physical volume of production	131.5	131.2	56.6	100.0	71.1	75.3	51.8	43.2	204.4
Number of persons engaged	95.6	102.1	65.5	100.0	68.2	58.3	46.3	38.9	145.8
Primary horse power	114.1	110.3	.....	100.0	71.1	59.1	43.0	28.0	307.5
Output per person engaged	137.6	128.5	86.4	100.0	104.3	129.2	111.9	111.1	23.9
Nonferrous metals:									
Physical volume of production	129.8	125.7	66.5	100.0	64.9	60.6	44.5	31.4	313.4
Number of persons engaged	81.2	91.2	53.6	100.0	66.4	61.2	51.6	43.3	87.5
Primary horse power	114.0	117.5	.....	100.0	53.8	44.1	28.3	19.8	475.8
Output per person engaged	159.9	137.8	124.1	100.0	97.7	99.0	86.2	72.5	120.6
Chemicals and allied products:									
Physical volume of production	140.6	125.1	94.5	100.0	70.7	58.8	42.9	30.2	365.6
Number of persons engaged	91.8	95.7	77.6	100.0	70.3	60.5	49.5	42.3	117.0
Primary horse power	147.1	134.8	.....	100.0	72.6	49.6	35.0	21.9	571.7
Output per person engaged	153.2	130.7	121.8	100.0	100.6	97.2	86.7	71.4	114.6
Stone, clay, and glass products:									
Physical volume of production	179.1	155.6	93.3	100.0	113.5	104.3	78.9	67.3	166.1
Number of persons engaged	115.1	115.7	84.1	100.0	110.4	95.4	81.8	68.4	68.3
Primary horse power	151.5	124.7	.....	100.0	98.4	74.9	44.6	28.0	441.1
Output per person engaged	155.6	134.5	110.9	100.0	102.8	109.3	96.5	98.4	58.1
Lumber:									
Physical volume of production	113.6	110.1	79.9	100.0	110.6	137.3	104.0	106.4	6.8
Number of persons engaged	94.1	98.9	73.9	100.0	99.5	113.9	83.0	87.4	7.7
Primary horse power	86.9	81.9	.....	100.0	92.9	98.2	63.2	58.3	49.1
Output per person engaged	120.7	111.3	108.1	100.0	111.2	120.5	125.3	121.7	−0.8
Paper and printing:									
Physical volume of production	152.8	137.1	93.4	100.0	87.5	69.8	51.9	36.6	317.5
Number of persons engaged	108.8	106.5	92.4	100.0	76.5	65.2	56.1	42.4	156.6
Primary horse power	131.1	117.7	.....	100.0	87.6	70.5	59.1	41.2	218.2
Output per person engaged	140.4	128.7	101.1	100.0	114.4	107.1	92.5	86.3	62.7
Textiles:									
Physical volume of production	119.3	122.9	96.8	100.0	96.8	91.9	71.9	60.7	96.5
Number of persons engaged	104.5	111.1	95.0	100.0	89.3	85.2	71.7	63.9	63.5
Primary horse power	126.6	116.7	.....	100.0	83.7	70.0	53.9	43.6	190.4
Output per person engaged	114.2	110.6	101.9	100.0	108.4	107.9	100.3	95.0	20.2
Leather and its remanufactures:									
Physical volume of production	93.4	105.6	85.2	100.0	87.4	87.7	81.5	69.8	33.8
Number of persons engaged	90.6	99.8	81.8	100.0	85.7	84.7	70.1	65.4	38.5
Primary horse power	106.9	105.9	.....	100.0	80.5	69.1	51.2	40.8	162.0
Output per person engaged	103.1	105.8	104.2	100.0	102.0	103.5	116.3	106.7	−3.4
Food and kindred products:									
Physical volume of production	116.4	111.6	93.5	100.0	80.8	74.8	65.1	53.0	119.6
Number of persons engaged	81.3	83.5	76.1	100.0	71.1	62.7	53.8	49.2	65.2
Primary horse power	115.8	107.6	.....	100.0	81.5	70.4	60.7	49.1	135.8
Output per person engaged	143.2	133.7	122.9	100.0	113.6	119.3	121.0	107.7	33.0
Tobacco manufactures:									
Physical volume of production	124.4	109.8	95.3	100.0	76.4	66.6	57.8	46.3	168.7
Number of persons engaged	79.9	91.2	93.4	100.0	116.3	108.9	103.4	86.6	−7.7
Primary horse power	97.0	100.3	.....	100.0	80.5	65.7	56.7	51.4	88.7
Output per person engaged	155.7	120.4	102.0	100.0	65.7	61.2	55.9	53.5	191.0
Rubber products:									
Physical volume of production	158.8	130.8	80.0	100.0	32.3	21.0	.....	.....	......
Number of persons engaged	79.7	80.5	62.7	100.0	41.5	25.2	21.9	18.7	326.2
Primary horse power	152.8	140.9	.....	100.0	46.4	28.5	20.2	16.6	820.5
Output per person engaged	199.2	162.5	127.6	100.0	77.8	83.3	.....	.....	......
Vehicles for land transportation:									
Physical volume of production	238.3	199.5	76.8	100.0	36.0	15.6	8.2	4.4	5,315.9
Number of persons engaged	108.3	114.8	65.2	100.0	42.5	29.9	25.4	25.4	326.4
Primary horse power	182.5	148.9	.....	100.0	51.2	35.6	19.5	13.4	1,261.9
Output per person engaged	220.0	173.8	117.8	100.0	65.6	36.7	27.4	17.3	1,171.7
Ship building:									
Physical volume of production	7.0	7.9	30.7	100.0	7.3	7.2	10.0	9.0	−22.2
Number of persons engaged	13.5	16.5	27.8	100.0	11.8	10.9	13.2	11.9	13.4
Primary horse power	54.8	57.4	.....	100.0	20.8	15.9	14.1	11.2	389.3
Output per person engaged	51.9	47.9	110.4	100.0	61.9	66.1	75.8	75.6	−31.3

leather, chemicals, and stone, clay, and glass groups are more representative of their whole groups than the indexes for iron and steel, food products, lumber, and paper and printing.[34]

In Table 24 changes in the productivity of these groups of industries during various periods of time are shown. No comparisons are made with the years 1904, 1914, and 1921 because they were years of industrial recession in which production per worker was temporarily reduced. From the beginning of the century to 1925, the greatest advances came in the automobile, tobacco, smelting and refining, and chemical industries.

TABLE 24.—CHANGES IN PRODUCTIVITY OF MANUFACTURE, BY INDUSTRIAL GROUPS, FOR SELECTED CENSUS PERIODS, 1899–1925

(Per cent of increase or decrease (−))

	1899 to 1925	1923 to 1925	1909 to 1925	1919 to 1925	1909 to 1919	1899 to 1909
All industries	45.3	9.7	32.6	39.1	− 4.7	9.6
Iron and steel	23.9	7.1	6.5	37.6	−22.6	16.3
Nonferrous metals	120.6	16.0	61.5	59.9	1.0	36.6
Chemicals and allied products	114.6	17.2	57.6	53.2	2.9	36.1
Stone, clay, and glass products	58.1	15.7	42.4	55.6	− 8.5	11.1
Lumber	−0.8	8.4	0.2	20.7	−17.0	−1.0
Paper and printing	62.7	9.1	31.1	40.4	− 6.6	24.1
Textiles	20.2	3.3	5.8	14.2	− 7.3	13.6
Leather and its remanufactures	−3.4	−2.6	− 0.4	3.1	− 3.4	−3.0
Food and kindred products	33.0	7.1	20.0	43.2	−16.2	10.8
Tobacco manufactures	191.0	29.3	154.4	55.7	63.4	14.4
Rubber products	......	22.6	139.1	99.2	20.0	......
Vehicles for land transportation	1,171.7	26.6	499.5	120.0	172.5	112.1
Shipbuilding	−31.3	8.4	−21.5	−48.1	51.3	−12.6

If the changes from 1909 to 1925 and from 1923 to 1925 are examined, it is clear that rubber products should be included among the industries showing the most rapid rise in productivity. Out of these five industrial groups, then, three (automobiles, rubber products, and chemicals) are directly or indirectly associated with the automobile industry, since much of the growth of the chemical industry may be attributed to the development of the industry of petroleum refining. The striking increase in the tobacco group reflects the growth of cigarette production and the substitution in consumption of the machine-made cigarette for the hand-made cigar. The rise in the group of stone, clay, and glass products is, no doubt, associated with the great increase in building construction

---

[34] Representativeness is here tested by comparing the change, in census periods, in the number of wage earners employed in the industries included in the index with corresponding changes in the industries in the group not included in the index. This is not necessarily a conclusive test, particularly where increased elaboration of manufacture or improved technique has characterized the excluded industries, as, for instance, in the iron and steel group.

and consequently in the use of building materials. Thus, in the period from 1909 to 1919, both the total and per capita output of lumber and stone, glass, and clay products decreased because of Government restrictions on building during the war. But in the following years, 1919 to 1925, the per capita output of both increased.

The advance of nearly 40 per cent in productivity for all manufacturing from 1919 to 1925 was shared by all industries, except leather and shipbuilding. But the shipbuilding industry, which had grown to large proportions during the war, was, of course, violently reduced in size after the war. For the rest, the greatest growth was in those industries—nonferrous metals, chemicals, paper and printing, tobacco, rubber, and vehicles—which had been growing rapidly in all other periods. It is interesting to note that, in the period of general decline in per capita output from 1909 to 1919, productivity increased 63 per cent in tobacco manufactures, 20 per cent in rubber products, and 173 per cent in vehicles for land transportation. Again, from 1923 to 1925, when the per capita output for all manufactures advanced by 9.7 per cent, tobacco manufactures increased 29 per cent, rubber products 23, automobiles 27, and chemical and allied products 17 per cent.

The Period 1925 to 1927.—Until the statistics from the census of manufactures of 1927 are available, it would be unwise to place too much weight on the estimates of manufacturing production in those years and on the changes in per capita output by industry, recorded in Table 25. It appears from the figures in this table, which represent an approximation of the course of productivity after 1925, that the precipitate rate of advance, begun in 1922 and continued through 1925, has perceptibly slackened and in the latest two-year period was 4 per cent. This was due, in large measure, to the fact that total production declined toward the end of 1927 and was, for the whole of the year, only slightly greater than in 1925.

Most of the decrease in output occurred in automobiles, lumber, and iron and steel. The textile and leather industries were more active in 1927. The expansion in the production of cigarettes and of petroleum products continued. Employment declined in every group shown except shipbuilding, paper and printing, and petroleum refining. Output per worker rose for most of the groups, with the largest increases in the shipbuilding, tobacco, and petroleum industries. The altogether surprising drop of more than 12 per cent in per capita output in the automobile industry is unquestionably to be explained by the existence of an unusual condition in the industry. During most of the last half of 1927, the Ford plants were not producing automobiles. Although the number of employees was then reduced, many were retained in the manufacture of parts, which do not appear in the available records of production. The operations of many other automobile companies were also considerably curtailed in the last part of the year and the marked recession in the activity of this industry had its customary depressive effect on productivity.

TABLE 25.—PRODUCTION AND EMPLOYMENT, BY INDUSTRIAL GROUPS

(Percentage of increase or decrease (−) 1925 to 1927)

	Production	Employment	Output per wage earner
Total manufacturing....................	[a]0.8	[a]− 3.0	[a]4.0
Iron and steel—group.........................	[b]− 2.5	− 1.8	[b]− 0.7
Iron and steel industry.....................	− 2.5	− 5.1	2.6
Nonferrous metals............................	2.0	− 6.4	8.0
Petroleum refining...........................	18.2	0.6	17.4
Stone, clay, and glass.......................	− 0.4	− 3.6	3.3
Lumber—group.................................	[b]11.2	−10.4	[b]− 0.9
Lumber industry............................	−11.2	−12.1	0.9
Paper and printing...........................	7.1	2.9	4.0
Paper and pulp.............................	3.7	− 1.1	4.9
Textiles.....................................	[b]8.7	− 2.4	[b]11.5
Fabrics....................................	8.7	− 1.1	10.0
Products...................................	....	− 4.6	......
Leather......................................	6.8	− 4.4	11.7
Food...	− 1.5	− 1.8	0.3
Tobacco......................................	12.8	− 8.7	28.5
Automobile tires and tubes...................	4.5	− 4.9	10.0
Automobiles..................................	−19.6	− 7.9	−12.7
Shipbuilding.................................	70.4	13.1	50.5

[a] Without adjustment for bias shown in Table 23.
[b] Comprehensive group indexes of production not available.

The Nature of the Data.—It has already been noted that the raw statistical materials used in measuring productivity possess inherent limitations and peculiarities which merit further consideration. In general, the indexes of productivity appear to be considerably affected by temporary factors, particularly by cyclical swings in production. When total output in industry is relatively large, output per worker is usually also large. While this concurrence is partly the result of full-time operation and the free flow of work, it is in larger measure due to the failure to allow for changes in the number of working hours.[35] The unit of employment is the individual worker whose name appears on the pay roll, regardless of the amount or nature of the work he does. As a result of this method of measuring productivity, the index of output per person tends to fluctuate with the index of production. In long-time comparisons the effect of temporary influences relative to the total change that has occurred may be small, but in short periods the temporary effects are probably dominant. Considerable evidence of this

[35] Investigations have been made by the United States Bureau of Labor Statistics of changes in the productivity of labor in specific industries, with allowances for changes in working hours. See *Monthly Labor Review*, January, 1927, pp. 35–49.

peculiarity of the method can be found in the variations in productivity for many industries over periods of only several years. Wherever there are measures of production per man-hour, the increase in productivity is almost invariably greater than the increase in productivity measured by the rise in output per man-year. This is universally the case in the United States, since the number of working hours for all American manufacturing industry has had a great decline in the past quarter-century.

Inherent in the preceding measures of productivity are evidences of the changing structure of industry which, on the one hand, account for the increases in productivity in the past and, on the other, forecast like advances in the future. For those industries in which total output and output per worker have grown most rapidly in the past decades, such as motor vehicles, petroleum refining, rubber tires, cigarettes, cement, chemicals, electrical machinery, printing and publishing, butter, cheese, condensed milk, and manufactured ice, the actual value added to output for each worker by the processes of manufacture is greater than in those industries that have expanded more slowly. Expansion in output in these types of industries, therefore, requires a relatively smaller addition to the total number of workers than in the others. If, at the same time, the first group of industries, or others like them, become relatively more important in the total industry of the country, their influence on raising the productivity of all industry becomes correspondingly greater. This is, in substance, what has happened. Measured by value of product, the motor vehicles industry was the most important of all manufacturing industries in 1925; in 1919 it was third; and in 1909, twenty-second. In 1909 petroleum refining ranked twenty-fourth in the list of manufacturing industries; in 1919 it ranked seventh, and in 1925 fourth. Similar striking changes have taken place in the position of the rubber tire, electrical machinery and supply, canning and preserving, chemical, and cement industries.

The Causes of Changing Productivity.—Aside from factors such as have been just discussed, whose effects are clear and determining, there remain many circumstances that influence the course of total and per capita production. The prevailing systems of wage payment, the relations between management and employed, the state of the industrial arts, and the cost of investment funds are only a few of the many factors that deserve to be studied and weighed. But they are hard to disentangle and, when separated, to measure. Even such an apparently simple concept as the mechanization of industry does not yet lend itself to satisfactory statistical analysis. According to the census of manufactures, for example, the amount of primary horse power installed in factories showed a relatively smaller increase between 1919 and 1925 than in any previous census period, and the expansion from 1923 to 1925 was not unusual. The record of machinery production for the same periods, likewise, fails to show any noteworthy increase. In fact, decreases were common in some lines, although the manufacture of electrical machinery, apparatus, and supplies did increase. None of these figures, however, indicates changes in the degree of utilization of either machines or existing power equipment. With this as with other central economic problems, the supply of the available statistical materials must be progressively increased; but at the same time, the statistical analysis needs to be supplemented by detailed field examinations of the processes of industry.[36]

IV. EMPLOYMENT AND UNEMPLOYMENT

The extent of fluctuation in what are generally called employment and unemployment depends often on the definition of these terms. If employment be defined as the number of people attached to an industry, or the number seeking a livelihood in an industry, the movement in employment may vary markedly from the employment that registers changes in the number of people actually on the pay rolls of an industry. This latter figure, in turn, may, and often does, differ substantially from employment, expressed in terms of the number of man-hours worked by those on the pay roll. Comprehensive data for the comparison of three such series are not available, but it is known from the observation of samples that their range of fluctuation is unequal and that they move generally, but not necessarily always, in the same direction.

Obviously, each of these three series may be put to different uses. Attempts have been made to estimate unemployment from changes in the number on pay rolls. In the section on productivity, the average number employed each year was used in estimating per capita output. For more elaborate estimates of unemployment, it is sometimes the practice to compare the numbers attached to an industry with the numbers on pay rolls. Most frequently, however, monthly statistics of the numbers on pay rolls have been used as measures of the stability of employment, and monthly statistics of the total wages paid to those on pay rolls as measures of the stability of the purchasing power of wage earners. It is in this last sense that the statistics of employment and income are used in this section.[37]

Employment since 1919.[38]—Discussion of the monthly fluctuations of employment and pay roll must be confined to factory and railroad

[36] For an example of this type of inquiry, see forthcoming study by Harry Jerome on the mechanization of industry in the series of the National Bureau of Economic Research.

[37] For more comprehensive discussions of the employment data, see W. A. Berridge, "What the Present Statistics of Employment Show," in *Business Cycles and Unemployment*, 1923, Chap. IV; R. G. Hurlin and W. A. Berridge, *Employment Statistics for the United States*, Russell Sage Foundation, 1926.

[38] The material for this section on employment was prepared by W. A. Berridge, of the Metropolitan Life Insurance Co.

employees. In the other important branches of industry, mining and quarrying and building construction, in retail and wholesale trade, in the group of personal services, and in agriculture there are at present no adequate data for the study of employment and income. While this is a serious gap, the railroad and particularly the manufacturing data are important enough to be valuable in themselves.

The great instability in both the employment and income of factory workers from 1920 to 1922 is shown in Chart 3.[39] Income dropped from its high in March, 1920, to its low in January, 1922, by 42 per cent, while employment declined from a high in March, 1920 to a low in July, 1921, by 31 per cent, the variations in the two series being due, of course, to a

CHART 3.—FACTORY EMPLOYMENT AND PAY ROLLS

Base: 1923–1925 average = 100 per cent

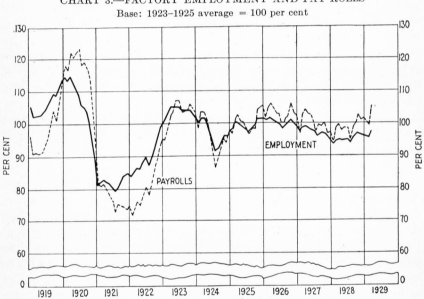

drop in wages during the period and to the further reduction in income from short time, not revealed in the employment index. Thereafter, both curves move within a much narrower range. Employment drops 14 per cent from the high in May and June, 1923, to the low in July, 1924; and again approximately 8 per cent from March, 1926 to January, 1928.

Comparisons of the prewar and postwar course of employment in manufacturing industries are impaired by changes in the character of the underlying data over a long period of time. The rough comparisons in Table 26, however, would appear to show no startling differences

[39] Both series charted here have been adjusted to all four censuses (1919, 1921, 1923, and 1925) by Woodlief Thomas. For individual industries, Mr. Thomas has thus far worked out such adjustments only through the Census of 1923.

between the normal stability of employment before the war and the condition after the collapse in 1920.[40]

TABLE 26.—COURSE OF EMPLOYMENT IN MANUFACTURING INDUSTRIES

Peak of boom	Bottom of depression	Approximate decline of employment
		Per cent
Middle of 1903	Middle of 1904	5
Middle of 1907	First quarter, 1908	15
Early 1910	Middle of 1911	5
Early 1913	Late 1914 and early 1915	10
Third quarter, 1918	Second quarter, 1919	15
March, 1920	July, 1921	30
May and June, 1923	July, 1924	13
March, 1926	January, 1928	8

Measures of labor turnover[41] in manufacturing industries, available for the period since 1919 but not before the war, confirm the impression of stability shown by the indexes of employment and income. Since 1921, and particularly since 1923, both the accession or hiring rates and the lay-off rates, corrected for differences in the length of the month, have fluctuated much less violently than in the first part of the postwar period. In the 1919–20 boom, accession rates rose in some months as high as 220 per cent; while the average[42] lay-off rate was at or near zero. In the following severe depression, accessions fell to about 15 per cent, and lay-offs rose to a peak of 50 per cent.

In the strong revival of industry in 1922–23, accession rates rose, but this time only to about 155 per cent, lay-offs falling meanwhile to about 1 per cent. The depression of 1924, and the ups and downs since then, have at no time forced accession rates below 25 or above 85 per cent; lay-off rates in these five years have been confined within the range of 3 to 12 per cent.

Monthly statistics of railroad employment and wages paid were not available until July, 1921. The great decline in employment and pay rolls of manufacturing industries between 1920 and 1922 was matched in the experience of the railroads. During the busiest quarter of 1920, the monthly income of railroad workers was $350,000,000. This fell to the rate of $190,000,000 per month in the early part of 1922. Since

[40] See Berridge, *op. cit.*, p. 59.

[41] Published by the Policyholders' Service Bureau of the Metropolitan Life Insurance Co. The canvass is not limited to group policyholders. Although the figures cover no more than 10 per cent of the factory workers of the country, they are obtained from a wide variety of factory industries and are regarded as a sound sample. For a description of the measures, see W. A. Berridge, "A New Set of Labor Turnover Indexes," *Personnel Journal*, Vol. VI, No. 1, June, 1927.

[42] The form of average used in constructing these indexes is the median.

CHART 4.—HIRING AND LAY-OFF RATES, 1919–1928

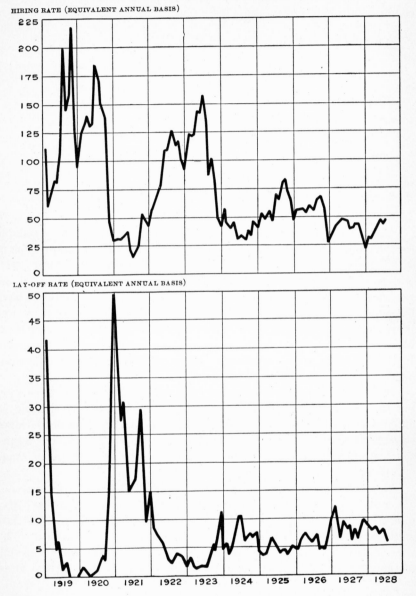

HIRING RATE (EQUIVALENT ANNUAL BASIS)

LAY-OFF RATE (EQUIVALENT ANNUAL BASIS)

early 1922, these money incomes have fluctuated within the range from $220,000,000 to $270,000,000 per month, being for three-fourths of this last period within a range one-half as great.

An interesting measure of the stability of employment is one derived from statistics published monthly[43] since 1920 by the National Industrial

[43] For the last seven months of 1920 and for the last six months of 1922.

Conference Board. This presents for more than twenty representative manufacturing industries the average per capita full-time hours per week and the average per capita hours actually worked. Comparison between these two figures should yield a useful measure of what may be described as unemployment within employment. Such measures were computed by taking the percentages that the number of hours lost are of the nominal hours per week. Where these percentages are positive, the actual work-week fell short of the nominal; where negative, the actual work-week exceeded the nominal, probably due to overtime. The average percentages for all of the manufacturing industries included in these computations are, of course, always positive, but individual industries occasionally show a negative percentage. The averages for all industries and for those showing the best and worst employment are given in Table 27.

TABLE 27.—PER CENT HOURS LOST ARE OF NOMINAL HOURS PER WEEK

Year	Best industry	Worst industry	Average all industries
1920	−0.8 (paper and pulp).	12.9 (woolens and silk).	5.7
1921	2.7 (meat packing).	18.4 (agricultural implements).	10.4
1922	−2.5 (chemicals).	16.6 (fertilizers).	3.6
1923	−2.1 (chemicals).	11.0 (fertilizers).	3.3
1924	−1.6 (meat packing).	15.6 (cotton, North).	6.6
1925	−2.9 (chemicals).	11.6 (hosiery and knit goods).	4.8
1926	−5.0 (paper and pulp).	11.6 (hosiery and knit goods).	5.2
1927	−3.6 (paper and pulp).	9.6 (hosiery and knit goods).	5.1

The averages for all industries unquestionably give the impression of greater stability than was to have been expected, and confirm in a measure the findings of an earlier investigation by W. I. King, covering the period from 1920 to 1922.[44] In both 1920 and 1922, however, the averages for the year might have been modified if the statistics for all 12 months had been available.

Unemployment.[45]—Estimates of the volume of unemployment will vary, as we have often seen in this country, with the method of measurement used and with the definition of unemployment.[46]

[44] "Changes in Employment in the Principal Industrial Fields," in *Business Cycles and Unemployment*, 1923, p. 95.

[45] All of the material in this section was prepared by Meredith B. Givens, of the Social Science Research Council, and of the National Bureau of Economic Research, formerly of the United States Bureau of Labor Statistics.

[46] For this reason, some general machinery for registering the unemployed is likely to yield the most satisfactory statistics of unemployment; first, because such an agency of registration can make use of a definition of unemployment that is simple and universally understood, and second, because registration, if compulsory, catches the great bulk of the unemployed. These are, indeed, the characteristics of the

In the United States, where there is virtually no adequate, continuous registration of the unemployed, measures of unemployment have been derived in one way or another from the statistics of employment. Where this procedure has been used, it may be said to measure not unemployment, but the shrinkage in employment. Under limited ideal conditions, the two may amount to the same thing, but under the conditions of measurement prevailing in this country, as will be seen later, they are usually not the same thing; they may, indeed, be very far apart. The possible divergencies can be best seen by examining recent estimates of the volume of unemployment in the United States for either the year 1927 or for early 1928.

An estimate by the United States Bureau of Labor Statistics places the numbers laid off the pay roll by early 1928 at 1,874,500.[47] This number is described as "a shrinkage between the average of 1925 and January, 1928." It was assumed in making this estimate that there was no "noticeable unemployment question" in 1925. The estimated shrinkage, moreover, was derived from the known reduction in railroad employment, taken from the reports of the Interstate Commerce Commission and from the drop in manufacturing employment reflected in the monthly employment statistics compiled by the Bureau.

TABLE 28.—UNEMPLOYMENT ESTIMATED BY LABOR BUREAU, INC.

		Plus	Minus
Estimated number unemployed in 1923		1,000,000	
Estimated increase in supply of employable persons through population growth		3,000,000	
Estimated number of farm workers moved to town		1,000,000	
Estimated possible increases of employment in certain lines		....	2,100,000
Professions	200,000		
Amusements	100,000		
Public utilities	200,000		
Automobile sales and service	750,000		
Other distribution	500,000		
Building	300,000		
Miscellaneous	100,000		
Estimated declines in employment		1,200,000	
Manufactures	1,000,000		
Railways	100,000		
Coal mining	100,000		
Net unemployment, 1927		4,000,000	

statistics of unemployment wherever there is an inclusive machinery of registration, either as a part of the system of unemployment insurance or in the form of a comprehensive chain of public employment bureaus. Even such estimates of unemployment may be defective in not indicating the volume of short time or in omitting important occupations whose employment experience is not recorded, but in spite of their shortcomings they are generally superior to measures of unemployment that rest on no registration basis whatsoever.

[47] United States Sen. Doc., No. 77, 70th Cong., 1st sess., pp. 3, 5.

A second estimate, by the Labor Bureau, Inc., rests not only on shrinkage in employment but involves measures of increases in employment in expanding industries and in the total number of persons available for work. The various steps in this estimate are shown in Table 28.

The Brookmire Economic Service, following a still different method, has estimated the number unemployed each year from 1910 to 1928. These estimates are shown in Table 29. They represent the difference in each year between actual employment and probable maximum employment. Five years during this period, 1912, 1917, 1920, 1923, and 1926, have been regarded as years of exceptionally high business activity and, therefore, of full employment. In such years, there is assumed to be no unemployment.

TABLE 29.— UNEMPLOYMENT SHOWN AS THE DIFFERENCE BETWEEN PROBABLE MAXIMUM EMPLOYMENT AND ACTUAL EMPLOYMENT

(In thousands)

Year	United States population	Full employment[a]		Actual[b] employment	Un-employed[c]
		Per cent	Number		
1910[d]	92,267	41.5	38,167	38,167	.....
1911	93,628	41.5	38,856	38,360	496
1912[d]	95,097	41.5	39,445	39,445	.....
1913	96,512	41.6	40,149	39,882	267
1914	97,928	41.7	40,875	38,848	2,027
1915	99,343	41.9	41,585	40,106	1,479
1916	100,758	42.0	42,318	42,206	112
1917[d]	102,173	42.1	43,016	43,016	.....
1918	103,588	41.5	42,989	42,931	58
1919	105,003	40.8	42,841	42,766	75
1920[d]	106,422	40.2	42,809	42,809	.....
1921	108,445	39.8	43,161	39,508	3,653
1922	109,893	39.3	43,189	40,622	2,567
1923[d]	111,693	38.8	43,284	43,284	.....
1924	113,727	38.0	43,216	41,826	1,390
1925	115,378	37.1	42,805	42,418	387
1926[d]	117,136	36.2	42,433	42,433	.....
1927	118,628	36.2	42,943	41,477	1,466
1928 (March)	120,013	36.2	43,445	40,813	2,632

[a] The percentage of total population employed was computed for the years of full employment, and percentages for intervening years interpolated on a straight line and used in computing full employment for those years.

[b] Actual employment, for each year, was computed by the Brookmire staff from official data taken from the following sources: Census; Department of Agriculture; Department of Labor; Interstate Commerce Commission; Bureau of Mines; and the Federal Reserve Board; also National Industrial Conference Board, Russell Sage Foundation, New York Times Annalist, and Paul Douglas in the *American Economic Review*.

[c] Unemployment, as shown, is the difference between probable maximum employment and actual employment. It does not allow for numbers idle, even during years of exceptionally high business activity.

[d] Assumed to be years of full employment owing to the high level of business as shown by the Brookmire Business Index.

Lewis Corey,[48] finally, estimates total unemployment in 1927 at 3,500,000. His estimates rest on the assumption that a surplus of industrial workers was created during the period from 1919 to 1926 as the result of technological improvements in industry.[49] The size of this surplus is determined by the estimates of the number of gainfully occupied persons reported by the National Bureau of Economic Research, by the reduction in farm employment, and by the decline in the average number of persons employed in manufacturing, mining, and transportation, as shown by the current indexes. The depression of 1927 is estimated to be responsible for a further reduction in employment of 1,000,000 persons. To the aggregate so obtained are further added an estimated permanent labor reserve of 750,000.

No check of the underlying data in the elaborate estimates of Corey, the Labor Bureau, and the Brookmire Service is possible because the details of the methods and assumptions used are not available. In the first two of these estimates it is clear that much of the basic material is in the form of round numbers and that more refined methods might materially modify the totals. They both also neglect or underestimate the extent of diversion of employment and such an item as the increase in school attendance. The Brookmire assumption that there are years of no unemployment is one rarely held. Finally, the method employed by the United States Bureau of Labor Statistics is too obviously limited to constitute an acceptable measure of unemployment.

A New Estimate of Unemployment.—This latest estimate is based on the definition of the volume of unemployment as the difference between the number of persons actually employed and the number desiring and habitually dependent upon employment. In making· this measure, accordingly, the average number of persons actually employed annually in the United States has been determined by aggregating the number so employed in the various occupational and industrial groups composing the total. This average annual employment has been compared to the estimated total number of persons dependent upon employment, or "attached" to industry; and the difference between the two sets of figures has been defined as the estimated average annual unemployment. Such estimates were made for each year, beginning in 1920 and ending in 1927.

The resultant measures of the volume of unemployment are probably minimum estimates. Actual unemployment during any year has doubtless exceeded the figure shown. The material on which this and other estimates of unemployment rest is not all of the same quality and a large

[48] Lewis Corey, "An Estimate of Unemployment: Cyclical Idleness Added to Technological," *The Annalist*, March 9, 1928.

[49] See Technological Unemployment, Chap. II, Industry, Part 1, p. 92; Chap. V, Marketing, p. 328; Chap. VII, Management, p. 514.

amount of inference and estimate is unavoidable. Only additional information to be collected in the future, such as a comprehensive census of distribution, can uncover the errors hidden in the material now available. With the information we now have, the present estimates may be held to throw light on the direction and structure of total employment and unemployment since the war, and no more. They could hardly serve as the actuarial basis for the fixing of unemployment insurance premiums.

The basic figures of the numbers gainfully employed in agriculture, industry, trade, service, and the professions, and in their major subdivisions are taken from the elaborate estimates made by W. I. King in connection with the inquiries of the National Bureau of Economic Research into the national income. Substantially, King's estimates of the numbers attached to industry are made by discovering in each year the highest month of employment and by inflating this figure by an arbitrary percentage to allow for illness and other known factors.

In the present study, those forces that are believed to have affected the structure of the working population of the country since 1920 have been examined, and King's estimates have been slightly revised in several particulars to allow for certain changes. The total school population of the country has, for example, increased by 4,000,000 from 1919 to 1926, exclusive of kindergarten enrollment. One-fifth of the total population were in school in 1919. Assuming the percentage in school to have remained constant, the King estimates have allowed for a normal increase of 2,500,000 in school enrollment during this period as a result of an increase of 12,000,000 in the total population of the United States. This leaves 1,500,000 to be accounted for as growth owing to greater popularity of schooling. This figure, which represents pupils of all ages from primary age through the colleges, has been prorated to determine what fraction of the increase not accounted for by King's estimates is composed of full-time students of 16 years of age and over. It is thus discovered that about 500,000 students have been withdrawn from the ranks of the employed, beyond the number accounted for in the normal growth of population and school enrollment according to the trends during the preceding decade.

The King estimates were made on the assumption that the increased school enrollment was offset by the increased employment of women. This was true during the years 1909 to 1919, but what evidence there is for the more recent period indicates that the proportion of women among the gainfully occupied has remained about constant. Statistics on the matter are available only for limited samples. In Ohio, the proportion of women gainfully occupied has increased by 2 per cent from 1919 to 1926. Conditions in Ohio should be representative of conditions in the country, since Ohio is a large agricultural and also a highly diversified industrial state. Scattered data for Iowa and Illinois fail to reveal any trend, and while women have strengthened their position as a permanent factor in the industrial and commercial life of the country, it appears that they have not increased in relative numerical importance in gainful pursuits during the postwar period. While definite evidence must be delayed until the census of 1930, the King estimates have been here modified for increased school enrollment on the assumption that the proportion of women gainfully occupied has not canceled the effect of more popular education.

There are no data with which to test the general impression that the average age of industrial employees has been declining during the past decade. A small sample, covering some 14,000 employees carrying group insurance with a large insurance company, appears to show that the average age is slightly higher in 1925–1927 than in 1917–1920. In the absence of accurate data, this factor is not considered in the estimates.

Since 1920 the cumulative loss in farm population has been more than 3,000,000 persons. Of this number, certainly a large part should be added to the available supply of nonagricultural labor, since many farmers, migrating to the cities, are in search of jobs in industry and trade. It has been here estimated that at least as large a proportion of those leaving the farm will be gainfully occupied as among those remaining.[50] While this procedure probably leads to an underestimate of the farm population absorbed in urban employment, the discrepancy is not likely to be large. King's estimates of gainfully occupied agricultural population, while showing an appreciable shrinkage, do not drop so rapidly as the farm population, as estimated by the Bureau of Agricultural Economics. A correction has therefore been made in King's estimates to allow for migration from farm to city of those desiring nonagricultural employment. This correction and the allowance for increased school enrollment partially offset each other.

The most interesting and probably one of the most important changes in employment since the war has been the expansion in nonindustrial employment. This trend is examined with reference to the fields of public and mercantile employment and in a category of miscellaneous occupations. The total number of public employees is much less in 1927 than in 1919, but slightly greater than in 1920. Federal civil service employees were in 1927 more than 100,000 fewer than in 1920, but in the same period the number of state and municipal employees increased by more than 200,000, owing largely to the increase in the number of teachers. Mercantile employment, as shown in Table

[50] Bureau of Agricultural Economics, *Bulletin*, "The Agricultural Situation," Vol. XII, No. 4, pp. 22–24, April 1, 1928, Washington, D. C.

30,[51] was roughly 1,500,000 greater in 1927 than in 1920. Very little information on the growth of employment in particular lines of mercantile enterprise is available and the figures in the table are the best, and sometimes the only, estimates that could be had.

TABLE 30.—MERCANTILE EMPLOYMENT

(In thousands)

	1920	1921	1922	1923	1924	1925	1926	1927
Attached to mercantile pursuits, total employees (King)	3,215	3,298	3,694	4,237	4,015	4,297	4,412	4,623
Employees in specified groups (included above):								
Two large mail order houses	24	.....	.....	.....	.....	.....	.....	32
Tire dealers and salesmen[a]	.....	.....	.....	.....	.....	95	95	95
Auto dealers and salesmen[a]	.....	.....	.....	181	181	196	225	363
Automobile supplies, parts, etc.[a]	.....	.....	.....	135	135	140	135	160
Oil heating[b]	c	.....	.....	.....	.....	.....	.....	10
Radio[b]	c	.....	.....	.....	.....	.....	.....	40
Electric refrigeration[b]	c	.....	.....	.....	.....	.....	.....	20

[a] Estimate taken from *Facts and Figures of the Automobile Industry*, National Automobile Chamber of Commerce.

[b] Estimates for radio distribution obtained from Department of Commerce.

[c] Negligible.

The group of miscellaneous occupations likewise shows a great increase over the period under discussion. The details are shown in Table 31. The estimates for artists, authors, and musicians are probably a gross understatement. They were made on the assumption that these groups increased at least as rapidly as the number of teachers and professors. The increase in the number of insurance agents, estimated from reports of insurance companies, represents the only approximation of employment in the financial group aside from banking. There is no method available for estimating the numbers employed in real estate, home insurance offices, brokerage, mortgage, loan, and specialty financing companies, although it is a commonplace of everyday experience that many more persons are so engaged than before the war. The large growth of the medical and allied professions has come not through a material increase in the number of physicians and surgeons, but through the great growth in the number of nurses, hospital attendants and those associated with public health activities.[52]

King's statistics of the gainfully occupied population of the country, with the modifications referred to above embodied in them, are shown in Table 32. The industrial groups of mining and quarrying, transportation, construction, and manufacturing are separated from the groups of public and mercantile employees and miscellaneous occupations, since

[51] The increment of gainfully employed from farms has been arbitrarily divided equally between the mercantile and miscellaneous groups.

[52] See Chap. I, Consumption, pp. 17–22.

TABLE 31.—MISCELLANEOUS OCCUPATIONAL GROUPS

(In thousands)

	1920	1921	1922	1923	1924	1925	1926	1927
Attached to miscellaneous groups,[a] total..........	5,876	6,028	6,851	6,682	8,030	8,316	8,310	8,338
Employees in specified groups (included above):								
Professional and allied groups[b]—								
Medical and allied professions...........	795	815	995	1,160	1,200	1,235	1,240	1,300
Lawyers and judges....................	125	128	131	134	136	139	142	145
Clergymen[c]...........................	195	199	214	220	218	216	[d]216	[d]215
Religious, charitable, penal workers[d].....	53	....	....	....	....	....	....	55
Librarians and assistants[d]...............	18	....	....	....	....	....	....	22
Artists, authors, musicians[d].............	210	....	....	....	....	....	....	250
Financial groups—								
Banking.............................	232	246	252	265	271	277	287	291
Insurance agents[e].....................	120	....	....	....	....	....	....	216
Miscellaneous—								
Hotels, restaurants, etc.[f]................	1,500	....	....	....	....	....	....	2,025
Barbers, hairdressers, manicurists[f].......	216	....	....	....	....	....	....	385
Moving pictures[f]......................	200	....	....	....	....	....	....	350
Amusements, lodges[g]..................	85	....	....	....	....	....	....	135
Garage employees[h]....................	....	....	....	110	110	115	125	125
Automobile, repair shops[h]...............	....	....	....	....	....	480	450	300
Dyers and cleaners[i]....................	18	....	....	....	....	....	....	33

[a] These figures are not adjusted for the slight revisions of King's estimates made in this study. Entrepreneurs as well as employees are included.

[b] Teachers should logically be included here, but they cannot conveniently be separated from the public employees group.

[c] Figures published in *Yearbook of the Churches.* Estimates are doubtless too high, including ministers otherwise gainfully employed, and otherwise classified in the *United States Census of Occupations.*

[d] Groups taken according to *United States Census of Occupations,* 1920, and increased slightly over the period.

[e] Increase since *Census of Occupations,* estimated by Lawrence B. Mann, Department of Commerce.

[f] Estimated by Lawrence B. Mann, Department of Commerce.

[g] Number shown in *United States Census of Occupations,* 1920, increased to correspond with moving pictures.

[h] Rough estimates given in *Facts and Figures of the Automobile Industry,* N. A. C. C., New York (published annually).

[i] Estimated by Lawrence B. Mann, Department of Commerce.

it is in the former that the problem of unemployment is generally regarded as significant. There is, moreover, no method for estimating the volume of unemployment among public employees, those of mercantile establishments, and those engaged in professional or personal service. The estimates of the number unemployed in these categories are, therefore, largely arbitrary minimum estimates, and are regarded as underestimating the actual volume of unemployment.

Estimates of the numbers attached to industry and the average numbers employed or unemployed for each of the four industrial groups are shown in Tables 33, 34, 35, and 36. For each group there is a considerable mass of statistical material which cannot be described in detail here. It should be noted, in connection with Table 33, that the employment figures for metal mining and quarrying represent the total number

TABLE 32.—CLASSIFICATION OF GAINFULLY OCCUPIED PERSONS IN THE UNITED STATES[a]

(In thousands)

	1920	1921	1922	1923	1924	1925	1926	1927
Total population	106,422	108,370	109,742	111,478	113,466	115,004	116,442	117,980
Cumulative increase in school attendance, pupils sixteen years of age and older		390	629	843	1,028	1,185	1,342	1,430
Total gainfully occupied	40,008	40,429	40,701	41,313	42,095	42,659	43,218	43,943
Cumulative increase in nonagricultural gainfully occupied, resulting from migration from farms		112	224	336	486	608	802	861
Total nonagricultural gainfully occupied	31,137	31,681	32,382	33,024	33,909	34,621	36,491	36,372
Total employees attached to nonagricultural pursuits (entrepreneurs omitted)	27,558	27,989	28,505	29,293	30,234	30,941	31,808	32,695
Public employees	2,719	2,689	2,618	2,633	2,674	2,736	2,785	2,819
Mercantile employees	3,215	3,298	3,694	4,237	4,015	4,297	4,412	4,623
Miscellaneous groups[b]	4,057	4,931	4,576	4,488	5,852	6,043	6,318	6,603
Employees attached to major industrial groups	17,567	17,071	17,617	17,935	17,693	17,865	18,293	18,650
Mines, quarries, oil wells	1,217	1,234	1,250	1,254	1,196	1,182	1,278	1,285
Transportation and communication[c]	4,235	4,151	4,431	4,691	4,658	4,582	4,744	5,204
Construction (excluding highways)	932	932	1,199	1,277	1,352	1,613	1,594	1,563
Manufacturing	11,183	10,754	10,737	10,713	10,487	10,488	10,677	10,598

[a] This table represents a slight revision and an array of the King estimates of the number of persons gainfully occupied and attached to various industrial and occupational groups.

[b] Including banking and other financial employments, the professions, etc.

[c] Bus, truck, and taxi transportation have been added to the original King estimates, and deducted from items for miscellaneous groups.

TABLE 33.—EMPLOYEES—MINES, QUARRIES, OIL WELLS

	1920	1921	1922	1923	1924	1925	1926	1927
Attached to the industries (King):								
Salaried	75,000	74,000	75,000	65,000	68,000	70,000	70,000	70,000
Wage earners	1,142,000	1,160,000	1,175,000	1,189,000	1,128,000	1,112,000	1,208,000	1,215,000
Total	1,217,000	1,234,000	1,250,000	1,254,000	1,196,000	1,182,000	1,278,000	1,285,000
Employed:								
Coal mines[a]	590,000	465,000	400,000	550,000	490,000	470,000	547,000	495,000
Metal mines[b]	137,000	94,000	106,000	123,000	123,000	127,000	128,000	120,000
Quarries[b]	86,000	77,000	79,000	92,000	94,000	92,000	91,000	92,000
Oil and gas	130,000							
Unemployed	274,000	470,000	520,000	329,000	326,000	308,000	323,000	380,000
Average number days worked by mines:								
Bituminous	220	149	142	179	171	195	215	191
Anthracite	271	271	151	268	274	182	244	225
Production: Coal (thousands of net tons)—								
Bituminous	569,000	416,000	422,000	565,000	484,000	520,000	573,000	518,000
Anthracite	90,000	90,000	55,000	93,000	88,000	62,000	84,000	80,000
Petroleum (thousands of barrels)	443,000	472,000	558,000	732,000	714,000	764,000	767,000	901,000
Natural gas (thousands of cubic feet)	798,000	662,000	762,000	1,007,000	1,142,000	1,189,000	1,313,000	1,445,000
Indexes of production:[c]								
Bituminous[d]	109	79	78	108	92	100	110	98
Anthracite[d]	110	112	65	115	108	77	105	100
Petroleum[d]	61	64	75	100	97	103	104	122
Natural gas	72	60	69	91	103	107	118	130

[a] Averages of estimated monthly employment based upon available production and employment statistics for both bituminous and anthracite mines.

[b] Figures compiled from reports of the United States Bureau of Mines.

[c] 1923–1925 base.

[d] Federal Reserve Board.

of workers employed at any time during the year rather than the average monthly employment, as, for example, in the case of manufacturing industries. Therefore the employment totals for these groups are somewhat too high. The figures for coal mining represent the best approximation of the average number of men actually at work daily. This means that men employed at a given mine are regarded as out of work whenever the mine is not operating.[53]

TABLE 34.—TRANSPORTATION AND COMMUNICATION—NUMBER OF EMPLOYEES ATTACHED TO THE INDUSTRIES[a]

(In thousands)

	1920	1921	1922	1923	1924	1925	1926	1927
Total employees attached to the industries[b]	4,235	4,149	4,431	4,691	4,658	4,582	4,744	5,204
Subdivision of the industries:								
Steam railroads, switching and terminal companies	2,163	2,122	2,097	2,080	2,041	1,891	1,903	1,856
Street railways	307	308	308	319	318	317	319	322
Pullman	23	23	21	22	25	26	27	28
Express companies	91	82	77	75	70	68	68	65
Water transportation	399	394	392	388	369	355	354	341
Bus and truck transportation[c]	750	700	1,000	1,220	1,220	1,275	1,400	1,900
Telephone	311	318	322	350	370	377	381	385
Telegraph	75	75	75	76	77	86	86	86
Electric light and power	116	127	139	161	168	187	206	221

[a] Based principally upon King's estimates.
[b] Including bus transportation.
[c] Estimates from *Bus Facts*, 1927 and 1928, Bus Division, American Automobile Association. Includes bus drivers and professional chauffeurs.

The results of the various steps in the process of estimating unemployment are shown in Table 37. These figures are limited to unemployment among the nonagricultural employed, since it is impossible to estimate the agricultural unemployed. As has been pointed out before, the figures of unemployment in the mercantile, public service, and miscel-

[53] In all cases, estimates of average employment and unemployment have been arrived at by the study of employment and unemployment data and, in many cases, of other series, such as indexes of production or of value of output. It is impossible to reproduce all of the relevant data involved in estimating the numbers occupied and unemployed in the industrial category of transportation and communication. A great variety of data is used for both estimates: for steam railroads, the reports of the Interstate Commerce Commission; for street railways, local reports on numbers employed; for the Pullman Co., the number of revenue passengers; for the telephone industry, the United States Census of Electrical Industries and figures from the American Telephone and Telegraph Co.; and so on. The percentages of unemployment used in computing the number of unemployed in the building trades were derived from comparisons of the value of building contracts and statistics of unemployment for Ohio and Massachusetts, and for the whole country from the reports of trade union unemployment as compiled by the American Federation of Labor, in relation, of course to the King estimates.

TABLE 35.—EMPLOYEES IN THE CONSTRUCTION INDUSTRY (EXCLUDING HIGHWAY CONSTRUCTION)

	1920	1921	1922	1923	1924	1925	1926	1927
Attached to the industry (King):								
Salaried	82,000	83,000	108,000	115,000	122,000	146,000	145,000	142,000
Wage earners	850,000	849,000	1,091,000	1,162,000	1,230,000	1,467,000	1,449,000	1,421,000
Total	932,000	932,000	1,199,000	1,277,000	1,352,000	1,613,000	1,594,000	1,563,000
Employed[a]	702,000	684,000	969,000	1,057,000	1,002,000	1,268,000	1,314,000	1,141,000
Unemployed[b]	230,000	248,000	230,000	220,000	350,000	345,000	280,000	422,000
Total value of building contracts awarded in the United States[c] (000 omitted)	$3,337,647	$3,068,983	$4,329,750	$4,768,100	$5,237,080	$6,662,000	$6,901,580	$6,786,580

[a] Estimates obtained by subtracting the estimated number of unemployed from the estimate of the number attached, except 1924–1926 inclusive, for which years the estimates were interpolated on the basis of fluctuations in total value of building contracts.

[b] Estimates obtained by applying the following estimated percentages of unemployment to the number attached: 1919, 25 per cent; 1920, 24.60 per cent; 1921, 26.7 per cent; 1922, 19.0 per cent; 1923, 17.2 per cent; 1927, 27.0 per cent. Figures for 1924–1926 inclusive were derived by subtracting estimated actual employment from the number attached.

[c] Figures furnished by the F. W. Dodge Corporation.

TABLE 36.—EMPLOYEES IN MANUFACTURING INDUSTRY[a]

(In thousands)

	1920	1921	1922	1923	1924	1925	1926	1927
Attached to manufacturing (King):								
Wage earners.............	9,735	9,330	9,334	9,328	9,112	9,118	9,290	9,100
Salaried.................	1,448	1,424	1,403	1,385	1,375	1,370	1,387	1,498
Total..................	11,183	10,754	10,737	10,713	10,487	10,488	10,677	10,598
Employed:[b]								
Wage earners.............	[c]9,207	7,042	[c]7,744	8,909	[c]8,266	8,544	[c]8,729	[c]8,510
Salaried.................	[d]1,489	1,158	[d]1,232	1,372	[d]1,297	1,366	[d]1,396	[d]1,361
Total..................	[d]10,696	8,200	[d]8,976	10,281	[d]9,563	9,910	[d]10,125	[d]9,871
Unemployed.................	487	2,554	1,761	432	924	578	552	727

[a] Including grist mills, custom saw mills, and power laundries.
[b] Based upon United States Census of Manufactures.
[c] Estimates and extrapolations based upon computations by Woodlief Thomas.
[d] Number of salaried persons estimated on basis of percentage of salaried in total employment for adjacent years.

laneous groups are the least reliable of all and are probably much too low. All of the estimates are approximate measures of the average annual minimum volume of unemployment and are more adequate as indicators of the trend of unemployment than as measures of the actual number unemployed in any year.

By these estimates it appears that unemployment in 1927 was less than half that of 1921 and considerably below 1922. The depression of 1927, measured by the volume of unemployment, appears to have been not so severe as the recession in 1924. Throughout the whole period it is surprising to find a persistent and large volume of unemployment even in the very active years, 1920, 1923, and 1926.

TABLE 37.—ESTIMATED AVERAGE MINIMUM VOLUME OF UNEMPLOYMENT, 1920–1927

(In thousands)

	1920	1921	1922	1923	1924	1925	1926	1927
Total employees attached to nonagricultural pursuits....................	27,558	27,989	28,505	29,293	30,234	30,941	31,808	32,695
Minimum number of unemployed:								
Manufacturing...................	487	2,554	1,761	432	924	578	552	727
Construction.....................	230	248	230	220	350	345	280	422
Transportation and communication..	170	598	580	251	340	184	144	152
Mines, quarries, oil wells...........	274	470	520	329	326	308	323	380
Public service, mercantile, miscellaneous........................	240	400	350	300	375	360	370	374
Minimum total unemployed.............	1,401	4,270	3,441	1,532	2,315	1,775	1,669	2,055

V. ORGANIZED LABOR

The historical development of trade unionism in the United States follows in its essentials much the same course as that pursued by foreign labor movements. Beginning with small spontaneous uprisings and becoming gradually a systematic movement for the spread of organization, labor unions here, as elsewhere, have grown with the rise of modern industry. They have made use of the weapons of the strike, picketing, and boycott, either in defense against attack or in carrying organization into unorganized areas, and have thus slowly and over a long period added to their numbers and influence. From 1900 to 1910, American labor unions gained nearly 1,200,000 members and, from 1910 to 1915, a half million more. Immediately before the war their total membership was two and three-quarters millions.

This moderate trend upward, which has persisted with only slight occasional recessions since 1897, became greatly accelerated during the war. American unions, in common with labor organizations all over the world, responded promptly to the economic and political forces associated with the World War and rose to new heights. By 1920 union membership was nearly double that of 1914 and stood at 5,100,000. The gains of the period, moreover, were scattered over a wide industrial area. Not only did the old, strong organizations grow, but unions were established where there had before been little or no organization at all. Effective trade unions sprang up among the shopcraft and maintenance-of-way employees on the railroads; in the manufacturing industries unorganized strongholds like the textile, metal and machinery, leather, food, and men's clothing industries were all unionized; and organization took root among many clerical and semiprofessional occupations in both public service and private business.

Labor organization proved to be as sensitive to the business depression and unemployment of the period following the middle of 1920 as it had just been to prosperity and a favorable labor market. By 1924 the American labor movement had lost nearly 1,500,000 members. The bulk of these losses was precisely in those occupations and industries in which the growth during the war had been greatest. Of a total drop in membership from 1920 to 1923 of 1,330,000, the transportation and metal unions together lost 800,000 members.[54]

With the turn in the business situation in 1922, followed by years of considerable business activity and prosperity, the labor movement was commonly expected to retrieve its early postwar losses. This expectation was not realized. Although the statistics of membership show a

[54] For a detailed discussion of the movement of trade union membership in the United States, see Leo Wolman, *The Growth of American Trade Unions, 1880–1923*, National Bureau of Economic Research, 1924.

TABLE 38.—MEMBERSHIP OF AMERICAN TRADE UNIONS[a]

Year	Membership	Year	Membership	Year	Membership
1897	447,000	1908	2,130,600	1918	3,508,400
1898	500,700	1909	2,047,400	1919	4,169,100
1899	611,000	1910	2,184,200	1920	5,110,800
1900	868,500	1911	2,382,800	1921	4,815,000
1901	1,124,700	1912	2,483,500	1922	4,059,400
1902	1,375,900	1913	2,753,400	1923	3,747,200
1903	1,913,900	1914	2,716,900	1924	3,746,600
1904	2,072,700	1915	2,607,700	1925	3,817,900
1905	2,022,300	1916	2,808,000	1926	3,900,500
1906	1,958,700	1917	3,104,600	1927	3,903,800
1907	2,122,800				

[a] The figures since 1923 were collected by Ruth Budinoff, of the Labor Bureau, Inc.

rise of about 150,000 from the low point in 1924, a considerable portion of the increase may be attributed to overstatement by many of the smaller unions and in particular by the large United Mine Workers. This organization reports its membership in 1927 as 400,000, or about 64,000 in excess of its membership in 1920. It is common knowledge that the United Mine Workers have lost heavily since 1920, not only in the non-union areas of Kentucky and West Virginia, but in the union fields of Pennsylvania, Ohio, and Indiana, as well. It would do no violence to the facts, therefore, to consider the present membership of the United Mine Workers as closer to 300,000 than to 400,000. When these factors are taken into consideration, it is clear that the downward movement which began late in 1920 has not yet been effectively stopped.

As matters stand now, the movement has about 1,000,000 more members than it had in 1913. Very little of this increase, however, represents the war growth in manufacturing industries, where, in fact, trade union membership is probably less now than it was before the war. As Table 39 shows, the net increase of 1,000,000 is made up almost

TABLE 39.—INCREASE IN MEMBERSHIP OF TRADE UNIONS

Industry	Membership		Gain
	1913	1927	
Building trades	553,000	1,014,000	461,000
Clothing	164,000	283,000	119,000
Theaters and music	82,000	171,000	89,000
Transportation	557,000	950,000	393,000
Paper, printing, and bookbinding	107,000	161,000	54,000
Total	1,463,000	2,579,000	1,116,000

exclusively of gains in the nonmanufacturing industries. Only in the printing and clothing industries, in the manufacturing group, is there a steady growth over 1913. The rest of the unions in the manufacturing industries either show slight increases, like 6,000 in the textile industry and 14,000 in metals, machinery, and shipbuilding, or actual decreases, like 6,000 in leather, 57,000 in food, liquor, and tobacco, and 15,000 in the chemical, clay, glass, and stone industries. Meanwhile, the great basic manufacturing industries of the country, iron and steel, metals and machinery, food, automobiles, and textiles, are less organized now than they were before or during the war.

In the absence of a new Census of Occupations, little would be gained by attempting to convert these figures of growth and decline into more precise estimates of the present strength of the American labor movement.[53] Allowing for some increase in the total working population of the country since 1920, it is probable that all American wage earners, excluding agricultural labor, were roughly one-fifth organized. In view of the marked increases in membership in the building trades and the transportation industry, organization in both has probably grown to nearly 50 per cent. In coal mining, on the other hand, the extent of organization has dropped from about 50 per cent in 1920 to well below 40 in 1927; and in the general category of manufacturing industries, from a bit more than one-fifth in 1920 to a figure closer to one-sixth at the present time. Women membership is difficult to measure. But such figures as there are indicate that most of the gains of the war have been lost and that there is substantial organization among women only in the clothing industry and among the railway clerks.

The uneven growth of trade unions has profoundly affected the internal constitution of the American labor movement. From 1913, and even from 1920 to 1927, the position of the transportation and building unions has become increasingly important in the movement. In 1927, the two groups represented one-half of the total membership of American trade unions. In the next years their relative position is likely to improve, both because they show signs of continuing to grow and because the remaining groups in the movement show no signs of swift recovery. It is interesting to observe that, in the main, American unions have grown in those industries where the conditions of business competition are quite different from those prevailing throughout the manufacturing and coal industries. The rail transportation industry is under extensive public control, while the competitive area of the building industry is, by its very nature, highly restricted.

In consequence, perhaps, of this experience since the war, many parts of the labor movement have devoted serious attention to their economic policy and have, in some instances, subjected it to drastic revision.

[55] Wolman, *op. cit.*, Chaps. III and IV.

TABLE 40.—PER CENT OF TOTAL MEMBERSHIP IN EACH GROUP

Group	1913	1920	1927
All groups..	100.0	100.0	100.0
Transportation..	20.2	24.6	24.0
Building..	20.1	17.4	26.0
Metal, machinery, and shipbuilding........................	8.0	16.8	6.0
Food, liquor, and tobacco.................................	4.9	2.3	2.0
Paper, printing, and bookbinding..........................	3.9	3.2	4.1
Chemicals, clay, glass, and stone.........................	2.0	1.0	1.1
Mining and quarrying......................................	15.7	8.2	10.4
Leather..	2.0	2.2	1.3
Clothing...	5.9	7.1	7.3
Public service..	3.1	3.2	6.1
Textiles...	1.1	2.9	1.0
Theaters and music.......................................	3.0	1.9	4.4
Restaurant and trade.....................................	3.3	2.8	1.6
Lumber and woodworking.................................	0.9	0.5	0.4
Miscellaneous..	5.9	5.9	4.3

Substantially, changing trade union policy has manifested itself in a greater preoccupation with the problems of production. In the widely heralded experiment in union-management co-operation, known as the "B and O Plan," the essence of the experiment is the assumption by the union of responsibility for efficiency and output. The developments in the men's clothing industry have been even more far-reaching. Here the Amalgamated Clothing Workers has gone so far as to undertake for manufacturers the opening of new units of manufacture and to share with the management, in both the new and the old shops, the burdens of supervision, thus reducing overhead costs directly and many items of labor cost indirectly. Similar beginnings are said to be taking place in the full-fashioned hosiery industry. The latest arrangement of this nature was recently made through an agreement between the Mitten Management and the Amalgamated Association of Street and Electric Railway Employees, whereby the Mitten Management may agree to union recognition on its properties if, by secret ballot, the employees choose the union as their representative, and if the same co-operation and efficiency is achieved as now prevails within the Mitten Management enterprises in the cities of Philadelphia and Buffalo.

Traditional trade union attitudes toward restriction of output and the introduction of machinery have unquestionably been severely modified in these past years. A growing number of unions have come to a clearer notion of their stake in the prosperity of the industry over which they claim jurisdiction; and the recent experience of the United Mine Workers will no doubt contribute to strengthen the view that labor organizations cannot successfully and to their own ultimate benefit obstruct technical progress in industry. At the same time, the American Federation of Labor and its constituent unions have sought to adapt organized labor's principles of wage fixing to the conditions of a mechanized and more efficient industry, by enunciating the doctrine that wages should rise proportionately with the increased productivity of labor.

The course of American industry since the war has, likewise, given a new turn to labor's concern with unemployment. The belief that the introduction of machinery has led to extensive displacement of labor and to persistent unemployment has led organized labor to demand the progressive shortening of the work-week and the acceptance by industry of its responsibility for such displaced labor. Except in its discussion of the five-day week and of the device of a public works reserve for times of unemployment, the proposals of the labor movement for handling the problem of industrial unemployment have not yet passed much beyond the elementary stage. In the various branches of the needle trades, several unions, by agreement with the organized manufacturers, have, since 1920, set up unemployment insurance funds, that are based on contributions made either by the manufacturer and union together, or by the manufacturer alone. The contributions to these funds run from 1½ per cent to 4½ per cent of the total weekly union pay roll of the firms under agreement with the union. At present the largest of the unemployment funds is that under the Amalgamated Clothing Workers of America, which covers some 70,000 workers in the men's clothing industry of Chicago, Rochester, and New York.

These postwar developments in trade union policy and in the methods of collective bargaining have been accompanied by the widening of the general economic activities of organized labor. While the experiments in workers' control, born during the war in the form of workers' management in the Rock Island Arsenal or of the Plumb Plan on the railroads, have since been abandoned, American unions have shown an inclination to engage in collateral enterprises quite novel in the history of American labor. The first of these began in 1920 with the organization of banks owned by unions and their members. It was assumed at the outset that these institutions would be limited dividend corporations, owned or controlled by organized labor. The movement of labor banking grew rapidly until it reached its peak in December, 1926, when 36 labor banks had accumulated resources of $127,000,000. Meanwhile the banks of the Brotherhood of Locomotive Engineers, the largest link in the movement, ran into difficulties of management and were forced to dispose of a part of their large holdings. Several of the smaller banks changed hands or closed down. At the last accounting, on December 31, 1928, there remained 27 labor banks with combined resources of $116,300,000.

The method of the limited dividend corporation has also been carried by organized labor into the business of life and health insurance. Both the Electrical Workers' Union and the American Federation of Labor itself, have organized life insurance companies, whose ownership is entirely in the hands of unions and of union members, to sell all forms of insurance to the general public as well as to members of labor organizations.[56] Finally, the same principles of business organization and labor control have been adopted by various unions for creating investment trusts and for the building of co-operative houses for working men.

Whatever promise these new activities of labor hold, and what influence they will have on the position of American labor in the future, it is too early to estimate. The enterprises are all young. Some have already changed their character and retain hardly any of the distinctive features with which they started; while a few have gone far in exploiting the potentialities of labor enterprises. At the moment, however, they are no more than an evidence of a fresh orientation in the outlook of the labor movement.

Much of this new attitude of organized labor may be attributed to the peculiar industrial situation that has prevailed in the United States since 1922. The quick recovery of business in 1922, and its comparative stability since, failed to have the anticipated effects on the growth of trade unions. In the light of all past experience it was to have been expected that the labor movement would, by 1928, more than have recovered its earlier losses. This it has not done, and the failure to do so has, without doubt, turned the attention of the movement toward an estimate of its own methods and outlook.

Adding further complexity to the situation has been the growth of devices and institutions which, in their present magnitude at least, are quite foreign to the American scene. The foremost of these is the company union, or employee representation plan, or works council. While such organizations of labor are not all alike, they all differ from the trade union in fundamental respects. They are organized through the initiative of the employer. Their jurisdiction is not spread over the whole of a competitive area, as is that of a labor union, but is limited to a single plant or single ownership. They do not, therefore, regard the standardization of wages and working conditions throughout a competitive area as one of their principal functions. They differ from the trade union, and among themselves, in the degree in which they enjoy freedom of action. They are not a new institution in American industrial relations, but they have grown very rapidly since the war and may at the present time claim considerably more than 1,000,000 members. Organized in some instances to replace existing labor unions, either during or after a strike, and set up elsewhere in plants where there has been no trade union, these plans

---

[56] On August 31, 1928, the Union Labor Life Insurance Co. had insurance outstanding of $37,523,000, of which less than $2,000,000 was ordinary and the balance group insurance. At the same time, the Union Co-operative Life Insurance Co., the Electrical Workers' company, had written more than $50,000,000 of insurance.

of employee representation have so far had the effect of retarding the growth of organized labor.

Of like effect have been the so-called welfare features established in many industries, either in connection with company unions or independent of them. The content of welfare plans differs widely, but nearly all now make some provision for workers' insurance, principally against death, but in increasing measure against total disability, sickness, and old age, as well. The form of workers' insurance which is most significant in this connection is that commonly known as group insurance, which is clearly distinguishable from other existing forms of personal insurance. The coverage is a group and not an individual; membership in the group, for insurance purposes, begins and terminates with the acquisition or loss of a job; the term of the insurance is usually one year; contracts are made without physical examination; the rates are low; insurance ceases with the loss of a job, except that the individual may, without physical examination, buy ordinary life insurance at the regular rate for his age; and the premium is paid either in whole or in part by the employer. Group insurance of this type, a very small item in the insurance business before the war, is now a business of very considerable magnitude.

Both the plans of employee representation and group insurance are assumed to tie workingmen closer to their shops and factories and to establish a new and more binding relationship between them and their jobs. The same ends, it is believed, are being served by the increase in workers' purchases of industrial investments. In view of the importance which is now generally attached to these developments in the United States and of their significance on their own account, it is essential to examine their size and rate of growth.

Workers' Insurance.[57]—It is impossible among the many types of life insurance sold in this country to segregate the precise amount bought by workingmen. Some examination of the total volume of life insurance now in force and of the distribution of this total among the various classes of insurance will, however, yield a rough measure of the order of magnitude of workers' insurance and throw considerable light on its growing importance.

Life insurance as a whole has, in the United States, been growing without interruption and at a rate much faster than the population of the country. Table 41, which shows the total and per capita amount of life insurance in force in commercial companies from 1911 to 1927, reveals the striking rate of increase for all of the combined forms of life insurance and the contrast between the growth before and after the World War. In the five years from 1911 to 1915, the increase in per capita insurance

---

[57] The material on this subject was compiled by Elizabeth Steele, of the Metropolitan Life Insurance Co.

in force was 19 per cent; in the next five years, 62 per cent; from 1921 to 1925, 47 per cent; and from 1926 to 1927, 9 per cent.

TABLE 41.—TOTAL AND PER CAPITA LIFE INSURANCE IN FORCE

Year	Population, continental United States	Amount in force—all classes	
		Total insurance	Per capita
1911	93,682,189	$17,730,128,000	$189
1912	95,097,298	18,955,471,000	199
1913	96,512,407	20,204,437,000	209
1914	97,927,516	21,202,140,000	217
1915	99,342,625	22,360,475,000	225
1916	100,757,735	24,211,590,000	240
1917	102,172,845	26,659,071,000	261
1918	103,587,955	29,250,471,000	282
1919	105,003,065	35,120,630,000	334
1920	106,421,621	41,364,115,000	389
1921	108,444,777	44,991,807,000	415
1922	109,893,003	49,225,064,000	448
1923	111,693,474	55,653,480,000	498
1924	113,727,432	62,531,016,000	550
1925	115,378,094	70,261,274,000	609
1926	117,136,000	76,973,268,000	657
1927	118,628,000	84,801,409,000	715

Ordinary life insurance is still the most popular form and accounted in 1927 for roughly three-fourths of the total amount in force. It appears also to be growing at no diminished rate, and its present absolute annual increase is greater than that of group and industrial life insurance combined. No material is available that would permit the distribution of the ordinary life insurance now in force among wage earners and low-salaried workers, and other economic classes. But it is known that a substantial and growing volume of ordinary insurance is held by the former group.[58]

[58] A study of the average amount of ordinary life insurance held in 1927 by the members of various occupations was recently made by the Phoenix Mutual Life Insurance Co., of Hartford, Conn. Their analysis, based on some 20,000 cases, shows the following very interesting figures:

Occupation	Average per capita insurance held, 1927
Office employees	$4,043
Retail clerks in stores	3,450
Skilled workers in manufacturing	4,594
Unskilled workers in transportation	3,163

While these amounts appear large, they are for the past few years by no means improbable.

TABLE 42.—AMOUNTS OF LIFE INSURANCE IN FORCE, BY CLASSES

(In thousands of dollars)

Year	Amounts of life insurance in force		
	Ordinary	Group	Industrial
1911	14,374,539	....	3,355,589
1912	15,315,802	13,172	3,626,497
1913	16,304,966	31,202	3,868,269
1914	17,091,561	64,468	4,046,111
1915	17,956,463	99,049	4,304,963
1916	19,396,661	152,859	4,662,070
1917	21,261,234	346,525	5,031,312
1918	23,122,510	627,008	5,500,953
1919	27,611,252	1,135,036	6,374,342
1920	32,827,156	1,614,387	6,922,572
1921	35,710,348	1,575,821	7,705,638
1922	38,861,734	1,808,211	8,555,119
1923	43,476,206	2,430,829	9,746,445
1924	48,457,565	3,133,620	10,939,831
1925	53,671,545	4,228,345	12,361,384
1926	58,117,778	5,338,655	13,516,835
1927	64,052,576	6,274,636	14,474,197

With this growth in insurance outstanding, the income arising out of the payment of death claims, matured endowments, annuities paid, and

TABLE 43.—PAYMENTS TO POLICYHOLDERS

Year	Total payments to policyholders			
	Industrial	Group	Fraternal and assessment	Total
1911	$ 74,275,662	....	$ 89,665,297	$163,940,959
1912	81,287,041	....	101,163,921	182,450,962
1913	89,138,370	....	105,919,898	195,058,268
1914	102,711,514	....	103,033,658	205,745,172
1915	113,591,045	....	102,863,175	216,454,220
1916	119,843,381	....	111,874,449	231,717,830
1917	131,107,031	....	102,088,575	233,195,606
1918	187,170,711	....	124,010,149	311,180,860
1919	168,962,217	$ 6,595,261	148,366,992	323,924,470
1920	172,743,541	10,762,470	114,440,177	297,946,188
1921	195,494,551	10,591,889	112,794,046	318,880,486
1922	244,029,395	11,498,920	115,264,376	370,792,691
1923	292,322,353	15,544,620	115,091,446	422,958,419
1924	331,342,194	19,415,437	125,612,037	476,369,668
1925	385,572,212	25,772,140	131,426,104	542,770,456
1926	441,449,574	34,462,608	134,355,300	610,267,482
1927	505,166,137	40,749,476	184,758,547	730,674,160

disability, dividends, and payments for lapsed, surrendered, and purchased policies has become a substantial addition to the incomes of
policyholders. The known streams of insurance income are shown in
Table 43. All fraternal and assessment insurance may not be workers'
insurance, but since the average amount of such insurance held is small,
the bulk of it must be insurance of the lower income groups. The
figures for workers' health insurance and old age pensions cannot be
segregated, but they are said to be small. Adding to the figures that
are clearly workers' income from insurance the further income that flows
to workers from their holdings of ordinary life insurance and from
workmen's compensation, it is clear that the present annual income to
the wage-earning and lower-salaried groups from insurance must be
more than one billion dollars.

Workers' Investments.—The growth of personal insurance in all of
its forms finds its counterpart in the widening diffusion of corporate stock
ownership in this country. In part, this phenomenon is nothing more
than one of many features in the development of the American investment market; in part it is the result of the deliberate policy of many
business enterprises designed to encourage their workingmen to share
in the ownership of the business. Particularly since 1920 a growing
number of large and small businesses have made arrangements with
their employees whereby they may purchase a limited number of the
firm's shares of stock, usually on the condition that the shares so purchased are paid for by weekly or monthly installments deducted from
wages.[59]

On the whole matter of the diffusion of stock ownership it is still
difficult to obtain reliable and useful information. That ownership is
more general than it used to be, and is constantly becoming more so, is
reasonably clear. But that this movement has radically affected the
distribution of wealth and income in the country, or that it is an evidence
of marked changes in distribution, is doubtful. An elaborate investigation by the Federal Trade Commission of the situation in this regard
in 1922 led that agency to the conclusion that the "data indicate a very
wide distribution of corporate stock among individuals" but "it was not
possible from the information supplied by the corporations (4,367
corporations were studied by the Commission) to analyze the proportions
owned by different individual stockholders or the extent to which stock
was held by a few individuals." The Commission did find, however,

---

[59] There are a great number of such arrangements now in force in American indus-
try and they are described in detail in R. F. Foerster and E. H. Dietel, *Employee
Stock Ownership in the United States*, Princeton University, 1926, and in *Employee
Stock Purchase Plans in the United States*, National Industrial Conference Board,
New York, 1928.

that "nearly one-third of all corporate stockholders in 1922 held not more than $500 worth of stock each."[60]

In estimating the volume of securities held by employees, there are two fundamental statistical difficulties; first, that it is impossible to procure a frequency distribution of individuals' holdings of securities, and second, that the term employees is so used as to include not only wage earners and lower-salaried employees, but executives and higher-salaried employees, as well. Thus when the Federal Trade Commission found for the year 1922 that the "average holdings per person for employees" was $1,419 of common stock and $2,803 of preferred stock, the group of employees must obviously have included many in the higher income classes.[61]

But the evidence that there has been a marked growth in stock ownership by workingmen is too strong to be disregarded. A recent study of plans of employee stock ownership, made by the National Industrial Conference Board, comes to the conclusion that a minimum estimate of such employee holdings would place their volume in 1927 at more than a billion dollars. A summary of their findings on stock ownership is given in Table 44, taken from the Board's report. But with reference

TABLE 44.—EXTENT OF EMPLOYEE STOCK OWNERSHIP AMONG 315 COMPANIES IN THE UNITED STATES, 1927[a]

Type of plan and eligibility of employees	Number of companies	Number of employees		Market value of shares[b]
		Total	Stock-holders and subscribers	
Active purchase plan....................	[c]253	2,439,844	736,641	$936,140,941
Rank and file of employees...........	[d]230	2,397,298	733,112	909,134,425
Selected employees.................	23	42,551	3,529	27,066,516
Inactive purchase plan[c].................	51	236,207	30,582	60,466,372
Rank and file of employees...........	46	230,788	30,322	59,327,862
Selected employees.................	5	5,419	260	1,138,510
Profit sharing, bonuses, etc..............	11	60,392	38,845	[e]48,543,097
All plans........................	[d]315	2,736,448	806,068	[e]$1,045,150,410

[a] This estimate is probably a minimum. Moreover, it does not include $10,825,000 worth of securities of two companies known to be owned by the employees jointly, in addition to those which are owned by them individually.

[b] These values relate for the most part to the middle of 1927, when prices of some shares were unusually high. In many other cases, however, there had been no such unusual inflation. For thirty-five companies, book or par value was used, in the absence of data regarding market value.

[c] Plans that have been discontinued.

[d] Includes four companies, whose plans were not analyzed in detail.

[e] Includes $11,550,000 jointly owned by 11,500 employes of the Philadelphia Rapid Transit Co.

[60] *National Wealth and Income*, United States Sen. Doc., No. 126, 69th Congress, 1st session, Washington, 1926, pp. 148, 151.

[61] *Ibid.*, p. 148.

to the degree of control exercised by these stockholders, the Board comes to much the same conclusions as those reached by the Federal Trade Commission for its study of the year 1922. At that time the Commission found that while "employees comprised 7.5 per cent of the common stockholders reported and 3.5 per cent of the preferred stockholders," they "had only 1.5 per cent of the common stock and 2 per cent of the preferred."[62] Similarly, the Industrial Relations Section of Princeton University, reviewing employee stock ownership in 20 large corporations in 1926, found that employee stockholders comprised 21 per cent of all of the stockholders of these companies, but that their holdings represented only 4.3 per cent of the market value of the total stock outstanding.[63]

VI. INDUSTRIAL DISPUTES

The bare statistical records of strikes and lockouts cannot always give a true picture of the prevalence of peace or conflict in industry. Industrial disputes differ in intensity, in the degree to which they succeed in interrupting production, and in the effects produced by their settlement. Considerations such as these are not measurable, but a knowledge of them will qualify many patent conclusions drawn from a study of the number of industrial disputes.

Measured by any standard, the period since 1922 has been remarkably free of upheavals in industrial relations.[64] Although the reporting of the number of persons involved in disputes was more inclusive after 1922 than before, yet in the six-year period from 1922 to 1927 both the number of disputes and the number of strikers show a sharp decline over the preceding years from 1916 to 1921. These average figures, moreover,

TABLE 45.—NUMBER OF DISPUTES AND EMPLOYEES INVOLVED

Period	Annual average	
	All disputes	Number of employees involved
1916–1921	3,503	1,798,301
1922–1926	1,164	688,538

distort the picture somewhat, partly because the year 1922, one of large strikes, more properly belongs in the earlier period, and partly because

[62] *Ibid.*, p. 160.

[63] *Employee Stock Purchase Plans in the United States*, National Industrial Conference Board, p. 39.

[64] The statistical material in this section was compiled, from the reports of the United States Bureau of Labor Statistics, by Ben M. Selekman.

they conceal the steady decrease in disputes since 1922. This decline is shown in Table 46. Unfortunately, the record of industrial disputes is not available for the years immediately before the war, but comparison of these war and postwar figures with the elaborate statistics from 1881 to 1905 would appear to indicate that the number of disputes has since 1922 been less than then, whereas the number of employees involved was relatively slightly greater in the late than in the early period.

TABLE 46.—INDEX NUMBERS OF INDUSTRIAL DISPUTES AND NUMBER OF EMPLOYEES

(1916 = 100)

Year	Industrial disputes	Employees involved	Year	Industrial disputes	Employees involved
1916	100	100	1922	29	101
1917	117	77	1923	41	47
1918	88	78	1924	33	41
1919	96	260	1925	34	27
1920	90	91	1926	27	21
1921	63	69	1927	19	22

The comparative quiet of these last years is all the more marked in contrast with the state of affairs before 1923, when there took place some of the largest and longest strikes in the history of the country. In 1919, more than 1,000,000 workers were involved in strikes in the coal, steel, and railroad industries; disputes in the building trades of Chicago and New York resulted in a strike of 250,000; 100,000 longshoremen along the Atlantic Coast stopped work; a strike in the stockyards of Chicago brought out 65,000 strikers; and strikes in the clothing and textile industries several hundred thousand more. Altogether, the reports to the United States Bureau of Labor Statistics indicate more than 4,000,000 persons involved in industrial disputes in 1919. The following years were quieter but by no means free of strikes. In 1920 there were the large "outlaw" strikes of railway switchmen and yardmen and the strike of the anthracite miners; in the year following, a strike of the marine workers in all principal ports, and conflicts in the clothing, building, and packing industries; and in 1922, when the number of reported strikers rose to 1,600,000, there took place the great strikes of the coal miners and of the railroad shopmen.

Major industrial disputes during these latest years have been largely localized in the coal, textile, and clothing industries. In the coal industry, strikes have been almost continuous and appear now to be stopping, at least temporarily, with the abandonment by the United Mine Workers of the Jacksonville agreement and with a recent decision of the union authorizing the district organizations to negotiate their own agreements with the operators. Unsettled conditions in all branches of the New

England textile industry, accompanied by frequent attempts to cut wages, have precipitated bitter strikes, particularly in Passaic and New Bedford; while the movement to introduce the 40-hour week, organization campaigns against non-union manufacturers, and a struggle for control of unions between the administrations of several organizations and the Workers' Party have been the principal causes of conflict in the many branches of the clothing industry.

VII. SUMMARY

Since 1920, the most striking changes in the supply of labor have been associated with the policy of immigration restriction, the growth of industry in the South, and the falling birth and mortality rates. Wage rates are a useful measure of the changing position of labor. The most striking feature is the slight decline in wage rates during the severe depression from 1920 to 1922 and the recovery since 1922.

In manufacturing industries there has been a reduction in the nominal work-week of roughly five hours from 1914 to the present, and the prevailing hours of labor are now around 50 a week.   Since 1922 it seems likely that labor costs have continued to fall.

Production per capita is now nearly 60 per cent greater than it was in the closing years of the nineteenth century.   The output per worker engaged directly in production has increased 80 per cent during the same period.   The precipitate rate of advance in productivity, which began in 1922 and continued through 1925, has slackened.

Comparisons of prewar and postwar employment in manufacturing industries show no startling differences between the normal stability of employment before the war and the condition after the recovery from the depression of 1920–21.   Measures of labor turnover in manufacturing industries confirm the impression of stability shown by the index of employment and income.

Lack of machinery for compulsory registration makes difficult a determination of the amount of unemployment.   Estimated average unemployment, is arrived at by taking the difference between the number of persons actually employed and the number desiring and habitually dependent upon employment.   The most interesting and probably one of the most important changes in postwar employment has been the expansion of nonindustrial employment.   Measured by the volume of unemployment, the recession of 1927 does not appear to have been so severe as that in 1924.   Throughout the whole period there is a large and persistent volume of unemployment, even in the very active years.

It is probable that American wage earners, excluding agricultural labor, are about one-fifth organized.   Since 1920, the position of the transportation and building unions has become increasingly important. In 1927, these two groups represented one-half of the total union membership.   In general, American unions have grown in those industries where the conditions of business competition are quite different from those prevailing throughout the manufacturing and coal industries.

Union policy is much more preoccupied with problems of production, as shown by the experiments in co-operation and the relaxation of the traditional trade union attitude toward the introduction of machinery. The American Federation of Labor has initiated the doctrine that wages should rise proportionately with the increased productivity of labor. Labor is much more preoccupied with unemployment, and has demanded the progressive shortening of the work-week and the acceptance by industry of its responsibility for labor displaced by improved machinery and methods.   Unemployment reserve funds of various sorts have been set up.   Unions have shown an inclination to engage in such enterprises as banking, and life and health insurance.   Company unions have grown rapidly and claim more than one million members.   The increased number of corporate stockowners has been important.

The period since 1922 has been remarkably free from strikes and lockouts.

CHAPTER VII

MANAGEMENT

By Henry S. Dennison

In this chapter[1] are recorded the methods of management found in a survey of American manufacturing and marketing. For the most part, they represent what can be called average good practice, though in some cases methods too significant to omit entirely, but used in too few companies to warrant the broader title, are described as methods of the exceptional few.

The survey first examined managerial methods used in keeping up and building up the organization itself; then in meeting the problems of manufacturing, marketing, selling, merchandising, and clerical control. The order followed in this chapter is the order of the topics in the Field Interview Schedule printed in Appendix A.

To get the facts upon which this chapter is based, some 500 people, employed by 100 different companies, were interviewed. Advice was sought from professional consultants, bankers, and other men in contact with the business world. Advantage was taken of many public and private inquiries which have been carried out during the past few years into special phases of managerial technique. And close study was made of business articles and books, going back in many cases, for purposes of comparison, to those of a dozen years ago to give indication of the important trends of effort and attention. By these means it was sought to present as broad and true a picture as possible.

From a list of several thousand companies, out of which the most nearly typical were selected by trade association officials and others well-acquainted with the field, 100 were chosen as nearly as possible to be fair samples of normally successful, established businesses.

The sampling, therefore, and the chapter do not actually cover the whole field of American business. They leave out the failures and that large group of the Babbittry of business, whose methods are safe and dependable, but whose ways change slowly and only after learning of the well-tested practices and of the more aggressively successful. They leave out also those not yet settled-down enough to have established management practices.

[1] The author was assisted in the direction of the survey and the drafting of this chapter by Ernest R. Burton, John S. Keir, Richard H. Lansburgh, Erwin H. Schell, and Donald S. Tucker.

The survey, however, did not confine itself merely to the ultra-successful; it included small and large companies making moderate to notable successes in a variety of businesses in different sections of the country. Among them, all the main divisions of the census, except lumber, tobacco manufacture, musical instruments, and railroad repair shops, are represented by two or more companies. It is believed to be a fair sample of the group of American business men whose management practices would by any practical man be considered the "prevailing" practices. Its results check well with the considerable number of surveys into specific methods which have been made in the last few years.

Earlier standards were characterized by the phrase "business is business," with the implication that whatever means succeeded were right ones. Muckraking and regulative law followed, not only as the effects of the first changes of attitude but also as the causes of further changes. A specific and widespread assertion that modern business has obligations beyond the law appeared in July, 1915, as the "Rotary Code of Ethics." In 1921, 1922, and 1923, dozens of trade associations adopted ethical codes;[2] in 1924 came publications of the United States Chamber of Commerce code and of Hoover's *Principles of Business Conduct;* and in 1926 there was almost an epidemic of books on business ethics.

But the course is no more run when codes are formulated than when evils are first exposed. Codes may be little more than words or may, on the other hand, through their effect on consciousness and subconsciousness, develop a professional pride or a powerful social demand for decency.

This survey gave evidence that a growing number of business men care a great deal for something more than what they can get out of business for themselves. To the organization itself, and to its investors, there is a decided sense of responsibility. Toward customers, also, there is such a sense; at least, *caveat emptor* as an alibi is dead. Toward employees there is less feeling of responsibility; yet there is some. Business morals may be called more or less rudimentary according to the standards by which they are judged; they certainly exist and seem to be evolving. Progress toward higher intellectual standards for management is clearly indicated by the survey. The values of training in the material sciences are widely granted.

A large majority of the companies in this survey expressed it as their aim to work for progress in the next few years through perfection of physical facilities; only 20 per cent included the bettering of the skill and morale of the employee. It is, therefore, obvious that there are as yet only the beginnings of scientific thinking on the more human problems. But the marked tendency toward the scientific rather than

[2] For many examples, see *Codes of Ethics* by E. L. Heermance, 1924.

the opportunist type of mind, and the growing belief that training for general business management is worth while, make it possible that the human problems will some day get a larger share.

Of characteristic and weighty influence upon American business management as a whole, and often of saving influence upon those who prefer to follow rather than to pioneer, are the business publications and the business meetings which, each in its own way, lift managerial noses off grindstones and help each manager to see his problem as one of a group of problems from a study of which he may learn much.   A considerable majority of companies belong to one or several sorts of business associations, and a much larger number take one or many of the business publications whose circulation aggregates 11,000,000.[3]

The Department of Commerce published, in 1926, a list of nearly 9,000 business associations, 6,500 of which were local, 1,100 state-wide, and 1,200 interstate, national, or international.   Their activities ranged over almost the whole field of management, including especially statistical service, cost accounting, industrial and commercial research, simplification, standardization, credit information, traffic and transportation studies, and trade ethics.   It is significant that several hundred business executives are members of some national association of the social sciences.[4]

The last few years have been extremely favorable in many ways for the development of those intellectual, moral, and social attitudes which lead toward high professional standing.   The situation of to-day holds all the opportunity any one could desire for the wholesome development of business management into a great profession.

I. ORGANIZATION

To find the better forms of internal structure has commanded the increasing attention of American business during the last few years. The natural course of evolution away from absolute one-man management, aided by the financial shake-ups of 1921, gave to good organization structure a growing importance.   A mere increase in the number of the departments and divisions of a straight line organization has not been sufficient to meet the demands of modern complexity, since it has required of each of a large number of executives too wide a range of knowledge. Certain especially difficult and important functions have, therefore, been more and more set aside for the particular consideration of one man or a group of men, who are expected, in one way or another, to guide, direct, or supplement the actions of line executives in these fields.   It has been

[3] The *Market Data Book* lists 1,111 business and 524 professional publications. The total of such circulation figures as *are there given for business publications* is 11,333,078.

[4] See details of membership in the American Statistical Association in their *Journal*, June, 1927.

more and more generally recognized that the conquest of a special problem requires not only the ability and will to win, but also the devotion of men who have sufficient time for its solution.

Functionalization.—When the word is used in its strictest sense there can be found few organizations which are not formed partly along "functional" lines; to separate selling, or accounting, or buying, is to departmentalize with respect to the type of activity or function rather than the type of goods to be handled, equipment to be used, or territory to be covered, and hence to functionalize. These more obvious and inescapable divisions of labor, however, have been so long settled as to be considered normal "line" departments; an organization must have gone somewhat deeper in its specialization of types of activity to be generally described as "functionalized."

The more fully functionalized type of organization has been experimented with and written about for more than a score of years, but until recently its significant applications have not been many. To-day there is to be found a definite trend toward the development of such functional departments as "Planning," "Material Control," "Personnel," "Methods," "Sales Promotion," "Styling," and "Merchandising," as well as some less sharply defined advisory positions like "Economist" and "Statistician." Companies well-functionalized some years ago have continued to develop their organizations in the direction of further functionalization. New companies have often set up their organizations along functional lines, while new general managers of old companies, when they have reorganized, have almost uniformly done so on a functional basis. Many of the organizations which do not use the functional structure are operated by heads who have held their positions for a long time. That the trend is the result of a broad change in the ideas of management is indicated by the fact that the size of the company, or the nature of its work, bears little relation to the extent of its functionalization.

Managers have found that, when functions are newly set off, their performance usually requires more personnel than when they have been fully developed. When the work is better known it can be simplified, and sometimes certain functional and line responsibilities may both be assigned to the same executive. Or a functional responsibility may reside in a committee of line executives. The more important and exacting functions, however, remain in charge of a staff executive, sometimes aided by a large number of assistants.

In marketing, the employment of functional specialists is new and hence its development to-day is extensive rather than intensive. Among the separate functions which have evolved, are the development of merchandising policies and practices, sales promotion, marketing research, style bureaus, and product improvement. With rare exceptions, all have been created since the war, and show a marked acceleration during the last five years. Particularly noticeable are the undertakings of the Association of National Advertisers and of some advertising agencies in market analysis, and the extension of the field of management consultants into marketing.

An important by-product value of the use of functional specialists has been found in the chance it offers for making fuller use of the widely ranging variety of natural aptitudes among executives. The kind of man too "one-sided" to make a good line executive has been found capable of excellent work in a functional or staff position.

Research.—Research through the material sciences got a great start during the war, and much support during the days of excess profits taxation which followed. It has now progressed so far that many kinds of organization have been set up for it;[5] there are company, joint, consulting, and trade association[6] laboratories, and co-operating research services in universities. Some manufacturers have combined in maintaining laboratories to conduct researches covering basic process problems interesting to all. It is widely believed by business managers that the research activities of leading companies are among the primary causes of their success. Prosperity has really come to mean a rate of advance rather than a state of affairs. Even pure research—formerly thought uncommercial because related to no designated commercial purpose—is now supported by a few American concerns.

Functionalizing and the establishment of organized research both arise to meet the same need—that of finding out more about some parts of the total job of management than can be found out in the odd moments of a line executive's life. There has been rapid progress by chemical and physical research into processes generally believed twenty years ago to be understandable only by practical men "skilled in the art." Since 1921, a similar invasion into those business processes which are more subject to human than to mechanistic influence has been begun by departments of methods research, statistical research, and market analysis.

Co-ordination.—The greater complexity of business problems, and of the organization necessary to cope with them, have forced attention upon better methods of co-ordinating the plans and the work of specialists and executives. Where there are research men, staff men, and operating men, a close mutual understanding and counseling among them has been found necessary, whether it is effected by formally arranged conferences and committees or, as one executive put it, "by a great use of shoe

---

[5] There are 999 listed in the *Bulletin* of the National Research Council, July, 1927, No. 60, as compared with 300 in *Bulletin*, No. 16 of 1920.

[6] The United States Chamber of Commerce, in November, 1925, published a list of 527 specific research projects of 68 different trade associations.

leather." Under a pervasive one-man control, where the chief executive disposes of all important questions, such co-ordination is, in theory, effected through that man. But the trend is definitely away from control by one man; and, even where it exists, his absences may force department heads into conferences so frequently that they have, in effect, a system of regular operating committees.

The use of the conference as a co-ordinating device is widespread. Conferences, occasional or frequent, and systematic interchange of information among executives, form the two steps first taken by those companies which are tending away from one-man control. They do not change the responsibilities of men or departments, or affect in any way the visible structure of the organization, but often become slowly crystallized into committees. Committees seem to be a normal evolution of the consultation necessary to co-ordinate a complex organization. Irregular conferences among executives and their subordinates, however, are still the most common means of co-ordination.

After first trials, committees have often seemed wasteful of time, and frequently first trials are ill adapted to their ends or are led by unskillful chairmen. Some companies have found committees too unwieldy and have returned to the appointment of an operating head, who calls such conferences or consultations as he desires. Yet for every plant abandoning them, there were found eight which added to their number. Committees, where favorably regarded, are looked upon as methods of education and cross-fertilization of ideas, as valuable sources of counsel, and as opportunities to gain co-operation in the effecting of constructive changes.

There seems to be less use of committees in very large and very small companies than in the medium-sized. So-called "executive committees," or committees dealing with general matters, are the most frequent type found. In a few companies, such committees actually control the operations of the business, but there is evidence to indicate that committees which are clearly understood as advisory to a responsible executive survive better than those whose votes constitute in themselves executive decisions. Where complete committee control is found, the reason for it seems to be that some leading executive has passed out of the company, no choice to succeed him seems possible among the remaining executives, and to bring a man in from the outside is not desired.

A list of typical committees most commonly found in the survey follows:

SMALL PLANTS, UP TO 500 EMPLOYEES	PLANTS EMPLOYING 500 TO 1,000 EMPLOYEES
General Committee.	
Quality Committee.	General Committee.
Scheduling Committee.	Cost Committee.
Committee for Purchasing Control.	Budgeting Committee.

Estimate Committee.
Finance Committee.

MEDIUM PLANTS, 1,000 TO 5,000 EMPLOYEES

General Manager's Staff.
Advertising Council.
Competition Committee.
Cost Committee.
Budget Committee.
Design Committee.
Executive Committee.
Foremen's Committee.
Manufacturing Betterments Committee.
Merchandising Council.
Management Committee.
Inventory Control Committee.
Personnel Committee.
Safety Committee.
Service Committee.
Standards Committee.
Sales Committee.
Production Meeting.

Scrap Committee.
Labor Committee.
Wages Committee.
Power Committee.
Suggestion Committee.

LARGE PLANTS, 5,000 TO 10,000 EMPLOYEES

Intercompany Committee.
Waste of Material Committee.
Usual committees above.

VERY LARGE PLANTS, ABOUT 10,000 EMPLOYEES

Future Demands Committee.
Public Relations Committee.
Industrial Relations Committee.
New Work Committee.
Special Committee for Parts Problems.
Co-ordination Committee.
Works Committee.
Usual committees above.

Organization charts are maintained by relatively few companies, and fewer still keep them up to date. Yet the interest in developing effective organization is much alive. The chart as an aid seems to have its principal value to each company in the earlier stages, and to picture the status of organization rather than its living relationships. In business literature of ten years ago it was frequently to be found, but seldom indeed to-day. Careful job specifications, including the beginnings of a description of the working relationships among jobs, seem to be taking the place which the chart once held as an aid to organization building. The setting forth of an organization form, as if it were capable of being fitted down over a going concern, hardly appears now in the business publications in which it was common fifteen years ago. It is the principles of organization rather than the forms which are to-day being discussed.[7]

It might be assumed that increase in the size of an organization would demand that greater attention be given to organization form. This has, of course, occurred in some cases, but in general there is a striking lack of relation between the size of a business and the methods used to operate it. A dominating one-man control is to be found in one of the

[7] See, for example, Oliver Sheldon, *Philosophy of Management*, 1923; *Scientific Foundations of Business Administration*, by H. C. Metcalf, editor, 1926; *Psychological Foundations of Business Management* and *Business Management as a Profession*, by H. C. Metcalf, editor, 1927; David R. Craig, "Measuring Morale and Leadership Ability," *Personnel Journal*, October, 1927, p. 155 (publication of the Personnel Research Federation).

very large organizations of the country; and highly decentralized, functionalized, and co-ordinated forms are to be found in relatively small, though not, of course, the smallest companies. The characteristics and tendencies of the man or men "at the top" are still the pre-eminent influences in determining what shall be the form of an organization.

In these days of mergers, it is to be expected that many articles upon organization and reorganization would appear, but so far it would seem that the financial aspect rather than the structural aspect of mergers has held the center of attention.

Executive Technique.—Handling functional and research specialists—men who must themselves originate and create—has brought into prominence a technique of consultation, persuasion, and inspiration, as against a technique of order-giving. It is the man who can lead rather than domineer who is now chiefly desired in executive positions. The large organization needs an able head, but must have much more brains at the top than one head will hold; the organization pyramid is being rounded at the peak.

Just what the qualities of creative leadership are—just what is involved in the position of the chief executive—has been the subject of several discussions and articles in the past few years.[8] It appears in business publications, in the proceedings of the Taylor Society, the American Management Association, the Society of Industrial Engineers, the Personnel Research Federation, the American Society of Mechanical Engineers, and crops up in many discussions with business executives. The idea that even the chief executive's job admits of analysis and comparison of methods is in sharp contrast to the older ideas that its fulfillment could not be described further than as an expression of the personality of the holder, and that it was only results that could be counted.

It is impossible to know whether or not changes in managerial personnel have been more than normally rapid during the last decade. We must rest with the presumption that ups and downs among different lines of business, shifts in ownership since 1921, and changes in business technique have combined to make them so. The newcomers into each managerial grade appear to have come from outside the organization rather more often than one would expect who knew how common is the praise of "promotion from the ranks." But a majority still come from within; and in the larger and long established companies a big majority. The specialists who are being used in increasing numbers come more often from outside.

[8] For example: H. P. Kendall, "The Problem of the Chief Executive," Taylor Society *Bulletin*, April, 1922; M. P. Follett, "The Illusion of Final Authority," Taylor Society *Bulletin*, December, 1926; and Ordway Tead, "Nature and Uses of Creative Leadership," Taylor Society *Bulletin*, January, 1927.

There is probably a real increase in the care with which the younger men hired are being looked over for those qualities which fit them for later promotion. College graduates are being taken more frequently, as would almost necessarily be the case, since the numbers of baccalaureate degrees increased from 38,500 in 1920 to 71,500 in 1926; of professional degrees from 8,000 to 20,000; and of graduate degrees from 4,850 to 11,450.[9] Some prejudices against the college graduate still remain, but among an unimportant minority; the rating of technical graduates is generally high.

Selection for promotion rests as yet almost wholly upon the general judgment of "results." In a small but growing number of cases where budgets have been carried through in considerable detail, they have been found to furnish a useful standard against which "results" can be checked.

A considerable number of companies—in this survey as many as one-half—make bonus payments, in one form or another, to their executives. The bonuses are paid in cash, in stock, or the right to buy stock, and are apportioned according to individual or departmental showings, to salary, or to some combination of factors.[10] The amounts depend in most cases upon profits, but in a few are based on departmental showings independent of company profit, thus partaking rather of the nature of piece rates or commissions. They have come rapidly into vogue in recent years, supplementing the straight salary which is now to be found in a decreasing number of companies.

Planning.—Until recent years, it has not been at all the common practice among business concerns to attempt to plan their courses on paper in advance. The form of organization and quality of men had to be such as were best able to meet emergencies. The distinct trend now, begun in a small way well before the war, is to try to avoid emergencies, by making and examining pictures of the possibilities the future may contain. With some truth it can be said that modern hand-to-mouth buying has made hand-to-mouth thinking impossible. The length of time for which plans can be laid vary, of course, from style goods to staple goods, every step in simplification of product or standardization of parts allowing a longer planning period. In the factory, a manufacturing schedule based on orders has often of necessity been replaced by a schedule based on prospective business. The planning of sales effort, found necessary as manufacturing plans develop in accuracy and detail, has only begun.

Budgeting.—A plan for the whole organization is coming to be called the master plan, one condensation of which is the budget. Budgets, though known years ago, have made extraordinary progress in the

[9] Figures given by the American Council on Education, Washington, D. C.
[10] Many varieties described by C. C. Balderston, *Managerial Profit Sharing*, 1928.

business world since the publication of McKinsey's book[11] in 1922. They have come in more rapidly than any other management device of parallel complexity which has ever been introduced. Of the companies which now have budgets, it is estimated that four-fifths have introduced them since 1921, while many budgets which existed prior to that time have since then been bettered in operation or expanded to cover more phases of the business. Originally starting as expense budgets, they extend themselves almost necessarily to cover estimates of sales, of probable operating improvement, and of needed enlargements and replacements. Consulting accountants say that where they used to start with cost accounting, now, starting with budgeting, they find costing and planning follow naturally.

The first two or three years of budget making have been frequently reported as yielding unsatisfactory results, but usually by the fourth year enough lessons have been learned, and enough skill gained, to produce a good budget. From then on, it is not uncommon to hear stories of uncanny accuracy. The reponsibility for the preparation of the budget is ordinarily put into the hands of some special officer, who in a large organization will devote himself to the budget but in smaller ones will have other duties.   He gets department heads to work up their own figures, in close consultation with him; for the acceptance by operating officials of the budget as reasonable—in a word their consent to the budget figures—has been found essential to its most effective use. As might be expected, therefore, the budget is used chiefly in those companies which attempt to have an organized plan of operating take the place of a continuous issuance of orders from headquarters, and it forms for them a valuable addition to their methods of co-ordination.

The common period of budgets is a year, though they are made for as short a time as one month. In some companies both short- and long-time budgets are used, the one for routine operating, the other to aid in such problems as reinvestments and financing.

Bankers' Influence.—There are only a few banks in the United States which are as yet paying much attention to the budgets of the companies which are borrowing from them, and hence budgets so far have seldom been shown to the banks. In fact, the interest in and the influence of commercial bankers upon practices of business management have not been disclosed by these studies to be as strong as was thought at the beginning.   In a few cases they have taken over or greatly influenced management; in most they have not concerned themselves with management methods, or have confined their interest to the encouragement of better accounting and statistical information.

Investment bankers seldom interest themselves in the smaller companies. The fees and other gains of reorganization and merger,

[11] J. O. McKinsey, *Budgetary Control*, 1922.

however, have brought them to the forefront in hundreds of the large recent incorporations. In them, their influence upon management is often dominant, but the directions in which it is exerted vary so widely from banker to banker, and even from case to case, that no prevailing trend can be reported; the typical influences common to all radical financial changes are there, of course, but show few elements which are peculiar to the banker. There is a recent tendency among investment houses to employ men who are expert in different lines of business to look into possible opportunities for reorganization or merger, and to sit upon the board of directors of those companies in which the house has an important interest.

Upon the management of the older corporations the influence of the financial world seems to be growing less. There is, therefore, some evidence for the theory that financial domination increases when changes are rapid and decreases as business affairs stabilize.

Forecasting.—Forecasting services in the United States are many and varied. With the help of several institutions, a list of 132 was compiled, but there is no reason to believe it includes all there are. For the purposes of this chapter, however, many can be left out of consideration, for some carry only special trade information, and a large number have as their predominating purpose to serve those who want information concerning stock market investments or speculations. Those which relate themselves to business management reduce to small numbers. One of these was kind enough to analyze its circulation list and reported that even of these selected customers, 60 per cent were clearly using the service only as an aid to investment.

Two years ago, the combined circulation of five of the best-known forecasting services was reported as 35,000.[12] Allowing one-half for the large number who take more than one, and eliminating 60 per cent estimated as investors only, there remain about 7,000 which go to business managers. In addition to this relatively small number, there must be taken into account the great general circulation which reports of business facts have had in recent years. These reports appear in newspapers, trade papers, business magazines, reports of the Department of Commerce, and in monthly publications by banks. The combined monthly circulation of two among the best known of the bank bulletins is 275,000. The use of forecasting by business management cannot as yet be called widespread; but the knowledge of the facts upon which forecasting must be based would seem to be much larger, and growing.

Among the companies of this survey, the most serious use of forecasting, as an aid in management, was made by the few who had established a statistician to study all reports and information pertinent to their particular problems.

[12] Cox and Hardy, *Forecasting Business Conditions*, p. 41, 1927.

The organizations forecasting business conditions use principally the following three methods in different combinations:

(a) The setting forth of differences above and below the so-called normal and the use of the theory of business cycles.

(b) A study of recurring sequences, on the theory that what will happen will usually resemble what has happened under comparable conditions.

(c) A cross-section balance-sheet analysis of all the forces working either up or down at the moment.

No one of the larger organizations relies exclusively upon any one of these.

The business weather is, at any given moment, the resultant of a confusing combination of forces. At the present stage of our knowledge, it is sometimes difficult to say with preciseness what that weather is. Exactness in prediction can hardly be expected as yet, though careful forecasting should have chances in its favor over random guessing, just as weather forecasting has.

In testing accuracy, few services can be used, because, of the few which are left after investors' and speculators' services are eliminated, only a part are definite enough in their month-to-month statements to be checked by the outcome. Even then, there are logical and statistical difficulties in the way of a dependable test.

In 500 forecasts of general prices, just over one-half were found correct, just over one-quarter were incorrect, and about one-fifth negative, that is to say, neither harmful nor helpful in their results. The ratio of helpful to injurious predictions was 18 to 10. In 433 forecasts concerning the volume of general business, nearly two-thirds were correct, one-sixth incorrect, and one-sixth negative. The ratio here of the helpful to the injurious was 37 to 10. Five hundred forecasts on individual prices were tested. As with the predictions of general prices, these ranged a little better than one-half correct, a little better than one-quarter incorrect, and one-fifth negative.

The forecasts tested above were spread over the whole period from 1921 to 1927. Accuracy, however, does not run evenly over this period. It was distinctly better before 1923, during which year it suffered greatly. with the result that forecasters grew more and more cautious, and many qualified their predictions out of all definiteness. This whole period, moreover, was marked by relatively slight changes in total business volume or average prices. The prediction of "slight or no change," therefore, predominated during the period. When the few changes did come, accuracy of prediction was distinctly less.

It was as difficult a period on which to test forecasting as has recently occurred. The few general services that were issued in the extreme days of 1920 make a better showing. All of them gave general and early warnings, though not always as solemn as events proved warranted. One, which started early and emphasized its warnings strongly, was rewarded by a sharp though temporary drop in the number of its subscribers. At the opposite extreme there are to-day some fly-by-night services which make a specialty of enthusiastic and favorable prediction. All services must feel the pressure in this direction, and it is to their credit that so many are resisting it, and, against the difficulties of insufficient knowledge of facts and causes, are helping to develop what should some day become an important aid in business navigation.

However specific results in its chosen field may be judged, forecasting must be credited with having done a considerable share toward developing a desire in the American business manager to look farther and farther ahead, a growing faith in the possibilities of doing so, and, finally, a habit of mind which has shown its influence not merely in forecasting for the guidance of general management but in departmental budgeting, production planning, far-sighted research, and longer-range planning of capital expenditures.

II. MANAGEMENT OF MANUFACTURING

Purchasing.—Most manufacturing companies have a sharply differentiated purchasing department, with full and elaborate purchase records. Purchasing is naturally always in close contact with the manufacturing division, but is not often subordinate to it.

Orders may be placed through competitive bidding or exclusively with tested vendors. Quite commonly a combination of these methods is used by calling for competitive bids, from tested companies only. On account of the growing emphasis upon uniform quality, it is probable that there is a slight trend at the present moment toward buying of tested vendors, checking their service from time to time by placing orders out for competitive bids. A minority use competitive bidding only. The policy of splitting orders among two or more vendors and that of maintaining a single supply are found in about equal numbers, but those who use competitive bidding, added to the former group, definitely set the going practice against buying exclusively from a single supplying house.

The responsibility for buying certain principal materials is sometimes in the hands of other officials than the purchasing agent. In the smallest plants, particularly, is this true; while in the largest there are few cases to be found where the purchasing agent does not do all of the buying. Not uncommonly, however, the purchasing agent is strongly influenced by the selling department, or board of directors, toward certain customers, thus taking part in what is called reciprocal buying.

An interesting development of recent years is the attention given by some purchasers toward the saving of salesmen's time and convenience, and, in general, cultivating their constructive goodwill.   It was not to be expected that this sort of trend would occur in times like these, when the buyer controls the market, and yet it is to-day a trend and indicates that purchasers are developing a broader conception of their function than that which ruled some years ago.   Buyers are taking their part in working out annual contracts with price adjustments, and in placing repeat orders without salesman's call, each primarily for the purpose of saving time for the visiting salesman.   Sometimes this time is again used up, but in somewhat more productive ways, by asking intimate and con-structive assistance from the salesman himself, having him go into the plant, see its problems, and make such suggestions as he can toward their solution.   The changes in buyer-salesman relations are doing more to lower inventories and co-ordinate production without vertical combina-tion than is generally realized.   There is real evidence that a widening knowledge of facts is reducing the area of dickering.

In one company which takes its job of purchasing in a seriously professional spirit, there was appointed some years ago, at the request of the purchasing agent, a special "auditor," who reports directly to the executive officers.   He examines all orders, quite independently of the purchasing agent, being sure that the proper amount of competition has been secured, that no favorites are being played, and that consideration is given to all new sources of supply.   In general, there will be found among purchasing departments a drift away from the old notion that placing an order constitutes a great and personal favor.

Purchasing agents are more and more keeping in touch with the general market through commodity indexes and business publications, among which trade journals prevail.   The economic behavior of specific commodities in the last decade has varied so widely from the curves of average economic activity that general statistical services are not so widely used in purchasing departments as are the journals and reports which publish all of the significant facts concerning each of the separate important commodities.

Inventory Control.—The shortage of materials during the war and the boom, and their excess during the 1921 depression, both resulted in a great increase of concentration upon inventory control.   The wider use of planning and budgeting has since then added its influence.   Con-trol of raw materials, goods in process, and finished stock is obtained through a close checking of card records, or the use of maxima and minima, and in some companies is entrusted to an independent stores department, to special committees, or, in a few cases, to the budget department itself.   This control is not now chiefly for financial reasons, but rather more to reduce the risks of depreciation and obsolescence of material, which the lessons of 1921 proved to be considerable, and to save the wastes of carting materials unnecessarily in and out of warehouses,[13] which the more recent studies into production costs have disclosed.

One of the dramatic developments of the last year or two is to be found in some automobile plants, where the average inventory has actually decreased from several months' to a three or four days' supply. A reserve stock of all materials used in three or four days' production is placed in a convenient warehouse, but daily deliveries from vendors are arranged according to the production schedule. Materials are, therefore, planned to be taken directly from the freight cars and placed in the manufacturing departments where they are used, thus eliminating handling and the expense of stores control. Obviously, such a tight system can be successfully managed only with very dependable railway freight service and in a business where a large part of production is carried out on a uniform daily schedule.[14]

Production Management.—Production is managed either by sending all orders into the works as fast as received and leaving the sequence of their production to be arranged by each department head, or it is planned, to a greater or less degree, on the basis of known standards of output and quality, of known inventories of raw materials and parts, and known or estimated demand for finished products.

Complete production planning, as it is found to-day, includes routing, or the determination of the path of an order through the plant; scheduling, or the determination of the time at which each operation shall be done; dispatching, or the actual assignment of orders to the production agent for the work which he is to do next.[15] In this survey, the majority of plants was found to have functionalized their production planning. Most of them had done so under the spur of war times; some, especially in the metal trades, started even before that. Most of those which have not yet done so are laying plans to give it special attention. Like other functions, planning, when first isolated, was heavily centralized and over-elaborated, later it was simplified and partly decentralized.

Production planning varies greatly in complexity. In a jobbing shop with diversified product, large and expensive planning departments are to be found; in a one-product shop, making by continuous process a standardized quality, production planning once installed is simple of operation.

[13] Eugene G. Grace, in the *Saturday Evening Post*, September 6, 1926, traces broad and wholesome effects of close inventory control, emphasizing especially regularization of employment.

[14] See Inventory, Chap. II, Industry, Part 1, p. 91; Chap. III, Construction, p. 242; Chap. IV, Transportation, Part 1, p. 302; Chap. V, Marketing, p. 350; Chap. IX, Price Movements, p. 637.

[15] A fuller description can be found in the Production Control section (beginning p. 597) of *Management's Handbook*, L. P. Alford, editor, 1924.

Costing is found closely associated with planning. Both use much the same facts and both serve the needs of general management in controlling production. Like planning, costing is found in a majority of plants, but in a variety of forms. Until the last few years, costs were "actual costs" almost exclusively, though kept with great differences in accuracy and detail. Actual costs vary with each lot and with every season; their use as a check on selling prices or for budget purposes is, therefore, limited. A few years ago there was a strong movement toward standard costs[16] worked out either roughly from past averages, or more carefully from standards of quantity production per hour and of materials used. The purpose to which these costs are put, in the largest single number of cases, is to show profit margins, but an almost equal number use them to check departmental performance; some use is made of them to determine the actual losses involved in part-time operation, or as aids in working out special economies. Most companies using standard costs are also keeping actual costs, but much simplified in detail and reduced in expensiveness. Where production is fully serialized, costing as well as planning is greatly simplified.

Quality Standards.—One factor upon which production planning depends is uniformity in the quality of materials. If automatic machines are regularly to produce parts capable of being assembled without slow and painful hand fitting, the raw material or parts fed into them must be of standard and uniform quality. Or if effective systems of wage payment are to be installed, the materials furnished to the worker must have a dependable uniformity.

Buying upon specification and checking by testing laboratories has become the going practice. Most of the larger companies, and many of the smaller ones, have their own laboratories; and commercial laboratories are freely used by them, as well as by those which cannot afford their own. Practically all managers report that they are increasing the precision of their specifications, which in the larger companies comprise several printed volumes. Some work out their own specifications, as must be done in special cases; but, for the more staple items, the large majority are using the published standards which leading trade associations have been active for several years in developing. The American Society for Testing Materials and the American Engineering Standards Committee[17] have had large shares in this development, and a considerable number of companies are using to an increasing extent the specifications of the United States Bureau of Standards.[18]

---

[16] T. H. Sanders, *Problems of Industrial Accounting*, 1923, gives a chapter outlining in brief form the principles of standard costs. See also several bulletins of the National Association of Cost Accountants.

[17] See their *Year Book* for 1928.

[18] See *Standards Year Book*, 1928.

Uniform standard quality in parts to be assembled, and in final product, is being provided for by similar methods. Special inspection departments, often under or closely connected with the engineering department or the laboratory, are maintained in a considerable proportion of companies; and parts and product specifications are set up with the same care as material specifications. The processes themselves have been studied by engineers to eliminate chances of variation. Automatic thermostatic control, perfected mixing devices, elaborate jigs, highly accurate gauges, and electrical tempering are found in increasing numbers.[19] The field survey clearly showed the greater pressure for quality output which increasing competition has exerted upon manufacturers. Quality demands have, in fact, been giving executives more concern than have quantity demands. In some goods this machine-made age is giving us better and more dependable quality than was possible in the age of handicraft. The progress of engineering toward objectified control of quality is certainly one of the significant trends of our technical progress.

Since the publication of *Waste in Industry*, in 1921, more and more attention has been given to the problem of gaining continuous co-operation from the whole body of employees toward the maintenance of standard quality and the avoidance of the waste of rejections. Some form of financial incentive to this end has been set up in a fair number of plants, which has been supplemented in some of them by other influences intended to develop a favorable group habit of thought. Suggestion systems, periodical quality meetings, and publications have all been used, and the maintenance of quality and the elimination of material waste have been subjects frequently appearing in the consultations of employers and employees in union relationships or works councils. There is an increasing tendency to install special departments which study the causes of every sort of waste and the better utilization of such wastes of materials as cannot be prevented.

Maintenance Standards.—The maintenance of machinery in standard condition, which is as necessary to standard quality as is uniform material, has not been given the same attention. It is in the newer plants that more specific machine maintenance standards seem to be most often found. A few factories schedule maintenance, so planning as to get replacements made ahead of actual need and at such times as will least interrupt production. In most companies there is no such planning, and maintenance departments are expected to act only in response to the calls of producing department heads.[20]

[19] See Mechanization, Chap. I, Consumption, p. 52; Chap. II, Industry, Part 1, p. 84, Part 2, p. 104; Chap. III, Construction, p. 234; Chap. V, Marketing, p. 328; Chap. VI, Labor, p. 483; Chap. VIII, Agriculture, p. 557.

[20] The Society of Industrial Engineers, *Bulletin*, December, 1927, p. 7, and June, 1928. p. 5.

Quantity Standards.—Control of production is found to increase with the specification of standards of quality and quantity, and with the accuracy and fullness of planning. For many years after Frederick W. Taylor first set forth his ideal of a true control of production processes,[21] its acceptance as a practicable goal was slow, but of late years it has been rapid. It is now common practice to have some sort of quantity standards, and once established, even crudely, there is a distinct tendency toward their continuous improvement; for efforts toward the advance planning of production and the developing of incentive wage payments encourage progress toward greater accuracy of quantity standards.

Methods for determining standards range from a rough analysis of past records through the study of machine speeds and some crude and sometimes harmful over-all time studies, to careful elemental time and motion studies. The more laborious but more substantial methods seem to be gaining slowly.[22] Employers find that the cruder forms carry with them evils which become more serious as time goes on. Over-all time studies which fail to analyze and standardize the process, and which, therefore, set a time standard for an unstandardized process, result in piece or bonus rates only roughly accurate. Some are too high and some too low, causing fluctuations in earnings not corresponding to effort, and complaints of favoritism. Readjustment without analytical time study results in bickerings or feelings of resentment. Any readjustment, or threat of readjustment, of rates downward that is not convincingly supported by facts, and some that are, will inevitably result in output restriction. The full power of a standard of output is not realized unless the standard can be accepted as just.

A detailed report of scores of cases of restriction, which strikingly illustrates the variety of circumstances under which this practice will arise, is to be published by S. B. Mathewson and William Leiserson. This study finds incentives double-acting. Before, during, and after over-all time studies, there are strong influences at work to limit production, sometimes in most ingenious ways. Men commonly are convinced, and often correctly, that management has in mind a figure of "excessive earnings" at which it will cut rates or make other vital changes. These figures are played up to with great skill by employees in a wide variety of situations, not confined to the manufacturing field. The motives are, in a very large majority of cases, motives of simple self-protection.

Increased Output.—Within such limitations as individuals and groups have set for their protection, output per man per year has, nevertheless,

[21] See Frederick W. Taylor, *Shop Management*, pp. 94–124.

[22] See for Results of Society of Industrial Engineers' survey, "Development of Standard Practice for Time-Study Engineering," Society of Industrial Engineers, *Bulletin*, November, 1927.

increased notably. Such plants as could be found in this survey with man-hour productivity figures running back several years show considerable increases, but the fact that they were few, and that, because they were careful enough to keep such figures, they were probably among the most interested, precludes the use of their experience as anything more than corroborative evidence. Thirty-five, which furnished information going back to 1919, showed a man-hour productivity increase of 74 per cent; and a few who can compare 1927 with 1924 show an average increase of 39 per cent.[23]

This increase is the result of the interplay of several causes. Among them are the introduction of new machines,[24] the better internal arrangement of factories through which, by "serialization," supermachines are made out of groups of machines, production control, more rigid specification of quality of materials, change in methods of wage payment and in the basic attitude between employer and employee, shortened learning periods, and reduced labor turnover.[25] Many of the technological changes have been made possible by simplification of product or standardization of parts. In the companies where style has made the product less standard than before, there was less evidence of increased productivity.

There could be found no single impelling force which drove management to its recent rapid technical progress, though well up in the list stands the influence of higher wages. A great many changes have originated from attempts to get low costs in spite of high wage rates, and then have been continued and have spread into fields where wages were not high. Changes to reduce manufacturing costs have, in fact, become the fashion. They are becoming less and less casual, less dependent upon the good ideas and ingenuity of operating men, and more upon the work of research and accounting departments, specially set up to increase the frequency of improvements in method.

Whether and to what extent there is to-day an overexpansion of industrial facilities are questions which may be answered only by a determination of the correct amount of equipment for a given output and of the true extent of demand. The opinion of industrialists is about evenly divided on the subject. There is general agreement that the war times and 1920 saw heavy overexpansion, the lessons of which were costly

[23] For further details of output per man, see Chap. II, Industry, Part 1, p. 81, Part 2, p. 103; Chap. III, Construction, p. 248; Chap. IV, Transportation, p. 285; Chap. VI, Labor, p. 447; Chap. VII, Management, p. 512; Chap. VIII, Agriculture, p. 602.

[24] It must be noted that the production of machinery from 1922 to 1927 shows no noteworthy increase. For a complete description of mechanization in four industries, see G. E. Barnett, *Machinery and Labor*, 1927.

[25] A clear case of what can be done by management alone, with only slight changes in mechanization, is set forth in Chapter V, pp. 350–1.

and not easily forgotten; but few managers regard their own equipment as too extensive for normally active times. The Department of Commerce is at the present time making a survey of the industrial equipment of the country, which should constitute a sound beginning of better knowledge on this subject.

Effect upon Workers.—The effects of these great changes upon the worker is a matter of considerable controversy. Some men believe that the present changes are merely a continuation and accentuation of those which began with the Industrial Revolution, and that reabsorption of the unemployed into activities made possible by the increased producing power of the world has been constantly going on, though, of course, more slowly during the inactive sectors of the business cycle than during the active.

Others believe that we are facing a wholly new problem, which they call "technological unemployment," and that there is now and will continue to be an unemployment of serious proportions unless something is done about it.[26] The thing that is certain is that our information concerning the extent, nature, and reasons of unemployment in this country is inadequate.

The inadequacy of public information is, unfortunately, equaled by the inadequacy of information in individual companies. Few of them know exactly what numbers have been released or transferred on account of technical improvements; and almost none knows anything about what has happened to the men who were released.[27] It is not a new problem to industry, but in former times it was none of the manufacturer's business what happened to workers after he laid them off. He is now begin-

---

[26] Studies of the extent of unemployment will be found in Chap. VI, Labor, pp. 462–478, and reference to technological unemployment in Chap. II, Industry, Part 1, p. 92; and Chap. V, Marketing, pp. 321–331.

[27] A recent study of cutters in the Men's Clothing Industry in Chicago, by Robert J. Myers, a graduate student at the University of Chicago, shows what has happened to displaced workers in one industry. (Dr. B. M. Squires, Chairman of the Trade Board, Men's Clothing Industry, Chicago, and Professor at the University of Chicago, included a reading of the survey in an address before the American Association for Labor Legislation, December 26, 1928.) A detailed description appears in the accompanying table.

Further data on the problem appear in a study, "Measuring the Mobility of American Labor and The Absorptive Power of American Industry," made by Dr. Isador Lubin for the Institute of Economics of the Brookings Institute, Washington, D. C. (Part of the findings in this study were presented before the American Statistical Association at the December, 1928, meeting in Chicago.) The second tabulation here given, made by Dr. Lubin, shows the periods of unemployment of a sample of 754 discharged workers.

From a group of 820 discharged workers, of those who found jobs 273 went to work in new industries, and 221 in new jobs; 188 returned to their old jobs and 134 to the old industry. In this case, nearly half of the workers on new jobs received lower incomes than in their previous permanent employment.

NUMBER AND PER CENT OF TOTAL OF 217 CUTTERS FROM HART SCHAFFNER & MARX, AND 153 CUTTERS FROM OTHER FACTORIES ENGAGED IN SPECIFIED OCCUPATIONS, EARLY SUMMER, 1928

Occupation	Number		Per cent of total	
	Hart, Schaffner & Marx	Other	Hart, Schaffner & Marx	Other
Total.................................	217	153	100.0	100.0
Total cutters.................................	49	25	22.6	16.4
Men's clothing—				
Chicago, regular work, union..............	10	7	4.6	4.6
Chicago, regular work, non-union..........	4	3	1.8	2.0
Chicago, temporary work.................	16	2	7.4	1.3
Chicago, job permanence unknown........	0	9	0.0	5.9
Out of city.............................	6	3	2.8	2.0
Allied trades.............................	13	1	6.0	0.6
Professional men..............................	5	2	2.3	1.3
Tailors and cleaners...........................	3	14	1.4	9.2
Skilled workmen, not elsewhere classified............	14	10	6.4	6.5
Grocers, confectioners, etc........................	17	9	7.8	5.9
Politicians.......................................	6	4	2.8	2.6
Office clerks......................................	3	2	1.4	1.3
Real estate and insurance agents..................	13	11	6.0	7.2
Drivers, truckers, etc............................	17	24	7.8	15.0
Firemen, police and letter carriers.................	2	0	0.9	0.0
Farmers...	1	0	0.5	0.0
Salesmen, not elsewhere classified.................	34	20	15.7	13.1
Bartenders and bootleggers........................	4	1	1.8	0.6
Factory and industrial workers....................	9	7	4.2	4.6
Caretakers, janitors, messengers, etc...............	11	4	5.1	2.6
Day laborers....................................	4	4	1.8	2.6
Not employed...................................	25	16	11.5	10.4
Dead..	6	2	2.8	1.3
Retired......................................	2	3	0.9	2.0
Ill, unemployable..............................	3	1	1.4	0.6
Unemployed, seeking work...................	14	10	6.4	6.5

PERIOD OF UNEMPLOYMENT OF 754 DISCHARGED WORKERS

Length of time unemployed	Number who found jobs	Per cent who found jobs	Cumulative per cent who found jobs	Number still unemployed when interviewed	Per cent still unemployed when interviewed	Cumulative per cent still unemployed
Under 1 month.................	47	11.5	.....	43	12.5	.....
1 month – 2 months...........	66	16.1	27.6	40	11.6	24.1
2 months– 3 months...........	66	16.1	43.7	37	10.8	34.9
3 months– 4 months...........	60	14.6	58.3	34	9.9	44.8
4 months– 5 months...........	43	10.5	68.8	26	7.6	52.4
5 months– 6 months...........	30	7.3	76.1	22	6.4	58.8
6 months– 7 months...........	28	6.9	83.0	27	7.9	66.7
7 months– 8 months.....:....	23	5.6	88.6	18	5.2	71.9
8 months– 9 months...........	18	4.4	93.0	31	9.0	80.9
9 months–10 months...........	10	2.4	95.4	19	5.5	86.4
10 months–11 months...........	7	1.7	97.1	7	2.0	88.4
11 months–12 months...........	3	.7	97.8	8	2.3	90.7
Over 1 year...................	6	1.5	99.3	29	8.4	99.1
No data......................	3	.7	100.0	3	.9	100.0
	410			344		

ning to see the matter in another light.[28] The new attitude is well expressed by Ernest G. Draper, of Hills Bros. Co., who says,

It is now time for the modern business man to give up thinking of this hazard of industry (unemployment) as a charitable problem and begin thinking of it as a business problem which directly affects his company's net income . . . Unemployment is not only harmful from a social point of view. It is wasteful from a business point of view. When enough industrial leaders can become sufficiently interested in this serious maladjustment of society, the chances are that it will succumb to their ingenuity just as many other so-called insoluble situations have done in the past.[29]

A remark of Professor Tugwell is also to the point.[30]

One difficulty which runs all through attempts to get control of the modern forces in the interest of a better world is that the old rate of change has been superseded by a greatly accelerated one.

This comes close to the heart of the present problem. The *type* of to-day's change is, in its effect upon the workers, the same that we have been experiencing for nearly 200 years; the *rate* of change may now be such as to introduce new considerations and demand new measures.[31] The crucial factor may be the rate of invention of new consumers' goods, as compared with the rate of invention in machines and processes of manufacture.

Besides affecting workers through unemployment and shift of occupation, the last few years have brought important changes in the demand for skill. During the last century many special "skills" have been made worthless by process changes; more than once has the work of the skillful father been displaced by the untrained fingers of his wife and children. Where technical changes came slowly, the new occupations themselves soon allowed of the development of new special skills. But where these changes are as rapid as they are to-day, and bring with them such erratic fluctuations in market demands, there has been afforded to employers special reason to work out the newer processes in such form that they demand the least possible training and hence contain a low "skill content." Often by holding raw materials and parts to rigid standards, the old need of skill in detecting and manipulating variations has been entirely done away with. Some of the automobile plants in 1927 took farmers who had been driven out of their homes in Arkansas by the floods and put them not only on the assembly lines but on specialized machine tools. They claim that these men in a few days were among the best

[28] See, for example, article on the five-day week by Clarence W. Barron in *Dow's Financial Bulletin*, June 8, 1928. For a full analysis, see *Business Cycles and Unemployment*, National Bureau of Economic Research, 1923.

[29] *Personnel*, American Management Association, August, 1928.

[30] *Industry's Coming of Age*, 1927.

[31] The results reached by Dr. Wolman on page 478 indicate no immediately pressing problem of this sort.

workmen they had ever had. Many companies say they "would rather have green men with no preconceived notions."

As the great number of highly specialized machines increases, there is less and less carry-over of skill from one job to another, and fewer places to which a worker can put to use any special skills he has managed to gain, but there are more places in which he can reach average ability in a very few days.

An important influence in shortening the learning period has been the higher intelligence of the learners; more have finished grade school,[32] more have been in trade schools and high schools, and, since the restriction upon immigration, relatively more have understood English.

Any real knowledge of the extent to which skill has been displaced, or of the social consequences of such displacement, must wait upon some consensus of opinion as to what is to be taken as constituting skill. Miss Bezanson,[33] in 1922, made one of the earliest studies in the field, but little has been published since. Meanwhile, general opinion repeats that "there are fewer highly skilled jobs but fewer really unskilled jobs;" or that "all of the old really skilled workers can find high place in the new schemes of things as foremen, tool makers, machine fixers, and the like."[34]

Effects of the War on Management of Labor.—War times, with the difficulties in obtaining large numbers of employees, in getting them trained to wholly new jobs and holding them against temptations to shift, forced wider recognition of personnel management as a distinct function. The work of the Army itself in placing, training, and assimilating its millions had no small part in bringing about this recognition. Up to that time, the problem of personnel management had been recognized by few as one of importance. With free immigration, help was easy to get, and, though it was not easy to hold, to hold it seemed of no importance until a highly original article by Magnus W. Alexander, appearing just before the war, made a powerful case against the extravagances of a high labor turnover.

To meet the extreme war-time situation, men were called to personnel management who were new to the problem; necessarily so, since not a half dozen men in the country could be called old to it. Their experience was academic but their outlook fresh, their sympathies and earnestness were high, many of them had keen and well-trained minds, and they knew enough to begin at once to learn from each other by pooling their experiences. They overcentralized and overelaborated the job, as is always

---

[32] Between 1920 and 1924, the pupils in public high schools increased from 1,850,000 to 2,950,000; in private secondaries, from 117,000 to 216,000; in industrial trade schools, from 185,000 to 410,000; in percentage of total school population, from 2.1 to 3.3 per cent. *Statistical Abstract*, 1926.

[33] *Quarterly Journal of Economics*, August, 1922.

[34] From the field survey.

likely at the installation of a new functional department; and in this case all the more so because of the intense pressures.

With the business stagnation and glutted labor market of 1921, they were virtually swept away, but they left behind them new practices, and old ones modified: psychological and trade tests, job analyses and classifications, rating scales, systematic training, and shop committees. What is of more importance is that they left a habit in the business mind of considering personnel management as a difficult, distinct, and major function of business management. Previously, such little selection, training, health and safety work, insurance and social contacts, and joint relationships as had been attempted, had often been administered with no co-ordination, with disproportionate emphases and accidental and fluctuating interests—sometimes as frills, sometimes as personal whims of benevolence, seldom as serious projects of human engineering.

Subsequent Trends.—To-day, though unquestionably greater attention and interest is given to the materials and machines which an organization handles than to the humans of which it is made up,[35] attention to the problems of personnel management has by no means lapsed, but appears rather to be increasing. There is not so much said now in the field or in publications about the personnel manager himself or the centralizing of the personnel functions. From 1918 to 1920 there was a great deal, which dropped off into an almost complete silence by 1922. Since then, attention has been given more to the specific and practical measures of personnel management, with the implication that they are among the problems of general management rather than problems apart. Especially out of fashion to-day are the magazine articles which in 1919 and 1920 described "what we do for our employees."

Personnel management to-day is now tending to emphasize the responsibility of line officers—foremen and department heads—for sound relationships, but to give to staff personnel men the task of analyzing and criticising results, and devising and installing measures to make them progressively better.

Among different-sized companies, personnel work varies, there being naturally less of it in the smaller plants.[36] In plants of 2,000 employees, it is common to find it fully organized, and some smaller plants do very complete work. The results of this survey, arranged geographically, show considerably greater activity in the Middle West than in the Northeastern section.

Selection.—The routine parts of the job of personnel management, most widely recognized and functionalized, are selection and placement,

[35] Examples of a considerable variety of executives' attitudes toward labor are given by J. David Houser, *What the Employer Thinks*, 1927.

[36] See "Personnel Administration in Companies of 1,000 or Less," American Management Association Convention Address, Series No. 10, 1924.

maintenance of individual records, medical service, and supervision of transfers and separation.

The utilization of psychological and trade tests for selection and placement was given a big start during the war by the work of the Army Committee on Classification of Personnel. A great deal of the work which had been so rapidly undertaken, however, was given up during the depression of 1921; but, even before then, it had become evident that no single simple method would suffice to discover and test the subtle and varied qualifications of men. Most companies, therefore, have now dropped tests completely and only a small minority use them at all; many of these have specialized them greatly, attempting by tests to find particular trade skills and different types of aptitude, rather than general intelligence levels. An unexpected number of companies were found carrying on correlation studies to discover special uses to which information in application blanks might be put. They report fair success in their results so far.

There is a promising field within which the technique of testing is being developed in the selection of life insurance salesmen,[37] department store employees, and employees of street railway and taxicab companies. Steady work is being done by groups of psychologists,[38] and by the United States Civil Service Commission,[39] which, required by law to use examinations for selection, is doing outstanding work in inventing examinations which really examine. Universities which have student personnel officers, or which are experimenting with methods of meeting the admission problem, are also making their contributions to the discovery of less subjective, fluctuating, and capricious methods of selection.

Preceding psychological examination, and now extending in development far beyond it throughout industry, is medical examination.[40] The majority of companies, large enough to have a clinic of their own,[41] are using medical examinations and are steadily improving them in accuracy and detail. Few can be found which have dropped medical examination after once taking it up.

A systematic understanding of the jobs, among which an employee, once selected, has to be placed, has made slower headway. Job specifi-

---

[37] Grace E. Manson, "What Can the Application Blank Tell?—Records of 4,000 Life Insurance Salesmen," *Journal of Personnel Research*, July, 1925.

[38] For example, see Slocombe and Bingham, "Men Who Have Accidents; Individual Differences among Motormen and Bus Operators," *Personnel Journal*, December, 1927.

[39] L. J. O'Rourke, "Saving Dollars and Energy by Personnel Research," *Journal of Personnel Research*, January, February, and March, 1926.

[40] *Medical Care of Individual Workers*, National Industrial Conference Board, 1926.

[41] A few interesting cases of small companies running clinics jointly were found in the files of the National Industrial Conference Board.

cations are not common, and those which are more than hasty and informal generalizations, sufficient perhaps for the rough methods of selection used, are less common. In the rare cases in which they go beyond a roughly general description, they seem to have been prepared for the purposes of classification of wage and salary bases and standards, and worked out as a thorough-going job study by the personnel officer and the line officers concerned, in close collaboration.

Where there are functionalized employment departments, there is often to be found a systematic follow-up of new employees, used both as a means of checking correctness of selection and placement and as a means of developing good will during the difficult period of adjustment. Performance and attendance records and the pay changes of new employees are given special study and checked against standards. During the adjustment period, employees are frequently talked with in order to discover, if possible, any special difficulties in their way. Medical examiners, too, are more and more frequently following up their preliminary work. Few companies have compulsory periodic medical examination, but a growing number are offering facilities for examination, under such conditions as will enlist the confidence of the employees and persuade them to take voluntary advantage of it.

Training.—In spite of the obviously shorter learning periods required for many of the newer jobs, the interest in training[42] aroused at the time of the war has not materially abated. The actual training school, or vestibule school, has almost disappeared, but it is common to find functional supervisors who give attention to the training which now generally takes place in the producing departments, though often in special subdivisions of them. Apprentice training courses are still used in considerable numbers, though restricted for the most part to a few trades; but special training for aliens, so common ten years ago, has naturally fallen off, and, in the few cases in which it exists, is now provided for chiefly by the community rather than the factory.

For foreman training, there are to be found, and apparently in increasing numbers, foremen's conferences, co-operation with the Y. M. C. A.'s and State's departments of education, evening classes at the plant in special subjects, and discussion groups. A survey by the United States Chamber of Commerce gave the number of courses for foremanship training as 105 in 1925 and 933 in 1927. The old doctrine that a foreman was to learn his job on the job and from the job is not so often heard.

In a small and growing number of companies, educational opportunities are offered for those beyond foremanship grade; courses in cultural subjects having no direct relation to the business were found

[42] See H. G. Kenagy, "The Technique of Training on the Job," American Management Association, Annual Convention, Series No. 74, 1928.

in a little less than 10 per cent of the companies of this survey. Some of the larger corporations have carefully arranged job sequences to be followed through under the guidance of a training supervisor. These were especially designed for college graduates, but are usually open to others who can pass an appropriate examination.

An interesting special case of training has been developed by the public relations departments of some public service corporations. Their corps of "service samplers" continually test the contact of employees and public, reporting the especially good cases by name and the unsatisfactory cases without identification. These latter are made the subject of discussions by executives and of large group conferences of "contact employees," at which methods of improvement are considered.

As a means of general education, the company or plant magazine stood high ten years ago, but as such it has been quite widely discontinued. Few other activities related to personnel management have been so curtailed in recent years as the company magazine. Yet it remains in a significant number of cases,[43] ranking now as a method of fostering good will and promoting better acquaintance among all members of the organization rather than as a strictly educational device.

To assist in the orderly progress of employees, and to get such objective help as is possible in selecting men for promotion, a few companies have continued and developed the rating scales which came into use during the war. In themselves, rating scales have not gone far, but, even in some of the places where they are undeveloped or have been given up, they nevertheless have emphasized the double importance of correct selection for promotion and the consequent need of the utmost possible avoidance of the distortions of unaided personal judgment. It is more and more widely recognized that, while the importance of choosing the right person for promotion is great in so far as his work in the higher position will affect the company, it is many times greater in its effect on his fellow employees, who are bound to set the fashion of their performance by what his elevation led them to believe were the accomplishments upon which promotion depends. Rating scales, however imperfect, have shown an advantage in being a down-on-paper statement, usually with important qualities so listed that they cannot be overlooked. They have helped to avoid the day-to-day fluctuations of personal opinion.

Several companies provide a small special committee of department heads to review periodically the rating charts of the entire personnel. They discuss the relative qualifications of various individuals for eventual salary increase or for promotion to advanced positions. Then when a vacancy occurs, the work of this committee is first canvassed to find if

[43] The National Industrial Conference Board, in November, 1928, estimated about 700 in the United States.

any members of the organization can be considered in line for the position. In a few companies, such job and man classifications have grown after some years into a standard promotion schedule. with normal lines of progress extending on from each position.

Separations.—Discharge is in most companies still the exclusive prerogative of the foreman, though in some the approval of the personnel manager is necessary. In a considerable majority, on voluntary separation or discharge, an exit interview is carried out in order that special and remediable causes of misunderstanding may in the given case, or in future cases like it, be overcome. Many companies circulate the general information from these exit interviews among their executives, to disclose departmental differences or trends toward the better or worse.

In spite of reductions in labor turnover rates, indicated by the studies of the Metropolitan Life Insurance Co. to be not far from one-half,[44] interest in turnover does not seem to abate but rather to increase. This is probably because certain organizations of high standing, such as the Policyholders' Service Bureau of the Metropolitan Life Insurance Co., the Brown University Bureau of Business Research, the Bureau of Industrial Research of the University of Pennsylvania, the Ohio State University Bureau of Business Research, and some trade associations are issuing current and valuable information on the subject.[45] A great many companies are reporting to them. About two-thirds of the companies covered by this survey were tabulating turnover figures, and a little less than one-half were reporting their figures periodically to some outside organization.

Little evidence can be gathered from the field as to the age at which workers are being retired.[46] There seem to be more jobs on which the vigor of youth is demanded, and fewer on which the sort of skill is needed which would increase with age. Yet, in examining individual cases, there is seen to be still a considerable amount of work fit for older men. On the whole, it seems likely that during depressions there would now be a somewhat larger number of the men over 55 and a smaller number of the younger men laid off from factories than in days before the war. It is not clear as to whether or not this, if true, would result in increased social hardship.

Wages.—Rapid shifts in relative skills, new jobs, and new methods on old jobs, have led many companies to make critical comparisons among their wage rates and weekly earnings. Where this has been done thoroughly, it has disclosed the interest of the worker not only in the amount

---

[44] The highest rate, reported in their monthly medians for 1922, is 96 per cent; in 1923, 130 per cent; in 1927, 48.3 per cent; and in 1928 (7 months), 41.5 per cent.

[45] W. A. Berridge, *Personnel Journal*, June, 1927.

[46] A small sample of employees, carrying group insurance, showed average age slightly higher in 1925–1927 than in 1917–1920. See Chap. VI, sec. 4, p. 471.

he receives but in what he regards as the fairness of its relation to other amounts. As Whiting Williams found, the wage or salary is to its recipient not only an income but also a symbol of status.

Personnel departments and operating executives have considered it important to work toward the elimination of the more serious discrepancies in rates and, if possible, to develop orderly and rational systems of differentials. In nearly one-half the companies in this survey were found job and rate classifications, with various basic rates worked out from union scales or from comparable rates in the vicinity. Interchange of information on rates has been common for many years. Lately, in the larger centers, it has become still more common on account of the formation of local associations of employment managers.

Forms of incentive wages which take into account quantity or quality of output, or both, have come rapidly into use in recent years, although they cannot yet be estimated as covering a majority of the workers.[47] They are no longer merely piece rates, but have a variety of forms combining time rates, piece rates, premiums, and bonuses in many ways. Group rates are now being used increasingly.

Besides direct payments, there are to be found length-of-service bonuses, attendance bonuses, and suggestion awards.[48] Pay for vacations has also come into vogue to some extent during the last ten years. Of 199 vacation plans described by Mills, 75 had been adopted before 1919, 100 in the five years from 1919 to 1923 (inclusive), and 24 in the three following years.[49]

From the discussions of business managers, speeches at their conventions, and a considerable number of articles published by them, it is obvious that an economic doctrine quite different from that prevailing among them some years ago has gained a foothold. Instead of believing that every cent paid as increased wages must come from the investor's return, or else from ultimate consumers, it is now widely believed that, where an appropriate increase in productivity can go along with an increase in wages, the consequent increase in purchasing power results not only in higher standards of living and better states of health but also in increases in the quantities and varieties of goods which can be sold. These increased quantities, by helping to carry overhead and by making specialized operations possible, tend further to reduce cost and so again to increase wealth. In 1921, this theory as a business manager's doctrine cannot be said to have been born. The President's

[47] The National Metal Trades Association found in 672 member plants that 307 paid their employees on a straight time basis exclusively. Of the total employees in all 672 shops, 27.5 per cent were paid on incentive basis. It is wholly probable that the percentage for industry as a whole is higher than this.

[48] For details, see Z. C. Dickinson, "Suggestions from Employees," *University of Michigan Business Studies*, Vol. 1, No. 3, 1927.

[49] Charles M. Mills, *Vacations for Individual Workers*, 1927.

Unemployment Conference gave out its findings in the autumn, and one of its members, Roy Dickinson, an editor of *Printer's Ink*, wrote several articles on the relation of wages to the volume of trade. But among operating executives the most frequent subject for discussion was the necessity for "liquidating labor" before recovery could be expected from the depression. In 1921, more than 300 articles appeared telling of methods used in cutting wages and speculating as to how far they would fall. By 1922, articles of this sort had disappeared and those about wage incentives had taken their place. In 1923, Mr. Baum, in the *Paper Trade Journal*, wrote, "It is becoming a sign of poor management and a mark of disgrace to pay low wages." Since then even more emphatic statements have been made and by employers of national reputation.[50] The high wage doctrine by 1926 had gained its present standing. Nevertheless, no one can say whether its foothold is as yet strong enough to stand the strains of a long depression. Not many popular beliefs gain such strength in a half dozen years.[51]

Security.—Of all the problems of personnel management none has had so much attention as those which pertain to the workers' need for security—regularization of employment, accident prevention, group insurance, pensions, savings plans, and stock purchase plans.

To judge from the companies of this survey, the beginnings of substantial progress have been made, since the Unemployment Conference in 1921, in moderating the severities of seasonal irregularities. In about one-half of the companies it was found that definite measures had been put into effect; in 4 per cent especially trying conditions had increased irregularity; in 5 per cent nothing had been done to attempt to mitigate the effect of seasonal fluctuations; and in 40 per cent the problem had never been acute. Among the measures reported are increased standardization of products, better planning, scheduling production, inducing customers to buy more regularly, additional or specialized warehousing facilities, training employees to be versatile, manufacturing to stock, working repairs in with production, and adding complementary lines of goods. The ladies' garment industry in Cleveland in 1921, and the men's clothing plants in Chicago in 1923, took steps toward regularization of employment through guaranteed employment and unemployment insurance plans. In 1928, the garment industry in Rochester and in New York City began the establishment of unemployment insurance funds. All of these arrangements have been worked out through the co-operation of employers and unions. A few individual

[50] Among them, the article by Eugene G. Grace in the *Saturday Evening Post*, September 4, 1926, cited above.

[51] The birth of this doctrine has been a subject of much interest to foreign observers Most of them conclude that it gained its place by the force of economic circumstances rather than by reasoned adoption.

companies in various lines of manufacturing have established unemployment compensation plans[52] which have helped to regularize workers' incomes.

Under the combined influence of industrial medical departments, safety engineers, the National Safety Council, insurance companies, and factory legislation, a broad interest in physical working conditions has been aroused in the minds of manufacturing executives.[53] Special safety inspectors, sanitary inspectors, and committees on health and safety are often to be found in the factories, and within the past few years particular attention has been given to the designing of machinery so as to avoid serious hazards. Beginning at first merely with the posting of safety rules and the guarding of machinery, safety work has lately progressed into more difficult psychological fields, and is attempting through internal advertising, safety contests, and other forms of recurrent emphasis to establish throughout the whole plant a frame of mind alert to avoid all accidents whether arising from mechanical or nonmechanical sources.

Fatigue and monotony have been given some attention as causes of accidents and of injury to nerves and body structure as well.[54] Yet almost nothing is known about them or the conditions which bring them about. There is wide popular discussion of the effects of modern mechanization upon decreasing skill and increasing monotony, which is extremely difficult to bring down to cases even after the examination of many plants. This is likely to be true so long as we know no more than we do at present about what precisely constitutes fatigue and monotony and their relation to skill. The comprehensive changes of the past few years, running in many directions and in varying amounts, have made studies in this field peculiarly difficult. For a change in conditions of work may, merely as change, induce fatigue or interrupt monotony. There have been many displacements by highly simplified jobs of complex jobs which used to be called skilled and were therefore considered interesting; and there are jobs of tending new, elaborate, and expensive machines which are not now called skilled but which demand a high grade of general intelligence and care. There are thousands of jobs for the unskilled carrying with them a high interest content and greater opportunity for self-respect than most unskilled jobs of former days. And there are thousands of jobs calling for the simplest repetitive effort, concerning the interest-content or fatigue-effects of which we as yet know nothing.

[52] See Herman Feldman, *Regularization of Employment*, 1925; and *Business Cycles and Unemployment*, National Bureau of Economic Research, 1923.

[53] A close comparison of 359 companies by the American Engineering Council showed a drop of 10.4 per cent in accident frequency between 1922 and 1925.

[54] See "Mental Hygiene in Industry," in *Psychological Foundations of Management*, H. C. Metcalf, editor, 1927.

A considerably increased satisfaction in the job seems to be possible through working in teams.   Modern methods have greatly enlarged the use of workers teamed up into organized groups, and there is some evidence that a given job is less monotonous when it can be continually seen as a part of a more complex job done by the team of which one is a member.   At the moment nothing final can be said upon this extremely important subject of job interest.   From all the evidence available, it seems, however, wholly safe to guess that the total fatiguing effect of factory work has not increased, whether monotony has or not.

The hazards of accident are now generally met, in part at least, by state laws; the hazards of sickness are met quite commonly by employee mutual benefit associations, independent of or assisted by employers, and also to a growing extent by group insurance.   Group life insurance has had the most striking development in recent years—54 per cent of the companies in this survey, and 40 per cent of 4,655 companies reported on by the National Industrial Conference Board in 1927, had it in force. The Board estimates that, by the end of 1926, 4,700,000 employees were covered by group insurance totaling $5,500,000,000.   In October, 1928, Mr. Graham, of the Equitable Life Assurance Society, estimated 5,800,000 employees covered by $7,500,000,000 of insurance.[55]

Ten years ago, the argument was generally advanced for group insurance that it would reduce labor turnover, but it is doubtful if it ever did so in any significant number of cases.   To-day it is generally advocated upon the grounds that relieving the stable and responsible type of worker from some of the worries of death and sickness hazards results in benefit to the company through his released energies and enhanced goodwill. There has been a strong drift toward having employees share in the costs of those plans for life and sickness insurance which have been instituted in the last five years.   The Conference Board reports that, of the group insurance plans established in 1919, 6.7 per cent were contributory, and in 1925, 68 per cent.

Pension plans are rarer than group insurance, in spite of the fact that the pension idea is the older.   They are found in a great variety of forms, among which can be discovered little uniformity of idea.   Publications on the subject have increased since 1921, partly because the failure of certain pension plans called attention to the ease with which their true costs can be overlooked, and recently a few group insurance policies with annuity provisions have been taken out.   As the higher costs are realized, there is likewise a growth of contributory plans.   In the report of Bryce M. Stewart, of the Industrial Relations Counsellors, Inc., it is stated: "While only 16.7 per cent of the plans recorded in this study are contributory, the proportion of contributory plans has increased steadily from 10.5 per cent of the total number established in the five-year period

[55] Other and fuller figures are included in Chap. VI, pp. 484–487.

1906–1910 to 24.6 per cent in the period 1921–1925." Eighty-five per cent of the plans covered were set up after 1910. As the case for pensions from a purely business point of view, it is urged in Mr. Stewart's report:

That, in the absence of formal pension provisions, employees are likely to be retained on the pay roll beyond their efficient age; that the pension plan affords greater facility in the retirement of incapacitated employees, and that a modern pension scale is probably less costly than the retention of aged workers on the pay roll.[56]

The growing belief of workers that employers are opposed to hiring persons past middle age in order to keep their pension liability low, and discussions of the difficulties involved in developing adequate private industrial pension plans, have stimulated in a few states the movement to establish state pensions supported by taxation.

The study made by Dr. Lubin[57] shows an unexpectedly large proportion of younger men among the unemployed:

AGE DISTRIBUTION OF UNEMPLOYED

Age	Number	Per cent of unemployed	Cumulative per cent
15 to 20 years	72	9.5	9.5
21 to 25 years	118	15.7	25.2
26 to 30 years	122	16.2	41.4
31 to 35 years	157	20.8	62.2
36 to 40 years	111	14.7	76.9
41 to 45 years	77	10.2	87.1
46 to 50 years	30	4.0	91.1
51 to 55 years	26	3.4	94.5
56 to 60 years	14	1.9	96.4
Over 60 years	16	2.1	98.5
No data	11	1.5	100.0
Total	754		

Believing that financial and other difficulties will make adequate pensioning impossible, some companies, by instituting schemes which offer special incentives for cash savings, or which enable the employee to purchase the stock of the company upon an installment basis and at a price below the market, have in recent years encouraged employees to make provision for old age. Many companies promote thrift in co-operation with savings banks,[58] making it easier for employees to save by permitting them to authorize pay roll deductions to be credited to their

[56] See also, E. S. Cowdrick, "Pensions, A Problem of Management," American Management Association Convention Series No. 75, 1928, and a report on "Pensions in Trade Unions," by M. W. Latimer, Industrial Relations Counsellors, Inc.

[57] See footnote 27, p. 514.

[58] Employees' savings data from 1917 to 1925 can be found in "Trend of Wage Earners' Savings in Philadelphia" by Margaret Schoenfeld, published in the *Annals of the American Academy of Political and Social Science*, September, 1925.

accounts at the bank. Several varieties of savings plans, especially Christmas and vacation savings, have been known for many years, but, until the war period, were actually in effect in a very small number of companies. Thirty-three per cent of the companies covered in this survey have now established savings plans, or co-operate with banks, building and loan associations, and similar organizations in the effort to promote thrift among employees.

Stock purchase plans were found in one-quarter of the companies covered in this survey, appearing in one-third of those having functionalized employment work, and one-fifth of the others. While stock purchase plans have existed in a few companies for more than a quarter of a century, the movement as a whole is of comparatively recent origin. "During the war and the period of prosperity that followed, the movement increased with special rapidity. In 1921, when business was depressed, and in 1922, there was a distinct falling off in the number of companies making new or further offerings of stock. In 1923, however, the movement started with renewed vigor."[59] Of the 389 plans, considered in 1928 in the report of the National Industrial Conference Board, 273, or 70 per cent, were established during the period from 1916 to 1925, and 162, or 42 per cent of the total, during the five-year period from 1921 to 1925. There has been much discussion[60] as to the possible influence of such movements upon the future, but they are in fact too new as yet to afford decisive evidence as to their effects. A few failures which have wiped out employee savings have pointed the need of special caution.

Company loan funds seem to be of diminishing significance. In a few plants provision for making loans to employees from company funds will be found, but a mutual savings and loan fund, and, especially in some localities, credit unions, have made less frequent the calls of employees upon employers for emergency aid.

Credit unions, from European models, were adopted by Canada in 1900, through the influence and enthusiasm of M. Desjardins. In 1909 they were established in Massachusetts, with the help of Pierre Jay, who was then bank commissioner; and under the influence of Edward A. Filene have since then grown greatly. In 1927 there were 279 in Massachusetts with assets of $13,500,000; and in other states, with later starts, there has been similarly rapid growth. Being self-managed, they give training in business methods to many rank and file employees and hence are of a broader than financial significance.[61]

[59] R. F. Foerster and Else H. Dietel, *Employee Stock Ownership in the United States*, 1926, p. 7.

[60] See, for example, the *Proceedings of the Academy of Political Science*, Vol. II, No. 3, April, 1925.

[61] See R. F. Bergengren, *Cooperative Banking, a Credit Union Book*, 1923.

Other provisions aiming at financial benefit to employees are company stores and special buying privileges. They were found, in this survey, in one-fourth of the companies having functionalized personnel work, and in 6 per cent of all others. The movement to establish company stores was at its height during the war years and until 1921, but their importance from the standpoint of money savings has greatly diminished in recent years because of the decreased cost of living. In most companies where there are still special buying provisions, the list of goods handled has been greatly reduced; it includes sometimes only those articles regularly carried in stock by the company for its own use.

At one time, the social, athletic, and recreational activities known as "welfare work" were regarded as inducements which would attract the better class of employees. Company provisions for these activities, and opportunities of the same character afforded by various public and private organizations in most communities, are now so common that their differential value as special attractions is almost negligible. The results of this survey showed no recent development along these lines. On the contrary, there were several companies in which one type or another of such activities had been discontinued because of diminished interest on the part of employees and in order to reduce expense. Nevertheless, social activities, such as picnics, dances, and entertainment for employees and their families, were carried on in one-third of the plants visited; athletic teams, partly or wholly supported by the companies, in one-half; and recreational facilities, such as rest rooms and game rooms, in more than 40 per cent.

Joint Relations.—While there is no adequate measure of the changed and changing attitude of management toward joint relations, it is apparent from many indications that executives to-day are more ready than they were before the war to enter into organized schemes for regularly dealing with their employees. It is still undoubtedly true that in most establishments the relations of the management with employees are with individuals only, and based solely upon supervisory contact. This was the situation in well over one-half of the companies covered by this survey. About 20 per cent had active, formal employee representation plans, 10 per cent dealt occasionally with specially elected employee committees, and 6 per cent were working under union agreements.

The year 1921 saw the discontinuance of many arrangements for joint relations, both union agreements and independent employee representation plans. The serious unemployment at that time and the weakened position of the unions resulted in the abrogation of many arrangements made during the war and boom years. Many plants closed, and when they reopened the employee committees which had previously existed were not revived.

The figures in the following table of the National Industrial Conference Board show that there have been many changes and a slight net growth:

GROWTH OF EMPLOYEE REPRESENTATION[a]

	1919	1922	1924	1926
Number of companies with employee representation plans	145	385	421	432
Number of companies establishing new employee representation plans during the period between surveys	....	317	173	59
Number of companies discontinuing employee representation plans during the period between surveys	....	77	137	48
Number of workers covered by employee representation plans	403,765	690,000	1,240,704	1,369,078

[a] Adapted from table in *Service Letter*, No. 359, January 10, 1927.

It does not appear that the success or failure of an employee representation plan or of a co-operative relationship with a trade union is dependent upon the size or nature of an enterprise. The attitude of the managing officials has more to do with it. An analysis of the cases of abandonment of works councils[62] shows the causes reported by the companies to be "discussion of trivial matters," "lack of interest in elections," "poor selection of representatives," "plans too cumbersome," "improper candidates for representatives," "fluctuation of employment demoralized councils," "business conditions," "committee would not respect instructions from supervisor," and "more time spent in conference than in production." From these it is apparent that the executives in the companies which abandoned works councils had not seriously regarded joint committees as affording employees an opportunity to participate in the processes leading to decisions affecting them, or thought through many of the problems of operating in conjunction with them, but had continued traditional attitudes and methods of control.[63]

Most employee representation plans, adopted in the years of the war and the boom, came from mixed motives, ranging from sentimental to ulterior, and most of them failed.[64] It is as yet too soon for final judgments of the survivors or of the younger plans. But there is plenty of evidence that, where built soberly into consistent relationships with the whole organized structure, they are proving to have deep and many-sided values.

[62] National Industrial Conference Board, *Service Letter*, No. 364, February 14, 1927.
[63] For fuller description and discussion, see Burton, *Employee Representation*, Baltimore, 1926.
[64] See, also, Chap. VI, Labor, p. 484.

During recent years there has been an increasing amount of discussion[65] concerning the effectiveness, both from the standpoint of management and of labor, of union-management co-operation, under arrangements similar to those obtaining on the Baltimore & Ohio, Chicago Northwestern, Grank Trunk Western, Chicago, Minneapolis & St. Paul, and Canadian National Railroads. This idea, also, is too new to judge; with it, as with other radical changes, such as newly installed piece rates, mergers, and works councils, there is always danger of being misled by the clean sweeps of a new broom. But certain special areas of possibility for co-operation have been under test for a number of years by some of the printing trade unions, and similar work in the clothing trades is beginning to show something of the opportunities and limitations of unions as partners of management in working toward higher productivity.

III. MANAGEMENT OF MARKETING

Since 1920, it is pre-eminently the problem of marketing, and especially the creation of demand for the product and the development of new products, which has held the attention of business executives. It is often said that mass production is forcing selling; it is probably more accurate to say that the turn of the price curve in 1920, after a score of years of scarcely interrupted rise, has forced both mass production and intensive selling.

A widespread interest in marketing methods cannot be said to have come with the turn of prices, although at that time there was plenty of talk about the difficulties of getting sales. As early as October, 1920, however, articles suggesting a more scientific viewpoint on marketing appeared in the Taylor Society *Bulletin*. The Joint Committee on Agricultural Inquiry in 1922 issued a report which attracted attention to certain high costs of marketing. And the *Harvard Business Review*, since 1922, has persistently printed articles analyzing sales problems.

In recent years, interest has increased with great rapidity.[66] Distribution conferences were held by the United States Chamber of Commerce in 1925, and commercial surveys and special marketing censuses have recently been made by the Domestic Commerce Division of the Department of Commerce. As yet, however, marketing technique must be judged primitive both in its planning and in its control. There are a few important exceptions, but as a whole it must be said that manufacturers, wholesalers, and retailers alike, in their marketing thinking since 1920, having passed through the expletive stages, are only just entering the

[65] See, for example, *Bulletin* of the Taylor Society, February, 1926.

[66] Since 1922, a large number of books on all phases of marketing management have been published.

explorative.   Even to-day, more marketing executives are worrying than are analyzing conditions and inventing measures appropriate to them.

Among those companies which have made changes, there is appearing a tendency toward functionalization similar to the tendency which has been developed in manufacturing.   There are being introduced into their sales departments men to give centered attention to special problems of progress.   It is being found, as was found in the factory, that those men responsible for carrying on the daily routine of getting orders should not be solely depended upon to devise and improve the methods of getting them.

The department to devise methods of selling is most often the "sales promotion department."   For the development of new and improved goods to sell, there are engineering or design departments or committees who concentrate on merchandising.   These companies have sent an increasing number of specialists into the field, not chiefly to sell but rather to prepare the way for future sales by learning and teaching the best uses of the goods.   For those who have sold production equipment, this has meant sending men who have sometimes acted as consulting engineers for their customers; for those who have sold to retailers, it has meant sending men expert in display methods or in specialized retail salesmanship.   Measures of this sort have not usually been planned for permanency, but have been undertaken rather more often to develop a new market or to consolidate an old one.

Sales Personnel.—Even where, in these companies, special men have not been sent out into the field, attempts to serve a similar purpose have been made through an alteration of salesmen's methods or of personnel. Selection, training, and remuneration have been subjects of increasing interest in discussions and in business literature.[67]   Something like 50 per cent more articles appeared on these subjects in 1927 than in 1925. The companies which are reorganizing their sales efforts are taking more pains with selection, in an attempt to get men not merely of good manner and persuasive powers, but of quick intelligence.   For producers' goods, technically trained men have been increasingly sought, and to sell all sorts of goods there is a growing demand for college graduates.   Psychological tests were tried in many cases, but have persisted only with a few large companies; interest in them does not seem to have waned, but sales managers are rather holding off until more satisfactory tests have had a chance to be developed.

The training of salesman to meet the difficult conditions of the field is being carried on with increasing elaboration, and always with more emphasis upon knowledge of the product and its uses, and distinctly

[67] "Selection, training, and supervision" stood second on a list of 27 "outstanding problems of marketing management" in the answers to a questionnaire of the Taylor Society, published in its *Bulletin*, December, 1927.

less upon the technique of persuasion and what used to be called salesmanship.

Changed conditions have forced companies to give more and more consideration to the problems of salesmen's remuneration. Some years ago, certainly, and probably now, a straight commission on sales was the prevailing method. To-day, wherever missionary and educational work are important, this simple method is found inadequate. A number of other devices are being tried, some of which have been enthusiastically proclaimed as the one best method. Most of the sales executives who are working at this problem seem to believe that no one system will be found; that a variety of devices of remuneration will have to be combined in different ways to meet different conditions.

In the past, there has been a general lack of close management in the routing of salesmen and in studying their performance through frequent reports. One frequently heard the complaint that "men do not like to be held to a definite route," and "we can not get our older men to turn in any reports." This situation is closely parallel to those of an older day in factory departments, where piece rates or the "highly skilled workmen" were depended upon to keep the wheels going.

To-day, the attempts to get increased sales and more capable salesmanship, and yet to sell at a lower sales cost, have encouraged the analytical studies of quotas, which have been widely instituted during the past few years, and have led some companies to restrict the territories or lists of customers salesmen are expected to cover.

Sales Costs.—Sales expense is the center of increasing attention. A number of companies reported that they were now undertaking a study of this problem, and were setting up new statistical or accounting precedure for the purpose. The figures of 81 companies, widely distributed geographically and over different trades, have been carefully analyzed by Bigelow, Kent, Willard & Co., Inc., of Boston. They are for the first six months of 1926, 1927, and 1928, as shown in the tables on page 534.

The general trend of reduction in manufacturing costs has made selling relatively, even where not absolutely, of greater importance.[68]

With the encouragement of the Harvard Bureau of Business Research, accounting for sales *expense* has been greatly extended and improved. Sales *costing*, however, as it bears upon different lines of goods or classes of customer, has been little analyzed. There has been a certain degree of broad departmentalizing; but the prevailing custom has been to express the cost of selling as an over-all percentage applying equally to all goods and all transactions, thus losing any differentials of cost there may be

[68] The trends of sales expense among retailers, wholesalers, chains, and department stores are discussed in Chap. V, pp. 352–374.

Costs Analysis of 81 Companies

Item	Profit-making companies			Losing companies		
	1926	1927	1928	1926	1927	1928
Number............	68	62	51	13	19	30
Sales ratio...........	1.000	1.039	0.982	1.000	0.949	0.977
Sales..............	1.000	1.000	1.000	1.000	1.000	1.000
Manufacturing costs:						
Material........	0.491	0.476	0.475	0.602	0.591	0.588
Labor...........	0.182	0.180	0.179	0.191	0.190	0.188
Manufacturing ex- pense........	0.107	0.108	0.117	0.153	0.158	0.142
Total.........	0.780	0.764	0.771	0.946	0.939	0.918
Gross profit.........	0.220	0.236	0.229	0.054	0.061	0.082
Commercial costs:						
Selling..........	0.082	0.110	0.121	0.121	0.147	0.156
Administrative...	0.054	0.058	0.056	0.099	0.087	0.080
Total.........	0.136	0.168	0.177	0.220	0.234	0.236
Operating profit or loss	0.084	0.068	0.052	−0.166	−0.173	−0.154

Change in Ratios from 1926 Basis in Per Cent

Item	Profit-making companies		Losing companies	
	1927	1928	1927	1928
Materials..............................	− 3.06	− 3.26	− 1.83	− 2.33
Labor.................................	− 1.1	− 1.65	− 0.52	− 1.57
Manufacturing expense..................	+ 0.93	+ 9.3	+ 3.27	− 7.2
Selling expense........................	+34.1	+47.6	+21.5	+28.9
Administrative expense.................	+ 7.4	+ 3.7	−12.1	−19.1
Profits of profit-making companies........	−19.0	−38.1	......	......
Losses of losing companies...............	.....	.....	+ 4.2	− 7.2

among them. Significant of a change are two recent articles,[69] published by the Department of Commerce at the request of its Advisory Committee on Distribution.

Reorganizations of the sales force cause temporary extra expenditures by selling departments, much of the sort which, when spent for tangible assets, are counted as investments. Those manufacturers who are so reorganizing know this, and count it as a special expenditure. But they expect it, when fully completed, to reduce their cost of sales even in spite of hard market conditions.

[69] J. W. Millard, *Analyzing Wholesale Distribution Costs*, and G. E. Bitner, *Analyzing Retail Selling Costs*.

Advertising —It was commonly believed that, in its day, the excess profits tax was the cause of a tremendous increase in advertising. During the depression of 1921, advertising was greatly curtailed, but the indications of this survey are that, between 1922 and 1924, the amounts spent in advertising increased at nearly double the rate of other increases in sales expense.[70] Since 1924, this rate of increase has materially diminished.

High pressure selling efforts of the producers of various forms of advertising accompanied these great increases in expenditures, and a large number of advertisers allowed themselves to be governed by plans originated by the sellers, without taking the trouble to find out for themselves all the factors involved in this important part of their marketing management. As a result, many advertisers have been spending their money with no definite goal or, if they have one, without knowing whether they are hitting the mark or not. Among the sellers of advertising are many highly efficient men, who approach their tasks in a conscientious frame of mind, who believe that the future of advertising will depend upon the analytical intelligence with which it is used, and who are working energetically toward sound practices. There were definite general indications in the first part of 1928 that advertising appropriations were going to be looked at with a more discriminating eye, either to reduce the total amount or to apply it in more effective ways.

Merchandising.—By far the most important occurrences in American marketing have been the invention and introduction of a wide variety of new consumers' goods. These well-known inventions, and the national success of those who have sold them, easily give the general impression that every business man in this country is altering his merchandise and inventing new. As a matter of fact, it is hard to discover in a field survey that the job of analyzing merchandise and its uses, the every day part of the job of merchandise invention, is adequately arranged for. The progressive development of the quality and utility of merchandise, and its continuously closer adaptation to both market needs and manufacturing facilities, have been the responsibilities of no one in particular and everyone in general. They were usually found to be expected of the chief executive or the board of management, in addition to their other duties. The result has been that such improvements as did occur were often strokes of good fortune or the consequence of insistent market pressure. Final results are, therefore, spotty. The known cases of organized systematic merchandise inventing, outside of the engineering industries, are few in number as compared to the total business organizations of the country.

---

[70] For 1927 the total spent on advertising, as estimated by Dr. Copeland, was $1,500,000,000. See Chap. V, p. 402.

Those who have taken definite steps to meet the need are specializing upon research into the make-up of the merchandise and the needs of the market, and toward a closer co-ordination of the designing, engineering, manufacturing, and sales departments. They are trying to find out how to make their products accord in quantity and kind more nearly with the desire and capacity of consumers to buy, and hence to find savings in simplifying the movement of goods from shipping platforms to ultimate consumers, comparable with the savings which have been made in manufacturing them. The influence of field specialists, demonstrators and instructors, upon this work is notable. The creation of most merchandise is, in fact, found to be more effectively carried out in contact with the place where it is used than shut up in a manufacturing laboratory.

The function of merchandising is only partly the developing of new goods. An integral part of it is eliminating items and standardizing parts. This task, which under the influence of the Department of Commerce has gained the name "simplification," has won a definite standing in American industry. It is being carried on both by trade associations and by individual employers. Where merchandising is to be found thoroughly organized, the simplification process is being worked out continuously, going along with the development processes of adding new goods and improving old. By persistence in pruning out the least desirable and adding the better, progressive improvement of the lines to be sold is accomplished.

Determining the price at which goods were to be sold has, in the past, been a responsibility of the sales department in most companies. Pricing is now showing a trend away from exclusive selling influence. It is carried on in a variety of ways, which most often lead up to an ultimate board of management for approval; but in the discussions and determinations of price bases there are more and more appearing such other influences as that of the accounting department or the field specialist.

During the years of greatest upheaval, many manufacturers, to determine their sales possibilities, undertook thoroughgoing market analyses which were, however, too expensive to be carried on generally. Some market analyses of wide usefulness, available to all, have been instituted by some of the larger advertising agencies. More recently the Department of Commerce has undertaken, for the first time in the history of this country, a census of retail and wholesale distribution. It is experimental only, covering 11 cities, but has proved to be of such interest that it is expected to be the forerunner of the first complete national Census of Distribution to be taken in 1930. While the variety of information required by different companies is great, there is certain basic information for the setting of quotas, the allocation of sales territories, the evaluation of competition, and the checking of performance, which is of definite value to all.

Trade Channels.—The general pressure for sales, intensified and complicated by the rapid rise of chain stores, has given to those manufacturers who sell to distributors for resale some special problems, the definite solutions for which are as yet hardly to be found. Whether to try to distribute identical products through all the different trade channels, or whether to sell through the jobber, or direct, or exclusively to chain stores, are problems being tried out in many ways. Those manufacturers who have experimented the longest believe that the answer does not lie in any one alternative, but in some nicer adjustment of means to ends. To them, to rely exclusively upon the chain store, or jobber, or to eliminate either, offers no solution. They are experimenting to find what parts of their business are best adapted to the one means or the other.

Almost any close study of the market reveals one tendency which must necessarily run with low inventories and hand-to-mouth buying. Speed and dependability of delivery are of increasing importance in getting orders. This tendency has worked with the cost of selling as an influence, slight as yet but probably significant, toward so delimiting sales areas as to make the most of territorial advantages.

Wholesalers.—Developments in transportation, in availability of capital, in advertising, in merchandise, and in chain store and mail order retailing have combined to change greatly the traditional management problems of the wholesaler—the "jobber" of former days. His markets are not the same, nor is the competition he must meet. Skill in making a good "trade" is taking second place before skill in a nice fitting of varied means to ends. He is accommodating himself but slowly to these changes; in general it may be said that he has attempted rather to trade his way out of his troubles. But in February, 1928, a Wholesalers' Conference, held in Washington, sought to stimulate frank analysis, research, and constructive action.

Constructive methods are being tried in a few significant cases. Line analyses have resulted in lessening unprofitable sales pressures and removing slow movers and duplicate items. The Department of Commerce reported one case where 42 per cent of the sales were accountable for 14 per cent of inventory, and 17 per cent of the sales for 49 per cent of inventory.[71] Analysis of sales by regions and delivery costs have resulted in radical revisions of territory. Headway has been made in a few instances, even against the influence of hand-to-mouth buying, in reducing the number of those orders which are so small that merely entering and handling them use up their margin of profit.

In specific response to the chain store threat, a few wholesalers began, with chosen groups of retailers, to work out experiments in joint and

[71] J. W. Millard, *Analyzing Wholesale Distribution Costs*, 1928.

regular buying to save selling and handling cost, and in advisory specialist services for window display, store arrangement, accounting, and stock control. During the last three years, moves of this sort have spread with great rapidity,[72] especially in groceries and drugs. Group buying by wholesalers themselves has also been started, to enable them to hold their own with chain stores in buying power.

Small Retailers.—Dr. Julius Klein, of the Department of Commerce, reported, in his radio talk of September 8, 1928, an estimate of 750,000 retailer in the United States doing an average business of less than $25,000 each per year. In one of the trial census cities, "over a third of the retail stores are each doing less than an average of $7 worth of business a day." A great many have been and are being hard hit or actually knocked out[73] by chain stores. But it is not the smallest or those of any other size group which are losing; it seems rather to be those who have nothing but price to rely upon to make their appeal for patronage.

As offsetting the thousands of retail grocers who have been put out of business by the chains, the *Winnipeg and Western Grocer*, on May 15, 1928, calls attention to the "other thousands who have been spurred by chain competition into running better stores."

Little information is yet available from which any adequate picture of these hundreds of thousands of shops can be drawn, or anything more than a guess made as to their fate. When the department store came, and again the mail order house, their doom was proclaimed. Yet many survived and it is likely, therefore, that many will survive the coming of the chains. The crucial factor seems to be management ability rather than size or location. Failure stories seem to bear this out. A close study of 500 grocery failures found 65 per cent accounted for by beginners' handicaps—chiefly incompetence or lack of capital; 17 per cent were from character breakdowns; 16.6 per cent, from fire, flood, sickness, and robbery; and 1.4 per cent directly from competition.[74] Hardware stores, to judge from a survey of 1,330 of them, undertaken by the National Retail Hardware Association, do better in smaller communities than in large. Those located in towns of less than 1,000 population averaged 9.33 per cent profit on their investments in 1927, while those in cities of 50,000 and over made 5.96 per cent. Rent and salary expense in the smaller communities was 13.5 per cent of sales against 20.25 per cent in the larger.

[72] "Forty-two wholesale grocery firms, owned by a group of retailers representing 15,000 individual retail grocery stores throughout the United States, have organized the National Retail-Owned Wholesale Grocers' Association for the betterment of the individual retailer and the general improvement of trade conditions." *Journal of Commerce*, New York, January 27, 1928.

[73] But then they seem to be always getting knocked out by one thing or another, as an article by J. George Frederick in the *North American Review*, October, 1928, brilliantly and wittily sets forth.

[74] *Ibid.*

But even those independents left out of jobbers' chains are apparently not going to rest content without some of the advantages of group action. According to the New York *Journal of Commerce* of October 27, 1928, "thirteen buying groups of retailers in Canada with a total of 2,724 stores will do an estimated business of 54 millions in 1928. Buying groups did an estimated business of 42 millions in 1927, while chains did 49 millions." They claim that at least 50,000 United States retail grocers, who do a business nearly equal to the chains in their line, are affiliated in some way with co-operative groups.

With the settling down of chain store development, there has appeared evidence that a flowing in and out of managers and buyers between small independents, chains, and department stores, is taking place. To whatever extent this spreads, it seems likely to result in a better adaptation of special abilities to their appropriate jobs and a general raising of retail management technique. Without such outside influences, the intensely personal quality of the owner-merchant's job has made him slow to recognize any but its unique aspects and quick to reject ideas of change as reflections upon past performance.

To estimate conditions and trends among so large and varied a group of men is difficult. There would certainly not seem to be as yet sufficient grounds for the belief that the small, independent retailer is soon to be relegated to an insignificant share in the whole field of distribution.

Department Store Management.—The beginning of this decade found department store managers giving most of their attention to problems involving the procurement of goods and the maintenance of a satisfactory personnel. With the depression of 1920–21, interest turned to questions of stock control.[75] During subsequent years, increasing competition from other department stores, chain stores, and mail order houses, and the upward tendency of operating expenses have caused emphasis to be turned to problems of sales promotion, more precise control over expenses, and more careful selection of merchandise.

The past ten years have witnessed a definite trend toward great functionalization in department store organization. Many had attained their large size and volume of trade as the result of constantly adding departments, each under control of a department head or buyer who carried on the purchase, display, and sale of some new line of merchandise. During the period of abnormal business activity at the close of the World War, many of these departments were considerably enlarged, and a wide variety of burdens of administration were placed upon the buyers. In the general overhauling of organizations which occurred after the depression, departments were subdivided and buyers given control over more limited and specialized lines. Beginning with this period, there has been a small but growing tendency to introduce divisional

[75] See also M. P. McNair, *The Retail Method of Inventory*, 1925.

merchandise managers, who have been given charge of related departments to relieve the buyer of some of his co-ordinating responsibilities. Paralleling this trend has been a tendency to substitute, for the old-time floor walker, a section manager who has been given greater jurisdiction over personnel. Concentration of attention upon closer stock controls and increased rates of turnover has led to the functionalization of receiving, checking, and marking incoming goods. Justification has been found for giving greater power to such men as the comptroller, publicity manager, and general superintendent.

In addition to these trends, there has been during the past ten years, as in manufacturing, a tendency to introduce new functional activities, requiring the services of specialists, such as store display specialists, color experts, and traffic managers. Of predominant influence in the last few years has been the installation of "stylists."

All of these tendencies have combined to decrease the variety of responsibilities hitherto assigned to the buyer. In the last year or two there has been discussion among department store managers as to the desirability of even further subdivision of responsibility. Chain stores have always made it a practice to separate the functions of buying and selling. A similar separation is now being tried in a limited number of department stores.

In many stores, some of the complexities resulting from growth and the introduction of new departments have been avoided through the leasing of some specialty or service departments to syndicates composing a chain of such departments. A survey[76] of 88 stores in 1928 showed one-half the stores to have from one to three departments leased. Nearly two-thirds leased their millinery departments, and about the same number their beauty parlors; about one-third leased shoe departments, one-fifth their candy, and one-fifth their optical departments.

Recent years have witnessed a serious attempt on the part of some department store managers to standardize the quality of their merchandise. Testing laboratories have been introduced in many of the larger stores for the purpose of insuring proper quality of goods. Customer complaints have received attention of a more scientific nature, and specifications for purchases have been more rigidly defined. For example, during the last year or two, inspection of size has been increasingly undertaken.

A striking feature of the decade has been the rapid growth of resident buyers located permanently at foreign and domestic market centers, where they purchase for one or several department stores. This can be accounted for by the decreasing weight of a single department store buying power in comparison with that of other retailers since the advent

[76] By the National Retail Dry Goods Association, conducted bv Miss Grace J. Averall.

of the chain stores and mail order houses. The growing importance of style in an increasing number of articles, and the rapidity of style changes, have also forced closer contact with the markets. Style has, in fact, affected nearly every part of the technique of retail store management.

The increased pressure of competition during recent years has thrown a heavy emphasis upon sales promotion. This activity is being directed to a greater extent toward the bringing of people into the store and to a lesser extent toward the selling of specific merchandise. Institutional advertising is increasing, and there has been a rapid growth of "shoppers news," distributed from house to house, thus taking a new place midway between newspaper advertising and direct mail solicitation. Department store window displays are tending more toward beauty and less toward the presentation of specific merchandise.

The similarity of their problems, and the noncompetitive nature of those department stores which are situated in different localities, have made them a particularly fertile field for the development of co-operative relationships. During recent years, a number of associations of department stores have been formed for the purpose of group research through store comparisons, as well as for the practice of group buying. Another feature of the period has been the development, through the Harvard Bureau of Business Research, of comparative statistics of expense ratios drawn from figures regularly sent to the Bureau by a large number of stores. These tabulations have developed standards with which contributors can compare their own figures.

Personnel work in department stores has passed through approximately the same cycles as it has in manufacturing, except that it was not so generally allowed to drop during 1920–21. With the exception of the work of training, the trend during later years has been toward greater functionalization. Training departments, at first highly centralized, show now a tendency to limit their activity to brief courses in store systems and procedure and to supervision over the decentralized training activities in the various departments.

The employment function has been assigned to a specialist in a large number of stores. The use of psychological tests is showing a slow increase, and in at least one instance psychiatric studies[77] have been undertaken. Rating of employees is a practice which is generally increasing, and many stores have arranged for a periodical review of salaries in the light of the more recent ratings. College graduates are entering retail stores in increasing numbers, and the study of retailing is included in the curricula of our educational institutions.

Medical service has been for a considerable period quite fully functionalized in department stores, but physical examinations are required in a limited number of stores and there is little evidence of their increasing.

[77] See V. V. Anderson, "A Psychiatric Guide for Employment," *Personnel Journal*, April, 1928.

Wage incentives for selling employees are common, and a variety of salary and commission or salary and bonus plans are in use.[78] The seasonal character of the business renders the setting of quota bases for such plans rather intricate, and there are some experiments with simpler forms of payment, which, nevertheless, will still be based upon individual effort. In office work incentive plans are being used more often, and there has been a determined attempt to install such systems in the delivery departments, in spite of the difficulties of establishing proper standards and units of measure. The setting of standards in other nonselling departments through time and motion study has been undertaken by a few stores, and there is evidence that increasing attention is being given to improvements in all nonselling operations.

There seems to be no recent growth in employee representation, similar to that shown in manufacturing, although a few stores have had plans of this general nature for a considerable period.

Chain Stores.—The rapid growth of chain store systems,[79] due to the trading strength of concentrated buying, to their opportunities to weigh consumer preferences, to their handling of only quick selling items, and to their elimination of auxiliary services, forced them promptly to center attention upon certain special managerial problems and to functionalize for their continuous handling. The selection of store location, inventory control, accounting, window display, local advertising, and store management were among the earliest specializations, and purchasing was subdivided almost from the first.   Interchain competition and the adding of services and slower moving items have hastened the next stage in organization—the efforts to carry on the functionalized activities with closer economy and to blend them more thoroughly into the work of the line organization.

As chains increase in size, problems of warehousing and transportation come to the forefront, particularly in the cases of those chains which originated in large cities but whose expansion program is carrying them into the rural communities.   There is some indication that manufacturers selling to chains are growing less willing to accept warehousing responsibilities and small lot shipments.   Certain of the large chains have given much attention to this problem, with the result that their warehousing and transportation methods have been greatly refined.   In general, however, traffic and warehousing management still offers many problems to be solved.

[78] See D. R. Craig, *Payment Methods in Department Stores*, Retail Bureau, University of Pittsburgh.

[79] See Hayward & White, *Chain Stores, Their Management and Operation*, 1st ed. 1922, 2nd. ed. 1925; W. J. Baxter, *Chain Store Distribution and Management*, 1928; Paul H. Nystrom, *Retail Selling and Store Management*, 1914; also Chap. V, Marketing, pp. 362–369.

Chain store advertising, the absence of which was originally set forth as one of their chain store economies, is increasing. The significance to the consumer's mind of many manufacturers' brands is causing a retardation of what appeared to be, in earlier years, an overpowering trend toward the development of private chain brands. There is a growing number of instances of co-operative advertising between manufacturers of nationally branded goods and chain store systems.

Judging by articles in the chain store publications, there has long been a keen appreciation of the importance of the store manager and, on the other hand, of the difficulty of directing him. In the effort to find practical integration between the specialists' contributions and local managers' individual abilities, between consistency of service and local needs, and between central policies and decentralized administration, chain store systems have carried out many valuable experiments. They have used premium payments, profit sharing, rigidly classified salaries, and individual salaries unclassified; they have turned traveling inspectors into supervisors or into teachers; they have had fields in which the store manager's behavior is rigidly standardized, and fields within which their own judgment rules. Through it all, there runs a persistent tendency to raise the average level of ability of store managers.

The original simplifications of lines down to those which sold most freely allowed problems of sales personnel to become secondary. Now, wherever lines are becoming elaborate and services are being instituted, and especially where there are several stores of one chain in a single community, a few training classes, psychological tests, and sales manuals are appearing.

A special set of problems for the growing chain system arise out of the balancing of expansion with intensive development. With some, total sales have increased, but the sales per store have decreased. The value of priority in a new market has incited many to expand at a rate which has jeopardized their effectiveness and resulted in supersaturation of some markets. There appear to be optimum sizes of chain store organizations, dependent upon the capabilities of the management, which have in some cases been exceeded.

Within the last few years, there has been a growing tendency to develop chains through the simultaneous merging of a considerable number of independent stores. This method of development is different from that followed by the older chains, and materially increases management problems.

Close observers agree that management structures, practices, and abilities in the chain systems have yet to be tempered in the long, hot fires of extended and vigorous competition.

Office Management.—The number of people in clerical occupations is distinctly on the increase. The United States Census showed that from

1910 to 1920, of all men engaged in gainful occupations, male clerical workers increased from 3.8 to 5.1 per cent; among women, the increase was from 7.3 to 16.7 per cent. In Ohio, the percentage of males listed as clerical workers was 5.6 per cent in 1914 as against 6.8 per cent in 1926; of women, 17.6 per cent in 1914 and 26.2 per cent in 1926. These figures can indicate only a part of the growth of clerical service, since there has been, also, during these periods a great increase in the sale of mechanical office equipment[80] which has increased the output per worker.

The development of clerical service has not been accompanied by a similar growth in the status of clerical management. Frequently office management is not found to be a separate operating function at all, and seldom are its duties clearly defined. The title "office manager" is not common; of 145 members of the national association, only 55 are listed in the roster of 1926 as having that title. Office management can be found as a side line of the treasurer or assistant treasurer, the controller, chief accountant, secretary, production or sales manager, and even the purchasing agent. It is not, therefore, surprising that its co-ordination with other departments is seldom found to be well effected, in spite of the importance of its work in cost control and in a variety of other ways to both factory and selling departments.

In the limited way in which conditions allow it to operate, the National Association of Office Managers has been persistent in cultivating better management methods. A decade ago, in discussions and business literature, a standardization or simplification of forms held a prominent place. Work in this direction still continues, but has been elaborated to cover a wider field of standardization and to include lay-out of office, routing of work, salary classification,[81] standard instruction, and job analysis. The exchange of information on many detailed parts of office management goes on with considerable vitality.

The rapid introduction of office machinery has brought to office management a new problem, and has created, within the traditional office workers, a group comparable to those on light factory processes; in fact, measured production and payment by results have already been established in a small way among them.

IV. SUMMARY

The art of management, in almost all its aspects and activities, turned a corner in 1921. During the up-swing with which the century started, sheer power and drive could win almost every time over finesse. At the turn of the tide, amid the confused cross-currents, more depended upon skillful understandings of the whole situation and nice adjustment of

---

[80] Two books which are no less than encyclopedias have recently been issued, listing office mechanisms.

[81] See article by M. A. Bills in *Journal of Personnel Research*, March, 1923.

means to the immediate environment. The art of management to-day is in large part the progressive adjustment and integration of conflicting needs, conflicting influences, and conflicting purposes.

All managers, however, did not turn the corner in 1921. A reorganization of thought has had first to be brought about. Under the new charter, to manage is not a vested right but the exercise of a special skill which, through temperament or through training, some have and some have not. An English article expresses it strongly:

Nothing is more characteristic of modern business than the way in which control based on power and ownership is giving place to authority based on knowledge, qualifications, and skill. Management is no longer a preserve of the owners of capital, nor is it an hereditary right. Men of ability, without capital or family ties to assist them, are breaking into the hereditary ranks. Industrial conditions are in their favor . . . The leveling forces of Nature have been at work, producing the average except in cases where systematic selection has been exercised. But the average man is not equal to the strain of a day when conditions are uncertain, when business is growing more complex, and when nothing but competent administration can enable a firm to survive.[82]

To cope with the growing complexities, the manager type, through slow processes akin to natural selection, is changing. More men are being brought within managerial responsibilities, and the co-ordinated group, each member of which has his own share in the total of responsibilities, is replacing the absolute "big boss." To release and utilize all the creative and managerial abilities which any of their members may possess or develop is the definite goal of organization. There is to-day not only more production per man, more wages per man, and more horse power per man, but more management per man as well.

Reinforcing all the other influences which are pressing toward higher-grade management is the present prevailing doctrine of high wages. Management is the planning and directing of human efforts, and the more one has to pay for these efforts, the more worth while is high-grade direction. So long, then, as that doctrine prevails, it will continue to be a powerful influence toward progress in management. There are as yet no signs of its weakening.

The foundations of experience upon which management is built are broadening. No matter how rich it may be, the experience of one man or even of one company is seldom broad enough for to-day. Associations, periodicals, committees, luncheons are all antennae through which companies become sensitive to current progress. To no small degree it is co-operative thinking which is to be credited with the present state of American prosperity. Freer and freer exchange of information, constantly improving lines of communication, are keeping the body of the American business army marching behind its pioneers.

[82] In *Industrial Peace and Administration*, August, 1928, Oxford, England.

The speed at which changes have taken place and taken effect has varied as widely as human nature varies, and has varied, also, with the differences in the pressure of necessity. As a result, the present situation in the business world is more "spotty" than it perhaps has ever been. Within industries and among industries, there is a wide spread in methods of management. To the "prevailing practices," noted in this chapter, all sorts of exceptions can be found; in the directions of trend there is much more uniformity.

Business has, of course, always benefited from discovery, but it has mostly taken discovery where it found it—as a gift. It is now more often the case that, by research, discovery is specifically provided for and so accelerated. Business research does more than invite discovery; it gives to operating management a chance to base its decisions upon fact; and research and the habits of mind it engenders are extending beyond the applied physical sciences into the fields where conditions are determined chiefly by human desires, impulses, and frailties; into industrial psychology, labor management, marketing, sales management, merchandising, advertising.

Applied to general management, these habits of mind demand that long range plans be made, that jams and emergencies be avoided, and progress itself be scheduled. In a few companies there can be found now the germ of what is likely some day to be a full-fledged and functionalized Department of the Future, which will know how to forecast and to make provisions, within limits, and will know how to estimate those limits.

Finally, such mental habits will bring into business management an appreciation of the principle of balance, which centuries of military experience have taught the general staffs of all nations. A factory too good with relation to its selling force can be a source of weakness and is always a source of internal strain; a company or a community can devote itself to invention which reduces cost too much as compared with the degree to which it devotes itself to invention which increases consumption.

Any step in any direction of progress has so far brought with it an increased complexity; our economic mechanism is now intricate and delicate. During the last generation we have many times found that it pays to get men of better than average intelligence as operators of intricate machines, and to institute careful methods of training for them. We are seeing now more and more clearly that management—the continuous adjustment and steering of our business machinery—demands also its special intelligence and its careful and continuing training.

CHAPTER VIII

AGRICULTURE

By Edwin G. Nourse

The several chapters of this survey thus far have dealt with consumption, transportation, merchandising, manufacturing industries, labor and management, with only casual bearing on the situation in agriculture. In those chapters, great emphasis has been laid upon the radical adjustments, both in technique and in business organization and practices, which have been outstanding developments of the postwar period. Turning now from discussion of our national industry in general to the particular problem of agriculture, one must be struck with the fact that the adjustments there called for have been no less drastic in character. Circumstances, however, have conspired to accord to the farmer a less satisfactory meeting of his difficulties, and therefore a general situation as to prosperity with which he is by no means satisfied, and which practically all students of the problem agree leaves him on a lower level of prosperity than that being enjoyed by the majority of economic groups.

At intervals during the last few years, Congressional committees, private institutions, Government workers, and interested individuals have attempted to formulate quantitative statements of the farmer's situation, and to measure the extent of his distress or the degree of his economic disadvantage.[1] Comparisons have been made longitudinally

[1] One of the most common short-cut methods of statistical comparison has been to take the index numbers of farm-product prices and divide by the index of prices (wholesale) of nonagricultural commodities to produce a quotient which was often labeled "an index of farmers' purchasing power."

"This method of measuring the value of farm products," says C. M. Purves, of the United States Bureau of Agricultural Economics (*Index Numbers of Prices Farmers Pay for Commodities Purchased*, (mimeograph report)) "has not been entirely satisfactory because farmers do not buy at wholesale nor are index numbers of nonagricultural wholesale prices weighted according to the amount of farmers' purchases. . . . Index numbers of prices paid by farmers for what they buy have been constructed by the Bureau of Agricultural Economics, United States Department of Agriculture. These indexes show changes in prices since 1910 of commodities purchased by farmers for the family living and for operating the farm. They are constructed with the same base period and as nearly as possible in the same manner as the indexes of prices received for farm products. The ratio of the index number of prices received for products sold to the index number of prices paid for commodities farmers purchase will hereafter be used instead of the ratio of farm prices to nonagricultural wholesale prices as a measure of the purchasing power of farm products.

with conditions of agriculture in previous years, and in cross section as comparisons with other economic groups. Such nominally exact calculations have been impaired by innocent errors and partisan distortions to an extent which has caused them to produce more confusion than enlightenment. Professor Black has examined many of these difficulties, and says:[2]

If any conclusion at all can be safely drawn from these data, it is . . . that the real per capita incomes of farm people fell behind badly from 1870 to about 1895, improved

"Users of these index numbers of farm prices and of prices paid by farmers are cautioned against their misinterpretation and misuse. These price index numbers do not measure changes in farm receipts or in farm expenses, and the ratio of prices farmers receive to prices paid for purchases is not a measure of the purchasing power of the farmer. These index numbers do not take into account any variations in the quantities of crops sold or quantities of goods purchased. Furthermore, the prices used in constructing these index numbers do not represent all sources of receipts or all varieties of expenditures. The income from farming is spent not only for commodities purchased for the family living and for operating the farm but also for interest on mortgages and loans, rents, railroad fares, and other items which are not represented by these index numbers. Strictly speaking, the ratio of the index number of prices received for farm products to the index number of prices paid for commodities purchased merely represents the power of a fixed quantity of selected farm products to purchase a fixed quantity of goods in relation to the base period."

These index numbers of farm prices, prices paid by farmers, wages, and taxes (1910–1914 = 100) are presented in the following table:

Date	Prices received for farm products	Prices paid by farmers for commodities bought	Ratio of prices received to prices paid	Farm wages paid to hired labor	Taxes on farm property (1914 = 100)
1910.................	103	98	106	' 97	...
1911.................	95	101	93	97	...
1912.................	99	100	99	101	...
1913.................	100	100	99	104	...
1914.................	102	101	101	101	100
1915.................	100	106	95	102	102
1916.................	117	123	95	112	104
1917.................	176	150	118	140	106
1918.................	200	178	112	176	118
1919.................	209	205	102	206	130
1920.................	205	206	99	239	155
1921.................	116	156	75	150	217
1922.................	124	152	81	146	232
1923.................	135	153	88	166	246
1924.................	134	154	87	166	249
1925.................	147	159	92	168	250
1926.................	136	156	87	171	253
1927.................	131	154	85	170	258

[2] John D. Black, "Agriculture Now?" *Journal of Farm Economics*, April, 1927, pp. 151–161.

from then until 1919, especially during the last three of these years, and then fell with a crash in 1920 and 1921; and if farm people are badly off now, it is principally because of developments during the war, and the price *débâcle* since, but to some extent because agriculture *had not entirely recovered by* 1916 *from the severe retrogression of the* 1870–1895 *period.*[3] But it is doubtful even if such a conclusion is safe . . . It is still entirely possible, in spite of these figures, that agriculture's share in the general income relative to population was somewhat less in 1915 than in 1870. Agriculture made great progress during this period; but possibly the cities made more progress . . . [Amended data] strongly suggest that in 1918 and 1919 the per capita incomes of farm workers were at least equal in purchasing power to those of the average of all other workers in the same sections of the country, but that from 1909 to 1916 they were far from being so . . .

The Federal Reserve Board's data show that factory wage earners' buying power in 1925–26 was 16 per cent higher than in 1919–20, and that even their money incomes were 3 per cent higher. The difference between 16 per cent more for city labor and 19 per cent less for farmers is truly stupendous. The year 1926 was the best year that the corporations in the United States have ever had. Each year of late has shown a large increase in the number of million dollar incomes. The outward signs of this rapidly increasing well-being of the already well-to-do and of the somewhat improved condition of the city working classes are evident to farm people the moment they enter a city's gates. It is small wonder that they are discontented.

Thus, whatever our devotion to the statistical method, the inadequacy of data forces the careful student back to statements of the problem which are qualitative rather than quantitative in character. Whether a given farmer's reward, when translated from price returns to real wages, interest, and profits, and the latter suitably adjusted in the light of psychic income, is more than that of a city worker of equal ability and expending equal effort, we shall probably never know, nor would the information do us much good if we had it. Any reasonably acute observer who examines any large sample of American farm life is pretty sure to conclude that the price level of agricultural commodities does not pay production costs on the present plane of efficiency and leave to the majority of farmers a surplus large enough to maintain standards of living comparable to those of town and city dwellers, and provide adequate education, recreation, and insurance against sickness and old age. Whether this condition tends to grow better or worse, and what measures, if any, are practically available for its improvement, we shall discuss later in the chapter. First, however, we must get a general view of the forces which have operated to produce the conditions amidst which we now find ourselves.

I. DIFFICULTIES CONFRONTING AGRICULTURE

There is always danger of talking about "the farmer" and "American agriculture" as a unit. In a large and diversified country, differences in type, activity, and situation are numerous and extreme—so much so, in fact, that a properly specialized account of the several branches of our

[3] The italics are the author's.

agricultural industry involves a diversity of details quite unmanageable in a discussion of the present scope. We must content ourselves with the broad outlines of major factors which apply somewhat generally over the country.

Since most of the interest and attention with reference to the situation of agriculture during the last eight years has centered on the comparatively low level of prices for agricultural commodities, we should notice first the forces operating to create and prolong this unsatisfactory price equation.

On the demand side:

1. Since the war, several strong competitors, particularly in the field of cereals and livestock products, have become increasingly strong contenders for what had been our traditional export outlet.

2. The possibility of developing in foreign countries a satisfactory, expanding market for the more intensive types of agriculture, coming with the maturer development of our agricultural industry, has been seriously checked by the slow recovery of the industrial nations of Europe and the fact that internal disorders in Russia, China, Mexico, and elsewhere have retarded the progress of these countries toward the higher type of European commercial and industrial civilization.

3. Dietary habits, fashions in clothes, and other factors in domestic consumption have caused this department of market demand to yield rather disappointing results to the farmer.

4. The rapid and widespread substitution of mechanical power for draft animals has further curtailed the demand for products of the soil.[4]

On the supply side:

1. Additional land has come into use for the first time or land already in use has been advanced to a more intensive stage of utilization, while withdrawals have been too slight to afford an adequate offset.

2. The maturing of methods of disseminating knowledge of efficient farm practices is beginning to show clear results in the increase of farmers' efficiency as producers, while declining fertility, though pulling in the opposite direction, seems a factor of less significance at the moment, and is indeed checked by many of the improved methods just referred to.

[4] The writer has developed these points more fully in *American Agriculture and the European Market*, 1924; *Journal of Farm Economics*, January, 1927, p. 21; *Proceedings of the Academy of Political Science*, January, 1928, p. 116; *Journal of Political Economy*, June, 1928, p. 330.

3. The process of mechanization has "stepped up" the productivity of man labor applied in many parts of our agricultural industry, while the number of workers leaving agriculture has only partially offset this increase.[5]

And, finally, the market mechanism by which supplies and demands are brought together in terms of price has shown:

1. Higher freight rates—only partially offset by the development of water transportation or the use of the motor truck.

2. An increase in many handling and selling charges as a result of higher costs of operation, particularly in the matter of wages paid.

3. Higher costs of containers and of labor and facilities used in packing and repacking, storing, and processing products on their way to the consumer.

Let us now examine these factors in the order in which they have been listed.

II. THE DISAPPOINTING DEMAND

It is a matter of common knowledge that the development of western Canada, Argentina, Australasia, and other countries has contributed to the decline of American exports of cereals and animal products which was clearly under way before the opening of the World War, or has required us to meet a very low price basis in the world markets as the condition of our continuance in the business.

Canadian wheat supplies have risen from 52 million bushels in 1900 to 232 million in 1913, and 550 million (preliminary estimate) in 1928. Similarly, Argentina produced 239 million bushels of wheat in 1927–28 as against 169 million in 1913–14, and 78 million in 1899–1900. The Australasian figures moved up from 49 million to 108 million and 119 million, respectively, during the same years. America's exports of the five principal cereals declined from 530 million bushels in 1897–98 to

---

[5] In some localities, farmers have been constrained to work longer hours and use more labor of women and children in the hope that a larger output might offset the unsatisfactory unit price of their product. For example, the issue of *Wallaces' Farmer* for October 4, 1926, says editorially: "What part of our bumper crops are the product of the unpaid labor of women and children? An Iowa subscriber writes: 'As our boy of thirteen and I stopped to rest our teams in plowing this summer, I looked around and counted ten of us in sight cultivating. There were three grown men and seven children, one girl and six boys, all plowing corn. The ages ranged from eight to fourteen years.' Farmers like this man are not working their children because they want to. They are doing it because they see no other way of keeping the farm going and turning out the volume that seems to be necessary in order to get by. Child labor on the farms is one of the factors that put real fire into the farm relief movement. Men will fight harder to save their children from hardship than to save themselves."

168 million in 1913–14. From the war-stimulated peak of 533 million bushels in 1921–22, they again dropped to 210 million in 1925–26. From this low point, however, they have risen somewhat during the last two years of heavy production, but on a basis of price unsatisfactory to American producers, and indicating the outward thrust of heavy home production rather than the attractive pull of profitable foreign demand.

Beef exports from the Argentine have risen from 54 million pounds in 1900 to nearly 2 billion pounds as an annual average to-day, while American exports have become negligible.[6] Similarly, exports of pork products have shown a marked decline, although our pre-eminence in corn growing enables us to retain a position in the world market, particularly so far as lard is concerned. The postwar decline in the export of pork products has brought them to less than 40 per cent of the wartime peak, but they are still at a level slightly above the immediate prewar years. This is doubtless owing in part to the redundance of domestic corn supplies in the face of the sharply declining number of horses and mules. Great Britain is still our greatest agricultural export market, but the trend of her interest seems to lie toward fostering imports from within the immediate family circle of her own empire, or from nations whose trade relations fit better than those of the United States into this system of exchange.

Second, as American agriculture has in some sections turned its attention from the old staples toward newer specialties, such as dairy and horticultural products (see Table 1) which are in or near the luxury class, the possibility of developing for these products a profitable export market to take the place of that for cereals or meat has been curtailed by the shock suffered by European industrial life, where in the prewar period consumers for such classes of products were developing at a most satisfactory rate. The repercussions of Europe's difficulties upon other nations in a less advanced stage of economic development has tended to check their economic progress, and thus to prejudice the possibilities of developing such a market rapidly in non-European countries. Add to this the internal disturbances of such countries as China and Mexico, the general tendency for non-European civilization to move at its own pace rather than at the tempo which was being introduced through European influence at the height of the imperialistic period, and we have a situation which seems, in general, to present no very flattering outlook for export surpluses of the American farmer.

Turning now to the domestic situation, we find standards of lighter eating and drinking, the use of less voluminous clothing, and an expanded use of natural and artificial silk and of paper products, where formerly textiles of agricultural origin were employed, which has brought about a

---

[6] Except in the case of oleo oil, which amounts to about 90 million pounds a year.

by no means insignificant lightening of the public demand for the farmer's wares.[7]

Finally, in the past 13 years there has occurred a decline in the number of horses and mules on farms from 25.7 million to 19.5 million head, as an accompaniment of the increase of tractors and trucks. During the same period there has been an even greater decline in the number of horses and mules in towns and cities. Estimates vary as to the amount of pasture and crop acreage that has been thereby released, but it seems clear that demand for at least 15 to 18 million acres of hay and grain land has dropped away as a result of this transition from horse power to internal combustion motors. Obviously, there is some offset in the growth of the market for farm products among those who produce these machines and the gasoline and oil with which they are fed. Their purchasing power, however, is largely directed into other channels, and the disruption of prices owing to the inability to readjust types of farming has been severe. Throughout much of the corn belt, oats and hay have come over a long period of time to a very important and very firmly entrenched position in standard crop rotations. Farm equipment, the experience of workers, and the whole farming system have grown up around this rotation plan, and as yet no fully satisfactory substitutes have been found to meet the new ratio of demands anywhere nearly as well as did the old corn, oats, and meadow combination.

All in all, then, the farmer has been called upon to make drastic adjustments to altered purchasing power abroad, the competition of newer industrial lands, and several cumulative changes in the volume and character of domestic demand. The one mitigating circumstance has been that our domestic industrial population has, in general, been rather fully employed at comparatively good wages. The national policy, however, has looked toward restriction of immigration, and hence a smaller number of mouths to be fed. High wages go not so much to increase the takings of products raised on the farm as to create a demand for greater fabrication of products and additional forms of trade and professional service. The situation thus presented on the demand side has been one which, in order to keep the various branches of the agricultural industry stabilized and so far as possible prosperous, would have called for a large degree of control over the quantity and direction of producers' efforts. How fully this condition has been met, we must now see.

III. EXUBERANT PRODUCTION

In spite of the fact that the census of 1890 celebrated the passing of the American frontier, the decades since that time have continued to witness the bringing of additional farm land into use, and the process did

---

[7] Phases of this matter are discussed in considerable detail under the heading "Changes in Consumption" in Chap. I (see pp. 530–558).

not terminate at the outbreak of the World War or with the signing of the Armistice. Land utilization is not determined by broad policies of public welfare nor is it under comprehensive state control. It proceeds largely along lines of individual profit-seeking on the part of private landholders, reinforcing their own zeal for land exploitation by Government reclamation projects wherever possible. As a result of this, additional areas have been or are being drained, irrigated, or cleared of timber, brush, and stone to make farms for settlers. Likewise, the extension of railroads and highways and the coming of the motor truck have increased the utilization of certain areas of land previously inaccessible.

But more significant than so-called "reclamation" is the process by which a considerable amount of land, particularly in the western half of the country, has been raised from range use to that of crop cultivation, or from extensive crop growing to general farming, stock raising, or horticultural uses. Millions of acres of Texas, Oklahoma, and Kansas range land have, since 1920, gone into cotton and wheat, and the vineyards and orchards of California and other states have been recruited from one-time grain and hay fields at a rate which has threatened to swamp certain branches of the horticultural industry. Some of these developments are clearly apparent in Table 1.

TABLE 1.—ACREAGE OF SPECIFIED CROPS IN CALIFORNIA, 1920–1928

(In thousands of acres)

Commodity	1920	1921	1922	1923	1924	1925	1926	1927	1928[a]	Change since 1920
Extensive crops	4,439	4,181	4,259	4,223	3,316	3,729	3,738	3,749	3,840	−599
Wheat	714	557	712	748	377	603	653	812	796	
Barley	1,250	1,188	1,129	1,095	765	1,050	1,080	994	1,083	
Oats	155	140	150	162	86	151	156	147	144	
Hay (tame and wild)	2,320	2,296	2,268	2,218	2,088	1,925	1,849	1,796	1,817	
Intensive crops	1,356	1,295	1,447	1,546	1,714	1,934	2,090	2,155	2,306	+950
Truck	171	145	191	214	221	268	327	356	360	
Fruit (bearing)	1,035	1,095	1,189	1,249	1,364	1,494	1,601	1,671	1,725	
Cotton	150	55	67	83	129	172	162	128	221	

[a] Preliminary.

Obviously, there is another side to the picture, and some land, utilized during the World War or before, has been so unprofitable under postwar schedules of price as to be "abandoned," either literally or in the sense of reverting to less extensive uses. In certain of the northeastern states, some of this land is being reforested by state or private agencies. It would be futile to attempt to make a quantitative determination of the ratio which such subtractions bear to the additions already discussed. The point is that such withdrawals have ordinarily been in sections where the land is of poor quality, undesirable in climate or topography, or at a disadvantage in terms of transportation or other facilities for production or social life, whereas the accretions have been of land which is superior for some technological or economic reason.   Regardless of how the area of "abandoned" land would compare with that of new additions, it is evident that such withdrawals have not been sufficient to bring production into desirable balance with demand, while at the same time additions to land area or increases in intensity of cultivation have complicated the problem and tended to delay ultimate adjustment.   In spite of repeated protests from farmers and farm organizations against public reclamation enterprises during this period of adjustment, Government irrigation projects have made some addition to our productive plant, and local interests have pushed private developments wherever their immediate interest seemed to be served thereby.[8]

While this factor in the situation must not be exaggerated, an understanding of the problem requires that it be remembered that the agricultural resources of the country are by no means all in use, and· that changes in agricultural technique or in other branches of our economic life frequently result in tapping these latent resources in such a way as seriously to disturb the adjustment of existing agricultural enterprise.

Probably a larger factor, and certainly one more general in its application, is that of the advancing technique of agriculture as a fruition of efforts toward general dissemination of scientific farming methods throughout the agricultural group.   From the Civil War to the World War, we had a succession of developments of Federal and state departments of agriculture, agricultural colleges, agricultural experiment stations, extension service, and county demonstration agents or farm advisers.   The pressure of war needs and "food-will-win-the-war" campaigns resulted in a rapid development of the extension service and the putting of local educational agents in about 4,000 of the principal agricultural counties, from one end of the country to the other.   This has been followed by intensive development of boys' and girls' club work, with exhibitions and prizes provided by banks, chambers of commerce, and other interested bodies, with state and national championships rewarded with ribbons, cups, cash, tours, and even calls upon the President of the United States.   Farm bureaus have developed educational activities and systematic programs of work, and the teaching of agriculture has been widely extended in the high schools, a move facilitated

[8] One of the items in the agricultural referendum recently submitted to its members by the Chamber of Commerce of the United States reads as follows: "The Committee recommends that the bringing into cultivation of additional areas for agricultural production at public expense be delayed until such additional production of agricultural commodities as would result therefrom can be demonstrated to be an economic need of the nation."   There were, according to the preliminary canvass, 2,537½ votes in support of this proposition and 391½ opposed.   This commits the Chamber in favor of the proposition.

by the development of consolidated school districts in many sections. The pressure upon the farmer to make both ends meet, coinciding as it did with this forward thrust of educational effort in agriculture, has resulted in a widespread advance in sound and scientific farm practices, which, as such things go, has been phenomenally rapid. While quantitative measures of its effectiveness are out of the question, its qualitative significance is established in the testimony of agricultural leaders in all parts of the country.

These practices have included wider dissemination of good seed, better methods of tilling, drainage, terracing, and the like, better sanitation for livestock, with better breeding, more intelligent feeding, record keeping, and the culling of unprofitable animals from flocks and herds. Its details are almost endless, but in general it may be characterized as a move to bring the science of agriculture, as developed by two generations of laboratory and test-plot work, into the daily understanding and practice of the rank and file of farmers.

Finally, the most dramatic and probably the most significant single factor which has entered into the productive situation of agriculture within the last few years has come with the increased mechanization of the farm, primarily as a result of the development of the internal combustion engine. This represents the second wave of mechanical advance in American agriculture, the first having been the sweeping adoption of horse-drawn implements in the period between the Civil War and the World War. Some suggestive comparisons may be made between the two movements.

Prior to 1850, American agriculture, in common with that of all other countries, was carried on by hand labor, employing only a few simple tools, and differing but slightly from the methods of the Middle Ages or ancient times. During the latter years of this period, however, "Yankee ingenuity" had been busy on the problem of devising machines which would save labor and improve results in farming, so that from the steel moldboard plow of 1833 to the Marsh harvester of 1858 a fairly extensive line of horse-drawn implements had been made available to the American farmer. Actual adoption of this power equipment was extremely slow until the pressing demands and shrinking labor supply, which developed as the Civil War progressed, forced farmers in large numbers to turn to these labor-saving methods. Immediately after the war came the homestead movement, and an even more pressing demand for horse-drawn implements. These were perfected in great variety as the years went on, but, with few exceptions, were limited in size and character to the sort of machine which could be moved over the ground and derive its operating power from a team of from two to five horses or mules. "Big-team hitches" were developed in some parts of the West, but a one-horse or a two- or three-horse team was the norm of practically all farm operations up to the time of the World War.

The only notable exception in which the horse gave way to mechanical power in farming during the nineteenth century was the steam thresher, and there was a very slight application of steam engines to plowing. The development of dry-farming methods some twenty years ago accentuated the demand for mechanical power, and internal combustion engines were employed in tractors of a clumsy and none-too-reliable sort in the last few years just prior to the World War.

In all this, we see a situation rather strikingly similar to that of farming during the Civil War period. Technical developments of considerable potential significance had taken place, but pressure had not as yet been sufficient to force the general adoption of the newer methods. High war prices, the patriotic appeal that "food will win the war," the loss of farm labor through the draft, and the pushing of agriculture out into regions where extensive methods were employed, strongly stimulated the adoption of tractors, trucks, and stationary motors on our farms. The machines available were fairly crude, but they demonstrated the effectiveness of such forms of mechanical power on the farm and created a market outlet and a volume of field experience which enabled manufacturers to make rapid strides in the mechanical perfection of such equipment, and in furnishing it at prices and on credit terms which enabled the farmer to make the transition from the horse-power agriculture of his fathers to methods so largely dominated by power equipment that it is hardly an exaggeration to speak of present and prospective American agriculture broadly as "power farming." This phase of the situation now developing in American agricultural production is hardly less than revolutionary.

IV. THE ADVANCE OF POWER FARMING

The transition from horse power to mechanical power in agriculture, although it began about twenty years ago, shows its most striking development during the past ten years. This is revealed in Chart 1, which is based upon the statistics of horses and mules on farms, and of tractors in use during a series of recent years. Table 2 presents data covering the first of these points. It is noticeable that the pressure for large production caused the number of horses and mules to hold their own or even increase up to 1919. Thereafter the tide turned, and the decline in horses on farms has continued down to the present. Far from abating, it seems now to show signs of further acceleration. In the South, where mules are almost exclusively employed, the beginning of the decline was deferred until 1926, but the most recent figures show that the movement has now clearly begun. Other evidence suggests that it may proceed at a rapid pace.

CHART 1.—A COMPARISON OF THE NUMBER OF HORSES AND MULES WITH
THAT OF TRACTORS ON FARMS, 1910–1929

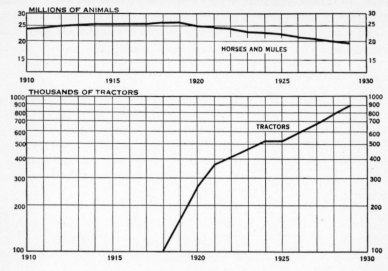

TABLE 2.—NUMBER OF HORSES AND MULES ON FARMS, 1910–1929

(Thousands)

January 1—	Horses	Mules	Total
1910	19,833	4,210	24,043
1911	20,277	4,323	24,600
1912	20,509	4,362	24,871
1913	20,567	4,386	24,953
1914	20,962	4,449	25,411
1915	21,195	4,479	25,674
1916	21,159	4,593	25,752
1917	21,210	4,723	25,933
1918	21,555	4,873	26,428
1919	21,482	4,954	26,436
1920	19,848	5,475	25,323
1921	19,134	5,586	24,720
1922	18,564	5,638	24,202
1923	17,943	5,702	23,645
1924	17,222	5,730	22,952
1925	16,489	5,725	22,214
1926	15,830	5,740	21,570
1927	15,145	5,679	20,824
1928	14,541	5,566	20,107
1929	14,029	5,447	19,476

The other side of the picture shows a sharply rising curve of tractor
use. Table 3 presents these data both from the standpoint of current
sales and of accumulating tractor equipment on farms, which is more
definitely comparable to the horse figures previously presented. This

table indicates a ratio of one tractor to each 7.8 farms of 50 acres or over in 1925, as against one tractor for each 16.9 farms of 50 acres or over in 1920. Such a figure is only roughly suggestive of the rapid advance of the tractor in a period of a very few years, and development has of course been most rapid in the years since the census of 1925 was taken. It is

TABLE 3.—TRACTORS MANUFACTURED, SOLD, AND IN USE ON FARMS, 1910–1929

Year	Manufactured	Sold in the United States	In use on farms, January 1
1910	4,000		
1911	7,000		
1912	11,000		
1913	7,000		
1914	10,000		
1915	21,000		
1916	29,670	27,819	
1917	62,742	49,504	
1918	132,697	96,470	80,100
1919	164,590	136,162	147,600
1920	203,207	162,988	a246,139
1921	73,198		354,600
1922	99,692	101,192	381,675
1923	134,590	117,701	447,000
1924	119,305	99,011	498,225
1925	167,553	121,998	a506,745
1926	181,995	126,725	585,068
1927	200,504	160,637	643,825
1928	171,137b	99,491	768,825
1929			852,989

a These figures are from the United States Census. The others are estimates of the National Association of Farm Equipment Manufacturers.
b Preliminary.

perhaps more significant to note the situation in particular states which bulk large in our agricultural industry, and whose type of farming is well suited to the utilization of the tractor.[9] Such a selected list is shown in Table 4. Obviously this method of presenting data has serious shortcomings, since tractors vary considerably in size and the larger farms ordinarily have more than one tractor each.

The snorting, balking marvels which first introduced the gas engine tractor to the farming community following 1902 were a nine days' wonder, but during the next decade they were rapidly perfected, and

[9] It is to be remembered, however, that the use of the tractor is by no means limited to wheat-farming states, the newer cotton region, and the comparatively large corn and livestock farms of the Middle West. It has been introduced into the potato fields of Aroostook County, Maine, and is to be found in respectable numbers in all the more important farming sections east as well as west of the Mississippi River.

general adoption proceeded swiftly and much as a matter of course. In fact, less thought has been given to the significance of the movement and its implications for the future of our whole agricultural industry than would have been desirable. The point alluded to earlier in this chapter may be here reiterated and developed in more detail, namely, that the introduction of the tractor implies and necessitates a sweeping revision of the whole character of our agricultural industry and of our ideas with reference to farm organization and management, land values, and other phases of rural economy.

TABLE 4.—NUMBER OF TRACTORS ON FARMS IN SELECTED STATES, 1918–1929

State	1918	1920	1922	1924	1926	1928	1929
Iowa	a8,940	a22,319	a26,876	a32,623	a40,612	b49,695	b59,609
Nebraska	c4,746	c8,888	c10,886	c11,457	c19,489	b24,486	b29,062
North Dakota	d	c13,006	d	b16,000	b18,177	b21,995	b24,156
Illinois	d	c23,102	d	b43,325	b47,893	f61,398	b69,973
Kansas	g5,415	c17,177	g21,717	g25,019	g33,853	b41,275	b49,681
Texas	d	c9,048	d	h16,905	b19,103	b23,114	b27,238
Montana	d	c7,647	d	h6,602	b6,700	b8,107	b14,000

a Iowa Monthly Crop Report.
b Estimate. The Montana estimate is clearly too low. There were probably 10,000 tractors in the state, Jan. 1, 1928.
c Nebraska Agricultural Statistics.
d Information not available.
e United States Census, 1920.
f Illinois Farm Equipment Survey, 1928.
g Reports of Kansas State Board of Agriculture.
h United States Census, 1925.

One reason that we have given so little attention to this grows, no doubt, out of the fact that the tractor was first thought of as a mechanical device which would take the place of the horse in existing methods of agriculture. But this iron horse, or "steel mule," as one manufacturer actually christened his tractor, does not merely take the place of horse-flesh in the traditional scheme of agricultural production. We are coming slowly to perceive that it sets a new pace and, rather than fitting itself unobtrusively into our agriculture, creates a demand that agriculture be quite drastically readjusted in accordance with its needs and potentialities.

It was but natural that the tractor in its early days should encounter a heavy weight of inertia—old methods and old ideas in what has always been regarded as a highly-traditionalized calling. It was born into a world of horse machinery, farmers trained to the handling of teams, and sizes of farms and methods of organization which had been worked out in response to the needs of horse farming.

As the tractor has established itself, however, farmers have with great rapidity learned to handle the new type of power with skill and enjoyment. Old implements have been adapted to the larger power made available through the tractor, or new implements devised to exploit its possibilities, and farm sizes and farming methods have begun to adapt themselves to the possibilities of the new source of motive power. Mutual adjustments of the internal combustion engine to farming and of farming to the internal combustion engine are now encountering less resistance, and are gathering such increasing momentum as to cause some agricultural engineers to predict that we stand on the threshold of a new agricultural era, which will be marked by revolutionary changes in the application of mechanical power to farming. Time alone will tell whether this is an exaggerated view, but at all events it appears that the period which we have just passed through is that of the relatively difficult initial introduction of something new and radically different, and that we are only now passing into the period of widespread adoption of improvements thus far developed by the leaders rather than the mass. To see the nature and appraise the significance of what is now under way, we should examine separately several of the major fields of agricultural production in which these changes have been taking place.

V. POWER FARMING AND WHEAT

Wheat growing easily takes its place at the head of the list in any discussion of mechanized farming. It was in this industry that bonanza farming developed in the latter part of the nineteenth century. Here also the steam thresher first blazed the trail of power machinery on the farm. It was the wheat growers of California, followed by those of the Pacific Northwest, who developed the combine harvester, which is one of the most outstanding features of the present development of power farming.

During the World War, when wheat was a commodity of prime importance, every effort was directed toward making the most of our productive possibilities; the now famous Campbell Farming Corporation of Montana had its inception, and showed what a man trained as an engineer could make of mechanical methods on some 100,000 acres of dry-farming land. Since the war, with the vigorous competition of Australia and Argentina returned to the market, our wheat industry has been constrained to follow this same line of attack, through greater mechanization, in the effort to reduce production costs to a point where we can survive in this competition. With rapid improvement in tractor design and the development of smaller sizes of combines, this method of harvesting has become the standard of modern practice over a large part of the western wheat belt, and is rapidly pushing eastward, adding the other small grains to its sphere of operation.

The "combine," or harvester-thresher, is simply a small threshing outfit, or "separator," hooked up with a cutter-bar and elevating apron such as are used on the standard grain binder. The binding mechanism is omitted from the harvester and the grain passed direct from the cutter-bar to the cylinders of the separator in a loose condition. As first developed, these outfits were hauled by big teams of from 12 to 20 or more horses each. This is still done to some extent, but more and more the tractor has taken the place of the big team. The larger combines ordinarily derive their power from a separate gasoline motor mounted on the front of the separator, but smaller outfits often are operated by a power "take-off" from the tractor which hauls the apparatus.

In some types of this machine, the threshed grain is spouted directly into a wagon or truck which accompanies the combine harvester over the field. In other cases, a grain tank is added to the machine, and in this the grain is collected and dumped, in lots of 50 bushels or in larger or smaller amounts, into wagons or trucks at convenient points. In the matter of disposal of straw, practice differs. Where it is feasible to plow the straw under, a straw spreader attached at the rear of the combine will effectively distribute the straw and chaff over the land. In some cases, however, the growth of straw is so heavy that it is necessary to remove it from the land. In such event, attachments are available which will deposit the straw in a continuous windrow for burning or collection by a hay loader, or gather it into convenient piles or small stacks for burning, baling, or hauling in the loose state.

The method of converting standing grain into threshed wheat at one operation first developed in California, then in the Palouse Valley of Washington and Oregon, and in the Southwest. In all these places grain ripens uniformly, is not often beaten down by storms or subject to frost damage. In Montana, the Dakotas, and farther east, however, all these difficulties present themselves with more or less frequency. If these sections are to secure the benefits of this cost-reducing method, their ingenuity is challenged to adapt the combine harvester in such a manner as to minimize these difficulties and yet secure at least a substantial part of the economies made possible by eliminating the older method of binding and shocking wheat. This has resulted in the use of windrowing attachments, or "swathers." By this method, grain which is not sufficiently dry for immediate threshing can be cut and deposited unbound in a single windrow, where the grain from a swath of 10, 20, or even 25 feet in width may be held until it is in suitable condition and good weather is available for threshing. Then the combine, with a "pick-up" attach-ment, similar in principle to the standard hay loader, is drawn over the field, completing the operation.

Obviously, this method foregoes the saving obtained by completing the whole process by a single operation. It retains, however, the economy of twine and power required for binding the grain, and elimi-nates the heavy labor charge of shocking and handling the bundled grain to the thresher. It likewise leaves the straw distributed in the field when it is desired to plow it under and, if a bunching attachment is used, makes field baling or the hauling of straw for bedding an economical operation.

The extent to which the use of the windrowing method will permit of the economical use of the combine over the more humid sections of the country is still in the process of experimental determination. Such outfits are in use to-day as far east as the Atlantic coast, and seem to be establishing themselves as standard farm practice in all important grain-growing sections.[10] With the present trend of grain prices and the growth of production in areas where "direct combining" is practicable, it would seem a fair inference that sections which are not able to compete, at least to the extent of doing field threshing with the windrow method, are likely to be in large measure forced out of the business of growing grain commercially.

Some idea of the rapidity of the recent spread of the combine over the country may be gained from the figures giving the total number sold in the United States annually during the past six years. These are as follows:[11] 1923, 1,099; 1924, 1,590; 1925, 3,563; 1926, 6,277; 1927 11,221.

Likewise, the figures showing distribution by states are interesting from the point of view both of dispersion and of the apparent direction of growth. These figures are given in Table 5.

Figures which will show accurately the comparative cost of the three methods are difficult to secure, both because of the experimental stage in which the windrowing method still remains and also because of the diversity of conditions under which the various methods are employed. A Texas study,[12] however, computes the cost of harvesting with the combine as ranging from 14.7 cents per bushel with an 11-bushel yield down to 7 cents with a 23-bushel yield, and average costs of harvesting with the binder and stationary thresher at 33 cents per bushel. Nebraska studies[13] show combine costs of 9 to 12 cents per bushel with yields of 11.8 to 13.4 bushels, and estimate the cost of the binder method at about 31 cents per bushel. A report made by the United States Department of Agriculture[14] shows similar savings, and the writer found it to be the judgment of careful observers in Montana that the combine reduced

[10] More and more, as the combine has moved out of the wheat area, efforts have been made by manufacturers to increase its range of uses by developing appliances not merely to meet special conditions, but to facilitate its use on as wide a range of crops as possible, including particularly soy beans, clover, and peas.

[11] United States Bureau of Census figures.

[12] "Harvesting Grain with the Combine Harvester-Thresher," Texas Agricultural Experiment Station, *Bulletin*, No. 373.

[13] *Extension Circulars*, Nos. 811 and 814.

[14] *Technical Bulletin*, No. 70.

TABLE 5.—NUMBER OF COMBINES IN VARIOUS STATES[a]

States	1926	1927
California	2,000	2,100
Colorado	.....	800
Idaho	800	1,100
Illinois	64	310
Indiana	.....	72
Iowa	.....	27
Kansas	8,276	12,782
Michigan	.....	10
Minnesota	.....	11
Montana	550	1,100
Nebraska	.....	3,000
North Dakota	26	200
Ohio	.....	20
Oklahoma	3,189	5,746
Oregon	1,500	1,800
Pennsylvania	.....	26
South Dakota	.....	225
Texas	2,684	2,890
Virginia	.....	4
Washington	2,500	3,100
Utah, Nevada, and Arizona	350	500

[a] As calculated by the National Association of Farm Equipment Manufacturers.

production costs by about 15 to 20 cents per bushel. The cost under the windrowing method presumably gets about half the savings secured by direct combining, but has considerable advantage in meeting difficult conditions of harvesting without the wasting and spoiling of grain which is unavoidable where the binder method is used.

In order to secure maximum economies, it is necessary to use the combine outfit to nearly its maximum capacity. For a medium-sized machine, this means something like 1,000 acres during the season, and it is generally calculated that no economies are effected unless at least 300 acres of grain are to be handled each year. In the regions of general farming, this would necessitate custom work or some sort of co-operative arrangement by which the combine would be used on several farms each season. The other way of meeting the situation is through the growth of larger operating units, each capable of utilizing one or more combines and other machine equipment well up to its maximum capacity. In the heart of the wheat belt, operating units are so large that "in recent years many wider machines have been purchased, and 20-, 24-, and even 36- and 48-foot machines are to be found."[15] With even a 16-foot machine, 40 to 50 acres per day may be cut, and the speed with which the work is completed is an important factor in avoiding waste and getting the best quality of grain.

These direct savings of as much as 20 cents a bushel on production costs have brought more farm relief to the wheat grower than has actually

[15] W. E. Grimes, *Journal of Farm Economics*, April, 1928, p. 226.

resulted from tariff protection at a nominal rate of 42 cents per bushel. The development of the combine and other low-cost methods has enabled the Pacific coast states to survive in world-market competition, has made possible the relative stabilization of the wheat-growing industry of Montana[16] and western North Dakota, and has enabled the Gulf Southwest to expand its production.

Evidently these low-cost methods are particularly suited to a rather extensive method of producing rather moderate yields on land which ranges down to comparatively low grades. This introduces a factor of competition to be met, for a time at least, by the grain lands farther east not dissimilar to that which confronted the Northeastern states when the prairies of the Middle West were rushed into production as an accompaniment of the coming of the horse-drawn binder. To what extent and by what measures central and eastern farmers may meet this competition is one of the interesting phases of the present farm problem.

The prominence which has been given to the combine harvester should not cause us to overlook the fact that it is but one, though doubtless the most striking, phase of the mechanization of grain production. Its coming has been largely facilitated by the use of the tractor, and the tractor in turn has made possible many other economies and improvements in grain farming. One of the chief of these is that it largely mitigates the burden of seed-bed preparation, particularly in the winter wheat region. "Fall plowing," so-called, actually is to a large extent performed in the late summer when weather is hot, moisture not infrequently inadequate, and flies and other insects add the last straw to break the horse's back. The tractor manifests sublime indifference to temperature, flies, or the condition of the soil, and permits of timely and thorough preparation of the ground and seeding under the most favorable conditions. Whether for fall or winter seeding, also, the tractor can be pushed long hours, even all night with suitable lighting attachments, and thus overcome almost any crisis, presented by unfavorable weather or flood or frost damage, which necessitates reseeding.

In other types of equipment, also, there has been considerable progress. Ideas of the proper amount and kind of stirring of the soil which

---

[16] The accelerated speed of power-farming development in Montana is revealed in the following table of sales of tractors and combines in that state during the last four years:

Year	Tractors	Combines
1925	1,160	112
1926	1,749	220
1927	3,607	968
1928 (estimate)	4,925	2,720

should take place in the annual plowing and in summer fallow operations have changed considerably, and the one-way disk, or "wheat-land plow," and the "duck-foot" cultivator have been devised to meet this situation, producing optimum condition with less labor than required by the older methods.[17] With a tractor of suitable power, the ground can be covered very rapidly with these appliances. These implements go far toward solving problems of weed eradication and control of soil-blowing in the land of summer fallow.

Finally, it should be remembered that the achievements of the internal combustion motor include the development of the farm truck, which scuttles about over the fields, taking on grain as it is discharged from the combine harvester and putting it swiftly on its way to market, at costs which would have been unbelievable in the old days of horse teams. Even the so-called "pleasure car" is an important machine, transporting the farmer and his laborers rapidly over the distance between home and fields, or between the farm and the town where repairs must be secured in case of a breakdown. As a matter of fact, the development of the automobile must be regarded as a condition precedent to much that has happened in the recently rapid progress of farm equipment. Air strainers, methods of sealing-in the motor, heat-treating of metal, the development of alloy steels, and methods of precision as developed in the automobile factory have been carried over in the making of farm tractors and trucks to the end that costs have been reduced, performance immeasurably improved, and the working life prolonged to a truly remarkable extent. In a modern tractor factory, methods of testing are as exact and exacting, and the speed, precision, and economy of the process by which an evolving machine advances down the assembly line until it moves off under its own power are as highly perfected as those found in any first-rate automobile factory.

It has already been suggested that the application of machine methods introduces new complexities as to the size and organization of the farm. The acceleration of the harvest period resulting from the use of the combine has likewise created new problems of marketing—of storage, car supply, glut prices, and moisture damage. The last is being attacked vigorously through methods of bin ventilation and weed removal attachments on the combine. The issue as to physical movement and price behavior challenges the farmer to tackle a whole series of problems.

[17] F. A. Wirt, agricultural engineer with the J. I. Case Co., supplies the author with figures of comparative cost (based in large part on cost studies made by the United States Department of Agriculture), which indicate that the cost of growing wheat, using the one-way disk plow and combine, amounts to barely 45 per cent of the total cost by the old method of plow, harrow, binder, and thresher, and that the cost of seed-bed preparation with this "wheat-land plow" is only about 55 per cent of the cost of plowing and harrowing. This implement might itself be called a "combine," since it results in telescoping two tillage operations into one.

How much and what kind of storage must he provide on the farm or (through organization) at the local shipping point or terminal market? Must he, through co-operative organization, secure a more orderly marketing of the crop, or can the machinery of future trading work out a scheme of differentials between the different months, weeks, and days, which is just and reasonable in view of the cost of effecting the necessary time distribution of a highly seasonal crop? Can farms of the present sizes and types of organization secure an effective and economical utilization of the size and number of machine units which will secure minimum production costs? Must problems such as the elimination of moisture damage and avoidance of the cost of windrowing be met by changes in cultural methods, designed to secure more adequate weed control, or by the popularization of varieties which have shorter and stiffer straw, earlier ripening, or less tendency to "shatter" when ripe?

The plant breeder and the agronomist seem disposed to match the brisk pace set by the agricultural engineer and implement manufacturer, and, at perhaps a somewhat more conservative rate, the actual farmer and professional students of farm organization and management are effecting an evolution in the size and set-up of operating units. In both the northwest and southwest wheat belts, farms 5,000, 10,000, and even 50,000 acres in extent are being operated, some of them with striking results in the way of efficiency and low unit costs. The subhumid region was originally granted to settlers in homesteads of 160 acres, and such grants were only slowly increased to the half-section and finally the section. Experience shows that in much of this region such a holding gives a family nothing but a chance at starvation, whereas a block of four sections, with modern equipment, will produce a very satisfactory family income, and can, in the region of summer fallow, be handled by two men suitably equipped with modern machinery, and the possible addition of a little seasonal labor. Farmers who had sufficient resources or skill or courage to "stick it out" in the years following the price decline of 1920 are building up such business units, through the lease or purchase of lands given up by their neighbors. One four-section farm in Montana is made up of eight parcels, seven of which went through foreclosure proceedings. These seven include the farm of the present operator, who is managing the larger enterprise with so much success as to be fairly on the way toward eventually owning the whole tract.

The present trend toward modern agricultural efficiency in the wheat belt gives assurance that America can supply itself with an abundance of grain at costs commensurate with modern industrial standards, and even send a considerable surplus abroad over cheap water routes from the Pacific Northwest and the Gulf Southwest. It is, however, a condition which affords ruinous competition to wheat enterprise in many of the older sections of the central and eastern states,[18] and rocks the foundations of land values in some of these older sections, much as they in their turn forced a revision in the agricultural utilization and land prices of the New England states.

It must be remembered that the very force which is contributing to the increase of low-cost wheat supplies in the Great Plains of the United States is also strengthening the chief competing regions in other countries. Farm implement manufacturers have been aggressive in developing the foreign market for the new power machinery even as they developed the export market for horse-drawn implements a generation ago. It goes without saying that wheat production in the prairie provinces of Canada is carried on by efficient machinery methods practically identical with those used in our own western wheat belt. It is perhaps not so well known that Argentina, Australia, and other wheat-producing countries are taking our tractors, combines, and tillage implements in considerable numbers, and seem to be entirely capable of duplicating the same sort of power-farming efficiency which we have so strikingly developed. Both these countries, as well as Canada, have considerable areas of level subhumid land, comparable to our own Great Plains region, among their advantages for low-cost grain farming.

Sparseness of population has been something of a brake upon the development of these competing sections, but it is just such a condition which promotes the rapid introduction of power machinery, and gives labor and investment such a high productivity as to attract new operators into the field. Furthermore, Great Britain is definitely attempting to direct some of her redundant population to the most favored agricultural

TABLE 6.—DOMESTIC AND EXPORT SALES OF SPECIFIED FARM MACHINERY, 1922–1927[a]

Year	Two-bottom plows		Disk plows		Combines		Tractors	
	Domestic	For export	Domestic	For export	Domestic	For export	Domestic	For export
1922	54,876	6,435	13,841	1,100	1,608	854	100,092	10,223
1923	67,211	19,060	15,591	2,985	1,099	2,986	115,040	16,608
1924	45,866	16,681	12,043	3,694	1,590	3,671	96,539	25,585
1925	60,937	30,290	16,296	6,712	3,563	1,878	118,739	46,627
1926	75,132	44,617	17,237	6,981	6,277	4,707	122,940	47,605
1927	62,952	25,925	15,174	5,346	11,221	4,701	155,843	43,761

[a] Bureau of the Census, Department of Commerce, *Manufacture and Sale of Farm Equipment.*

[18] For example, the state of Nebraska straddles the 100th meridian, and thus exemplifies both types of farming. The study cited above shows a cost of 38 cents for the production of wheat in Perkins County in the western end of the state, as against an average of 86 cents in four of the eastern counties.

regions of her outlying dominions,[19] and much of the immigration of Europe turns toward undermanned regions, now that the immigration policy of the United States restricts entry here. The preceeding table of exports of certain types of agricultural machinery as compared with sales in the United States shows to some extent the manner in which the strong foreign competitors of the United States are keeping step with the march of our own technological progress.

VI. THE CORN FARMER

Several of the changes already discussed with reference to wheat enter into the present situation of the corn industry. Excellent and moderate-priced tractors, in sizes smaller than those which are ordinarily used for hauling the combine and doing other wheat-farm work, are available to the corn grower in the general farming regions where corn is the backbone of the cropping system. Even with horses, some of the most progressive corn belt farmers developed efficient methods of economizing man labor, such as driving a five-horse team on a two-bottom riding plow and leading a three-horse team, which followed the plow with a disc or harrow. Two-row cultivators were first introduced for horse use, and corn binders and pickers were handled by four- or five-horse teams.

With high-grade tractors of 12 or 15 drawbar horse power, the corn farmer can prepare his land for planting at a rate practically twice as fast as was possible even with his efficient team methods. This is because a tractor can pull an equal or greater load and move at a speed about twice that of a good farm team. As an experimental beginning, two double-row planters were hooked together behind the tractor, and now implement manufacturers are putting out both four-row and three-row planters. When it comes to cultivation, a similar adaptation of the two-row riding cultivator to a four-row or three-row cultivator, with tractor power, is rapidly coming into use. One man with a two-horse team and riding cultivator could cover 8 to 10 acres a day. With a tractor and four-row cultivator he can cover 60 to 65 acres.

Corn-husking has always been a labor-consuming operation, frequently calling for outside seasonal help similar to that of shocking and threshing in the wheat belt. For some years back, this situation has been partially modified by the increasing use of the silo and the "hogging down" of corn. The horse-drawn corn picker was introduced nearly twenty years ago, and showed a constant though moderate increase in use. The number sold during the last five years about doubles the previous rate of adoption. Its employment is somewhat facilitated by the availability of greater horse power under tractor-farming conditions, and also

[19] "It is officially expected that 6,500 of the 8,500 harvesters sent to Canada will remain as a permanent addition to the British citizenship of the Dominion." *Britannia*, September 28, 1928, p. 9.

the change of corn sheller design, which makes possible satisfactory shelling of corn which has a considerable amount of husk remaining.

The silo has become standard equipment on livestock and dairy farms, and has done much toward extending the corn belt to the north. The corn binder and the silo filler applied machine power to this process. The handling of corn, however, from the field to the silage cutter has always been a disagreeable task because of the heavy labor involved in handling the corn bundles. Progress is now being made toward lightening this work by the introduction of tractor-drawn corn harvesters which gather and shred the stalks directly in the field, dumping the cut silage into wagons or trucks which haul it to the barnyard. There it is simply dumped on the feed platform of a silo filler, which blows it into the silo. This eliminates one of the most costly and disagreeable tasks of the corn farmer.

Where corn must be husked for dry feeding or cash sale, the modern type of corn sheller, run by belt power from the tractor engine, makes possible rapid and economical handling of the work, and permits of speed and economy in husking, owing to the lessened necessity for complete removal of the husks. Portable elevators and moderate-priced feed grinders carry the mechanization of the corn farmer's labors through to the final disposal of his product.

The tendency of the tractor to displace horse power is at its maximum in such a one-crop area as the wheat belt, where there is a heavy seasonal demand for labor, and the maintenance of horses over a 12-month period presents many and serious difficulties. As we go into the corn belt and the region of general farming, we find farmers who expect to remain on the job 12 months in the year and who can provide pasturage on the rougher parts of their farms and raise feed crops at a minimum of expense in connection with their other farm operations. While, of course, the demand for horse labor is not uniform throughout the year, it is fairly heavy for more than half the year, and teams, if properly managed, can be maintained quite cheaply during the rest of the time. Those who are interested in the horse industry are now carrying on an active campaign to teach farmers the most economical methods of horse management and to instruct them in the use of "big team hitches," whereby the savings in man labor secured by the use of the tractor can be realized without turning from horse power. Thus a 10-horse farm might range from 250 to 320 acres and furnish 8-horse teams for big machinery, such as is drawn by tractors of the type most popular in this region. Even 12-horse teams are advocated and used to some extent. But eight horses driven four abreast will handle a three-bottom plow with a harrow attached behind, preparing $8\frac{1}{2}$ acres of ground per day with the labor of one man. The extent to which this transition is taking place in the Mississippi Valley is indicated by the figures in the following table, furnished by Prof. O. G. Lloyd, of Purdue University, showing percentage of acreage worked by teams of various sizes in recent years as compared with the situation six years earlier.

Size of team	Discing		Plowing		Cultivating corn	
	1919 to 1921	1925 to 1927	1919 to 1921	1925 to 1927	1919 to 1921	1925 to 1927
	Per cent	*Per cent*	*Per cent*	*Per cent*	*Per cent*	*Per cent*
2-horse...............	....	....	1.8	0.2	80.0	72.4
3-horse...............	1.7	1.0	60.6	40.1	19.1	20.7
4-horse...............	88.9	67.8	27.6	33.3	0.9	6.9
5-horse...............	2.7	10.1	7.3	16.7	....	....
6-horse...............	6.7	19.4	2.7	9.1	....	....
8-horse...............	....	1.7	....	0.6	....	....

The repercussions of all this upon the economic organization of farming in the corn belt are somewhat less striking than the changes in wheat growing. The type of farming is much more intensive, with livestock occupying a large place in the program. And yet the effects of the development of larger power and machine units are highly significant. Even under general farm conditions, the 160-acre farm has become a small farm rather than a large one. The grain and livestock farm of the corn belt has been able to grow by the addition of "an 80" or a quarter section at the same time that it has reduced its demand for hired labor. Close observers of these developments are looking with more and more favor on the 640-acre tract as a family farm, and even coming to the conclusion that the better type of business farmers in this section can and should, for maximum efficiency, operate units of 1,000 to perhaps 2,500 acres. Such a farm permits a reasonable specialization in the labor force, a full line of modern equipment without excessive overhead, and the services of a practical manager who devotes his time fully to supervision of the technical and business operations of the farm without himself engaging in much, if any, manual labor.

As in the case of wheat, we find in the corn and livestock region of the great Middle West the gradual evolution of a type of skillful and adequately powered farming, which follows closely the developments of scientific research in the agricultural experiment stations. This will assure an abundant and moderate-priced supply of corn and livestock for home consumption, and will furnish for export those products for which this country offers superior advantage, such as lard, cured pork products, and oleo oil. Under such methods, farming will offer satisfactory returns to a declining number of workers, each performing the necessary labor on an increasing acreage with relatively large machine equipment.

The transition is being effected only at the expense of considerable recasting of the structure of land values and at a great deal of personal cost to those who are being forced to change their residence and occupation in the process. The farmers upon whom the demand falls for increasing their investment in equipment are finding difficulty in meeting the situation in a period when farm produce prices are low as compared to operating and overhead costs. It is extremely unfortunate that the war profits of the section could not have been more fully diverted into this channel. In far too many instances they were dissipated in unwise investments before those who had secured them as a legitimate incident of war-time developments realized the trend of events which lay just ahead of them. If a magic wand could restore to Iowa alone the wealth which was taken out of the state in the years immediately following the war by fake promoters, oil stock salesmen, and the yeggs who garnered millions in Liberty Bonds from the none-too-strong-boxes of the country banks where farmer buyers had left them for safe-keeping, it would make an appreciable contribution toward equipping farmers adequately for taking advantage of the possibilities for more efficient production which lie technically within their reach.

VII. THE COTTON BELT

For a century after the invention of the cotton gin, the cotton industry expanded itself steadily but with negligible change in its basis of organization. While the Civil War marked the passing of slavery, it did not significantly change the methods or equipment by which cotton land was cultivated and the crop harvested.

It was the boll weevil, introduced about 1892 but not producing widespread infestation until more than a decade later, that marked the beginning of the period of rapid adjustment and readjustment within the industry. The depredations of the boll weevil, as it spread into the eastern, moister regions of the cotton belt, were so severe as to call for additional acreage elsewhere, and this was forthcoming in the western part of the belt. Expansion was particularly noticeable in Texas and Oklahoma (Table 7). The World War, of course, produced serious derangement of the world cotton market, with curtailment in several important

TABLE 7.—CHANGES IN COTTON ACREAGE IN SELECTED STATES, 1918–1928[a]

(In thousands of acres)

State	1918	1920	1922	1924	1925	1926	1927	1928[b]
South Carolina	3,001	2,964	1,912	2,404	2,654	2,648	2,356	2,487
Georgia	5,341	4,900	3,418	3,046	3,589	3,965	3,413	3,798
Oklahoma	2,998	2,749	2,915	3,861	5,214	4,676	3,601	4,630
Texas	11,233	11,898	11,874	17,175	17,608	18,374	16,176	17,631
Arizona, New Mexico, and California	180	380	168	411	438	449	362	527

[a] United States Department of Agriculture, *Yearbooks.*
[b] Preliminary estimates.

consuming countries. These years were the period, likewise, in which boll weevil damage attained its full force. The resultant curtailment of the crop and high war and postwar prices stimulated such expansion of the producing area that the present size of the industry induces keen competition between two sections which show marked diversity in natural conditions, producing methods, and general economic organization.

The less simple and routine methods of farming called for in the eastern states under boll weevil conditions have brought out sharply the inadequacy of old methods and the shortcomings of negro labor. Meanwhile, the strong demand for unskilled labor in industrial towns and cities of the North and, in increasing degree, in the southeastern states, together with our policy of immigration restriction, has created such a pull upon plantation labor[3] as to bring about the abandonment of considerable areas previously given over to cotton growing. A study, conducted by the Georgia experiment station, showed that between 1910 and 1925 whole counties in that state had lost from 60 to 75 per cent of their negro farmers.

At the same time, the westward spread of cotton growing had been effected largely by white farmers of a vigorous pioneer type, who were vigorously exploiting the possibilities of their topography and climate to produce cotton with much less man labor, and at a cost which would yield them a profit even with the decline of prices which has recently been taking place. The westward movement of the cotton industry brought it into a region of comparatively cheap and very level land upon which machine methods could be introduced with a lowering of production costs and satisfactory net returns, even where yields were relatively low and methods of gathering the crop not such as to produce the highest quality.

The standard of the old cotton belt was an 8-inch plow, pulled by a single mule and manned by a negro field hand, who worked hard with crude methods over short periods but who, with his beast, had to be maintained for a 12-month period both on food and feed products which were largely imported from outside the cotton-growing section. This system was hardly conducive to high returns to land, capital, or management, or to a minimum cost of production. War-time demand and boll weevil scarcity put cotton prices at a point which made prosperous years for the cotton grower, but prices which were disproportionately high in an age of scientific achievement, mechanical advance, and high-pressure management.

Then the stone rejected by the builders became the head of the corner. The formerly submarginal lands of the Texas Panhandle and nearby Oklahoma, and the level coastal plain farther south which had yielded a sparse return as cattle range, were cut up into cotton farms. Moderate-sized tractors and appropriate tillage implements took the place of the mule and 8-inch plow. Cotton was gathered by swifter and "dirtier" methods, and the product was cleaned by a special apparatus which was promptly added to the standard gin equipment. In extreme conditions of late crop or short labor supply, this section even makes extensive use of the cotton "sled," which strips the cotton bolls, opened and unopened, at a single operation. The first crude types of this implement are gradually being perfected, and have apparently made a permanent place for themselves in the practice of this region, though by no means taking the place of hand picking even in West Texas and Oklahoma. The enormous saving in time effected is indicated by the fact that the cotton necessary to make a bale can be "sledded" in seven hours,[20] whereas hand picking would take at least ten times as long. Making proper allowance for the cost of cleaning and for some lowering of quality, the saving still is enormous. And even where this extreme labor-saving method is not resorted to, the general installation of cleaning equipment at the gins permits of much quicker and cheaper methods of snapping and hand picking.

The general mechanization movement has spread itself in varying degrees over the whole South,[21] and old methods have been discarded or modified in a variety of ways. Mechanical cotton choppers of several types have been introduced. Some cotton is being "checked in," according to the long-established custom for corn, so that it can be cross culti-vated. Mechanical cotton pickers of both the suction and the spindle type have been aggressively experimented with for some years, and it seems probable that commercially practicable machines will, within a few years at least, be available and economically feasible on at least the high-grade types of cotton. Their coming would tend to restore the competitive position of the eastern cotton section, in which the "sledding" method of the subhumid West cannot be used because of climatic difficulties.

What has happened in the cotton industry seems to reveal cotton-growing resources so abundant under modern methods of cultivation and harvesting as to put us in a position to continue our predominance among the world's sources of supply for many years to come. It has already forced the abandonment of a very considerable acreage in the

[20] United States Department of Agriculture, *Yearbook*, 1927, p. 224.

[21] "Tractor farming is rapidly coming to the front in the South . . . Last year a solid trainload of tractors went into the Delta section of Mississippi, and they are being operated successfully all over the South. In many small towns it is nothing unusual to see a carload of them driven down the streets in different directions and all of them headed for cotton farms. On a recent trip to a number of cotton farms where tractors are being operated, I was pleased to learn that every man interviewed was well pleased with the results. And in every instance the owners expect to cultivate larger areas with tractors and to get rid of some of the mules." *The Progressive Farmer*, November 3, 1928.

eastern part of the cotton belt, and challenged much of the district east of middle Texas to revise their methods and recast farm organization if they are to survive in competition with the new born western cotton belt. This new cotton region presents striking examples of tractor cultivation and mechanical harvesting on moderate-priced land with mile-long or half-mile rows, and a 160- to 320-acre family farm in lieu of the 10-acre patch, planted, chopped by hand, and hand-picked by the immemorial methods of the old cotton belt.[22]

Although large areas in the southern and eastern portion of the old cotton belt have gone out of cotton production, it is too much to assume that cotton growing will pass or become a minor factor in this region. Even though belatedly, the planters and farmers of the section are adjusting themselves to meet the new competition. Long-established traditions of economic organization must overcome a good deal of friction in such readjustment. There is a large area in the West which still can be turned to cotton production, if prices are maintained on present or higher levels. On the other hand, if the eastern part of the cotton belt can get production costs down to a point where that section can persist in competition with newer areas, the prices for the quantity of cotton which will come forward from the present area of production will probably discourage any rapid taking over of these new lands.

The South has always maintained a large stock of mules, mainly on expensive purchased feed, to deliver a small amount of power annually. Hence, any general introduction of tractors must have an enormous effect on production costs and incidentally on the northern farmer's feed market. Likewise, where cotton growing is displaced in the older sections there is considerable pressure toward the growing of forage crops, peanuts, and truck, and the development of dairy and livestock enterprises. Much of the coastal plain section is well adapted to the use of tractors. Among other things, they have great adaptability to the work of terracing—an undertaking of much importance in southern agriculture. All in all, it would seem that the coming of power farming holds as much promise, both of betterment and of disruption, in the South as in any other section.

VIII. OTHER BRANCHES OF AGRICULTURE

What has been said of the sweeping changes coming about in the production of cereals and cotton applies in varying, though generally in

[22] See L. P. Gabbard and F. R. Jones, "Large-scale Cotton Production in Texas," Texas Agricultural Experiment Station, *Bulletin*, No. 362.

Professor Gabbard writes the author (October 25, 1928): "I was in the Corpus Christi area recently, and an interview with dealers showed that at least 1,000 tractors of the farmall type will be in operation for that area this season. Four-row planters and four-row cultivators are fast becoming standard equipment with tractors. One dealer had taken up and shipped out eight carloads of mules."

less, degree to the other branches of American agriculture. Tractors, trucks, and other forms of mechanical equipment are widespread in their sphere of operation. Such appliances (including notably the milking machine, cream separator, and equipment for making silage) have been influential in the field of dairying, and it seems possible that, with the spread of rural electric lines, artificial refrigeration may before long achieve a rather important place in the picture. Likewise, in local milk plants, many of them co-operative, the installation of better equipment permitting the utilization of by-products in the form of dried or powdered skim milk and buttermilk, the building up of the ice cream business, and the transportation of fresh milk and cream economically and over long distances in glass-lined railroad tank cars is improving quality and reducing costs.

In the horticultural field, the introduction of certain new insulating materials and the development of small electric refrigerating units have resulted in eliminating a considerable amount of waste and permitting a longer season of marketing in many instances. The orchardist and truck grower are likewise benefiting from the use of tractors and better tillage implements and spray outfits, and from the use of the motor truck.

In the case of tobacco, sugar beets, and other products which have always required a large amount of hand labor, relatively little change has thus far been found possible, although mechanical "blockers" and the employment of the tractor in tillage, and the truck in harvesting, have had some value.

In recent years, the producers of electric current have become very much interested in the possibilities of "rural electrification."[23] This move has two major objectives. One looks to the supplying of power for pumps, feed grinders, and other light farm machinery. The other is concerned with domestic lighting and household appliances. Where population density in a country community is fairly high, and the type of farming such as to make numerous or heavy demands for the use of the current, service can be delivered at a moderate price and very satisfactory results obtained. This seems particularly to apply to regions of intensive agriculture where heavy machine work in the field is at a minimum and stationary power important. Artificial lighting of poultry houses, or artificial refrigeration of fruit or vegetables prior to marketing, are important operating factors in commercial poultry or truck raising districts, and cause a comparatively large demand for current. In general farming sections, however, the cost of distribution is ordinarily so high as to militate against the widespread use of electricity on American farms at the present time.

[23] See Guy E. Tripp, *Electric Development as an Aid to Agriculture*, 1926.

IX. ADJUSTMENTS OF PRODUCTION TO MARKET DEMAND

It is true that, in the past eight years, American farmers have been waging a courageous and resourceful battle to readjust their industry to new and rapidly-changing conditions. In this they have been rendered a splendid service by the Department of Agriculture, the state experiment stations, the extension service, and other educational agencies. Even with full appreciation of this effort, and admiration for those who have made it, the writer cannot find much cause for optimism or a belief that satisfactory adjustment will speedily be attained. It is difficult to move men from the farms, to adjust their property interests, and to absorb them into reasonably satisfactory industrial positions at a rate fast enough to balance the increase in technical efficiency and the spread of labor-saving appliances on the farm.

Farmers in a large number of lines have come to the decision that it is desirable to adjust downward from the present scale of production, but find it very difficult to select a substitute product or the crop to be adjusted upward. Shall the livestock man shift from unprosperous swine production to cattle growing or feeding because for the moment that industry is enjoying a touch of long-deferred prosperity? Many have already shifted toward dairying and poultry production, but poultry profits to-day are precarious, and the dairy industry, in spite of having developed an astonishing increase in the consumption of butter, fluid milk, and ice cream, finds itself facing the possibility of an export surplus and impairment of its whole price structure. Grain farmers have been struggling to find a profitable substitute for their redundant oats and corn acreage, while the expansion in wheat is forcing us further into a low-price world market instead of permitting our withdrawal. The horticulturist's problem of adjustment is complicated by the fact that prune acreage is excessive, peaches overdone, vineyard area outrunning the absorptive power of the market, grapefruit far in excess of profitable demand, and most other branches of the industry so close to market saturation that the advent of newcomers threatens the prosperity of all. Not all the surplus cotton acreage can be put into peanuts, and the raising of corn and livestock in the South introduces bitter competition for the harassed farmers of the corn belt.

On the production side, it seems at least dubious whether the American farmer is making or can make, during the next few years, his adjustments fast enough to catch up or keep up with the rate of change in technique and market situation.

X. COSTS OF DISTRIBUTION

Much is heard of the reduction of distribution costs as a possible means of improving the situation as to agricultural income. Considerable agitation and experimentation has turned in this direction during the past few years, but without fully satisfactory results. Even those recent changes which have produced positive economies seem to have a somewhat ambiguous meaning as applied to the farmer's problem.

The speed and economy of truck hauling in certain instances has already been referred to. As an offset to this, however, the development of automotive vehicles and the coming of hard roads has resulted in the abandonment of a considerable mileage of branch line railways, and in the disappearance or dwindling activity of many small country villages such as formerly afforded a local market for many farmers' products. While this may ultimately effect such a reduction in the cost of handling goods as to redound to the benefit of the producer, the first benefits seem to go largely to the carrying agencies, and the effects most noticeable for the farmer are to require further readjustment of his business to meet these changed transportation conditions. Frequently the change in our transportation system means remoter markets to which a farmer may perhaps not find it feasible to go at all with a small quantity of his product, or which he must expend additional time and effort to reach if he does go. On the other hand, it is doubtless true, in some cases at least, that the concentration of business in the larger towns tends to give a brisker, more competitive primary market, which reflects more accurately the trend of values at the terminal.[24]

In many sections the loss of railroad service through the closing of stations where business was small, or the entire abandonment of lines, has worked a hardship on the farmers. They have also complained that the general level of freight rates upon farm products is unduly high in view of the present prices of many agricultural products and in comparison with rates charged on other classes of railway traffic. In the final analysis, they agree that the quality of service is so important that the roads must have earnings which will defray not merely operating costs but permit the installation of facilities which will give to agricultural products a service of maximum speed and minimum possibility of deterioration.

While the Hoch-Smith resolution has called for a complete review of this situation, the whole question of the rate structure is so intricate and involves such controversial issues between economic groups and geographic localities as to afford little hope of extensive reductions on the farmer's product. The railroads are already at a level of technical efficiency which precludes any sweeping changes from that direction, and the lowering of labor charges, which would be the other chief avenue of approach, seems clearly out of the range of possibilities.

[24] The exact character of the shift in town and village population is extremely difficult to ascertain. A good deal of light is shed on the movement by the discussion contained in Sect. II, Chap. V, of this volume.

The real question at issue involves theories of rate-making on the one side and some very fundamental issues of agricultural economics on the other. Traditionally we have leaned toward the idea of making freight rates on the rather low-priced and bulky products of the farm which would stimulate the most rapid development of resources, no matter how remote from consuming centers. Farmers, especially in this period of agricultural distress, are inclined to urge this traditional policy. Some serious thought, however, needs to be given to the implications of this theory under present conditions. Since wheat and cotton are both depressed industries, and the competition is from the geographically more remote fringes of the producing areas, it is at least interesting to speculate on what would be the effect of a stricter application of the cost-of-service theory of rate making. If, as has been suggested earlier in the chapter, the present trend of events threatens to undermine values in the older sections, cost-of-service rates might tend to conserve the interests of a rather large agricultural section. On the other hand, so far as higher freight rates on food commodities and agricultural raw materials impose a burden on the distant consuming centers, the maintenance of higher rates might conceivably tend to stimulate the decentralization of population toward the agricultural producing sections to their ultimate benefit. As a single example, low freight rates on cotton would inure to the advantage of the New England mills; high rates, to the southern mills. Which do the cotton-growing states want?

Co-operative marketing has been widely turned to as a solution of the farm marketing problem.[25] In cotton, dairy products, livestock, and numerous horticultural commodities, these efforts have been productive of results of relative and in some cases striking value. Considerable improvement in standardization, processing, transportation, market distribution, and merchandising have been effected. In one important particular, however, co-operative effort has been signally unsuccessful. This is in the perception of the relation of supplies to prices and in the devising of any means by which such supplies could be adjusted upon a satisfactory price basis.

In the case of certain small and strongly-placed groups, the problem has been reasonably well met, temporarily at least. On the other hand, it must be recognized that the attempt to organize any large group of scattered independent producers so as to achieve any effective adjustment of supplies to market needs is almost out of the question. Co-operation in agriculture is therefore faced by a serious dilemma. Certain definitely discernible economies in marketing and increases in efficiency in the market process can be attained only through the adherence of a rather large percentage of the producer group. So long, however, as prices of the commodity remain on a generally unsatisfactory level, and the

[25] See, on co-operative buying and selling, Chap. V, Marketing, pp. 374-389.

co-operative organization shows no clear ability to better the farmer's situation, it appears to be humanly impossible to secure the adhesion and permanently constructive support of the very farmers who need the half loaf of more economical and efficient marketing, just in proportion as they are unable to get the whole loaf of market-price enhancement.

Conceivably, the trends which apparently exist, toward a smaller number of farm operating units under a higher type of management, and toward a higher degree of commercial specialization in agricultural production, will lead to improved distributive conditions for both the producer and the consumer. Both these trends would facilitate the progress of co-operative organization, with the added benefits that such a group movement would make possible. The development, during the last few years, of buying departments or subsidiaries of chain-store systems, and the movement toward mergers of distributing concerns, notably in the dairy industry, sharply raise the question whether whatever improvements in condition are destined to take place may not come mainly with the spread in efficient business organization from the central markets out to the smaller centers, absorbing many of the petty buyers, brokers, and traders now operating at local shipping points. That such a move might be productive of savings in the distributive process seems quite possible, but to what extent such gains would inure to the benefit of the consumer, the producer, or of the promoter and stockholders of the distributive organization itself, is a matter on which little more than snap judgment is possible at the present time. Many farmers are awaiting the outcome of events with no little trepidation. Ordinarily, the producer occupies an uncomfortable position in a buyers' market, and the persistent tendency toward overproduction which has characterized the postwar years in American agriculture puts a considerable number of farm producers recurrently or persistently into a buyers' market.

With the growth of large manufacturing and merchandising units and a general merger tendency in the market in which they sell, farmers have become increasingly impressed with the importance of effecting organizations on the selling side, which would be large enough to secure the maximum economy in handling, storage, and processing, the highest degree of skill in market distribution and salesmanship, and a bargaining power which might cope with that which they must meet on the buying side. More and more the objective has come to be an organization coextensive with the boundaries of the given industry. In default of such organization purely along lines of producer co-operation, efforts have in the last few years turned toward a horizontal integration of shipping and selling interests which would embrace private dealers as well as co-operative associations. Since the initial phases of the plan emphasize the assembling of the fullest possible information as to market supplies and movements, and contemplate the equalization of supplies through co-ordinated action in the best interests of the whole group, these organizations pass under the attractive title of "clearing houses."

How fully they will meet the hopes of their organizers, or how long their component elements will subordinate individual interest to the welfare of the whole group, is a question still in the stage of practical determination. They constitute, however, the latest thrust of organizational effort. If they fail, it seems a reasonable supposition to expect that they will be followed by a more determined effort than has thus far been witnessed to secure legislative authorization for marketing arrangements which would remedy the impotence of voluntary co-operation by requiring all those engaged in a given line of production to participate in a common scheme of market distribution.

XI. RURAL CREDITS AND FARM CAPITAL

Great emphasis has been laid on the farmer's credit situation as a factor in his problem. The question is no doubt important, and yet much that has been said on the subject has been ill considered. Undoubtedly, many rural districts were inadequately served with credit in the years shortly before the World War, when the rural credit agitation first came to an acute stage. With the passing of the Federal Reserve Act, the Federal Farm Loan Act, and the Intermediate Credit Act, the way has been paved for the removal of many of these difficulties, though obviously no mere piece of legislation can create a desired volume of credit or suitable administration of its extension. In practice, "sympathetic" officials in some of these institutions have extended lines of credit not justified by subsequent events, and credit losses of some magnitude have resulted. Such losses, however, have had the effect of cushioning, for certain unfortunate individuals, the shock of a distressing period in our agricultural history, and will doubtless be absorbed in our credit structure without serious harm, distributing scarcely avoidable losses to shoulders more able to bear them than those upon which they originally fell.

The main point, however, is how the extension of credits is to be suitably adjusted to the productive organization of our agriculture in the future. Perhaps we may grant in a broad way that the several pieces of rural credit legislation already enacted have tended to put the credit resources of the country at the disposal of the agricultural industry, upon terms as advantageous as those available to other industries, and adapted to the peculiar requirements of the business and those who are engaged in it. We must not, however, put the cart before the horse. Adequate credit facilities will not create a satisfactory credit situation for agriculture, but on the other hand a satisfactory basis of credit must precede the extension of loans. Even those farmers who, in the years just following the war, laid stress on the ability of liberal credit extension to serve them in the deflation period have seen the limitations of such relief measures and coined the phrase, "You can't borrow yourself out of debt."

The modern farmer is more of a capitalist than his predecessor, and needs to develop the art of financial management along with his general business education.   Likewise, the growing mechanization of agriculture and the tendency toward larger operating units is constantly enlarging the size of individual requirements, and presumably the business capacity of individual operators.   The passing of many small villages as marketing centers tends to bring the farmer more in contact with banks which serve the general business public, which are ordinarily larger in size, and which are manned by officials who are better trained and are closer students of the general business situation than is likely to be the case with the small country banker.[26]   The farmer who shifts to this sort of banking connection is likely to find himself held to a stricter standard of procedure in producing a credit rating and making a showing as to the financial plan under which he expects to employ the funds which he comes to borrow.

What seems to producers at times a Bourbon attitude on credit extension has sometimes proved merely the reflection of a sounder analysis of the trend of market values than that which the interested borrower could bring himself to accept.   The farmer's dependence upon banks of a general commercial character is likely to curtail the liberality of credit lines which he can secure, unless these larger town and city banks include within their executive staff officers who are sufficiently acquainted with crop and livestock operations to enable them to judge, without too great conservatism or too slavish adherence to mercantile banking principles, what are the liquidating possibilities of the prospective farm operations which are presented to them for financing.

To some extent, there has been a revival of "dealer credit" during the last few years to enable farmers to purchase machinery, fertilizer, or the like to an amount which their own resources or their bank credit would not permit.   This is particularly true in connection with the sale of tractors, combines, and other large machinery equipment.   In sections of the Great Plains states, the tangible basis for bank credit was severely constricted at the same time that heavy expenditures for power machinery were needed, if production costs were to be so reduced as to enable farmers to re-establish themselves on a sound basis.   The great farm implement companies had been going through a period of rather lean sales, and needed to stimulate demand in every way possible.   Under these conditions, they backed their faith in the section and in the new methods of power farming to the extent of placing such equipment in the hands of a large number of farmers on extremely small initial payments.   Since dealers in the locality were not much better able than farmers to carry

[26] Cf. Chap. V, p. 335.

this credit load, it was passed back directly to the implement companies who, in the main at least, handled it as a part of their general business rather than by forming subsidiary finance corporations after the manner of the automobile companies. In general, the method was to take initial payments of as little as 15 or 20 per cent of the purchase price, the buyer obligating himself to pay the balance from the proceeds of the crops of the two following years. The agricultural recovery of the section, under its new technique of farming, has been such as to justify the faith of the manufacturers and to reinforce their belief, often proved in the past, that the farmer is an excellent risk on a "character loan."

In both the implement and the fertilizer field, it is evident that the seller, with the profitable operation of his business at stake, may in difficult times like this be expected to go farther in the extension of credit than commercial banking agencies. This calls attention to the fact that a large element in the extension of credit to farmers is the knowledge which the lender has of technical aspects of the business, and the faith which he has in the profit-making possibilities of the given line of agriculture. This point is of considerable importance in connection with the discussions of branch banking as a possible improvement in our rural credit situation. In California, where the system has been tried, it seems clear that a branch banking system tends to be strictly run on formal rules which make it safe but not very elastic in adapting itself to the expansion of new sections or types of production. The line between technically safe banking and aggressive financing of worthy new developments is finely drawn.

Farmers in general, and not a few of the bankers who serve rural constituencies, are unable to wrench their minds free of traditional attitudes with reference to the profitableness of particular farm operations and to the accepted scale of land values. The number of rural banks which failed during the deflation period reflects somewhat sadly upon the professional competence of the officials in charge, or their ability to keep their minds undisturbed by popular sentiment through the changing stages of the economic cycle.

Agricultural financing appears to be in a transition period. Federal legislation has paved the way for agriculture to attain a more advantageous position in the financial structure of the country as a whole. Banks likewise have manifested considerable interest in better adapting their practices to the needs of agriculture, at the same time that they encourage agriculture to put its operations on a sounder business basis. A third constructive possibility emerges from the side of the co-operative organizations. They have been influential in mobilizing large blocks of farm products for safe and economical financing. This in itself tends to give the farmer a more flexible and advantageous position with reference to his commercial farm operations. The co-operatives, however, have gone still farther in becoming the agency through which production credit could be made available to their members, at a cost much below that which had generally been required in the past.

These movements are as yet hardly past their experimental stages. It would seem, however, that the legislative modification of our credit institutions, the constructive attitude of many bankers, the progress in the economic organization of agriculture, and the growth of co-operative groups should produce substantial improvement in conditions of rural financing during the coming years.

XII. CREDIT AND LAND VALUES

The sweeping readjustment process now under way in agriculture challenges the whole capital structure of the industry. Formerly, the farmer was a man of terrific industry and grinding thrift. Land was his bank, and an unencumbered title the heaven he sought to attain. In the process, the right to be his own boss was capitalized at an inordinately high rate, and frequently residence values of a sentimental and almost ancestor-worshiping kind were spread over the whole farm, no matter how meager the yield as a matter of plant operation. The time appears to be at last drawing near when we shall cease to view land in this exaggerated speculative-investment light, when adequate outlays for equipment and working capital become of prime importance in determining the return to labor and management, and when current income commensurate with that obtainable in other callings will be insisted upon by farmers and their families. "The fact that we cannot expect a complete recovery of farm land prices does not necessarily mean that agriculture will not be prosperous. Prosperity and high land prices do not necessarily go together. It does mean that in the future we shall have to look to annual profits rather than to increases in land value for farm prosperity."[27]

One of the most striking features of the postwar development of agriculture has been its spread into comparatively low-grade lands with fairly extensive methods of use, while land values in the older sections have ceased to advance through the capitalization of a scarcity value of such sections under the intensive piling up of large amounts of poorly-paid human labor. For this development to have followed so swiftly on the heels of the war-time inflation of farm prices has of course involved a rather lengthy muddle of foreclosure proceedings, credit losses, and uncertainty as to the equilibrium points toward which the readjustment was tending. If it has done nothing else, however, it should shake faith in the time-worn slogan prevalent in many parts of the country that "our land values have always gone up and they always will," and induce a rechecking, on the part both of farmers and of lending agencies,

[27] Editorial in *The Prairie Farmer*, August 18, 1928.

of the relations, respectively, of land and of capital goods to the production of net farm income.

There is in most quarters only very inadequate realization of the nature and extent of the decline in land values which has taken place in the Middle West. Furthermore, the implications and results of this price decline are still less understood. The land boom broke in 1920, but many circumstances contributed to prolong its effect through a series of subsequent disturbances and settlings. Much of the land had been transferred under contracts, or with second and third mortgages on which first payments were not due for anywhere up to five years. As settlement under these contracts or mortgages came due, there was a succession of defaults which strung along over several years. Land went back to the seller or to the mortgagee, and in this way banks, trust companies, insurance companies, and other investors found themselves the involuntary holders of land on which payments were in arrears.

For some years during the early nineteen twenties, the tendency was very strongly toward granting extensions and helping the nominal owner or mortgagor to retain title and, with it, the burden of ultimately paying up on the capitalization established during the boom period. More and more, such efforts became ineffective as the period of unsatisfactory prices for farm products and income to farmers lengthened. Eventually, supervisory agencies required banks to divest themselves of such properties or to go into complete liquidation. This brought a wave of foreclosures, bank failures, and forced selling of lands, which drove prices to a half or even a quarter of what they had been at the peak. The significant thing in all this, however, is that prices have shown but little tendency to recover, and meanwhile a very large number of involuntary owners are still holding on to this property, uncertain what policy to pursue. There is probably not a single large insurance company, if it loaned on real estate in the Middle West, which does not have substantial holdings of farm land in some of these states, and the total runs to many millions. That the Federal Farm Loan system has also become deeply involved in the situation is shown by the following table of farms which have come completely or practically into their ownership, the data being gleaned from annual reports of the Federal Farm Loan Board:

Banks	Jan. 1, 1926	Jan. 1, 1927	Jan. 1, 1928
Federal Land Banks:			
Farms owned outright..........................	1,598	2,763	4,086
Sheriffs' certificates...........................	1,160	1,260	1,088
Joint Stock Land Banks:			
Farms owned outright..........................	211	440	533
Sheriffs' certificates...........................	176	222	357
Total number of farms owned outright and subject to redemption........................	3,145	4,685	6,064

Such distress selling as has already taken place has enabled the more provident, well-financed farmers to increase the size of their farms at reasonable prices. But a large number of the larger holders are unwilling to take the losses which would be involved in disposing of all of their land in the present market situation. Should they attempt to do it, it is inevitable that values would again crumble and their losses be even greater than they now appear. As a result, many of them are renting these properties to such advantage as they can and, in order to bolster up the situation, are not infrequently appointing farm managers or supervisors to work with the tenants on these farms to assist their efforts sufficiently so that rent payments may be met and the farm kept in reasonably good condition.

In some areas, also, individual investors or companies, formed for the purpose, have looked upon this as a favorable opportunity for securing lands at bargain prices, to be held speculatively for the "return" of values. Generally speaking, the farms are too small and too widely scattered to permit of effective joint operation or any distinctive economies such as might conceivably be introduced under modern conditions of machine operation. The situation, at the moment, seems to be that these optimistic purchasers or holders of lands are supporting the general level of land values, have somewhat cushioned the shock of distress selling, and are supplying farms to tenants on fairly liberal terms. To some extent, even, such properties are obliged to go tenantless.

As we said at the beginning, the whole structure of capitalization of the agricultural industry over considerable parts of our country has been shaken by the events of the last few years, and it can by no means be said that such recovery as has taken place has yet given a clear indication of future trends or a firm foundation on which to re-erect any reasonably permanent and dependable scale of values. This can be clearly seen in the accompanying table of index numbers of land values in certain selected states (Table 8). This shows the comparative height to which prices rose during the war-time boom and the fact that these values are still declining in some states most severely affected by the advance. On the other hand, Kansas appears to have stabilized values, and Montana is one of the few states which shows a slight upturn.

If the changes in technique which are now upon us prove to be of as revolutionary a character as has been suggested in the present chapter, the result would apparently be to alter permanently the schemes of valuation in different agricultural sections, which were built up under the older traditions of American farming. From the immemorial past, the predominance of hand-labor methods in farming has given great differential superiority to those well-watered and fertile lands which showed the greatest capacity to absorb large amounts of human toil. But much as in the field of mining the progress of scientific metallurgy and

TABLE 8.—INDEX NUMBERS OF LAND VALUES[a]

State	1912	1913	1914	1915	1916	1917	1918	1919	1920	1921	1922	1923	1924	1925	1926	1927	1928
Connecticut	98	100	102	100	102	110	116	121	137	134	140	137	140	137	137	138	139
Indiana	98	100	102	101	110	116	128	135	161	147	119	115	108	102	95	87	84
Illinois	97	100	103	102	105	111	119	130	160	153	126	123	116	115	109	99	96
Iowa	96	99	104	112	128	134	145	160	213	197	162	156	143	136	130	121	117
North Dakota	97	100	103	103	112	118	124	130	145	141	136	128	114	109	105	100	99
Nebraska	98	100	102	101	104	110	127	145	179	166	144	139	128	123	123	119	117
Kansas	101	99	99	103	109	115	122	132	151	149	130	127	118	115	113	113	113
Montana	97	100	103	100	94	100	106	114	126	105	96	87	81	75	72	70	71
South Carolina	101	98	101	94	98	107	122	162	230	186	126	128	136	138	128	113	110
Georgia	98	101	101	94	105	116	131	172	217	172	136	125	123	116	112	104	102
Mississippi	97	102	102	97	111	121	131	155	218	150	148	143	134	136	134	126	123
Kentucky	97	100	103	100	111	127	146	170	200	172	151	147	141	140	139	134	130
Oklahoma	98	101	101	95	104	114	130	140	166	160	139	133	125	131	130	128	127
Texas	95	100	105	103	103	115	133	141	174	156	133	128	137	146	146	141	139
California	93	99	108	111	116	130	136	142	167	168	166	165	164	164	163	162	161

[a] "The Farm Real Estate Situation, 1927–28," United States Department of Agriculture, *Circular*, No. 60.

heavy power machinery have made profitable the utilization of low-grade ores, so the development of scientific and machine agriculture have brought into cultivation considerable areas of formerly submarginal land, and have indeed put a premium upon extensive methods of utilizing lighter soils, the remoter agricultural areas, and regions of scanty rainfall. Profits are being found by going rapidly over large areas of comparatively low-yield land, and the scarcity value of lands in the older sections has quite possibly lessened as a result. Their differential superiority has shrunk under the new technique, and market values must ultimately establish themselves in the light of this fact.

One other factor which tends to affect land values very widely is the heavier burden which taxation now bears upon farming land. Costs of government have risen not only with the advance of the general price level, but in response to the enlarged activities in road building or the amplification of services in the way of education or otherwise. With the continued reliance upon the general property tax, these burdens tend to fall heavily on agriculture.

The farmer's property is of a sort that is readily discoverable by the assessor and that bears a heavier proportional share of the general property tax than do many other classes of property. In some sections of the country, an almost intolerable tax burden rests on the farmer   Figures recently compiled for a number of rented farms in several Michigan counties show that for the last seven years taxes have taken about 90 per cent of what otherwise would have been the net return to the owners of these farms. It is believed that this is an exceptionally bad condition, but other studies in various sections indicate that in recent years a tax burden which takes from one-third to two-thirds of the return is by no means unusual.[28]

As long as this situation continues, it tends to hold down the net income from land, and hence the sum at which it is capitalized as a purchase price.

XIII. THE COMPARATIVE IMMOBILITY OF AGRICULTURE

With the basic problem of agriculture to-day one of drastic adjustment to a new technique and an altered commercial situation, one must be impressed with the fact that these sweeping adjustments are rendered difficult by reason of the immobility which, to a large degree, always has characterized the farmer's calling. There are several reasons why this immobility may be expected to continue.

In the first place, farmers to a much greater extent than mechanics, clerks, or other wage and salaried workers have their property, whether large or small, invested in the business in which they are working. They practically always must be owners of equipment, and almost universally desire to hold an equity in the plant with which they work. Since such

[28] United States Department of Agriculture, *Yearbook*, 1926, p. 698.

investments can be liquidated only slowly, or at heavy sacrifice, the farmer is peculiarly tied to his job as well as to his locality.

Furthermore, his technical training and experience have always been wrapped up in a particular type of farming to an extraordinarily high degree. The carpenter, machinist, salesman, or low-skilled factory worker can move from one line of city employment to another with much less struggle of readjustment than farmers as a class can switch from one branch of farming to another or from farming to town employment. Agriculture is to many of its followers a whole scheme of life and not a business in the ordinary commercial sense. A not inconsiderable number of farmers are concerned with the primary job of producing subsistence for themselves and their families. Such operators continue to farm whether prices be good or bad, and their operations tend to yield persistent but rather unpredictable surpluses of product which are marketed in competition with the products of those who are attempting to organize their operations on the basis of reasonable returns to labor, management, and invested capital. Any attempt to make significant readjustments in such lines of agricultural production encounters sufficient difficulty before it can get a rationalization of operations on the part of commercial producers, but even their efforts may be checkmated by the uncontrollable fringe of operators whose activities cannot be brought within any such scheme of organization. The very success of the better grade of producers to adjust on the basis of prices which will yield a reasonable return to that class of operators tends to peg prices at a level sufficiently satisfactory to attract still more of the cutthroat competition of the squatter type of farmer.

In the second place, the fact that actual direction of agricultural enterprise is determined by the decision of a number of operators, which embraces about 60 per cent of the total number of workers in the industry and whose capital resources are rather rigidly limited, means that neither the decision nor the means of making changes rapidly may be expected. If it had been left to a majority vote of the craftsmen in any industrial line to decide when they would abandon the tools or the character of product which they had been accustomed to make in favor of the manufactured products and the tools and machines by which they are made to-day, is it reasonable to expect that changes would have been made with any such celerity as has been the case under the capitalistic and managerial system which we have in industry?

To-day we are recognizing that "agriculture must be organized as other industries have been," but, beyond this platitude, thought divides sharply as to the direction this process of organization should or can take. Shall we strive for a maximum of efficiency under a system of decentralization and individual autonomy, or shall we direct our energies toward seeing how fully and skillfully efficiency through centralization may be brought to the solution of certain of our agricultural difficulties? Already an enormous number of tasks, which originally were classed as part of agriculture, are performed in town under industrial methods. The passing of milling, butchering, and churning from the farm to the city was long ago effected. The coming of the combine and the truck are now raising the question whether any storage and processing received by the grain between harvest and ultimate use can be done economically and effectively on the farm, or whether cleaning, drying, and storing shall be centralized at the terminal markets and milling centers. The supplanting of horse power by internal combustion engines has been a striking transfer from country to town of an important process in the task of getting our living from nature.

The struggle of the older farm management was toward filling up the valleys between seedtime and harvest peaks of the labor load. It seems quite conceivable that the newer agriculture will tend to maintain a skeleton force on the land, and transfer labor from town to country to meet seasonal requirements. Since the farmer more and more tends to require labor skillful in the handling of machinery or capable of performing manual tasks of the most routine character rather than to require those trained in the ancient lore of farming, the easier way seems the shift of tractor men and practically unskilled harvest hands into the country during short periods of special need, with the same groups productively fitted into industrial callings of the town during agriculture's slack season.

All in all, it seems that the hard and fast line between agriculture and other industries, and between rural and urban residence, will tend to disappear with the program of changes now under way in agriculture. A tendency is noticeable among some manufacturers to get their plants distributed in towns and villages adjacent to agricultural land, where their food requirements can be more cheaply met, where living quarters are better and lower priced, and where the factory can draw upon the rural population for part of its labor requirements. The truck and automobile make it possible for industry thus to supply its needs, and at the same time afford an opportunity for a considerable number of both men and women to make profitable use of the time which can be spared from farm work under modern methods of production. It is impossible to show this approach of manufacturing toward the agricultural regions by statistical methods with as much clearness as would be desired. But it is apparent from the census of manufactures over the last few years that a drift away from the highly industrialized centers in the Northeast and toward the smaller towns and villages in the central, southern, and western states has been under way. In Table 9 there is shown a marked decline in manufacturing in the larger cities and in states which we have been accustomed to class as industrial, with a clearly discernible growth of manufacturing in what have been regarded as agricultural states and in towns of less than 25,000 population.

TABLE 9.—PER CENT OF INCREASE AND DECREASE IN MANUFACTURING, IN SPECIFIED STATES, 1919–1925

Size group	New England States		Middle Atlantic States		Indiana	
	Number of establishments	Number of wage earners	Number of establishments	Number of wage earners	Number of establishments	Number of wage earners
Total................	− 11.7	− 16.7	− 17.5	− 13.0	− 19.9	+ 1.7
Over 250,000	− 3.3	− 12.6	− 16.6	− 15.5	− 10.7	− 16.3
250,000–100,000.............	− 10.7	− 20.0	− 5.4	− 16.8	......	......
100,000–25,000.............	− 5.4	− 18.2	− 14.7	− 13.6	− 15.6	+ 5.0
25,000–10,000.............	− 7.4	− 15.1	− 19.3	− 7.6	− 10.6	− 6.7
Less than 10,000...........	− 22.6	− 14.8	− 23.5	− 9.2	− 27.2	+15.0

Size group	Michigan		North Carolina		South Carolina	
	Number of establishments	Number of wage earners	Number of establishments	Number of wage earners	Number of establishments	Number of wage earners
Total................	− 17.6	+ 9.6	− 40.5	+17.1	− 21.0	+27 2
Over 250,000...............	− 16.9	+ 3.5	......	......	......	......
250,000–100,000.............	− 5.0	+ 8.5	......	......	......	......
100,000–25,000.............	− 9.4	− 0.2	− 1.8	+ 1.1	− 34.7	− 20 6
25,000–10,000.............	− 11.1	− 15.5	− 10.7	+46.0	− 24.0	+ 1 2
Less than 10,000...........	− 24.5	+44.0	− 47.2	+ 7.5	− 17.7	+37.0

In this connection, it may be mentioned that the washing machine and numerous other farm appliances, together with the use of more store products in the country home, tend to release the labor of women in a way somewhat comparable to that which we have discussed with reference to the labor of men. Furthermore, paved roads tend to enable city population to move farther away from their places of employment, and to cause the main roads connecting cities and larger towns in our industrial districts to become practically continuous residence streets, lined with dwellings to which are attached small plots of ground from one-quarter of an acre to 5, 10, or even 20 acres in extent. It seems reasonable to suppose that, at least in important agricultural states from Ohio to Iowa, and including southern Michigan, Wisconsin, and Minnesota, this process may result in rather considerable diminution of population in the open country without any undesirable sacrifice in the quantity of the product, but with a very satisfactory lowering of production costs and more effective utilization of our total labor power.

In certain geographic regions and in various branches of agricultural production, there has been a quiet and very gradual increase in the number of large farming operations.   In conformity with general business practice, such undertakings, if they pass the size compatible with individual proprietorship, tend to be organized as commercial corporations.   This has aroused in some quarters unreasonable expectations, and in others unwarranted fears, of a rapid spread of corporation farming.   It is much too early to attempt to prove conclusively just what this movement may amount to.   Likewise, the space limitations of the present volume do not permit any extended analysis of what the author believes to be its possibilities and limitations.   It is a matter of common knowledge, however, that corporate farming enterprises have demonstrated their ability to organize farming undertakings of moderately large size with efficiency and economy, and it would hardly be conceivable that agriculture, even with its peculiar needs, could completely escape the consolidation tendency of the age.   Obviously, the technique of corporate organization and management must undergo considerable adaptation, if it is to spread in the field of agriculture.   It would seem imperative also that, for its economic success as well as its social value, great attention must be given at each step of its development to seeing that conditions of domestic living, hours of labor, wages, opportunity for advancement, and conditions of community life be better rather than worse than those obtaining prior to the coming of the agricultural corporation.   So much progress has been made along these lines in other fields of corporate endeavor that there would seem no real reason why, with alterations to conform to the somewhat different situation, these lessons should not be effectively put in practice in agriculture.

Even at its best, however, any trend toward the industrialization of agriculture is regarded in some quarters as a social loss and political danger, because of the decay of that "sturdy yeomanry" which is held to be the "last bulwark of true democracy."   It is asserted also that such a transition would bring a larger proportion of our population into living conditions unsatisfactory from the standpoint of health as well as morals. But does not this rather sentimental reaction to the problem tend to idealize the best of country living conditions and to forget its flagrant shortcomings; to emphasize the city's evil repute in the matter of slum and sweatshop, without giving full weight to the achievements and potentialities of modern city efforts for better housing, health, entertainment, and regulation of working conditions?

The farmer may come to take as militant a stand with reference to an "American standard of living" as the trade unionist has done, and possibly to invoke the machinery of Government regulation toward this end.   In such a move, the binding power of his own individualistic traditions would doubtless prove a serious obstacle, if any importance may be attached to his repudiation of the child-labor law and his reaction to daylight saving. However this may be, it seems to the present writer that the *rapprochement* of city and country, which appears to be under way in response to new conditions of auto transportation, and to the organization of both farm and factory work, holds the possibilities for improved conditions on both sides. How far we shall fight the tendency, or how far we shall studiously endeavor to facilitate its constructive development, remains to be seen.

We have already referred to the sentimental attachment of the farmer to the soil and his unwillingness to abandon a highly traditionalized training for types of city employment which are strange to his habits of thought and mode of life. Even under unsatisfactory conditions, a farmer is likely to feel that he is in a position at least to provide his living from the soil where he is already established, and to shrink from the drastic changes necessary in any throughgoing move toward readjustment. Somewhat anomalously, there is a radical or pioneering group still to be found, at least in the western part of rural America, which, after a certain amount of dissatisfaction, is ready to jump to distant pastures which look green, with only a shoestring on which to operate, and nothing much more than vague optimism as the basis of its hopes of prosperity. This ultra group, like the ultra conservatives, gives us marginal or submarginal areas always offering cutthroat competition to operators who are attempting to organize their industry on a more stable and rational basis.

XIV. THE MOVEMENT FROM THE FARM

The process of adjustment to changed conditions which has been going on since 1920 has stimulated the rate of movement from farms to cities. Of course, there is a certain amount of movement in this direction all the time, owing to the excess of the country birth rate over the death rate and the gradual urbanization of our country which has been under way for 150 years. During the World War and the two years immediately following it, this process was temporarily reversed, only to be resumed at an accelerated rate which even yet has slackened but little.

The most careful studies of the whole matter have been made by Dr. C. J. Galpin, of the United States Department of Agriculture,[29] and his conclusions are summarized as follows:

During 1920 there was a net gain in total farm population of approximately 500,000 people . . . The unusual prosperity attending the farm occupation during 1920 apparently restrained considerably the customary flow to cities of young people between the ages of 18 and 24, while the annual movement of prosperous retiring farmers to town was offset by the arrival of persons from cities, drawn to farming by its prosperous condition. The excess of births over deaths on farms resulted in a natural increase.

[29] United States Department of Agriculture, *Yearbook*, 1926, p. 592; 1927, pp. 28–29.

The year 1921 saw the beginnings of an unusual movement from farms to cities. While many persons who were tempted to leave farming stayed on farms in the hope that soon the tide of prosperous times would turn and flow farmward, others who were close to the margin of livelihood were compelled to go where there was profitable employment. The result was that though there was a net increase of farm population, it was only 200,000 instead of 500,000 as during 1920. In 1922 the department survey indicated . . . a net loss in the farm population of 460,000 persons. In 1923 the loss to cities continued in full force, causing a net decline in the farm population equal to or possibly somewhat exceeding that of the previous year. In 1924 forces were at work sending back from cities to farms a larger number than formerly. The result was a net loss to the farm population of 182,000. For 1925 a continued decrease in farm population was reported to the effect that 479,000 fewer people were on farms January 1, 1926, than January 1, 1925.

The large gross movement from farms to cities apparently still overbalances the gross movement from cities to farms even when the increase on farms by births over deaths is added in. In the last seven years the farm population of the United States has probably declined more than 3 million . . . But the loss is in large measure a product of natural conditions, which do not necessarily indicate that agriculture is a declining business but which are quite compatible with its progress in prosperity . . . As a matter of fact, it is a sign of progress when a given economic result can be achieved with fewer workers.

In some quarters there has been considerable fear lest the better classes of the rural population would be driven from the farms by the recent unprosperous condition, leaving an inferior population to carry on the industry. Many strident assertions to this effect have been made, but no statistical proof has been forthcoming, nor would it be easy to adduce conclusive evidence either in support or in refutation. A few suggestive phases of the matter, however, are apparent to anyone who examines actual farming conditions at all widely.

In the South, it is quite evident that the pronounced loss of negro farmers has taken a relatively poor rather than a relatively good class of agricultural workers out of the industry. At the opposite end of the cotton belt, it is equally apparent that those who have entrenched their position in the reorganized cotton industry of the last few years are a hardy, resourceful white American stock whose pertinacity in continuing in the industry and whose ingenuity in devising ways of meeting a critical situation revive the finest tradition of the American pioneer. In between these extremes one may find, let us say in the Mississippi delta region, a splendid group of business men continuing to operate their properties and holding to their position as successful cotton planters by adopting machine methods, dispensing with superfluous hand labor, and organizing their selling through an extremely well-managed co-operative association.

Certainly those who have remained in the business of growing wheat and are fighting their way back to prosperity are the men who have shown ability to handle larger farms, reduce costs, and put their finances on a stable basis. In the general farming region of the Mississippi Valley the phrase is frequently heard, "You've got to be a pretty good farmer to stay in the game these days." But the good farmers of that section are staying in the business, are working with extension and experiment station specialists to keep financial records, analyzing their business with growing skill and understanding, and adjusting farm enterprises and operating methods in a manner calculated to win the highest respect.

It is obviously true that the man of highest qualifications for agriculture is likely to be a man whose opportunities for profitable employment elsewhere are likewise good, and that in the considerable reduction of the labor force in agriculture many instances will be found where the better-than-average farm operator is drawn away to some other calling. However, the writer could not look farmers, as he knows them in all parts of the country, straight in the face and give assent for a moment to the oft-reiterated statement that the quality of our farmer class generally is being lowered or that they are becoming peasants. Those who subscribe to such an idea must have known only particular groups in certain of the by-waters of agriculture where the industry as a whole was going distinctly backward. There are such spots, but a true appraisal must take into account the main body of the industry where it is effecting necessary adjustments, and also the inspiring frontier where expansion is taking place, not merely those spots where the process of adjustment is inevitably downward.

XV. THE EXPANSION OF NEW USES FOR AGRICULTURAL PRODUCTS

With the unsatisfactory prices which have followed the break of 1920, the suggestion has come forward from many sources that the farmer's difficulty is, in general, that he has been producing merely to fill the human stomach or to cover human backs—a highly inelastic market demand as compared with the expansible field of culture wants to which manufacturing industry so largely caters. We have already shown in this chapter that food and clothing wants, so far as they express themselves in a demand for agricultural products, have tended during the last few years to shrink rather than to expand. Industrial chemistry has been a potent factor in substituting raw materials of nonagricultural origin for those which were formerly produced on the farm. Indeed, the chemist is regarded not a little in the light of a wonder worker in the present age, and he is still looked to as the magician whose wand may yet open a new, expanding, and profitable outlet for farm products in other than food and clothing uses.

It has been suggested, for example, that the rapid rate of consumption of print paper might so outrun the rate of forest growth as to create a demand for paper-making materials from fibrous plants now produced or which might easily be produced on farms. Experiments along this line have met with reasonable success, and it has been demonstrated on a small commercial scale that excellent paper and insulating material may be made from cornstalks, and quite striking success has been made in the utilization of bagasse, or sugar cane fiber from which the juice has been extracted. This takes the form of a lumber substitute of exceptional insulating qualities and great tensile strength. As a nonconductor of both sound and heat, it is finding a rapidly expanding market in connection with the growth of the radio and artificial refrigeration. It is argued that its general introduction for use as a building material would lighten in a substantial way the burden on our coal resources, and might pave the way for practicable cooling, during the warm season, of even private residences over the southern half of the United States and in tropical or subtropical countries elsewhere.

Waterproof glue is now made from both casein and soy bean cake, and the growth of the ply-wood industry and veneering have opened an encouraging market for these products. The automobile created a rapidly expanding new demand for linseed oil, but our tariff situation is such that about half the product used in this country is imported. Likewise, the ingenuity of the industrial chemist has developed paint formulas which introduce many substitutes for linseed oil, and a similar result has followed in the case of artificial leather, rayon, and numerous other products. The chairman of the division of chemistry of the National Research Council says:[30]

The increased use of pulp from wood of almost the same cellulose content as cotton will make itself felt all the more seriously during the coming year. We may estimate that in 1927, for example, the equivalent of possibly a million bales of cotton will have been replaced in our American markets by the cheaper cellulose from spruce. Evidently the cotton crisis is yet before us . . . Up to the present the home use of cotton has been dropping, but its somewhat increased industrial use maintains the per capita consumption of cotton at about normal. New uses of cotton must be developed if we are successfully to counter the sudden and unexpected rise in the use of silk and the new form of artificial leather. In this respect the cotton planter dare not run ahead of the wheels of progress. He must abide that time when the demand for cotton asserts itself. This may or may not develop soon.

The harassed corn grower has looked with longing toward any one of half a dozen by-product uses. Technically a number of roads lie open, but commercially they lead nowhere, or come to an abrupt end after a very short distance. The chemist just quoted refers to these varied possibilities of the corn plant in the following words:

The growing of corn for the kernel, whereby only about one-fifth of the total weight of the corn and stalk in the field is utilized, smacks of mediaevalism . . . The greater portion of both corn and stalk must be diverted to industrial use before we can consider this staple as secure for the future.

The real future for the corn kernel itself lies in its adaptation, on the one hand, for the manufacture of starch and dextrose (corn sugar) together with corn oil and other

[30] *The Tariff Review*, May, 1927, p. 155.

by-products; and on the other hand, after degerminating, for direct fermentation into alcoholic compounds; the germ in this case also finding employment in production of corn oil. The residual material will be returned to the farmer as food for livestock.

The use of corn sugar, sometimes termed dextrose, glucose, or bearing the trade name of cerelose, is rapidly increasing. Over 300,000 pounds of this pure sugar is being manufactured daily in this country. Most of it finds use in bread and candies. In 1926, the corn products industry consumed only 76,000,000 bushels of corn, representing, however, an increase of 10 per cent over the year 1925. Our total corn crop averages 2,714,000,000 bushels annually; but only about 260,000,000 bushels reach the primary markets. Of this latter only 28 per cent enters the corn products industry.

With the coming into prominence of industrial alcohol, much hope was entertained by the corn farmers and also by potato and fruit growers that this might provide a profitable outlet for surplus and low-grade products. Such hopes have by no means been fully realized, largely owing to the low cost at which blackstrap molasses, a residue from the sugar mills of Cuba, can be imported for purposes of distillation. This provides a concentrated product of uniform quality from a single large and reliable source, whereas the waste and surplus products of this country which seek to compete for this market are of rather dilute character, uneven quality, and are widely scattered in such small quantities as to require undue costs of gathering and transportation, and to be processed in plants so small as not to compete effectively with the enormous tidewater plants now engaged in the business.

This, in fact, is one of the most serious problems in connection with the whole problem of by-product utilization. To gather straw or corn-stalks from the field, bale them, and transport them to a plant for making strawboard, insulating material, or similar products, involves a cost generally disproportionate to their value in competition with other raw materials already available in great quantity. This type of problem has been solved in certain instances, notably the sugar cane bagasse already mentioned, and experimental work is being done in the corn belt with a fair measure of success.

The department of chemical engineering of the Iowa State College of Agriculture is operating a good-sized laboratory for experimental work on the industrial uses of cornstalks and cobs, and the agricultural engineering department of the same institution is working industriously on the problem of economical harvesting, baling, and delivery to the commercial user. In that state, and also in Illinois, commercial plants for the making of cornstalk paper, insulation, and other products, are in operation. The manager of one of these plants reports[31] progress as follows:

We have proved on a commercial scale that the process used by this company can produce from cornstalks all the pulp required for paper consumed in the Middle West. We have demonstrated that this new industry, now in its infancy, can in time become a source of sound economic relief to a large part of the corn-growing area . . .

[31] Frank K. Gardner, "Paper from Cornstalks," *American Farming*, July, 1928.

Our first output is going into high-grade paper. A little later the company will be equipped to supply part of the requirements of the chemical cellulose industries—the raw material for manufacture of rayon or artificial silk, celluloid, motion picture and photographic film, lacquer, artificial leather, etc. This is a limited but rapidly expanding market . . .

Our first season's operations have taught us much concerning corn stalks as industrial raw material. We were told they could not be assembled at a price to compete with wood as raw material for pulp. We have proved, by gathering 10,000 tons of stalks, that it can be done . . .

The farmer will receive for his stalks all they are worth as fertilizer and a reasonable amount for his profit, besides a fair wage for his labor in harvesting them. What cornstalks are actually worth has become a much-debated question since science and industry discovered for the farmer a better outlet than burning cornstalks or turning them under for their doubtful soil-building value.

In the case of corncobs, oat hulls, and other milling by-products, the matter is somewhat simplified by the fact that such products accumulate in large quantities as a mill waste, and special appliances have been developed for burning them. Frequently, even in such cases, however, where the raw material cost is low and the process of reclamation is commercially feasible, the market for the product is so limited as to afford little relief to the farm producer. Furfural is readily produced from either oat hulls or corncobs, but "at the present time a few pounds of xylose, the parent substance of furfural, will satisfy the entire annual needs of the United States and, while the market for its derivative furfural is much wider, the present total demands of the entire world are not sufficient to make a dent in the available supplies of raw materials."[32] On this same point, the view expressed by experimental workers in Iowa stresses in somewhat more optimistic vein the future possibilities of expanding demand. They say[33] that furfural bids fair to become an important commercial chemical, and that quantity production and efficient by-product recovery will lower the price much below the cost estimates given by the various workers in the field.

Summarizing the situation, the chief of the bureau of chemistry of the United States Department of Agriculture says: "Many of the plans advocated to-day for the use of agricultural surpluses and residues are simply revivals of former agitations, dressed perhaps in new clothes, which often tend to hide the economic facts which must be recognized and be favorable if the industry is to survive."[34]

One of the outstanding cases in which the market demand has been sufficient in proportion to the more restricted volume of raw material

[32] Henry G. Knight, "A Survey of the Industrial Utilization of Farm Products for Other Uses Than Food and Clothing," a paper delivered before the Institute of Chemistry at Northwestern University, July 22, 1928.

[33] O. R. Sweeney, "The Commercial Utilization of Corncobs," Iowa Engineering Experiment Station, *Bulletin*, No. 73, pp. 41–42.

[34] Henry G. Knight, in the paper cited above.

to be turned to by-product use is that of the citrus industry. The California Fruit Growers' Exchange has developed very successful salvage plants for off-grade and surplus fruits. They yield a variety of products, including lemon and orange oil, concentrated juice, citric acid, pectin, and a residue fertilizer, and yield returns to the grower at rates of $10, $12, or occasionally even more per ton.

Undoubtedly the labor of the chemist, subsidized to some extent by both Federal and state funds, will produce further results in this line. But it is obvious that as an adequate program of immediate agricultural relief it cannot be much relied upon.

XVI. THE OUTLOOK FOR AGRICULTURE

With these several lines of analysis before us, a few words may perhaps be hazarded as to their significance for the general situation of agriculture to-day and to-morrow. What may the rest of the country expect from its agricultural group, and what may farmers expect for themselves?

We are told that agriculture is the paramount national problem, and that a fundamental remedy must shortly be forthcoming or the collapse of this industry will involve the whole nation in economic disaster. Mark Twain observed that everybody was always talking about the weather but that no one ever seemed to do anything about it. Agriculture threatens to rival the weather as a perennial topic of dolorous conversation. Obviously, farmers have suffered severely in the years since 1920 and are still finding recovery slow and rather unsatisfactory. The process of readjustment is too fundamental and far-reaching to be accomplished in any short period of time. Furthermore, we must not forget that the so-called depression of agriculture is not merely a phenomenon of the United States, but is an international problem, and many another country is as sorely perplexed as ours.

However great our sympathy with either the individual or the group during this trying period, it must be recognized that after ten years we can hardly think of the situation as an "emergency," but must address ourselves rather to the question of what sort of permanent organization of agriculture the nation demands and should expect in the modern economic age. What is actually happening is the slow adjustment of our farming to drastically changed conditions, a process in which the efficiency of agriculture bids fair to be sharply advanced, and the prosperity of those who can measure up to the larger needs of this new technique should be proportionately raised. The better farmers, who have adopted the modern methods, are in a large number of cases already enjoying this prosperity. For those, however, who are less adaptable to the new situation and in excess of numerical requirements, there is the serious problem of writing off their losses, effecting a shift in residence, and fitting into new lines of employment. Both public and private interest should be taken in studying this problem and assisting the necessary movement and relocation.

Meanwhile, however, the country as a whole has been profiting by prices of farm products which were too low to remunerate the producer adequately, and, if the views expressed above are sound, it bids fair to continue to enjoy relatively low prices for farm products produced from rich natural resources by a skillful, well-equipped, and constantly better-organized farming class.

XVII. SUMMARY

While no single measure of the present depression in agriculture is possible, some idea is conveyed by the ratio of prices received to prices paid by farmers, as prepared by the Bureau of Agricultural Economics of the United States Department of Agriculture. With the average index number of the years 1910 to 1914 taken as 100, this index of rural prosperity rose to 118 in 1917, from which peak it dropped to 75 in 1921. Recovering from that point to 92 in 1925, it dropped to 87 in 1926 and 85 in 1927. Of course there is great diversity between commodity and commodity and section and section, but certain major influences may be discerned as being responsible for the rather generally unsatisfactory economic position of our farmers. These are: (1) Disruptions of demand through the impairment of foreign purchasing power, the competition of rival producing countries, and, in the domestic market, changes in consumers' habits and industrial processes and substitution of the gasoline engine for horse power; (2) the disproportionate rate of supply in many lines of agriculture owing to war stimulation, increased technical mechanical efficiency, and the unregulated exploitation of land resources; (3) expense factors, such as freight and wages, which keep distribution costs high in spite of the decline in farm prices.

Possibly the most outstanding factor in the whole situation is the rapid advance in power farming during and since the end of the World War. To some extent the use of larger machinery and the development of labor-saving methods has come through the introduction of "big-team hitches," but to a more striking extent this has been an accompaniment of the rapid increase in the number of tractors. In the decade since the war, the number of horses and mules has dropped from 26.4 millions to 19.5, and tractors have risen from 80,000 to 853,000. This change has been particularly pronounced in the western end of the cotton belt and in the Great Plains wheat-producing areas, but it calls for a sweeping recasting in the economic as well as technological organization of American farming. It permits enormous economies in the production of staple agricultural products, but its effective utilization demands larger operating units and a more specialized type of economic organization; it permits also of a considerable release of man power.

Naturally, in an industry with as slow a turnover as agriculture, it has been difficult to effect these changes with sufficient rapidity to avoid distress. Business reorganization on sound lines has made substantial progress, and this seems now to be accelerating in its rate. A considerable shift of population from sections where it had become redundant has also been effected. Neither process is complete, and it has not been possible to make these changes without acute distress in individual instances and widespread and severe depression in regions scattered practically over the whole country.

Inevitably the impairment of current income has been reflected both in the ability of the farmer to meet his operating charges and living costs and of the farm to meet capital charges. This has resulted in an unprecedented rate of farm bankruptcies and financial embarrassments which have involved a large number of banks in difficulties. It has also rocked the foundations of the farm land market, and has entangled mortgagees, insurance companies, and land banks, both Federal and joint stock, in a baffling problem of revising the structure of farm land values in accordance with the changed and still changing conditions of agricultural production.

In spite of faith in the ability of our farmers eventually to work themselves out of this situation, the prospect of swift or comprehensive relief of the situation does not seem bright. Individuals are showing their ability to make profits, and some localities are conspicuously prosperous. But there does not seem to be in prospect any such sweeping rise of prices or decline of production costs as will take care of the badly-located or less efficient producer or of the section which finds itself maladjusted to the present trend of economic developments. Basic difficulties have not yet been removed, whereas new complications are continually being thrust into the situation.

Considerable helpful legislation has already been enacted, and in only minor details can the program of legislative help be looked to for further assistance. On the other hand, an aggressive and sympathetic, but at the same time conservative and intelligent, administrative attitude within the limits of existing legislation would go far toward facilitating the continued process of readjustment. Meanwhile, a continuation and improvement of the extensive educational attack upon the problem, already highly developed by Federal, state, and private agencies, will be productive of important results. Farmers themselves will continue to give a good account of themselves in working out their individual problems within the possibilities, helpful or harmful, which are supplied by the general institutional setting.

The country as a whole has been profiting by prices of farm products too low to remunerate the producer adequately. How long this differential in favor of the nonagricultural classes will continue, it is impossible to say. Obviously, the depression of the country has not paralyzed the town. On the other hand, abundant and low-priced food and raw materials of agricultural origin have had a stimulative effect. Inasmuch as the progress made since 1919 gives promise for the future of even greater efficiency and lower costs in agriculture,[35] accompanied by better economic organization and rising prosperity in the country, it would seem that the long-run prospect for the nation as a whole is distinctly favorable.

[35] The Secretary of Agriculture, in his annual report for 1927 (United States Department of Agriculture, *Yearbook*, 1927, p. 8), discusses the manner in which "the agricultural industry as a whole has been better adapted to market conditions," and sees in this "an augury of its future prosperity." The report also summarizes the factors which have contributed to the increased productivity of American farming.

"Technical progress in American agriculture has taken place at an extraordinary rate since the close of the World War, and in consequence the productivity of the individual farmer has increased . . . More productive crops have been planted. Livestock of increased productivity has become widely dispersed. Farm management has become more efficient, a better balance has been established among agricultural enterprises, and progress has been made in adjusting production to market requirements. The result is an increase in farm production more rapid than the rise in the country's population.

"This augmented production has been obtained on a decreased crop acreage and with fewer farm workers . . . From 1919 to 1924 there was a decrease of 13 million acres in crop land in the United States—the first decrease ever shown by census statistics in the agricultural area of the nation. There occurred at the same time a decrease in the number of farm animals, a decrease in the number of farms, and a decrease of farm population. Under such circumstances, one would hardly expect an increase in the volume of farm production. Yet an increase took place, and a very substantial one. It is estimated that crop production in the period 1922–1926 was nearly 5 per cent greater than in the period 1917–1921, although the aggregate acreage in crops decreased slightly. Likewise, the output of animal products is estimated to have increased fully 15 per cent. The increased productivity of the farm worker is estimated at about 15 per cent. This increase in labor efficiency, probably never before equalled, is attributable in part to the utilization of more productive livestock and crops, in part to the increased use of machinery and power on the farm."

CHAPTER IX

PRICE MOVEMENTS AND RELATED INDUSTRIAL CHANGES[1]

By Frederick C. Mills

There are three points of obvious difference between the price conditions prevailing during the years which have elapsed since the deflation of 1920–21 and the conditions which characterized the period immediately preceding the war. The level of wholesale prices is approximately 50 per cent higher. The trend of wholesale prices has not been rising, as in prewar years; the net movement has been slightly downward during the last seven years. The slightly declining trend of wholesale prices has been associated with increasing physical productivity, rising wages, and increasing profits, an association with but few precedents in prewar experience. It is the purpose of this chapter to investigate some of the details of the postwar price situation, to consider the relations among different elements in the postwar price structure, and to compare tendencies prevailing among these elements. In making such a study, account must be taken, of course, of the relation of prices to industrial and business changes.

The Postwar Price Situation—International Comparisons.—Economic conditions in the United States parallel, to some extent, conditions in other industrial countries. The data upon which international price comparisons must be based are not in all respects satisfactory, but a rough comparison will furnish a background for the study of developments in the United States. We may compare different countries, first, in respect to present price levels (measured from a prewar base), and secondly, in respect to postwar price trends.

It is not possible accurately to compare price levels and price trends in different countries. Official index numbers differ in their technical construction and in the lists of commodities upon which they are based. Certain countries are upon gold bases, while in other countries paper currencies prevail or have prevailed during part of the period to be studied. Accordingly, the comparison will not be as accurate as the quoted figures might indicate.

Table 1 shows 18 countries ranked according to the degree of price rise between 1913[2] and 1927. The indexes for countries in which paper

[1] W. E. Dunkman and Miss Mabel Lewis rendered valuable assistance in the preparation of this chapter.

[2] In a few cases the base is a month, or several months, in 1914.

prices prevailed in 1927 have been expressed in terms of gold prices, the correction being made in each case by applying the exchange rate on New York.

TABLE 1.—RANK OF 18 COUNTRIES ACCORDING TO LEVEL OF GOLD PRICES, WHOLE-SALE, 1927, WITH REFERENCE TO PREWAR BASES[a]

Country	Index of wholesale prices	Country	Index of wholesale prices
Russia......................	171	Sweden...................	146
Japan......................	170	Switzerland...............	[b]142
Norway....................	167	Great Britain.............	141
Australia..................	167	Germany..................	138
Denmark...................	152	Austria...................	[c]133
Canada....................	151	Italy.....................	[d]133
Netherlands...............	148	France...................	[d]126
United States.............	147	South Africa..............	124
New Zealand..............	147	Belgium..................	[e]123

[a] The base is 1913, except where otherwise noted.
[b] Base: July, 1914.
[c] Base: first half 1914. The index, as given, is on a gold basis.
[d] Gold basis.
[e] Base: April, 1914. Gold basis.

NOTE.—Following are descriptions of the index numbers quoted in the table: Russia, Central Bureau of Statistics, 69 commodities; Japan, Bank of Japan, 56 commodities; Norway, Central Bureau of Statistics, 95 commodities; Australia, Commonwealth Bureau of Census and Statistics, 92 commodities; Denmark, Department of Statistics, 118 commodities; Canada, Dominion Bureau of Statistics, 236 commodities; Netherlands, Central Bureau of Statistics, 48 commodities; United States, Bureau of Labor Statistics, 404 commodities; New Zealand, Census and Statistics Office, 180 commodities; Sweden, Chamber of Commerce, 160 commodities; Switzerland, Department of Public Economy, 118 commodities; Great Britain, Board of Trade, 150 commodities; Germany, Federal Statistical Bureau, 400 commodities; Austria, Statistical Bureau, 47 commodities; Italy, Riccardo Bachi, 120 commodities; France, General Statistical Bureau, 45 commodities; South Africa, Office of Census and Statistics, 188 commodities; Belgium, Ministry of Industry and Labor, 128 commodities.

Accepting these indexes as they stand, they show that the increase in the level of wholesale prices between 1913 (or early in 1914) and 1927 ranged from 23 per cent for Belgium to 71 per cent for Russia. With the exception of South Africa, the countries having the smallest increases in terms of gold prices are those which were in 1927 on a paper currency basis. (In terms of prevailing currencies these countries showed the greatest increases.) The indexes for the nine central countries in the list fall between 138 and 152, a small range of variation. For the 18 countries here included, the median value of the indexes is 146.5, a figure almost exactly equal to the index for the United States.[3]

[3] The figure employed for the United States is the unrevised index of the United States Bureau of Labor Statistics. The revised index, when the base is shifted to 1913, gives a figure of 137 for 1927. This is substantially lower than the figure of 147 which is cited in the text. Perhaps the chief reason for the difference is that heavier weight is given to fabricated industrial products in the new index than was given in the old. For purposes of international comparison it is considered advisable to employ the old index. In the construction of most of the foreign index numbers highly fabri-

Perhaps of greater practical importance than the degree of price rise in the last fifteen years is the direction in which wholesale prices are now moving. World economic conditions during the several decades before the war were vitally affected by the rising tendency in commodity prices, a tendency common to all industrial countries. Postwar trends are of equal importance. The period which has elapsed since a condition of relative price stability was generally achieved is too short to enable the trend of postwar prices to be definitely determined, but tendencies prevailing during the six years from 1922 to 1927 are of considerable interest. The nature of these tendencies is indicated by the figures in Table 2. The movement of the official price index in each country has been expressed in terms of the average annual rate of increase, or of decrease, during the period 1922–1927.[4]

The only two countries which show pronounced price increases during the period 1922–1927 were on paper bases. When the indexes for these countries are computed in terms of gold prices, the figure for France is changed from 14.1 to −2.1, and that for Belgium is changed from 16.4

cated industrial products are omitted. If they were given as much weight, relatively, as they are given in the revised index of the United States Bureau of Labor Statistics, the general level of foreign index numbers would doubtless be lower than it is.

A somewhat more exact comparison of price changes in certain fields is made possible by the use of the special index numbers of wholesale prices in 11 countries constructed by A. L. Bowley and K. C. Smith (London and Cambridge Economic Service, *Special Memorandum* No. 24, "Comparative Price Index Numbers for Eleven Principal Countries"). The same technical methods were employed throughout, in the construction of these index numbers, and nearly identical lists of commodities were used. (The index numbers are based on quotations for 35 commodities—food products and raw or semiprocessed industrial material.) In the following table these countries are grouped according to the values of the index numbers in the first month of 1927:

(1913 = 100)

Country	Index, January, 1927	Country	Index, January, 1927
New Zealand...............	151	Italy, gold prices..........	136
United States...............	145	Germany..................	132
Canada....................	143	Sweden...................	132
United Kingdom............	141	Holland...................	131
South Africa...............	[a]139	France, gold prices.........	123
Belgium, gold prices.........	[b]136		

[a] Base, January, 1914. [b] Base, July, 1914.

[4] Extensive use is made in the present study of figures which measure the average annual rates of change in economic series. Each of these figures is obtained from the value r, derived when a curve of the type $y = ar^x$ is fitted to the series in question. This is a curve which appears as a straight line on ratio paper. In evaluating r, use has been made of the mean value table constructed by Glover (*Tables of Applied Mathematics*, Ann Arbor, Mich., 1923, p. 468).

to −3.   In terms of gold prices only four of the 19 countries listed in the table showed rising levels of wholesale prices between 1922 and 1927. In fifteen countries wholesale prices declined, the rate of decline ranging from −0.1 to −6.5 per cent per year.   The most pronounced declines occurred in the Scandinavian countries, Czechoslovakia, Switzerland, and India.   Prices were approximately stable in Spain, Canada, the United States, Australia, and South Africa, though the tendency was slightly downward in the last three of these.

TABLE 2.—RANK OF 19 COUNTRIES ACCORDING TO AVERAGE ANNUAL RATE OF CHANGE IN INDEX NUMBERS OF WHOLESALE PRICES, 1922–1927[a]

Country	Average annual rate of change 1922–1927	Country	Average annual rate of change 1922–1927
	Per cent		*Per cent*
Belgium	[b]+16.4	New Zealand	−1.9
France	[c]+14.1	Great Britain	−2.4
China	+ 2.8	Japan	−2.9
Italy	[d]+ 2.2	Sweden	−3.2
Spain	+ 0.3	Switzerland	−3.8
Canada	+ 0.2	Czechoslovakia	−5.2
United States	− 0.1	India	−5.6
Australia	− 0.2	Denmark	−6.2
South Africa	− 0.7	Norway	−6.5
Netherlands	− 1.5		

[a] The index numbers from which these measures are derived are those described in the footnote to Table 1, with the following exceptions and additions: China, Bureau of Markets, Treasury Department, Shanghai, 147 commodities; Italy, Chamber of Commerce, Milan, 125 commodities; Spain, Institute of Geography and Statistics, 74 commodities; Switzerland, Dr. Lorenz, 71 commodities; Czechoslovakia, Central Bureau of Statistics, 69 commodities; India, Labor Office, Bombay, 42 commodities; Norway, Economic Review, 100 commodities.

[b] In gold prices, −3.   [c] In gold prices, −2.1.   [d] In gold prices, +1.5.

It is clear that during the years which have elapsed since the drastic liquidation of 1920–21 the general drift of world prices has been downward.   Belgium and France have resisted this tendency by the emission of paper currency, and China seems not to have felt it.   In half a dozen countries the net movement has been slight, while in 10 of the 19 countries listed the decline has proceeded at a rate of 1.5 per cent a year, or greater.

This movement stands in sharp contrast to the trend of wholesale prices in the chief industrial countries between 1896 and 1913.   During this period, wholesale prices in the United States rose at an average annual rate of 2.3 per cent; in Great Britain the rate of increase was 1.7 per cent a year, while in Germany prices advanced at a rate of 1.8 per cent each year.   The declining tendency observed in recent years has, of course, been a factor of great importance in the postwar economic situation. The wide extent of the decline indicates how pervasive has been the influence of the forces working toward lower gold prices.

Postwar Price Movements and Business Processes in the United States—A General Survey.—Price movements have no particular significance as detached phenomena. They must be considered in relation to general industrial movements and business processes. Recent price movements should be studied, therefore, in relation to general economic tendencies of the postwar period. In this brief survey, we may disregard month-to-month and year-to-year fluctuations and center attention on the persistent tendencies which have characterized this period.[5]

The measure most convenient for the comparison of such tendencies among miscellaneous economic series is the average annual rate of change, which was employed in Table 2. Certain of the distinctive features of the postwar period are summarized in Table 3.

TABLE 3.—ECONOMIC MOVEMENTS IN THE UNITED STATES, 1922–1927

Series[a]	Average annual rate of change 1922–1927
	Per cent
Primary production...	+ 2.5
Production of manufactured goods..............................	+ 4.0
Ton-miles of freight carried..................................	+ 4.0
Employment in factories.......................................	− 0.7
Factory pay rolls...	+ 1.7
Per capita earnings, factory employees........................	+ 2.4
Wholesale prices, all commodities.............................	− 0.1
Wholesale prices, products of American farms in raw state.....	+ 1.2
Prices of commodities at the farm.............................	+ 1.1
Wholesale prices, nonagricultural products....................	− 1.8
Profits, industrial corporations..............................	[b]+ 9.0
Dividend payments, industrial and miscellaneous corporations......	+ 6.8
Prices, industrial stocks.....................................	+14.1

[a] The indexes from which the measures in this table are derived are described in later sections of this chapter.

[b] Computed from data for the period 1923–1927.

The first three indexes reflect the sustained increase in the physical volume of production, which has been the basic factor in the economic well-being characteristic of this postwar era in the United States. Disregarding cyclical and other fluctuations, the volume of primary production (the output of raw vegetable, animal, forest, and mineral products)

[5] Strictly speaking, the period 1922–1927 is too brief to justify the use of the word "trend." Nevertheless, the purposes of the present investigation are served by measures of the tendencies which have been evident during the fairly well-defined period beginning in 1922. It is possible that certain of these apparent trends will be reversed in the near future, but it is the tendencies which are measured by the figures in Table 3 which have given this postwar period its characteristic economic features.

has gone up at an average rate of 2.5 per cent a year. The volume of manufacture has increased at a rate of 4 per cent a year, and freight movements (measured in ton-miles) have increased at the same rate.[6] (The rate of growth of population during this period has been about 1.4 per cent a year.) But accompanying this increase has come a definite decline in the volume of manufacturing employment, a decline at the rate of 0.7 per cent a year. Here is one of the anomalies of the postwar situation—increasing production with declining employment. This condition is at least in part explained by the next two figures. In the face of declining employment, factory pay rolls have gone up at a rate of 1.7 per cent a year, and per capita earnings of factory employees have increased at a rate of 2.4 per cent a year. (Employment, pay roll, and per capita earnings figures relate to identical establishments.) Output per man in manufacturing establishments has advanced at a rate of approximately 3.5 per cent a year[7] during the period 1922–1927, and it is, presumably, this gain in output which has permitted the increase in pay rolls to accompany declining employment.

The next set of figures in Table 3 relates to price movements, and here again we find a peculiar feature of the postwar economy. The increase in production and the changes which have been noted in factory employment and in per capita earnings have accompanied a slightly declining general price level. This decline has been felt chiefly by nonagricultural products, which have dropped at a rate of 1.8 per cent a year. Farm products have risen in price, at a rate slightly above 1 per cent a year. This is true both of prices at the farm and of prices of raw farm products in wholesale markets.

The summary account of postwar tendencies which is provided by these figures is completed by the last three measures in Table 3. Here are shown the remarkable increase in the profits of industrial corporations (at a rate of 9 per cent a year), the somewhat smaller increase in dividend payments, and the unprecedented advance in the prices of industrial stocks (at a rate of 14.1 per cent a year), an advance which has materially exceeded the gain in dividend payments and the increase in profits.

---

[6] The significance of these measures is, of course, dependent upon the adequacy of the index numbers from which they are derived. All the index numbers represented in the above table are based upon comprehensive data, and there is no reason to doubt that they give a substantially correct account of economic developments during this period. It may be noted that the difference between the rates of increase in primary production and in the volume of manufacture is not a necessary indication of inconsistency. Many primary products are consumed in a raw state. Moreover, the various raw materials enter in different degrees into manufacturing operations. Thus the production of raw minerals, most of which are subject to processing operations, increased at an average annual rate of 5.7 per cent during this period, a figure greatly exceeding the corresponding measures for the other classes of raw materials.

[7] This figure is based upon Dr. Wolman's statistics (Chap. VI).

Here, then, are certain of the broad features of the postwar economic situation. It will be the task of subsequent sections to break up certain of the averages upon which the above measures are based, and to examine in greater detail the movements of prices and of other economic series.

I. PREWAR PRICE TENDENCIES IN THE UNITED STATES[8]

Postwar price movements in the United States can be best interpreted in the light of tendencies which prevailed during the period preceding the war. The price revolution which occurred between 1914 and 1921 was an incident, though a violent one. The effects of this revolution have not yet entirely worn off, but, for an understanding of enduring tendencies in American economic life, it is probable that more is to be learned from a study of prewar movements than from an analysis of conditions during the disturbed years following 1914.

Among the conditions and tendencies in the field of prices which gave to the two decades preceding the war their distinguishing economic characteristics, the following were of major importance.[9]

1. A rising price level.

2. A considerable degree of internal disturbance in price relations, a degree of disturbance which tended to decline.

3. Relatively high variability of prices of individual commodities, marked again by a tendency to decline.

4. The existence, between 1896 and 1913, of clearly defined trends in the prices of most commodities at wholesale and in certain prices in other fields, trends which differed materially as among different elements in the price system. (This point will be discussed in a later section.)

The rising tendency in the level of prices during the two decades prior to the war, a tendency shared by every important commodity group in the United States, provided one of the most fundamental of the conditions under which business men of that era worked. It affected manufacturing methods and buying and selling habits, and was reflected in numerous business practices which business men found hard to change when conditions were altered. But the economic consequences of a rising price level have been discussed in considerable detail, and require no elaboration here.

[8] Some of the materials presented in this and the following sections have been published in *The Behavior of Prices*, National Bureau of Economic Research, 1927, and in a paper by the author on "Postwar Prices and Prewar Trends," *Proceedings* of the American Statistical Association, 1928. This paper has been drawn upon freely in the preparation of the present section of this chapter.

[9] These were not necessarily causal factors. Certain of the price conditions noted may merely have reflected other economic conditions.

The general price index does not tell the whole story of the main price movements of this period. Such an index measures the intensity of the force, or combination of forces, which is affecting the purchasing power of the dollar. There are many specific price-making forces which affect, primarily, the prices of individual commodities. These forces operate to change individual commodity prices unequally, and to prevent the prices of individual commodities from accommodating themselves promptly to changes in the purchasing power of the dollar. The influence of these disruptive forces is reflected in the dispersion of prices. The less direct the incidence of the force which is acting upon the price level, and the greater the relative importance of specific price-making factors, the more widely dispersed will prices be. These disruptive forces possess considerable economic significance, for every inequality of movement affects the buying and selling relations upon which the movement of goods depends. Every inequality of movement introduces some element of instability into the price system.

The index employed in measuring the dispersion of prices defines, in percentage form, the approximate limits of the zone within which would fall 50 per cent of the price relatives at a given date, and on a given base.[10] Thus a value of 10 for a given date means that, on that date, approximately half the price relatives deviated from the geometric mean of all the relatives by less than 10 per cent. Such measures, computed from annual link relatives, weighted, for the period 1891–1927, are given in Table 4, together with geometric means of the link relatives.[11]

Two facts concerning these measures are of immediate significance. The first is that this prewar period, particularly the early part of the period, was marked by a relatively high degree of dispersion, that is, by relatively severe disturbances in price relations.[12] The second point of

---

[10] This measure is the antilogarithm of a fractional part (.6745) of the logarithmic standard deviation. The logarithmic standard deviation was first used as a measure of dispersion by Professor Irving Fisher.

[11] The commodities employed are those for which wholesale price quotations are published by the United States Bureau of Labor Statistics. The weights are based upon the values of the quantities marketed during the period 1920–1923.

[12] Severe, that is, relatively to similar disturbances at other times and in other lands. That it was severe during the early part of this period, in comparison with disturbances in other periods, is shown by certain measures, not given above, defining the degree of dispersion of fixed base relatives in different periods. The dispersion, in 1902, of relatives on the 1891 base is measured by an index of 17.6; in 1913 the index of dispersion of relatives on the 1902 base was 14.1; in 1926, the index of dispersion of relatives on the 1913 base was 17.4. (The figures for intermediate years of this last period were considerably higher, but at the end of the period the dispersion was less than it was in 1902, on the 1891 base.)

That the disturbance was severe in comparison with similar disturbances in other lands is suggested by certain figures of Lucien March (*Metron*, Vol. 1, No. 4,

TABLE 4.—GEOMETRIC MEANS AND MEASURES OF DISPERSION COMPUTED FROM
LINK RELATIVES OF WHOLESALE PRICES, 1891–1927

Year	Number of price series	Geometric mean	Index of dispersion	Year	Number of price series	Geometric mean	Index of dispersion
1891	195	100.0	10.6	1910	205	102.9	7.9
1892	195	93.8	7.3	1911	205	94.5	8.7
1893	195	101.8	8.3	1912	205	106.8	7.3
1894	195	89.8	7.9	1913	205	101.1	8.4
1895	195	101.3	9.8	1914	391	97.9	7.4
1896	195	95.3	9.8	1915	391	101.1	10.6
1897	195	100.6	9.7	1916	391	125.8	13.7
1898	195	102.6	7.7	1917	391	138.6	12.4
1899	195	107.1	10.5	1918	389	111.7	14.2
1900	195	108.5	8.4	1919	389	106.8	11.9
1901	195	99.2	7.9	1920	391	110.2	15.7
1902	195	107.3	8.6	1921	391	65.4	18.3
1903	205	100.8	9.2	1922	391	101.0	11.7
1904	205	99.6	10.2	1923	390	105.0	11.0
1905	205	100.6	7.4	1924	390	97.4	8.3
1906	205	103.6	7.7	1925	387	105.8	11.5
1907	205	106.4	5.7	1926	385	94.5	8.9
1908	205	96.0	8.7	1927	372	97.1	9.2
1909	205	106.1	7.6				

importance is that during the 24 years prior to the war there was a
sustained downward tendency in the degree of dispersion of link relatives.
The disturbances of which such dispersion is a reflection were definitely

p. 83). Using relatives on the 1890–1899 base in each case, March gives the
following figures:

Number of commodities	Country and year	Standard deviation of price relatives
203	United States, in 1909	31.8
55	France, in 1913	22.5
42	Great Britain, in 1913	20.0

Although the period was four years longer for France and Great Britain than for
the United States (a condition which would tend to increase the dispersion), the degree
of dispersion was materially greater in the United States than in either of these countries. Differences in the commodities used, and in the number of quotations employed,
lessen the comparability of the results, but the same general tendencies would probably be revealed by other samples.

Both these examples relate, not to year-to-year dispersion of the type referred to
in the text, but to the dispersion of prices over much longer periods. The records of
the war years support the reasonable assumption that exceptional disturbance of
fixed base relatives will be associated with high dispersion of link relatives.

diminishing. I shall discuss the economic significance of these facts in connection with the next point considered.

The third important characteristic of prewar price behavior is the high variability of the prices of individual commodities. Such variability may not be registered at all in changes in the price level. Though price-level changes and the variability of individual prices are not unrelated, the one furnishes no accurate index of the other. For each of more than 200 commodities, we have, for each year from 1890 to 1927, a measure of the variability of its prices within the year.[13] The averages of these annual measures are given in Table 5.

TABLE 5.—MONTHLY VARIABILITY OF WHOLESALE PRICES. AVERAGES COMPUTED FROM MEASURES OF PRICE VARIABILITY FOR INDIVIDUAL COMMODITIES, 1890–1927

Year	Number of price series	Arithmetic mean of measures of variability	ear	Number of price series	Arithmetic mean of measures of variability
1890	204	4.8	1909	214	4.6
1891	204	4.4	1910	214	4.3
1892	204	4.5	1911	214	4.3
1893	206	4.9	1912	214	4.6
1894	206	4.6	1913	213	3.7
1895	206	6.3	1914	214	4.4
1896	206	4.7	1915	214	5.9
1897	206	4.8	1916	214	8.7
1898	206	4.1	1917	214	10.6
1899	206	6.0	1918	213	7.3
1900	206	5.5	1919	212	9.7
1901	205	4.3	1920	214	10.8
1902	214	4.7	1921	214	8.5
1903	214	4.8	1922	213	6.5
1904	214	4.1	1923	214	4.9
1905	214	4.5	1924	213	5.4
1906	214	3.5	1925	211	4.7
1907	214	4.5	1926	211	4.2
1908	214	4.7	1927	209	4.7

The points noted in connection with the dispersion of prices appear to be true of these measures of price variability. The wholesale prices of individual commodities in the United States during this period, as a whole, were highly variable;[14] this variability was tending to decline.

[13] This measure is the mean deviation, expressed as a percentage of the mean price for the year.

[14] We have, unfortunately, no similar set of averages for other countries covering this period, but some indication of the relative variability of American prices and prices in other countries is afforded by a comparison of measures of variability relating to individual commodities. In 24 out of 31 such comparisons of individual price series in the United States and in other countries (Great Britain, France, and Ger-

A consideration of these measures of dispersion and of price variability throws some light on the economic characteristics of the prewar period.

1. The prices of individual commodities were subject to relatively abrupt changes from month to month and from year to year. (There were, of course, many individual exceptions to this general condition.) These changes introduced a considerable degree of uncertainty into business operations, and enhanced the speculative features of business operations.

2. The relatively high degree of dispersion from year to year represents a condition of rapidly changing price relations. The specific price-making forces which affected individual commodities differed materially in their intensity; the disruptive forces which tended to alter existing price relations were relatively strong. Here, again, we have a condition which introduces uncertainty into business dealings, and intensifies the speculative element in business.[15]

3. The preceding points may be summed up in the statement that there was a high degree of price instability in the prewar era. Individual prices and the relations among the prices of individual commodities were both relatively unstable.

4. Finally, and perhaps most important, during the quarter century preceding the war these measures of instability showed a definite tendency to decline. The variability of individual commodity prices was diminishing, and there was less disturbance in price relations. The movement toward greater stability of individual prices and of price relations was broken and uneven, but it is clearly present as a sustained trend.[16] This downward trend is the more significant in that it accompanied a rising price level.

In the high variability of individual prices prior to the war, and in all that that implies, we have, I think, one of the most significant of the conditions which gave to prewar economic life its characteristic tone, and in the downward trend of this variability we have one of the most

---

many), American prices were found to be more variable. Again, measures of price variability for seven important commodities (coal, iron, sugar, silk, rice, barley, and wheat) in five countries, for the period 1890–1913, were averaged. The average was highest for the United States, with Japan, France, Great Britain, and Germany coming next in order. These are only scattered cases, yet they indicate that our prewar price system was characterized by a relatively high degree of variability of individual commodity prices.

[15] Points 1 and 2 represent different aspects of essentially the same phenomena. The first depicts the condition with reference to the behavior of individual commodities; the second involves the relations among commodity prices and the degree of difference in their changes.

[16] This trend is apparent not only in the two sets of measures given above, but also in certain measures of the frequency of changes in the prices of individual commodities which, because of space limitations, can not be here discussed.

important of the tendencies which marked the economic development of this period. The conditions of high price variability and marked disturbance in price relations offer opportunities to business men for those conjunctural profits which result from faulty economic adjustments and temporary dislocations. A rising price level, coupled with variable individual prices, represents a happy hunting ground, indeed, for the speculative elements in the business world.[17]

II. THE BEHAVIOR OF PRICES IN THE UNITED STATES, 1922–1928 : GENERAL MEASURES

The upward trend of the price level during the period 1896–1913, a movement which carried the general index up by 2.3 per cent each year, gave to that period certain of its most pronounced economic characteristics. It is apparent from the data in Table 2 that the trend of world prices, in wholesale markets, has been declining since 1922, and there is no present evidence that the prewar rise will be resumed. In the United States there was a slight downward movement (at an average rate of one-tenth of 1 per cent a year) between 1922 and 1927, but the degree of departure from actual stability has been negligible. The significance of this approximate stability need not be discussed here, except to emphasize its obvious bearing upon the buying and selling operations of business men. The world in which the business man of to-day functions is different in many respects from that in which business was done during the two decades prior to the war. Perhaps the most important of these differences is found in the changed trend of the level of prices.

War-time developments gave a sharp check to the downward trend in the variability of individual commodity prices which was in evidence before the war. The range of fluctuations of individual prices was unprecedentedly large during the war years, and this high variability persisted even after the recession of 1920–21. The average of all the individual measures of variability for the six years 1922–1927 was 5. The average for the 14 years from 1901 to 1914 was 4.4. But to judge postwar conditions by this average alone is to ignore the significant decline in price variability in recent years as shown by the averages of the variability measures for individual commodities. From 1920 to 1927, the average declined from 10.8 to 4.7. (See Table 5 for the figures for intervening years.)

It is clear that the prewar tendency toward greater stability in the prices of individual commodities is still present. The average for 1927 is about equal to that prevailing at the close of the prewar period. We may, of course, expect fluctuations in these annual averages, with move-

---

[17] There is, it is true, a dark side to the picture, for highly variable prices will present opportunities for conjunctural losses, as well as for profits.

ments above the 1927 figure, but the existence of the declining trend in price variability before the war strengthens the assumption that the degree of variability to be expected in the future will be no greater than that which prevailed at the end of the prewar period, with some possibility that the downward movement will continue. If we may anticipate approximate stability in the price level in the future, the expectation of greater stability in the prices of individual commodities is strengthened.[18]

Recent movements of the index of dispersion tell somewhat the same story as do the averages of the variability measures. The well-defined downward movement in the degree of year-to-year dispersion which was in evidence prior to the war was reversed during the disturbances of the period from 1915 to 1921. (See Table 4.) Since 1922, however, the average degree of dispersion has been much lower, although somewhat above the prewar average. The average for the years 1922–1927 is 10.1; that for the years 1901–1914 is 8.7. The figures for 1924, 1926, and 1927 represent a degree of year-to-year disturbance about equal to that which prevailed during the decade before the war.

In respect, then, to the internal disturbances which are defined by the above measures, we appear to stand to-day approximately where we did in 1913. The excessive disturbances of the war years served only temporarily to check the tendencies toward increased stability of individual commodity prices and of internal relations among prices which were operative before the war. In the last several years, there have been fewer of those abrupt changes in prices and in price relations which characterized the nineties of the last century, and which gave the war and immediate postwar years their distinctive business flavor.

These tendencies toward price stability, which have so definitely reasserted themselves after the disturbances of the war years, will, if they persist, materially affect the economic complexion of the years before us. All that has been said above concerning the slow change that was taking place in the price conditions under which business was transacted during the quarter century preceding the war may be applied to the present and future. A tendency toward greater stability of prices and of price relations must involve some change in the direction in which business men look for profits. Something of the speculative element goes out of business when such a tendency prevails. Profits made from the fluctuations of individual commodity prices, and from changes in the relations among prices, tend to diminish. The high conjunctural profits and the great losses which go with extreme fluctuations in the prices of individual commodities alike tend to disappear. Business and prices

---

[18] Changes in the purchasing power of the dollar are not, of course, the sole factor affecting the movements of individual commodities, but this factor becomes of dominant importance during periods of violent change in the price level.

both become more stable. There is evidence that our economic system is moving in this direction.[19]

In this general survey, attention should be given to the cycles which have been reflected in prices and in related economic series, as well as to general tendencies prevailing during this period. Certain postwar tendencies in industry have been so pronounced that they have in part overshadowed the cyclical fluctuations, and in much of the current discussion it is these tendencies to which chief attention has been given.[20] Important as these have been, and important as they will be if they continue, the persistence of cyclical fluctuations is of equal importance.

Such fluctuations in prices and in several related series during postwar years are shown by the curves in Charts 1 to 15. These charts have been constructed in such a way as to reveal cyclical movements, rather than trends. Each of these curves portrays changes in the values of monthly relatives, these being secured by expressing each monthly value of the series in question as a percentage of its value at a date 12 months preceding.[21]

In Charts 1 to 5 appear curves, representing the movements of 12-month link indexes of this type during the period 1920–1928. The measures plotted are derived from indexes of general wholesale prices,

---

[19] Such tendencies, it is understood, operate slowly, and are subject to numerous interruptions. New inventions, new processes, may offset these tendencies for shorter or for longer intervals.

[20] As to the nature of these tendencies, more is said in the several sections next following.

[21] Thus the price (or production) index for January, 1920, is expressed as a percentage of the index value for January, 1919; the index value for February, 1920, is expressed as a percentage of the index value for February, 1919, and so on. These charts thus differ materially from the usual type, on which are plotted absolute values or relatives on a constant base, and they call for a somewhat different interpretation. Seasonal fluctuations, if they are constant, will not appear in the curve. Again, the measurement of changes with reference to a date 12 months preceding means that the curve of such an index fluctuates about the base line (*i.e.* the 100 line). When the curve crosses the 100 line, it means, of course, that the series has precisely the same value as it had 12 months before. Points above the 100 line represent rising values of the original series. If the curve is above the 100 line and rising, it represents a series which is increasing at an increasing rate; if it is above the 100 line and falling, it represents a series which is increasing at a decreasing rate. Changes below the 100 line are to be interpreted in a similar fashion. The effect of a consistent trend is not, of course, eliminated, but it appears in a form somewhat different from that to which we are accustomed. An upward trend serves to increase the number of entries above 100, intensifying and lengthening the swings of the index above the base line. A downward trend would have the reverse effect. Such an index, based on 12-month link relatives, has distinct advantages in the following of cyclical fluctuations. Its use conforms with the common practice of comparing monthly values with the values prevailing 12 months before. (A more detailed discussion of the nature of measures of this type will be found in *The Behavior of Prices*, National Bureau of Economic Research, 1927, pp. 247–251.)

CHART 1.—FLUCTUATIONS IN COMMODITY PRICES, AT WHOLESALE

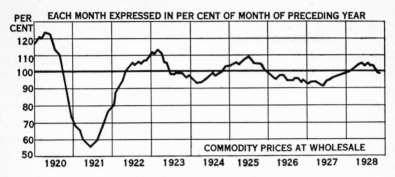

CHART 2.—FLUCTUATIONS IN PRICES OF NONAGRICULTURAL PRODUCTS, AT WHOLESALE

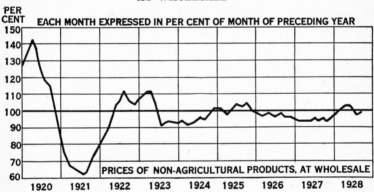

CHART 3.—FLUCTUATIONS IN VOLUME OF MANUFACTURING PRODUCTION

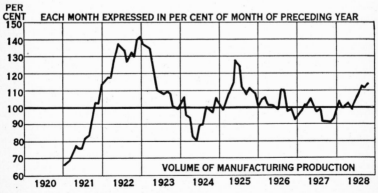

CHART 4.—FLUCTUATIONS IN VOLUME OF INDUSTRIAL EMPLOYMENT

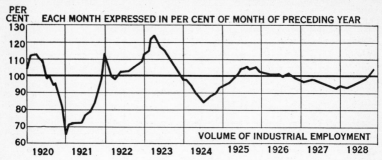

CHART 5.—FLUCTUATIONS IN PAY ROLLS OF MANUFACTURING INDUS-
TRIES

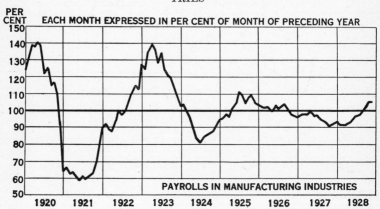

CHART 6.—FLUCTUATIONS IN COMMODITY STOCKS

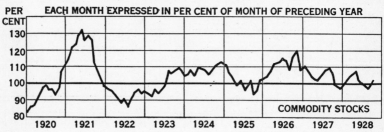

CHART 7.—FLUCTUATIONS IN UNFILLED ORDERS

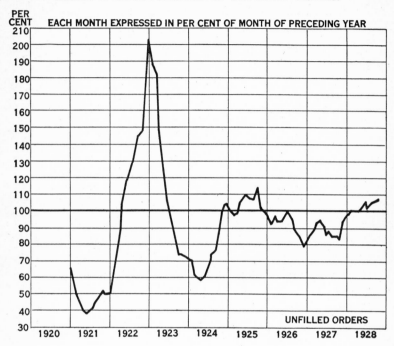

CHART 8.—FLUCTUATIONS IN VOLUME OF TRADE

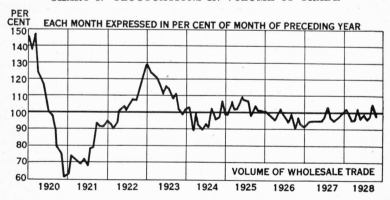

CHART 9.—FLUCTUATIONS IN PRICES OF FARM PRODUCTS

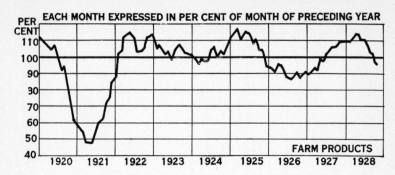

CHART 10.—FLUCTUATIONS IN PRICES OF FOODS

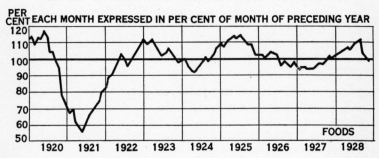

CHART 11.—FLUCTUATIONS IN PRICES OF HIDES AND LEATHER PROD-
UCTS

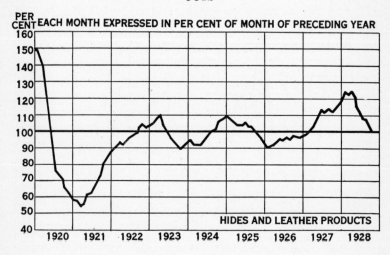

CHART 12.—FLUCTUATIONS IN PRICES OF TEXTILE PRODUCTS

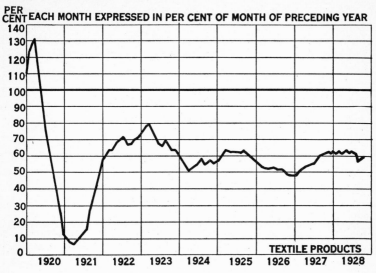

CHART 13.—FLUCTUATIONS IN PRICES OF FUEL AND LIGHTING

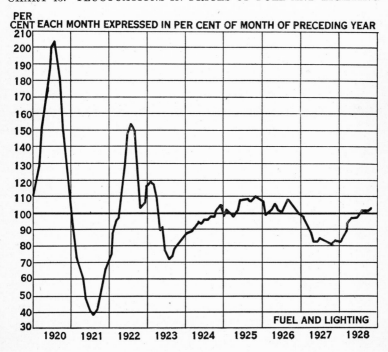

CHART 14.—FLUCTUATIONS IN PRICES OF METAL AND METAL PRODUCTS

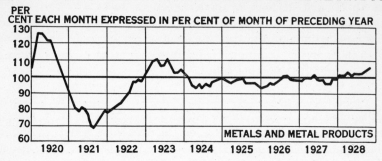

CHART 15.—FLUCTUATIONS IN PRICES OF BUILDING MATERIALS

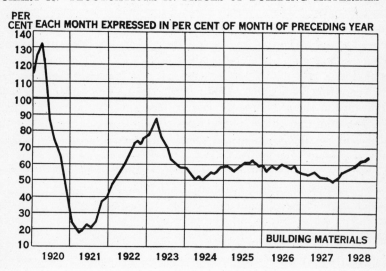

of the prices, at wholesale, of nonagricultural (*i.e.*, industrial) commodities, of manufacturing production, of industrial employment, and of pay rolls in manufacturing industries. The recession of 1920–21 and the subsequent business recovery are clearly apparent in all the indexes.[22]   Thereafter, we find in all series a clear cyclical peak in 1923, a recession in 1924, a peak in 1925, and a slow but appreciable decline from 1925 to 1927. The index of manufacturing production has been above the base line during almost all of the last three and a half years, which means that the trend of such production has been almost unbrokenly upward. But the *rate* of such advance has declined appreciably since the peak of the cycle in 1925, and it is in this decline that the influence of cyclical forces has been apparent. All the other series,

[22] The index of manufacturing production shows only the recovery since, in this link form, it goes back only to the beginning of 1921.

notably the prices of industrial commodities at wholesale, have suffered more appreciable declines in their absolute values.

In Charts 6 to 8 there are shown similar curves relating to commodity stocks, unfilled orders, and the volume of wholesale trade, and in Charts 9 to 15 there are plotted, in the same form, price indexes of a number of commodity groups, at wholesale.[23]

III. TRENDS OF PRICE GROUPS, PREWAR AND POSTWAR

Reference has been made to the fact that between 1896 and 1913 there existed material differences among the price trends of different commodities, and it was suggested that a key to certain of the distinctive economic characteristics of the prewar period could be found in these differences. Thus, during the 18-year period between 1896 and 1913, rosin rose in price at an average annual rate of 10.2 per cent, print cloths rose at a rate of 2.8 per cent, and wood alcohol declined at a rate of 3.4 per cent a year. During the period 1922–1927, hogs rose in price at an average annual rate of 6.9 per cent a year, while the price of pig iron declined at a rate of 7.3 per cent a year. It is such differences which reflect enduring changes in economic relations. The nature and economic significance of these differences may be best appreciated when attention is shifted from individual commodities to important commodity groups, and it is in the differences among groups, in respect to their price trends, that our present interest lies. The discussion of recent price tendencies may be introduced by a brief summary of the movements of prices during the two decades preceding the war.

The relative movements of the commodity groups for which the Bureau of Labor Statistics has constructed index numbers for prewar years are shown in Table 6.

TABLE 6.—PREWAR TRENDS OF COMMODITY PRICES, AT WHOLESALE
(Groups of the United States Bureau of Labor Statistics)

Commodity groups	Average annual rate of price increase, 1896–1913	Commodity groups	Average annual rate of price increase, 1896–1913
	Per cent		*Per cent*
Farm products............	+3.4	Cloths and clothing........	+1.8
Building materials.........	+2.4	House furnishings..........	+1.4
Foods....................	+2.3	Metals and metal products..	+0.8
All commodities...........	*+2.3*	Chemicals and drugs........	+0.5
Fuel and lighting..........	+2.1		

These measures afford one view of the fundamental changes that were taking place during the years preceding the war. The sustained improve-

[23] The group index numbers plotted are selected from those computed by the United States Bureau of Labor Statistics.

ment in agricultural conditions is reflected in the margin of more than 1 per cent between the rates at which farm products and all commodities were rising in price. Five of the eight groups rose less rapidly in price than did the all-commodities index. That is, fuels, clothing, furnishings, metal products, and chemicals and drugs were becoming relatively cheaper during this period.

Additional information concerning prewar economic tendencies may be gleaned from other classifications of commodities.

TABLE 7.—PREWAR TRENDS OF COMMODITY PRICES, AT WHOLESALE
(Various groupings)

Commodity group	Number of commodities	Average annual rate of price increase, 1896–1913a
		Per cent
Cultivated products..............................	128	+2.3
Noncultivated products...........................	98	+1.5
Products of American farms.......................	117	+2.4
All other commodities............................	109	+1.5
Raw materials....................................	49	+2.6
Processed materials..............................	177	+1.8
Foods...	67	+2.5
Nonfoods..	159	+1.7
Producers' goods.................................	115	+1.9
Consumers' goods................................	111	+1.9
Forest products..................................	22	+3.3
Animal products.................................	51	+2.4
Cultivated vegetable products.....................	74	+2.1
Mineral products.................................	70	+0.9
Domestic products...............................	161	+2.0
Foreign products.................................	13	+1.6
Products from both domestic and foreign sources......	52	+1.7
All commodities..................................	226	+1.9

a The measures in this table have been derived by averaging equally weighted rates of change in the prices of individual commodities. The commodities included are those for which the Bureau of Labor Statistics compiles and publishes price quotations. The difference between the rates of change for "all commodities," as given in this and in the preceding table, is due chiefly to the fact that one is the average of measures for individual commodities, while the other is derived from an index number.

The classifications upon which these measures rest differ materially, it may be noted, from those employed in the construction of currently published index numbers, even from certain ones having the same group names. This accounts for certain differences between the rates here given and those cited in the paper to which reference has been made, "Postwar Prices and Prewar Trends." In a later publication of the National Bureau of Economic Research, detailed information will be given concerning the present classifications.

Certain fairly sharp differences are revealed in Table 7. Products of cultivation were becoming relatively dearer in prewar years, while non-cultivated products were becoming progressively cheaper in price.[24] Raw

[24] The comparison runs in relative terms, of course. The value of a commodity, with reference to other commodities, was declining if the rate of its price increase were less than the average increase for all commodities.

materials were rising in price more rapidly than processed goods. Foods were becoming dearer and nonfoods cheaper, in relative terms. The greatest differences are found in the next to the last division of the table. Forest products were rising in price at a relatively rapid rate, while the prices of animal products and of cultivated vegetable products were gaining on the general average. The relative value of mineral products, in terms of all commodities, was declining at a rate of 1 per cent a year.

Much information is concealed by such broad averages as the above. Within each of the groups there distinguished, we may expect to find differences among individual commodities and among minor groups. With reference to the farm situation, the trend of the prices of raw farm products is more significant than the movement of the entire group of commodities which are classed as products of American farms. Here we find raw materials rising at a much more rapid rate than processed materials (3.2, as against 2.2). Again, a striking margin is found between the trends of raw minerals and of processed minerals. The raw minerals rose at a rate of 1.8 per cent a year, while the processed goods rose at 0.6 per cent. The value, in terms of other commodities, of processed mineral products declined more rapidly during this prewar period than did the value of any other important commodity group. This progressive cheapening of major industrial products played an important part in the economic development of the United States during this era.

In Table 8 is shown a final picture of prewar movements in the field of living costs and wages.

TABLE 8.—PREWAR TRENDS, COST OF LIVING, AND EARNINGS OF LABOR

Index[a]	Average annual rate of increase, 1896–1913
	Per cent
Cost of living..	+1.9
Earnings, all groups of employees........................	+2.4
Earnings, factory employees.............................	+2.0
Purchasing power of earnings, all groups................	+0.5
Purchasing power of earnings, factory employees...........	+0.1

[a] The indexes of living costs and of earnings from which these measures have been derived are those constructed by Prof. Paul H. Douglas. The rates of change in purchasing power, *i.e.*, in real earnings, are derived from the rates for cost of living and money earnings.

Costs of living were rising, during the two decades before the war, at a rate not materially different from that of wholesale prices. The earnings of all labor, as these are measured by the indexes constructed by Prof. Paul H. Douglas, were rising at a rate of 2.4 per cent a year, while the earnings of factory labor rose at a rate of 2 per cent a year between 1896 and 1913. In terms of purchasing power, or real wages, the gains of labor are not so impressive. For all workers, the gain was at a rate of one-half of 1 per cent each year, representing a slow but sustained improvement in well-being. The corresponding figure for employees of manufacturing plants is one-tenth of 1 per cent a year. The earnings of these workers barely kept ahead of living costs during this period.

The twenty-odd years preceding the war constituted, from an economic viewpoint, a fairly homogeneous period, a period of rising prices, increasing production, expanding commerce. The brief account preceding has dealt with the tendencies in the field of prices which helped to give to this period its distinctive economic complexion. We may turn now to the period in which our chief interest lies, the period which began with the recovery following the drastic liquidation of 1920–21. We are at a disadvantage in attempting to define the tendencies characteristic of this postwar era, for this period has by no means run its course. There will doubtless be many reversals of present trends before we arrive at a point marking a decisive termination of this era. Nevertheless, it is instructive to consider the tendencies which may now be observed, and to contrast these with the tendencies which were operative before the war.

In Tables 1 and 2 of Appendix B there will be found numerous measures of the price changes which have occurred since 1922. From the groups there represented, certain of the more significant figures may be selected for comment here (Table 9). The first set correspond to the prewar figures shown in Table 6.

TABLE 9.—TENDENCIES AMONG COMMODITY PRICES, AT WHOLESALE
(Groups of the United States Bureau of Labor Statistics)

Commodity group	Average annual rate of change, 1922–1927[a]	Commodity group	Average annual rate of change, 1922–1927[a]
	Per cent		Per cent
Foods......................	+2.3	Building materials..........	−1.3
Farm products..............	+1.2	Textile products...........	−1.5
Hides and leather products....	+0.2	Metals and metal products..	−1.5
All commodities..............	−0.1	House furnishings..........	−1.5
Chemicals and drugs.........	−0.5	Fuel and lighting..........	−2.7

[a] The index numbers from which these rates of change have been computed are the revised measures, on the 1926 base.

The net movement of the prices of all commodities, at wholesale, has been slightly downward during this period, but the differences between the movements of the major commodity groups have been even greater than those which developed during the prewar era (see Table 6). As for the earlier period, farm products and foods have gained, relatively, while metals, fuels, and house furnishings have lost. Building materials and chemicals and drugs have reversed their relative positions. Of the nine groups, six have declined (five substantially), two have risen appreciably, and one has remained practically on a level.*

TABLE 10.—TENDENCIES AMONG COMMODITY PRICES, AT WHOLESALE

(Minor groups of the United States Bureau of Labor Statistics)

Commodity group	Average annual rate of change, 1922–1927[a]
	Per cent
Rubber, crude..	+16.8
Textile products (other than cotton, silk, and wool)........	+ 6.0
Livestock and poultry.................................	+ 5.5
Meats...	+ 5.1
Drugs and pharmaceuticals[b]...........................	+ 4.6
Grains...	+ 3.5
Essential oils[b].......................................	+ 2.7
Butter, cheese, and milk..............................	+ 1.9
Nonferrous metals....................................	+ 1.9
Crude drugs[b]..	+ 1.2
Boots and shoes......................................	+ 0.8
Chemicals..	+ 0.6
Leather..	+ 0.4
Foods (other than butter, cheese, milk, and meats)........	+ 0.3
Cattle feed...	+ 0.1
Furnishings..	+ 0.1
Woolens and worsted goods............................	0.0
All commodities.....................................	*– 0.1*
Anthracite coal.......................................	– 0.2
Paper and pulp.......................................	– 0.5
Brick..	– 1.1
Farm products (other than grains, livestock, and poultry)..	– 1.2
Structural steel......................................	– 1.4
Hides and skins......................................	– 1.5
Portland cement......................................	– 1.7
Petroleum products...................................	– 1.8
Cotton goods...	– 1.8
Lumber..	– 1.9
Iron and steel..	– 1.9
Furniture..	– 3.7
Bituminous coal......................................	– 4.5
Coke..	– 5.6
Silk and rayon.......................................	– 5.8

[a] The index numbers from which these rates of change have been computed are the revised measures on the 1926 base.

[b] Index numbers of the *Oil, Paint and Drug Reporter*.

* Relative changes in the prices of different commodities are influenced most strongly by the possibilities that exist, with respect to particular commodities, of applying to their production mechanical aids and scientific discoveries. To the ordinary individual, the most significant recent change in price levels is the relative cheapness of those things that can be turned out in quantity by mechanical processes, and the high price of personal service and of those things that can be turned out only by crude hand labor. This differentiation can be seen in traveling from country to country, when it is observed that in mechanically backward countries, those things are relatively cheap which are produced by crude hand labor, and those things are dear which require skilled and highly mechanized production. Note by M. C. Rorty.

These movements reflect the changes which are generally understood to have been characteristic of the postwar period. Farm products have risen in price, while industrial goods have tended to decline. But the figures for these nine major groups leave untold much of the story of the price changes characteristic of this postwar period. More detailed measures, and measures representing classifications other than that employed by the Bureau of Labor Statistics, are needed to supplement those there given. Some of the details of the picture are filled in by the measures in Table 10, defining the average annual rates of change in the index numbers for minor commodity groups, as constructed (with three exceptions) by the Bureau of Labor Statistics.

Here we have, as is to be expected, a much wider range of variation, extending from the crude rubber group, which increased in price at an average rate of 16.8 per cent a year, to the silk and rayon group, which declined in price at an average rate of 5.8 per cent a year. The ranking of groups does not permit such a relatively simple interpretation as did the division of nine major groups. Something of the complexity of the general economic situation is revealed by these detailed figures. The subclasses of certain of the broad groups are found to have differed widely from each other in their price trends during the past six years. Thus we find the general group of textile products broken into four smaller groups, one of which is second from the top, one approximately at the center of the list, one seventh from the bottom, and one at the bottom of the entire list of 32 minor groups. From a study of this table, much may be learned concerning the character of the forces which were affecting economic processes during this period.

Certain of the broader tendencies of the period may be discerned when the general list of commodities is divided into groups on different bases. A number of classifications have been applied by the National Bureau of Economic Research to the commodities in the Bureau of Labor Statistics' list, and from the index numbers thus constructed certain of the measures in Table 11 have been computed.[25]

The various index numbers measuring the movements of agricultural and nonagricultural products agree in showing both an absolute and a relative gain in the prices of the former group.[26]

[25] These index numbers will be published at a later date, and details of the various classifications will be given at that time. The index numbers, from which the rates of change in the present chapter have been computed, are unweighted geometric averages of relative prices, on the 1913 base.

[26] In the discussion of the postwar trends of these groups, one point of some general importance must be borne in mind. The discussion of prewar trends dealt with the period from 1896 to 1913; the treatment of post-war trends is restricted to the period 1922–1927. Developments during the intervening years have been ignored. There is justification for considering developments during the period 1914–1921 as so much water under the bridge, and for neglecting these in attempting to trace postwar

TABLE 11.—TENDENCIES AMONG COMMODITY PRICES, AT WHOLESALE

(Various groupings)

Commodity group	Number of commodities	Average annual rate of price change, 1922–1927
		Per cent
Agricultural products[a]	141	+0.7
Nonagricultural products[a]	263	−1.8
Cultivated products	230	+1.0
Noncultivated products	174	−1.1
Products of American farms	201	+0.7
All other commodities	203	−0.5
Raw materials	106	+1.4
Processed materials	298	−0.4
Foods	136	+2.0
Nonfoods	268	−0.9
Consumers' goods	172	+0.3
Producers' goods	232	+0.0
Animal products	96	+1.2
Cultivated vegetable products	127	+0.5
Mineral products	128	−0.9
Forest products	40	−1.6
Foreign products	34	+3.4
Domestic products	294	−0.4
Commodities from both domestic and foreign sources	76	+0.5

[a] These index numbers are compiled by the Bureau of Labor Statistics. Agricultural products include all the commodities classed as "Farm Products," and "Foods," except that hides and skins, cocoa beans, coffee, copra, fish, pepper, salt, tea, and cocoanut oil are excluded, and bran, cottonseed meal, linseed meal, and mill feed middlings are included. All other commodities are classed as "nonagricultural."

The margin between the two rates of change has been somewhat greater for the period since 1922 than it was during the prewar period, for which figures were given in Table 7. As in the prewar period, raw materials have been gaining, in relation to processed materials, and foods have been rising in relation to nonfoods. For these three major groups, recent tendencies have resembled those prevailing in the earlier period. Animal, vegetable, and mineral products stand also in the same relative positions, but forest products, which in prewar days rose most rapidly, have declined at the sharpest rate in recent years. There has been a slight, but hardly significant, change in the relative positions of producers' and consumers' goods. The price trends of foreign and domestic products have been reversed. Within the last six years, foreign products (a rela-

trends. Yet events during this disturbed period have influenced recent trends. The fact that agricultural prices have risen in recent years, while nonagricultural prices have declined, is in part a result of the more severe recession in agricultural prices in 1920–21. Therefore, although we deal with trends since 1922, it is well to remember that these trends are not set off sharply from the developments of the preceding period.

tively small group, it should be noted) have risen at a rate of 3.4 per cent a year, in the face of a practically stable price level.[27]

More direct evidence concerning the change in agricultural conditions is afforded by the index numbers of prices at the farm, which are compiled by the Bureau of Agricultural Economics. In Table 12 are given rates of change in these indexes, together with rates relating to raw and processed products of American farms at wholesale, and rates of change in the prices of commodities purchased by farmers.

TABLE 12.—PRICE TENDENCIES AMONG AGRICULTURAL PRODUCTS AND AMONG COMMODITIES PURCHASED BY FARMERS

Commodity group	Number of commodities	Average annual rate of change, 1922–1927
		Per cent
Products of American farms, at wholesale:		
Raw materials...................	58	+1.2
Processed materials...............	143	+0.4
Farm products, prices at the farm.........	30	+1.1
Meat animals....................	5	+6.6
Grains..........................	6	+4.3
Fruits and vegetables.............	8	+4.0
Dairy and poultry products..........	4	+0.2
Unclassified commodities...........	5	−3.7
Cotton and cottonseed.............	2	−7.5
Commodities purchased by farmers:		
For use in production..............	...	+0.6
For family maintenance............	...	+0.3

The chief gain in the prices, at wholesale, of farm products, has been recorded by raw materials. Prices at the farm, as averaged for all farm products, have gained at a rate of 1.1 per cent a year. This average conceals important differences between groups. Substantial gains have been made by meat animals, grains, fruits, and vegetables. Dairy and poultry products have just held their own, while the unclassified commodities (which include horses, hay, flaxseed, wool, and tobacco) and cotton and cottonseed have declined materially. The agricultural improvement which is shown by these figures has been spotty. A survey of the figures for individual commodities, which are given in Table 2 of Appendix B, reveals similar differences between the rates at which the prices of individual commodities have changed.

Table 13, relating to various subdivisions of raw and processed materials, sheds further light on the price changes which have occurred in recent years.

[27] The "all commodities" index, constructed in the same way as the index numbers in Table 11, shows a gain at the rate of 0.08 per cent a year between 1922 and 1927.

TABLE 13.—PRICE TENDENCIES, RAW AND PROCESSED MATERIALS

Commodity group	Number of commodities	Average annual rate of change, 1922-1927
		Per cent
Raw materials..........................	106	+1.4
Commodities not products of American farms.............................	48	+1.7
Products of American farms..........	58	+1.2
Foods...............................	53	+3.0
Nonfoods...........................	53	−0.1
Consumers' goods...................	22	+2.3
Producers' goods...................	84	+1.3
Processed materials.....................	298	−0.4
Products of American farms.........	143	+0.4
Commodities not products of American farms.............................	155	−1.1
Foods...............................	83	+1.4
Nonfoods...........................	215	−1.0
Consumers' goods...................	150	0.0
Producers' goods...................	148	−0.7

The rise in raw material prices has already been commented upon. Among raw materials, foods have gained materially over nonfoods, and consumers' goods have gone up more rapidly than producers' goods. Of the processed materials, foods have risen, while nonfoods have declined, consumers' goods have held steady and producers' goods have declined.[28]

A broader picture of the conflicting movements within the price system is afforded by Table 14, giving the rates of change of the various indexes from which the index of the general price level is constructed by the Federal Reserve Bank of New York.

The movement of the general index has been upward in recent years, as opposed to the slight declining tendency of the index of wholesale prices. Among the various group indexes, security prices have shown a quite phenomenal gain since 1922, the rate far exceeding those at which other elements of the price system have changed. Wages, as measured by the present index, come next, having gained at a rate only slightly below 3 per cent a year. The only material declines are found in transportation costs and the prices of industrial commodities at wholesale. The relation between the movement of wages, industrial commodity prices, and certain other price groups has already been commented upon.

[28] The revised index numbers of the Bureau of Labor Statistics include indexes of the prices of raw materials, semimanufactured articles, and finished products. Average annual rates of change, 1923–1927, have been as follows: Raw materials, +0.5; semimanufactured articles, −1.9; finished products, −0.4.

Raw materials and finished products stand in the same relative position as in Table 13. A considerable decline is shown in the prices of semimanufactured articles.

TABLE 14.—MOVEMENTS OF WAGES, RENTS, AND PRICES[a]

Group	Average annual rate of change, 1922–1927
	Per cent
Security prices	+9.1
Wages	+2.8
Food prices, retail	+2.4
Equipment and machinery	+1.3
Prices at the farm	+1.1
Automobile prices	+0.9
Hardware prices, wholesale	+0.3
Rents	0.0
Realty values	−0.1
Cost of living items, other than food and rents	−0.3
Transportation costs	−1.5
Industrial commodity prices, at wholesale	−1.8
Total (index of general price level)	+1.5

[a] Following are descriptions of the items entering into the general index:

Security Prices.—Preferred stock (weight 1); common stock (weight 4); inverted yield on 60 high-grade bonds (weight 5). Federal Reserve Bank of New York, from data of Standard Statistics Co.

Wages, Composite.—Based on agricultural wages (rate), weight 5; railroad wages (earnings), weight 10; teachers' salaries (rate), weight 5; factory wages (earnings), weight 40; building wages (rate), weight 15; clerical wages (earnings), weight 15; unskilled labor wages (rate), weight 10. Federal Reserve Bank of New York.

Retail Food Prices.—43 articles of food in 51 cities, United States Department of Labor.

Equipment and Machinery.—Federal Reserve Bank of New York.

Farm Prices at the Farm.—Farm prices of 30 commodities, United States Department of Agriculture.

Automobile Prices.—Weighted price index of six makes of passenger cars. Data from Raymond B. Prescott.

Wholesale Hardware Prices.—Index of National Retail Hardware Association.

Rents.—Cost of housing in 32 cities, United States Department of Labor (monthly changes interpolated arithmetically).

Realty Values.—Urban, Federal Reserve Bank of New York (weight 4). Farm, estimated value per acre, United States Department of Agriculture (weight 1).

Other Cost of Living Items.—Cost in 32 cities of clothing (weight 4), fuel and light (weight 1), house furnishing goods (weight 1), and miscellaneous (weight 4). United States Department of Labor (monthly changes interpolated arithmetically).

Transportation Costs.—Federal Reserve Bank of New York. Railway Freight Receipts per ton-mile, United States Interstate Commerce Commission (1913–1919, inclusive monthly average only, and current data from United States Department of Commerce, "Survey of Current Business").

Industrial Commodity Prices, at Wholesale.—*Nonagricultural Prices*, United States Department of Labor.

Finally, we may summarize certain figures, comparable to those given in Table 8 for prewar years, relating to living costs and the earnings of labor.

It is noteworthy that the average annual rates of increase in earnings, as shown by these various indexes, fall very close to the rates at which money earnings were increasing during the two decades preceding the war. (See Table 8.) The great difference between prewar and postwar conditions, in respect to the present set of measures, is owing to the difference between the trends of living costs in prewar and in postwar days. The rise in living costs between 1896 and 1913 accounted for substantially all of the increase in the earnings of factory labor, and left only a small margin of gain for all groups of employees. But in postwar years living costs have increased at a rate of less than 1 per cent a year, while money earnings (except for women employees in manufacturing

TABLE 15.—POSTWAR TENDENCIES, COST OF LIVING, AND THE EARNINGS OF LABOR

Index[a]	Average annual rate of change, 1922–1927
	Per cent
Cost of living....................................	+0.7
Wages (general).................................	+2.8
Per capita earnings of factory labor................	+2.4
Earnings of factory labor, New York State..........	+2.8
Earnings of factory labor, Massachussetts...........	+2.4
Earnings of factory labor, total, 23 industries[b].......	+2.0
Men..	+2.6
Unskilled...............................	+3.0
Skilled..................................	+2.2
Women......................................	+1.1

[a] The measures given are based upon the movements of the following indexes and compilations:
Cost of living.—Index of the United States Bureau of Labor Statistics.
Wages (general).—Index of the Federal Reserve Bank of New York. (See footnote to Table 14.)
Per capita earnings of factory labor.—Derived from data on employment and pay rolls, compiled by the United States Bureau of Labor Statistics.
Earnings of factory labor, New York.—Compiled by the New York State Department of Labor.
Earnings of factory labor, Massachusetts.—Compiled by Massachusetts Department of Labor and Industries, Division of Statistics.
Earnings of factory labor, 23 Industries.—Compiled by the National Industrial Conference Board.
[b] The data upon which these rates are based cover the period July, 1922—December, 1927.

plants) have gone up at rates varying from 2 to 3 per cent. The gain in well-being is measured, of course, by the margin between the two. Accepting the measures in the above table as accurate, they show a gain in the purchasing power of wages in general at a rate of 2.1 per cent a year, between 1922 and 1927. For factory employees, the purchasing power of per capita earnings has gone up at a rate of 1.7 per cent.[29] These are materially greater than the corresponding values of 0.5 and 0.1, for prewar years.

The figures in the various tables above give some indication of the nature of the forces which have been in operation in the United States in recent years. For a more complete picture, the measures relating to price movements should be supplemented by corresponding measures relating to the production and distribution of goods, and certain measures of this type will be given in the next section. Some of the conclusions suggested by a survey of the price figures are summarized below:

1. During the period 1922–1927, the general level of wholesale prices showed a slight declining tendency, but there were pronounced differences among commodity groups in the direction and degree of price change.

[29] These rates relate to the actual earnings of employed workers. They should be read with reference to the unemployment figures cited in Chapter VI, pp. 462–478.

2. The prices of building materials, textiles, house furnishings, metal products, and fuels declined substantially.

3. Raw materials rose in price, while processed materials declined; foods gained, while nonfoods declined; consumers' goods advanced slightly while producers' goods remained substantially at a level. The small group of products of exclusively foreign origin rose materially in price, while products of exclusively domestic origin declined.

4. Cultivated products advanced in price; noncultivated, or industrial, products declined. In the general advance of cultivated products, the products of American farms shared. The advance in the prices of cultivated products was greater for raw materials than for fabricated goods made from such materials.

5. Prices of farm products at the farm advanced at a rate slightly exceeding 1 per cent a year. There were, however, great inequalities in the movements of different types of farm products. Meat animals, grains, and fruits and vegetables scored the greatest advances, gaining at rates varying from 4 per cent to more than 6 per cent a year. Cotton and cottonseed declined at a rate of 7.5 per cent a year.

6. When other price fields are included in this survey, still more pronounced differences are found. Security prices have leaped upward at an average rate of 9 per cent a year.[30] Important declines were registered in transportation costs, and cost of living items, other than food, fell somewhat.

7. The rate of gain in money wages in postwar years has been very close to that which prevailed during the two decades before the war. The advance in the earnings of factory labor has been at a rate of from 2 to 2.5 per cent a year; the advance in general wages has been slightly above this figure. The postwar gain in the purchasing power of labor has been at an appreciably higher rate than it was between 1896 and 1913, for living costs have gone up since 1922 at a rate much lower than that measuring the change in earnings. The purchasing power of earnings in recent years appears to have increased at a rate slightly below 2 per cent a year.

IV. POSTWAR TENDENCIES IN AMERICAN BUSINESS

It is an incomplete view of economic developments which takes account only of movements in the field of prices. In the tables which follow, are shown a number of measures defining postwar economic movements over a much broader field. Space limitations make it necessary to leave

---

[30] This figure serves to emphasize the need of caution in speaking of these postwar movements as "trends." They are not trends in the accepted sense of that word, for the period covers but six years. The measures given are significant as indexes of tendencies which have been operating during this six-year period, but not as measures of trends.

almost entirely to the tables the task of telling the story of recent economic tendencies. Considerable information may be gleaned from a detailed study of these tables, and of additional tables given in the Appendix.

The first table deals with general tendencies in the field of production.

TABLE 16.—INDEXES OF PRODUCTION

Index[a]	Average annual rate of change, 1922–1927
	Per cent
Production of raw materials	+ 2.5
Minerals (9 commodities)	+ 5.7
Crop marketings[b] (26 commodities)	+ 2.4
Animal products, marketings[b] (9 commodities)	+ 1.1
Forest products (13 commodities)	+ 0.6
Production of manufactured goods	+ 4.0
Chemicals, oils, etc	+ 9.9
Miscellaneous	+ 6.3
Stone and clay products	+ 5.6
Tobacco	+ 5.1
Metals, excepting iron and steel	+ 4.0
Iron and steel	+ 3.6
Lumber	+ 2.3
Foodstuffs	+ 2.0
Paper and printing	+ 1.5
Textiles	+ 0.8
Leather	− 1.1
Supplementary indexes:	
Petroleum refining	+12.6
Electric power production	+10.5
Rubber tires	+ 9.8
Automobiles	+ 4.2

[a] The indexes, with the exception of the last four, are those of the Department of Commerce. Descriptions and current values of these indexes are to be found in the *Survey of Current Business.* Three of the supplementary indexes are taken from those constructed by the Federal Reserve Board, appearing currently in the *Federal Reserve Bulletin.*

[b] The measures relating to crop marketings and the marketings of animal products are here employed as indexes of production, although they deal with the distribution, rather than the production, of goods.

Measures of change in the constituent series, from which the above indexes are derived, together with measures for certain additional production series, will be found in Table 3, in Appendix B.

The differences among the rates of change of the various production groups are greater, for the list as a whole, than the differences found in the study of price groups.

Table 17 shows the changes occurring during the last six years in the transportation and distribution of goods, and in series directly related to commercial transactions.[31]

[31] Additional measures relating to the movements of goods are given in Table 4, Appendix B.

TABLE 17.—THE DISTRIBUTION OF GOODS

Series	Average annual rate of change, 1922–1927
	Per cent
General indexes:	
Check payments outside New York City[a]	+ 7.0
Ton-miles of freight carried	+ 4.0
Freight car loadings	+ 3.2
Agricultural movements[b]	+ 1.5
Sales, wholesale[a,b]	+ 0.7
Freight car loadings:	
Miscellaneous	+ 4.9
Coal and coke	+ 3.5
Merchandise and l.c.l	+ 2.6
Ore	+ 1.9
Forest products	+ 1.9
Grain and grain products	− 0.4
Livestock	− 1.8
Crops, marketings:[c]	
Cotton products	+ 9.2
Fruits	+ 2.8
Vegetables	+ 1.5
Grains	− 2.6
Wholesale distribution—sales in wholesale establishments:[a,d]	
Meat	+ 5.9
Drugs	+ 4.1
Furniture	+ 2.6
Men's clothing	+ 2.2
Hardware	+ 1.3
Boots and shoes	+ 0.7
Groceries	− 0.1
Dry goods	− 0.7
Women's clothing	− 7.4
Jobbers' sales of iron, steel and other heavy hardware[e]	+ 7.4
Retail distribution:[a,f]	
Mail order house sales (4 houses)	+ 9.2
Ten-cent chain store sales (4 chains, average per store)	+ 4.5
Department store sales (359 stores)	+ 3.9
Chain store sales (number of chains constant, but number of stores not constant)—	
Groceries (27 chains)	+20.6
Five and ten (5 chains)	+12.0
Drug (9 chains)	+11.7
Candy (5 chains)	+ 8.0
Shoe (6 chains)	+ 5.7
Cigar (3 chains)	+ 3.9
Music (4 chains)	+ 2.9
Imports[a]	+ 6.0
Foodstuffs, crude, and food animals	+10.0
Crude materials	+ 7.9
Semimanufactures	+ 5.6
Finished manufactures	+ 5.3
Manufactured foodstuffs	− 0.7
Exports[a]	+ 4.7
Finished manufactures	+ 9.1
Semimanufactures	+ 8.1
Crude materials	+ 3.1
Foodstuffs, crude, and food animals	− 0.2
Manufactured foodstuffs	− 4.4

[a] Dollar value series.
[b] Indexes of the Federal Reserve Board.
[c] Indexes of the Department of Commerce.
[d] The indexes, as compiled by the Federal Reserve Board, are based upon sales in wholesale establishments, as follows: Meat—61 firms in 51 cities; drugs—92 firms in 60 cities; furniture—87 firms in 36 cities; men's clothing—13 firms in 5 cities; hardware—186 firms in 114 cities; boots and shoes—89 firms in 52 cities; groceries—362 firms in 213 cities; dry goods—146 firms in 84 cities; women's clothing—40 firms in 1 city.
[e] Based upon data compiled by the American Iron, Steel, and Heavy Hardware Association. The index is published in the *Survey of Current Business.*
[f] Indexes compiled by the Federal Reserve Board.

The different index numbers from which the above measures have been derived represent their fields with varying degrees of accuracy.

Some are based upon exhaustive data, some upon samples of questionable adequacy. Accordingly, the different measures brought together in Table 17, and in other tables of the present section, must be compared with caution.

With few exceptions, the measures indicate that goods have been moving from producer to consumer in a steadily growing volume. However, the measures relating to retail distribution do not necessarily indicate an increasing volume of total retail sales. In considerable part, they reflect the shifts in channels of retail distribution characteristic of recent years. This is particularly true of the chain store sales, where the number of stores is not constant. The figures indicate how rapid the increase in volume of business has been for certain of the chain stores. The sales (dollar value) of 27 grocery chains, for example, have increased during the period 1922–1927 at an average annual rate slightly in excess of 20 per cent.

TABLE 18.—COMMODITY STOCKS AND UNFILLED ORDERS

Series	Average annual rate of change, 1922–1927
	Per cent
Commodity stocks, all commodities[a]	+ 5.4
Raw materials, total	+ 5.9
Textiles	+ 7.0
Foodstuffs	+ 6.6
Chemicals and oils	+ 4.3
Metals	− 4.1
Manufactured goods, total	+ 4.6
Rubber	+13.8
Stone, clay, and glass	+13.6
Iron and steel	+ 9.2
Lumber	+ 5.8
Chemicals and oils	+ 5.8
Nonferrous metals	+ 3.3
Textiles	+ 1.0
Foodstuffs	+ 0.8
Paper	− 1.1
Leather	−10.1
Unfilled orders, all groups[b]	− 7.9
Lumber	− 3.1
Brick and glass	− 3.1
Textiles	− 4.7
Vehicles	− 8.5
Iron and steel	− 9.4

[a] Weighted indexes of stocks of commodities held at the end of each month, as compiled by the Bureau of the Census from data on 65 commodities. The indexes are published in the *Survey of Current Business*. Measures relating to the stocks of a number of individual commodities are given in Table 5, Appendix B.

[b] Compiled by the Bureau of the Census from data on 17 commodities, weighted. In addition to the groups named, data are also included in the total for one class of paper. The indexes are published in the *Survey of Current Business*.

The measures showing the changes in the volume and character of our foreign trade indicate that imports have been growing at a somewhat more rapid rate than exports, and that our exports of manufactured articles, other than foodstuffs, have been expanding rapidly. The only decline among the broad import groups here shown is found among manufactured foodstuffs.

Because of recent shifts in marketing methods, considerable interest attaches to changes in the volume of unfilled orders and in commodity stocks. Measures relating to these series appear in Table 18. It should be noted that the data on commodity stocks do not relate to mercantile stocks, but, primarily, to stocks in the hands of producers and manufacturers.

In spite of the emphasis upon hand-to-mouth buying, stocks of both raw materials and manufactured goods have increased steadily in recent years. The only three groups to show declines are raw metals, leather, and paper (in the case of the latter group, the decline occurred in wood

TABLE 19.—BUILDING ACTIVITY AND BUILDING COSTS

Series	Average annual rate of change, 1922–1927
	Per cent
Construction volume (actual installations)[a]	+6.2
Contracts awarded for building construction[b]	+5.7
Residential buildings	+7.4
Public and semipublic buildings	+7.2
Commercial buildings	+5.4
Industrial buildings	−0.5
Educational buildings	−4.2
Building costs:	
Building material prices[c].—	
Frame buildings	−0.2
Brick buildings	−0.5
Construction costs (including labor costs)—	
Index of Engineering News Record[d]	+1.8
Index of Associated General Contractors of America[e]	+0.9
Factory building costs, Aberthaw index	+1.4
Indexes of the American Appraisal Co.—	
Brick building, wood frame	+0.9
Frame building	+0.8
Reinforced concrete building	+0.4
Brick building, steel frame	+0.2

[a] From index compiled by the Associated General Contractors of America.

[b] From the data compiled by the F. W. Dodge Corporation. The original data are in thousands of square feet.

[c] Measures based upon price compilations by the Bureau of Standards. For detailed explanation, see *Survey of Current Business.*

[d] Index based upon the costs of steel, cement, and lumber, and the wages of common labor in a number of cities.

[e] An index combining wage and material costs, in the proportion of 40 per cent for wages and 60 per cent for materials.

pulp). It is possible that there have been changes since prewar days in the agencies holding the stocks, but there is no general tendency for the total volume of commodity stocks to decline.

In contrast to the increase in stocks is the pronounced decline in unfilled orders, a decline to which there is no exception among the major groups listed above. This decline is the more notable in that it has occurred during a period when the volume of production and the volume of trade have been increasing steadily.

The volume of building, which is measured in Table 19, increased at an average annual rate of about 6 per cent between 1922 and 1927, a figure materially higher than the 2.5 and 4.0 which measure, respectively, the rates of increase in primary production and in the production of manufactured goods during the same period. This increase has been owing entirely to marked increases in the volume of residential, public, and commercial building. The volume of industrial and educational building has declined. This increase in the volume of building has been accompanied by declining prices of building materials, but general construction costs, which include labor costs, have gone up slightly during this period.[32]

The measures in Table 20 relate to another and highly important aspect of the postwar economic scene.

TABLE 20.—EMPLOYMENT, PAY ROLLS, AND PER CAPITA EARNINGS IN MANUFACTURING INDUSTRIES[a]

Industrial group	Average annual rate of change, 1922–1927		
	Employment	Pay rolls	Per capita earnings
	Per cent	*Per cent*	*Per cent*
Lumber and its products	−2.8	+0.2	+3.1
Stone, clay, and glass products	−0.3	+2.7	+3.0
Iron and steel and their products	−0.6	+2.1	+2.6
Miscellaneous industries	+0.8	+3.5	+2.6
Paper and printing	+1.6	+3.9	+2.3
Food and kindred products	−1.4	+0.8	+2.2
Chemicals and allied products	+0.3	+1.9	+1.6
Vehicles for land transportation	−0.9	+0.6	+1.5
Textiles and their products	−2.6	−1.4	+1.2
Tobacco products	−4.7	−4.5	+0.2
Metal products other than iron and steel	−1.5	−1.3	+0.2
Leather and its products	−2.3	−2.6	−0.3
All industries	−0.7	+1.7	+2.4

[a] The data from which these rates have been computed were compiled by the United States Bureau of Labor Statistics. The rates of change in employment and pay rolls were derived from the data as compiled; the rates of change in per capita earnings were computed from the employment and pay roll figures. The data cover the period July, 1922–December, 1927.

[32] See Chap. III, Construction.

The measures for "all industries" bring out certain important characteristics of the postwar period. There has been a slight but significant decline in the volume of employment in manufacturing industries in the United States, accompanied by a material increase in pay rolls and a somewhat greater increase in the per capita earnings of factory employees. In interpreting these figures, it must be remembered that during this period there has been an increase in per capita production in manufacturing industries at a rate not far below 4 per cent a year. And these movements have accompanied a steady decline in the prices of industrial commodities.

In nine of the twelve major industrial groups there has been a decline in the volume of employment; in four of the twelve there has been a decline in pay rolls; and in only one of the twelve has there been a decline in the per capita earnings of employees. A more detailed view of these tendencies is given by Table 6, Appendix B, where there appear figures for the 54 industries from which the group totals have been secured.[33] Employment has declined in 37 of these 54 industries, pay rolls have declined in 26, and per capita earnings have declined in only six industries.

In these conflicting movements is found a partial explanation of the industrial distress which has been felt in some industries and among some groups of workers, although general wages and production have been steadily increasing. The decline in employment in 37 of the 54 industries is an obvious cause of such distress. Important, too, is the fact that actual wage disbursements have declined in almost half the industries (in 26 of the 54). It is true that the total volume of wage disbursements has gone up, but it is the changes in employment and in wage payments in specific industries which affect individual workers.[34]

Changes in corporation profits during the postwar period under review are shown in Table 21.

An important qualification to be borne in mind in interpreting the figures in Table 21, and, particularly, in comparing them with the measures given in other tables, is that the profits figures relate only to the years 1923–1927. Data precisely corresponding to those here employed were not available for 1922. It is probable that, for most of the groups represented in the above table, the rates of change would be somewhat greater if 1922 had been included, for general profits in that year were not as high as in the following years. Again, it is to be noted that the

---

[33] The data for certain industries do not cover the entire period, and figures for these industries, accordingly, are not fully comparable with the measures for the other industries.

[34] There is reason to suspect a downward bias in the factory employment and factory pay roll compilations from which the above measures have been divided. Since each comparison of employment or of pay roll disbursements at different dates relates to identical establishments, figures relating to new plants are excluded.

rates of change are based upon the aggregate profits in each of the groups. In the computing of such aggregates, large corporations dwarf the smaller ones. For certain purposes it is desirable that aggregate figures should be used and that the large corporations should be given predominant weight. If the data permitted, it would be well to supplement these figures with others, in which changes in the profits of smaller corporations could be followed.

TABLE 21.—CORPORATION PROFITS[a]

Industrial group	Number of corporations	Average annual rate of change, 1923–1927
		Per cent
Public utilities	129	+14.7
Public utilities other than telephone	51	+15.0
Telephone companies	[b]78	+14.2
Industrial and miscellaneous corporations	381	+ 9.0
Leather and shoes	9	+28.8
Motors	22	+22.5
Amusement	6	+18.2
Miscellaneous industries	58	+15.0
Machine and machine manufacturing	18	+14.9
Metals and mining	19	+13.9
Stores	19	+12.4
Chemicals and drugs	14	+12.3
Rubber	11	+11.3
Tobacco	16	+ 9.2
Oils	31	+ 6.7
Food and food products	39	+ 4.7
Steel companies	26	+ 0.4
Motor accessories	18	− 1.0
Building supplies	19	− 2.2
Paper	9	− 4.4
Railroad equipment	12	− 6.1
Clothing and textiles	24	−10.5
Coal	11	−48.6
Class I railroads	[b]183	+ 4.2

[a] The data from which these rates have been computed were compiled by the Federal Reserve Bank of New York.

[b] The number of telephone companies and the number of railroads represented vary somewhat as a result of consolidations.

Taken as they stand, these figures reveal an extraordinary increase in the profits of certain corporate groups. Profits of public utilities have grown at a rate of 14.7 per cent a year; for nine of the nineteen industrial and miscellaneous corporations, the rate of increase has exceeded 10 per cent a year. Six corporate groups have shown declining profits, the most severe losses having occurred in the clothing and textile and coal industries.

The tendencies in respect to profits which are shown in this table are in part explained by a comparison of the rates of change in prices, production, and other economic series which were given in earlier tables.[35] Some of the difficulties in the way of such comparison have already been suggested. To these may be added the final point that the figures for prices, production, stocks, profits, etc., are representative in varying degrees of the industries to which they relate. In spite of these limitations, the comparison is instructive.

Supplementary to the data on profits are measures of changes in the volume of disbursements by corporations, in the form of dividend and interest payments.

TABLE 22.—DIVIDEND AND INTEREST PAYMENTS[a]

Series	Average annual rate of change, 1922–1927
	Per cent
Total dividend and interest payments	+ 7.0
Total dividend payments	+ 6.7
Street railways	+12.5
Industrial and miscellaneous corporations	+ 6.8
Steam railroads	+ 4.5

[a] The measures in this table are derived from data compiled by the *New York Journal of Commerce.*

These payments have increased, as is to be expected, at rates somewhat lower than aggregate corporate profits. Yet the rates of growth in disbursements to bond and stockholders during this period of industrial recovery and business prosperity have been rapid.

One other aspect of the economic situation in recent years is revealed by measures relating to bankruptcies among business concerns.

TABLE 23.—BUSINESS FAILURES, COMMERCIAL ENTERPRISES[a]

Series	Average annual rate of change, 1922–1927	Series	Average annual rate of change, 1922–1927
	Per cent		Per cent
Number of business failures	+0.9	Liabilities of business failures	−5.5
Agents and brokers	+8.0	Trade establishments	−2.9
Manufacturing establishments	+0.7	Manufacturing establishments	−6.4
Trade establishments	+0.6	Agents and brokers	−8.4

[a] Measures derived from data compiled by *Dun's Review.*

[35] The highest of these figures, that for corporations engaged in the production of leather and shoes, is rather difficult to explain, in view of the tendencies in production and prices in this industry. In part, the increase is owing to the fact that 1923 was a year of very low profits for this group of corporations. The profit figures cover only 9 corporations, it may be noted, and are probably not representative of the industry as a whole.

In the difference between the tendencies measured above in regard to the *number* of business failures and the *liabilities* of business failures is found a key to one important aspect of the postwar economic situation which has not been brought out by the measures in earlier tables. In this period of expanding production and rising profits, the number of business failures has increased about 1 per cent a year, yet the liabilities of business failures have declined at a rate in excess of 5 per cent a year.[36]

TABLE 24.—INTEREST RATES, STOCK AND BOND PRICES, AND RELATED SERIES

Series	Average annual rate of change, 1922–1927
	Per cent
Bond prices and interest rates:	
Combined index of 40 bond prices[a]	+ 2.9
Interest rates on commercial paper[b]	− 2.3
Volume of sales:	
New York Stock Exchange sales—	
Stocks[c]	+20.5
Bonds[d]	− 1.1
Check payments in New York City[d,e]	+11.3
Stock prices:[d,f]	
Total stocks (229)	+13.4
Railroad stocks (31)	+11.3
Industrial stocks (198)	+14.1
Automobile stocks (10)	+42.5
Chain store stocks (11)	+30.7
Food stocks (9)	+20.8
Theater stocks (3)	+19.2
Utilities stocks (16)	+16.8
Tobacco stocks (7)	+14.9
Railroad equipment stocks (10)	+12.0
Steel stocks (9)	+ 8.9
Machinery stocks (5)	+ 8.3
Copper stocks (11)	+ 7.3
Rubber stocks (7)	+ 2.4
Petroleum stocks (17)	+ 1.5
Textile stocks (5)	− 14.4

[a] Quoted as per cent of par value of 4 per cent bond. Index compiled by Dow, Jones & Co., from the yields of the average prices of the bonds for each day of the month. Average yields of component classes capitalized at 4 per cent to give the combined index.

[b] Interest rates on 4 to 6 months paper. Data are averages of weekly ranges in the New York market as published by the *Commercial and Financial Chronicle*.

[c] Data refer to number of shares.

[d] Dollar value series.

[e] Check payments are represented by debits to individual accounts as compiled by the Federal Reserve Board.

[f] Compiled by the Standard Statistics Co. Indexes are of common stock market values, weighted by the number of shares of each stock outstanding. The monthly figures are averages of weekly closing prices or last previous sale prices.

[36] Business failures during 1922 reflected, in part, the effects of the preceding business recession. For the period 1923–1927, the rates of change were: number of business failures, +4.9; liabilities of business failures, −3.4. These are probably better indexes of recent tendencies than are the measures which include 1922.

The failures of large concerns, that is, have decreased materially, but for the rank and file of business it would appear the stress of competition has not relaxed. These conditions stand in sharp contrast to those prevailing during the period of war-time prosperity. Between 1915 and 1919, both the liabilities and the number of business failures declined materially, the former by 63 per cent, the latter by 71 per cent.

A final set of measures, in Table 24, depicts certain financial movements, and reflects tendencies peculiarly characteristic of the period.

The decline in interest rates, the corresponding rise in bond prices, the great increase in speculative activity and the extraordinary advance in stock prices—these have been outstanding features of the period since 1922. They are summarized, and the several movements are given definite measures, in the preceding table, to facilitate comparison with the economic series already presented. As in treating many of the other sets of figures given in this survey, comparisons must be made with caution, for precisely the same corporate groups are not represented in the tables relating to employment, production, profits, and stock prices.

V. COMPARISON OF ECONOMIC TENDENCIES, 1902-1907, 1922-1927

Some interest attaches to a comparison, with respect to prevailing economic tendencies, of two periods which happen to be just 20 years removed—the periods from 1902 to 1907 and from 1922 to 1927. Each of these six-year periods was a time of rapid industrial growth. In these periods the physical volume of production and trade was expanding at rates which were exceptionally high. Yet in other respects there were fundamental differences between the economic conditions prevailing during these periods. That which gives chief interest to the comparison is the fact that the expansion of 1902–1907 ended in a major industrial collapse, while the growth of 1922–1927 appears to have been a sounder and more normal development. Certain of the resemblances and differences are revealed in Table 25.

Although the eighteen series listed therein are not in all respects comparable, they furnish the material for a general comparison. The increase in the physical volume of production, which was an outstanding characteristic of each of these periods, is clearly revealed. The rate of increase in agricultural production was slightly higher in the recent period (an advantage owing primarily to the pronounced rise in cotton production), but in the production of raw materials and of manufactured goods the earlier period shows distinctly higher rates of increase. This is true, also, in respect to each of the individual commodities listed, with the single exception of copper. The rates of increase in the production of cement, petroleum, anthracite and bituminous coal, pig iron, and coke ranged from 8 to 24 per cent a year during the period of remarkable industrial growth between 1902 and 1907. Check transactions outside

TABLE 25.—ECONOMIC MOVEMENTS IN THE UNITED STATES, 1902–1907, 1922–1927

Series[a]	Average annual rate of change	
	1902–1907	1922–1927
	Per cent	*Per cent*
Indexes of production:		
Agricultural products (crops)	+ 1.4	+1.8
Mineral products, raw	+ 8.8	+5.7
Manufactured products	+ 5.8	+4.0
Production of individual commodities:		
Raw and semiprocessed materials—		
Crude petroleum	+12.0	+7.4
Pig iron	+ 9.7	+4.1
Anthracite coal	+ 9.2	+3.3
Bituminous coal	+ 8.5	+3.5
Copper	+ 6.5	+8.4
Processed materials—		
Portland cement	+23.9	+7.5
Coke	+11.8	+4.5
Check transactions outside New York	+ 7.5	+7.0
Business failures:		
Number of concerns failing	− 1.1	+0.9
Liabilities of concerns failing	+ 5.2	−5.5
Earnings of labor and living costs:		
Cost of living	+ 2.1	+0.7
Money earnings, manufacturing industries	+ 1.9	+2.4
Money earnings, all groups	+ 2.4	+2.8
Purchasing power of earnings, manufacturing industries	− 0.2	+1.7
Purchasing power of earnings, all groups	+ 0.3	+2.1

[a] The series from which the rates of change between 1922 and 1927 are derived are those cited in the general tables appearing elsewhere in this chapter.

In computing rates of change between 1902 and 1907, use has been made of the following series: Indexes of the physical volume of production compiled by Edmund E. Day, *Review of Economic Statistics,* September, 1920, January, 1921; bank clearings outside New York; wages and cost of living indexes of Paul H. Douglas.

New York, which furnish a fairly accurate index of the volume of commercial transactions, were rising at practically the same rate during the two periods here considered—a rate of about 7 per cent a year.

The last two sets of items in the table present sharp contrasts. In the earlier period, the number of business failures showed a net decline, at an average annual rate of 1.1 per cent.[37] The liabilities of business failures increased between 1902 and 1907, however, at a rate slightly in excess of 5 per cent a year. In the period preceding the recession of 1908, the figures indicate that the mortality of smaller concerns was declining, while that of larger concerns was rising. Each of these figures is reversed in the recent period. The number of concerns failing increased

[37] There was, of course, a great increase in the number of failures in 1908, a year not included in deriving the above figure.

at a rate of almost 1 per cent a year between 1922 and 1927, while the liabilities of bankrupt enterprises declined at an average rate in excess of 5 per cent a year. It would appear that the recent period was one marked by fairly severe competition, with increasing failures among smaller concerns, while the larger enterprises secured the lion's share of the profits and showed a corresponding decline in business mortality.

More significant are the figures relating to the earnings of labor and living costs. In the recent period, as we have seen, living costs were rising slightly, money wages were increasing much more rapidly, and there was a net gain in the purchasing power of wages at a rate of about 2 per cent a year for all wage-earning groups, and at a rate of 1.7 per cent a year for labor in manufacturing industries. During the years from 1902 to 1907, the cost of living (Douglas's index) rose at a rate of 2.1 per cent a year, while the money earnings of all groups of wage workers rose at a rate of about 2.4 per cent a year and the money earnings of workers in manufacturing industries rose at a rate of about 1.9 per cent a year.

TABLE 26.—PRICE TENDENCIES IN THE UNITED STATES, 1902–1907, 1922–1927

Commodity group	Average annual rate of change	
	1902–1907	1922–1927
	Per cent	*Per cent*
All commodities	+2.5	−0.1
Cultivated commodities and their products	+2.5	+1.0
Noncultivated products	+2.6	−1.1
Cultivated commodities and their products, excluding rubber, processed textiles, leather and shoes	+1.2	+1.8
All other commodities (*i.e.*, all industrial goods)	+3.2	−0.9
Products of American farms in raw state	+1.0	+1.2
Raw materials	+1.8	+1.4
Processed materials	+2.7	−0.4
Consumers' goods	+2.4	+0.3
Raw	+0.3	+2.3
Processed	+2.7	+0.0
Producers' goods	+2.6	+0.0
Raw	+2.3	+1.3
Processed	+2.8	−0.7
Foods	+1.2	+2.0
Nonfoods	+3.1	−0.9
Building materials	+4.9	−1.2
Clothing	+4.6	−1.8
Metals and metal products	+4.4	−1.5
House furnishings	+1.7	−2.6
Foods	+1.3	+1.8
Farm products	+1.2	+1.4
Fuels	−0.8	−4.4
Chemicals and drugs	−2.2	−0.2

The purchasing power of earnings for all groups of workers showed a slight increase, while the purchasing power of the earnings of manufacturing labor declined at a rate of about two-tenths of 1 per cent a year during that period of general industrial prosperity.

Here, perhaps, is the most striking difference between the period which culminated in the great recession of 1908 and the period extending from 1922 to 1927. In the earlier period, general wages barely kept pace with living costs, while the earnings of factory workers actually fell behind living costs. The purchasing power of employed workers in this large group of consumers was being impaired, while the volume of production was increasing at a rate without precedent in recent times.[38] In the period following 1922, the volume of production increased, but at a somewhat lower rate than that prevailing between 1902 and 1907, and the purchasing power of the earnings of labor has continued to advance at a rate of from 1.5 to 2 per cent a year.[39]

The comparison of the two periods may be extended to include tendencies prevailing within the field of prices. Rates of change in wholesale prices for a number of commodity groups are shown in Table 26.

---

[38] It is important to note that Douglas's index, from which the rate of change in earnings for the period 1902–1907 has been computed, is based upon the earnings of *employed workers*. Prof. Paul F. Brissenden has constructed an index of the incomes of manufacturing labor, in which account is taken of changes in the volume of employment. Brissenden's index shows that the purchasing power of the incomes of manufacturing labor increased at an average annual rate of 1.6 per cent between 1902 and 1907. The volume of employment was, of course, increasing during this period, and it is this fact which accounts for the difference between the rates of change of Douglas's and Brissenden's index numbers.

[39] A revealing comparison of the two periods is afforded by certain data given in Dr. Wolman's chapter on Labor. The following rates of change have been computed from his figures.

	Average annual rate of increase	
	1902–1907	1922–1927
	Per cent	*Per cent*
Persons engaged in manufacturing industries......	+3.7	+0.9
Volume of manufacturing production............	+5.7	+4.3
Output per person............................	+2.0	+3.5

During the earlier period there was a much greater increase in the number of employed workers and a somewhat higher rate of increase in volume of production, but the increase in output per person was much lower than it was between 1922 and 1927.

The rates of change given above are not based upon the same original sources as were those cited in earlier pages. This accounts for the slight differences between the rates quoted.

The general resemblances between the two periods, which were found when quantity series were compared, is not found when attention is turned to price movements. The drift of the general price level was slightly downward between 1922 and 1927; the movement was upward at a relatively rapid rate between 1902 and 1907. But the differences go much deeper. Within each of the twofold classifications set up above, the relative movements between 1902 and 1907 are exactly the reverse of those prevailing between 1922 and 1927. In the earlier period, non-cultivated products rose in price at a slightly higher rate than cultivated commodities and their products (this group includes all products of cultivation, animal and vegetable); in the period beginning in 1922, noncultivated products declined and products of cultivation rose in price. The contrast is the sharper, if we exclude from cultivated com-modities and their products, rubber, processed textiles, leather, and shoes, placing these commodities with noncultivated products in a general group which may be designated *industrial goods*. Between 1902 and 1907, these industrial goods rose at a rate of 3.2 per cent a year, as com-pared with 1.2 per cent for the restricted group of cultivated commodities. Between 1922 and 1927, the group of industrial goods declined at a rate just short of 1 per cent a year (−0.9), while cultivated commodities and their products (with the exceptions noted) rose at a rate of 1.8 per cent a year. The sharp rise in the volume of industrial production in the early period was accompanied by an almost equally pronounced advance in the prices of industrial products. The increase in production in the later period has been accompanied by declining prices of industrial products. In the first period, products of cultivation lost in relative position; in the second period, they gained materially.

One aspect of this last condition is of considerable importance in relation to the continuation of the state of prosperity. In the earlier period, the general level of wholesale prices (as measured by the index at present under review) was increasing at a rate of 2.5 per cent a year; the prices of products of American farms in raw state (prices which reflect most closely the receipts of agricultural producers) were increasing at a rate of 1 per cent a year. The purchasing power of these products was declining. Between 1922 and 1927, the general price level (wholesale) was declining at a rate of 0.1 per cent a year; the prices of products of American farms in raw state were advancing at an average annual rate of 1.2 per cent a year. It is true that the postwar recession left farmers' purchasing power relatively low, but for this class of producers as a whole purchasing power was increasing steadily between 1922 and 1927.

It is not difficult to find roots of trouble in the situation which was developing between 1902 and 1907. The general purchasing power of agricultural producers, as a class, was being steadily impaired during that six-year period, and the real earnings of employed workers in manufacturing industries were declining.[40]   In the corresponding postwar period, the purchasing power of these two groups was steadily advancing. In this difference is found one explanation of the relative soundness of recent economic growth.

The contrast between the two periods here under review might be elaborated by a discussion of price tendencies among the other groups listed in Table 26, but this comparison must be left to the reader.   The fundamental difference between the periods in respect to price movements is revealed in each of the classifications cited.   The similarity of quantity movements in these periods finds no parallel in the field of prices.   In these differing price tendencies, and in the factors lying back of them, is to be found one key to an explanation of the important economic differences between these periods, one of which ended in economic collapse, the other of which has brought a condition of sustained well-being perhaps never before attained in our economic history.

VI. POSTWAR AND PREWAR PRICE RELATIONS

There is a final question concerning price relations in prewar and postwar years which is not answered by any of the measures discussed above.   This has to do with the relations among the prices of commodities, and of groups of commodities, in postwar years, as compared with the relations prevailing at an earlier date.   When we speak of the "structure of prices," we have in mind a more or less enduring system, in which the prices of individual commodities and of commodity groups stand in fairly well-defined relations to each other.   It is obvious that there can be no such set of relationships in any absolute sense, that is, with reference to absolute prices.   But *relative prices*, measured from a uniform base, may be thought of as constituting a system, and there may be economic significance to such a system.   During a period of fairly regular economic growth, unmarked by such cataclysms as that which occurred between 1914 and 1921, there prevail important differences among the rates at which different commodities and groups of commodities are changing in price.[41]   Certain commodities are declining in price (relatively to the movements of the general price level) because of lowered costs of production, lessened demand, or other causes, and other commodities are rising in price because of changes in extractive or demand conditions.   These sustained and differing drifts of various elements in the price system are affecting economic relations, slowly but appreciably, and it is reasonable to think of the relative prices which reflect these differing movements as constituting a system of prices at a

---

[40] Because of the increase in the volume of manufacturing employment, the purchasing power of manufacturing labor as a group increased during this period.

[41] These movements, and their bearing upon the concept of "normal" price relations among commodities, are discussed in *The Behavior of Prices*, pp. 165–176.

given date. Such a "system" has meaning, of course, only with reference to the particular base from which the relative prices are measured, and its significance is conditioned by the choice of the base period, and by the economic significance of the changes which have occurred between the base year and the year, or years, in which the structure of prices is being studied.

If, now, we wish to study the relation of the postwar structure of prices to the prewar structure, we must define the base with reference to which all price changes are to be studied, and we must bear in mind the meaning which can be given to the "structure of prices." The first problem is that of defining the prewar structure of prices. If we adopt the base common to most index numbers measuring price changes, we might base our relatives on the year 1913, and assume that the ranking of these relatives in the year 1914 served to define a price system typical of prewar conditions. Strong objections may be brought against this procedure. The changes of prices between 1913 and 1914 reflected only in small part enduring changes, resulting from fundamental shifts in economic relations. Such changes from one year to the next are due, primarily, to accidental movements, or to phases of cyclical changes, which have no significance as symptoms of fundamental changes. The system of prices which may be accepted as typical of prewar conditions should represent changes over a longer period. In the present study two different standards have been employed and two sets of measures derived.

In the first of these, the base year used in the derivation of price relatives is 1891. The system taken to be representative of prewar price relations is defined by the ranking of these relatives in the year 1914. By 1914, the relatives on the 1891 base may be assumed to have reached fairly stable positions in relation to each other. The differences among them would reflect, to some extent, temporary dislocations owing to current cyclical and accidental movements, but the chief cause for differences among relatives on a base 23 years distant would be variations in underlying trends. Long-time changes in cost of production, enduring shifts in consumer demand, changes in styles and habits—all these would be reflected in the ranking of relatives on a base so many years removed.

But there are some objections to the use of a distant base, and accordingly a second set of measures has been computed. In this case, relatives on the 1909 base have been used, and a prewar price system has been defined by the ranking of these relatives, as averaged for the four years 1911–1914. This is, perhaps, more truly representative of the conditions prevailing at the close of the prewar epoch than is the system derived from relatives on the earlier base.

Changes in systems of prices as defined above are measured by *indexes of price displacement*.[42] The measure of price displacement (the term here used to define shifts in the relative positions of commodity prices) is one which fluctuates between values of 0 and 2. The value is zero if, between two dates, there has been no shift in the ranking of a set of price relatives. (That is, if the commodity which was lowest relatively, at the first date, is lowest relatively, at the second date, and if all the other commodities stand in precisely the same relative positions at the two dates.) The

[42] The index of price displacement is the value $1 - \rho$ where ρ is the coefficient of rank correlation.

$$\rho = 1 - \frac{6\Sigma d^2}{N(N^2 - 1)}$$

The significance of this index, as employed for the present purpose, is discussed more fully in *The Behavior of Prices*, pp. 286–311.

value of the measure is 1, if there is no correlation whatsoever between the relative positions of the various commodities at the two dates.   In this case, the set of relations prevailing at the first date has been completely shattered by the second date.   A value of 2 for the index of price displacement would indicate an exact reversal of the rankings throughout, the commodity which was lowest, relatively, at the first date being highest at the second date, and all the other commodities having reversed their relative positions in the same way.   Such an exact reversal is not, of course, to be expected when dealing with price relatives.

Annual changes, during the period 1915–1927, in the two systems of prices described above, are measured by the indexes in Table 27.

TABLE 27.—MEASURES OF PRICE DISPLACEMENT, 1915–1927[a]

1	2	3	4
Years compared	Index of displacement computed from relatives, 1891 base	Periods compared	Index of displacement computed from relatives on 1909 base
1915–1914................	.14	1915—av. 1911–1914	.43
1916–1914................	.28	1916—av. 1911–1914	.57
1917–1914................	.42	1917—av. 1911–1914	.79
1918–1914................	.38	1918—av. 1911–1914	.75
1919–1914................	.28	1919—av. 1911–1914	.62
1920–1914................	.44	1920—av. 1911–1914	.76
1921–1914................	.42	1921—av. 1911–1914	.78
1922–1914................	.41	1922—av. 1911–1914	.75
1923–1914................	.47	1923—av. 1911–1914	.78
1924–1914................	.41	1924—av. 1911–1914	.72
1925–1914................	.33	1925—av. 1911–1914	.66
1926–1914................	.31	1926—av. 1911–1914	.64
1927–1914................	.29	1927—av. 1911–1914	.63

[a] The indexes in column 2 were computed from 195 series, except for the years 1925, 1926, and 1927. In these years, 194, 193, and 189 series, respectively, were used.

The indexes in column 4 of this table were computed from 216 price series, except for the years 1925, 1926, and 1927.   In these years, 213, 212 and 208 series, respectively, were used.

As is to be expected, the indexes of displacement computed from relatives on the 1891 base are distinctly lower than those on the 1909 base.   The system of prices defined by the ranking in 1914 of relatives on the 1891 base was much more deeply seated, much more difficult to disrupt, than was the system defined by the ranking of relatives on the much more recent base, 1909.

The changes in the indexes of displacement, recorded in Table 27, are of considerable interest.   The transition to the war economy brought a definite swing away from the prewar ranking, a swing measured by an index of 0.42 in the case of the 1891 relatives, and by an index of 0.79 in the case of the 1909 relatives.   These represent fundamental shifts in price relations.   (A value of 1, it will be recalled, would indicate the complete destruction of relations prevailing at the date serving as criterion.)   In 1918 there was a minor movement back toward prewar relations, a movement which was much more pronounced in 1919.   The first effect of the end of the war, it is apparent, was to initiate a return to prewar price relations. (It is possible that this movement is in part a reflection of Federal price regulation from 1917 to 1919.) Between 1919 and 1923 there was another clear swing away from the relationships of prewar days. One of the indexes (that on the 1891 base) shows the situation in 1923 to be farther removed than that in 1917 from prewar relations. The movements of both indexes between 1923 and 1927 indicate an uninterrupted return toward the relationships prevailing before the war. The index constructed from 1891 relatives declined in four years from 0.47 to 0.29, and that based on 1909 relatives fell from 0.78 to 0.63.

Two noteworthy facts are revealed by these figures. The first is that the postwar price structure differs in important respects from that prevailing before the war. The decade which included the war and immediate postwar years witnessed fundamental shifts in the relative positions of different commodities and of different commodity groups. Measures of the degree of difference between prewar and postwar price structures vary in magnitude according to the standard selected as typical of prewar conditions. The system of price relations which embodied the results of changes during the five years from 1909 to 1914 has been substantially modified. The price structure which was built up during the quarter century preceding the war suffered less drastic changes, although it was materially altered by the price revolution which accompanied the war. The second point of importance is that during the period 1923–1927 there was a distinct return toward the relations which had been built up in prewar years, a tendency of considerable economic significance. Whether this tendency will continue to prevail is a question the future must answer.

VII. SUMMARY

This chapter deals with price changes and related industrial movements in the United States during the period 1922–1927. As a background for the general discussion, brief reference is made to price levels and price tendencies in other countries, and to prewar price tendencies in the United States. It is impossible effectively to summarize the various statistical measures which have been employed in this study, but certain of the results may be indicated.

1. The degree of increase in commodity prices, at wholesale, in gold, between 1913 and 1927 ranged, for 18 countries, between 23 per cent and 71 per cent. In the United States, wholesale prices increased 47 per cent during this period, a figure which is approximately equal to the median of the measures for the 18 countries.

2. Between 1922 and 1927, the general drift of world prices was downward. Of 19 countries for which measures were computed, the

net movement was downward for 15. The rates of decline varied from 0.1 to 6.5 per cent a year.

3. In many respects the postwar price situation stands in sharp contrast to that prevailing before the war, but recent tendencies should be considered in the light of prewar trends:

a. During the two decades before the war, the level of wholesale prices in the United States was rising at an average rate of 2.3 per cent per year. This rising tendency affected manufacturing methods and buying and selling habits, and confirmed business men in many practices not adapted to conditions under a stable price level or under declining prices.

b. During the quarter century preceding the war, commodity prices and the relations among such prices were relatively unstable. The prices of individual commodities were subject to relatively abrupt changes from month to month and from year to year, and the forces tending to alter existing price relations were strong. Both these conditions served to introduce a considerable degree of uncertainty into business operations, and to enhance the speculative features of business operations.

c. Perhaps more important, however, is the fact that these various measures of economic instability showed a definite tendency to decline during this prewar period. The variability of individual commodity prices was diminishing, and there was less disturbance in price relations. This downward trend is the more significant in that it accompanied a rising price level.

4. Certain of the general economic characteristics of the postwar period in the United States are suggested by the following figures, measuring average annual rates of change, between 1922 and 1927:

a. There was a sustained increase in the physical volume of production and in the rate of distribution. Primary production increased at a rate of 2.5 per cent a year, production of manufactured goods increased at a rate of 4 per cent a year, and volume of distribution, as measured by ton-miles of freight carried, rose at a rate of 4 per cent a year. These changes accompanied a population increase of about 1.4 per cent a year.

b. This increase in manufacturing production was accompanied by a definite decline in the volume of factory employment, a decline at the rate of 0.7 per cent a year. Per capita earnings of factory employees increased, however, at a rate of 2.4 per cent a year. During the same period, output per man in manufacturing establishments rose at a rate of 3.5 per cent a year.

c. The increase in production and in wages noted above accompanied a slightly declining level of wholesale prices. The rate of fall averaged 0.1 per cent a year. The decline occurred chiefly in the prices of nonagricultural products, which fell at a rate of 1.8 per cent a year.

Farm prices rose during this period at an average annual rate of 1.1 per cent.

d. Profits of industrial corporations increased, between 1923 and 1927, at an average rate of 9 per cent a year. Industrial stock prices rose, between 1922 and 1927, at a rate of 14.1 per cent a year.

5. The following are important general features of the postwar price situation:

a. The level of wholesale prices in the United States has shown no definite tendency either to rise or to fall since 1922. The net movement has been slightly downward. There is no present evidence, either in domestic or in world conditions, that the prewar rise will be resumed.

b. Important differences among commodity groups in respect to price trends are developing in the postwar era, differences which are in many cases more pronounced than those which prevailed before the war. These group tendencies are shown in detail in the various tables relating to price movements. Among the differences to be noted are the following (all statements relate to tendencies during the period 1922–1927):

Agricultural products have been rising in price; non-agricultural products have declined.

Raw materials have been rising in price; processed materials have fallen.

Foods have risen and nonfoods have fallen in price.

Consumers' goods have risen slightly; producers' goods as a class have neither fallen nor risen.

Prices of animal products and of cultivated vegetable products have shown a rising tendency; mineral products and forest products have declined in price.

Foreign products have risen in price; domestic products have declined slightly.

Among farm products, the chief gains in prices received by producers have been recorded for meat animals, grains, and fruits and vegetables. Cotton and cottonseed have declined materially in price.

c. War-time developments gave a sharp check to the prewar tendency toward economic stability, as reflected in the declining variability of individual prices and the greater stability of price relations. The extreme war-time disturbances persisted for several years after the close of the war, but since 1922 there have been fewer of those abrupt changes in prices and in price relations which characterized the nineties of the last century, and which gave to the war and immediate postwar years their distinctive business flavor. These tendencies toward price stability which have reasserted themselves after the disturbances of the war years will, if they persist, materially affect the economic complexion of the years before us. A tendency toward greater stability of prices and of price relations involves a change in the direction in which business men look for profits.   Something of the speculative element goes out of business when such a tendency prevails.   The high profits and the great losses which go with extreme fluctuations in the prices of individual commodities and with changes in the relations among prices, alike tend to disappear.   Business and prices both become more stable.   There is evidence that our economic system is moving in this direction.

If we may anticipate approximate stability in the price level in the future, the expectation of greater stability in the prices of individual commodities and in price relations is strengthened.

CHAPTER X

MONEY AND CREDIT AND THEIR EFFECT ON BUSINESS

By O. M. W. Sprague and W. Randolph Burgess

It is the purpose of this chapter to examine the monetary changes of the past six years, with a view to discovering the direction, not the extent, of their influence on business. The examination of the monetary conditions of the period takes two forms: first, a fact-finding study attempting to measure the availability of credit and capital for business use as compared with previous periods in the past; and second, a description of particular influences which have operated upon monetary conditions, such, for example, as Treasury financing, changes in banking organization, and the influence of the Federal Reserve System.

I. THE MEASUREMENT OF INTEREST RATES

The general characteristics of the period are illustrated by Charts 1 and 2, giving the movement of interest rates. Rates for short-time money show, in general, a slightly declining tendency through 1927, followed by a sharp upturn in 1928. Rates for long-time money show an almost continuous downward trend.

The significance of these tendencies will appear more clearly from a comparison with the interest rates of preceding periods, both as to the average level of rates and their direction of movement.

The Average Level of Rates.—The first rough measure of the cheapness or dearness of money during the period may be found in a comparison of the average level of money rates for 1922–1928, with the average level for the preceding 24 years. Such a comparison is made in Table 1.[1]

TABLE 1.—AVERAGE LEVEL OF MONEY RATES

Item	1890–1913	1922–1928
	Per cent	Per cent
Corporation bond yields	4.47	4.72
Common industrial stock yields	[a]5.43	5.97
Commercial paper	4.72	4.35
Time money	4.04	4.58
Call money	3.58	4.43

[a] 1900–1913.

NOTE.—Sections I, II, VIII, and X of this chapter were prepared by Dr. W. Randolph Burgess; and Sections III, IV, V, VI, VII, and IX by Dr. O. M. W. Sprague.

[1] The selection of somewhat different prewar periods of similar length would not affect the comparison materially.

CHART 1.—MOVEMENT OF INTEREST RATES IN THE UNITED STATES, 1922–1928

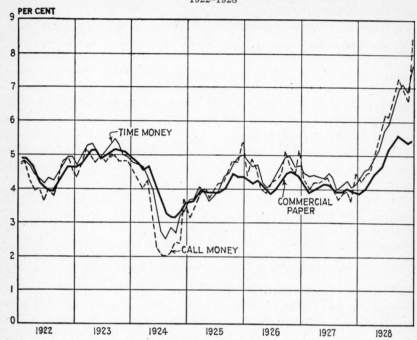

CHART 2.—BOND AND INDUSTRIAL COMMON STOCK YIELDS, 1922–1928

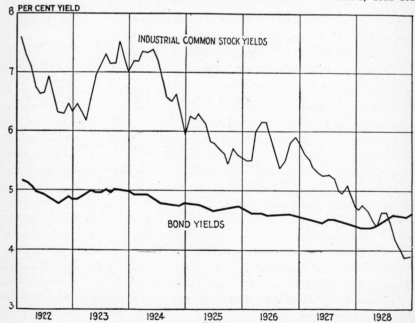

For the period as a whole, commercial paper rates were somewhat lower than in the preceding 24 years, but rates for time and call loans against stock exchange collateral (used primarily in speculation) and yields on both bonds and common stocks were higher than the average for preceding years. Rates for bankers' acceptances cannot be quoted, because the drawing of such bills was not permissible under the law before the passage of the Federal Reserve Act. Also it is not possible, because of inadequacy of data, to include completely reliable figures for the rates at which banks loaned money directly to their customers. From the scattered data which are available, it seems probable that rates charged bank customers are represented more nearly by open market commercial paper rates than the other rates quoted in Table 1, and such rates have been somewhat lower than the average for preceding years.

The lower level of rates for business money compared with higher rates for what might be called speculative money—call and time loans—is

CHART 3.—VOLUME OF COMMERCIAL PAPER, 1922–1928

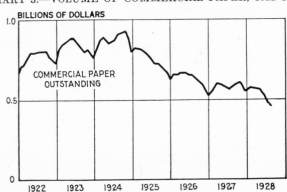

perhaps worthy of comment. Two possible explanations are offered. The first is that under the terms of the Federal Reserve Act commercial paper is eligible for rediscount at Federal Reserve banks, whereas loans on stock exchange collateral are not eligible, and under these conditions it is natural that member banks should discriminate in favor of commercial paper. The second explanation is found in the relative demand for these two types of loans in recent years. By reason of considerable acquisitions of funds through the issuance of securities, business concerns have reduced relatively their requirements for short-term credit. For this and other reasons, the amount of funds borrowed through the open market for commercial paper has been much reduced. This is indicated in Chart 3, which shows the amount of commercial paper outstanding through principal dealers reporting to the Federal Reserve Bank of New York.

In contrast with a less active demand for commercial loans, the demand for time and call money has been very great, accompanying active security markets, rising security prices, and a large volume of new financing.

Direction of Rate Movement.—Of more significance than the average rates shown in the preceding table is the direction of movement of rates. This is particularly true of yields on bonds and common stocks, which

CHART 4.—AVERAGE CALL LOAN DATES, 1890–1914 AND 1922–1928

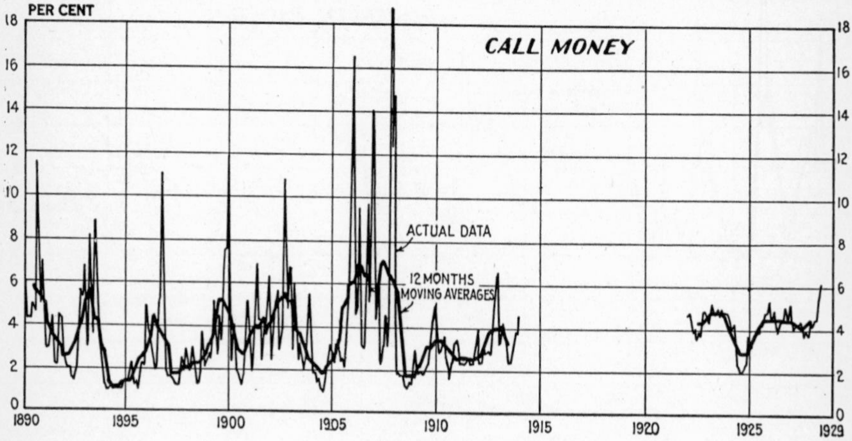

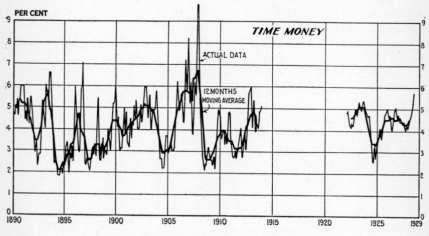

CHART 5.—AVERAGE TIME LOAN RATES, 1890–1914 AND 1922–1928

have moved sharply downward, so that the average is not fairly representative of the period.

Charts 4 to 8 show the monthly movement of rates since 1890 of call money, time money, commercial paper, and bond yields, and since 1900 of stock yields.[2]

[2] The figures on stock yields were computed by Col. Leonard P. Ayres.

In each of the charts the actual averages for each month are shown by light lines, and a heavier line shows the 12-month moving averages centered on the sixth month. These averages indicate the tendencies of the movements, and smooth out many of the seasonal and irregular

CHART 6.—AVERAGE COMMERCIAL PAPER RATES, 1890–1914 AND 1922–1928

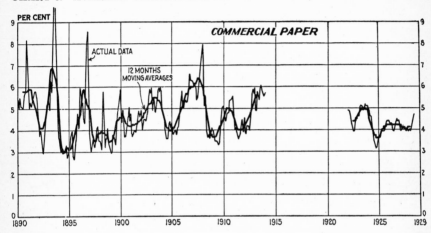

fluctuations. Call money, time money, and commercial paper rates show something of a downward movement during the period, although this movement was terminated in 1928, when rates rose to the highest figures of the period. The relative increase in call and time money during 1928 was much larger than that in commercial paper. Bond

CHART 7.—AVERAGE BOND YIELDS, 1890–1914 AND 1922–1928

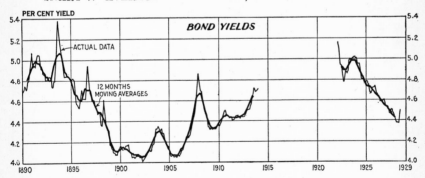

yields and stock yields (representing long-time rates) show a much clearer and sharper downward tendency. In the case of bonds, the figures for the end of 1927 are slightly below the average of the years from 1890 to 1913, and in the case of stocks the yields in 1928 are well below, not only the average, but also the lowest yields for any of the months from 1900 to

1913. These downward movements of bond and stock yields and the corresponding increases in prices which they represent, continuing for so long a period, have been accompanied by the purchase of securities on a large scale. Under these conditions, it has been possible to sell new issues of stocks and bonds at low rates, and in this way industry has been in a position to secure funds in the capital markets at rates, in many instances, lower than the rates at which these same concerns could borrow money at their banks.

From the foregoing charts, it is possible by inspection to compare recent rate movements with those of somewhat similar periods in the past. While comparisons of this sort should not be forced to carry too

CHART 8.—AVERAGE STOCK YIELDS, 1900–1914 AND 1922–1928

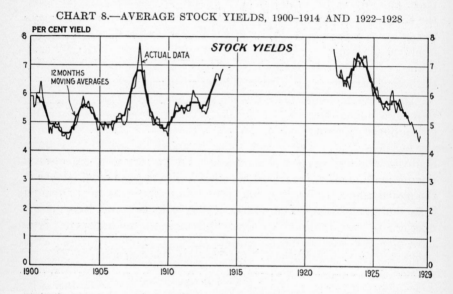

heavy a load of analogy, they at least indicate that the recent rate movement has not been unique.

Variation in Interest Rates.—The foregoing charts illustrate also the month-to-month fluctuations in rates. From an inspection of the charts, the general conclusion may be drawn that rates in this recent period have been considerably more stable than was the case in the years from 1890 to 1913. The comparative variability of rates in the two periods may be measured somewhat more precisely by computing average per cent deviations of the actual monthly data from the 12-month moving averages. This gives a measure of the month-to-month fluctuations in rates, as compared with the general tendency. The figures in Table 2 are the result of such a computation.

The figures in Table 2 indicate that the fluctuation of bond and stock yields has been considerably reduced, that the fluctuation of commercial

TABLE 2.—AVERAGE DEVIATIONS FROM 12-MONTH MOVING AVERAGES

Item	1890–1913	1922–1928
	Per cent	*Per cent*
Corporation bond yields..............	0.77	0.62
Common industrial stock yields.........	*a*3.00	2.60
Commercial paper....................	10.82	4.33
Time money.......................	16.91	6.12
Call money.......................	33.10	8.39

a 1900–1913.

paper and time money rates has been reduced to less than half, and that the fluctuation in call money rates has been only a fourth as much as in the earlier years. The reduction in rate fluctuations is in part a result of improvements in the credit mechanism, and particularly the influence of the Federal Reserve System, but it is also partly due to the absence in the recent period of any considerable credit disturbance.

The above measure of variability thus gives us a record of month-to-month fluctuations, but it does not attempt to measure the relative extent of the longer fluctuations, which in the past have been a feature of the business cycle. The period under review is so brief that it seems doubtful whether any valid conclusions can be drawn as to cyclical fluctuations. It is, in fact, possible to select a number of other periods in the past in which the cyclical fluctuations of interest rates were no larger than during the years from 1922 to 1928, but, so far as the monthly fluctuations are concerned, the evidence is clear that recent interest rates have been more stable, and, as a result, the business man or other user of credit has been more certain as to the price he was likely to pay for funds in succeeding months.

This discussion of the measurement of interest rates may be summarized by saying that the average level of rates from 1922 to 1928 has been lower for commercial funds and higher for speculative funds than in the years from 1890 to 1913, that the direction of movement of rates has in general been somewhat downward, but that the most marked change is in variability. The fluctuation of rates has been much reduced; rates have been more stable.[3]

II. THE SUPPLY OF BANK FUNDS

The preceding section has pointed out, among other things, that interest rates in general have shown a downward tendency during the period. The question may now be asked: What have been the causes of this decline, and what has been the effect upon business? There are two principal media through which credit is extended, known roughly as

[3] See also Chap. IX, Price Movements, p. 643.

capital funds (funds derived from saving), and bank funds (funds made available through the commercial banks). It is the purpose of this section to summarize the evidence as to the supply of funds made available through the last mentioned medium, the commercial banks.

There are several kinds of evidence which may be introduced. The data as to interest rates have already been given and they indicate that the supply of bank credit was well able to take care of the demand. From the side of practical experience, the testimony of competent observers is that the period, for the most part, was one of extremely vigorous competition between banks to lend funds. It was a "borrowers' market." This condition, as well as declining interest rates, may, however, have been due to a reduced demand for bank funds rather than to an unusually ample supply of bank credit. Data, which will be introduced later, indicate that business in this period has been financed less by borrowing from banks and more by borrowing in the capital market through issues of securities. In this way, individual lenders of funds have loaned unusually large sums directly to industry and commerce without the funds going through the form of bank deposits. Industrial requirements for bank loans have also been lessened by the prevailing custom of reducing inventories to the lowest possible levels.[4]

For further light as to whether the comparatively easy bank credit of the period may be ascribed to reduced demand for bank funds or to an ample supply, it will be profitable to examine the data for the actual growth of bank credit during the 1922–1928 period, as compared with other periods, and also the data as to the supply of bank reserves, which are the basis for all bank credit.

Growth of Bank Funds.—Chart 9 shows the growth of bank funds in the United States since 1875. The figures plotted are those for the loans and investments of all banks, excluding savings banks, on or about June 30 of each year, as reported by the Comptroller of the Currency. An inspection of this line shows that some distorting factors have influenced the actual figures, for there is little consistency of movement. This is particularly noticeable from 1915 to 1922, when a period of unprecedented increase was followed by a substantial decline. When it is remembered that this was also a period of violent price movements, it will be seen that these movements have been the distorting factors. Before conclusions can be drawn as to the volume of credit available for business, some consideration must be given to the effect of changes in prices; and as bank credit is extended for trade in other lines than commodities, study must be made of the changes in prices not only for goods, but for services, rents, and securities as well. For this reason, an additional line has been added to Chart 9, to show the volume of credit

---

[4] See Size of Inventory, Chap. II, Industry, Part 1; Chap. III, Construction, p. 242; Chap. IV, Transportation, Part 1, p. 302; Chap. V, p. 332; Chap. VII, p. 508; Chap. IX, Price Movements, p. 637.

adjusted to eliminate the influence of price changes. The adjusted figures were derived by dividing the bank loan and investment data by the index of the general price level,[5] which includes prices of commodities both at wholesale and retail, rents, wages, securities, and other prices affecting the value at which exchanges of goods or services are made.

CHARTS 9–10.—LOANS AND INVESTMENTS OF ALL BANKS IN THE UNITED STATES AND BY GEOGRAPHICAL DIVISIONS, 1875–1928

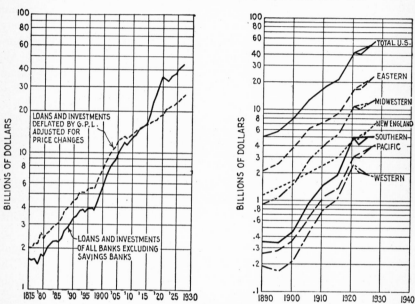

The adjusted line shows the recent period to be one of rapid growth in bank credit, though not more rapid than a number of other periods in the past fifty years. The recent growth was notably less rapid than in the years from 1897 to 1907, when there was an unusually high rate of

TABLE 3.—ANNUAL RATES OF INCREASE IN BANK CREDIT, BY PERIODS

Fiscal years ended June 30 or nearest call date	Unadjusted figures	Adjusted for price changes
	Per cent	Per cent
1875–1880.....................	0 75	2.79
1880–1892.....................	6.65	6.89
1892–1897................... ..	0.56	1.39
1897–1907.....................	11.53	9.04
1907–1914.....................	4.57	2.85
1914–1920	4.56	2.67
1922–1928.....................	16.25	4.36

[5] Prepared by the Federal Reserve Bank of New York.

increase, accompanied by rising prices, and culminating in the panic of 1907.

Increase by Geographical Areas.—One feature of the growth in bank credit since 1922 has been its uneven distribution geographically. This is shown in Chart 10. The most rapid increases in credit have been in the Eastern, New England, and Pacific districts, whereas in the Middle Western and Southern districts there has been only a moderate growth, and in the Western district a decline.[6] These results are perhaps to be expected in view of unfavorable economic conditions in a number of the agricultural states, which have been accompanied by bank failures and in some cases by public loss of confidence in certain of the country banks.

The retarded growth of bank credit in the three predominantly agricultural districts followed an extended period of rapid growth from 1900 to 1920, much more rapid than that which characterized the Eastern or New England districts. A close examination of Chart 10 will raise the question in many minds whether the rural financial disturbances of 1921 and following years may not have been partly the result of over-expansion from 1900 to 1920, a period during which too many banks were organized and during which there may have been a considerable overexpansion of bank credit.[7] Unfortunately, overexpansion of credit is very difficult to diagnose, not only at the time of its occurrence, but even after the event.

Timing of the Increase.—Chart 9 is not on a large enough scale to allow a close analysis by short periods of the changes in bank credit since 1922. For that purpose there has been added Chart 11, which shows by months the total loans and investments and total deposits of the reporting member banks of the Federal Reserve System. These banks at present include more than 600 of the large banks in principal cities, and have in the aggregate nearly 40 per cent of the total banking resources of the country. They are the only banks for which monthly figures for loans and investments are available, but changes in their condition are sufficiently typical of changes for the country as a whole to make their figures a useful index of the month-to-month fluctuations of bank credit.

[6] The states included in each of the several regions mentioned above are as follows:

New England.—Maine, New Hampshire, Vermont, Massachusetts, Rhode Island, and Connecticut.

Eastern.—New York, New Jersey, Pennsylvania, Delaware, Maryland, and District of Columbia.

Southern.—Virginia, West Virginia, North Carolina, South Carolina, Georgia, Florida, Alabama, Mississippi, Louisiana, Texas, Arkansas, Kentucky, and Tennessee.

Middle Western.—Ohio, Indiana, Illinois, Michigan, Wisconsin, Minnesota, Iowa, and Missouri.

Western.—North Dakota, South Dakota, Nebraska, Kansas, Montana, Wyoming, Colorado, New Mexico, and Oklahoma (including Indian Territory in earlier years).

Pacific.—Washington, Oregon, California, Idaho, Utah, Nevada, and Arizona.

[7] See Chap. VIII, Agriculture, p. 582.

This chart shows that the increase of bank credit since 1922 has been far from steady and continuous. It was particularly rapid in 1922, 1924, and 1927, with little or no gain in 1923 and 1926. The increase in 1922 was at a time of business recovery from depression, and the increases in 1924 and 1927–28 were at times of business uncertainty. In general, the most rapid increases of credit during the period were at times when business was most in need of the stimulus of easily available credit, and, contrariwise, the periods of slowest growth were when business was in large volume and perhaps in some danger from overstimulation. The

CHART 11.—LOANS AND INVESTMENTS, AND DEPOSITS OF REPORTING MEMBER BANKS, 1922–1928

influence of the Federal Reserve System on the timing of changes in the volume of credit will be discussed later.

Movement of Reserve Funds.—The rate of growth of bank credit is primarily determined by the supply of what may be called reserve funds —that is, funds which are available for use as bank reserves. In the last analysis, gold is the reserve upon which the bank credit of any gold standard country is based, and changes in a country's gold stock are usually the most important influences upon the volume of bank credit. This has been true in the United States since 1922; in this period the flow of gold has been extraordinary. The effect of gold movements has, however, been modified by other important influences. These modifying influences include changes in the amount of currency in use, changes in practices as to bank reserves, and changes in the position of the Federal Reserve System.

Between the beginning of the year 1922 and the middle of 1927, there were gold imports into the United States of $885,000,000, and, when domestic production and changes in the amount of gold under earmark are taken account of, there was an increase of about $902,000,000 in the total gold stock of the country. The increase in the gold supply in this five and a half year period was greater than in the fourteen years from 1900 to 1914, and it followed substantial net gains from 1915 to 1921, which had already greatly enlarged the gold basis of our bank credit. These gold accessions were added directly to the reserves of banks. Table 4, showing the changes from 1922 to 1927 in the factors affecting reserve funds, indicates how the banks of the country made use of the gold they acquired.

TABLE 4.—FACTORS IN SUPPLY AND DEMAND FOR RESERVE FUNDS, JANUARY, 1922 TO JULY, 1927

(In millions of dollars)

Item	January, 1922	July, 1927	Net change
Increase in supply through:			
Monetary gold stock..............................	3,673	4,575	902
Monetary silver stock.............................	630	834	204
Miscellaneous items...............................	.....	.....	50
Total..	.....	.....	1,156
Increase in demand through:			
Member bank reserve balances......................	1,707	2,289	582
Money in circulation.....	4,566	4,851	285
Total..	.....	.....	867
Estimated net decrease in demand for reserve bank credit....	.....	.....	289
Actual decrease in reserve bank credit...................	1,304	1,026	278
Difference, due to errors and omissions..............	.....	.....	11

The banks used a part of the additions to their reserves, resulting from gold imports, to obtain currency from the Reserve banks to put into circulation, as indicated by an increase of $285,000,000 in money in circulation; they used part of it to repay borrowing at the Federal Reserve banks, as shown by a decrease of $278,000,000 in Federal Reserve credit in use; but the major part, $582,000,000, went to increase the reserve deposits of the member banks at the Reserve banks. Since each dollar of these reserves supports on the average well over $10 of commercial bank deposits (including both time and demand), this increase in reserves, resulting largely from gold imports, was the basis for the increase of deposits in the member banks over the period.

The effect of gold imports was accentuated by an important change in practice as to bank reserves. Before the Reserve System was established, the law required the same bank reserves against time as against demand deposits, but under the Federal Reserve Act the requirement was reduced to 5 per cent in 1914, and to 3 per cent, by amendment, in 1917. Under this encouragement, there has been a rapid growth in time deposits, including probably some transference of deposits from the demand to time classification. There was also a reduction in the reserve required against demand deposits. These changes have allowed a given amount of reserves to support an increased amount of bank credit; consequently the imported gold has gone further in supporting credit expansion than would otherwise have been possible.

These changes may be summarized by saying that the principal influence from 1922 to 1927 toward rapid growth of bank credit and easy credit conditions was gold imports, an abnormal influence which cannot be expected to continue in the future, for the causes which brought us so much gold are no longer operative. The gold came to this country primarily because this was the only large country which was operating on the gold standard with a free gold market. Most paper currencies elsewhere were subject to wide and unpredictable fluctuations, and in the endeavor to gain greater security, the citizens of many countries created and maintained large balances in New York. But now the monetary affairs of the world are again stabilized, and other countries are again takers of gold, and may be expected not only to retain their present gold stocks but to seek to increase them.

TABLE 5.—FACTORS IN SUPPLY AND DEMAND FOR RESERVE FUNDS, JULY, 1927 TO JULY, 1928

(In millions of dollars)

	July, 1927	July, 1928	Net change
Increase in supply through:			
Money in circulation..............................	4,851	4,746	105
Monetary silver stock............................	834	839	5
Total.......................................	.....	.....	110
Increase in demand through:			
Monetary gold stock.............................	4,575	4,113	462
Member bank reserve balances.......................	2,289	2,324	35
Miscellaneous items............................	.....	.....	72
Total.......................................	.....	.....	569
Estimated net increase in demand for reserve bank credit.....	.....	.....	459
Actual increase in reserve bank credit....................	1,026	1,488	462
Difference, due to errors and omissions.................	.....	.....	3

This change in affairs has been illustrated since the middle of 1927. France and other countries have withdrawn in gold a part of the huge balances accumulated here. In the 12 months ended July, 1928, this country lost more than half as much gold as was imported in the preceding five and one-half years, making it necessary to call into use about $462,000,000 of additional Federal Reserve credit.

This reversal in the gold movement has changed materially the outlook for the supply of bank funds. In the first place it has greatly reduced the country's supply of what may be called "free gold"—that is, gold in excess of legal requirements as banking reserves and as collateral for note issues. In 1927, the country's holdings of free gold amounted to approximately $900,000,000. A calculation of excess gold above legal requirements of Federal Reserve banks, June 29, 1927, in thousands of dollars, is shown in the following statement:

Total cash reserves (gold and lawful money)......................... 3,183,809
Federal reserve notes issued to Federal Reserve banks....... 2,076,382
Eligible paper held as collateral.......................... 647,180

Gold collateral required against notes..................... 1,429,202
Gold redemption fund (equaling 5 per cent of those notes
  secured by eligible paper)............................. 32,359

Total gold required against notes................... 1,461,561
Gold and lawful money required against deposits (equaling 35
  per cent of total deposits of 2,398,952).................. 839,633
Total gold and lawful money required against notes and deposits.... 2,301,194

Excess of gold over requirements ("free gold")...................... 882,615

In addition to the gold in the Reserve banks, there has been about one billion dollars of gold in circulation in the form of gold certificates, which are often thought of as a potential future gold reserve. These certificates could be replaced in circulation by Federal Reserve notes, and the gold be added to the reserves of the Reserve System, thus raising the reserve ratio. This operation, however, would not release any free gold. The reason is that the Federal Reserve notes, issued in place of the gold certificates, would have to be collateral dollar for dollar with gold. The amount of collateral, other than gold, back of Federal Reserve notes has not been large enough to cover the total of Federal Reserve notes outstanding, and many of the notes are in effect gold notes—secured dollar for dollar by gold. Any additional reserve note circulation would perforce be so secured, unless there were a large increase in the amount of borrowing by the member banks at the Reserve banks, or an increase in holdings of bankers' acceptances, furnishing additional collateral. But any such borrowing would put a strain on the credit situation and tighten money rates. For the experience of the Federal

Reserve System shows a direct correlation between the amount of member bank borrowings and interest rates. The member banks properly regard borrowing as a measure for emergencies and for busy seasons, and not for continuous use. Hence, when a large number of banks are forced to remain continuously in debt for considerable periods, bankers tend to restrict their lending, and money rates rise. Gold released only at the price of increased rediscounts cannot properly be termed "free" gold.

Of the $900,000,000 of free gold in June, 1927, about one-half has been lost, leaving at present (September, 1928) about $500,000,000 of free gold, assuming a normal amount of member bank borrowing of about $500,000,000. The present amount of borrowing is larger and makes possible the release of more gold, but at the price of somewhat strained credit conditions.

As we look forward to what may be considered normal credit conditions, we cannot safely figure much more than about $500,000,000 of free gold, under present laws and with moderately easy credit conditions.

In considering the problem of the future supply of bank reserves in this country, the following are among the factors of importance:

1. Although no withdrawal is in sight as large as the recent French movement, other countries still hold in this country large liquid balances, which are subject to withdrawal.

2. With other countries eager takers of gold, it is uncertain how much, if any, of each year's new output of gold will flow here.

3. The normal growth of credit and currency in the country, to care for the increasing needs of trade, calls for additions to our reserves of about $50,000,000 to $100,000,000 a year, although this is very difficult to forecast.

4. If the $650,000,000 of National Bank notes now in circulation were retired and replaced by Federal Reserve notes, with gold collateral, this operation would lock up over $600,000,000 of gold.

5. If the unsecured issue of legal tender notes were retired and replaced by Federal Reserve notes, with gold collateral, an additional $150,000,000 would be required.

It seems probable that this country must adjust itself to a smaller annual increase in bank reserves than has been available recently. The method of adjustment cannot be predicted in advance but may well be given careful study. It may be that continued economy of currency circulation will help to solve the problem; perhaps a revision of the law is desirable to liberalize the provisions of the Reserve Act concerning collateral for Federal Reserve notes. If these notes were secured by the general assets of the Reserve banks, rather than specific types of assets, considerable amounts of gold would be released. It may be that a less rapid increase in bank credit than in the past five years would be eventually more wholesome; for it is yet to be seen whether the recent increase has sowed seeds of trouble which have not yet fully grown.

III. THE SUPPLY OF FUNDS DERIVED FROM SAVINGS

Preceding sections of this chapter have discussed various aspects of the question of how far business has been aided by ease in obtaining funds. The first and perhaps the most convincing evidence introduced was the data for interest rates, which showed that rates for commercial money have been reasonable and declining during most of the period. The next section examined the supply of bank funds, and found that the available evidence would indicate a larger surplus than in most preceding periods, though in recent months the supply has been somewhat restricted. It is the purpose of this section to summarize the evidence as to the supply of capital funds, that is, of funds derived from savings.

Savings by individuals are made with a variety of motives; they tend to increase with the growth of real income, and are facilitated by the diffusion of agencies and recognized opportunities for investment. Profits retained in both individual and corporate enterprises are also a large factor in capital formation, and are properly included in the aggregate of savings. During recent years, it is certain that conditions have been highly favorable to the rapid increase of capital through saving, both by individuals and by corporations. Real income as well as money income of the community, taken as a whole, has increased. Saving motives and habits have become more general. Business profits in many instances have been large, and investment opportunities and agencies have been readily at hand.

In the absence of any comprehensive measure of capital accumulation, it is necessary to rely upon a number of individual series of figures, some of which extend over a considerable period of time and may be thought of as a sampling of the trend. Even though they are an imperfect measure, they will help us somewhat in attempting to answer the question as to whether the rate of capital accumulation has been more than ordinarily helpful to business in the recent period. A number of these series are shown in Chart 12.

The assets of life insurance companies and of building and loan associations, and the time and savings deposits of banks, represent a considerable part of the savings of individuals, though no one can say accurately just how large a part.

The actual dollar figures show a rather steady rate of growth until 1915, after which the growth becomes steeper. It is at once evident that some allowance must be made for price changes, as, for example, a dollar savings deposit in 1920 represents considerably less purchasing power than a dollar in 1913. In making allowance for changes in purchasing power, an index of the cost of living has been used; this index

CHART 12.—SAVINGS AND TIME DEPOSITS, LIFE INSURANCE, AND BUILDING AND LOAN ASSOCIATION ASSETS, ACTUAL AND ADJUSTED TO PRICE CHANGES, 1900–1927

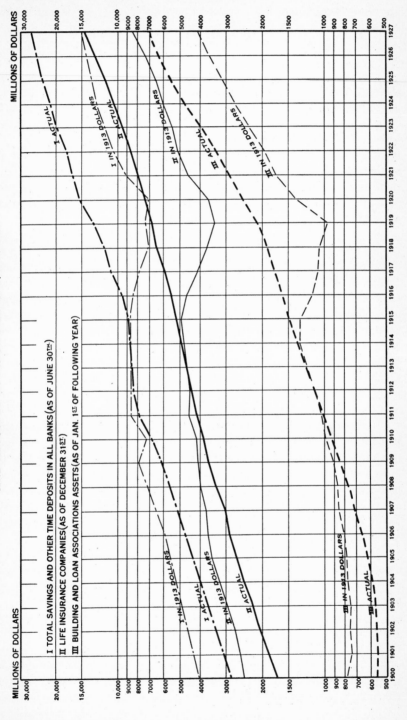

I TOTAL SAVINGS AND OTHER TIME DEPOSITS IN ALL BANKS (AS OF JUNE 30ᵀᴴ)

II LIFE INSURANCE COMPANIES (AS OF DECEMBER 31ˢᵀ)

III BUILDING AND LOAN ASSOCIATIONS ASSETS (AS OF JAN. 1ˢᵀ OF FOLLOWING YEAR)

was chosen rather than the general price level, previously described because it more nearly represents changes in the prices of the varied uses to which the savings might have been put by the individual savers. The figures, adjusted to eliminate the influence of price changes, show, in general, an increase at a diminishing rate from 1900 through 1915, with a decline until 1920. From 1920 to date, there follows a sharper rate of increase than characterized any of the preceding periods.

In the form as given, the figures may be a little misleading, for they show what amounts to a cumulation of savings of all previous years. For example, the 1927 figure represents not the total savings for that particular year but the net accumulation of savings for that and all

CHART 13.—ANNUAL INCREASE OF SAVINGS AND TIME DEPOSITS, LIFE INSURANCE, BUILDING AND LOAN FUNDS, ADJUSTED TO COST OF LIVING, 1900–1927

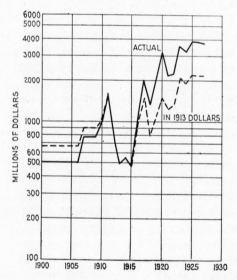

preceding years as well. While it is correct from the point of view of its purchasing power, at any one time, to use the total divided by a price index, a misleading picture of each year's accumulation may result.

In order to show the annual net amounts of savings through these institutions, the year to year addition to the total figures was computed, and the latter figures divided by the cost of living. The result is shown in Chart 13.

It appears that annual savings, in terms of dollars with a constant purchasing power, from 1900 through 1913, averaged considerably less than one billion dollars a year, while, from 1922 to 1927, savings averaged nearly two billions, and for the three years ended with 1927 held steady at a level somewhat above two billions. Of course, these figures are not inclusive of all types of saving, but at least they give a fair sample. This, together with evidence that the public has been a heavy investor in the security markets during recent years, leaves little doubt that savings have been in unusually large volume.

Other convincing evidence of abundant savings is to be found in the field of bank credit itself. The volume of bank credit, or of aggregate deposits, with a possible exception to be noted presently, is, indeed, not directly related to savings. It expands and contracts with changes in reserves. But the use which depositors make of bank balances is profoundly influenced by the volume of savings relative to demand for capital, by the course of interest rates, and by the choice which is made of investment methods or arrangements. When fears of credit inflation are expressed, it is not solely the rapid increase in bank deposits that is in question. There is at least an implication that the increase in deposits will be accompanied by a corresponding increase in the volume of checks drawn, and the further implication that this increase in the purchasing medium will be more considerable than the growth in the physical volume of trade, and so tend to induce an unhealthy advance in the level of commodity prices, speculation in inventories, rapid labor turnover, and extravagant consumption. These are familiar incidents of rapid credit expansion, but they did not appear during the period under survey.

Although there was a notable increase in the aggregate amount of bank deposits, there was no corresponding rise in the level of wholesale commodity prices. In June, 1920, when the wholesale price index of the Bureau of Labor Statistics registered 167 (on the basis of 1926 prices as 100), individual deposits of all banks in the United States amounted to 37 billions of dollars. A decline to 35 billions in June, 1921, accompanied the severe depression of the intervening months, but this decline was followed by a continued upward movement that brought the aggregate of individual deposits in June, 1928 to more than 53 billions. In spite of this 50 per cent increase in deposits, wholesale prices were not only far below the 1920 maximum, but were less than 5 per cent above the level to which they had fallen in 1921.

It is evident that if the larger volume of deposits of 1928 had been used in the same fashion and to the same extent as those of 1920, there would have been a condition of inflation of bank credit which would have been patent in its effects. But deposits were certainly not being employed similarly in the two years, and the nature of the difference can be readily indicated.

When banks make additional loans or investments, checks are ordinarily soon drawn against the balances thus created. But after the initial use, such deposits become merged with the general mass of deposits, the use of which is determined by the multitude of influences that shape the employment of its free funds by the community. One of these influences is the abundance of savings relative to the demand for capital. Many individuals, saving from current money income, rather than make investments on their own account, prefer to maintain larger balances than formerly with banks, either as savings or time deposits, or in the form of larger checking balances, *i.e.*, demand deposits. Corporations do the same thing with some part of current profits, or perhaps the funds released by a reduction in inventories.

This tendency is further accentuated if, as has happened during the period under survey, interest rates have declined. Influenced by the ease with which issues of securities have been marketed, and by the possibility that rates may turn upward, many enterprises are financed in excess of current requirements, maintaining for longer or shorter periods exceptionally large bank balances, either on demand or as time deposits. Again, when interest rates decline, all readily saleable securities, yielding a fairly certain return, appreciate in value, and not a few owners convert their holdings into inactive bank balances in the expectation of lower quotations at some future time.

Funds in excess of adequate checking balances, which depositors elect either temporarily or permanently to entrust to banks, appear mainly in the item of savings or time deposits in bank statements. These statements indicate that the growth of this class of deposits accounts for a large part of the increase in total deposits.

When savings or the proceeds of security issues are used to maintain larger checking balances, the lending power of the banks is unaffected. But when demand deposits are transferred into time or savings deposits, the lending and investment power of the banks is enlarged, together with some coincident reduction of ability to support demand deposits. For banks that are members of the Reserve System, reserves of 7, 10, or 13 per cent (according to the location of the bank) are required against demand deposits, and a uniform 3 per cent reserve against time or savings deposits. A transfer, say, of a million dollars, from demand to time deposits reduces the reserve requirement from an average of $100,000 to $30,000, leaving $70,000 available to support additional credit. Under the conditions assumed, the total deposits might be materially increased, but demand deposits would be reduced from $1,000,000 to $700,000. A further complication should not be overlooked. Increasingly, general recognition of the facility with which deposits may be transferred from one category to the other must tend in some measure to reduce demand deposits to a minimum and increase the activity of such balances.

Summing up the influence of widespread saving upon the banking position, it may be said that it has tended to increase the aggregate loans and investments and total deposits of the banks, at the same time reducing somewhat the amount of demand deposits. Thanks, at least in part, to saving, active business and large additional supplies of bank credit have not brought about a rapid advance in commodity prices; and the community has not experienced intense competition for labor and materials in the production of consumers' and capital goods, analogous to that between civilian and military demand during the World War, which in times of peace has appeared in periods of prosperity.*

If now we ask ourselves in what respects the financial situation would have been otherwise during this period if banks had acquired smaller reserves, no precise and complete answer can be given. Total bank loans and investments would have been smaller, and total deposits as well. But it does not follow that the total amount of funds seeking employment would have been reduced by the difference between actual bank loans and investments and the smaller aggregate that would have obtained with lower reserves. In the earlier years of the period, on the assumption of a smaller supply of bank funds, the decline in interest rates would have been less precipitate, particularly on those classes of loans and investments favored by banks for the employment of surplus funds. With somewhat less of pronounced ease in the money market, security issues would have been more exactly related to current requirements, and a less spectacular advance in bond and share quotations would have reduced the volume of sales by holders seeking to realize profits. In

---

* I should question the fact that increased savings have been the primary reason for the failure of prices to rise. Increased savings involve fundamentally a shift of purchasing power from consumption goods to buildings, new machinery, etc. They do not involve a decrease in total purchasing power. It is quite possible that the large increase in thrift accounts during recent years has been due, in considerable part, to the prosperity of workers who are as yet not fully accustomed to making direct investments in mortgages or otherwise on their own account. This has perhaps to an increasing extent made the commercial banks investing agents for such depositors, but it is difficult for me to see how this trend or the shift from demand to time deposits has any material effect on the price level.

It is perhaps necessary to distinguish between true savings and that accumulation of excess deposits that is characteristic of the later stages of a business depression. This latter phenomenon is, however, merely an evidence of the fact that prices and business activity are on low levels—it is not the cause of such low levels. Similarly, even without a business depression, an excess of money beyond current needs (free gold) will almost of necessity reveal itself as excess deposits, which may appear to be, but in reality are not, true savings. These again are the effect rather than the cause of the price level being below that which the credit machinery could accommodate.

A further comment, with respect to the relation of the volume of savings to the general price level and to credit conditions, is that it is almost impossible to measure the volume of savings over short periods. Actual money movements may be quite deceptive in this respect, and the only safe index of the volume of savings is the accumulation of capital goods, buildings, etc., measured over periods long enough to eliminate the major elements of error in the computations.—Note by M. C. Rorty.

consequence, there would have been a smaller increase in the amount of funds derived from these sources placed with banks as inactive balances. A similar result may be presumed in the case of savings from individual money incomes. If quotations had advanced less abruptly, the attractiveness of a purchase of securities relative to that of a time deposit would have been enhanced for the cautious type of investor. Although it is not possible to measure the effect of such influences upon the financial situation, they are not less real on that account. An abundance of bank credit, in conjunction with ample savings, creates conditions which tend to modify the character of bank deposits, rendering them less active, and so, at least in some measure, neutralizing the potential effect of an enlargement of funds furnished by banks upon the acquisition of larger reserves. This tendency is greatly accentuated by the inelasticity of the rates of interest which banks pay on deposits. These rates are not adjusted quickly to changes in the yield on current purchases of securities. In any period marked by declining interest rates, therefore, it becomes relatively more and more advantageous to leave funds with banks rather than to purchase securities.

While large and widespread saving has been an influence in counteracting the upward price tendency of an abundant supply of bank credit, a number of supporting influences of diverse character have also been present during the period of the survey. Vivid memories of losses incurred in 1920 have certainly exerted a persistent restraining influence against the accumulation of inventories in order to reap profits or to escape losses from advancing prices. Efficient transportation service has removed fears of delays in shipment. For many products, style has become a factor of increasing importance, and there has been growing recognition of the economy and elimination of risks that may be secured in merchandising through a rapid rate of turnover.[8]

These moderating price influences have not been absent in the field of manufacturing, in which still other influences tending to produce the same result are also to be observed. In not a few industries, existing facilities have been available for the production of larger supplies of goods than could be sold at profitable prices. For industries in this situation, even a sudden and considerable increase in demand has not been followed by a decided and maintained price advance. In perhaps a wider range of industries, increased output, resulting from greater efficiency of management and labor and improved equipment, has made necessary additional sales effort to stimulate or even create a demand among wider circles of consumers. The practice of adjusting production to changes in demand, actual or anticipated, has spread from certain basic industries, such as iron and steel where it has long been practiced, into other fields of production.

[8] See Chap. V, Marketing.

A further price-restraining factor has been the unbalanced economic situation of the country, evident when account is taken of all of its various activities. The process of agricultural adjustment has been slow and painful, and is not yet completed, while producers of such important products as coal and many of the textiles have experienced upon the whole a highly unsatisfactory demand.

Finally, the restraining influence of the situation in other countries on prices in this country must not be overlooked. The advance of gold prices in any single country is inevitably impeded and finally checked if prices do not advance elsewhere. Throughout the entire period of this survey, no sustained general advance of gold prices in the more important trading countries has been possible. Sufficient supplies of bank credit were not available to provide large additions to the purchasing medium, and in any event the dislocation of industry and markets would have proved an insuperable obstacle.

These influences, in conjunction with large savings, furnish an explanation of the failure of commodity prices to respond with a decided upward swing to the impact of an abundant supply of bank credit available at declining rates during recent years of generally active business. Evidently, there is no automatic or close mechanical relationship between the volume of bank credit and the course of commodity prices. Herein is perhaps to be found the chief significance, both theoretical and practical, of our financial experience during this period.

IV. GOVERNMENT DEBT REDUCTION AND THE SUPPLY OF CAPITAL

In addition to the supply of funds derived from saving and the extension of bank credit during the period of this survey, a further supply of indeterminate amount may be properly attributed to the rapid reduction of debt by the Federal Government. The amount to be credited to this policy is by no means to be taken as the full amount of debt reduction. Had taxes rather than debt been reduced, it is certain that taxpayers would have saved some part of the larger incomes which would have been at their disposal. And it may safely be assumed that the amount thus saved would have been a large part of the total, in view of the high percentage of Federal revenue that is derived from those in enjoyment of large incomes—from that group in the community which regularly contributes largely to the supply of capital. The relationship between debt retirement and the supply of investment funds is set forth in the following statement from the *Bulletin* of the Federal Reserve Board of July, 1928:

Under existing conditions, the effect of Treasury disbursements in reduction of debt on the volume of investment funds is relatively limited, except to the extent that purchases or cancellations of securities are made by the Government with funds obtained under foreign debt settlements. Under a system of taxation where a large number of taxpayers turn over to the Government a part of their income, which otherwise would have been expended in the purchase of goods, and the Government uses funds thus obtained in the retirement of securities held mainly by large investors, the retirement of public debt would result in the conversion of a considerable volume of current income into investment funds. But since under the system of taxation in the United States a large part of the contributions to the Government comes from persons with large incomes, which would normally be available in part for investment purposes, a relatively small amount of new investment funds is created by debt retirement. No precise data are available covering the incidence of the various taxes with reference to the distribution of Government securities. Customs and miscellaneous internal revenue and corporation taxes are widely diffused in their incidence, but returns of the individual income tax, from which about one-fifth of the Government revenue is derived, indicate that more than one-half of the taxes on individual incomes are paid on incomes in excess of $100,000 and less than 5 per cent on incomes of $10,000 or less. In these circumstances funds collected through taxation would be available in large part for investment, whether they previously passed through the hands of the Government or were used in the first instance by the investing public.

V. FOREIGN INVESTMENTS[9]

Foreign investments are a manifestation of an abundant supply of investment funds in a country, and of possibilities or expectations of securing a higher return elsewhere. They widen the area and opportunities for the employment of capital, and by so doing tend to equalize and render more stable interest rates throughout the world. There are certain financial risks incident to foreign investments, in addition to those to which investments of all sorts are subject, but there is no fundamental economic difference between foreign investments and those that are made within the investor's own country. When the savings of citizens of the New England states are invested in municipal bonds, or the securities of corporations, or farm mortgages of communities in the western states, the economic effects are essentially the same as when foreign government or private securities are purchased. In both instances, the purchasing power of the regions in which the funds are invested is immediately increased, supporting, in one case exports, and in the other domestic trade. In both instances there are similar possibilities of unwise and excessive investment with similar unfortunate consequences. Foreign investments are indeed subject to certain special risks, in particular those arising from war, revolution, and disordered currencies and dislocated exchange, and on account of these risks, as well as from unfamiliarity with foreign conditions, the investor may demand a higher return than upon similar domestic investments. But qualifications of this character obviously do not involve an essential economic differentiation between the two classes of investments.

[9] See Chap. XI, pp. 725–736.

In the absence of the foreign demand of recent years, interest rates in the United States probably would have declined more sharply, the problem of placing all funds seeking employment would have been more difficult, but in some way or other it is certain that uses would have been found. The employment of a larger part of these funds at home might have entailed greater industrial readjustments and so have affected business unfavorably, but the same might be said if some important domestic demand for funds had not materialized, as, for example, that for the construction of urban dwellings.

And finally, we may say of recent foreign as of domestic investments that only the future can determine whether or not they have been shrewdly made, with advantage to borrowers and with but negligible losses to those who have supplied the funds.

VI. THE EMPLOYMENT OF INVESTMENT FUNDS

The abundant supply of funds, seeking investment at declining rates, seems to have exerted an influence favorable to the strengthening of the financial structure of business during the course of the period covered by the survey. A larger proportion of the assets of business enterprises has come to be financed by means of the resources of owners and long-term obligations; a smaller proportion through current obligations to banks and merchandise creditors. At the same time, there has been a wide diffusion of ownership through the sale of securities in many enterprises that were formerly closely held by a few individuals, in addition to those that had long been available for purchase by the public. In some instances, the capital structure in the course of time will doubtless prove defective. Initial issues of shares have been so large as to cast doubt upon the ability of some corporations to secure additional capital in the future through the sale of stock, and, though less frequently, there has been a seemingly disproportionate reliance upon bonds. There is also the possibility that unfortunate results, in the long run, may follow the separation of management and control from ownership which, whether by design or not, is apt to be found when a business is owned by wide circles of investors. But, with all the diversity in policies exhibited in recent changes in corporate financial structure, there is to be noted general agreement in a desire and purpose to reduce the volume of current obligations.

Direct evidence of such a change in corporation financing is obtained from a study of the statements of a number of large corporations, which was made by the credit department of the Federal Reserve Bank of New York. Some of the results are indicated in the following tabulation:

Companies	Bank debt (thousands of dollars)	
	1922	1927
Six wholesale grocers......................	9,755	9,235
Seven cotton goods manufacturers...........	17,725	6,560
Eight shoe manufacturers..................	4,458	5,674
Five dry goods, wholesale.................	14,890	12,296
Seven lumber.............................	3,168	5,021
Six drug manufacturers...................	1,618	902
Total 39 companies.................	51,614	39,688

Companies	Ratio, capital funds to current debt		Ratio, total debt to current debt		Ratio, net worth to total debt	
	1922	1927	1922	1927	1922	1927
Six wholesale grocers....................	2.24	2.40	1.01	1.05	2.18	2.22
Seven cotton goods manufacturers.........	2.58	5.26	1.09	1.18	2.26	4.27
Eight shoe manufacturers...............	4.33	3.42	1.42	1.32	2.73	2.34
Five dry goods, wholesale...............	1.23	2.17	1.02	1.10	1.19	1.88
Seven lumber..........................	2.42	4.65	1.09	1.35	2.12	3.18
Six drug manufacturers.................	5.30	12.82	1.46	2.35	3.31	4.86

These figures, while not offering conclusive evidence, at least indicate the general tendency of corporate financing. The first part of the table shows that, notwithstanding a variation in the different lines, total bank loans of these companies were reduced about 25 per cent. The second part indicates that, in a majority of the six lines of business, the tendency has been away from the employment of bank funds and toward capital funds.

This preference for permanent methods of financing business is also reflected in the relatively small increase in the commercial loans of the banks in recent years, as contrasted with the increase in security holdings and collateral loans. Between June 30, 1922 and June 30, 1927, in the case of the national banks, for which alone data regarding the various classes of loans are available, investments increased from $4,563,000,000 to $7,147,000,000, and collateral loans from $2,907,000,000 to $5,114,000,000, a combined increase of $4,791,000,000, or 64.1 per cent. During the same years, unsecured loans and those secured by merchandise and warehouse receipts—loans that are mainly commercial in character— increased only from $7,859,000,000 to $8,575,000,000, or 9.1 per cent.

From the standpoint of those securing capital for actual use, it makes little difference whether funds are forthcoming through the purchase of securities with cash resources by banks and others, or through purchases consummated by means of collateral loans. A given investor may either purchase securities outright or leave funds with a bank, thus enabling it to purchase the securities or grant loans to would-be buyers. In all three instances the obligation incurred by the corporation or government securing the funds is the same. Indirectly, collateral loans facilitate the acquisition of bank credit for business purposes on a stock basis, a type of direct investment by banks that is subject to legal and traditional restrictions. Thus, it may be said that some portion, of constantly varying amount, of the capital of the United States Steel Corporation throughout its entire history has been supplied by the banks, to the extent that steel stock has been accepted as security for collateral loans. Since, by and large, a business becomes stronger as the proportion of its assets financed by shareholders increases relative to its indebtedness, collateral loans in contributing to this result are performing a most useful service to the community.

The increase in collateral loans and security holdings relative to commercial loans may reflect a permanent tendency in the employment of bank credit. Improvements in methods of production, in general, involve the employment of increasing amounts of capital in fixed forms; seasonal peaks in industry are being reduced, and business organizations of large size are occupying a widening area in the field of production and merchandising. These developments favor the financing of the resources of business in permanent ways, through the issue of stocks and bonds, and the wide distribution of such securities among investors. This is a merchandising activity which requires large funds that are mainly secured from banks by means of collateral loans. When secured for this purpose, the collateral loan is strictly analogous to a commercial loan. It is serving to finance an operation of the borrower which, in the ordinary course of his business, will shortly be completed, and followed by a succession of similar operations in the future.

But the collateral loan performs another, less obvious though quite as indispensable, function in the security field. It makes possible the development of a continuing market for outstanding securities, in the absence of which the attractiveness of securities as investments would be seriously reduced. As the volume of securities in the hands of the public increases, organized markets and a coincident increase in collateral loans are needed, if holders are to find a ready sale for such securities as they may wish from time to time to convert into cash.

From the point of view of the banker, collateral loans possess conspicuous attractions. When made against a variety of securities, less trouble and care are requisite than are involved in making unsecured loans to borrowers engaged in different lines of business. And further, collateral loans are not, as is often assumed, less liquid than commercial loans. For a given bank, a loan is liquid if it can be readily shifted to another lender, and, aside from discounting from Reserve banks, this possibility is present for a larger proportion of collateral than of commercial loans. On the other hand, sudden contraction on a large scale is possible with no class of loans, and under a well-organized banking system is never necessary.

With the accumulation of wealth and the acquisition of funds from a widening circle of investors by governments and business enterprises, banks and banking houses of the larger cities become the agencies through which an increasing proportion of the savings of the community reach those who use them. It does not necessarily follow on this account that bankers are exercising an increasing measure of control over industry and trade. Doubtless, greater responsibility rests upon bankers for the placement of capital in capable hands, and for its balanced distribution among various uses. But the positive control over the conduct of industry that bankers may exercise is determined more by the abundance or scarcity of capital relative to demand than by the actual amount of funds that are made available. A business that is in a weak position, whether from poor earnings or faulty financial structure, may be obliged to follow implicitly the suggestions of bankers. When investment funds are in ample supply, a strong business enterprise occupies a position of satisfactory independence.

It is, of course, entirely possible that much of the ample supply of capital may have been placed in feeble hands, and that certain industries may prove to have been overdeveloped. But when capital is secured on the basis of more or less permanent financial arrangements, the consequences of errors of judgment disclose themselves slowly with the lapse of time. For this reason, the years from 1922 to 1928 cannot be considered a complete or even well-defined period of experience. It would doubtless have been otherwise, if bank credit had been employed in active speculation in the commodity markets with a rapidly rising price level. For the full round of changes in a business cycle in which trading activities are the major factor, six years may be ample time. A longer period may be required when the investing of additional capital takes the leading rôle in the activities of the business world.

VII. STOCK EXCHANGE OPERATIONS

Securities held by the general public are commonly listed on one or more of the stock exchanges of the country, and this practice has led, in recent years, to a noteworthy increase in the number and variety of issues readily available for active trading purposes. Although the business handled on other exchanges has increased, the overshadowing importance of the New York Stock Exchange has suffered no diminution. The obvious advantages of nation-wide connections and publicity inevitably exert a potent influence toward centralization, and, measured either by the value of securities listed or by the volume of trading, the New York Stock Exchange greatly exceeds all the other stock exchanges in the United States, including its active neighbor, the New York Curb Market.

The scope of operations on the New York Stock Exchange is evident from the following table which gives, for the years 1919 to 1928, the number of issues of bonds and shares listed and the annual volume of trading measured by the value of bonds and number of shares sold.

SEPARATE ISSUES LISTED, 1919 TO 1928

(At the beginning of each year)

Year	Bonds	Stocks	Totals
1919	1,131	612	1,743
1920	1,114	691	1,805
1921	1,115	756	1,871
1922	1,156	792	1,948
1923	1,234	778	2,012
1924	1,262	889	2,151
1925	1,332	927	2,259
1926	1,367	1,043	2,410
1927	1,420	1,081	2,501
1928	1,491	1,097	2,588
a1928	1,513	1,131	2,644

a As of October 1.

VOLUME OF TRADING

(000,000 omitted)

Year	Stocks (Number of shares)	Bonds (Face value)
1919	312	$3,771
1920	223	3,955
1921	171	3,504
1922	260	4,098
1923	237	2,753
1924	282	3,828
1925	452	3,398
1926	449	3,029
1927	576	3,321
1928	920	2,939

It may first be noted that dealings in bonds play a minor rôle on the Exchange and that, in spite of a considerable increase in listings, they have manifested little or no tendency to increase. Purchases and sales of outstanding and new issues of bonds, as well as of inactive stocks, continue to be arranged in large measure directly between investors and dealers in securities. It is only securities that, for whatever reason, exhibit decided changes in value that are the objects of Stock Exchange transactions.

During the first six years covered by the table, the volume of dealings in shares was comparatively steady. A shrinkage in 1921, a year of depression, illustrates the proposition that prolonged activity in security dealing is always associated with rising quotations. After an initial stage of more or less enforced liquidation, a declining market becomes stagnant until an upward movement is inaugurated. It was not until 1925 that the annual volume of dealings in shares exceeded the total for 1919. A record was then made which was practically maintained in the following year, was greatly exceeded in 1927, and more than doubled in 1928.

Unquestionably, Stock Exchange transactions have been the most conspicuous financial development of the later years of the period under review, and the causes of the unexampled expansion in trading and its economic, as well as financial, significance and effects deserve careful examination.

On the basis of the movement of industrial security quotations, the years since 1921 divide into two periods; one, of moderate change until the summer of 1924, and a subsequent period of persistent advances continuing to the end of 1928. A similar division appears in the case of brokers' loans, no decided increase in the first period, very great expansion in the second. The course of call loan rates does not, however, follow this division. A sharp decline in 1922 was followed by fairly stable rates until the beginning of 1928. Thereafter, rates advanced sharply, with, it is to be noted, no accompanying decline but rather a further increase in the volume of brokers' loans.

Many influences of varying degrees of importance contributed to bring about the marked upward movement of security prices and to induce an exceptional volume of trading. Leaving out of account an initial advance incident to the recovery of business following the depression in 1921, the abundance of funds seeking investment and the decline in interest rates provided the basis for a general advance in security quotations. Other factors have been the more general recognition of the possibilities of appreciation of common stocks in a growing country, the organization of many investment trusts, a large increase in the number of branch offices of Stock Exchange houses, the listing of shares of many additional enterprises and, above all, the impressively large profits of a considerable number of companies, giving rise to anticipations of a further increase in earnings of these and other undertakings. Discounting the future in the security market may be carried to excess with resulting unhappy consequences, and it is an important limitation upon the significance of this survey that it covers a period that witnessed only the economic, social, and financial effects of a rising market for securities.

The effects of rising security prices during the period of advance may here be generally indicated. A rising stock market has a psychological influence favorable to business activity. It also serves to facilitate the marketing of securities among investors, and lessens the cost of additional capital secured through the issue of new stock by many enterprises. In such markets, large and sudden gains are realized, and some part of these gains doubtless serves to increase the demand for many commodities, particularly articles of luxury. Finally, a rising security market tends to transfer ownership of some part of the accumulated wealth of the country from the cautious to the farsighted and venturesome.

An active stock market always involves an increasing volume of loans to brokers. The rate of increase in these loans since 1923 has been rapidly accelerated. The funds that are borrowed to finance Stock Exchange transactions, it should perhaps be noted, are not withdrawn from use and held in the market. Brokers' loans are simply one of the various channels through which funds enter into general use throughout the community. The broker incurs an obligation to make payment, but the funds he borrows are at once turned over to those from whom securities are purchased and are thereafter employed for every kind of purpose, as are the funds borrowed to finance real estate, the production and marketing of goods or other transactions. Here and there, it may indeed happen that a particular borrower has been unable to secure accommodation because those lenders to whom he had access had employed all their available resources in brokers' loans, but such cases must have been exceptional, since the funds thus employed have come almost exclusively from urban sources,—city banks, and other large lenders. Valid criticism of brokers' loans must rather be concerned with the more direct effects of this use of financial resources.

In view of the moderate rates on all classes of loans that obtained between 1922 and the close of 1927, it would appear that the growth in brokers' loans in these years served to provide a reasonably safe and liquid avenue for the employment of surplus funds. It was not until 1928 that the stock market demand for additional funds became so intense as to exert an influence tending to bring about an advance in rates on all other classes of loans. That security prices should have further advanced in 1928, with an accompanying increase in brokers' loans and in spite of a sharp advance in rates, may perhaps be regarded as symptomatic of unrestrained speculation. But even though an over-extended situation in the security market should not develop and be followed by a disastrous reaction, it may be said that the recent experience in the functioning of the money market, as it is affected by the Stock Exchange demand for credit, raises new and perplexing problems. In the past, the bulk of brokers' loans has been furnished by banks and bankers.   Under the influence of rates for call loans ruling generally above rates on all other classes of loans, the funds of investors and surplus funds of business enterprises have been attracted into the market in such volume that they now provide very nearly one-half of the total supply. The outcome of this practice remains for the future to disclose.

The recent development of a stock market demand for loans that seems almost without limit and is impervious to moderate advances in rates, and the possibility of the recurrence of a similar situation from time to time in the future, cannot fail to affect unfavorably the development and functioning of the New York money market as a great and reasonably stable national and world financial center.   The issue and marketing of bonds, the granting of acceptance credits and the functioning of the bill market, have been unfavorably affected by the instability of rates, occasioned by the absorption of credit in connection with Stock Exchange operations.   The volume of transactions on the Stock Exchange is immensely greater than that on the exchange in any other country. Customers are far more numerous and, above all, daily settlements are a unique feature of trading.   The adoption of term settlements has been suggested, but the proposition has met with but little favor in Stock Exchange circles.   The only other means of securing a reasonable measure of stability in the functioning of the New York money market would seem to be through the exercise of a restraining influence by the Federal Reserve System.

During 1928, efforts to restrain the absorption of credit in the security markets were indeed made by the Reserve banks, and the conclusion should not be drawn from the lack of success that attended the measures taken that restraint could not be made effective through the Reserve System.   Early in 1928, the Reserve banks initiated a policy of restraint through the exercise of very gradual pressure upon the market.   Government securities were sold and discount rates were increased by three successive advances of $\frac{1}{2}$ of 1 per cent, at intervals separated by from two to three months.   The possibilities of effectually restraining intense speculative activity through sharp and even drastic action have not been tested.

VIII. INVESTMENT TRUSTS

The investment trust is a development of recent years in American finance.   While this type of financial organization is, in large measure, a copy of British investment trusts, its rapid growth in this country appears to be due in part to a new recognition of the value of common stocks as investments.   Statistical studies during the past few years, showing the relative advantages of investments in stocks as compared with bonds, together with the recent rise in stock prices, and the unfortunate experience during the war with the purchasing power of fixed interest securities, have led to widespread buying of common stocks, not simply by speculators but by conservative investors as well.

Since the junior securities of a corporation, in general, carry greater risks along with the possibility of a larger return, diversification becomes of increasing importance, and thus for the small investor considerable advantage is offered by some type of organization which gathers funds from many sources and invests them over a widely distributed list of securities. Moreover, an organization of this sort can command information not available to the individual.

The investment trust is not dissimilar in principle from the savings bank, in that it gathers funds from many sources and employs them in a diversified list of securities selected by a management group. The principal differences are (1) that the investment trust is not limited in its choice of securities by the legal restrictions which surround savings banks, (2) that the investment trust is not under such close governmental supervision, and (3) that the investment trust, unlike the savings bank, usually makes no promise of a fixed rate of return, and indeed has no set limit of return.

Since the investment trust management exercises a much wider discretion than the savings bank, and since it deals in securities of much more speculative character, the important question with regard to its safety and efficiency relates to the character of management. It offers an opportunity for small investors to enjoy some of the same advantages of investment which have heretofore been mainly restricted to investors with large resources, but it faces the dangers of concentrated control in the hands of a few men, without, at the present time, any very close supervision.

The creation of investment trusts has been so rapid in recent months that it is difficult to estimate the total amount of paid-in capital funds of these companies, but they are probably in excess of one billion dollars.

The effects of the growth of investment trusts are similarly difficult to estimate. It has probably furthered the movement toward the purchase of common stock, though, to a considerable extent, purchases by investment trusts have simply meant buying in a block securities which investors might otherwise buy as individuals.

If the investment trust under competent management purchases stocks when they are cheap and sells them when they are dear, a stabilizing influence upon the security market would result, though the question on this point is whether the investment trust would conduct its operations more or less wisely than individual investors.

Another effect would appear to be the placing of large amounts of funds in the stock exchange money market. The small individual investor with funds awaiting investment ordinarily carries these funds on deposit with his bank, whereas the investment trust is more apt to carry such funds in the form of loans in the stock exchange money market. Since such loans tend to support a security market at times when security prices are high, this activity of investment trusts frequently may have an inflationary rather than a stabilizing influence upon stock prices.

The investment trust movement, however, is too new to justify comprehensive conclusions, and the total size of the trusts has not been large enough to warrant belief that they have exercised any very large influence upon American finance.

IX. BANKING ORGANIZATION AND PRACTICE

While there have been no changes of great moment in banking organization and practice during the period of this survey, a number of tendencies are to be observed that may prove to be the initial stages of significant modification and development. Particular interest attaches to the decline in the number of commercial banks throughout the country, the growth of branch banking and chains of banks, and the widening range of functions and activities undertaken by a steadily increasing number of banks.

During the first two decades of the century, to go no further back, there had been a continuous and accelerating increase in the number of banks in the United States, the amazing total of more than 30,000 being in operation in 1921. A conspicuous reversal of this tendency has now continued for more than seven years, and, taking the country as a whole, there has been a decided reduction—4,000—in the number of banks. But with over 26,000 banks still in operation, this reduction still leaves the banking system of the country unchanged in this its most characteristic and fundamental feature. It remains a system constituted by a multiplicity of local banks, exhibiting extreme diversity in size, in character and experience of management, and in the surrounding economic conditions of the communties to be served.

Whether there will be a further material decline in the number of banks cannot be positively predicted, though it seems by no means improbable. In any event, it may be confidently anticipated that the decline will be at a far less rapid rate, since the major cause of the disappearance of banks in recent years—numerous bank failures—reflects conditions abnormally unfavorable to banking solvency in many localities, conditions unlikely to reappear with any like severity in the near future. But other less potent influences tending to bring about a reduction in the number of banks have also been present, and these influences may be expected to persist and perhaps assume greater significance. As the analysis of these influences will throw some light upon the bank failure problem, they will be given prior consideration.

Branch and Chain Banking.—Under a system of independent unit banks, the accommodation that is available to the great mass of borrowers is limited to the amount of funds at the disposal of the local banks. But as any particular business undertaking grows in size, the geographical range of its borrowing possibilities widens. It is able to resort to the nearest urban center, and, with further growth, to banks in the larger cities throughout the country, including New York. The services of dealers in commercial paper may also be utilized to secure funds from a large and changing number of scattered banks. Under a unit banking system, in contrast with a highly developed branch banking system, the borrower seeks distant supplies of funds, as supplies of funds are not sent to his neighborhood for employment.

Resort to the money centers by large borrowers is by no means a recent practice, but it is certain that the practice is being more and more generally employed and by a widening range of individuals and corporations. When a number of small producing or merchandising units are combined into a single organization, dependence on local supplies of bank credit is eliminated. Finance companies, utilizing credit lines established with many city banks, relieve local dealers from some portion of the obligations which they could only finance through local banks. Co-operative marketing associations of farmers secure acceptance credits from distant metropolitan banks whose assistance could not possibly be enlisted by any considerable number of the individual members. Legislation that fosters this particular development is to be noted in the system of intermediate credit banks, the resources of which are especially designed to assist co-operative marketing.[10] In the farm mortgage field, also, the same situation is to be observed. The Federal Land Bank System provides a standardized security resting upon hundreds of thousands of first mortgages, which enables farmers to tap distant sources of funds, but necessarily at the same time removes from the portfolio of the local banker a security of the best obtainable character.

Taking all these tendencies into account, it is evident that the character of the business that many local banks retain must have undergone not a little deterioration. And these are not the only difficulties with which in many instances they are beset. The bank in the small village or rural hamlet, like the neighboring storekeeper, is unfavorably affected by improvements in transportation, which have greatly widened the area that is conveniently adjacent to the larger cities and towns.[11] Banks in the larger centers have been gaining deposits, and seem likely to continue to gain, at the expense of the small rural bank in surrounding territory. Exceptionally capable management will doubtless enable many to surmount these various obstacles, but these conditions are not favorable to the maintenance of solvency, to say nothing of satisfactory earnings.

[10] See Co-operative Buying and Selling, Chap. V, Marketing, pp. 374–390; Chap. VIII, Agriculture, pp. 579–581.
[11] See Chap. V, Marketing, p. 335.

To depositors and borrowers alike, a further decline in the number of banks, in agricultural sections particularly, would involve no appreciable inconvenience, and would result in a decided gain in security. But mergers and voluntary liquidation are the desirable means of accomplishing this result rather than bank failures, and it is satisfactory to note that these more desirable methods are being freely employed. More than 50 mergers and voluntary liquidations, during the first seven months of 1928, in the over-banked state of Missouri furnished a notable instance of this desirable tendency.

There is also evidence of not a little concentration in banking where weak and excessively numerous banks are not in question, where the initiative is taken by strong banks which acquire prosperous neighbors in order to become still larger and, at times also, in order to secure the services of experienced and capable officers. Concentration of this general character is limited by legal restrictions upon the operation of branches by banks, and one of the notable developments of the period under review has been the settlement, at least for the time being, of the vexing and contentious controversy which had arisen over this form of banking organization. Many of the states prohibit branch banking entirely; others allowed it within city or county limits; still others, of which California is the most striking example, impose no restrictions. In states which allowed branches, national banks were at a disadvantage, since they were practically limited in this field to the branches of such state banks as they might absorb. A change in the national banking law, giving them branch powers similar to those enjoyed by state banks in their respective states, would have been satisfactory to national bankers, but this remedy encountered opposition from states in which branch banking was either prohibited or restricted, since, upon its adoption, national banks would no longer have unitedly opposed further liberalization of legislation regarding branches in those states. Finally, a compromise measure was adopted, under which national banks are permitted to open branches in cities in which state banks enjoyed that privilege at the time of the passage of the act, but not in wider areas, and not in cities that might subsequently be opened to branches by state law. And further, in order to curb the spread of branch banking under state law, it was provided that state bank members of the Federal Reserve System might establish additional branches only in localities in which the act permitted national banks to open branches. This measure places no obstacle in the way of a nonmember state bank, but it was assumed that any large bank, operating numerous branches, would desire to retain its membership in the System.

With the operation of branches narrowly restricted by legislation, the tendency toward concentration in banking is manifesting itself to an increasing extent, in a slightly different and decidedly more unsatisfactory fashion—in the formation, under a bewildering variety of arrangements, of chains of banks. Investment in a limited number of shares in scattered banks does not constitute a chain of banks. Some measure of control and management is involved. Chain banking overleaps state boundaries, and may, and commonly does, include both state and national banks. Chains lack the internal controls of a unified accounting system, and they escape the simultaneous examinations to which banks with branches are subject. In spite of these defects, with management in honest and capable hands, good results will be attained, but it is obviously a form of organization which lends itself to grave abuse.

Bank Failures.—During the seven years, 1921–1927, according to information gathered by the Federal Reserve Board, 4,513 banks suspended payment, of which 559 were subsequently reopened. The total deposits of these failed banks were $1,151,000,000, an average of but $291,000 for each bank. Even if large allowance is made for heavy withdrawals of deposits shortly before failure, it is evident that this epidemic of failures has been confined almost entirely to small banks with resources of less than $500,000. Since the business of such banks is ordinarily circumscribed within narrow local areas, these numerous failures, however grievous to the communities in which the banks were established, have not been a large factor in the general financial situation of the country.

These failures do not imply a weak condition and poor management of the banks generally, but they indicate, as does experience in earlier periods, that large numbers of banks, which seem to be in a flourishing condition during years of business activity, are unable to withstand the stress and strain incident to depression and a downward adjustment of values in the communities in which they are established. In the territory served by the Federal Reserve Banks of Boston, New York, and Philadelphia, a section which speedily recovered from the industrial reverses of 1920, bank failures were relatively few—only 43 during the seven years, 1921–1927. The Cleveland district with 61 failures, and the San Francisco district with 187, also show a comparatively low casualty rate. In the four southern districts of Richmond, Atlanta, St. Louis, and Dallas, on the other hand, there were 1,321 failures during this seven-year period. The three remaining districts present a still less favorable record; the Chicago district shows 550 failures, Kansas City shows 685, and finally there is the astounding number of 1,097 failures in the Minneapolis district.

Dishonesty and gross mismanagement account for a small number of these failures. The suspension of a larger number was precipitated by adverse conditions of a purely local character, such as a succession of crop failures or the sudden collapse of real estate booms in particular towns and cities. But the great majority of banks failed because they were unable to withstand the stress exerted by the persistence of unprofitable prices for the products of agriculture and animal husbandry—stress that was particularly severe because it was experienced after years of abounding prosperity and extreme appreciation in the value of farm property, and a large increase in the number of farms mortgaged and the amount of mortgage indebtedness.

These adverse conditions alone, it can hardly be too strongly emphasized, do not furnish a complete explanation of the numerous bank failures of the last seven years. By no means all, or even a majority, of the banks in the localities most seriously affected have been obliged to suspend operations. Financially weak and unskillfully managed banks have been weeded out; strong, well-managed banks have no doubt experienced heavy losses, but they survive. Great significance in this connection attaches to the findings of a special committee on the banking situation, appointed in 1927 by the legislature of Minnesota, a state in which adverse conditions have been particularly severe and the number of bank failures numerous. Analyzing the causes of bank failures, the committee says:

A survey of the closed bank situation in Minnesota presents an interesting picture. Certain communities of the state seem to have escaped entirely, or almost entirely, this epidemic of closed banks, while in other parts of the state the proportion of closed banks to the number of banks chartered in the community is very great, nor is this unequal distribution of closed banks due in large measure to different conditions of soil or condition of the farmers, for in parts of the state where the farming conditions are almost identical one part shows a large percentage of failed banks and another part almost none. The cause lies deeper than that.

Unqualified agreement with this view of the matter, as seen by the Minnesota committee, is not inconsistent with recognition that external conditions during the last ten years, in certain parts of the country, have been most unfavorable to the conduct of banking along safe lines. In the agricultural development of the country, however, the stage is apparently being more generally reached in which farm values will be more closely related to current net income. Except in the event of a war of major magnitude, it is not probable that commodity prices will again exhibit the extreme fluctuations of the last decade, or that we shall again witness the number of bank failures that has marked the last seven years. If this anticipation is realized, the bank failure problem assumes more manageable proportions, but, in the absence of improvements in organization and practice, it is not to be doubted that a discreditable number of failures will continue to occur, mainly concentrated in periods of trade reaction.

There are hundreds of small banks throughout the country which are ably managed and abundantly strong, and which overcome the handicap of an absence of industrial diversity in the communities which they serve by the exercise of exceptional judgment and caution. On the other hand, while there is no exact relationship between the number and size of the entire group of banks in a locality and the strength of its banking position, it is certain that no community can hope to enjoy the benefits of safety in banking if the business is organized in units so numerous as to exceed the available supply of competent officers and responsible directors, and with insufficient earning power to be able to absorb inevitable losses. Ample evidence of the unhappy consequences of excessive numbers and inadequate size in banking is clearly to be found in the geographical distribution of the failures of the last seven years.

In the Federal Reserve districts of Boston, New York, and Philadelphia, there were only 43 failures during these years. These districts have an area of 150,000 square miles with a population of 33,000,000, and were served in 1927 by less than 3,300 banks (3,287). The Chicago district, with a somewhat larger area, 190,000 square miles, but with a population of only 17,000,000, was still provided with a number of banks larger by nearly 2,000 (5,175) and had a record of 550 failures between 1921 and 1928. Again, the Minneapolis district, it is true with a much greater area, 414,000 square miles, but with a population of only 3,500,000, still had 2,633 banks in operation after 1,087 failures in the same period.

Comparison by states tells the same story only the more forcibly. The 11,000,000 people of the state of New York, with an area of 47,000 square miles, appear to have been adequately supplied with banking facilities in 1920 by 1,056 banks, and there were only 10 failures in the seven subsequent years, while the 2,500,000 people occupying an area of 55,000 square miles in Iowa were served by 1,763 banks, of which 329 failed. North Dakota supplies an even more extreme instance of the overdevelopment of banks and its inevitable sequel—349 failures among 898 banks that had been established to meet the need of a population of 650,000 on an area of 70,000 square miles.

No community can possibly provide adequate resources, competent officers, and experienced directors for one bank to every 750 of its inhabitants as in North Dakota, or to 1,400 as in Iowa. And the situation in these states was not exceptional; on the contrary, an excessive number of banks have been established throughout those sections of the country that are mainly devoted to agriculture. Banking troubles were inevitable with the advent of adverse conditions, and for the severity of these conditions the unwise use of credit administered by an inordinate multiplicity of banks was in no small degree responsible.

As in earlier periods marked by numerous bank failures, an insistent demand for greater safety in banking is to be anticipated, and this demand is not rendered less reasonable by the presence of strong and well-managed banks in every locality. The public must make use of banks, but few are in position to distinguish between the strong and the weak.

Bank statements and other external information relating to banks do not furnish an adequate basis for intelligent discrimination. Unless failures become infrequent, it may be expected that all banks will be subjected to an increasing range of restrictions, restrictions which are quite superfluous for well-managed banks, but which are adopted to curb the weak and incompetent minority.

But safety in banking will never be secured if reliance continues to be placed primarily and almost exclusively upon legislative restrictions covering the details of banking operations. A more immediate enforcement of existing legislation would do much, but remedies for bank failures, to be effective, must be designed to reduce the number of financially weak banks, secure more competent officers and directors, and above all to insure that unsound policies will be checked long before solvency is threatened.

X. INFLUENCE OF THE FEDERAL RESERVE SYSTEM

The assigning of a place in the economic developments of recent years to the Federal Reserve System can only be done tentatively. The Reserve System has been one of many influences, and it is impossible to segregate these various influences. Nor is it easy in dealing with this question to write without bias for or against the System. Before satisfactory conclusions can be drawn, more perspective will be required and longer experience.

Perhaps the most valuable approach to the discussion of the contribution of the Federal Reserve System to business in this period is to consider it in terms of the major monetary problems of the period with which the Reserve System has had to deal. Two unusual problems were, first, that created by huge gold movements, and second, the problem of international monetary stability. In addition, there were the continuing problems relating to stability in the money market and the attitude of the Reserve System to those business fluctuations summarized under the term "business cycle."

Gold Movements and Inflation.—As already noted earlier in this chapter, there was a net gold import into the United States of nearly $900,000,000 from the beginning of 1922 to the middle of 1927, and, in the 12 months following, a gold export of about $500,000,000. These were larger movements of gold than in any period of the past, except for the abnormal flow during the war and immediate postwar period.

A huge gold import, such as that from 1922 to 1927, ordinarily carries with it a threat of inflation of credit and of prices. It might have been expected that the inflationary effect of the gold imports would be accentuated because they followed a huge import movement, in the closing months of 1920 and during 1921, which totaled over $800,000,000. This movement of gold had fortunately been absorbed without inflation, by reason of the fact that the incoming gold was used by member banks to liquidate their indebtedness at the Federal Reserve banks. The gold import, from 1922 to 1927, was not absorbed in any such fashion, save to a very limited extent, but, on the contrary, was used as the basis for an expansion in credit and in currency, as was indicated in Table 4 in this chapter, which shows the changes in the reserve position of the country over that period. Of the $900,000,000 in gold (plus about $200,000,000 derived from an increase in the silver stock, and $50,000,000 from other sources), roughly $600,000,000 was used to increase the reserve balances of the member banks at the Reserve banks, and thus support expansion in credit of more than $6,000,000,000. About $300,000,000 was used in an expansion of currency, and the balance of $250,000,000 was used to decrease the amount of Federal Reserve credit in use. Thus it may be said that gold imports from 1922 to 1927 exercised much their normal influence toward credit expansion. This credit expansion was large and rapid; it was accompanied by an increase in the general level of prices, as shown by an increase of 9 per cent (14 points) in the general price index of the Federal Reserve Bank of New York. It is true that there was no inflation of commodity prices. The change in the price index of the Bureau of Labor Statistics from January, 1922 to July, 1927, shows an increase of 3 per cent. That the large increase in bank credit, that is in purchasing power, was not accompanied by a large increase in commodity prices may be explained in a number of different ways, some of which have already been dealt with in this report.

1. It was a period of rapid accumulation of savings, and much of the increase in bank deposits took the form of an increase in savings deposits, which have a relatively slow rate of turnover.

2. Commodity prices in other important countries of the world were tending to decline during this period, and hence commodity prices in this country, which are greatly influenced by conditions in world commodity markets, met resistance against any upward movement.

3. The general prosperity of large business corporations made the securities of those corporations attractive to investors, and much of the additional credit was employed to finance active dealings in a growing volume of securities at rising price levels.

4. The period was characterized by increases in wages and salaries, and additional amounts of credit were employed for this purpose.

5. Considerable amounts of credit found their way into other employment, such as financing a huge volume of building and financing real estate transfers at appreciating prices.

The Federal Reserve System during this period did not prevent a very large expansion in bank credit which might perhaps be described in some part as inflationary, to the extent that it was accompanied by increases in prices of various kinds. The principal influence of the Federal

Reserve System upon this credit expansion related to the timing of the
expansion.   As was indicated earlier in this chapter, the increase in credit
during these years was not continuous, but was more rapid at certain times
than at others.   It was more rapid, for example, in the years 1922, 1924,
and 1927, than in 1923 and 1926.   The differences among these years, as to
the rate of credit expansion, may be ascribed, in part at least, to the operation of Federal Reserve policy for, during 1922, 1924, and 1927, Federal
Reserve policy was such as to encourage credit expansion, whereas, in
1923 and 1926, Federal Reserve operations had a tendency to discourage
expansion.   The nature of Federal Reserve operations which would
presumably have this effect is illustrated in Chart 14.

CHART 14.—FEDERAL RESERVE BANK CREDIT, 1922–1928

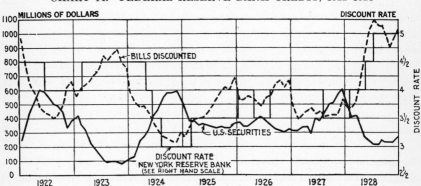

It will be seen from this chart that during the first few months of
1922, and considerable parts of 1924 and 1927, the Federal Reserve banks
were purchasing government securities.   These purchases had the effect
of putting money into the money market.   The money thus made
available was deposited promptly in member banks, and, in 1922 and
1924, was used by them in repaying their indebtedness at the Federal
Reserve banks, as shown by decreases in the total amounts of bills discounted.   In 1927, the money made available by security purchases was
used chiefly to offset losses through gold exports.   The member banks,
as they found themselves freed from indebtedness at the Federal Reserve
banks, were in a position to extend credit to their customers or to the
market more freely, and as they received additions to their reserves
through gold imports they were able to employ these funds in an expansion of credit.

During the latter part of 1922 and the early months of 1923, the
latter part of 1924 and early in 1925, and to some extent in 1926, the
Federal Reserve banks were selling Government securities.   This had
the effect of withdrawing funds from the market and of compelling the
member banks to increase their indebtedness at the Reserve banks.

Member banks thus found themselves in a position to lend or invest their funds less freely, and there was a tendency to check the rapid expansion of credit. Thus the timing of the employment of gold imports was determined in some measure at least by Federal Reserve policy.

It is not easy to summarize the purposes toward which this policy was directed. Any decision of Federal Reserve policy is made from a consideration of the whole of the credit situation, and it is difficult to interpret the relative importance of the different phases of that situation, as they enter into the decisions of the groups of men who determine policy. But among the factors were certainly the movement of domestic business and prices, the world credit situation, and the movement of gold itself.

The relation of the Federal Reserve System to the gold imports of this period may be summarized by saying that the Reserve System did not sterilize the imported gold, but allowed the gold to have much its usual effect in bringing about an increase in the volume of credit. This increase was limited to a primary credit expansion; that is, the gold was used only once for a credit expansion at the time when the member banks deposited it in the Reserve banks. It was not used for a secondary expansion; that is, the Reserve banks did not utilize the additional lending power which they derived through their receipts of gold during the period.

In the last year of the period under discussion, from July 1, 1927 to the middle of 1928, the gold movement was reversed, and more than $500,000,000 of gold was exported. Under the monetary mechanism of the country prior to the establishment of the Reserve System, any such export of gold in a single year would have brought widespread disaster; for so large a reduction in bank reserves would have been reflected immediately in curtailment of the credit based upon those reserves to an amount many times as large as the gold reserves themselves. The mechanism of the Federal Reserve System provided means by which the loss to reserves from this cause could be repaired by drawing into use Federal Reserve credit. As their reserves were depleted through gold exports, the member banks restored their reserves by borrowing from the Reserve banks against their eligible paper. This increase in member bank borrowing from the Reserve banks did not take place without an effect upon the credit situation. The member banks are always reluctant to remain continuously in debt to the Reserve banks and, as usual in such circumstances, they endeavored to get out of debt by the sale of securities and by some reduction in their advances, particularly for speculative purposes. As a consequence money rates rose. This tendency was accentuated rather than diminished by Federal Reserve policy. By selling securities in the early part of 1928, the Reserve banks made necessary a still further increase in the amount of member bank borrowing, which, in turn, tended to accentuate the firmness of money conditions. The firming of money conditions had the effect of impeding the further export of gold, and gradually checking the rapid increase in the volume of credit, though in the year from June 30, 1927 to June 30, 1928, the increase in credit was larger than in any other year since 1924, despite the loss of gold.

These events may be summarized by saying that the mechanism of the Reserve System made possible a huge export of gold without serious consequences to business or monetary conditions, though at the price of firmer money conditions. In view of the huge growth in credit for speculative uses, the Reserve System did nothing to prevent the gold from exerting something of its normal influence in tightening credit conditions.

International Monetary Stability.—The beginning of the period under survey found the nations of the world with generally unstable currencies. War had forced them into such large issues of paper currency that gold payments were suspended, and currencies were depreciated from their par values. Under these conditions, world trade had shrunk to about two-thirds of its prewar volume, and European purchases of American commodities tended to be restricted. American trade with other nations was made more precarious by the fluctuations of the foreign exchanges. Gold, detached from the currencies of these countries, tended to flow in a steady stream to the United States, and threatened, if long continued, to bring about credit and price inflation.

Under these circumstances, it was to the interest of the United States that every possible assistance be rendered to the countries of Europe in their effort to re-establish themselves on the gold standard as promptly as possible. The investment bankers and the investors of this country played an important rôle in this recovery by lending to European countries as much as $1,000,000,000 a year for several years. The loans furnished the means for these countries gradually to rebuild their industries and reorganize their monetary systems and, at the same time, to continue their purchases of American products during an interval when they were unable to make payment for goods purchased here.

In two specific ways the Federal Reserve System has been able to aid in the European financial recovery. First, the Federal Reserve banks extended credits to the Bank of England, the National Bank of Belgium, the Bank of Italy, and the Bank of Poland at the times when these countries were prepared to announce their legal stabilization programs. In the cases of Belgium, Italy, and Poland, the Federal Reserve credit was a part of a larger credit participated in by many of the European banks of issue. The credits took the form of an agreement on the part of the Reserve banks to purchase bankers' acceptances from those three banks of issue, at stipulated rates and in specified amounts, if the need should arise. In the case of the Bank of England, the credit took the form of an agreement to sell gold to that bank, if desired. In none of these four cases was the credit utilized, but the public announcement that the Federal Reserve banks were prepared to extend this support to the banks of issue of the different countries provided an important psychological influence toward the success of the stabilization programs.

The other method, by which the Reserve System exerted some influence toward facilitating the return of world monetary stability, was its consideration of world conditions in the determination of its credit policy at certain periods. While at all times domestic conditions have of necessity received first consideration in the determination of Federal Reserve discount rates and open market operations, there have been periods when some modification of Federal Reserve policy, with the world situation in view, was not incompatible with domestic conditions.

The two principal occasions of this sort were in 1924 and 1927. The year 1924 was one of somewhat reduced business activity in the United States, so that, as far as domestic conditions were concerned, a policy of low discount rates, supplemented by open market purchases of securities, was likely to be beneficial rather than otherwise. It was at least a time when easy money might be expected to do little harm.

For the international money markets, 1924 was a critical year. London had always been the world's principal money market, and the stability of the pound sterling was prerequisite to a return of international monetary stability. While sterling had returned within 4 per cent of parity early in 1923, it had then receded to 4.25 in January of 1924, partly because of high money rates in this country.

With every desire to bring their currency to a stable position as promptly as possible, the British found themselves with their exchange 13 per cent below parity in January, 1924. The other exchanges of the world were so closely related to sterling that it was almost hopeless to expect their recovery until the important step had been taken in England. The experts were working on the Dawes Plan, and a solution was hoped for.

In the United States, the need for high money rates had passed with the subsidence of the speculative and business boom of early 1923. Under these circumstances, the Federal Reserve System, toward the close of 1923, adopted a policy of placing additional funds in the money market through the purchase of Government securities, and, between that time and September, 1924, purchases amounted to $500,000,000. The first result of this action was that the member banks were enabled to repay the Reserve banks much of their indebtedness, so that, by the middle of 1924, the member banks in principal cities had practically liquidated their borrowings. This placed the banks in a position to advance funds more freely, and money rates declined steadily. Consequently, money rates in New York, for the first time in some months, became cheaper than money rates in London. The amount of new financing in New

York was increased, and there was a tendency for funds to flow from New York to London. Sterling exchange began a steady climb, so that, in the spring of 1925, when Great Britain passed her stabilization legislation, sterling was within a few cents of parity, and the transition to gold payments could be made without serious economic disturbance. The return to gold payments by Great Britain opened the way for similar action by many other countries.

It is not possible to determine to what extent the climb in sterling was due to action by the Federal Reserve banks in making money easier in New York and to what extent it was due to other causes, but certainly the recovery would have been more difficult without this Federal Reserve action. In any such vigorous attempt to ease the money market, banking authorities always assume the risk of credit and price inflation, and it may be that there was some inflation as a consequence of the action taken by the Reserve System in 1924, but the generally retarded condition of American business in 1924 made this action appear less dangerous than it might have been at other times. In fact, the probability is that easy money in 1924 was an influence toward preventing a more serious business depression at that time and toward stimulating the rapid business recovery which ensued.

Another occasion when the world monetary situation was an important factor in Federal Reserve policy decisions was in 1927, when the rates of a number of the Reserve banks were reduced in August and September, and purchases of Government securities were made. On that occasion, as in 1924, certain results appeared to be ascribable to the action taken. As money rates receded, following Federal Reserve action, and reached lower points than prevailed in London, the gold movement reversed itself, the exchange on London and a number of other centers moved upward, and a threatened money stringency abroad, which would have hampered world trade, was averted.

The economic situations, both in 1924 and 1927, were so nicely balanced that Federal Reserve policy was probably more effective than might ordinarily be expected. It is hardly to be expected in the future that the influence of Federal Reserve policy will be so dramatic or so effective; nor, in fact, is it likely that, now that the currencies of Europe are stabilized, Reserve policy need concern itself so much with conditions abroad. But in the return of the world monetary stability, it seems clear that the Reserve System, both by its action in granting credits to the banks of issue in foreign countries and by its credit policy, has exercised an important and beneficial influence which has reacted favorably upon American foreign trade.

Stability of the Money Market.—The best thing that the Federal Reserve System could do for business would probably be to exert its influence toward a steady flow of funds readily available for business use at moderate rates. High rates discourage business, while, on the other hand, low rates tend to overstimulate business and prepare the way for business disorganization and depression. But it is clear also, from any study of the course of business over past years, that a rate which may seem low at one time may seem high at another, or *vice versa*. Business does not move forward in a steady continuous stream but moves by long fluctuations, and its psychology differs greatly from one period to another. Business is forever tending to be under- or overstimulated. The problem then, for the Reserve System and for other factors which influence credit, is not one of preserving rates at a uniform level but of exerting an influence so that money rates may be adapted to the economic swing of business. High money rates at times of overstimulation and low money rates at times of understimulation should, in the long run, assist in flattening out the fluctuations of business and in bringing about a more even prosperity.

This may be summarized by saying that the Reserve System's direct contribution to business stability consists of adjusting interest rates to the movement of the business cycle, so as, in some measure, to mollify business booms or depressions.

One marked result of the operations of the Federal Reserve System is demonstrated by the figures for the average deviation of money rates from their moving averages, which were shown in Table 2 of this chapter. The figures appear to indicate that, since the Reserve System has been operating under anything like normal conditions, the fluctuations in money rates have been greatly reduced.

A sufficient period has now been covered by the operations of the System, so that the evidence seems reasonably conclusive that the presence of the Reserve System has made a substantial improvement in the stability of the money market. This is in accordance with what one would expect theoretically, for the Reserve System has provided a method never before available in this country, by means of which reserve funds can be drawn into use or drawn out of use in accordance with the necessity of the money market.

Influence on the Business Cycle.—Since 1922, the fluctuations of business, which might be termed the movements of the business cycle, have been moderate, and there have been no long continued booms nor have there been any deep depressions. It is even difficult to determine how many business cycles we have had. The best guess is perhaps that one cycle extended from the middle of 1921 to the middle of 1924, and another from the middle of 1924 to the end of 1927.[12] But some students believe that we have had during this entire period one continuous business cycle. No matter which conclusion is adopted, it is clear that the experiment has not been sufficiently long to justify passing judgment as

[12] See the concluding Review, pp. 890–909.

to the influence of the Federal Reserve System upon the business cycle. Many other causes have been in operation which may account for the moderation of the movement of business in this period. About all that one can do, in attempting to draw a conclusion as to the influence of the System, is to analyze the action which the System has taken at different times to discover, if possible, whether this action was of a character which would tend to mollify the fluctuations.

Such an analysis appears to show that Federal Reserve influence was toward firm money when business was most active, and toward easy money when business was most depressed. This appears most definitely exhibited in open market operations. We reached the bottom of a business cycle in the summer of 1921 and then started up. At about that time the Federal Reserve System began to purchase Government securities in large amounts. From the funds thus obtained, member banks were able to liquidate some of their indebtedness, and were able to loan somewhat more freely, so that the recovery from depression was stimulated somewhat by Federal Reserve action. As the cycle began to reach its peak in the latter part of 1922 and the early part of 1923, the Reserve System reversed its policy and sold securities, making it necessary for the member banks to borrow more heavily, this condition, in turn, making them less ready to lend in large amounts. In the spring of 1923, discount rates were increased and the Reserve System discussed in its publications the dangers of overexpansion of credit. The peak of expansion was soon passed. Near the end of 1923, business had begun to decline toward the low point of the middle of 1924. In December, 1923, the Reserve banks began to purchase Government securities, and between that date and the middle of the following September they purchased $500,000,000. The funds, thus made available, enabled member banks to reduce their indebtedness, and placed them in a position to lend somewhat more freely to their customers. Accompanying purchases of securities, Federal Reserve discount rates were reduced. Business recovered rapidly from this period of depression, and by the early part of 1925 it reached a new high peak. This movement of business was accompanied by a vigorous speculative movement, and in the early months of 1925 the Federal Reserve System sold $200,-000,000 of the securities purchased in 1924. During 1925 and 1926 and the early part of 1927, business went forward confidently, with the possible exception of a few months in 1926, when a brief period of hesitation was accompanied by small purchases of securities by the Reserve banks and the lowering of the discount rate at New York for a few months.

In 1927, there was again some evidence of business hesitation, particularly in the second half of the year. This coincided, as it had in 1924, with monetary stringency abroad, and the Reserve System purchased

$300,000,000 in securities between May and December, and the discount rates of the reserve banks were reduced. Business again recovered promptly from a period of depression.

Accompanying an outburst of speculation in early 1928, and large increase in the volume of credit, the Reserve System sold $400,000,000 of securities between the end of December, 1927 and June, 1928. The outcome of this latest movement both in business and speculation has not yet become apparent.

This recital of facts carries with it no convincing proof that the presence of the Reserve System has reduced the swing of the business cycle, but it does appear to justify the assertion that its influence has been in that direction.

Test Not Yet Complete.—With regard to all this evidence, it seems important to emphasize the need for suspending judgment as to final conclusions. The period has been one of many unusual economic developments. Business has continued for extended periods above any computed normal growth line, with only brief recessions. There has been an extraordinarily large volume of building, of new financing, of automobile production, and of consumption. There has been a huge volume of speculation, accompanied by striking increases in prices of securities. This has been made possible, in part, by gold imports and the resulting comparatively easy money conditions.

It is possible that in some one or more of these directions an unsound economic structure has been built up, the dangers of which are not now obvious. Only the test of a longer period of time can yield convincing results.

XI. SUMMARY

The average level of money rates from 1922 to 1928 has been lower for commercial funds and higher for speculative funds than in the years before the war. Month-by-month fluctuations of rates have been much reduced. Business has been financed less by borrowing from banks and more by borrowing in the capital market through issues of securities. The growth in bank credit has shown more rapid increases in the Eastern, New England, and Pacific districts; in the Middle Western and Southern districts there has been only a moderate growth, and in the Western district a decline. In general, the most rapid increases of bank credit occurred when business was most in need of the stimulus of easily available credit, and the periods of slowest growth occurred when business was in large volume and, perhaps, in some danger from overstimulation.

The effect of gold movements on the volume of bank credit has been modified by changes in the amount of currency in use, changes in practice as to bank reserves, and changes in the position of the Federal Reserve System.

The principal influence in the period 1922 to 1928 toward rapid growth of bank credit and easy credit conditions was gold imports—an abnormal influence which cannot be expected to continue in the future. The reversal in the gold movement has materially changed the outlook for the supply of bank funds. It may be that a less rapid increase in bank credit than in the past five years would eventually be more wholesome.

Savings have been in unusually large volume. Widespread savings have tended to increase aggregate loans and investments and total deposits, at the same time reducing somewhat the amount of demand deposits. Thanks, at least in part, to saving, large additional supplies of bank credit have not brought about a rapid advance in commodity prices, and the community has not experienced intense competition between consumers and capital for goods and services. Large and widespread savings have been a primary influence in counteracting the upward price tendency of an abundant supply of bank credit. Vivid memories of 1920 have certainly tended to restrain the accumulation of inventories. Efficient transportation has removed fears of delays in shipment. Style has become a factor of importance in many lines, and there has been growing recognition of the economy and elimination of risks that may be secured in merchandising through a rapid rate of turnover. Declining commodity prices in other countries also have been a restraining factor. These and other influences, in conjunction with large savings, furnish an explanation of the failure of commodity prices to respond with a decided upward swing to the impact of an abundant supply of bank credit available at declining rates during recent years of generally active business.

Government debt reduction also has contributed to the abundant supply of capital. Foreign investments have served to widen the opportunities for funds seeking employment. In general, the abundant supply of funds seeking investment at declining rates seems to have strengthened the financial structure of business.

For more than seven years, there has been a progressive decrease in the number of commercial banks in the United States. This tendency probably will continue. Banks in large centers have been gaining, and seem likely to continue to gain, at the expense of small rural banks. Mergers and voluntary liquidations, rather than bank failures, are bringing about this result.

The Federal Reserve System, during the period under review, has had to deal with two unusual problems; first, that created by huge gold movements, and second, the problem of international monetary stability. In addition, there were the continuing problems relating to stability in the money market, and the attitude of the Federal Reserve System to those business fluctuations called "business cycles." The mechanism of the Federal Reserve System made possible a great export of gold in the past year without serious consequences to business or monetary conditions, though at the price of firmer money conditions. In view of the huge growth in credit for speculative purposes, the Federal Reserve System did not prevent the gold from exercising something of its normal influence in tightening credit conditions.

Investment bankers and investors played an important part in European recovery, by lending as much as one billion dollars a year for several years. Federal Reserve banks extended credits to the Bank of England, the National Bank of Belgium, the bank of Italy, and the Bank of Poland. In none of these four cases was the credit utilized, but public announcement that the Federal Reserve banks were prepared to extend this support created an important psychological influence.

The problem for the Federal Reserve System and other factors which influence credit is not one of preserving money rates at a uniform level, but of exerting an influence so that rates may be adapted to the economic swing of business. High money rates at times of overstimulation and low money rates at times of understimulation should, in the long run, assist in flattening out the fluctuations of business and bringing about a more even prosperity. There is no convincing proof that the Reserve System has reduced the fluctuations of the business cycle, but its influence has been in that direction.

CHAPTER XI

FOREIGN MARKETS AND FOREIGN CREDITS

By James Harvey Rogers

I. FOREIGN MARKETS

Exports.—The value of American exports, which increased greatly each year from 1922 to 1925, declined slightly in 1926; and in 1927, while undergoing a mild increase, it still remained a little below the maximum reached in 1925. In 1928, however, the rapid increase was resumed and during that year reached a total 34 per cent greater than in 1922. When changes in the aggregate weight of exports are considered instead of changes in value, the results are different. Thus measured, the volume of our outgoing trade rose during the period, but showed considerable declines both in 1925 and 1927.

The explanation of the divergence in 1925 seems to lie in variations in both prices and quantities, spread over a considerable number of articles.

TABLE 1.—TOTAL ANNUAL EXPORTS OF THE UNITED STATES, 1922–1928

(Value in millions of dollars; volume in millions of tons)

Year	Value	Volume in cargo tonnage of water-borne exports	Value with important price changes eliminated[a]
1922	3,971	42.5	4,009
1923	4,343	49.1	4,213
1924	4,772	52.3	4,676
1925	5,093	49.7	4,976
1926	5,002	67.7	5,245
1927	5,067	56.9	5,467
1928	5,321	....	.....

[a] For exact description of character of the data of this column, see footnote 1.

Sources: Values are taken from *Monthly Summary of Foreign Commerce*, Bureau of Foreign and Domestic Commerce, United States Department of Commerce. Cargo tonnage figures for 1922–1925, inclusive, are taken from the *Statistical Abstract of the United States*, compiled on the basis of data gathered by United States Shipping Board, Bureau of Research, Division of Statistics. Data for 1926 and 1927 are taken from *Special Report*, Division of Statistics, No. 298 of the United States Shipping Board.

Description of data: Value data were gathered by the United States Customs Service and compiled by the United States Department of Commerce. They are subject to errors of valuation and of other accidents of declaration.

Data of value in Table 1 include the trade of the United States Customs Area (which includes continental United States, Alaska, Hawaii, and Porto Rico) with other countries (including the Philippine Islands and the Virgin Islands) plus shipments from continental United States to Alaska, Hawaii, Porto Rico, Guam, and American Samoa. To give the trade of continental United States alone, it would be necessary to deduct the small exports of Alaska, Hawaii, and Porto Rico to foreign countries.

In 1926, on the other hand, while a major explanation of the divergence between weight and value is to be found in the increase of approximately 16,000,000 tons in the export of coal, largely to Great Britain and presumably to some of its European coal customers, occasioned during that year by the British coal strike, perhaps just as potent a separating influence is found in the drastic decline in the price of our largest export, raw cotton.

In order to get another approximate measure of the physical volume of our export trade, as well as for other purposes which will appear later, price changes of a number of important exports have been eliminated. This has been accomplished by computing the annual value of each such export at its average price for the period.[1] The resulting total value, with the prices of a number of important exports thus kept constant, are given in the third column of Table 1. So measured, our total exports, instead of showing a slight decline in 1926 and 1927, increased regularly throughout the period. This conclusion is confirmed by the calculations of the Department of Commerce, using a more elaborate method for eliminating price changes.

The geographic distribution of our outgoing trade has varied considerably during the period from 1922 to 1928. Table 2 gives the total value of exports, by large geographic divisions and by important subdivisions, for the seven years under discussion.

Of our total exports, substantially one-half goes to Europe. The remaining one-half is divided into three roughly equal parts—one going to Canada, another to Latin America, and the third to all the rest of the world combined. Of our exports to Europe, somewhat more than a third goes to the United Kingdom, about one-fifth to Germany, and considerably less to France, the next in order of importance of our European customers. Of our total sales to Latin America, Cuba, Argentina, and Mexico account for considerably more than half; and of those to the rest of the world, Japan, Australia, and China take the largest portions.

But during the last seven years, the proportions of our total exports going to various parts of the world have changed greatly among them-

---

[1] The exact method used was the following: Of every commodity for which both values and quantities are given in Table 3, the total value each year was divided by the corresponding total quantity. Of the resulting prices, simple arithmetic averages were computed for the six years 1922–1927. These average prices were then multiplied by the quantities exported each year. The resulting products were used as the revised total values of each export thus treated. To get the grand totals by years and by geographical divisions, these revised values were in turn added to the actual values of exports of lesser importance and of those for which no quantities are available. The method is little more than a makeshift but would seem to be generally valid for procuring the approximate results desired. The results agree fairly well with those yielded by the more refined index method employed by the Bureau of Foreign and Domestic Commerce for determining year to year changes in like magnitudes.

TABLE 2.—ANNUAL EXPORTS OF THE UNITED STATES, 1922–1928

(In millions of dollars)

Division	Average 1910–1914	1922	1923	1924	1925	1926	1927	1928
Grand total......................	2,243	3,971	4,343	4,772	5,093	5,002	5,067	5,321
Europe.................................	1,350	2,083	2,093	2,445	2,602	2,310	2,314	2,375
United Kingdom and Irish Free State...	568	856	882	983	1,039	990	851	861
Germany..........................	304	316	317	440	470	364	482	467
France............................	139	267	272	282	280	264	229	241
Italy..............................	66	151	168	187	205	157	132	162
Netherlands.......................	105	118	109	152	142	136	148	142
Belgium...........................	53	102	101	116	120	99	116	112
Spain.............................	26	71	62	71	79	68	74	87
Denmark..........................	15	36	39	43	56	51	59	47
Soviet Russia in Europe.............	24	20	4	41	68	48	64	73
Remainder of Europe................	50	146	139	130	143	133	159	183
Canada, Newfoundland, and Labrador.......	320	583	660	634	660	747	844	925
Latin America.......................	302	558	695	770	882	872	846	878
Cuba.............................	63	128	192	200	199	160	155	128
Argentina.........................	47	96	113	117	149	144	163	179
Mexico............................	53	110	121	135	145	135	109	116
Brazil............................	32	43	46	65	87	95	89	100
Caribbean Region[a].................	74	122	143	163	200	219	223	247
Remainder of Latin America..........	33	59	80	90	102	119	107	108
Rest of the World......................	271	747	895	923	949	1,073	1,063	1,143
Total Asia included above............	121	449	511	515	487	565	560	654
Japan.............................	45	218	264	250	228	261	258	288
Australia..........................	39	81	120	125	149	169	159	141
China.............................	22	100	109	109	94	110	84	137
Africa............................	25	56	61	70	89	101	107	117
Porto Rico[b]......................	33	58	77	78	78	85	86	82
Hawaii............................	25	54	66	70	73	76	80	78
Philippine Islands....................	23	43	49	60	61	69	70	80
British India.......................	11	31	30	35	38	50	63	54
Remainder of rest of the World.........	48	106	119	126	139	152	156	166

[a] Includes Central America, West Indies (except Cuba), Colombia, and Venezuela.

[b] Includes only exports from continental United States to the Territory.

Source: *Monthly Summary of Foreign Commerce*, Bureau of Foreign and Domestic Commerce, United States Department of Commerce.

selves. In order to bring out the more significant of these relative changes, the device of the logarithmic chart has been introduced. By plotting, for each territorial division, the logarithm of its total takings of our export trade each year instead of the total takings themselves, graphs showing the relative changes in the proportions taken by each of the geographical areas will result.[2] In Chart 1 are represented on such a logarithmic scale, (1) the total value of our exports distributed according to the major geographic divisions to which they were sent; and (2) the

[2] Since the logarithm of any multiple of a given number is equal to the logarithm of the number plus the logarithm of the multiplier, equal proportional changes in the original items are represented by equal absolute changes in the logarithms.

totals going to each major division in turn distributed among the principal receiving countries.

CHART 1.—EXPORTS OF THE UNITED STATES ANNUALLY, 1922–1927

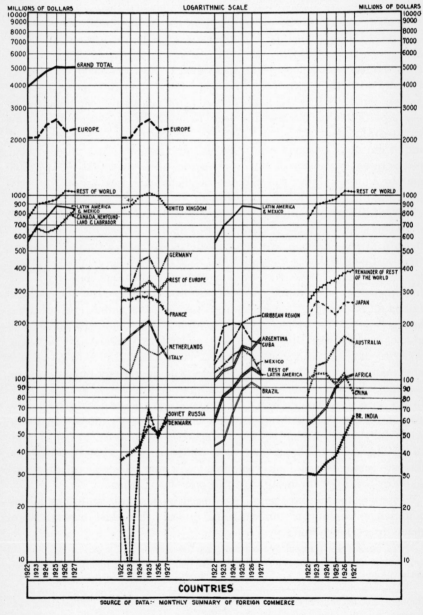

By reference to this chart, it will be seen that, during the period under discussion, exports to all three of the other main divisions gained more largely than did those to Europe. Also, of those to Europe, it will be seen that, while the United Kingdom, France, and Italy hardly maintained their takings, the portions taken by Germany—which, even when price changes are allowed for, have already reached their prewar level— increased rapidly, as did those taken by the Netherlands. Meanwhile, exports to all the rest of Europe moved gradually upward. Of our exports to Latin America, the increases in the purchases of two of our three largest customers—Cuba and Mexico—did not keep up proportionally with the increases of the rest of the countries, most of which greatly enlarged their takings. Finally, an analysis of the changes in our exports to other parts of the world shows, with the exception of those to Australia, that the chief increases have come not in the takings of important old customers but rather in those of new ones. Much, then, of the recent expansion of our export trade, other than that to Australia and to Canada, came through the development of new and formerly little-used markets, rather than through the extension of old ones.

When important price changes are eliminated[3] (see Chart 2), many differences appear in the movements.[4] Exports to the United Kingdom, instead of showing a nearly horizontal trend, carry a marked upward trend Likewise those to France and to Italy no longer show declining trends. In the Pacific, too, the nearly horizontal trend formerly found for Japan has shot rapidly upward, showing clearly that the general falling off of our sales in that country was fictitious and a result of price changes only. Nevertheless, confirmation is found for the conclusion above reached: that, in volume, our exports to Canada and to Latin America—as well as to outlying parts of the world including Oceania and many parts of Asia—have increased more rapidly than those to Europe. Within Europe, the elimination of important price changes brings into even bolder relief the preponderant increases to Germany and to Russia as contrasted with those to our former allies. In Latin America, the great increases of our exports to Argentina, to Brazil, and to certain of the smaller countries, as compared with those to two of our largest customers of long standing, Cuba and Mexico, are in every sense real and not the results of mere price fluctuations.[5]

Of more direct importance for American business conditions is the commodity content of our outgoing trade. Our chief exports were made up as shown in Table 3.

[3] For exact description of method used, see footnote 1.

[4] Reference is here made to the period 1922–1927 only. The data for 1928 are not yet available.

[5] This conclusion cannot be drawn directly from the chart, for the reason that price changes have actually been eliminated only in the case of a small proportion of the exports to Latin American countries. It is known, however, that the prices of the highly varied manufactured goods which make up the bulk of the trade have not fluctuated sharply, and such changes as have occurred have affected the several countries in roughly similar measure.

"King Cotton" still holds first place.　Nor has there yet appeared
an aspiring rival to dispute its position.　In spite of the much-vaunted

CHART 2.—EXPORTS OF THE UNITED STATES ANNUALLY, WITH IMPOR-
TANT PRICE CHANGES ELIMINATED, 1922–1927

Inserted figures indicate per cents actual value of adjusted items are of original total values.

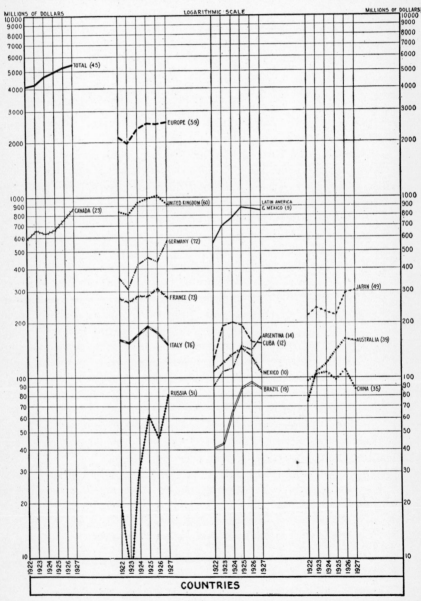

Americanization of world industry, the exports of machinery of all types
combined prove but a poor second to cotton, totaling in value a scant

TABLE 3.—ANNUAL EXPORTS OF DOMESTIC GOODS OF THE UNITED STATES, BY COMMODITIES, 1922–1928

(Value in millions of dollars; quantity in millions of unit specified. For basis of totals, see description of data in note to Table 1. The figures for individual commodities do not include shipments to Alaska, Hawaii, and Porto Rico)

Commodity	1910–14 Value	1910–14 Quantity	1922 Value	1922 Quantity	1923 Value	1923 Quantity	1924 Value	1924 Quantity	1925 Value	1925 Quantity	1926 Value	1926 Quantity	1927 Value	1927 Quantity	1928 Value	1928 Quantity
Total..................	2,243	.....	3,971	.....	4,343	.....	4,772	.....	5,093	.....	5,002	.....	5,067	.....	5,321	.....
1. Cotton, raw—pounds.........	552	4,420	673	3,153	807	2,743	951	3,483	1,060	4,384	814	4,692	826	4,897	920	4,579
2. Machinery..............	154	.....	239	.....	288	.....	317	.....	385	.....	400	.....	435	.....	497	.....
3. Wheat—bushels...........	55	57	206	165	116	99	237	166	149	87	202	138	240	168	120	96
4. Iron and steel..........	142	.....	189	.....	234	.....	221	.....	224	.....	250	.....	234	.....	262	.....
5. Gasoline, naphtha, and other finished light products—gallons....	17	147	127	579	138	846	167	1,186	198	1,290	263	1,784	210	1,824	232	2,174
6. Passenger automobiles^a...	17	19	51	67	91	127	113	151	185	244	176	239	208	279	264	368
7. Leaf tobacco—pounds.......	45	388	146	431	152	474	163	547	153	468	137	479	139	506	154	575
8. Cotton manufactures.......	45	.....	139	.....	138	.....	133	.....	148	.....	131	.....	132	.....	135	.....
9. Copper, (refined)—pounds...	b118	.....	89	653	110	729	138	1,010	140	968	121	856	125	922	140	948
10. Fruits................	28	.....	74	.....	67	.....	96	.....	101	.....	110	.....	120	.....	128	.....
11. Boards and timber—board feet...	62	2,709	67	1,882	103	2,368	102	2,638	99	2,508	97	2,694	107	2,951	108	3,119
12. Lard—pounds............	56	501	91	767	130	1,035	126	944	118	689	109	699	92	681	99	760
13. Lubricating oil—gallons...	25	191	77	331	77	348	87	379	91	403	86	389	89	404	92	456
14. Wheat flour—barrels.......	51	11	86	15	88	16	91	16	85	11	83	12	85	13	74	12
15. Kerosene—gallons.........	64	1,056	83	895	77	848	89	916	84	877	100	925	79	810	93	918
16. Chemicals..............	20	.....	52	.....	57	.....	53	.....	58	.....	65	.....	73	.....	75	.....
17. Bituminous coal—tons.....	34	14	66	11	105	19	71	15	68	16	156	31	71	16	59	14
18. Meats—pounds...........	63	.....	135	799	150	1,037	114	803	118	612	99	481	64	356	61	365
19. All other to outside customs area.	617	.....	1,242	.....	1,240	.....	1,322	.....	1,446	.....	1,410	.....	1,536	.....	1,616	.....
20. Total shipments to Alaska, Hawaii, and Porto Rico.	78	.....	139	.....	175	.....	181	.....	183	.....	193	.....	202	.....	192	.....

Source: *Monthly Summary of Foreign Commerce*, Bureau of Foreign and Domestic Commerce, United States Department of Commerce. Only items aggregating $50,000,000 in at least one year are included.

a Quantity in thousands (passenger cars except electric).
All copper (not stated separately).

half.   Nevertheless, the path of cotton has not been consistently upward. Severe declines below the 1925 level appeared in 1926 and in 1927. Both are explained by price recessions, as the physical volume of the exports increased considerably during those years.   In 1923 and again in 1928, when the total value increased considerably, the actual quantities exported were substantially reduced.

Of significance for American manufactures, as contrasted with agriculture, are the extraordinary and almost uninterrupted increases in the value of our exports of machinery and automobiles.   Since 1922, total values of machinery have doubled and those of passenger automobiles more than quintupled, and the quantities exported have increased in similar proportion.   Exports of gasoline and of fruits have also increased greatly and almost continuously throughout the period, while those of meats have declined, until in 1928 they were below their prewar level in value despite much higher prices.

Many shifts in the relative positions of our exports have taken place in the short period under consideration.   In certain cases, the changes have resulted largely from variations in prices of important articles; but in others, equally important fluctuations in physical volume have appeared.   In order to distinguish between the two types of changes, values of each of the major exports, so far as quantities are available, have been computed at the average price[6] at which it sold during the period.   These values, with price fluctuations thus largely eliminated, are plotted along with the actual values in Chart 3.

How much the variations in prices have affected the total value of our exports is seen in the graphs.   The volume of foreign sales of cotton increased yearly from 1923 to 1927, but declined somewhat in 1928; on the other hand, the values in both 1926 and 1927 were much below those of 1924 and 1925, and even in 1928, despite an increase in price, the value remained somewhat below the values in those years.   Exports of gasoline and allied products increased greatly in quantity throughout the entire period, but the values in 1927 and 1928 were considerably less than in 1926.   With meats, the quantities from 1923 to 1927 declined even more rapidly than values, while with automobiles, the rises (temporarily halting in 1926) appear almost equally rapid in quantities and in values throughout the entire period 1922–1928.

The destinations of the chief items of our export trade are also shown in Chart 3.   Among the foreign purchasers of our cotton, the first place, formerly held by the British, in 1927 passed to the Germans.   The purchases by the Japanese increased greatly throughout the period up to

_____

[6] This method of measuring quantities has an advantage over the usual one in that it facilitates comparisons with corresponding values at the same time that the relative importance of the export is kept automatically in the mind of the reader.   Also the effects of price changes are brought out more clearly.

CHART 3.—EXPORTS OF THE UNITED STATES ANNUALLY, 1922–1927, COM-
MODITY DISTRIBUTION

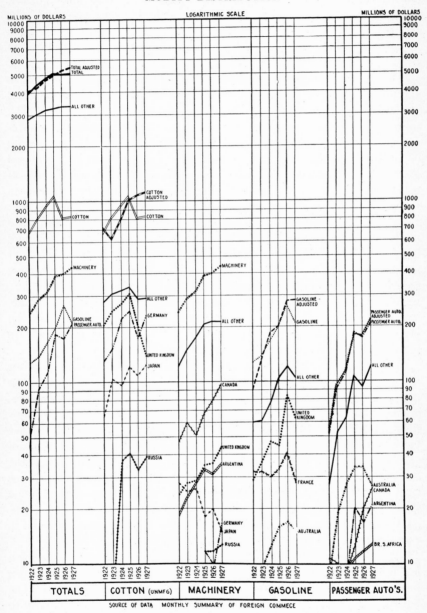

SOURCE OF DATA   MONTHLY SUMMARY OF FOREIGN COMMECE

1927, but fell off in 1928.   Of machinery, the wide geographic distribution
of our sales is clearly evident.   Canada naturally holds first place.
In spite of its tariff walls, industrially it has long been a part of the
United States; and recently, on account of those same trade barriers

combined with the "imperial preference" policy of the British Empire, it has attracted an ever increasing number of American branch plants. The notable increase in its takings of American machinery during the period under discussion is to be remarked. Curiously enough, the United Kingdom, with its pre-eminence in machinery manufacture, takes second place in our exports of machinery, as a result of an increase throughout the period hardly less rapid than that of Canada. The rapid increases to Argentina, especially in the early part of the period, are to be noted, as are those to Australia. But above all, attention is called to the extraordinarily rapid advance in machinery sales to the many and diverse countries included under the caption "All other." Of automobiles, the greatly enlarged sales to Argentina, Australia, and British South Africa (though in the case of Australia some decrease occurred in 1927 and 1928) constitute probably the most phenomenal development, though the steep incline of the "All other" curve indicates the rapid increase in exports of these, as of machinery, to all other parts of the world.

Imports.—While the value of American merchandise imports was one-third larger in 1928 than in 1922, considerable declines appeared both in 1924 and in 1927 and a small decline also in 1928. The aggregate weight, as given by the cargo tonnage, showed similar declines. When changes in the prices of important articles are eliminated, although the decline of 1924 again appears, the imports of 1927 remain almost exactly equal to those of 1926. (There was, moreover, an increase in 1928, although precise computations are not yet available.)

TABLE 4.—TOTAL ANNUAL IMPORTS OF THE UNITED STATES, 1922–1928

(Value in millions of dollars; volume in millions of tons)

Year	Value	Volume in cargo tonnage of water-borne imports	Value with important price changes eliminated[a]
1922	3,298	44.7	3,745
1923	4,027	43.3	3,990
1924	3,851	40.9	3,755
1925	4,479	43.1	4,291
1926	4,693	44.0	4,546
1927	4,442	42.0	4,551
1928	4,372	....	.....

[a] For exact description of character of the data of this column, see footnote 1.

Source: Values are taken from *Monthly Summary of Foreign Commerce*, Bureau of Foreign and Domestic Commerce, United States Department of Commerce. Cargo tonnage figures for 1922–1925, inclusive, are taken from the *Statistical Abstract of the United States* compiled on basis of data gathered by United States Shipping Board, Bureau of Research, Division of Statistics. Data for 1926 and 1927 are taken from *Special Report* No. 298 Division of Statistics of the United States Shipping Board.

Description of data: See footnotes to Table 1.

The geographic distribution of our import trade shows many interesting characteristics. In Table 5 is shown the total value distributed, first by major geographic divisions and then by important countries making up the larger areas. Europe continues to supply the largest single portion, which, although it shows a considerable decline from the full one-half of prewar years, still makes up somewhat more than one-fourth of the total. Latin America comes second with a supply but slightly less in value than that of Europe. Canada, on the other hand, is responsible for less than half as much as that originating either in Latin

TABLE 5.—ANNUAL IMPORTS OF THE UNITED STATES, 1922–1928

(In millions of dollars. See also description of data in note to Table 1)

Division	1910–14	1922	1923	1924	1925	1926	1927	1928
Grand total..........................	1,790	3,298	4,027	3,851	4,479	4,693	4,442	4,372
Europe................................	837	991	1,157	1,096	1,238	1,286	1,276	1,249
United Kingdom and Irish Free State......	279	357	404	366	414	385	360	350
Germany.............................	177	117	161	139	164	198	201	222
France...............................	130	143	150	148	157	152	168	159
Italy.................................	51	64	92	75	102	103	109	102
Netherlands...........................	35	64	78	74	93	102	87	84
Belgium..............................	40	54	68	66	69	78	72	75
Remainder of Europe...................	125	192	204	228	239	268	279	257
Canada, Newfoundland, and Labrador..........	119	366	418	402	458	485	484	499
Latin America...........................	434	815	1,050	1,059	1,041	1,094	1,019	1,030
Cuba.................................	122	268	376	362	262	251	257	203
Brazil................................	111	120	143	179	222	235	203	221
Mexico...............................	71	132	140	167	179	169	138	125
Argentina............................	33	86	115	75	80	88	97	99
Chile................................	23	60	92	98	89	81	62	75
Caribbean Areas[a]...................	57	105	124	137	163	219	222	266
Remainder of Latin America.............	17	44	60	41	46	51	40	41
Rest of World...........................	400	1,126	1,402	1,294	1,742	1,828	1,663	1,594
Total Asia, included above..............	259	827	1,020	931	1,319	1,401	1,257	1,169
Japan................................	85	354	347	340	384	401	402	384
Straits Settlements.....................	25	94	154	148	314	384	278	204
China................................	35	135	188	118	170	143	152	140
British India..........................	56	91	128	103	144	151	131	149
Hawaii...............................	45	73	101	108	103	98	109	117
Philippine Islands......................	19	62	78	97	112	104	116	115
Porto Rico............................	37	60	80	77	93	90	97	97
Africa................................	23	65	87	73	92	96	93	90
Dutch East Indies......................	9	34	55	58	96	120	92	86
Alaska...............................	19	51	54	55	55	73	51	68
Australia.............................	12	36	41	33	55	46	39	32
Ceylon...............................	10	20	28	25	48	56	41	31
Remainder of rest of the World...........	25	51	61	59	76	66	62	81

[a] Includes Central America, West Indies (except Cuba), Colombia, and Venezuela.

Source: *Monthly Summary of Foreign Commerce*, Bureau of Foreign and Domestic Commerce, United States Department of Commerce.

America or in Europe.   All the rest of the world together accounts for but little more than that already attributed to Europe.

Within the main geographic areas in Europe, it is the United Kingdom which purveys the largest single portion of our import trade; and while before the war and still in 1922 France accounted for the next larger portion, more recently her part has been greatly exceeded by that of Germany.   In Latin America, Cuba with its great sugar plantations continues our largest supplier, but, by the end of the period, accounted for only a slightly larger proportion of our imports than did Brazil with its vast production of coffee.   Mexico, which in 1922 surpassed Brazil in the value of its exports to the United States, showed in 1928 an actual decline as compared with 1922, having thus dropped back to its prewar position.   The Caribbean States during each year have shown an increase, usually very marked.   In the rest of the world, while Japan continues our most important supplier, our great demands for rubber have brought, during several recent years, the combined imports from the Straits Settlements, Ceylon, and the Dutch East Indies into a position of even greater importance.   China, on the other hand, has little more than maintained the position which it held in 1922.

In order to bring out more clearly the relative changes in the proportions of our imports coming from the various parts of the world, the device of the logarithmic chart will again be resorted to.   In Chart 4, the logarithms of the value of our imports from various parts of the world, instead of the actual value, are represented.   Hence, in the various graphs, equal absolute changes represent equal proportional changes in the values of the imports.

The values of our imports thus represented and distributed according to geographic sources show many changes during the period since 1922. It is immediately evident that, of our incoming trade from Europe and from Latin America, the values have increased proportionally less than those from Canada and much less than those from the rest of the world. Also, of those from Europe, the rapid increase in the value of imports from Germany, Italy, and from most of the other countries, as contrasted with those from the United Kingdom and from France, are extremely noticeable.

In Latin America, the rapid increases of our imports from the newer and smaller countries, especially from the Caribbean area, as compared with those from the older and more established markets, are especially to be noted.   And as regards the rest of the world, the extraordinary increases from the Straits Settlements and other rubber producing countries, from our territorial possessions, from British India, and from Africa are to be contrasted with the smaller increases from our older suppliers, such as China, Japan, and Australia.

CHART 4.—IMPORTS OF THE UNITED STATES ANNUALLY, 1922–1927

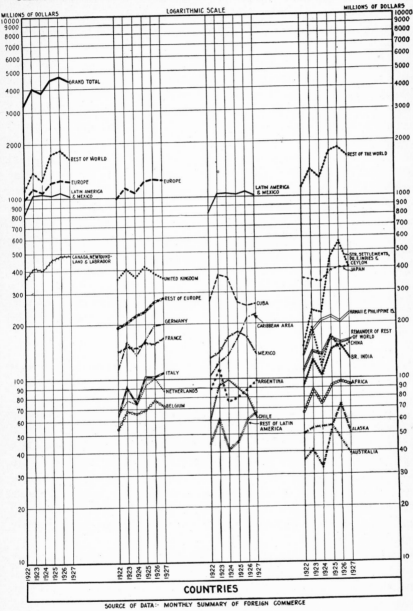

SOURCE OF DATA:- MONTHLY SUMMARY OF FOREIGN COMMERCE

With imports, then, as with exports, much of the recent increase has come from the development of new and formerly little-known markets rather than through the extension of older ones.

CHART 5.—IMPORTS OF THE UNITED STATES ANNUALLY, WITH IMPOR-
TANT PRICE CHANGES ELIMINATED, 1922–1927

Inserted figures indicate per cents actual values of adjusted items are of original total
values

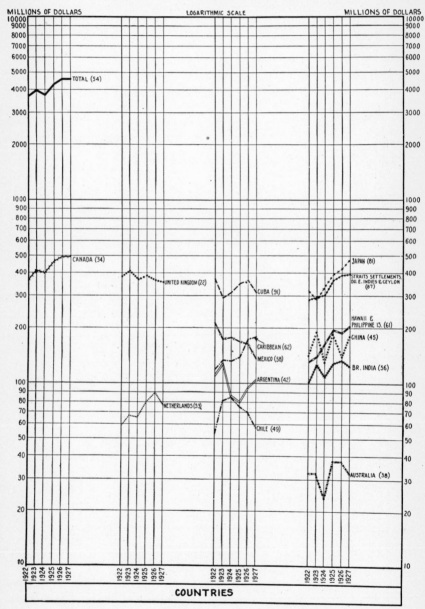

When important price changes are eliminated (see Chart 5), certain
changes in the above conclusions appear, especially in connection with

TABLE 6.—ANNUAL IMPORTS OF FOREIGN MERCHANDISE BY THE UNITED STATES BY COMMODITIES, 1922–1928

(Value in millions of dollars; quantity in millions of units specified. For the basis of totals see description of data in note to Table 1. The figures for individual commodities, except sugar, fruits, and nuts, do not include imports from Alaska, Hawaii, and Porto Rico)

Commodity	1910-14 Value	1910-14 Quantity	1922 Value	1922 Quantity	1923 Value	1923 Quantity	1924 Value	1924 Quantity	1925 Value	1925 Quantity	1926 Value	1926 Quantity	1927 Value	1927 Quantity	1928 Value	1928 Quantity
Total	1,790		3,298		4,027		3,851		4,479		4,693		4,442		4,372	
1. Raw silk—pounds	77	24	366	51	392	50	328	51	396	64	393	66	390	74	368	75
2. Cane sugar[a]	169	612	329	1,156	498	942	489	1,040	362	1,163	337	1,201	382	1,111	337	1,080
3. Crude rubber—pounds	86	106	102	674	185	692	174	735	430	888	506	926	340	955	245	978
4. Coffee—pounds	102	899	161	1,246	190	1,408	249	1,421	286	1,284	323	1,493	264	1,433	310	1,457
5. Newsprint paper—pounds	5	238	72	2,059	98	2,618	101	2,714	104	2,897	124	3,701	131	3,974	139	4,314
6. Fruits and nuts	48		99		101		102		129		128		126		134	
7. Furs	23		68		88		88		115		118		124		109	
8. Hides and skins—pounds	105	531	107	551	119	532	75	357	97	362	105	369	113	447	151	506
9. Tin—pounds	42	106	41	135	61	154	69	146	95	172	102	173	101	159	87	175
10. Wood and manufactures	42		97		121		112		120		107		93		80	
11. Raw wool—pounds	39	208	87	376	130	394	93	268	142	329	107	310	83	267	80	245
12. Tobacco—pounds	37	58	74	81	67	63	84	72	81	82	70	72	84	106	63	78
13. Wool manufactures	22		59		69		74		74		71		79		78	
14. Petroleum—gallons	5		70	5,347	54	3,445	74	3,267	75	2,597	79	2,536	78	2,451	90	3,350
15. Burlaps—pounds	29	421	49	521	67	598	59	576	85	626	82	599	67	570	80	620
16. Cotton manufactures	67		44		68		62		80		67		66		69	
17. Oil seeds	15		58		61		50		75		72		64		61	
18. Vegetable oils	27		45		64		62		78		65		61		63	
19. Fertilizers[b]	41	863	40	1,340	49	1,858	67	1,893	54	2,268	69	2,082	59	1,819	78	2,533
20. Pulp (sulphite)[b]	15	472	32	636	34	712	51	834	38	866	61	924	58	925	56	948
21. Cocoa—pounds	16	142	49	345	48	414	29	378	52	382	43	426	57	425	47	379
22. Flax and hemp	32		38		56		57		49		53		54		51	
23. Copper, unrefined	28	111	48	303	49	395	59	471	53	379	56	444	52	439	68	543
24. Raw cotton—pounds	21		43	186	52	187	47	161	50	157	46	181	46	206	43	172
25. Diamonds[c]	35		23	454	32	540	38	502	57	514	51	555	41	446	42	440
26. Vegetable fibers[b]				187		244		226		238	50	223	39	206	36	216
27. All other outside customs area	632		931		1,088		1,001		1,142		1,302		1,299		1,300	
28. All other receipts from Alaska, Hawaii, and Porto Rico, other than sugar, fruits, and nuts	30		79		86		84		95		116		91		107	

Source: *Monthly Summary of Foreign Commerce*, Bureau of Foreign and Domestic Commerce, United States Department of Commerce.

[a] Tens of millions of pounds.

[b] Thousands of tons.

[c] Thousands of carats (cut but not set).

CHART 6.—IMPORTS OF THE UNITED STATES ANNUALLY, 1922–1927

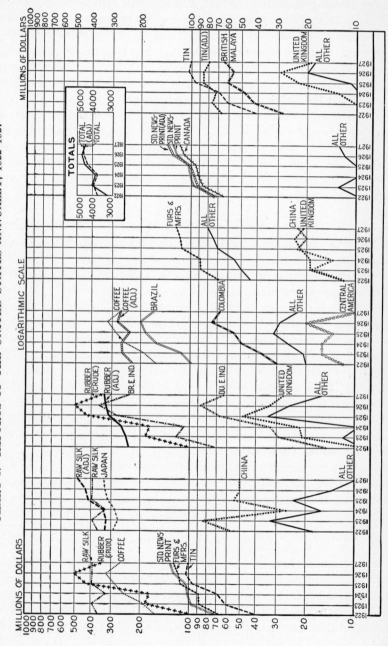

our trade with the Far East. Thus measured, our imports from the rubber-growing countries no longer rose more rapidly after 1922 than did those from Japan and from our insular possessions. The rapidity of the rise in imports from British India is considerably reduced. It is evident that the drastic fluctuations in the price of rubber served greatly to distort the changes in the values of our imports from certain rubber-producing countries, while the smaller fluctuations in the prices of silk affected the value of our large imports from Japan.

Of more significance in its bearing on American industry is the commodity content of our import trade. The principal items are enumerated in Table 6.

It will be noted immediately what prominent proportions of the total are made up of silk, sugar, rubber, and coffee. In fact, in 1926, these four articles alone made up in value one-third of the total of our imports, and in 1928, in spite of a drastic decline in the price of rubber, more than one-fourth. Most of the remainder of those which bulk high in value are, like three of the above, raw materials admitted with little or no tariff restriction.

During the period since 1922, important changes have occurred in the relative proportions made up by the various components. Chart 6, in which the logarithms of the values of each import, instead of the values themselves, are plotted, makes clear the relative movements of the values of the various items. Especially to be noted are the enormous increases in rubber and in tin down to 1926, and the rapid increase, scarcely broken to 1928, in copper, newsprint, furs, and cocoa. When important price changes are eliminated, many of the most pronounced inclines are much reduced. Rubber and tin show almost unbroken upward trends throughout the period, but with slopes much less than those of newsprint and fertilizers, or only about the same as that of raw silk, the actual value of which followed an almost horizontal trend throughout the period. Petroleum, although its actual value showed an upward trend, has, until 1927, a pronounced downward slope when the changes in its price are eliminated; and although a marked rise occurred in 1928, the total import was still much below that for 1922.

II. FOREIGN LOANS

Extension of Idea to All Investments.—Any discussion of foreign loans in their relationships to international trade or to business conditions in the lending country must necessarily involve the broader consideration of all credit transactions with the outside world. Whether the advance of funds takes the form of a public flotation of security issues, a direct investment in the construction of a foreign plant, or a temporary loan by a finance institution, there are so many elements of similarity in the resulting influences set into operation that few advantages and many disadvantages might be expected to arise from more narrowly limiting the problem. Consequently, in this study of the effects of foreign loans on business conditions in the United States, all kinds of credits will be considered.

In securing any worthwhile estimate of the volume of such credits, almost insuperable difficulties are encountered. Although several compilations by independent investigators are published periodically, all are subject to grave error. In fact, it is only of the publicly floated issues that many of the outstanding details ever become generally known. And even with regard to such credits, important uncertainties inevitably arise. That an issue was floated in New York may not mean that all the securities were sold to Americans even in the first instance. This is especially true in cases of issues by Canadian firms, which are beginning to use New York's financial facilities much as businesses do which are located in Michigan or in Ohio. And even when securities are originally sold here, there is nothing to prevent their being rapidly resold to people in other countries. Statistics of both these types of "backwash" are as yet extremely inaccurate.

Our statistical information is even more rudimentary on other types of credits. Privately granted credits and direct investment, once they reach the public press, are "caught" as they appear. But what proportion of them receives publicity? And what fraction or multiple of the actual cash involved in those which do, gets mention in the press dispatches? Indeed, in certain direct investments, it is difficult to determine even theoretically what should be included. For example, an oil company incorporated in New Jersey, but conducting extensive operations in Latin America, floats a loan in New York City to provide funds for the purchase of barges and loading machinery necessary for the transport of crude oil to its refineries here. What proportion of the loan represents an investment in Latin America? Finally, credits of extremely informal character are doubtless continually arranged between head offices and branches of banks and of other finance institutions both American and foreign, as well as between banks only partially interconnected by stock ownership, and between important correspondents. Informal credits, too, are likely to be contracted between head offices and branch manufacturing plants which American firms are fast constructing in many parts of the world. Of the amounts of such credits, little more than the wildest guesses are available.

In the face of all these obstacles, the Finance and Investment Division, Bureau of Foreign and Domestic Commerce, United States Department of Commerce, has compiled a series of estimates of the various types of the foreign credits of the United States. While admittedly subject to a wide margin of error, so many cross-checks have been used in their compilation, that the gross estimates, which alone are presented in this study, cannot but command respect.   On account of his interest in the subject, Dr. Ray O. Hall, who for the last two years has been in charge of the compilation of the *Balance of International Payments of the United States,* has kindly consented to reconstruct for this study the estimates for earlier years, using the method which has apparently given such excellent results in the handling of the 1926 and 1927 data.   His revised estimates are used throughout the remainder of this chapter.

Facts of Foreign Loans.—Outstanding at the end of each of the years 1922–1927 our total foreign investments are estimated[7] as shown in the following statement:

1922	$ 8,522,000,000
1923	8,775,000,000
1924	9,589,000,000
1925	10,405,000,000
1926	11,195,000,000
1927	12,187,000,000

Similar estimates of the investments of foreigners in American securities and properties at year-end dates are given in the following statement:[8]

1922	$2,808,000,000
1923	3,052,000,000
1924	3,096,000,000
1925	3,301,000,000
1926	3,469,000,000
1927	3,700,000,000

The estimated service actually paid to Americans by foreigners and to foreigners by Americans are given in Table 7.   In the same table are added the amounts of the service on inter-government war debts, and the estimated amounts of service on short-term obligations of all sorts. The final balances represent estimates of the net sums entering into our balance of international payments for each year on account of indebtedness outstanding during that year.

[7] Estimate by Ray O. Hall, Assistant Chief of the Finance and Investment Division, Bureau of Foreign and Domestic Commerce, United States Department of Commerce, Washington, D.C.   At the ends of 1926 and 1927, range estimates are given as follows: 1926, $10,500,000,000 to $12,500,000,000; 1927, $11,500,000,000 to $13,500,000,000.   Estimates for other years are probably not more accurate.

Description of data.   In making the estimates of this table the following method was used: The estimated value of the total American investments abroad at the end of the calendar year 1925, as given on page 15 of the *Balance of International Payments of the United States in 1925,* was taken as a base.   For the other years, cumulative additions to and subtractions from this base were made on the basis of the yearly investments of Americans abroad, as given in the first "Balance" column of Table 8.

[8] Description of data.   In making the estimates of this table the following method was used: From the total investments of foreigners in the United States at the end of 1927, as given on page 25 of the *Balance of International Payments of the United States in 1927,* have been subtracted the cumulative flotations each year as given in the "Balance" of "Investments of Foreigners in the United States" in Table 8.

TABLE 7.—INTEREST AND COMMISSION

(In millions of dollars)

Year	Received from foreigners			Paid to foreigners		
	Interest on long-term private investments	Short-term interest and commissions	War-debt receipts of United States Treasury	Interest on long-term private investments	Short-term interest and commissions	Balance
1922	526	25	158	120	24	565
1923	560	30	259	140	40	669
1924	596	35	183	150	42	622
1925	639	45	186	165	64	641
1926	678	57	195	190	78	662
1927	738	57	206	203	78	720

Source: Revised estimates of balance of international payments of the United States for calendar years 1922–1927, inclusive, by Ray O. Hall. Hereafter this reference will be condensed to: Revised estimates by Ray O. Hall. War-debt receipts of United States Treasury include interest and principal.

TABLE 8.—ANNUAL CHANGES IN PRIVATE FUNDED CAPITAL ITEMS, 1922–1927

(In millions of dollars)

Year	American investments abroad, new long-term	Refunding and backwash	Balance	Investments of foreigners in United States securities	Refunding and backwash	Balance	Net export of long-term capital
1922	1,220	478	742	80	74	6	736
1923	581	328	253	308	64	244	9
1924	1,424	610	814	131	87	44	770
1925	1,593	777	816	283	78	205	611
1926	1,653	863	790	709	541	168	622
1927	1,974	982	992	931	700	231	761

Source: Revised estimates by Ray O. Hall.

Descriptions of data: "United States investments abroad, new long-term" is the sum of "Foreign security investments of Americans" and "Direct foreign investments of Americans."

"Refunding and backwash" is the sum of "Refunding to Americans," "Bond redemption and sinking-fund payments from foreigners" and "Resale of investments to foreigners."

No allowance has been made for "Discounts on investments abroad."

Net annual increases in our long-term foreign investments, divided into "publicly floated" and "direct investments," are given in Table 9.

Estimates of the reverse items, of purchases by foreigners each year of American properties and securities, are given in Table 10.

In Table 11 are given estimates of the yearly net balances of the movements of funded and unfunded credits and direct investments.[9]

[9] In the first column are entered the direct estimates made by Ray O. Hall. In view of the admitted unreliability of the "unfunded items" entering into these estimates, the same balances have been recompiled with a method similar to the one in general use in the British balance of payments. More explicitly, the combined estimates of the movements in the balance of payments of all items—visible and invisible—except credits of all sorts, are assumed to be accurate in the sense that errors are

TABLE 9.—LONG-TERM FOREIGN INVESTMENTS OF AMERICANS

(In millions of dollars)

Year	Publicly floated	Direct investments	Total
1922	626	116	742
1923	206	47	253
1924	701	113	814
1925	597	219	816
1926	550	240	790
1927	735	257	992

Source: Revised estimates by Ray O. Hall.

Description of data: "Publicly floated" is the balance of "Foreign security investments of Americans," "Refunding to Americans," "Bond redemption and sinking-fund payments from foreigners" and "Resale of investments to foreigners."

TABLE 10.—LONG-TERM INVESTMENTS IN THE UNITED STATES BY FOREIGNERS

(In millions of dollars)

Year	Net investments by foreigners in U. S. securities	Direct investments	Balance
1922	−4	10	6
1923	234	10	244
1924	24	20	44
1925	175	30	205
1926	136	32	168
1927	203	28	231

Source: Revised estimates by Ray O. Hall.

TABLE 11.—NET AMERICAN INVESTMENTS AND SHORT-TERM CREDITS ABROAD

(In millions of dollars)

Year	Estimate of Ray O. Hall of net balance of funded and unfunded credits	Estimate based on British balance of payments method
1922	260	198
1923	−42	−54
1924	458	521
1925	539	443
1926	119	34
1927	641	621

Source: Revised estimates by Ray O. Hall.

Description of data: The estimate of Ray O. Hall is the balance of net "Private, funded capital items" and net "Unfunded items." The estimate based on the British balance of payments method is the balance of the net "Commodity and miscellaneous items" and the "Pure cash items."

mutually counteracting. The remainder required to establish an equilibrium of payments each year is accordingly regarded as a net balance of credits extended. Since the basic assumption upon which the method rests is subject to grave inaccuracies both theoretical and practical, only to the extent that all the errors are counteracting in character will the final balance prove valid.

Data are not available for determining the distribution of our foreign investments, either according to the uses to which the derived funds have been put, or even according to the geographic locations of the borrowers. *For publicly floated issues alone* these data are available, and in Table 12 such a distribution is given. The reader is warned that no deductions have been made either for issues only nominally placed in New York or for repurchases by foreigners of large blocks of issues, the bulk of which have remained in this country.

TABLE 12.—GEOGRAPHIC DISTRIBUTION OF FOREIGN CAPITAL ISSUES PUBLICLY OFFERED IN THE UNITED STATES FROM 1922 TO 1928; NEW NOMINAL CAPITAL

(In millions of dollars)

Item	1922	1923	1924	1925	1926	1927	1928
Total..	682	414	928	1,085	1,135	1,376	1,191
Government and official guaranteed...............	486	295	777	649	583	852	624
Corporate....................................	197	118	152	437	551	524	568
Europe, total.................................	214	108	530	652	495	571	597
Government and guaranteed.....................	136	78	508	409	188	289	231
Corporate....................................	78	30	22	242	307	282	366
Latin America, total.............................	223	114	148	133	355	359	268
Government and guaranteed.....................	161	63	75	87	284	296	238
Corporate....................................	63	52	74	46	71	63	29
Canada, total..................................	129	118	146	150	238	268	188
Government and guaranteed.....................	77	81	105	70	80	142	73
Corporate....................................	52	37	40	80	158	127	115
Far East, total.................................	113	71	96	142	32	145	131
Government and guaranteed.....................	111	71	81	75	20	113	76
Corporate....................................	3	...	15	67	12	32	54
United States territories and possessions, total...........	3	3	8	10	14	32	9
Government and guaranteed.....................	1	3	8	9	12	11	5
Corporate....................................	2	...	...	1	3	21	4

Source: Special circulars on foreign security offerings, Finance and Investment Division, Bureau of Foreign and Domestic Commerce, Department of Commerce.

Description.—The above data are subject to serious inaccuracies. From the total nominal capital of foreign issues have been subtracted only the estimated refunding to Americans. Thus, no allowance is made for purchases at a price other than par, or for purchases by foreigners of capital issues publicly offered in the United States.

In spite of the undependability of the estimates of many of the individual items which have appeared in the foregoing tables, the outstanding fact remains that the expansion of American foreign investments during the period under discussion has been very large and generally increasing. What is the explanation of this comparatively new phenomenon in American economic life? And how important are its effects on American business?

Reasons for Expansion.—To answer the first question, a comparison will be made between the interest rates in New York and in the other large investment centers of the world, during the period under discussion. In Chart 7 are represented the best estimates available of both long- and short-term interest rates in New York, London, Amsterdam, and Berlin, together with long-term interest rates in New York.

Not only were both long- and short-term rates in New York generally declining throughout the period, but they were usually lower than those prevailing in other investment markets. In fact, Paris and Berlin have been completely out of the investment competition, and London, the long-established center of most of such financing, has generally had the handicap of tighter money.

TABLE 13.—SHORT-TERM INTEREST RATES IN IMPORTANT MONEY CENTERS

Year and month	New York	London	Berlin	Amsterdam	Long-term bond yield, New York
1922					
January	4.50	3.60	....	....	5.17
February	4.13	3.26	....	....	5.13
March	4.13	3.28	....	....	5.07
April	4.00	2.62	....	....	4.97
May	3.38	2.34	....	....	4.94
June	3.25	2.40	....	....	4.93
July	3.38	1.97	....	....	4.87
August	3.25	2.27	....	....	4.81
September	3.50	2.50	....	....	4.77
October	3.75	2.41	....	....	4.82
November	4.00	2.52	....	....	4.90
December	4.00	2.55	....	....	4.87
1923					
January	4.00	2.27	....	....	4.86
February	4.00	2.48	....	....	4.89
March	4.00	2.28	....	....	4.97
April	4.13	2.11	....	....	5.00
May	4.13	2.01	....	....	4.98
June	4.13	2.10	....	....	4.98
July	4.13	3.24	....	....	5.01
August	4.13	3.18	....	....	4.99
September	4.13	3.18	....	....	5.02
October	4.13	3.29	....	....	5.02
November	4.13	3.30	....	....	5.01
December	4.13	3.27	....	....	5.01
1924					
January	4.13	3.29	....	4.88	4.95
February	4.13	3.54	....	5.19	4.95
March	4.00	3.20	....	5.13	4.96
April	3.88	3.07	....	5.06	4.95
May	3.25	3.05	....	4.19	4.90
June	2.25	3.03	....	3.56	4.84
July	2.00	3.59	....	3.13	4.80
August	2.13	3.79	....	2.88	4.80
September	2.13	3.74	....	.25	4.78
October	2.25	3.72	....	4.63	4.77
November	2.36	3.72	....	4.44	4.76
December	2.88	3.73	....	4.00	4.78

TABLE 13.—(*Continued*)

Year and month	New York	London	Berlin	Amsterdam	Long-term bond yield, New York
1925					
January	3.00	3.80	8.38	2.63	4.78
February	3.13	3.83	8.00	2.14	4.76
March	3.25	4.48	8.00	2.34	4.76
April	3.13	4.30	8.00	3.23	4.72
May	3.25	4.59	8.00	3.45	4.67
June	3.25	4.44	7.83	3.08	4.66
July	3.25	4.35	7.83	2.72	4.69
August	3.25	3.94	7.78	3.72	4.72
September	3.50	3.68	7.27	3.63	4.72
October	3.50	3.57	7.16	3.47	4.73
November	3.50	3.92	6.78	3.34	4.74
December	3.50	4.67	6.75	3.43	4.70
1926					
January	3.63	4.76	6.28	2.95	4.66
February	3.63	4.31	5.46	2.19	4.63
March	3.66	4.37	5.00	2.67	4.63
April	3.38	4.33	4.88	2.90	4.61
May	3.25	4.37	4.69	2.95	4.58
June	3.25	4.27	4.53	2.83	4.58
July	3.38	4.26	4.54	2.74	4.60
August	3.50	4.45	4.61	2.63	4.59
September	3.88	4.54	4.88	2.78	4.60
October	3.88	4.69	4.82	2.83	4.60
November	3.82	4.57	4.63	3.21	4.56
December	3.82	4.53	4.72	3.39	4.55
1927					
January	3.75	4.17	4.20	2.97	4.54
February	3.63	4.19	4.23	3.47	4.53
March	3.63	4.33	4.59	3.50	4.51
April	3.63	4.04	4.61	3.47	4.47
May	3.63	3.88	4.90	3.46	4.46
June	3.63	4.34	5.39	3.57	4.51
July	3.50	4.33	5.90	3.53	4.51
August	3.13	4.33	5.82	3.45	4.48
September	3.13	4.32	5.90	3.56	4.45
October	3.25	4.32	6.69	4.11	4.43
November	3.25	4.33	6.76	4.50	4.42
December	3.25	4.31	6.87	4.49	4.40
1928					
January	3.38	4.19	6.27	4.29	4.38
February	3.50	4.18	6.20	3.97	4.38
March	3.50	4.12	6.72	3.97	4.37
April	3.75	4.02	6.71	4.18	4.38
May	4.00	3.97	6.66	4.27	4.42
June	4.13	3.82	6.59	4.18	4.50
July	4.25	3.99	6.74	4.10	4.54
August	4.63	4.27	6.68	4.13	4.59
September	4.50	4.23	6.65	4.39	4.57
October	4.50	4.35	6.57	4.40	4.57
November	4.50	4.38	6.28	4.44	4.55
December	4.50	....	....	....	4.59

Source: London rates for 1922 and 1923 are taken from the *London Economist*. All others are from the *Federal Reserve Bulletin*.

Description of Data.—The rates used are the open-market rates for prime bankers' acceptances. Although the London rates for 1922 and 1923 are not available in the *Bulletin*, the same method of computation has been employed. The rates given are monthly averages of the daily quotations that are published in the *London Economist*. The data for the long-term bond yield are taken from the "Statistical Bulletin" of the *Standard Trade and Securities Service*, published by the Standard Statistics Co., Inc.

With regard to long-term interest rates in absolute values, little can be said. Bond yields depend so completely on the types of bonds for which they are computed that, for absolute comparisons, little confidence can be placed in any of those at present published. There seems little doubt that during most of the period, long-term funds could be borrowed in New York more easily than in London. Not only was the available supply almost always greater, but the stronger competition among American investment bankers in turn enhanced the position of the borrowers. Under such circumstances, the plentiful supply of investment

CHART 7.—SHORT-TERM INTEREST RATES IN IMPORTANT MONEY
CENTERS, 1922–1928

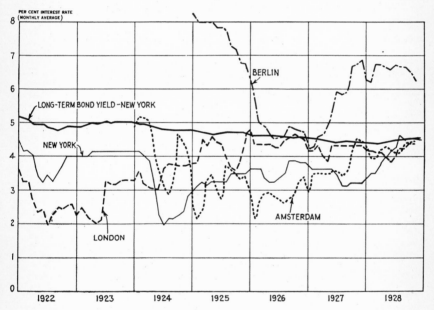

funds in this country has been sought by eligible borrowers in many parts of the world. Borrowers in a position to do so have sought the market where capital could be secured in the amounts desired at the cheapest cost.[10]

Analysis of Anticipated Effects of Foreign Loans.—The effects of a flotation of foreign loans or other forms of foreign investments in this country will differ much according to the disposition of the proceeds of the sale of the securities. In general, they may be divided into three cases.

[10] The abrupt decline in borrowings in this country by foreigners with the rapid increase in interest rates after the middle of 1928 lends support to this thesis. Also, it is an open secret that many foreign flotations have already been arranged for and that their public announcement awaits only more favorable money and investment conditions.

Case I.—When all or a large portion of the derived funds are used for the purchase of American products, the effect is direct and immediate. The resulting stimulus to business, spreading forward, backward, and sidewise, while varying in character and in importance according to the types of goods purchased, is obvious.

Case II.—When the proceeds are shipped in gold, the effects on American business are altogether different. Not only is there no direct stimulus, as is the case when an equivalent amount of American goods are sold, but the shipping of the gold is itself a deflationary influence, and, except to the extent that the Federal Reserve banks increase their credit expansion, proves a retarding rather than a stimulating influence.

Case III.—When the funds borrowed are largely transferred and spent in other countries, the effects on American business, while important, are less direct, less evident, and much less clearly defined than in the other two cases just discussed. Nevertheless, irrespective of their destination, the transfer of the funds acts directly not only on the international exchange value of the currency of the country receiving them but also on that of the currency of the lending country itself. The resulting movements in exchange rates, sometimes involving much of the world, are largely responsible for all the further indirect effects on American prosperity or depression.

To the extent that the international value of the currency of the borrowing country is improved, goods purchasable by its inhabitants in other countries are correspondingly reduced in price; and, to the extent that dollar rates are lowered by the transfer, a further impetus is given to the purchase by all outsiders of American rather than of other foreign wares, while exports to the United States are correspondingly discouraged.

Between gold standard and other stable exchange countries, these movements in exchange rates are relatively insignificant; consequently the resulting stimulus toward the purchase of American and other foreign goods is correspondingly slight. When the borrowing country is on a depreciating paper standard, the *main* influence—operating, as it does, on the unstable currency—while immediate and great, provides a stimulus toward the purchase of foreign goods almost as great as toward that of American goods in particular.

If the transfer of such borrowed funds is at any time so great as to depress dollar exchange rates to the gold-shipping points, naturally gold flows out to other countries in sufficient quantities to bring the rates back within their normal range of the gold parity. The effect of such an outflow, as explained under Case II, far from stimulating, tends to depress American trade.

On the other hand, to the extent that the fall in dollar exchange does not lead to an outflow of gold, purchases of American products are stimulated by the reduction of their prices in terms of other currencies.

But, as mentioned above, on account of the slightness of the reduction in exchange rates necessary in order to cause the flow of gold between gold standard countries, such an influence would necessarily prove slight in stimulating exports to any part of the world. However, it would normally be of greater importance in stimulating sales to inhabitants of borrowing countries on depreciating paper standards. In such cases, not only would the fund transfers reduce slightly dollar exchange rates with the rest of the world, but they would very likely improve substantially those of the borrowing country, whose inhabitants would find the prices of foreign products on that account correspondingly reduced. Their purchases in the United States and, to a slightly less extent, those in other countries would therefore normally increase.

The extensions of credit to silver standard countries have, in certain cases, other interesting consequences. When the new funds are used for the purchase of goods in the lending, or other nonsilver standard countries, or for the procuring of gold to be imported, the effects are not different from those already discussed in Cases I and II above. If the funds are transferred for expenditure in the borrowing or other silver standard country, however, the effects may be different from any of those above discussed. Virtually the sale of the dollar exchange in the silver standard country amounts to the "offer" of gold for silver or to the "bid" for silver with gold. If the size of the credit thus being transferred is large, it might cause the value of gold to fall considerably in terms of silver, or of silver to rise in terms of gold, and thus stimulate the buying of all silver standard countries in gold standard countries while discouraging that of the latter in the former.

Finally the effects in countries in which gold-exchange standards are operated may be different still. If the funds are transferred for expenditure at home, the resulting sales of dollar exchange, if large, causing as they would, rates on all gold standard countries—and with them, those on most other countries—to weaken, would make necessary the purchase by the home central bank or other control agency, of dollar, or other, gold exchange, to approximately the extent of the transfers. Thus credit would be inflated at home against an equivalent balance held abroad; whereas, under the gold standard, international shipments of the monetary metal would have automatically transferred from somewhere the foreign balance to the borrowing country.

Such a discussion as the above, however, is far too simplified even for the problem under discussion. As in most fields of economic research, not only are "cause and effect" relationships inadequate when quantitative results are sought, but very often even the oversimplified logical reasoning which is used to uncover them proves a perverting rather than a clarifying means of analysis. A special application of the general idea of economic equilibrium will therefore be introduced.

III. COMPARISON OF THE MOVEMENTS OF FOREIGN TRADE WITH THOSE OF FOREIGN INVESTMENTS

The General Idea of the Balance of Payments.—Even such an improved device as the statement, now available for the United States, cannot, for any chosen period, represent an actual balance of international payments. It is neither a balance sheet nor a profit and loss account.[11] In fact, even theoretically, its two sides do not balance. Many goods and services, and especially securities purchased on margin, are sold on open account, the required payments being made after varying periods have elapsed. Also, in certain cases, payments are arranged in advance of the proposed purchase of goods. Such lags, either way, may cause the goods, services, and securities exported to appear in the balance of payments of one year, while the corresponding credit or cash transfers connected with the payments may show in that of another. Provided the balances carried over from one year to the next are substantially equal, no great distortion would appear. Perhaps, with most goods and services, such as cotton and Canadian electrical power, for example, sold regularly and with standardized methods of delivery and of payment, such balances in general can be relied upon pretty nearly to cancel each other. With certain others, however, the situation is clearly very different. Securities bought on margin, for example, might be carried over the year-end in great or small volume, according to speculators' judgments as to their future values; and in years of rapidly rising prices, like 1926 and 1927, the original purchase prices might be entirely paid by the resale of comparatively small portions of the original totals, thus leaving a net transfer of securities with no counterbalancing item of payments. As to how great both these types of distortions may have proved in years like 1926 and 1927, only guesses can be made. Also, the question might be raised as to what should be done even theoretically with the huge stock-market operations of a great foreign branch bank located in New York. Are their holdings of securities exported? And, are the New York funds with which they are carried a form of international credits? If the securities are counted without the borrowed funds, the balance is "out" on one side; and if the funds transferred for margins are included without a corresponding proportion of the securities purchased, a reverse lack of balance appears.

But, what is perhaps of much greater importance, suspended accounts arising from various sorts of credit transactions provide an additional source of error even in the theoretical balance. Certain securities are issued and sold to the American public months in advance even of the deposit of the derived funds to the accounts of the foreign borrowers, who

---

[11] *The Balance of International Payments of the United States in 1927*, p. 55.

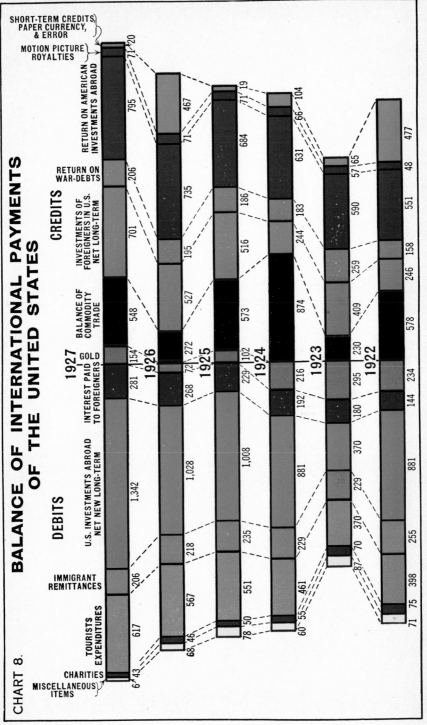

CHART 8.

BALANCE OF INTERNATIONAL PAYMENTS
OF THE UNITED STATES

may further delay their transfer. Other flotations, on the contrary, are made for no other purpose than to fund, at varying and extended intervals, outstanding credits granted earlier, the proceeds of which have already been expended or transferred. Of neither of these types of lags can the balance of payments, as at present compiled, take account.

Finally, all the "finance bills" and international money-market loans made through the drawing and sale of long bills—important as they have come to be in the adjustment of both exchange and interest rates—are at present so inaccurately reported as automatically to be eliminated from consideration.

When all of these untabulated items are added to the necessarily extremely informal credit arrangements between head offices and branches of many business firms—as well as of banks, both American and foreign, and the but slightly less informal ones between industrial and financial institutions only partially owned one by another—it is seen that even a theoretically accurate balance could not be expected. And when, in addition, allowances are made for the inaccuracies necessarily appearing in the estimates of the amounts of even the visible items of our international trade, the statement cannot be regarded as holding except within very wide limits of error.

Nevertheless, the device, as an instrument of analysis, represents a great advance over those previously in use, and consequently will be used in this study. In Table 14 are represented, for each year of the period, the estimated value of each of the major items included in the balance of international payments of the United States.

In order that the relative magnitudes of the various items may be more readily seen, the data of this table, in simplified and combined form, are further represented in Chart 8.[12]

The statement, it will be seen, has a debit and a credit side. On the left (or debit) side are entered all items requiring payments to be made outside the country during the year; and on the right (or credit) side, all those requiring for their accomplishment payments from outside to persons living within the country.

Facts—Balance of International Payments.—Reference to either the table or the chart shows how completely the entire balance is dominated by the loan and investment items. True, either merchandise exports or imports alone are each year much larger than any other single item. Nevertheless, the commodity balances of trade, although they have varied within comparatively wide limits, make up only small portions of the totals. In fact, if tourists' expenditures, which in a very real sense are to be regarded as a type of commodity imports, are included in the

[12] This method of presentation is taken from the *Monthly Bulletin* of The National City Bank of New York, entitled "Economic Conditions, Governmental Finance, United States Securities," Sept., 1927.

TABLE 14.—CONDENSED BALANCE OF INTERNATIONAL PAYMENTS OF THE UNITED STATES, CALENDAR YEARS, 1922–1927

Class of transaction	1922			1923			1924			1925			1926			1927		
	Credit	Debit	Bal.	Credit	Debit	Bal.	Credit	Debit	Bal.	Credit	Debit	Bal.	Credit	Debit	Bal.	Credit	Debit	Bal.
Commodity trade except silver	3,927	3,341	+586	4,264	4,032	+232	4,691	3,853	+838	5,009	4,471	+538	4,918	4,668	+250	4,961	4,434	+527
Silver	63	71	-8	72	74	-2	110	74	+36	99	64	+35	92	70	+22	76	55	+21
Total of commodity trade	3,990	3,412	+578	4,336	4,106	+230	4,801	3,927	+874	5,108	4,535	+573	5,010	4,738	+272	5,037	4,489	+548
Tourist expenditures	95	493	-398	114	493	-379	115	576	-461	110	661	-551	142	709	-567	153	770	-617
Return on American investment abroad:																		
(a) Long-term	526		+526	560		+560	596		+596	639		+639	678		+678	738		+738
(b) Short-term	25		+25	30		+30	35		+35	45		+45	57		+57	57		+57
Interest paid to foreigners:																		
(a) Long-term		120	-120		140	-140		150	-150		165	-165		190	-190		203	-203
(b) Short-term		24	-24		40	-40		42	-42		64	-64		78	-78		78	-78
Return on war debt	158		+158	259		+259	183		+183	186		+186	195		+195	206		+206
Immigrant remittances	45	300	-255	66	295	-229	56	285	-229	40	275	-235	35	253	-218	35	241	-206
Charitable and missionary contributions		75	-75		70	-70		55	-55		50	-50		46	-46		43	-43
Motion picture royalties	50	2	+48	60	3	+57	70	4	+66	75	4	+71	75	4	+71	75	4	+71
Miscellaneous invisible items	329	400	-71	316	403	-87	346	406	-60	332	410	-78	366	434	-68	410	416	-6
Total commodity and miscellaneous items	5,218	4,826	+392	5,741	5,550	+191	6,202	5,445	+757	6,535	6,164	+371	6,558	6,452	+106	6,711	6,244	+467
Foreign security investments of Americans		1,104	-1,104		534	-534		1,311	-1,311		1,374	-1,374		1,413	-1,413		1,717	-1,717
Refunding to Americans	146		+146	82		+82	291		+291	245		+245	182		+182	208		+208
Discount on investments abroad	101		+101	48		+48	125		+125	119		+119	121		+121	120		+120
Direct foreign investments by Americans		116	-116		47	-47		113	-113		219	-219		240	-240		257	-257
Bond redemptions and sinking fund payments from foreigners	92		+92	81		+81	119		+119	221		+221	322		+322	304		+304
Resale of investments to foreigners	240		+240	165		+165	200		+200	311		+311	359		+359	470		+470
Investments of foreigners in United States securities	70	74	-4	298	64	+234	111	87	+24	253	78	+175	677	541	+136	903	700	+203
Direct investments by foreigners	10		+10	20	10	+10	20		+20	30		+30	32		+32	28		+28
Total private, funded capital items	659	1,294	-635	684	645	+39	866	1,511	-645	1,179	1,671	-492	1,693	2,194	-501	2,033	2,674	-641
Unfunded capital items (short-term credit)	375		+375	3		+3	187		+187	47		+47	382		+382			

Pure cash items:

Gold	37	275	—	238	29	323	—294	62	320	—	258	262	128	+134	116	214	—	98	201	207	—	6
Changes in ear-marked gold	4	.....	+	4	5	6	— 1	46	4	+	42	15	47	— 32	50	24	+	26	183	23	+	160
Currency	40	.....	+	40	50	.....	+ 50	.....	20	—	20	.....	30	— 30	.....	.....	.....	.....	.....	.....	.....	20
Grand total	6,333	6,395	—	62	6,512	6,524	— 12	7,363	7,300	+	63	7,991	8,087	— 96	8,799	8,884	—	85	9,128	9,148	—	20

Description of data: In this combined balance Hall's "Commodity trade except silver" has replaced the sum of "Merchandise exports and imports (as reported)," "Bunker coal and oil sales to foreign vessels," "Ship chandling, ship repairs, and tonnage dues," "Sale of vessels," "Unrecorded parcel-post shipments (adjusted for gifts)," and "Other merchandise adjustments;" "Return on American investments abroad—long-term" has replaced "Yield of long-term private investments received from American investments abroad;" "Return on investments abroad—short-term," the "yield of short-term interest and commissions collected from foreigners abroad;" "Interest paid to foreigners long-term," the "Yield of long-term private investments—paid to foreign investors in the United States;" "Interest paid to foreigners—short-term," the "Yield of short-term interest and commissions—paid to foreigners abroad;" "Return on War-debt" the sum of the items "Principal" and "Interest" under "War-debt receipts of United States Treasury;" "Miscellaneous invisible items," the sum of "Freight payments and receipts," "Ocean-borne passenger traffic (by 'substitution')," "Other United States Government receipts; United States Government payments; and foreign representations here," "Insurance transactions" and "Miscellaneous minor items;" "Foreign security investments of Americans," the sum of "Foreign securities publicly offered here (par value)" and "Foreign stocks and bonds bought from foreigners in small lots;" "Discount on investments abroad," the sum of "American underwriters' commissions" and "Securities issued below par;" "Resale of investments to foreigners," the sum of "Resale to foreigners of direct investments" and "Foreign stocks and bonds resold to foreigners;" "Investments of foreigners in United States securities," the sum of "American stocks and bonds sold to foreigners," "Redemption and sinking-fund payments to foreigners" and "American stocks and bonds bought back from foreigners." The other items, whose titles are identical in both tables, are identical in content also.

"In the present survey the geographic limits of the United States . . . include continental United States, Alaska, Hawaii, and Porto Rico. They exclude the Philippines, the Panama Canal Zone, Guam, Samoa, and Virgin Islands; these are counted as foreign countries."—*Balance of International Payments of the United States in 1927*, by Ray O. Hall, p. 56.

Source: Estimated Balance of International Payments of the United States, Calendar Years 1922–1927, Inclusive, as revised for this study by Ray O. Hall, Assistant Chief, Finance and Investment Division, Bureau of Foreign and Domestic Commerce, U. S. Department of Commerce:

balance of trade, in three of the six years under discussion the balance becomes adverse, while in the other three it remains but mildly favorable. In fact, our numerous travelers abroad furnish almost enough funds for the payment of the entire interest on all our outstanding foreign investments.

The largest single item[13] on either side of the balance for every year, except 1923, is that of our new investments abroad. Likewise on the opposite side of the balance the largest item, except for two years, 1922 and 1924, is the interest received on outstanding obligations held abroad. Both sides of the account, therefore, are in general dominated by items growing out of our large foreign investments. Relatively insignificant in size, when compared with the return on such investments, is the item made up of both principal and interest payments on the war debt to the United States of various foreign governments. Gold movements, on the other hand, make up only minute portions of the totals.

But far more important even than the relative magnitudes of the various items of the balance is the degree of their adjustability. In other words, which are the magnitudes following independent courses dominated largely by influences unconnected with the balance or lack of balance in international payments? And which, on the other hand, are those readily and sensitively adapting their movements to changes in exchange rates and related phenomena directly connected with disturbances in such a balance?

The older theory of international trade assumed that between gold standard countries, as between other countries on the same metallic standard, the money metal supplied the one and only immediately adjustable element in the balance. Whatever other adjustments appeared might be traced directly to influences set in motion by the international movements of the precious metals. The movements of gold out of a country with that metal as a standard led ultimately to a corresponding reduction in prices and consequently to an increase in sales (and a decrease in purchases) abroad of goods and of services sufficient not only to restore the balance but in general also to recover much of the lost gold. Conversely, when gold was shipped into a country, prices would rise by an amount sufficient to re-establish the balance and to get rid of much of the unsought gold so recently shipped in. Possible credit adjustments did not pass unmentioned by the more careful writers, but, even by them, were usually relegated to a minor position.

In recent years it has been learned that, at least in the United States, prices are not nearly so responsive to gold movements as had been supposed.

---

[13] It should be noted, however, that if only balances were represented, as in the cases of merchandise trade, tourists' expenditures, and gold, this statement would not hold.

The adjustability of these various items is difficult to test statistically. Considerable variations are to be noted in the merchandise balance of trade; but, as already pointed out, wide differences in the values both of imports and of exports frequently appear on account of almost purely accidental movements of prices of such important articles as cotton, silk, or rubber. Certainly, by no stretching of the imagination could such adjustments be interpreted as being in any important way connected with restorations of international balances of payments. Moreover, payers of international, as of domestic interest, except in the cases of governments, fortunately continue to pay according to what they owe rather than according to the effects of their actions on various international balances of payments; and the declarations of dividends, as always, depend on boards of directors, if not on the affairs of their companies. Little adjustment in such items can accordingly be expected.[14] Furthermore, recently arrived immigrants continue to send money to their relatives at home, and American tourists continue their expenditures without regard to the effects of their actions on the American balance of payments.

A similar review of the numerous items entering into our international accounts yields the presumption that all except credit items, securities, and gold are either relatively fixed in magnitude or else move largely under the influence of forces *temporarily* almost completely independent of balance-of-payments considerations.

In total value, the gold movements have been seen to be relatively very small indeed. Their influence in adjusting disturbed equilibria, however, is unquestionably great. Nevertheless, in all countries with highly developed money markets and modern lending institutions, there is little doubt that it is the operations of the credit mechanisms—sometimes as a result of gold movements, sometimes in anticipation of them, but perhaps often in response to still other influences—which provide the most sensitive adjustments in our balance of international payments. Even when gold is ultimately to be moved, the effects on credit conditions are apt to precede by months the actual shipments.

With a general tightening of credit conditions, foreign borrowing in this country is discouraged while American borrowing abroad is stimulated, and *vice versa*. In general, it is largely through such credit influ-

---

[14] Even in the case of private borrowers in Germany, no disturbance of their own international accounts can be expected to affect their payments. In spite of laborious legal opinions to the contrary, such payments take automatic precedence over all payments by the Reparations' Agent, for the simple reason that there is no way of stopping them. So long as German exchange is sold freely in any part of the world, and so long as the German Government does not make illegal the discharge of honestly contracted obligations, such payments will be made whether international accounts are thereby thrown out of equilibrium or not.

ences, combined with the movements of the monetary metals, that the equilibrium of payments can be maintained.

Nor does the force of the above considerations apply exclusively to short-term credits. As has been frequently demonstrated, a tightening of money rates almost invariably[15] carries with it a rise in interest rates, a fall in bond prices, and a consequent curbing of security flotations. Reverse monetary conditions provide a corresponding stimulus to security flotations.

Moreover, in certain countries, special credits have at times been arranged for the avowed purpose of correcting exchange or of otherwise relieving the effects of an adverse balance of payments.

Far from being a fixed item in our balance of international accounts, credit transactions are usually the most sensitively adjustable of any. Prices, it is true, tend to adjust themselves, but usually with a considerable lag. Only prices of securities, which in the final analysis are an integral part of the credit structure, and to a much less extent those of commodities sold on the speculative exchanges, move quickly and rapidly enough to play any immediately important part in restoring a disturbed balance of international payments.

Unfortunately, the results just arrived at analytically cannot be tested satisfactorily with statistics. While the amounts of most of the long-term obligations are fairly accurately determined, it is not they which furnish the element most quickly responsive to changes in credit conditions. Of the short-term credits, on the other hand, which seemingly furnish the most highly sensitive of all the adjustments, available estimates are the least dependable.[16] Consequently, the wide fluctuations observable in the magnitude of this item may be as much a result of inaccurate estimates as of changes in the amounts of the credits themselves. Nevertheless, the large variations would seem to indicate, in their magnitudes at least, a high degree of flexibility.

But what of the long-run effects? Can adverse balances over an indefinite period of time be continually adjusted by a resort to borrowing? Evidently not. Credit represents postponement of payment with a

---

[15] Notable exceptions have occurred, especially in periods of great currency disturbance.

[16] An exact description of the questionnaire upon which the estimates were based is given in *The Balance of International Payments of the United States in 1925,* p. 45. It includes year-end estimates of total deposits with foreign banks, and of foreigners with American banks; total loans and advances to foreign banks, and by foreigners to American banks; and short-term international investments for the account either of the bank or of its customers.

In 1927 the returns, which were received from 167 leading international banks and investment houses, proved irreconcilable with certain known facts. The results, therefore, were ignored in that year. For a full account, see *The Balance of International Payments of the United States in 1927,* p. 45.

charge in the meantime for the privilege of delaying the day of reckoning. Defaulted debts must be paid, with interest, and, in the final analysis, such payments, except for insignificant amounts of the monetary metals utilizable for such purposes, are largely based upon the excess of exports over imports of goods and services. The same is evidently true of interest charges on debts and returns of all sorts on other kinds of investments. The analysis upon which such deductions are based is irrefutable, and the validity of the results themselves is no longer seriously questioned. Slowly but surely, and usually very gradually, far-reaching changes—yet to be described—in the economic systems of both the lending and borrowing countries make their appearance. New equilibria are established. Certain elements giving rise to a change in trade balances make their entrance.

The very accumulation itself of long-continued adverse balances, thus corrected by ever increasing credits, often sets up powerful forces operating not only to prevent current maladjustments, but also to correct the cumulated deficits. The stimulus to increased tourists' expenditures and to the migration of American industry are explained in detail below. Furthermore, if a rare and entirely different sort of influence may be cited, to certain countries of former greatness and wealth, for which the adverse balances of trade are but indications of a process of gradual impoverishment and of chronic business depression, not only are charities and immigrant remittances stimulated, but in them the incentive for the sale of international securities as well as of shares in their own enterprises and in their properties becomes ever stronger. It is under just such a stimulus that, over a long period of time, a continued import of capital may take care, for the borrowing countries, of an equally long series of otherwise adverse balances of payments; and besides, during the interim, may provide the means of payment of the interest and dividends on the securities which have been but recently exported. It is in such a period for certain countries that the United States is playing the rôle of chief lender and chief purchaser of an ever increasing volume of exported securities.

There is a danger, however, of overemphasizing the *international* character of the transactions under discussion. In essential elements, an international credit is not different from a domestic one. A primitive and remote state like Florida begins to develop. Funds are borrowed in the wealthier states to finance the development. Essentially, the exchange problem is the same as though Florida were a foreign country under a stable and enlightened government and with a well-regulated currency system of its own. The credits which are secured in New York and elsewhere, if wisely granted, will have to be paid. And in order for payment to be made, money, goods, and services must be exported (or taken by tourists) from Florida in sufficient amounts to provide the sums required, or else new credits must be raised. The raising of credits at home, for use in making payments outside, would drain the country of an equivalent amount of cash and would consequently fall under the first alternative, above cited, of exporting money, goods, and services. Since, however, the currency available for export could make up but an insignificant portion of the total outside obligations, payments in this case, as in those in which foreign countries are involved, would rest in the final analysis on an equivalent export of goods and of services from the borrowing state.

Comparison of Movements of Foreign Trade and Foreign Credits.— In order to test statistically whether or not any observable relationships seem to exist between the movements of our international trade on the one hand and those of our foreign loans and investments on the other, a number of comparisons will be made.* The following are the foreign loan items:

> Annual total of new foreign loans and investments[17] in excess of refunding and commissions.
> Annual total of new *long-term*[17] foreign loans and investments in excess of refunding and commissions.
> Net[18] annual new foreign loans, investments, and credits of all sorts in excess of refunding, commissions, repurchases by foreigners, and purchases by foreigners of American securities and properties.
> Net[17] annual new foreign *long-term* loans and investments in excess of refunding, commissions, backwash, and of net purchases by foreigners of American securities and properties.

These will each in turn be compared with the following foreign trade items:

> Annual total of commodity exports.
> Annual total of exports (visible and invisible).[19]
> Annual balance of commodity trade.
> Annual balance of trade (visible and invisible).
> Annual balance of commodity trade, including gold movements.
> Annual balance of trade (visible and invisible), including gold movements.

In Chart 9 are represented the total trade and total credit items. Reference to this chart shows, for commodity exports, little observable likeness either to total or to long-term loans and investments. When invisible as well as visible items are included in exports, however, the

---

* An additional comparison of interest is between the net foreign investment in any year and the estimated yield in the same year from previous investment. Such a comparison will show that, particularly in the last three years, the relationship between the two figures is close, but it is too early as yet to determine whether this is likely to be a continuing relationship.—Note by George O. May, Director.

[17] Revised estimates by Ray O. Hall.

[18] Compiled with the use of the British method.

[19] Includes "total commodity trade," "tourist expenditures," "motion picture royalties," and "miscellaneous invisible items."

series shows considerable similarity in movement (though not in the absolute magnitudes of the yearly items) with that of total new American loans and investments abroad. It likewise shows some rough similarity in movement to new long-term investments.

Comparisons of *net* new long-term foreign investments and *net* foreign investments and credits of all sorts with each of the series of exports in turn yield less noticeable similarities.

CHART 9.—FOREIGN CREDIT AND EXPORT, 1922–1927

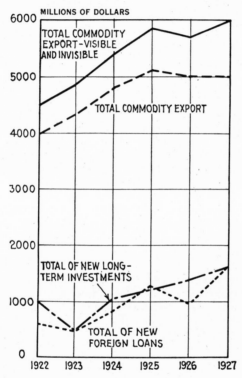

If, instead of total exports, export *balances* are considered, as in Chart 10, much more clear-cut similarities make their appearance. Net long-term foreign credits show, especially in the earlier years, considerable likeness in movement to balances of commodity trade, both when invisible items of trade are included and when they are excluded. If gold shipments are included in the visible trade balances, the similarity of the two series, not only in movements, but in the absolute magnitudes of their items, becomes somewhat enhanced.

Much more evident, and apparently even more significant, is the high correspondence in the movements of the *two types of balances of trade* on

CHART 10.—COMPARISON OF TRADE BALANCES AND FOREIGN CREDITS, 1922–1927

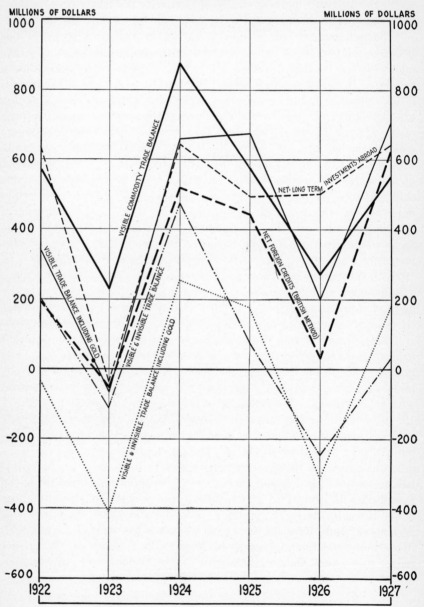

the one hand and those of the *net foreign credits of all sorts* placed in the United States on the other. Moreover, the correspondence is almost equally high whether the visible balance alone is used or whether invisible items are also included.

Finally, whether the net credits series is compiled by the American[20] or by the British[21] method, the great similarity persists. A more thorough study of these and allied series would therefore seem warranted.

The net credits[22] curve always (except in 1922 and in 1927) lies between the two trade balance curves, with the visible balances larger and with the combined visible and invisible balances correspondingly smaller. It will be noted, however, that, in the earlier part of the period, it was with the items of the lower series that the credit items almost exactly coincided; while, in the latter part of the period, it was with those of the upper. In fact, in the year 1922 it was slightly below the lower, while in the last year, 1927, even the visible commodity balance of trade was exceeded by the net foreign credits floated. Thus, at the beginning of the period, American credits were used only in amounts not quite sufficient to cover our net balance of trade when all of our big invisible imports were included, while in 1927 they were taken in amounts slightly greater even than the net commodity balance alone. And when it is further borne in mind that the spread of the two balances has gradually increased from approximately $375,000,000 in 1922 to $517,000,000 in 1927, the probable significance of the change becomes even more striking. The question naturally arises: "How much, if the present extraordinary method of financing exports continues, shall we lend at the end of another six years in order to continue our favorable commodity balances of trade?"

The influence of gold shipments has been significant. To understand its character and importance, two further series have been compiled. The monetary metal has been regarded as simply another article of international commerce, and the two types of trade balances have been recompiled with its inclusion. The resulting series have been inserted in Chart 10. Reference to this chart will show that, while the inclusion of the gold has made the fluctuations of each of the balances in turn correspond more closely with those of the net foreign credits series, it has had very different effects on the absolute magnitudes of the items. In the visible balance series, its inclusion has almost invariably tended to bring the magnitudes of the items of that series into correspondence with those of the items in the credits series. Its combination with the more comprehensive trade balances, on the other hand, has yielded a series with items more widely different in magnitudes from those of the credits series than were the original ones. What deductions, if any, can be drawn from these observations?

[20] The American method is that of direct estimates of all constituent items.

[21] For detailed description of the British method see p. 728, note 9.

[22] On account of the admitted undependability of several important constituent items used in the compilations according to the American method, these credits have been computed according to the British method.

Evidently, during the six year period under discussion, gold generally moved in such ways as to adjust balances in *visible* trade to correspondence with the net credit balances. The one exception in 1925, when there was a net export of gold, seems to be only a partial one; for, although the recorded shipments increased the difference in the magnitudes of the items of the two series, it brought into somewhat closer correspondence the directions of their movements. Is there any plausible explanation for the high similarity in absolute magnitudes, as well as in movements, of the two series of net foreign credits and balances of commodity trade, including gold? Superficially, the most obvious reply is that, otherwise than with gold shipments, our favorable balances of commodity trade may be regarded as being largely financed by the new foreign credits and other investments placed each year in this country. In fact, in 1922, 1923, 1924, and 1926, when new net credits alone were not sufficient to pay for the balance of commodity trade, gold was imported in quantities sufficient to make up much of the deficits. Again in 1927, when net foreign credits were somewhat more than enough to pay for the commodity balance, gold was exported in sufficiently large quantities to take up the excess, and to reverse the relative sizes of the items. In 1925, on the other hand, a net export of gold widened an otherwise very narrow difference in the items of the two series.

While the adjustment of the two series is far from complete, and while the comparatively near approach to equality of most of the individual items may be accidental and passing, the high correlation of the movement of the two series, even for so short a period as six years, would seem to indicate some sort of causal interconnection. The question arises, as to whether the export balances are adjusting themselves to the volume of foreign credits, or whether, reversely, it is the volume of foreign credits which is adjusting itself to an otherwise favorable balance of payments. The fact that, in most of the years, gold moved in such ways as to take up much, but not all, of the differences indicates that neither trade nor credits will adjust themselves completely without friction. On the other hand, the trade balance is the wider mover of the two. And it may be held, in fact, that the bulk of international commodity exchanges cannot be regarded as really voluntary. We must, in effect, export cotton and copper and we must import sugar and coffee. Nor is the situation very different with many types of highly manufactured articles. But the narrower, and at times apparently lagging, fluctuations in the net credits series would seem to lend support to the analytical conclusion that it is in the net foreign credits rather than in the commodity balances of trade that much of the year-to-year adjustment of our balances of international payments makes its appearance.

Whether or not such a conclusion is valid, the close correspondence in the movements of the two series from year to year seems to leave little doubt that our favorable trade balances are dependent on a continuation of increasing net foreign lendings.

The question may legitimately be asked whether the close correspondence found between trade balances and net foreign credits is not a purely mechanical result. At first glance, it might appear to be nothing else—especially when the net credits are compiled with the use of the British method. The gross commodity trade items are by great odds the largest in the balance. But, to get the foreign credits balance each year, these large dominating items of commodity trade are combined with the much smaller ones of invisible trade, purely financial items such as interest, dividends, etc., and gold and currency. The remainder required to establish an equilibrium each year is, by definition, the net foreign credit item for that year. If, therefore, errors of a type to affect net balances of commodity trade were made, while all other errors occurring in the estimated items of invisible trade, those purely financial, and all others except credits, were either nonexistent or were counteracted by one another, the identical errors would appear in the net foreign credits items. On the other hand, the net foreign credits items also absorb all the errors in the items other than those of commodity trade. The answer to the question, whether the correspondence between trade balances and net foreign credits is mechanical or not, depends, therefore, upon whether the errors in the estimates of commodity trade or those to be found elsewhere are the dominating ones. It would seem that the greater accuracy of the estimates of the commodity trade balances would more than compensate for their larger size; but upon this question, the writer is unable to pass judgment. It will be assumed, however, with considerable confidence, that the correspondence is not mechanical.

IV. SUMMARY

1. The value of our visible exports makes up approximately 10 per cent of our domestic production of *exportable commodities*. Of our total production, the percentage is much less. (Visible imports throughout the period have been slightly less valuable.)

2. While the values, both of exports and of imports, have shown a general tendency to increase during the past six years, the proportions which they make up of our total production have, on the contrary, maintained a gradual downward trend.

3. Our largest exports, with the proportion which the value of each makes of total exports, from 1922 to 1927 inclusive, are shown in the following tabulation:

Commodity	Value	Per cent
Total....................	$28,247,000,000	100.0
Cotton (unmanufactured)........	5,131,000,000	18.1
Machinery....................	2,064,000,000	7.3
Iron and steel..................	1,352,000,000	4.8
Wheat........................	1,150,000,000	4.1
Gasoline and allied products......	1,103,000,000	3.9
Leaf tobacco...	890,000,000	3.2
Passenger autos................	824,000,000	2.9
Cotton (manufactured).........	821,000,000	2.9
Copper (refined)...............	723,000,000	2.6
Meats........................	680,000,000	2.4
Lard.........................	666,000,000	2.4
Fruits.......................	568,000,000	2.0
Coal (bituminous)..............	537,000,000	1.9
Kerosene.....................	512,000,000	1.8
Lubricating oil................	507,000,000	1.8

4. Our largest imports, with the proportion which the value of each makes of the total imports, during the period under consideration, are shown in the following tabulation:

Commodity	Value	Per cent
Total....................	$24,789,000,000	100.0
Cane sugar	2,397,000,000	9.7
Raw silk......................	2,265,000,000	9.1
Crude rubber..................	1,737,000,000	7.0
Coffee.......................	1,473,000,000	6.0
Fruits and nuts................	685,000,000	2.8
Wood and manufactories.........	645,000,000	2.6
Raw wool.....................	642,000,000	2.6
Newsprint....................	630,000,000	2.5
Hides and skins................	608,000,000	2.5
Furs.........................	601,000,000	2.4
Cotton manufactures...........	491,000,000	2.0
Tin..........................	472,000,000	1.9
Tobacco......................	455,000,000	1.8
Petroleum....................	430,000,000	1.7
Wool manufactures.............	421,000,000	1.7
Burlaps......................	409,000,000	1.7
Vegetable oils.................	382,000,000	1.5
Fertilizers....................	382,000,000	1.5
Oil seeds.....................	363,000,000	1.5
Pulp (sulphite)................	313,000,000	1.4
Flax and hemp.................	313,000,000	1.4
Copper (refined)...............	310,000,000	1.4
Cotton (unmanufactured)........	291,000,000	1.2
Diamonds.....................	284,000,000	1.1
Cocoa........................	233,000,000	0.9
Vegetable fibers................	233,000,000	0.9

5. But perhaps the outstanding change in our foreign commerce in recent years has been the exportation of American industries themselves.

Because of the extreme difficulty of exporting to countries with high tariff walls, many American firms have constructed branch manufacturing or assembling plants behind the walls. Moreover, the lower and gradually decreasing foreign price levels have encouraged the migration.

6. The foreign capital issues publicly offered in the United States have tended to increase from year to year since 1922 absolutely, but not in proportion to total capital issues so offered.

7. In certain years, especially toward the latter part of the period under discussion, foreign purchases of American securities and the placing of foreign funds in the New York money market have largely counterbalanced the larger foreign lendings of Americans.

8. A striking similarity in the amounts as well as in the movements of our balance of commodity trade with net foreign credits and other investments is discovered. These likenesses, while noticeable in the comparison between long-term investments and commodity balances of trade, became closer when short-term credits were included in investments and gold movements in commodity balances of trade.

9. No evidently significant correspondences appear between foreign credits or investments and the total exports of the United States, though a slight correlation appears between total merchandise exports to Canada and Europe, respectively, and the corresponding net nominal long-term publicly floated credits to each.

10. In the balance of international payments of the United States, the dominating positions held by credits of various sorts, by interest payments, and by tourist expenditures were observed.

11. The readily adjustable items—other than gold—in our balances of payments seem to be largely included in the investment and credit items rather than in the balances of commodity trade.

In general outlines, the picture seems to be about as follows: In a period of the world's history characterized by the most extraordinary technical advances which have yet been known, the United States holds perhaps the dominating position. Not only have its scientists been responsible for a large share of the recent mechanical inventions and its business executives for an even larger contribution of effective operating organizations, but its citizens as a whole, on account of their wealth and savings, have been prepared and eager to finance the ever advancing changes.

In direct contrast to the healthy and stimulating conditions in this country during the period under consideration are the general poverty and dejection in many of the countries of central and eastern Europe, the social and economic unrest and business depression almost uniformly prevalent in the domain of our former allies, and the disturbed currency, banking, and debt conditions, only gradually being corrected, in almost all of the western European countries alike. Finally, in the newer parts of the world, as always, are vast regions with their great but perhaps largely undiscovered resources, many untouched and others in all the various stages of development, awaiting alike the transforming influence of modern business organization. Under such circumstances, our plentiful and generally excellent products have naturally tended to flow to other parts of the world, while our large supplies of savings have naturally been pulled away to the countries of central Europe and to the new and undeveloped countries to the north and to the south.

The flow of goods, however, has met with many obstacles, while the outflow of capital from the United States to other parts of the globe has been greatly stimulated by an unusual combination of circumstances. The resulting flood of new American capital has in turn temporarily lifted the most formidable barrier to the outflow of goods.

Many of our otherwise best customers live behind high tariff walls, and most of the rest of them are fast building up theirs. Besides, even if we succeed in scaling their walls, we require of many of them, in order to repay us, that they bring their wares over the much higher wall which surrounds us. Even under such discouraging circumstances, our export trade during the past six years has in general continued to increase. What is the explanation? How has the double obstacle been surmounted? The answer is clear and significant.

The second obstacle, that of our own tariff walls, by the extraordinary set of circumstances already referred to and to be further amplified, has been temporarily removed for us.

In order to make payments for the surplus of our exports over imports, our customers have not been required in the normal way to scale our high tariff walls with excessively dutiable articles. Whatever portion of the balance has not been taken care of by the steady growth of our tourists' expenditures has been automatically handled in another way. The low interest rates and the supply of funds in our great money market have made of New York the cheapest international market, where funds are sufficiently plentiful for all to borrow. The resulting large flotations of foreign loans, and of all other kinds of foreign investments and foreign credits placed in this country, have been sufficient not only to take care of any excess of exports over imports but, also, when combined with tourists' expenditures, immigrant remittances, and relatively small shipments of gold, to provide means of making to us all other necessary payments.

The first type of barrier, the high tariff walls erected against American products, are in some cases being scaled; but, what is vastly more disconcerting, many of these are being permanently avoided by the establishment of American controlled factories on the other side. Thus, substantial portions of our most highly developed and most profitable industries are actually migrating to foreign countries, carrying with them not only American organization and methods but also American talent, with all the resultant loss of purchasing of American domestic products and of the stimulus to American business in general.

Besides being an era of extraordinary technical advance, the present is likewise, as in no other stage of history, a money and credit age. In such a financial world, the rôle of the United States, and of New York in particular, while not a dominant but rather an aspiring one, is shared by but a single serious competitor. Moreover, during the special six-year period under discussion, the older rival has labored under so many serious domestic handicaps that the younger aspirant has, at least temporarily, taken first place. Along with the assumption of so prominent and so powerful a rôle, many significant and perhaps unexpected changes have occurred.

Because of the unquestioned stability of the dollar in the foreign exchange markets of the world, and because of the broad and active markets for securities and investments of all sorts as well as for short-term paper and bank credits, New York gradually became a safe and otherwise desirable place for the deposit, by central banks and other foreign financial institutions, of temporarily idle but readily available funds; and, with the deposit of such funds, the breadth and activity of the New York market in liquid paper of all types inevitably grew. With this added prestige and with the larger deposit of foreign funds, came further imports of gold, further loosening of the money market and an easing of longer-term interest rates. And with the loosening of the capital market, came larger flotations of borrowers living in all parts of the world; and with the increase in foreign flotations, New York's position as an international financial center became even more firmly established. Of the more significant financial happenings of the period, many have seemingly been associated with this extraordinary and ever cumulating financial development of our great monetary center.

Out of this unusual situation have come many by-products of especial significance for the purposes of this study. Because of our low interest rates and plentiful funds available in an indisputably stable monetary unit, credits to many parts of the world and in almost all approved forms have been granted in generally increasing amounts. Along with the increase in foreign credits have come larger purchases of American securities, larger foreign bank balances maintained in New York, and a favorable balance of commodity trade actually in excess of the remainder of the net credits granted. The excess, meanwhile, in a curiously equivalent amount—if the questionable accuracy of the data permits their use—has been made up by a net import of gold, which, far from shutting off merchandise exports, seems temporarily to have stimulated them further. The large imports of gold not only have failed to raise American commodity prices, but in the past five years have not even kept them from taking a mildly downward trend.

Further, since it is only through price changes that gold movements directly affect merchandise trade balances, the normal checks to American exports have simply failed to operate. On the other hand, as has already been mentioned, the gold imports, by further loosening rates in the New York market, have generally stimulated the placing in this country of increased foreign credits. These, in turn, have largely removed, both in this country and abroad, the chief monetary influence toward further price changes.

Meanwhile, this new situation, because of the failure of the normal correctives to operate, becomes even more extraordinary. Should our foreign credits cease now, and with them our entire favorable balance of merchandise trade, not only would gold probably not cease to come in, but its import very likely would increase in volume—so great has become the interest charge annually required.

In conclusion, the outstanding effects on American industry of the happenings, above outlined, can be summarized under the following heads:

1. Large exports made possible by the great volume of foreign credits placed in this country.

2. Resulting stimulus to export industries.

3. The continuance of easy money rates in New York resulting from its developing financial prestige and from the uncertain currency conditions abroad, causing foreign balances substantially to increase and gold imports to grow.

4. A resulting stimulus to speculation and to business, arising from easy and plentiful short-time money.

5. A further lowering of interest rates throughout the country, and a resulting stimulus to business and to investment in domestic as well as in foreign securities.

6. Finally, the heavy and rapidly increasing payments required of foreigners, combined with the maintenance of our high tariff policy, are forcing slowly and gradually, but none the less surely, an ever wider separation in prices at home and abroad, with a resulting rapid increase in the expenditures of American tourists abroad and the migration of American industry to many foreign countries.

The close correlation between the movements of the foreign credits placed in this country and those of our balances of commodity trade seems to indicate a close interconnection between the two—*even from year to year*. Even if the estimates, upon which the comparisons are based, were sufficiently accurate to assure the validity of the high correlation discovered, the question as to whether trade followed automatically the loan or whether, on the contrary, the credits were placed in order to relieve otherwise severe maladjustments in our international balances of payments, remains unanswered. During a period when prices in this country and those in many others were being artificially restrained from *separating,* relatively low interest rates prevailed in the United States. Under such circumstances, the plentiful, generally excellent, and cheap American products and capital were urgently demanded by the less fortunate but recovering countries of Europe and also by the rapidly developing countries which make up much of the rest of the world. Between credits and trade, seemingly minor adjustments took place in both directions.

What is of outstanding importance is that the large foreign borrowings in the United States made unnecessary for the borrowing countries a larger export of gold and consequently, in spite of large purchases abroad, enabled them the more easily to restrict the fall of prices; while to the United States, the resulting reduced imports of gold made generally unnecessary the restrictions against a further general price rise. And it was the failure of prices, in the borrowing countries and others, to fall sufficiently, and of those in the lending country to rise sufficiently, which in turn made possible the continued large balances of exports from the United States. It is clear, therefore, that in the last resort, our foreign loans and investments, combined with heavy and increasing tourists' expenditures, were making possible the continuance of our favorable balances of trade.

The resulting stimulus to export industries during the period is qualitatively immediately evident, though the ultimate effects on American business as a whole are quantitatively obviously impossible to trace.

It must be continually borne in mind that our exports aggregate in value but little more than 10 per cent of our output of exportable articles and a much smaller proportion still of our entire production. What then, it may reasonably be asked, can be the importance to American industry as a whole of a very large absolute increase in so small a proportion of the total?

In certain industries, it is true, a large increase in the consumption of its products signifies comparatively little. In others, such as the growing of cotton, an increase of 10 per cent in consumption might often mean, for a whole section of the country, the difference between genuine prosperity and deep depression. Furthermore, the stimulus to the business of mail-order houses, and of their suppliers and others throughout the country, resulting from "good times" in the South, while quantitatively impossible to evaluate, is beyond question, great. Similarly, an increase in the foreign sales of machinery or of automobiles, by stimulating activity in those industries and in turn in those of their suppliers, might confidently be expected to bring important, but as yet unmeasured, prosperity to a considerable portion of American industry.

The influences operating through the money and investment markets are even more difficult to evaluate quantitatively. A comparatively small import of gold, for example, serving, as it usually does, as a direct inflationary force, and also as a net increase in the reserves of our Federal Reserve banks, may lead to a manifold expansion of bank credit throughout the country. Moreover, the extent of the possible, or even probable, expansion depends very much upon the uses to which the proceeds are put. Should they be used continually for stock speculation alone, their influence might be very great indeed. On the other hand, the more they flow away to less active *business* uses, the less become the credit expansion possibilities. It is nevertheless true that, whatever their use through our banking and credit machinery, the possibilities of their expansion is several fold.[23] So long, in fact, as the operations growing out of the credit expansion do not so upset the balance of international payments as to cause a reverse outflow of gold or its equivalent, the expansion in business lending may be at least four, perhaps ten, times the gold import, while that in lending for speculative purposes might be much greater still.

The annual imports of gold, therefore, continuing throughout much of the period, and its exports during 1925 and 1927, in their influence on American business, may perhaps be ranked as of *primary* importance.

[23] For more complete analysis of this subject, the reader is referred to an earlier publication of the writer, *Stock Speculation and the Money Market*, 1927.

CHAPTER XII

THE NATIONAL INCOME AND ITS DISTRIBUTION[1]

BY MORRIS A. COPELAND

I. THE NATIONAL TOTALS

Estimates of the national income are useful for many purposes, but they need to be used with care, both because they are not perfectly accurate, and because the term "national income" has several different meanings. The present estimate of the income of the people of the United States may be in error by as much as 5 per cent; in some years the error may be slightly more than that. The constituent streams that combine to make the national income are known less accurately than the total.

The sense in which the national income will be chiefly considered here has been called "total realized income." This includes (1) all pay rolls (including value of board and lodging furnished), (2) pensions, benefits, and compensation for accidents received by employees and ex-employees, (3) net rent (including both cash and payments in kind, less maintenance and depreciation), royalties, interest, and dividends received by individuals, (4) profits withdrawn from businesses by individual enterprisers, (5) the net rental value of owned homes and imputed interest on investment in other durable consumption goods, (6) the value of certain commodities produced by families for their own consumption. It does not include paper profits, profits from the sale of capital assets, or the value of housewives' services. In 1928, the total realized income probably reached the stupendous total of about 89 billion dollars or about $745 per capita.

The reason for excluding profits from the sale of capital assets and such paper profits as additions to corporate surplus and changes in value of real estate is that these items depend upon arbitrary accounting methods or are subject to fluctuations with business optimism and pessimism. Logically they should be included, but practically their inclusion may give rise to year-to-year changes in national income which do not correspond to any changes in the production of goods and services

---

[1] The author desires to make full acknowledgment to Dr. Willford I. King, of the National Bureau of Economic Research, upon whose estimates of national income and related items this study is based. Where other sources have been employed they have been so noted.

or the capacity of our resources to produce them.* A rough estimate
indicates that the inclusion of these items would increase the national
income for 1925 from 82 to 85 or 86 billions,[2] but in some years it is
probable that total accrued income (i.e. realized income plus these profit
items) has been less than total realized income. The value of housewives'
services has not been included in any of the estimates because of the
difficulties of determining a satisfactory basis of valuation.

Another important meaning for the term "national income" is total
income received in money. This excludes items (5) and (6) and also compensation for labor or leased property received in kind. Total money
income in 1925 amounted to about 74 billions.

In none of these three senses does national income measure the welfare
of the population. Only income actually consumed should be included
for this purpose. In years of great depression and depreciation in values,
such consumed income may conceivably be greater than total accrued

---

* Additions to corporate surplus should be added to "total realized capital." The
surplus thus set aside is a very definite and permanent addition to the income of
property owners. The relative share of the property-income group and the wage-
earning and salaried group in the product of industry from year to year cannot be
adequately determined when these additions to surplus are not included. I am not
convinced that the reasons set forth above are sufficient to justify the exclusion of these
figures.—Note by H. W. Laidler, Director.

I do not agree with the treatment of corporate surplus. It should be included in
realized income. I do agree with exclusion of profits from sale of capital assets and
exclusion of changes in value of real estate. "Logically" these should be excluded,
whereas Mr. Copeland says logically they should be included. On the contrary,
corporate surplus should logically be included and practically it should be estimated,
like other estimates. He omits it apparently because it fluctuates, and might be a
deduction instead of an addition. This reason is inconsistent. Other quantities
might be excluded on this ground. By taking one year, 1925, he should treat that
year on its own showing, and let other years go off on their own showing. This addition of corporate surplus would make considerable difference in many parts of his
treatment, especially in comparing corporate income which he hereby minimizes,
with other incomes not minimized.—Note by John R. Commons, Director.

[2] Total accrued income was estimated from the realized income total for 1925 by
adding estimates of business savings and gain in value of real estate held by individuals.
The estimates of change in urban real estate values are King's. King also has estimates of corporate and individual profits in the merchandizing and unclassified
groups and of total profits in construction and banking. These, and his estimates of
profits withdrawn, yield estimates of business savings for these three groups. Corporate business savings in manufacturing, mining, and the transportation and public
utility group were estimated by assuming that they bore the same ratio to cash dividends in the income tax returns. For mining and manufacturing, individual business
savings (or withdrawals of surplus) were estimated on the assumption that the ratios
to profits withdrawn were the same as for corporations. Changes in the value of
agricultural real estate, including improvements, were estimated by nine regions from
the 1920 census values and the value indexes, for March 1, of the Bureau of Agricultural
Economics, United States Department of Agriculture, *Circular* No. 15, October, 1927.

CHART 1.—TOTAL REALIZED INCOME, INCOME DISBURSED IN MONEY
AND BANK DEBITS TO INDIVIDUAL ACCOUNTS (WITH BANK CLEAR-
INGS SPLICED AT 1919), UNITED STATES OUTSIDE NEW YORK
CITY, 1913 TO 1927

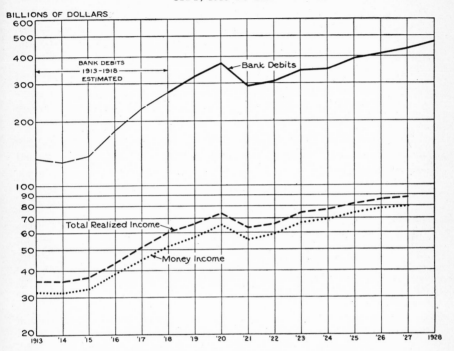

income, although ordinarily it is substantially less than the latter.
For 1925 it may be set down roughly at 74 to 75 billions, that is, about
one-sixth of total accrued income was "saved."[3] There are still other
meanings for national income, some of which will be noted shortly.

The total realized income of the United States and the total income
disbursed in money[4] are shown in Chart 1 and also in Table 1. The

---

[3] Consumed income was estimated by deducting from accrued income an estimate
of savings in 1925, made by J. S. Taylor, of the Department of Commerce, revised in
the light of the 1925 tax returns, and with a correction in the capital flotations item to
allow for stock dividends.

[4] Money income was estimated by deducting from total realized income (1) value
of farm produce consumed by farm population, (2) profits from cow keeping in towns,
(3) profits from urban poultry and gardens, (4) rental value of urban homes, (5) rental
value of owned farm homes, (6) imputed interest on other durable consumption goods,
(7) payments in kind to Army and Navy. Item (1) was a two-year moving average of
Bureau of Agricultural Economics' estimate, 1919–1928. To estimate other years,
farm population was multiplied by an index of farm prices (1927 *Agricultural Year
Book*, p. 1149), and the ratio of the resulting series to value of produce consumed 1919–
1927 was calculated. The average of these ratios was assumed to be the ratio for the
earlier years. Item (7) was assumed to be the same proportion of total Army and
Navy pay in 1926–27 as in 1925.

prosperity of the past few years is shown in the rapid growth of national income since 1921. There is only a slight check in the growth of income in 1924. The year 1927 also shows a slowing down in the rate of growth. As a basis of comparison for the income estimates, an estimate of total debits to individual accounts in commercial and savings banks in the United States outside New York City[5] is shown also, together with data for bank clearings spliced on to debits in 1919. One might expect the cyclical fluctuations of money income to be more marked than those of total income, but the difference between the two series in this respect is small. Both rise to a sharp peak in 1920, and fall in 1921 below the 1919 level. Neither series shows more than a slight check in 1924. One interesting feature of the relation between these two series is that the income disbursed in money forms a gradually increasing percentage of total realized income—88.2 per cent at the beginning of the period and 91.1 per cent at the end. In other words, an increasing proportion of economic activity is passing through the market place. It should be noted, however, that the important item, value of housewives' services, is not included in the total, so that the picture is incomplete. The increase shown is largely because of the increasing proportion of all homes that are rented and so receive an annual market valuation.

The volume of bank debits outside New York is nearly five times the national income. The debits-clearings curve is distinctly more sensitive to business depressions in 1914, 1921, and 1924, and the upward swings from 1914 to 1920 and 1921 to 1927 are steeper. There is, indeed, a general resemblance between the movements of debits (and clearings) and total income disbursed in money, but not anything approaching a precise agreement. Debits represent chiefly settlements by check, and partly because of the large volume of check payments connected with speculative transactions, partly because collections are slower at some times than at others, and partly because commodities change hands more frequently at some times than at others, debits fluctuate quite differently from national income. But whatever their disagreements, the trends since 1921 are strikingly alike; both income and debits have shown a most remarkable growth in the past seven years. The national income increased by about three-eighths from 1921 to 1927, as against a little over 100 per cent from 1914 to 1920, and in 1927 it was about one-sixth greater than in the high year 1920.

During this period there have been tremendous changes in prices. How far do these fluctuations of national income represent changes in the physical volume of flow of goods and services? How far do they reflect changes in prices and in the amount of goods which a given sum of money will buy? We may, following King's method, correct each of the constituent income streams that go to make up the national income

[5] *Journal of the American Statistical Association*, September, 1928, p. 301.

CHART 2.—TOTAL REALIZED INCOME IN DEFLATED DOLLARS RELATIVE
TO 1913 AS 100 PER CENT, AND AN INDEX OF COMMODITY PRODUC-
TION (1913 = 100 PER CENT), UNITED STATES, 1913 TO 1927

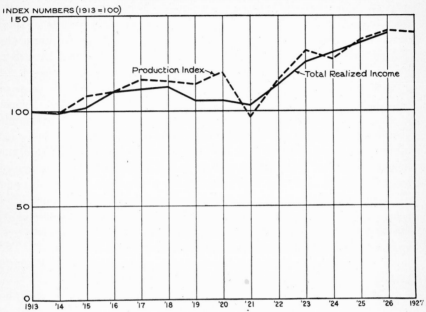

for changes in the prices of goods purchased by the recipients of that
income stream, so that instead of the number of dollars received, say
in 1920, the figure for 1920 will be the number of dollars, at 1925 prices,
that would be required to purchase the same bill of goods the actual
1920 income would purchase for the recipients. In this way we may
correct the total realized income, and express it in dollars of 1925 purchasing power to the income recipients.[6] Thus, in a sense, income
expressed in 1925 dollars represents the physical volume of flow of goods
and services. Chart 2 compares the total realized income, so corrected,
with an index of commodity production.[7] The two series, expressed as

[6] King's indexes were converted to 1925 as 100, and each income stream was divided
by the index representing cost of living to the income recipient. The basic indexes
represent living costs for: (1) farmers, (2) farm employees, (3) urban employees,
(4) those spending $5,000 on consumption goods in 1919, (5) those spending $25,000
on consumption goods in 1919.

[7] The index of the physical volume of commodities produced was prepared jointly
by Dr. Woodlief Thomas and the writer. The annual indexes of the *Review of Economic Statistics* for crops and animal husbandry, indexes of mineral and manufacturing production constructed from annual data by Dr. Thomas, and the Department
of Commerce estimate of total lumber cut, were combined by the aggregative method.
Three overlapping sets of indexes were computed: (1) 1909–1919 on the basis of 1909
aggregate values, (2) 1909–1927 on the basis of 1919 aggregate values, and (3) 1918–
1927 on the basis of 1925 aggregate values. In each case the value aggregates are for
value added by the industry. The three overlapping sets of indexes were combined in
such a way as to approximate Fisher's ideal formula with 1919 as the base year.

relatives to 1913 as 100 per cent, are close together at the end of the period, but certainly they behave very differently between 1914 and 1925. Commodity production shows a rapid growth in 1917 and 1920, a sharp drop in 1921, and a distinct fall in 1924. "Deflated" income shows declines in 1914 and 1921, but none in 1924.[8]

Whatever the qualifications that are required in interpreting "deflated income," it seems clear that there has been a real and considerable gain in national income every year since 1921, quite apart from any changes in prices.

Any estimate of income measured in "corrected dollars" is likely to give rise to misleading interpretations. None the less, we may risk a further estimate of this sort. Has the national income increased per capita, changes in prices being allowed for? Table 1, column (6), shows per capita realized income, in dollars of 1925 purchasing power to the recipients. There is a decline in 1914, and a peak in 1916–17, followed by a decline to 1921. The recovery in 1922 brings per capita income back to the prewar level, and since then there has been a steady gain. Per capita realized income is not a satisfactory measure of consumers' welfare, though it gives some indication of what might be done with the productive power of our present economic system, were it not for voluntary and involuntary savings. It is difficult, with present data, to estimate consumed income per capita, but we are probably justified in inferring from the fluctuations of realized income that consumed income per capita also increased during the war, then declined (not necessarily as sharply as total realized income), has been showing a marked yearly increase now for several years past, and was considerably higher in 1927 than during the war.

Conditions in different countries are so dissimilar that international comparisons are fraught with danger. And the United Kingdom alone

---

[8] Because production indexes corrected for price changes have been used to estimate the national income, the striking differences between these two series are significant. For one thing, it should be borne in mind that commodity production does not include all production. Indeed, only a little more than one-third of our national income is disbursed by enterprises engaged in commodity production in agriculture, mineral extractive industries, and manufacturing. It is not surprising, since goods can be stored more easily than services, that commodity production should fluctuate more widely than service production. Another possible explanation of the differences between the two series lies in the process of "deflating" the income. The prices used in converting income to "1925 dollars" were for consumption goods used by the income recipients, not prices or costs for the producing enterprises. Deflation is a process that requires cautious use. The method of deflation employed by King, which we have just discussed, is probably the most generally useful type for correcting the national income, but it is not well adapted to the particular purpose of comparing income with output. And it is possible, even for general purposes, that some of the years are overcorrected. For example, both 1919 and 1920 have probably been made too low, relatively to 1918, by the deflation.

TABLE 1.—TOTAL REALIZED INCOME OF THE UNITED STATES COMPARED TO CERTAIN
RELATED SERIES, 1913 TO 1927

	(1)	(2)	(3)	(4)	(5)	(6)	(7)	(8)
Year	Total realized income	Money income	Bank clearings (U. S. outside New York City)	Bank debits (U. S. outside New York City)	Realized income in 1925 dollars		Production index (1913 = 100 per cent)	Ratio of money to total income (per cent)
					Total	Per capita		
			Billions of dollars					
1913........	35.7	31.5	75.4	. . .	60.3	$621	100	88.2
1914........	35.6	31.3	72.2	. . .	59.5	601	99	87.9
1915........	37.2	32.8	77.3	. . .	61.7	615	108	88.2
1916........	43.3	38.5	102.2	. . .	66.7	655	111	89.0
1917........	51.3	44.9	129.5	. . .	67.7	656	117	87.4
1918........	60.4	51.9	153.8	. . .	67.9	651	116	85.9
1919........	65.9	57.2	181.9	322	64.2	611	114	86.7
1920........	74.0	65.5	209.0	370	63.9	600	121	88.5
1921........	63.4	55.8	161.9	293	62.4	576	97	88.0
1922........	65.9	59.0	.....	305	68.6	625	117	89.6
1923........	74.3	67.1	.....	344	75.7	679	132	90.2
1924........	77.1	69.6	.....	348	79.1	697	127	90.3
1925........	81.9	74.3	.....	391	81.9	712	137	90.6
1926........	a85.7	a77.9	.....	411	a85.3	a733	142	90.8
1927........	a87.5	a79.7	.....	431	.....	....	141	91.1
1928........	a89.0	a81.0	.....	468	.....	....	...	....

a Preliminary estimates.—The preliminary estimates for 1926–1928 in this and the following tables
were prepared, so far as possible, on a basis to make them comparable with King's estimates for preceding years. The general procedure was to select some standard series which could be taken as a yearly
index for the years 1925, 1926, 1927 and 1928 of each item or group of items to be estimated, and, with
King's 1925 estimate as a base, to estimate the other two years. Income tax data were available for
estimating income in 1926 but not in 1927 and 1928. The estimates for 1926 are therefore distinctly
more reliable than those for 1927 and 1928.

among the great European powers affords a satisfactory postwar estimate
to make comparison possible. The attempt at such a comparison raises
two further questions regarding the meaning of national income: (1)
Is interest on the war debt properly a part of national income? (2) Are
we speaking of income received in the country, or income produced in
the country?

Stamp has argued that interest on internal national war debts should
be excluded in reckoning national income:

> Suppose that we had not elected to tax ourselves severely during the war, but had
> borrowed a very much larger sum, then the interest to be paid on the debt to-day
> would be very much greater. Are we to assume, therefore, that the "invisible income"
> that we shall each receive in future years, in the way of services in conquering the
> Germans many years ago, would have been greater than it is under present actual
> conditions?[9]

[9] Sir Josiah Stamp, *Current Problems in Government and Finance*, London, 1925,
p. 138.

In other words, to include interest on war debts is to include an item the size of which depends upon a past policy of government finance—an item which might have been a great deal larger without producing any material increase in present flow of goods and services. The point is a disputed one, and it is by no means clear that the entire interest on the national debt is, as Stamp seems to imply, a mere transfer from one individual to another, being precisely offset by tax payments and so not properly included in the consolidated national income total. But it will probably improve the comparability of the income totals for the two countries, if we eliminate interest on the national debt. We shall call the balance "accrued social income."

With regard to the second question, it seems obvious that both income received and income produced are of interest. Table 2 sets forth a comparison of the national income of the United Kingdom and the United States. The English estimates are those of Bowley and Stamp. The American figures, for gross accrued income received, represent King's estimates of realized income plus a crude allowance for the profit items, added in order to make the totals comparable with those for the United

TABLE 2.—NATIONAL INCOME OF THE UNITED STATES AND THE UNITED KINGDOM COMPARED, 1914 AND 1924

Item	United Kingdom[a]		United States	
	1914	1924	1914	1924
Gross income produced at home (billions of dollars)	9.7	17.7	37.2	79.4
Interest on national debt (billions of dollars).........	.1	1.2	.0	.9
Accrued social income produced at home (billions of dollars)......................................	9.6	16.5	37.2	78.5
Net received from abroad (billions of dollars)........	+ 1.1	.7	− .1	.6
Accrued social income received (billions of dollars)...	− 10.7	17.2	37.1	79.1
Accrued social income received per capita (dollars)...	248	384	375	697

  [a] The income estimates for the United Kingdom are from Bowley and Stamp, *The National Income, 1924*, Oxford, 1927, especially pp. 45 and 46. "Accrued social income" includes pensions (Bowley and Stamp have excluded this item). The 1914 figures were estimated by multiplying the 1911 data by 2,250 divided by 2,090 (see Stamp, *Current Problems in Finance and Government*, p. 291). The conversions to dollars were made at the average daily rate for cable exchange. In making allowances for the exclusion of southern Ireland in 1914, it was assumed that this section received none of the income from foreign investments and 4 per cent of other income. The deduction for net interest received from abroad by the United States includes interest received by the Federal Government, banks, and insurance companies, and is therefore larger than the item in the miscellaneous income statement. For the estimates of accrued and saved income for the United States, see footnote 2, p. 758.

Kingdom. The total accrued social income of the United States is apparently about four and one-half times that of the United Kingdom for 1924. Making allowance for price changes, our national income has increased about one-third in the decade, while, according to the estimates of Bowley and Stamp (whose method of deflation is not entirely comparable to King's), the income of the United Kingdom was approximately the same in 1924 as in 1911, and so possibly a trifle smaller than in 1914. According to Bowley and Stamp, the deflated total accrued social income of the United Kingdom per capita declined 5 to 10 per cent in this 13-year interval, while the deflated per capita income of the United States shows an increase of about one-seventh in the decade 1914–1924. The English estimates indicate that about one-eighth of the total social income was "saved" in 1924, as against nearly one-sixth in 1911.   According to J. S. Taylor's estimate of savings in this country, the proportion was about one-tenth in 1924 (a mild depression year), and one-sixth in 1925.   About three-fourths of 1 per cent of our income came from abroad in 1924, while 4 per cent of the income of the United Kingdom came from outside, and an even larger percentage before the war.   In using these comparisons, it should be remembered that the year 1914 was one of depression in this country, and partly so in England.   In 1924 there was a mild depression in the United States, while in England there was a slight lessening of a prolonged depression.   But in spite of these and other qualifications,[10] it seems clear that the average individual is considerably better off in this country than in England, and that the difference to-day is distinctly greater than before the war.

For further light upon recent changes in the national income, we may turn to a consideration of the major income streams of which it consists. First of all, we may analyze the national income on a functional basis into wages, salaries, and pensions; rent, interest, and dividends; and profits withdrawn by individual enterprisers.   It may be broken up also among the principal disbursing industry groups, agriculture, construction, mineral extractive industries, manufacturing, public utilities, merchandising, commercial and savings banks, all branches of government, and unclassified enterprises and occupations.   The national income was estimated by adding together wages, salaries, etc., for each of these groups, so that it is fairly easy to obtain estimates for each of these streams of income.   But when we come to assign the national income to different parts of the country, we encounter a great many·difficulties. And the attempt to determine how the national income is distributed among the higher and lower income classes will prove even less satisfactory, but some light can be shed upon this problem.   We shall consider these four types of income distribution in order.

[10] Especially in comparing the absolute amounts of the national totals or per capita incomes, a number of qualifications are necessary.   Price differences between countries are more difficult to allow for than price differences between two dates for the same country, but the allowance would presumably make the showing appreciably less favorable to the United States.   A factor suggesting an opposite correction is that nearly 23 per cent of all English females were gainfully employed in 1921, as against 16½ per cent of American females in 1920; a smaller proportion of women's services are priced in this country.

It has already been noted that the total realized income of the United States is known more accurately than are many of the income streams that make it up, for it is improbable that all the errors of estimate for the constituents are in the same direction. In dealing with the constituent income streams, then, we shall do well to remember that we are on less secure ground. There is one redeeming feature. An estimate, say, of mining wages, may be wrong in absolute amount, and still the year-to-year percentage changes in the estimate may be approximately correct. Again, we may not have an accurate estimate of total pay rolls, but if the ratio of estimated pay roll to all income shows a decrease between 1923 and 1925, that decrease may still be a correct portrayal of events. Since the basis of estimate from year to year is similar, it is likely to lead to similar errors in each year. Our information about year-to-year fluctuations in income streams, then, is more reliable than our information about the absolute amounts of those streams.[11]

II. THE SHARES OF LABOR AND PROPERTY

The bulk of the national income falls into two chief classes, income going to labor and income going to property holders. But there is an important part of the national income which the available data do not permit us to apportion between these classes with any great confidence. Profits withdrawn by individual business enterprisers represents a mixture of labor income and income from property. Labor income of employees may be subdivided into wages; salaries; and pensions, benefits, and compensation for accidents. Property income includes rents and royalties, interest, and dividends. Table 3 shows total realized income for 1925 and 1913, and total money income for 1925 apportioned to these classes.

It appears that employees received about 57 per cent of realized income and 63 per cent of money income in 1925, and that their share in the national dividend has increased over the prewar figure. About two-thirds of the employees' share goes to wage workers. The chief gain as against prewar proportions has, however, come in the field of the salaried employees, which, according to King's classification, includes all of govern-

[11] A general word of caution should perhaps be entered at this point regarding the interpretation of year to-year variations in many of the income streams. One would expect that the variable income streams, particularly, would fluctuate up and down with the ups and downs of business conditions. But to find that a given income stream does fluctuate as one expects it to, is not always precisely an empirical verification of one's hypothesis. This hypothesis may have been used in making the estimate. For example, there are no satisfactory annual data on pay rolls in merchandising, and the pay roll estimates depend on estimates of number of employees on the pay roll. In making this estimate, a fluctuation with business conditions was assumed. In certain other lines, manufacturing and railroads, for example, there are annual pay roll figures, and the fluctuations of these income streams are not due to the method of estimate.

TABLE 3.—DISTRIBUTION OF TOTAL REALIZED INCOME OF THE UNITED STATES IN 1925 AND 1913 AMONG VARIOUS LABOR AND PROPERTY GROUPS[a]

Item	(1)	(2)	(3)	(4)	(5)	(6)
	Total realized income		Money income, 1925	Total realized income		Money income, 1925
	1925	1913		1925	1913	
	Billions of dollars			Per cent		
1. Wages.........................	30.8	13.0	30.8	38	37	42
2. Salaries........................	15.0	5.5	14.9	18	15	20
3. Pensions, benefits, and compensations	1.1	.3	1.1	1	1	1
4. Total share of employees.......	46.8	18.8	46.8	57	53	63
5. Rents and royalties.................	10.6	5.2	5.8	13	15	8
6. Interest.........................	3.9	1.5	3.9	5	4	5
7. Dividends........................	4.1	2.2	4.1	5	6	6
8. Property income..............	18.6	8.9	13.8	23	25	19
9. Entrepreneurial profits withdrawn.....	16.4	8.0	13.7	20	22	18
10. Total realized income..........	81.8	35.7	74.3	100	100	100

[a] On the extent to which the omission of additions to corporate surplus, etc. understates the share of property, see Table 4, note a.

ment and banking.   The growth of pay rolls in these two lines has been extremely rapid, but the increase of salaries in the public utility, merchandising, and unclassified groups of industries has been large also.[12]

With the increasing importance of labor and of plant and equipment, financed by the issue of securities as the country has developed industrially, rents became a smaller proportion of the national income in 1925 than they were in 1913.   While there have been definite declines in the importance of the interest item in several of the industry groups, this item has shown a great increase in the case of the government group (an increase measured in per cent of the total national income) nearly equal

[12] The chief differences between total realized income and income disbursed in money are brought out in Table 3.   Item 5 includes the most important noncash items, net rental value of owned homes and "interest" on the value of other consumers' durable goods.   No attempt has been made to exclude agricultural "share rents" in estimating money rents, although this would have been desirable, if the basic data had permitted it.   Item 9 includes profits withdrawn by farmers in the form of agricultural produce consumed, and urban garden produce and "profits" from cow and poultry keeping.   The only important nonmoney employees' labor income included in these estimates are those for food and board of the Army and Navy and of agricultural employees.   In calculating money wage income, only the former of these two has been deducted from total disbursed income, the entire amount of agricultural produce consumed by the farm population being deducted from farmers' profits because of the difficulty of apportioning it between farmers and employees.

to the net increase of the interest percentage of total national income for all groups combined. The decline in the proportion of total realized income going to stockholders is fairly evenly distributed among the different types of enterprise. In the case of profits withdrawn by individual enterprisers, the decline in relative importance is partly owing to the shift from the individual to the corporate form of organization, but the chief decline is in agriculture, where this factor is not of consequence.

Considerable interest attaches to determining the proportion of total realized income which goes to labor and that which goes to property. If we attempt to estimate the amount of labor income included in profits withdrawn by individual enterprisers, on the assumption that the average enterpriser in each of the nine industry groups (except the unclassified) receives for his services the same annual income as the average wage earner in that group, and that in the unclassified group, where lawyers, doctors, and stockbrokers are among the most important types of enterprisers, the average enterpriser's labor income equals the average salary, the figure for enterprisers' labor income in 1925 is well over nine and a half billion dollars. No satisfactory basis for a direct estimate of enterprisers' property income is available. As a rough check upon the estimate of total property income which the nine and a half billion estimate leaves, we may note that in 1922 the corresponding estimate would mean a total realized property income of over 21 billion dollars, or about 6 per cent on 353 billion dollars of national wealth.[13]

But this comparison is not especially useful as a check on the estimate of enterprisers' property income. Moreover, the check of the total property income estimate is subject to the qualification that realized property income is not the same as accrued property income. About all that can be said is that the property income estimate is of an order of magnitude which shows no striking disagreement with the estimate of wealth.

If we take enterprisers' labor income at nine and a half billion dollars in 1925, all labor income represents nearly 69 per cent of total realized income, and property income represents about 31 per cent.

Another figure of general interest is the proportion of what has been called "earned income" to the total. "Earned income" includes employees' labor income and enterprisers' profits. In both the United Kingdom and the United States in 1924, "earned income" was about three-fourths of the total "social accrued income."[14] In both countries the proportion is larger in 1924 than before the war, the proportion for the United Kingdom in 1911 being about two-thirds, and for the United States in 1914 about 73 per cent, as against 76 per cent in 1924.

---

[13] As estimated by the Federal Trade Commission, *Sen. Doc.* No. 126, 69th Cong., 1st Sess. p. 50.

[14] As defined in footnote to Table 2.

If we examine the year-to-year changes in the distribution of total realized income (Table 4), it appears that the gain in the employees' share came largely in 1919 and 1920, and that the chief change after that was a slight rise in 1923, followed by a dip in 1925. The preliminary estimates for 1926 and 1927 do not substantiate the contention that the share of employees in the national income has been declining. This share has been practically constant since 1920. The share of property—rent, interest, and dividends—reaches its peak in 1921 and 1922, during the postwar depression period. There has been no significant variation since 1923. The share of individual enterprisers rose during the war, declined sharply in 1920 and 1921, and has since then increased slightly but is still below the prewar figure.

TABLE 4.—THE PROPORTIONS OF LABOR AND PROPERTY AND ENTERPRISERS' INCOME,[a] AND THE RELATION BETWEEN CORPORATE DIVIDENDS AND NONAGRICULTURAL WAGE PAYMENTS, UNITED STATES, 1913–14 AND 1918–1926

	(1)	(2)	(3)	(4)	(5)	(6)
Year	Total share of employees	Rent, interest, dividends	Profits withdrawn	Corporation dividends on common stock	Nonagri-cultural wage pay-ments	Ratio of dividends to wages (per cent)
	Per cent of total realized income			1913 = 100 per cent		
1913................	53	25	22	100	100	13
1914................	52	25	23	93	95	13
1918................	54	22	24	172	157	15
1919................	54	22	24	155	176	12
1920................	57	22	21	143	228	8
1921................	57	25	18	136	179	10
1922................	57	24	19	124	190	9
1923................	58	23	19	164	224	10
1924................	58	23	19	176	227	10
1925................	57	23	20	205	241	11
1926................	b59	b23	b19	b230	b255	b12
1927................	b59	...	...	....	b258	....

[a] A rough idea of the effect of using realized income instead of accrued social income in analyzing distribution may be gained from the following estimates. Accrued social income includes additions to surplus and certain real estate appreciation, and excludes interest on the Federal debt.

	1914	1924	1925
	Per cent	*Per cent*	*Per cent*
Proportion of accrued social income going to			
Employees..	50	56	56
Enterprisers and property................................	50	44	44

b Preliminary.

The changes in the share of employees are largely accounted for by changes in the two chief constituent industry groups, manufacturing and the unclassified enterprises and occupations, labor income of which represents over one-half of total labor income. The proportion of realized income included in the unclassified pay rolls was less than half the prewar figure in 1918 and has increased since, reinforcing the increase in manufacturing in 1920 and offsetting the 1921 decline.

The fluctuations in the share going to employees show little correspondence with the ups and downs of business. If money incomes of employees are compared with total money income, it appears that the share of employees rises in the depression period of 1921 and 1922. But this is, in part at least, a result of differing fluctuations in different industry groups. Agriculture, for example, has a large proportion of property and enterprisers' income, and the total realized income of agriculture drops sharply in these years. It may be well, therefore, to compare money wages outside of agriculture (salaries being excluded as being a more stable form of income) with corporate cash dividends paid to individuals. Dividends appear, on the whole, to be about as stable a form of income as wages. Columns (4) and (5) of Table 4 show total cash dividends paid to individuals on common stock, and total money wages (except in agriculture) relative to 1913, and column (6) gives the ratio of dividends to wages. The greater drop of wages in 1921 is reflected in the increase of the ratio of dividends to wages. In 1922–23, however, estimated dividends to individuals show a continued decline, while wages do not. Of course, stockholders' accrued income (that is, cash dividends plus additions to, or minus withdrawals from, the stockholders' equity) drops sharply in 1921 (by about 90 per cent, according to the income tax returns), even if their cash dividend income shows only a slight decline.

But percentage shares in the national dividend are perhaps less important from the point of view of the employee than his average annual labor income. Table 5 shows the changes in wages and in salaries per employee attached to industry, that is, total wages or salaries, divided by the total number of wage or salary workers, including those who may be temporarily out of employment. In order to facilitate comparison, wages and salaries are expressed as percentages of the 1913 figures, and the changes are shown both for actual dollars and for dollars corrected for changes in the workers' costs of living.[15] It appears that real annual wages per employee (that is, wages corrected for price changes) were about the same in 1918 and 1920 as in 1913, that they declined appreciably in 1919 and more sharply in 1921, and have risen considerably since, though there was a setback in 1924. Real annual salaries per employee, on the other hand, were considerably lower in

[15] See Chap. IX, Price Movements, p. 604; Chap. VI, Labor, pp. 430–445.

TABLE 5.—AVERAGE ANNUAL COMPENSATION OF WAGE EMPLOYEES, SALARIED EMPLOYEES, AND ALL EMPLOYEES, RELATIVE TO 1913 AS 100 PER CENT, AND NUMBER OF EMPLOYEES, UNITED STATES, 1913–14 AND 1918–1926

Year	Average annual wages per wage employee		Average annual salary per salaried employee		Average labor income per employee		Number of wage workers	Number of salaried employees
	Current dollars	1925 dollars	Current dollars	1925 dollars	Current dollars	1925 dollars		
	Relative to 1913 as 100 per cent						Millions of persons	
1913.............	100	100	100	100	100	100	21.9	5.2
1914.............	93	92	102	101	96	94	22.5	5.3
1918.............	158	101	119	76	152	97	21.7	8.9
1919.............	173	95	136	75	168	92	22.4	8.0
1920.............	214	103	163	79	203	98	23.2	6.7
1921.............	165	93	159	89	169	95	23.8	7.0
1922.............	170	103	161	97	173	104	24.3	7.0
1923.............	194	114	172	102	192	113	24.9	7.2
1924.............	191	113	178	105	193	114	25.6	7.5
1925.............	198	115	183	106	199	115	26.2	7.7
1926.............	a201	a118	a190	a109	a205	a119	26.8	7.9
1927.............	a203	a119	a196	a114	a208	a122	27.3	8.3

a Preliminary.

1918 than in 1913, declined still further in 1919, and have risen every year since, not even excepting 1921. Since 1923 they have apparently been above the prewar level. The decline in real wages in 1919, and to some extent also the decline in real salaries in 1918 and 1919, were owing to price changes, but the latter was due in part also to the temporary war-time increase in the number of Government employees receiving low salaries. As we should expect, wages are evidently more responsive to price changes and business conditions than salaries. On the whole, real wages have risen considerably more than real salaries in the interval from 1913 to 1926, 18 per cent as compared to 9 per cent, and even since 1922 real wages have gained 15 per cent as against a gain of 11 per cent for real salaries. The number of salary workers has, however, grown more rapidly from 1913 to 1926 than the number of wage workers, according to King's estimate.

It may be interesting as a comment on the development of the wage system to note whether the proportion of total money income derived from pensions, benefits, and compensation for accidents is changing. The estimates for this item are not very complete, but, so far as the available evidence goes, there is no very appreciable trend in the proportion of money income taking this form. Both in 1913 and in 1925 it was slightly less than 1 per cent.

We have considered the changes in the proportion of total disbursed income going to property. This income consists of three principal parts—rent, interest, and dividends. While rent accounts for a gradually decreasing proportion of the income in this period, the proportion going to interest, after a slight drop in 1917 and 1918, rises with the increase in Government financing and remains above the prewar figure (Table 6). These two income streams are alike in being a larger proportion of total income in years of poor business. Dividends, on the other hand, represent a slightly larger proportion of total income in 1921 than in adjoining years, and a slightly smaller proportion in 1914 and 1924. The proportion shows a downward trend to 1919–1922, and an upward trend since, but the 1926 percentage is still considerably below that of 1913.

TABLE 6.—RENTS AND ROYALTIES, INTEREST, AND DIVIDENDS EXPRESSED AS PERCENTAGES OF TOTAL REALIZED INCOME; THE RELATION OF FIXED TO TOTAL MONEY INCOME; RETURN TO RAILROAD BONDHOLDERS CORRECTED FOR PRICE CHANGES; AND THE RELATION OF DIVIDENDS AND PROFITS WITHDRAWN TO INTEREST PAYMENTS BY DOMESTIC BUSINESSES, UNITED STATES, 1913–14 AND 1918–1926

Year	(1) Rents	(2) Inter-est	(3) Divi-dends	(4) Fixed money incomes (billions of dollars)	(5) Ratio of fixed money income to total money income (per cent)	(6) Railroad bond yields corrected for price changes[a] (per cent)	(7) Divi-dends on common stock	(8) Interest payments by domestic business	(9) Ratio of divi-dends etc., to inter-est
	Per cent of total disbursed income						Billions of 1925 dollars		
1913	14.5	4.1	6.1	10.1	32.1	[b]1.3	2.7	2.2	1.2
1914	15.0	4.2	5.8	10.6	33.9	[b]3.3	2.5	2.3	1.1
1918	12.5	3.6	5.9	16.7	32.2	−10.6	3.3	1.9	1.7
1919	12.7	4.3	4.9	18.6	32.5	− 8.8	2.6	1.8	1.5
1920	13.8	4.0	4.2	20.2	30.8	1.7	2.1	1.7	1.3
1921	15.7	4.8	4.7	20.7	37.1	16.2	2.2	2.0	1.1
1922	14.7	5.4	4.0	21.7	36.8	4.6	2.1	2.2	0.95
1923	13.4	4.9	4.5	22.8	34.0	4.2	2.7	2.3	1.2
1924	13.4	4.8	4.5	24.3	34.9	4.6	2.9	2.4	1.2
1925	13.0	4.7	5.1	25.3	34.1	2.3	3.3	2.5	1.4
1926	[c]13.2	[c]4.9	[c]5.3	[c]26.5	[c]34.1	6.4	...	2.7	...

[a] Data for funded debt beginning of year and interest paid on that during the year (fiscal years prior to 1916) for Class I roads (excluding nonoperating subsidiaries) were from the Interstate Commerce Commission. These were deflated by King's indexes to give: (1) deflated value of debt at beginning of year, (2) same deflated by index for end of year, (3) deflated interest paid. (1) minus (2) plus (3) equals annual return on investment. This divided by (1) equals rate of return.

[b] Year ended June 30.

[c] Preliminary.

It would be desirable if we could compare the year-to-year changes in the percentage of return on investment.   For rents, dividends, and profits, no satisfactory data are available to make possible such a comparison, but for one important group of interest payments such a comparison may be made, namely, interest on railroad bonds.   There are dangers in attempting to make corrections for price changes, but failure to make such correction is certainly worse.   Table 6 shows the rate of return to investors in the bonds of Class I railroads (nonoperating subsidiaries excluded) upon the par value of their investment at the beginning of the year.   The return is made up of interest received and of the change in the purchasing power of the par value of the bonds to the income recipiénts.   Table 6 shows clearly that, when price changes are allowed for, this type of investment yields anything but a stable return.   The year-to-year changes in the deflation index (cost of living of the higher income classes) may be open to question, but it is beyond dispute that there were losses in the years of rapidly rising living costs, and that bondholders who invested before the rise have fared badly, while those who invested at the peak of living costs profited considerably by the subsequent decline.   Table 6 also shows the ratio of dividends paid on common stock to all interest payments other than payments by government or by foreigners, when both are corrected for price changes. The high figures in 1918–1920 and the low figures in 1921 and 1922 suggest that, when price changes are taken into account, common stock may be a more stable type of investment than bonds and mortgages in a period of widespread and violent price changes.

A grouping of income streams which is less familiar than the classification into wages, salaries, interest, etc., but of great significance for national prosperity is shown in Table 6.   The more important "fixed money income" streams are assembled—disbursements to individuals which business enterprises cannot easily adjust to changes in volume of business: money salaries, pensions, and benefits;[16] rents (excepting rents and royalties in mining); and interest (short-term interest should logically be excluded, but it did not seem worth while to attempt this exclusion). Column (5), Table 6, gives the ratio of this stream of fixed incomes to total money income.   Two things stand out clearly: the ratio of fixed to total money income is highest in depression years, 1914, 1921, 1922, and 1924, and the ratio has an upward trend.   In interpreting these movements, it is well to bear in mind several qualifications.   The distinction between wages and salaries is not precisely a distinction between fixed and variable incomes, and none of the other constituent streams of our national income falls wholly in one of these two classes. Furthermore, an increasing proportion of corporate dividends might properly be regarded as forming a fixed income stream.   And there are

[16] Total salaries and pensions and benefits less Army and Navy pay in kind.

changes in the wage system in certain fields which might require a similar qualification with respect to wages; for example, the development of some types of unemployment insurance. If these factors are taken into account, the upward trend of fixed income is probably underestimated. From the point of view of the individual enterprise, the disbursement of a large proportion of fixed incomes is a disadvantage in meeting the cyclical fluctuations of business. From the point of view of a national economy, it is an advantage. The increase in proportion of fixed incomes is a factor making for increased stability of business.

III. THE PROSPERITY OF VARIOUS INDUSTRY GROUPS

The analysis of the national income into the shares contributed by the major industrial groups and types of industrial organization is important because it summarizes the chief changes that have been taking place in the structure of industry and at the same time throws light on some of the factors which have been responsible for these changes. Moreover, because the estimates of national income have been made by adding together these shares, it helps to make clear precisely what is included in the national income, and what reliance may be placed upon each constituent estimate in the light of the peculiar difficulties which have been encountered in making it.

Let us consider first the amounts of total income realized from each industry group in 1913, 1925, and 1926, 1913 being taken as representative of prewar conditions. These amounts and the percentages of total realized income coming from each industry group are shown in Table 7. The most important shifts among the industry groups which this table shows are the declining importance of agriculture and the increasing importance of government and of merchandising. The proportion of income from agriculture has decreased 3 per cent in the 13-year period under review. In interpreting these changes it is important to recognize that a change in percentage of income disbursed by a group may mean a change in the relative importance of the physical volume of its output. It may also mean a change in the remuneration which a given physical volume commands, relative to that in other lines. Furthermore a change in relative remuneration may represent either a change in economic efficiency or a change in relative bargaining power. This decline in agriculture is probably partly a matter of change in relative remuneration. But it is to be expected that the relative importance of this industry, measured in physical units of output, should decrease as the country becomes more highly industrialized. The increase in the percentage of income disbursed by government is doubtless partly a war phenomenon, interest payments by the Federal Government having been multiplied more than thirtyfold. But there has certainly been a great increase in the peace-time activity of government also.

TABLE 7.—AMOUNT AND PERCENTAGE OF TOTAL REALIZED INCOME DERIVED FROM EACH INDUSTRY GROUP,[a] UNITED STATES, 1913, 1925, AND 1926

	1913		1925		1926	
	Billions of dollars	Per cent	Billions of dollars	Per cent	Billions of dollars	Per cent
1. Agriculture............................	5.0	14	8.9	11	[a]8.9	[a]10
2. Mines, quarries, etc......................	1.2	3	˙2.2	3	[a]2.5	[a]3
3. Manufacturing..........................	7.3	21	16.9	21	[a]17.8	[a]21
4. Construction............................	1.5	4	3.5	4	[a]3.5	[a]4
5. Transportation and public utilities..........	3.2	9	6.7	8	[a]7.3	[a]8
6. Commercial and savings banks.............	.5	1	1.1	1	[a]1.2	[a]1
7. Merchandising..........................	4.5	13	12.0	15	[a]2.5	[a]15
8. Governments...........................	2.0	6	6.1	7	[a]6.6	[a]8
9. Unclassified industries and occupations[b].....	7.1	20	16.4	20	[a]17.3	[a]20
10. Miscellaneous income[b]....................	3.4	9	8.1	10	[a]8.2	[a]10
11. Total realized income...............	35.7	100	81.9	100	[a]85.7	100

[a] Preliminary estimate.

[b] Group 10 includes nonmoney income from nonfarm cows, poultry, and gardens, and interest on value of durable consumers' goods, net rentals for owned and leased homes, and net income from foreign investments. Group 9 includes income from all business enterprises, institutions, and gainful occupations not included in the first eight groups. For further information on the make-up of each group, see text.

The proportion of total governmental realized income disbursed by state and local governments was not much smaller in 1926 than in 1913, 61 per cent as against 66 per cent in the earlier year. It is difficult to be certain how far the increase in proportion of total income realized from retail and wholesale enterprises is a matter of physical volume and how far of relative remuneration. There is no satisfactory direct measure of the volume of goods marketed by wholesalers and retailers, but the fact that the percentage of income realized from the transportation group and also from the three groups, agriculture, mining, and manufacturing, has declined, lends color to the belief that merchandising is commanding a larger remuneration relative to other lines for handling a given physical volume of goods. The fact that the proportion of income realized from the construction industry shows no appreciable change between 1913 and 1925 appears to corroborate the contention advanced elsewhere[17] that the amount of construction in recent years may not have been so abnormally large as some have supposed.

A word may be said about the other years which do not appear in Table 7 (see Table 38, page 839). While they do not give reason to alter materially the statements regarding the trends of changes made above, they show certain interesting fluctuations. In 1918, when Government war-time activity was at its height, over 10 per cent of the national

[17] See Chap. III, Construction, p. 219.

income was derived from government. The government's percentage was also high in 1921–22, when it was 9 per cent. In 1919, the unclassified industries accounted for only 11.3 per cent of the national income, as compared to 20 per cent in 1926. In 1920, the percentage for manufacturing was high; it was 26½ per cent, while that for merchandising was only 11.8 per cent. But these fluctuations were largely the result of war and postwar temporary conditions.

Table 8 shows the amount and proportion of income disbursed by corporate enterprises. As might be expected, there is an increase in the importance of this type of organization, as an income-disbursing agency, between 1913 and 1925. But the increase is not a striking one and the

TABLE 8.—TOTAL INCOME DISBURSED BY CORPORATIONS, BY CORPORATIONS AND GOVERNMENT, AND TOTAL INCOME DISBURSED IN MONEY IN THE UNITED STATES IN 1913, 1925, AND SEVERAL INTERVENING YEARS

	(1)	(2)	(3)	(4)	(5)	(6)
	1913	1914	1919	1921	1923	1925
1. Total income disbursed by corporations[a] (billions of dollars)	13.0	12.4	25.2	23.6	28.9	31.1
2. Total income disbursed by corporations and government (billions of dollars)	15.0	14.5	31.3	29.3	34.6	37.2
3. Total money income (billions of dollars)	31.5	31.3	57.2	55.8	67.1	74.3
4. Per cent of total money income disbursed by corporations	41.3	39.6	44.0	42.4	43.0	41.9
5. Per cent of total money income disbursed by corporations and government	47.5	46.3	54.7	52.5	51.6	50.2

[a] These estimates of total income realized by United States corporations were made by industry groups and by types of income. King has estimates of interest and dividends of corporations No estimate of dividends or interest from foreign corporations is included in the totals given in Table 8. For manufacturing in 1919 and 1914, and for mining in 1919, the census affords a basis of estimate of pay roll, the number of employees in each type of establishment, for both corporations and all establishments, and the total wages for each type of establishment. It was assumed that the ratio of corporate to all wages for each type of establishment was the same as that of the number of corporate to all employees, and that the ratio of corporate to all wages in each of these two industry groups was the same as the ratio of corporate to all pay rolls (including pensions, etc.). Other years were estimated by assuming that the proportion of noncorporate pay rolls varied in proportion to the changes in the ratio of noncorporate to total value of product (mining) or noncorporate to total operating expenses (manufacturing). The merchandising and construction pay rolls were prorated on gross revenue from sales. All compensation of employees in the banking and transportation and public utility groups was arbitrarily assumed to be corporate. Since again the unclassified group is the most unsatisfactory, it seemed the best available expedient to prorate pay roll on King's estimate of profits, a procedure which presumably gives too small a figure, but one with an approximately correct trend.

Rents were apportioned between corporate and other enterprises on the basis of value of products for mining, merchandising, and manufacturing, and profits for the unclassified group.

decline in proportionate importance after 1919 is greater than the net increase for the entire period. Paradoxical as it may seem, the corporate form of organization has disbursed a steadily increasing proportion of income in the several industry groups taken one by one, and yet appears to have disbursed a smaller proportion of total income in 1925 than in 1919. The explanation appears to lie chiefly in manufacturing pay rolls. The pay rolls of manufacturing corporations, which make up about three-sevenths of the total income disbursed by corporations, have grown during these six years, but not as rapidly as total disbursed money income. We have already seen that the proportion of all realized income derived from the manufacturing group declined some 6.5 per cent in this six-year period, and it is not surprising that manufacturing corporation pay rolls have also failed to grow as rapidly as total income disbursed in money. If we eliminate this one item, the ratio of the remaining streams disbursed by corporations to total income disbursed in money increases from 22.7 per cent in 1919 to 23.4 per cent in 1925.

Corporate enterprises and government together accounted for about 47.5 per cent of the total income disbursed in money in 1913 and for almost 55 per cent in 1919, but by 1925 the percentage had declined again to about 50 per cent.

Table 9 shows the percentage of employees' income coming from each industry group, and average remuneration per employee by groups. Manufacturing accounts for about 30 per cent of all employees' labor income, and the unclassified occupations for nearly 25 per cent. These groups, together with merchandising, public utilities, and government, pay out nearly eight-ninths of all compensation paid to employees. On the average, banks appear to have the highest paid employees, with government and the construction industry next, and agriculture at the bottom of the list.

TABLE 9.—PER CENT DISTRIBUTION OF VARIOUS TYPES OF INCOME AND AVERAGE ANNUAL LABOR INCOME PER EMPLOYEE, BY INDUSTRY GROUPS, UNITED STATES, 1925

	(1)	(2)	(3)	(4)	(5)	(6)
	Share of employees	Average income per employee	Rents and royalties	Interest	Dividends	Individual profits withdrawn
	Per cent		Per cent	Per cent	Per cent	Per cent
1. Agriculture..............	2.7	$537	11.4	6.0	0.0	37.9
2. Mining................	3.3	1,318	2.4	1.8	6.5	.1
3. Manufacturing..........	30.5	1,362	1.9	7.0	46.4	1.1
4. Construction...........	5.4	1,574	0.0	.8	1.7	5.0
5. Transportation and public utilities............	10.9	1,554	.2	23.2	16.8	.....
6. Banking................	1.3	2,179	0.0	8.5	4.1	a
7. Merchandising..........	12.0	1,315	6.9	9.7	10.7	29.2
8. Government............	11.0	1,585	0.0	25.4	0.0	0.0
9. Unclassified industries....	22.9	1,408	7.2	6.7	13.8	25.1
10. Miscellaneous income....	0.0	......	70.0	b10.9	b	1.5
11. All groups combined.....	100.0	1,384	100.0	100.0	100.0	100.0

a Included with dividends.

b Dividends on foreign stocks included in miscellaneous interest.

It also appears from Table 9 that over two-thirds of the rents in 1925 (including here imputed interest on consumption goods) fall in the group of miscellaneous incomes, chiefly rental value of urban homes and that agriculture, merchandising, and the unclassified industries account for all but 4.5 per cent of the rest. The government and the public utility groups disbursed nearly half of all the 1925 interest payments, and nearly 30 per cent of the total comes from banking and trade, and from abroad. About 7 per cent comes from domestic manufacturing and about 6 per cent from agriculture. Of dividends in 1925, nearly one-half come from the manufacturing group, and about one-sixth from public utilities, while merchandising and the unclassified industries account for over 10 per cent each. Individual profits withdrawn are concentrated in three groups, agriculture, trade, and the unclassified industries.

A rough idea of the relative profitableness of the several industry groups may be gained from the corporation income tax returns. Table 10 shows (1) the capital, surplus, and undivided profits or book value of stockholders' equity for each group as of the close of the year 1926;[18] (2) the cash dividends paid; (3) the net profits after paying the tax; and (4) the ratio of profits to the book value of the stockholders' equity.[19]

Mining is distinctly the least profitable of the industry groups according to this showing, and construction the most profitable; but this and other comparisons, so far as the mining industry is concerned, may be vitiated by the different accounting for income tax returns in mining. It seems probable that the rate of return in mining is actually much higher than it appears.*

[18] Includes all fiscal years ended between July 1, 1926 and June 30, 1927.

[19] Among the qualifications to be considered in interpreting these figures may be noted the following: (a) The methods of valuing assets and determining such items as depreciation expenses are not uniform. This qualification is particularly important in the case of mining, where depletion changes and valuation of reserves may be quite arbitrarily determined. (b) The classifications are not precisely the same as King's, and the "all other" class has not been included with the unclassified groups, as it includes a considerable proportion of inactive concerns. (c) The income tax data classify a corporation according to the predominant character of its business; for example, the United States Steel Corporation, if it renders one return, would be classed as "manufacturing," although it is also engaged in mining and transportation. Consolidated returns are permitted for combinations. (d) Only about 79 per cent of all reporting corporations furnished balance sheets, though for the most part it was the smaller corporations and corporations showing a deficit that failed to file balance sheets. Balance sheets were filed by 97 per cent of corporations reporting a net income of over $10,000. (e) Sales prices of a mining corporation to a financially interested or parent company (and consequently its revenues) may be arbitrarily determined.

* In my opinion, the Statistics of Income published by the Bureau of Internal Revenue afford no indication of the profits of the mining and quarrying industries, for

TABLE 10.—RETURN TO STOCKHOLDERS ON INVESTMENT. UNITED STATES CORPORATION INCOME TAX RETURNS, 1926

	(1)	(2)	(3)	(4)
	Capital stock, surplus, and undivided profits as of end of year	Cash dividends	Profits after tax	Ratio of profits to capital investment
	Billions of dollars	Millions of dollars		Per cent
1. Unclassified group....................	ᵃ16.9	ᵃ678	ᵃ986	5.8
2. Mining..............................	8.3	403	305	3.7
3. Manufacturing.......................	46.2	2,544	3,640	7.9
4. Construction........................	1.0	55	105	11.0
5. Transportation and public utilities.......	26.5	1,277	1,849	7.0
6. Banking............................	ᵃ8.2	ᵃ458	ᵃ638	7.8
7. Trade..............................	12.1	525	761	6.3
8. All others (including inactive corporations).............................	.1	5	−3	−2.7
9. All corporations.....................	119.3	5,945	8,281	6.9

ᵃ The book value of the stockholders' equity as of June 30, 1927, for the banking groups is from the report of the Comptroller of the Currency. Profits are estimated for all banks as yielding the same rate of return on the stockholders' equity as for national banks. Dividends are estimated to bear the same ratio to profits for all banks as for national banks. The unclassified group represents the items listed in the tax returns as agriculture, public service, and finance less these banking group estimates.

Table 10 refers only to corporations. Table 11 shows the number of individual income tax returns reporting profits and the amount of reported profits in 1925.[20] The highest reported profits per return were in mining,

three reasons, which are noted by Mr. Copeland but not in my judgment sufficiently stressed; they are:

1. The practice of permitting consolidated returns and classifying them according to the character of the principal business.

2. The fact that the profits are arrived at after deducting statutory deductions for depletion, which to a large extent do not represent any actual cost incurred; for 1925, the total allowances under this heading were nearly 50 per cent greater than the reported net profits in the mining and quarrying group.

3. The practice, among certain classes of mining corporations, of transferring mine products to stockholders at cost, or other figures below fair value.

I think there is good reason to suppose that, making due allowance for these three items, the profits of the industry for the year 1925 were 100 per cent or more in excess of the figures quoted from *Statistics of Income.* I do not believe any satisfactory conclusions can be predicated upon statistics subject to so wide a margin of error.— Note by George O. May, Director.

[20] Profits here include labor income, and no satisfactory way of measuring rate of return is available. The estimated number of enterprisers in each group is shown, and the average reported profit per return. Less than half of all enterprisers in manufacturing are apparently reporting, and only a negligible proportion of farmers' incomes fall above the reporting limit. An unknown number of enterprisers in column (3), which is based on King's estimates, should be transfered from Item 7 to Item 5 in order to make King's classification comparable with the tax returns, for King does not include taxicabs and trucking under Item 5.

with banking and the unclassified group next, and agriculture at the bottom of the list. But these figures speak only for the most profitable portion of each group.

TABLE 11.—INDIVIDUAL ENTERPRISER'S BUSINESS PROFITS REPORTED IN INCOME
TAX RETURNS, AND NUMBER OF REPORTING AND OF ALL ENTERPRISERS,
UNITED STATES, 1925

Group	(1) Business profits (millions of dollars)	(2) Reporting	(3) Total	(4) Average profit per reporting enterpriser
		Number of enterprisers		
		Thousands of persons		
1. Agriculture.................................	250	83	6,317	$3,010
2. Mining, quarrying, etc.....................	25	5	17	5,520
3. Manufacturing.............................	268	69	159	3,900
4. Construction..............................	247	60	185	4,080
5. Transportation and public utilities...........	84	27	28	3,170
6. Trade....................................	1,217	367	1,484	3,320
7. Unclassified and banking groups.............	1,598	368	1,827	4,330
8. All enterprisers...........................	3,689	979	9,997	3,790

According to economic theory, our industrial system, which has no general manager to dictate how much of each commodity or service shall be produced each year, or how much of our available human or material resources shall be devoted to each form of production, is nicely articulated through a scheme of pecuniary incentives. Prices and profits exercise a guidance over production and the apportionment of resources. If too much of any commodity is being produced, prices and profits will fall, production will be curtailed, and resources will be withdrawn from this type of production for want of attractive remuneration. If too little is being produced, prices and profits will rise, and the increased remuneration of resources devoted to this kind of production will attract new employees and new capital, and output will increase. There are many qualifications to be put upon this theory, and it is not to be expected that the response to the guidance of price and profit will take place without lag. In particular, it should be noted that in lines where overhead costs are high, low profits or even losses are not necessarily incentives to withdraw from the industry. Withdrawal may be an even more poorly paying proposition.

As we examine each of the great industry groups of our economic system, it will be interesting to inquire how sure and prompt appears the responsiveness to the guidance of price and profit. We shall, of course, be dealing with broad averages, and these may conceal a responsiveness of our economic system which a more detailed analysis would bring to light. Moreover, the accuracy of the income estimates and of other statistical measures is probably not sufficient to yield more than crude results. Finally, in such economic changes as the growth of government enterprise, other than pecuniary considerations may be the determining factor.

Another hypothesis on which recent changes in our national income streams may throw some light is the productivity theory of the distribution of income. According to one formulation of this theory, the income realized from (or more strictly accruing from) any industry group, measured in dollars of constant purchasing power to the income recipients, might be expected to vary with the physical volume of its output of commodities or services. It will be worth while to test this hypothesis also, but again it will be a test which is subject to the qualification that our statistical measurements are not sufficiently accurate to yield more than crude results. And perhaps it should be added that the hypothesis is usually so qualified as to recognize that technological change may be a disturbing factor.

Agriculture.—The items which go to make up the total income disbursed by agriculture can best be seen by considering the following consolidated statement of income, in millions of dollars, for agriculture for the year ended June 30, 1927:

1. Revenue from sale of farm products......................... 9,537
2. Farm value of farm products consumed by farm population..... 2,590

3. Gross value of agricultural production....................... 12,127
4. Payments made to other industry groups.................... 3,697

5. Net current income realized from agriculture before deducting
   real estate depreciation................................... 8,430
6. Rental value to owners of farm houses..................... 161

7. Total income realized from agriculture and farm houses before
   deducting real estate depreciation........................ 8,591
8. Loss from change in property value (real estate and improvements) 2,160

9. Net income account of farms............................... 6,431
10. Wages and salaries (including value of board, etc.)............ 1,291
11. Rents paid to individuals (including other farmers)............ 1,428
12. Interest paid to individuals (including other farmers).......... 260

13. Total expenses paid to individuals........................ 2,979

14. Net profit to owners..................................... 3,452
15. Interest on market value of owners' equity at 4½ per cent...... 1,759
16. Labor income of independent enterprisers (owners and tenants
    at $540 a year, average annual wage per wage employee)..... 3,410

17. "Normal profit" for year................................. 5,169

18. Deficit in actual profit.................................. 1,717

NOTE.—Items 1 and 2 and the data for most of the other items are from *Crops and Markets* for July, 1928. Item 4 is the Bureau of Agricultural Economics estimate for operating costs plus 30 per cent of taxes, plus two-thirds of estimated interest paid. (The proportions follow King's estimates.) Item 6 is King's 1925 estimate. Item 8 was estimated by regions from 1925 census values and value indexes in Department of Agriculture *Circular* No. 15, October, 1927. Item 10 is the Bureau wage estimate, plus King's estimate of salaries (average for 1924 and 1925). Item 11 is the Bureau estimate for rent paid. Item 12 is one-half interest as above. Item 15 is the Bureau estimate less item 6. The number of entrepreneurs for item 16 is King's estimate.

Items 1 and 3 do not include for the most part the value of crops fed to livestock, since this part of agricultural production represents raw material for further production by the industry. Item 4 includes interest paid to banks and merchants; expenses for manufactured feed; business taxes; fertilizer expense; repairs and replacements for implements, automobiles, and buildings; cost of supplies; and some purchases of agricultural products from other farms. In agriculture and in each of the other industry groups, so far as practicable, the effort has been made to classify expenses as (*a*) those paid to other industry groups and (*b*) those paid to individuals. Disbursed income includes only those expenses paid to individuals plus cash dividends and other profits withdrawn by individuals.[21] To include expenses paid to other industry groups would involve double counting. As practically all of agriculture is organized on an individual basis, additions to surplus are not easily distinguished from new investment. All profits are treated as withdrawn, and the whole net value produced by agriculture (before deducting depreciation of real estate plus rental value of owner-occupied houses) is considered as realized income.[22] Items 2 and 6 necessarily involve somewhat arbitrary valuations. Consequently, item 7, total income realized from agriculture, in spite of the wealth of statistics on this industry, is at best a good guess. Even wages and salaries, which are, as in most other groups, the most accurately estimated items, include value of board, etc., received in kind, at a more or less arbitrary figure.

In spite of all possible errors, the showing can hardly be a favorable one in 1926–27, and the deficit in most of the immediately preceding

[21] This statement requires some qualification as applied to certain industry groups having interest and dividend income, but it holds as applied to the consolidated statement for all groups combined. In the groups where corporate enterprise is important, interest and dividends paid by one group to another have been deducted from the gross interest and dividends paid by the group receiving these intercorporate payments, rather than from the gross interest and dividends of the group paying them.

[22] Most of the items in this estimate are subject to a considerable margin of possible error. It is an extremely complicated problem to determine what proportion of gross agricultural produce—corn for example—is consumed by the industry itself as raw material for hog or other production. And the attempt to determine the amount of payments to other industry groups is equally difficult.

years was undoubtedly greater. If no allowance were made for loss on
real estate values due to market changes, the deficit for 1926–27 would
be converted into a surplus, but the estimated "normal" remuneration
to independent farm operators for their services (at the same rate as for
agricultural wage labor) and the 6 per cent return on value of owned
investment are modest allowances. In spite of continued agricultural
deficits, the census shows an increase in value of farm buildings between
1920 and 1925 of over 2 per cent and a decline in the number of independent farm operators of less than 1 per cent,[23] while crop acreage, according
to the Department of Agriculture, shows no material change. The
census value of implements and machinery does, however, show a sharp
decline of 25 per cent, which is certainly not primarily a price decline;
and the number of independent farm operators who are owners decreased
1.5 per cent, while tenant farmers increased during this five-year period.
On the other hand, in spite of the agricultural deficits in recent years,
production was probably larger in the period from 1923 to 1927, if animal
products as well as crops are included, than before or during the war, except
for 1915. An analysis of these various changes, by states and by types of
farming, would undoubtedly show a greater responsiveness of economic
activity to farming deficits, but on the whole it seems clear that agriculture responds slowly and imperfectly to the guidance which price and
profit are supposed to exercise over economic activity. In part, no
doubt, this is because overhead costs are heavy and capital assets cannot easily be converted to nonagricultural employment. In part also,
technological changes have been responsible for increased production in
spite of deficits.

Table 12 shows further facts about agriculture. As might be
expected, the proportion of total disbursed income going to individual
capitalists as rent and interest (column (1)) fluctuates inversely with the
prosperity of the industry. This item shows no upward trend, although
there has been an increase in farm tenancy since 1910. Indeed, the
amount of these rent and interest payments actually declined from about
$1,596,000,000 in 1920 to $1,386,000,000 in 1923, thus decreasing some
of the fixed charges in this overcapitalized industry.

The fact that, except during the war period, production has apparently
increased more rapidly than total income realized from agriculture,
corrected for changes in value of the dollar to income recipients, suggests
that the decline in the proportion of total national income disbursed by
agriculture is partly the result of a decreased relative remuneration per
unit of output.[24] How far this is due to increased efficiency, how far

[23] This decline might be slightly larger, if recreational farming could be excluded.
Similarly, the increase in building values may be partly suburban. The Dakotas,
Indiana, and a number of southern states showed declines in building values, while
states with large urban centers showed increases.

[24] Column (6) divided by column (7) may be said to afford a crude index of relative
remuneration per unit of output.

TABLE 12.—ANALYSIS OF AGRICULTURAL REALIZED INCOME IN THE UNITED STATES, 1913 AND 1914, AND 1918 TO 1927

Year	(1) Income from agriculture going to— Borrowed capital	(2) Hired labor	(3) Average annual earnings per wage worker — Nonagricultural industries	(4) Agriculture	(5) Number of wage workers (agriculture)	(6) Total realized income in 1913 dollars (agriculture)	(7) Index of agricultural production[a]	(8) Money income disbursed by agriculture	(9) Total money income disbursed in United States	(10) Per capita current income of farm population[b]	(11) Per capita income of United States
	Per cent of realized agricultural income				Relative to 1913 = 100					Current dollars	
1913	17.8	15.1	100	100	100	100	100	100	100	143	368
1914	18.4	14.9	92	98	99	99	111	97	99	141	360
1918	11.8	10.8	159	155	101	137	112	233	165	328	579
1919	12.6	12.2	173	185	104	129	114	258	181	356	628
1920	14.4	15.0	214	213	101	108	123	254	208	319	695
1921	22.1	20.2	164	180	100	87	103	137	177	196	585
1922	19.1	16.5	170	160	96	97	114	155	187	212	601
1923	17.3	15.3	193	167	95	108	117	175	213	239	667
1924	17.2	14.8	190	168	95	111	115	182	221	251	680
1925	16.0	13.8	197	172	95	113	118	203	236	281	712
1926	c17.7	c14.4	c204	175	96	...	121	c199	c247	...	736
1927	c17.5	c14.2	c201	174	95	...	c122	c196	c253	...	742

a See p. 759, footnote 5. The crops and animal products indexes were combined as then indicated on the basis of value added in process.

b Current income of farm population is wages and salaries in agriculture, plus "current income of farmers" (King). It includes property incomes of farmers from investments in agriculture and other lines. Farm population for noncensus years is estimated by linear interpolation.

c Preliminary estimate.

to decreased bargaining power, it is difficult to say. If the relation between these two series be accepted as a crude test of the productivity theory, it is clear that production and remuneration do not vary closely together, though the dependence of agriculture on weather and other uncontrolled conditions is a disturbing factor, and it may be doubted whether the series are sufficiently accurate to offer any satisfactory conclusions. Another interesting feature of the table is that money income disbursed by agriculture appears to vary far more closely with general business conditions, as reflected in total national income disbursed in money, than it does with agricultural production.

Columns (3) and (4) show that agricultural wage earners have probably received a steadier income than those attached to other industries,[25] but on the whole their wages have risen less as compared to the prewar figure. The decline in number of wage earners since 1919 suggests a greater mobility of labor than of capital in this industry.

One of the best measures of changes in the general welfare of the population is the average current income per capita. Current income includes wages, salaries, profits, income from investments both in agriculture and other lines, and rental value of homes to owners and tenants.[26] While not as well off in 1925 as in 1918 and 1919, even when price changes are allowed for, the average member of the farm community has apparently improved his condition as compared to 1913. An average of $281 a year compares unfavorably with $712, the average per capita for the entire country, but the unfavorableness of the comparison is, at least in part, apparent only. Living costs, especially rent and food, are higher in the city. While these averages include rental value of owned homes and value of agricultural produce consumed at home, the value of the housewife's services are not included, and allowance must be made for the greater extent to which such services have been replaced in the city by services that must be paid for in money. If we compare the 1925 averages with those of 1913,[27] it appears that the per capita current income of the farm population has increased 96 per cent, while that of the entire population (i.e., realized income) has increased 94 per cent.[28]

This unexpectedly favorable showing for agriculture may be partly due to errors of estimate. We have already noted that earnings of agricultural wage workers have lagged behind those of other wage earners.

[25] As here used, the expression "employees attached to an industry" means those actually employed plus those unemployed who look chiefly to that industry for employment.

[26] No estimate for income from trucking and other nonagricultural work is included, but some of the included wage income goes to persons not a part of the farm population.

[27] See Table 12, columns (10) and (11).

[28] Using King's deflation indexes, the showing in 1925 is even more favorable, 24 per cent for the farm population as compared to 14 per cent for the entire United States.

Moreover, the proportion of gross value of agricultural output paid to other industries is, according to the estimates, about the same in 1925 as in 1913 (consolidated statement of income for agriculture, page 781, item 4 divided by item 3). But farm population actually decreased about 10 per cent during this period, so that it represented only 24 per cent of the total population in 1925 as against 32 per cent in 1913. The corresponding decline in realized income was from 14 to 11 per cent. In section IV we shall see that in some parts of the country the change in agricultural per capita income, even between 1920 and 1925, is more favorable than that for the rest of the population.

Mining, Quarrying, and Oil and Gas Wells.—King's method of estimating income disbursed by other industries than agriculture is illustrated by the case of the mining, quarrying, and oil and gas well group. Dividends and profits withdrawn (and additions to surplus) are estimated independently of the value of products sold to other industry groups and to individuals. The item, expenses paid to other industry groups, is simply the difference between item 1 and item 3. The reliability of the item "added to surplus," which has been estimated on the basis of income tax returns to complete the income statement, is doubtful at best. In the case of the mining industry (where it is a minus quantity), the opportunities for accounting jugglery are peculiarly great. Item 3, total income produced by the industry, represents total realized income minus the doubtful item 11, withdrawn from surplus. Except for 1919, where the census forms a fairly secure basis of estimate, the pay roll figures are less dependable than for manufacturing or railroad transportation. Rents and royalties are the most doubtful items in noncensus years. The chief problem in the case of interest and dividends, in this and the other corporate industry groups, arises from the necessity of eliminating intercompany payments. The following is a consolidated statement of the income (in millions of dollars) for mining, quarrying, and oil and gas wells, 1925:

1. Estimated value of products	3,893
2. Expenses paid to other than individuals	1,783
3. Total income realized from industry less withdrawal of surplus	2,110
4. Wages	1,389
5. Salaries	169
6. Rent and royalties paid to individuals	255
7. Interest paid to individuals	70
8. Total expenses paid to individuals	1,883
9. Profits	227
10. Cash dividends (and estimated disbursements to individual proprietors)	285
11. Withdrawn from surplus	58

NOTE.—Item 1 is based on 1919 Census and Bureau of Mines annual data, and item 11 on income tax data; other items follow King. It is possible that more accurate data would turn the last item into an "addition to surplus." At all events, the relations between items 4 to 8 and item 10 (which make up realized income) do not depend upon the doubtful income tax data.

While the condition of the mining industry has not been so deplorable as that of agriculture, it was not a very profitable undertaking in 1925 and was distinctly less so in the four preceding years.[29] The bituminous coal industry, which is one of the chief constituents of this group, is probably the most like agriculture in its failure to respond closely to the guidance of price and profit.

A rough idea of the make-up of this group may be gained from Table 13. Except for the pay roll figures, the data are from the capital stock and corporation income tax returns for 1925, during which year corporations disbursed over 94 per cent of the income for this group. As already noted, vagaries of accounting practice (for example, in the valuation of

TABLE 13.—MINING PAY ROLLS AND RETURN TO STOCKHOLDERS OF MINING COR- PORATIONS, UNITED STATES, 1925[a]

Industry	(1)	(2)	(3)	(4)	(5)
	Stockholders' approximate equity in tangible assets as of end of year	Reported net income less tax and reported deficits	Rate of return (per cent)	Ratio of number of balance sheets filed to number of income statements (per cent)	Mining pay roll (millions of dollars)
	Millions of dollars				
Coal.....................	2,444	−28	−1	101	1,205
Metal....................	1,378	22	2	67	.....
Oil, gas, and nonmetal....	2,160	177	8	84	.....
Quarrying...............	271	27	10	86	.....
All other...............	1,372	−10	−1	60	593
All mining indus- tries...........	7,625	188	2.5	78	1,798

[a] Stockholders' equity in tangible assets for the several mining groups is cash, accounts and notes receivable, inventory, real estate, buildings, and machinery, less accounts and notes payable, bonded debt, and mortgages. These balance sheet items are from the capital stock tax returns. Each corporation was required to file a separate capital stock return, whereas, in the case of the income tax, consolidated returns are permitted. Column (2) is based on corporation income tax data. Columns (2) and (5) are not directly comparable. Column (2) is considerably less than reported net profits (see Table 14), which is not available for the subgroups.

[29] Mining corporations follow the practice of paying out considerably more in dividends than they earn in book profits as reported to the Bureau of Internal Revenue, this withdrawal of capital presumably representing, in a rough way, depletion of reserves. Possibly this practice serves to mislead investors, and possibly the unprofitableness is a matter of book-keeping valuations or nominal sales prices by subsidiaries of vertically integrated holding companies. At all events, this unprofitableness of the industry does not appear to have discouraged production, which has shown a sure but unsteady growth. (See Tables 14 and 29.)

reserves) are responsible to an unknown degree for the showing with regard to profits. The table strongly suggests that coal mining, which is distinctly the most important constituent industry, has been much less profitable than the average, while oil and gas and quarrying corporations have been doing fairly well, but different rates of return are partly owing to the varying proportion of income statements for which balance sheets are available.

One further feature of the mining income statement deserves a word of comment. The proportion of total pay roll going to salaries is only 9 per cent, whereas in manufacturing it was over 22 per cent in 1925. In part at least, this reflects an industrial organization in which the individual worker receives less in the way of supervision, and the rôle of management plays a relatively smaller part, than in other forms of corporate enterprise.

Several important phases of the development of the mining industries are shown in Table 14. A large proportion of the disbursed income goes to employees, slightly larger now than before the war. This proportion is smaller for mining than for manufacturing, 75 per cent as compared to 85 per cent for the latter. On the other hand, the return to hired capital (rent and interest) is larger than in manufacturing and even than in transportation, the percentage for the transportation group being only 13.3 in 1925. The importance of this item is interesting because of the high risks in this industry, as is also the fact that both royalties and interest on loans (which are largely short term) vary from year to year with the conditions of the industry. While the average annual earnings per wage employee attached to the industry also fluctuate considerably from year to year, mining wage employees in recent years, according to King's estimate, have been better off in comparison to prewar conditions than have those in all nonagricultural industries, in spite of considerable unemployment. This improvement has not attracted employees into the industry, the estimated number showing no material change in 1926 from the prewar figure. But averages are likely to be misleading. Earnings in certain portions of the bituminous coal industry have not been such in the last few years as to attract new workers.

The growth of mineral production in relation to profits has been noted. It is interesting to compare the growth of production with total income realized from the industry, corrected for changes in value of the dollar to the income recipients. The year-to-year changes here show a much closer correspondence than in the case of agriculture, but the trends show a wide divergence. Production has apparently grown much more rapidly than deflated income. This suggests that here also the decline in proportion of the total national income disbursed by this industry, as compared to 1913, is partly a matter of money remuneration per unit

Table 14.—Analysis of Income Realized from the Mineral Extractive Industries,[a] United States, 1913–1914 and 1918–1927

Year	Per cent of total income realized from mineral extractive industries			Average annual wage per wage employee		Number of wage workers in the mineral extractive industries (thousands of persons)	Mineral extractive industries, total realized income in 1913 dollars	Production index[b]	Corporate profit after deducting income tax (mines, quarries, and wells) (millions of dollars)[c]
	Wages and salaries	Rent and interest	Cash dividends and profits withdrawn	Mining	Nonagricultural industries				
				Relative to 1913 = 100		Relative to 1913 = 100	Relative to 1913 = 100	Relative to 1913 = 100	
1913	69.6	10.6	19.8	100	100	100	100	100	...
1914	71.7	11.5	16.8	87	92	98	85	94	...
1918	67.7	13.4	18.9	175	159	96	117	123	...
1919	75.5	12.7	11.8	177	173	97	92	109	...
1920	78.5	14.8	6.7	227	214	100	101	124	...
1921	76.7	12.7	10.6	167	164	101	90	102	...
1922	76.2	15.2	8.6	151	170	102	90	110	70
1923	76.4	13.7	9.9	218	193	104	124	151	9
1924	74.1	14.8	11.1	185	190	98	105	143	41
1925	71.8	15.0	13.2	194	197	97	110	150	266
1926	[d]71.6	[d]14.4	[d]14.0	[d]205	[d]204	105	...	161	305
1927			...	[d]188	[d]201	106	...	165	...

[a] For qualifications on the validity of data from income tax returns, see note 19. p. 778. [b] See footnote 7, p. 761. [c] Corporation income tax returns [d] Preliminary estimate.

of output. These results diverge from what the productivity theory, as formulated above, might lead one to expect, but technological change and discovery in this field have been disturbing factors.

Manufacturing.—From the point of view of volume of realized income, manufacturing is the most important of the nine industry groups, and, apart from the unclassified industries, the most complex. About half of the revenues which it collects from other groups it pays out to these groups again as expenses. Of the total realized income (item 3 minus item 15) labor received nearly 85 per cent in 1925. Salaries were 22.6 per cent of total pay roll, indicating a large attention to managerial activities. The preponderant importance of the corporate form of organization is evidenced by the profits items, as is also its more conservative management as compared with mining. The following is a consolidated statement of manufacturing income (in millions of dollars) for 1925:

1. Revenue from sales to others than manufacturing enterprises...		36,347
2. Expenses and dividends paid to other industry groups........		18,215
3. Net value produced by manufacturing (total realized income plus additions to surplus)................................		18,132
4. Wages..	10,898	
5. Salaries..	3,180	
6. Pensions, benefits, and compensation for accidents............	206	
7. Rents and royalties.....................................	205	
8. Interest paid to individuals..............................	271	
9. Total expenses paid to individuals........................		14,760
10. Net profits credited to individual stockholders and enterprisers.		3,372
11. Corporation cash dividends to individuals....................	1,958	
12. Individual profits withdrawn.............................	146	
13. Total dividends and profits disbursed to individuals...........		2,104
14. Corporate savings......................................	1,178	
15. Individual savings......................................	90	
16. Total added to surplus..................................		1,268

Note.—Item 1 was estimated by adding to the census "value added in manufacturing" the value of minerals (mining statement), agricultural products sold (Bureau of Agricultural Economics), value of imports of crude materials and foodstuffs and semimanufactured goods, and deducting the values of the chief raw products exported without manufacturing. Items 14 and 15 are from income tax data; other items are based on King's estimates.

In view of the wide differences among the types of enterprise which make up this group, some analysis of the chief constituent classes seems desirable before considering the changes which manufacturing income as a whole has undergone in the last few years. A rough attempt to apportion manufacturing disbursed income in 1925 among 11 classes of establishments is shown in Table 15. Much the largest group is that of metals

TABLE 15.—MANUFACTURING INDUSTRIES IN THE UNITED STATES: 1925 REALIZED INCOME, 1926 RETURN ON STOCKHOLDERS' EQUITY, AND GROWTH IN VALUE ADDED 1919–1925, BY GROUPS OF MANUFACTURING INDUSTRIES[a]

	1925						1926				
	(1)	(2)	(3)	(4)	(5)	(6)	(7)	(8)	(9)	(10)	(11)
	Pay rolls and pensions	Rents and royalties	Interest	Dividends and profits withdrawn	Total realized income	Value added in manufacturing (relative to 1919 = 100)	Stockholders equity as of end of year	Cash dividends	Profits after deducting tax	Per cent of total number of income statements with tabulated balance sheets	Ratio of profits to stockholders equity (per cent)
	Millions of dollars						Millions of dollars				
1. Food products, beverages, tobacco	1,213	38	59	308	1,618	103	6,058	327	482	87	8.0
2. Textiles and textile products	2,215	40	34	196	2,485	98	4,397	185	99	94	2.3
3. Leather and leather products	477	4	6	42	529	84	868	33	40	96	4.6
4. Rubber and rubber products	256	6	12	12	286	102	853	41	44	86	5.2
5. Lumber and lumber products	1,305	9	23	121	1,458	112	2,710	124	95	91	3.5
6. Paper, paper products, and pulp goods	352	5	10	67	434	117	1,444	56	101	95	7.0
7. Printing and publishing	733	38	8	97	876	162	1,509	122	177	88	11.7
8. Chemicals and allied products	678	18	38	352	1,086	120	9,090	545	824	88	9.1
9. Stone, clay, and glass	625	2	6	84	717	151	1,682	102	156	91	9.3
10. Metal and metal products	4,851	27	69	735	5,682	115	15,654	890	1,472	92	9.4
11. Other manufactures	1,579	18	6	90	1,693	91	2,009	119	150	88	7.6
12. Total manufactures	14,284	205	271	2,104	16,864	111	46,274	2,544	3,643	90	7.9

[a] In attempting to apportion the estimate of income in manufacturing to the chief constituent groups of industries (columns (1) to (5)), census data were used in the case of pay rolls and pensions, and rent; and income tax data in the case of interest and dividends. As a more detailed classification is available in the case of the census, the income tax classification was used. The census data were grouped as follows: 1, Food and tobacco manufactures; 2, textiles and their products; 3, leather and its products; 4, rubber and its products; 5, lumber and wood products, except pulp goods; 6, pulp goods, paper, and paper products; 7, printing and engraving; 8, chemicals; 9, stone, clay, and glass manufactures; 10, iron and steel, other metals, machinery, motor vehicles and their bodies, and locomotives; 11, other transportation equipment, musical instruments, railroad repairs, and miscellaneous manufactures. Following the income tax classification, ship construction was omitted, although it is included in manufacturing. The census data so grouped are only roughly comparable with the income tax data, since the former refer to separate "establishments," while in the latter a highly integrated corporation as a whole is put into the class in which the bulk of its output falls. Moreover, the income tax returns refer to corporations only, while the census includes all types of enterprise.

The procedure followed was to prorate King's estimates for pay roll, rent, interest, etc. on appropriate data. Pay roll was prorated on the census data for wages. Factory rent in 1919 for each of the 11 groups was estimated from rents for those constituent industries having a value-product (that is, value added by manufacture) of over $100,000,000, the unassigned portion of total rent being distributed on the basis of value added. Value added in 1925 and 1919 was then used to estimate 1925 factory rent by groups, and King's estimate of total rent was prorated on these estimates. Interest in 1925 was prorated on the income tax item interest paid, less interest on Government bonds received. Profits withdrawn was prorated on cash dividends less dividends received.

Column (6) is based on the census, and columns (7) to (11) are from the corporation income tax returns.

For qualifications on the validity of data from income tax returns, see note 19.

and their products. This group includes, in addition to raw and semi-finished metal products, machinery, motor vehicles, and locomotives. The textile and textile product industries disburse nearly half as much income as the metals group, while food, beverages, and tobacco manufactures, and lumber and wood products manufactures make up two groups, each about one-third the size of the metal industries. It is to be expected that the miscellaneous group of "all other manufactures" should rank highest in the proportion of income disbursed to labor, and lowest in that disbursed to capital, for it includes many small-scale enterprises which do not make use of elaborate plant and equipment. The leather, lumber, rubber, and textile industries also show a large ratio of pay roll to total income. The chemicals group is at the other extreme, petroleum refining and gas plants, with their heavy capital investment, being the two largest constituents of this group. The food, beverages, and tobacco group also shows a relatively high proportionate return to capital. The highest proportionate return to hired capital (that is, ratio of rent and interest to total realized income) are in the rubber and food industries, the former actually showing a larger return to hired than to owned capital. Accounting practices are far from uniform in this field, and any attempt to compare rates of profit is necessarily hazardous. But some of the vagaries of individual accounting are moderated by assembling figures for a large number of enterprises, and such a comparison for corporations is offered for what it may be worth. Printing and publishing have apparently been the most profitable, and their value product has grown the most rapidly, while the textile industries were least profitable in 1926, according to this showing, and their value product declined between 1919 and 1925.

Although manufacturing is commonly thought of as a type of business involving heavy capital investment, it is evident that property receives only a small proportion of total realized income. The share of hired labor has been over 80 per cent since the war. It showed a sharp drop in 1921, then rose again in 1922 to 86 per cent, and has since declined, except for 1924, but is still distinctly above the prewar level. Labor evidently bore more than a proportionate burden in the depression of 1921, but certainly did not do so in the 1924 decline. The increase in the share of hired labor over the prewar figure is at least partly accounted for by the increase in average annual earnings of wage workers, which doubled in 12 years. But annual earnings have risen since 1922, while labor's share has fallen. This paradox is hardly resolved by noting the movement of prices. Manufactures' sale prices for many products declined after 1923. All these circumstances point to an increase in the efficiency of management and improvement in processes of production during the last few years. The return to borrowed capital represents a small and declining proportion of total realized income, though there

TABLE 16.—ANALYSIS OF INCOME REALIZED FROM MANUFACTURING INDUSTRIES, BY TYPES OF INCOME RECIPIENT, UNITED STATES, 1913–14 AND 1918–1927

Year	Share of employees	Rents, royalties, interest	Dividends and profits withdrawn	Average annual wage per wage employee		Manufacturing production index[a]	Total manufacturing realized income (1913 dollars)	Manufacturing corporate profits after deducting tax (millions of dollars)[b]
				Manufacturing	Nonagricultural industries			
	Per cent of total realized income			Relative to 1913 = 100				
1913.........	80	4	16	100	100	100	100	.....
1914.........	79	5	16	90	92	92	93	.....
1918.........	83	2	15	168	159	119	132	.....
1919.........	85	2	13	180	173	116	124	.....
1920.........	88	2	10	235	214	120	131	.....
1921.........	84	3	13	149	164	92	103	.....
1922.........	86	3	11	167	170	120	115	2,528
1923.........	85	3	12	200	193	141	137	3,419
1924.........	86	3	11	193	190	132	132	2,649
1925.........	85	3	12	200	197	148	134	3,640
1926.........	[c]84	[c]3	[c]13	[c]206	[c]204	154	...	.....
1927.........	...	...	...	[c]203	[c]201	151	...	.....

[a] See footnote 7, p. 761.
[b] Corporation income tax returns.
[c] Preliminary estimate.

are temporary rises in bad years, 1914, 1921, and 1924. The war time increase of prices no doubt is partly responsible for this decline, which is chiefly in the interest payments going to bondholders—a fixed return that has not increased at the pace set by the other income-producing shares. The recent growth in the proportion of income disbursed to stockholders is a further evidence of improved efficiency, but it has not yet brought this share back to the prewar figure. There was a setback in 1924, but the growth of dividends, and of profits as shown by the income tax returns, does not confirm the theory that prosperity has been profitless.

Average annual wages per wage employee have kept close pace with annual wages of all nonagricultural wage workers, so far as their general trend is concerned, but they have fluctuated more widely. The 100 per cent rise above the prewar figure represents a distinct increase in the purchasing power of labor income, but security against year-to-year fluctuations has certainly not been achieved.

A comparison of the year-to-year movements of the physical volume of manufacturing production with those of total disbursed income, measured in dollars of constant purchasing power to the recipients, shows a fairly close agreement on the whole. The dip in the income index in 1919 is greater than that in the production index, while the 1922 rise in the latter is considerably greater, and so also is the dip of production in 1924. The longer-time movements do not agree so well. Deflated income rises more steeply to the 1918 peak, and from 1923 to 1925 it is only slightly above the war-time level, while production is distinctly higher. The rapid growth of ouput after 1921 seems a fairly convincing confirmation of the view that there has been a great improvement in efficiency, and suggests that while manufacturing accounts for about the same proportion of our national income in 1925 as in 1913, its importance in terms of physical output has increased relative to other industries, while its relative remuneration per unit of product has declined.

Construction.—The construction industry occupies an intermediate position between mining and manufacturing on the one hand and agriculture on the other, in that between one-half and two-thirds of the value of its output is produced by individual enterprises and other noncorporate forms of organization. As data for estimating both wages and profits withdrawn by individual enterprisers are not very satisfactory, the estimate is probably less accurate than that for agriculture. The return to borrowed capital is an extremely small part of total realized income in this industry—less than 1 per cent (except in the depression year 1921). This is presumably associated with the fact that the investment in fixed property for this industry is smaller than its current assets. The following is a consolidated statement of construction income (in millions of dollars) for 1925:

1. Corporate revenues	2,306	
2. Individual revenues	4,670	
3. Gross value of construction work		6,976
4. Expenses paid to other industry groups		3,408
5. Net value product of construction (realized income plus additions to surplus)		3,568
6. Wages	2,251	
7. Salaries	289	
8. Interest (other than that paid to banks)	30	
9. Total expenses paid to individuals		2,570
10. Profits		998
11. Cash dividends	70	
12. Enterprisers' profits withdrawn	819	
13. Total profits withdrawn		889
14. Business savings (added to surplus)		109

NOTE:—Data furnished by Willford I. King.

While salaries were only 11.4 per cent of total pay roll in 1925, a figure but slightly larger than for mining, it must be remembered that a large part of the reward for supervisory services is included in individual enterprisers' profits. This labor income element in individual profits also accounts for the fact that individual profits withdrawn are more than 10 times corporate cash dividends, although corporate enterprises did half as much business as the other types of enterprise.

The proportion of total realized income going to employees varies from year to year in a somewhat irregular manner, and shows a slight downward trend. The 1925 figure, 84.7 per cent, is somewhat smaller than the corresponding percentage for manufacturing, but a fairer comparison would again involve allowance for enterprisers' labor income. This would bring the proportion of labor to total realized income up to over 92 per cent, if we assume that the cash return to individual capital corresponding to corporate dividends bears the same ratio to value of construction by noncorporate enterprise as dividends bear to value of corporate construction. Labor income is probably a more important item in construction than in any of the other important industry groups, except perhaps the unclassified industries.

The average annual labor income per wage employee attached to the industry has risen more rapidly than has that for all nonagricultural industries, according to King's estimates. The fluctuations in wage income correspond on the whole with those of the volume of construction business, which was small during the World War and showed a rapid recovery from the postwar depression. The number of employees has varied in response to the fluctuations of wage income, but, according to King, the postwar increase in number of employees[30] still leaves a smaller number attached to the industry in 1927 than in 1913. This suggests, among other things, more regular employment and the resort to machine methods, but the estimates of pay rolls and number of employees may well be seriously in error. If the dependent estimates of average annual wages are to be relied upon, wage labor income has risen somewhat less rapidly than union labor costs per hour and both have outstripped the costs of materials since 1921.

Apparently the construction industry has been more profitable in the last few years than the average for all industries, if the income tax figures for corporations are to be depended upon as an index.[31] As already noted, the capital investment figures are incomplete, and they may be less complete for this industry than for others, but the indications are that construction has been fairly profitable.

[30] In this connection it should be borne in mind that the basic data for estimating pay rolls and number of employees (and consequently average annual wages) are far from satisfactory, so that these estimates are subject to the possibility of appreciable error.

[31] See Table 10.

TABLE 17.—ANALYSIS OF INCOME REALIZED FROM THE CONSTRUCTION INDUSTRIES, UNITED STATES 1913–14, AND 1918–1927

Year	(1) Total pay roll	(2) Interest	(3) Dividends and profits withdrawn	(4) Average annual wages per wage employee — Construction[a]	(5) Average annual wages per wage employee — Nonagricultural industries[a]	(6) Union wages per hour in building trades[a]	(7) Number of wage employees, construction	(8) Index of wholesale prices of building materials[a]	(9) Index of physical volume of construction (1919 = 100)[b]	(10) Total realized income in 1913 dollars, construction (1913 = 100)	(11) Corporation profits after deducting tax, construction (millions of dollars)[c]
	Per cent of total realized income, construction			Relative to 1913 = 100							
1913	76.8	.8	22.4	100	100	100	100	100	...	100	...
1914	62.0	1.3	36.7	71	92	102	100	93	...	91	...
1918	83.1	.6	16.3	160	159	126	53	174	...	51	...
1919	78.7	.6	20.7	169	173	145	72	204	100	68	...
1920	76.4	.8	22.8	216	214	197	77	264	80	61	...
1921	75.7	1.4	22.9	194	164	200	57	172	85	64	...
1922	76.6	.9	22.5	195	170	187	73	169	120	87	37
1923	76.3	.9	22.8	206	193	207	78	192	121	96	67
1924	70.5	.8	28.7	219	190	224	82	181	129	116	84
1925	73.4	.9	25.7	219	197	233	98	179	159	132	107
1926	d75.4	d.8	d23.8	d229	d204	248	97	176	158	...	105
1927	d73.8	d.7	d25.5	d235	d201	253	95	164	158	...	...

[a] United States Bureau of Labor Statistics.

[b] Columns (6) and (8) expressed as relatives to 1923 were combined with weights of 6 and 4, respectively, to give an index of building costs. The dollar volume of construction was deflated by this index. Deflated dollar volume, volume of floor space in construction contracts (Dodge), and an index of physical volume of building materials produced, constructed by the writer, expressed as relatives to 1923 were combined with weights of 50, 25, and 25, respectively, to make the index of the physical volume of construction.

[c] Corporation Income Tax Returns.

[d] Preliminary estimate.

No index of physical volume of construction is satisfactory. The composite index here offered shows a fairly close agreement in year-to-year changes with the total disbursed income measured in dollars of constant purchasing power to the income recipients. But if the physical volume index is to be relied upon, realized income measured in these corrected dollars has risen more rapidly than physical output. Probably this means, in part at least, an increase in the equipment of buildings with modern conveniences not represented in the physical volume index. In part also, it may be a reflection of the strong bargaining position which this industry occupies in our economic organization. The increase in wage rates and the high returns are consistent with such an hypothesis.

Privately Operated Transportation, Communication, and Electric Power Industries.—This group does not include the production and distribution of gas, which is included in mining and manufacturing, nor utility enterprises operated by the government. And a number of other privately operated utilities are treated in the unclassified group—pipe lines, water works, local carting and storage, and taxicabs. Yearly data for steam railroad transportation and for telephones and telegraphs are such as to make possible fairly accurate estimates of realized income for these industries. Census data at five-year intervals are available for street and electric railways, and for electric power. Except for the decennial census, the information about water transportation is about as unsatisfactory as that for merchandising and the unclassified industries discussed below.

The income statement shows a relatively small proportion of the total revenue for this group paid out to other groups. The proportion of total pay roll going to salaries is high as compared to other groups, 30 per cent in 1925, indicating the importance of managerial and technical labor and the keeping of records. The large return to borrowed capital is also characteristic of this group, dividends and additions to surplus being not much greater than rent and interest. The policy with regard to cash dividends is evidently conservative, if 1925 is at all typical. The following is a consolidated statement of income for the transportation and utilities group (in millions of dollars) for 1925:

1. Revenues...		11,601
2. Expenses and dividends paid to other industry groups..........		4,526

3. Net value produced by industry group (realized income plus addition to surplus).....................................		7,075
4. Wages..	3,545	
5. Salaries..	1,482	
6. Pensions...	66	
7. Rent paid to individuals.................................	18	
8. Interest paid to individuals..............................	897	

9. Total expenses paid to individuals..........................	6,008

10. Net profits for group credited to individuals..................	1,067
11. Net cash dividends paid and profits withdrawn by individual enterprisers...	709

12. Added to surplus..	358

Note.—Item 1 represents railroad, express, and net Pullman revenues; telegraph and telephone revenues estimated from Interstate Commerce Commission reports of revenues for 1922 and 1925, and 1922 census figures; electric power revenues estimated from revenues of companies reported in the *Electrical World*, 1922 and 1925, and 1922 census; water transportation revenues estimated from King's estimate of pay roll and the 1923 Federal Trade Commission estimates of revenues. Item 12 is based on income tax returns; other items are based on King's data.

Before proceeding to an analysis of the recent changes in the income streams for this group, it may be well to survey the realized income of the different constituent industries for 1925. It appears from Table 18 that steam railroads account for over 55 per cent of the total realized income and of wages and interest. The large figure for dividends of electric light and power companies suggests a less conservative policy for this rapidly expanding industry than that followed by other utilities. Water transportation is next to steam railroads in importance, though the incomes from power and street railways and telephones are nearly as large. The chief peculiarities of these industries are the large proportion of disbursed income going to labor in the case of water transportation, the express business, and the Pullman Co., and the large proportion going to capital in the case of electric power. The table also shows the rate of earnings on the book value of stockholders' equity for several of the groups, but it may be doubted whether book valuation is a reliable basis on which to calculate percentage of earnings, except in the case of the railroads.

The proportion of total realized income going to labor is lower for the transportation and utilities group of industries than for manufacturing or mining, on account of the large investment of capital. Property received about one-third of the total realized income in 1913, and a quarter in 1925. It is interesting to note, however, that if we prorate the deficit

TABLE 18.—INCOME REALIZED FROM SEVERAL PRIVATELY OPERATED TRANSPORTA-
TION AND PUBLIC UTILITY INDUSTRIES IN THE UNITED STATES IN 1925, AND
RETURN ON STOCKHOLDERS' EQUITY, 1926

(In millions of dollars)

	(1)	(2)	(3)	(4)	(5)	(6)	(7)	(8)
	Total share of employees	Rents and royalties	Interest	Dividends	Total realized income	Book value of stockholders' equity, Jan. 1, 1926	Profits, 1926	Ratio of profit to stock (per cent)
1. Steam railway companies	3,076	0	539	287	3,902	*a*11,503	*a*809	7.0
2. Pullman company........	34	0	0	5	39	*b*168	*b*14	8.5
3. Express companies........	116	3	0	1	120	*c*38	*c*2	5.8
4. Telegraph companies......	99	5	3	15	122	*d*395	*d*15	3.8
5. Telephone companies.....	452	7	50	88	597	*e*1,209	*e*155	12 8
6. Electric light and power companies.............	275	0	166	238	679	......	....	....
7. Street and electric railways	475	3	128	65	671	......	....	....
8. Water carriers...........	566	0	11	10	587	......	....	....
9. Total..................	*f*5,093	*f*18	*f*897	709	*f*6,717	......	....	....

a Class I steam railways.
b Pullman Co. profits for fiscal year ended July 31, 1926, book values as of July 31, 1925, annual reports.
c American Railway Express Co., annual reports.
d Western Union Telegraph Co., annual reports.
e American Telephone & Telegraph Co., annual reports.
f Cf. income statement for transportation and utilities group, items 4 plus 5 plus 6; 7; 8; 3 minus 12.
Data are furnished by Willford I. King.

for agriculture as between estimated normal return to the independent enterpriser's labor and that to his capital, the proportion of net realized income of agriculture going to property is nearly 36 per cent in 1926—a larger figure even than that for the public utility group. The increase in proportion of labor income for the public utility group to nearly 83 per cent in 1920 and its decline since, and the converse changes in proportion of property income, reflects the more rapid rise of wages than of rates before 1921, and their subsequent more prompt and rapid decline. Table 19 shows the proportion of labor to total income for the whole utility group, and indexes of hourly wages and transportation rates for steam railroads. Hourly wages probably fluctuate less widely with changes in business conditions than wages per unit of performance. The railroad transportation rate index here shown is subject to the limitation that it makes no allowance for changes in composition of traffic as between those kinds bearing high, and those bearing low, rates. The continued decline in proportion of disbursed income going to labor in the last few years may be due to an increase in operating efficiency and to additional investment. As might be expected, during a régime of rising prices, the proportion of return to borrowed capital declines until

1920.   The rise in this proportion from 1920 to 1922 is partly due to the decline in income disbursed to labor, but interest-bearing obligations have shown growth throughout the entire period.

TABLE 19.—ANALYSIS OF INCOME REALIZED FROM PUBLIC UTILITY ENTERPRISES, BY
TYPES OF INCOME RECIPIENT, UNITED STATES, 1913–14, AND 1918–1927

Year	Total share of employees	Rents, royalties, and interest	Dividends and profits withdrawn	Average annual wages per wage employee		Number of wage employees, utilities	Steam railways	
				Utilities	Nonagricultural industries		Average wages per hour (1916 = 100)	Rate index (1913 = 100)[a]
	Per cent of total income realized from utilities			Relative to 1913 = 100				
1913..............	67	19	14	100	100	100	...	100
1914..............	66	19	15	95	92	101	...	101
1916..............	....	....	....	....	....	...	100	101
1918..............	77	13	10	180	159	105	162	124
1919..............	79	12	9	189	173	112	200	143
1920..............	83	10	7	236	214	119	239	154
1921..............	80	13	7	184	164	117	236	182
1922..............	78	14	8	174	170	116	217	171
1923..............	79	13	8	197	193	117	215	161
1924..............	77	14	9	192	190	116	220	162
1925..............	75	14	11	205	197	110	223	160
1926..............	[b]73	[b]14	[b]13	[b]211	[b]204	111	223	158
1927..............	....	....	....	[b]212	[b]201	110	227	...

[a] See Table 20, footnote a.
[b] Preliminary estimate.

The average annual labor income per wage employee attached to this group of industries rose more rapidly up to 1920 and then declined further than the annual wages of all nonagricultural wage employees, so that since 1921 the net increase over 1913 has been only slightly greater in the utility group than in other lines.   The declines in depression years are only slightly less marked than for all nonagricultural wage workers, 1924 showing a definite setback in the upward movement since 1921. The fact that annual labor income in the utility group apparently rose from 1921 to 1923, while wage rates in the railroad industry declined, suggests a fuller employment of labor.   Conversely, the declines in 1921 and 1924 appear to be declines largely in employment, and labor was presumably less fully employed in 1925 than in the peak year 1920.   The number of wage employees attached to the industry fluctuates somewhat similarly to average annual earnings, except that it has declined considerably since 1923.   The growth in annual earnings and decline in number of employees in these last few years may mean a change in type of employee.

No satisfactory general index of production for this group of utility industries has been constructed, but we may compare realized income of two subgroups, measured in dollars of constant purchasing power to the recipients, with the production indexes for these two subgroups. Columns (1) and (2) of Table 20 show these data for steam railroads. It is to be expected that the physical volume of traffic should rise more rapidly

TABLE 20.—RAILROAD AND ELECTRIC POWER VOLUME OF SERVICE AND DEFLATED INCOME; AND RETURN TO RAILROAD STOCKHOLDERS, UNITED STATES, 1913–14, AND 1918–1927

	(1)	(2)	(3)	(4)	(5)	(6)	(7)
						Electric power companies	
Year	Total income realized from railroads (1913 dollars)	Index of railway traffic[a]	Capital stock and surplus of Class I railroads as of Jan. 1	Net income of Class I railroads[b]	Return on book value of stockholders' equity, Class I (per cent) 4 ÷ 3	Total realized income (1913 dollars)	Production index[c]
	Relative to 1913 = 100		Millions of dollars			Relative to 1912 = 100	
1912.............	...	96	....	....	....	100	100
1913.............	100	100	....	[d]486	....	108	...
1914.............	96	95	[d] 8,728	[d]351	[d]4.0	116	...
1917.............	...	...	....	....	....	127	220
1918.............	106	127	9,949	287	2.9	124	...
1919.............	98	116	10,643	448	4.2	123	...
1920.............	106	129	10,013	431	4.3	129	315
1921.............	96	98	10,228	314	3.1	164	295
1922.............	100	105	10,341	370	3.6	196	348
1923.............	110	126	10,370	555	5.4	225	407
1924.............	107	118	10,716	558	5.2	278	435
1925.............	107	124	11,141	701	6.3	303	487
1926.............	...	131	11,503	809	7.0	...	553
1927.............	...	125	11,921	....	....	...	...

a This index of physical volume of railroad traffic was compiled from three Interstate Commerce Commission series: (1) originating tons of revenue freight; (2) ton-miles of revenue freight; (3) passenger-miles. Weights of 4, 4, and 2, respectively, were applied to the figures expressed as relatives to 1919. The railroad rate index represents operating revenues divided by the traffic index, and expressed as relatives to 1913 as 100 per cent. The index of average hourly compensation of railroad employees is from Interstate Commerce Commission figures.

b Columns (3) and (4) are from the Interstate Commerce Commission. Nonoperating subsidiaries are excluded. The available data on income and stockholders' equity are only approximately comparable, partly because the balance sheets are only for concerns in operation at the end of the year and partly because of lack of uniformity in methods of handling depreciation.

c Represents kilowatt-hours produced according to the censuses for 1912, 1917, and 1922. Other years are by interpolation on data from the Geological Survey, published in the *Survey of Current Business*.

d Fiscal year ending June 30.

than deflated income during the war years. The discrepancy decreases after 1920, but traffic continues on a higher level than income, relative to the prewar figure. The yearly fluctuations agree fairly well except for 1925. The increased return on investment (column 5) and the declining or constant rates (Table 19) suggest a considerable improvement in operating efficiency, as well as in volume of traffic.

Columns (6) and (7) of Table 20 show deflated realized income for the electric power industry, and kilowatt hours produced by central stations. In this rapidly developing industry, output has increased considerably faster than realized income.

Banking.—The banking group includes only those enterprises doing a commercial or savings bank business. Revenue and expense statements are available yearly for national banks, and balance sheets for all banks, which afford a better basis for estimating realized income than is available for any of the other nine industry groups. The least reliable income item for this group is "interest paid to individuals," since it is difficult to separate this from interest paid to other industry groups. Banks follow a conservative practice with respect to the payment of dividends, so that the total income is considerably larger than disbursed income, some 16 per cent larger in 1925. The following is a consolidated income statement (in millions of dollars) for banking for the year 1925:

1. Interest on earning assets and miscellaneous income (includes some interbank interest on deposits).................................... 3,074
2. Interest, etc., and dividends paid to other industry groups.......... 1,690
3. Net value product of industry (realized income plus additions to surplus)... 1,384
4. Total pay roll... 596
5. Interest paid to individuals on savings accounts.................. 329

6. Total expenses paid to individuals.............................. 925

7. Net profit to individual stockholders............................ 459
8. Cash dividends paid to individuals.............................. 170

9. Added to surplus.. 289

NOTE.—Based on King except for items 1 and 9 which were estimated by following his methods.

The percentage of estimated total realized income paid to labor shows an increase in the war period, a falling off in 1922, followed by a gradual and partial recovery. The 1922 decline was relative only, for even pay roll increased as against 1921; both pay roll and average annual earnings have grown steadily since 1914. The growth of average annual earnings for this group outstrips that of all the others. It began with a modest figure, $925, but in 1926 was nearly $2,250 per annum, according to King's estimates.[32]

[32] Data for estimating number of employees are not very satisfactory.

TABLE 21.—ANALYSIS OF INCOME REALIZED FROM THE BANKING GROUP, UNITED STATES, 1913–14 AND 1918–1927

Year	(1)	(2)	(3)	(4)	(5)	(6)	(7)	(8)	(9)	(10)	(11)
	Salaries	Interest	Dividends	Average salary per salaried employee		Number of employees, banking	Total realized income in 1913 dollars, banking	Stockholders' equity as on July 1[a]	Profits	Dividends	Ratio of profits to stockholders' equity (per cent)[a]
				Banking	All industries				For year beginning July 1[a]	For year beginning July 1[a]	
	Per cent of total income realized from banking			Relative to 1913 = 100				Millions of dollars			
1913	35	38	27	100	100	100	100	.....	...	...	...
1914	36	39	25	99	102	103	99	2,046	127	114	6.2
1918	50	35	15	157	119	111	82	2,258	240	136	10.5
1919	56	33.5	10.5	187	136	120	79	2,357	282	148	12.0
1920	55	31	14	203	163	131	84	2,618	216	158	8.3
1921	57	26	17	214	159	140	105	2,795	184	166	6.6
1922	53	28	19	215	161	143	126	2,848	204	179	7.2
1923	53	29	18	218	172	151	131	2,876	196	164	6.8
1924	54	30	16	226	178	153	135	2,917	224	165	7.7
1925	54	30	16	236	183	157	140	2,970	249	174	8.4
1926	b54	b30	b16	b242	b190	163	...	3,090	252	181	8.2
1927	b55	b30	b15	b244	...	166	...	3,239	...	...	...

a Columns (8) to (11) are from the *Report* of the Comptroller of the Currency.
b Preliminary estimate.

There is no satisfactory index of the physical volume of production of banking services. The estimated number of employees may give some indication of this growth, though the estimate does not rest on a secure basis, and in so far as efficiency of bank operation has increased, it would suggest a smaller increase in services than has actually taken place. For the year-to-year changes it is probably a more satisfactory measure, though even here it is far from what might be desired. Certainly number of employees varies in little relation to the amount of realized income, measured in dollars of constant purchasing power to the recipients during the war, when the latter actually declined. Since 1920 they have risen together.

While the proportion of disbursed income going to stockholders in dividends falls off in 1914 and 1924, it actually increases in 1921 and 1922. With the rapid increase in salaries, the ratio of dividends to total income in 1925 is smaller than before the war. For national banks we have a complete and fairly statisfactory record not only of dividends but of the amount and rate of profits. The failure of dividends to drop in 1921 and 1922, when profits declined sharply, is striking evidence of the extent to which dividends have become a fixed charge upon this industry. The fiscal year 1924 appears to mark the inauguration of a more conservative policy with respect to dividends than that which had been inherited from the exceedingly profitable postwar years. The rate per cent of profit upon the book value of the stockholders' equity at the beginning of the fiscal year reached its peak in the fiscal year 1920, dropped sharply to about 6.5 per cent in the year ended June, 1922, and has since suffered declines from an upward trend in 1924 and 1927. For a public service industry, the accounts of which are carefully regulated, banking appears to be fairly profitable.

Wholesale and Retail Trade.—The approximate relations among the various income streams for merchandising in 1925 are shown in the income statement for this group of enterprises. A large proportion of total revenue from sales is paid to other industry groups; for the wholesale trade alone the proportion would be much higher. The doubtful item, additions to surplus, is small, so that practically the whole value product of the group represents realized income. Pay roll is slightly less than half of this total, while dividends and profits withdrawn are over 40 per cent of realized income. The large item, profits withdrawn by individual enterprisers, includes labor income to an extent not accurately determinable. The size of this item indicates the predominance of individual enterprise in this field. None of the items in this statement rests on a very secure basis, except perhaps corporate dividends. The following is a consolidated income statement (in millions of dollars) for mercantile enterprises in the year 1925:

1. Gross revenue from sales (retailers only)...................... 53,487
2. Expenses (cost of goods sold, etc.) and dividends paid to other
   industry groups... 41,115

3. Net value product of industry group (realized income plus additions to surplus).. 12,372
4. Wages... 4,358
5. Salaries... 1,292
6. Rent paid to individuals................................. 735
7. Interest paid to individuals.............................. 374

8. Total expenses paid to individuals..................... 6,759

9. Net profit credit to individuals............................ 5,613
10. Cash dividends to individuals............................. 440
11. Individual profits withdrawn.............................. 4,798

12. Total withdrawals...................................... 5,238

13. Added to surplus.. 375
NOTE.—Data furnished by Willford I. King.

No separate estimate of total income disbursed by wholesalers and retailers is available for 1925. In 1923, according to the Federal Trade Commission, retailers produced $6,100,000,000 of accrued income as against $2,500,000,000 produced by wholesalers.[33] Total sales in 1925 were $23,400,000,000 for wholesalers, according to King, and $53,500,000,-000 for retailers. Practically 60 per cent of the wholesale sales were estimated to be by corporations as against 67 per cent of the sales in the retail trade.

Table 22 shows that the share of disbursed income going to employees has been gradually increasing, though since the 1922 peak it has fallen off slightly. One factor making for this increase has been the integration of industry; individual enterprises have given place to hired employees. In 1913, corporate sales were only one-fourth of the total, while in 1925 they were over one-third. This increase has been most rapid in retailing, where labor is a more important factor. In 1913, corporate sales represented 30 per cent of the wholesale business and only 20 per cent of the retail business, according to King's estimates. The decline in the proportion of realized income going to labor since 1922, while average annual wages were rising, is reminiscent of a similar situation in manufacturing. In absolute amount, both the share of employees and that of borrowed capital increased during these years, but dividends and profits withdrawn have increased more rapidly. In some lines the margin between wholesale and retail prices has widened, but the rapid growth of profits (which on the whole have expanded along with dividends and individual with-

[33] Sen. Doc. No. 126, 69th Cong., 1st Sess., pp. 320, 324.

TABLE 22.—ANALYSIS OF INCOME REALIZED FROM WHOLESALE AND RETAIL TRADE, UNITED STATES, 1913–14 AND 1918–1926

Year	Share of employees	Rents, royalties, interest	Dividends and profits withdrawn	Average wages per wage employee		Number of wage employees, merchandizing	Total realized income in 1913 dollars, merchandizing	Deflated index of retail trade[a]	Mercantile corporation profits after deducting tax (millions of dollars)[b]
				Merchandizing	Non-agricultural industries				
	Per cent of total realized income from trade			Relative to 1913 = 100			Relative to 1913 = 100		
1913......	43	10	47	100	100	100	100	100	...
1914......	44	10	46	105	92	103	105	97	...
1918......	44	10	47	143	159	109	102	90	...
1919......	43	9	48	167	173	112	104	96	...
1920......	48	8	44	195	214	117	99	96	...
1921......	49	10	41	186	164	118	108	102	...
1922......	51	10	39	176	170	133	119	115	629
1923......	49	9	42	186	193	153	146	127	854
1924......	48	9	43	195	190	149	149	132	725
1925......	47	9	44	195	197	155	158	139	900
1926......	c49	10	c41	c208	c204	159	...	...	761
1927......	...	..	...	c202	c201	167	...	...	...

a Deflated index of retail trade is the writer's index (see *Harvard Business Review*, January, 1929) deflated by the United States Bureau of Labor Statistics index of living costs, rent excluded.

b Corporation income tax returns.

c Preliminary estimate.

drawals) must be due in part to a more rapid turnover of capital and the increased efficiency of distribution.

Perhaps the chief fact of interest about average annual wages per wage worker in this industry is its stability, if King's estimates may be relied upon. Annual wages for merchandising rose more slowly during the war than in other lines, but declined only slightly in 1921 and 1922, and have since increased steadily. The net increase over prewar is about the same as in all nonagricultural employments, according to King.

No satisfactory index of the physical volume of goods handled by middlemen is available. If retail trade, corrected for price changes, is to be relied upon as a rough upper limit index of such goods handled (and the physical volume of business handled by the wholesaler has almost certainly grown less rapidly than that of the retailer), realized income of middlemen, measured in dollars of constant purchasing power to their recipients, has increased more rapidly. This tends to confirm the suggestion already made that the increased proportion of total national income disbursed by this industry group represents an increased remuneration per unit of goods handled; for which increase a partial explanation may be found in the increase in hand-to-mouth, small-order buying by retailers.

Federal, State, and Local Governments, and Government Enterprises. While data for estimating income from governmental activities are far from satisfactory, these estimates are probably more reliable for year-to-year comparisons than those for any other industries except manufacturing, banking, and railroad transportation. In the statement, item 1 is simply a crude estimate to show the order of magnitude of all government revenues; item 5 includes interest on war loans. No item is included in these estimates for profit or loss in government enterprises; the total realized income is simply salaries plus pensions, etc., plus interest paid to individuals. The following is a consolidated income statement in millions of dollars for governments, 1925:

1. Approximate total revenues...............................	11,130
2. Paid to other industry groups............................	5,000
3. Salaries... 4,338	
4. Pensions, benefits, and compensation for injuries............... 813	
5. Interest paid to individuals................................. 979	
6. Total realized income disbursed by industry group.............	6,130

NOTE.—Data furnished by Willford I. King, except for item 1.

As might be expected, the proportion of realized income going to labor, past and present, is high for this industry group, 81.1 per cent as compared to 84.7 per cent for manufacturing. And Table 23 shows that it was considerably higher before the war than it is to-day, the decline being accounted for by the increase in the Federal interest-bearing debt. During the war, payments to labor increased rapidly, bringing the proportion of total realized income going to labor up to over 90 per cent. While payments to present employees are classed as salaries, because the labor contract is of a relatively long duration, it is probably better to compare the trend with urban wages. The average annual salary to government employees rose steadily, even during the depression years, but had not caught up to average annual nonagricultural wage income until 1926. The number of employees reached a minimum after the war peak in 1922 and has grown without setback since. The proportion of all income disbursed by municipal and other local governments naturally declined during the war but has increased since 1918, so that the proportions were not far from the same in 1925 as in 1913 for the several types of government organizations.

While government realized income per capita, in dollars of constant purchasing power to the income recipients, has fluctuated since the war, it was nearly as high in 1926 as in 1919 and shows an upward trend since 1920, which is likely to continue. Table 23A shows the distribution of income in 1925, by types of income and by divisions of government, and the Federal and local income in 1913. In 1925, interest comes to 21 per

TABLE 23.—ANALYSIS OF INCOME REALIZED FROM FEDERAL, STATE, AND LOCAL GOVERNMENTS, UNITED STATES, 1913-14 AND 1918-1927

Year	Salaries	Interest	Average annual labor income per—		City, village, and school district disbursed income	State and county disbursed income	Number of government employees	Government realized income per capita (in 1913 dollars)
	Per cent of total income realized from government		Government employee	Wage employee in non-agricultural industries	Federal disbursed income			
			Relative to 1913 = 100		Per cent of total income realized from government		Relative to 1913 = 100	
1913........	89	11	100	100	34	53	13	100	20
1914........	89	11	103	92	33	54	13	104	21
1918........	91	9	122	159	72	23	5	277	39
1919........	83	17	134	173	67	27	6	215	33
1920........	80	20	156	214	55	37	8	145	24
1921........	81	19	168	164	50	40	10	143	29
1922........	80	20	174	170	46	43	11	139	32
1923........	81	19	179	193	43	46	11	140	31
1924........	83	17	183	190	39	48	13	142	31
1925........	84	16	191	197	39	49	12	146	31
1926......	*a*85	*a*15	*a*206	*a*204	..	..	..	148	..
1927..	*a*86	*a*14	*a*214	*a*201	..	..	..	150	..

a Preliminary estimate.

TABLE 23A.—DISTRIBUTION OF INCOME FROM GOVERNMENT BY DIVISION OF GOVERNMENT AND TYPES OF INCOME, 1913 AND 1925

(In millions of dollars)

Item	1913		1925			
	Federal Government	Cities, villages, and school districts	Federal Government	State governments	Counties	Cities, villages, and school districts
Pay roll..........................	474	868	1,287	257	229	2,565
Pension........................	173	10	584	93	78	58
Interest.......................	17	175	499	51	19	410
Total.....................	664	1,053	2,370	401	326	3,033

cent of income realized from Federal Government. While city and other local governments devote a small sum annually to pensions and benefits, there has been a considerable increase in this item. The pension item for the Federal Government refers exclusively to the Army and Navy and

Veterans' Bureau. While Federal Government interest and pre-war pensions have been on the decline since 1922, pay roll is on the increase and all items for the other divisions of government have shown a consistent growth since 1913.

Unclassified Enterprises and Occupations.—All business enterprises, institutions, and "gainful" occupations, not classified with any of the eight groups already considered, have been lumped together as "unclassified." Many of these enterprises could best have been put into one of these eight groups, if adequate information about them were available, particularly certain transportation and financial enterprises. This group, then, represents the no-man's-land of income statistics. The basis for estimating pay rolls and rents is extremely unsatisfactory, and the same is true of the interest payments and profits of individual enterprisers.

The income statement for 1925 makes clear the importance of labor and of individual enterprisers for this group. The following is an income statement (in millions of dollars) of unclassified enterprises and occupations, 1925:

Wages	7,117
Salaries	3,614
Rent paid to individuals	767
Interest paid to individuals	257
Corporate cash dividends to individuals	572
Individual profits withdrawn	4,125
Total realized income	16,452

The proportion of salaries to wages is high, but far from all of salaries represent supervisory labor, since teachers in private institutions and ministers are included. While some enterprises have heavy investments and pay a large proportion of income to capital, other enterprises, like churches and colleges, disburse chiefly labor income. Moreover, some employees are employed directly by families. Some idea of the kinds of profit-making enterprises included may be gained from Table 24. Public service enterprises—professions, amusements, hotels, etc., and brokerage houses make up the bulk of these concerns. King estimates that there were 9,444,000 persons who looked to this unclassified group of enterprises and occupations for gainful employment in 1925: 6,033,000 wage workers, 1,587,000 salary workers, and 1,824,000 independent enterprisers.

The proportion of total realized income going to employees decreased during the war, but has since risen steadily, except for a slight check in 1925, to about two-thirds of the total. The percentage of total realized income going to borrowed capital (rent and interest), on the other hand,

TABLE 24.—ANALYSIS OF TYPES OF UNCLASSIFIED ENTERPRISES, 1925

(Income tax returns)

	Corporations net income		Reporting individuals	
	Reported gross income	Reported net income less tax deficits[a]	Thousands of returns	Business profits (millions of dollars)
	Millions of dollars			
1. Local transportation, cartage, and storage...	612	25	...	...
2. Miscellaneous transportation and public utilities.....:	......	...	[b]27	[b]84
3. Public service: Professions, amusements, hotels, etc.............	2,849	146	288	1,244
Finance:				
4. Stock and bond brokers.............	6,654	485	...	.....
5. Insurance..........................	1,980	58	...	.....
6. Other, multiplied by 16⅔ per cent (following King)......................	161	14	...	.....
7. Total...........................	8,795	557	[c]38	[c]222
8. "All other" (exclusive of inactive corporations)................................	322	3	43	152
9. Total "unclassified" returns........	12,578	731	396	1,702
10. Estimated total profits (King).............	......	731	...	5,123

[a] Net income, less deficit and tax, equals profits, less tax-exempt interest and dividends received.
[b] Includes individual enterprisers in transportation and public utility group.
[c] Includes individual enterprisers in finance group.

rose during the war and has gradually declined since. The proportion disbursed in dividends and profits withdrawn has fluctuated similarly to rent and interest.

Average annual wages in the unclassified occupations rose less rapidly during the war, according to King, than in all nonagricultural groups, and though they have risen steadily since the war they are still behind other wages in the increase over 1913. A similar and more striking discrepancy appears in the estimates for average annual salaries. Columns (7) and (10) in Table 25 show total realized income relative to 1913, corrected for price changes, and the number of all persons, including independent enterprisers, attached to the unclassified group for gainful employment. Up to 1920, deflated income increased more slowly than number of persons. Between 1920 and 1922, deflated income grew rapidly, so that in 1922 both series were about 4 per cent above the 1913 figures. And since that time, income has continued to grow more rapidly than number of persons attached to the group.

TABLE 25.—ANALYSIS OF INCOME REALIZED FROM THE UNCLASSIFIED INDUSTRIES AND OCCUPATIONS, UNITED STATES, 1913-14 AND 1918-1927

Year	(1)	(2)	(3)	(4)	(5)	(6)	(7)	(8)	(9)	(10)
	Share of employees	Rents, royalties, interest	Dividends and profits withdrawn	Average annual wage per wage employee		Total number of employees in the unclassified industries	Total number of employees and enterprisers attached to unclassified industries	Average annual salary per salaried employee		Total realized income in 1913 dollars, unclassified group
	Per cent of total income realized from unclassified group			Unclassified group	Nonagricultural industries			Unclassified industries	All industries	
				Relative to 1913 = 100						
1913	60	8	32	100	100	100	100	100	100	100
1914	61	8	31	97	92	108	106	99	102	101
1918	50	10	40	126	159	63	71	122	119	65
1919	53	9	38	145	173	63	71	124	136	59
1920	56	8	36	162	214	80	86	139	163	67
1921	62	7	31	164	164	102	102	140	159	90
1922	60	8	32	170	170	103	104	147	161	105
1923	61	7	32	177	193	107	106	151	172	109
1924	65	6	29	179	190	131	124	153	178	127
1925	65	6	29	186	197	136	128	158	183	134
1926	a66	a6	a28	a189	a204	143	132	a160	a190	....
1927	a68	a6	a26	a189	a201	157	143	a162	196	....

a Preliminary estimate.

Miscellaneous Income.—There remain a number of income streams not directly connected with any domestic industry. Two of these items represent cash receipts, and three are valuations of commodities and services consumed in whole or in part by the owners or purchasers. The following statement shows estimates of miscellaneous income (in millions of dollars) for the years 1925.

1. Income from urban gardens and poultry and cow keeping............... 243
2. Imputed interest on consumers' stocks of goods other than real estate..... 3,000
3. Rental value of urban owned homes (less depreciation and maintenance).. 1,760
4. Rent paid to individuals for leased urban homes (less depreciation and maintenance).. 2,517
5. Interest paid to individuals on long-term foreign investments............ 419

Total miscellaneous realized income............................. 7,939

Items 1 and 2 are presumably the least accurate, while item 5 is at least more accurate than the other four, although it cannot command a high degree of confidence. Item 1, income from village poultry, gardens, and cows, has been declining in relative importance and is only slightly larger than in 1920. Allowing for price changes and growth of population, it has declined absolutely. There has been a rapid growth in the rental

TABLE 26.—ANALYSIS OF MISCELLANEOUS REALIZED INCOME, UNITED STATES, 1913–14 AND 1918–1927

Year	Index of per capita income from poultry, gardens, and cows not on farms (1913 dollars) relative to 1913 as 100 per cent	Ratio of rental value of owned urban homes to rent paid for leased homes	Interest on investment in durable consumption goods other than homes (millions of current dollars)	Net income from foreign investment (millions of current dollars)
		Per cent		
1913.............................	100	86	1,070	−90
1914.............................	100	85	1,116	−85
1918.............................	167	80	2,302	−26
1919.............................	117	79	2,740	−17
1920.............................	101	76	3,717	− 8
1921.............................	77	75	3,015	− 7
1922.............................	78	74	2,596	354
1923.............................	82	73	2,834	369
1924.............................	81	71	2,923	390
1925.............................	84	70	3,000	419
1926.............................	83	69	3,022	a410
1927.............................	84	a68	a3,051	a410

a Preliminary estimate.

value of durable consumption goods, the automobile representing the largest of the consumer's investments in new types of mechanical and other modern devices. The ratio of rental value of owned urban homes to contract rents shows a very considerable decline. Net interest on investments abroad has changed from a minus quantity to an important and steadily growing item in the national income.

IV. HOW THE SEVERAL PARTS OF THE COUNTRY HAVE FARED[34]

We have seen that the United States as a whole has been enjoying an era of great prosperity, but that this prosperity has been far from evenly distributed among the various industries and occupations, and territorial specialization suggests that different parts of the country have fared very differently. In fact, most of the country has been less prosperous than the region which contains most of the population and receives most of the income. It will be helpful in interpreting the analysis of income for the several regions into which the Bureau of the Census has divided the United States, if we consider first the distribution of income in 1919,[35] as estimated by Leven. Since the prosperity of a region is largely a reflection of the prosperity of its industries, it would be desirable to know what proportion of its income comes from each industry group. Leven's estimates do not lend themselves to a complete answer to this question, but a partial answer will suffice for the purpose. Table 27 shows the percentage distribution of population in 1920 and of total realized income in 1919, by regions. It also shows for each region the percentage distribution of income received from various sources. Over 40 per cent of the population, and nearly 50 per cent of the income, are concentrated in the eight Middle Atlantic and East North Central states, which comprise only about one-ninth of the total area. On the other hand, the South Central and Mountain states, which include nearly half the area of the country, received less than one-fifth of the national income in 1919. The prosperity of the United States, measured in income, is largely determined by the prosperity of its northeastern corner. The predominance of agriculture in the income for four of the other regions, the West North Central and the Southern states, makes it easy to see why these parts of the country may have fared differently from the country as a whole.

One other fact, brought out by Table 27, is of considerable interest. The income is even more highly concentrated than the population. Per capita income is highest in the Pacific and Middle Atlantic states. New England and the East North Central states also have

[34] See Chap. II, Industry, Part 3, p. 206.

[35] A prewar year might be preferable to 1919, but no analysis is available for such a year. Since Leven's regional estimates were made, the national totals have been revised, hence Table 27 disagrees slightly with previous tables.

TABLE 27.—PER CENT DISTRIBUTION OF 1919 REALIZED INCOME RECEIVED FROM VARIOUS SOURCES FOR UNITED STATES AND NINE CENSUS REGIONS (PER CENT OF ALL INCOME)

(Based on Leven's estimates)

	United States	New England	Middle Atlantic	East North Central	West North Central	South Atlantic	East South Central	West South Central	Mountain	Pacific
1. Total income realized from agriculture	18.3	4.6	4.8	15.6	36.7	26.8	35.5	35.3	30.2	18.5
2. Rent, interest, and dividends paid, and profits withdrawn (except agriculture)	25.5	29.6	33.5	23.4	18.1	21.4	17.4	21.8	19.1	26.7
3. Construction (pay roll)	2.0	1.8	1.9	2.5	1.7	2.1	1.4	2.2	1.7	1.9
4. Mining (pay roll)	2.1	.2	2.5	1.8	1.3	2.6	3.5	2.2	7.0	1.0
5. Manufacturing (pay roll)	20.3	32.5	25.2	26.2	10.1	14.9	11.9	7.7	8.4	15.9
6. Other nonagricultural (pay roll)	25.1	24.6	26.1	23.3	24.8	25.5	23.5	24.4	26.7	29.1
7. Miscellaneous income[a]	6.7	6.7	6.0	7.2	7.3	6.7	6.8	6.4	6.9	6.9
8. Total realized income	100.0	100.0	100.0	100.0	100.0	100.0	100.0	100.0	100.0	100.0

Per cent distribution of total realized income in 1919 and of population as of Jan. 1, 1920, among the census regions (per cent of United States)

9. Total realized income	100	8.2	26.7	22.2	11.2	9.6	4.7	7.4	3.2	6.8
10. Population	100	7.0	21.0	20.3	11.9	13.2	8.4	9.7	3.2	5.3

Per capita realized income in 1919—United States and nine census regions

11. Per capita realized income	$614	$715	$781	$669	$582	$445	$345	$469	$634	$793

[a] Includes income from urban cows, gardens, and poultry; imputed rent of owned urban homes and farmers' homes; and imputed interest on value of durable consumption goods in hands of consumers.

high per capita incomes, while the per capita incomes in the Southern states, where the negro population is a large part of the total, are low.

In analyzing the national income into income received in each of the nine census regions, it has only been possible to assign about 60 per cent of the total income. We shall treat this assigned portion as an index of the income for each region, and consider the regions in order. The chief omissions in this index are a part of property incomes, and wages in mining (other than coal), public utilities, trade, government (except the schools), and the unclassified occupations, but in a sense these items are included indirectly, since the indexes for the nine regions were adjusted so that the combined index for the entire country would agree with the estimate of total realized income.[36]

[36] So far as possible, the methods developed and employed by Maurice Leven, in *Income in the Various States, 1919–1921*, have been followed, but the limitation of time has made it necessary to adopt various short cuts and to deal with only a part of the national income.

Because of the lack of classification of much of the basic income data on a geographical basis, it has only been possible in the time available to apportion about 60 per cent of total realized income to the nine census regions. The omitted items include: pay rolls in mining other than coal, in the transportation and public utility group, in government other than the public schools, and in merchandizing and the unclassified industries, and nonmoney incomes from property. About half of the money income from property is reported to the Bureau of Internal Revenue, and so only half of the estimated money income from property is included.

The national totals for 13 yearly series were apportioned to the nine census regions. These series fell into two groups: those having to do with agriculture, and those having to do with other types of income. The index of income for each district was made up by apportioning King's estimates for agricultural and nonagricultural income on the basis of these apportioned series. Five of the series referred to agriculture: (1) value of agricultural products—King's estimate of value of crops sold or eaten by the farm population plus the estimated value of crops fed to stock, used for seed, and wasted (two-year moving average of the Department of Agriculture estimate for fiscal years, *Crops and Markets*, Vol. 4, p. 252) plus value of animal products (King); (2) feed, seed, and waste cost as listed in (1) plus King's estimated cash feed cost; (3) expenditures for implements and autos and other machinery (King); (4) fertilizer expense (King); (5) interest paid to banks and merchants (King).

Following Leven's method, the apportioned items (2) plus (3) plus (4) plus (5) were deducted from (1) to approximate agricultural income for each region. The balance includes in addition to wages, rent, interest (to individuals), and profits, certain expenses which might have decreased the total current value product by 8 to 10 per cent.

Item (1) was apportioned by prorating on the value of crops and animal products estimated by Leven 1919–1921 and by the Department of Agriculture thereafter. Item (2) was prorated for 1924 on an estimate of its chief constituents for that year— cash, feed costs (census); value of wheat, corn, and oats not shipped out of country where grown; apples not marketed; Irish potatoes used for seed; other potatoes not sold prorated on total value of sweet and Irish potatoes separately; value of peaches wasted prorated on total value; value of hay and forage not sold prorated on total value, and dairy products not sold prorated on number of calves under one year of

It will be possible with each of these regions only to treat the region as a whole, but it is well to remember that none of these regions is par-

age (census). The data, except the two mentioned census items, were from *Crops and Markets*. For 1919, 1920, and 1921, item (2) was apportioned on the basis of Leven's estimates of feed and seed cost. This is the largest deduction item, and the percentage geographical distribution probably varies more from year to year than in the case of items (3) and (5). But none of these items shows a wide geographical variation from year to year, and the labor of making separate yearly estimates was so great that it seemed wise that the percentage of item (2) assigned to each region for the other years should be determined by interpolation. The fact that the results obtained by this process for 1920 and 1921 do not differ greatly from those which are obtained by using Leven's figures lends some support to this rough procedure.

The percentage distribution for item (3) for 1924 and 1925 was based on the census value of implements and machinery. For item (5) an estimate of agricultural loans and mortgages held by commercial banks and of interest rates charged as of December 31, 1923, formed the basis for the percentage distribution in 1923 and 1924. This estimate the Bureau of Agricultural Economics was kind enough to make, the basic data being from an unpublished study in which a questionnaire was answered by about one-half of the commercial banks of the country. The distribution of these two items for the other years was determined by interpolation. The distribution of fertilizer costs in 1919 and 1924 was that of the census. The 1920 and 1921 distributions were from Leven. For the three cotton-growing regions the other years were estimated on the basis of Department of Agriculture data for tons sold and their fertilizer price index. The percentages of total fertilizer expense for other regions were determined by interpolation and the totals adjusted to King's figures.

Finally, King's estimate of the net current income realized from agriculture was apportioned to each region by prorating it on item (1) minus items (2), (3), (4), and (5). The results of this method cannot be compared directly with Leven's regional estimates because the estimates of net current income realized from agriculture have been revised. The percentage distributions are compared for the three years in the following table:

	1919		1920		1921	
	Leven's estimate	Present estimate	Leven's estimate	Present estimate	Leven's estimate	Present estimate
New England	2	2	3	3	4	4
Middle Atlantic	7	7	9	9	11	10
East North Central	19	18	20	20	19	19
West North Central	23	22	18	19	16	16
South Atlantic	14	15	13	13	12	13
East South Central	9	9	8	8	9	9
West South Central	14	15	14	14	13	13
Mountain	5	5	6	5	6	6
Pacific	7	7	9	9	10	10
Total United States	100	100	100	100	100	100

The other items employed in constructing the geographical income indexes are: (6) bituminous coal wages; (7) anthracite wages; (8) manufacturing wages; (9)

ticularly homogeneous, and were each state in any one region considered separately, we might expect to find as wide divergences among those states as we shall find among the several regions that go to make up the United States.

---

construction wages; (10) bank salaries; (11) teachers' salaries; (12) salaries, except agriculture, banking, and government; (13) one-half of property and entrepreneurial income received in money—agricultural rent, interest, and profits being excluded. Item (7) falls entirely in the Middle Atlantic region. Item (6) for this region is wages as reported to the Pennsylvania Department of the Interior. The total for the other seven regions (New England's figures being zero throughout) is prorated on Leven's wage and salary estimate for 1919–1921 and on value of coal produced (Bureau of Mines estimate) for the next four years. The 1926 figures for each of the seven regions were estimated on the basis of percentage increase in tonnage over 1925, and the total was adjusted to King's wage estimate. (8) King's estimate of manufacturing wages for census years was prorated on the census figures for each region. For other years the percentage distribution was determined by interpola-tion. (9) Construction wages in 1925 were estimated on two bases: (a) relative wage rates on the 1919 base, relative construction dollar volume, and Leven's estimate of wages and salaries in 1919 (in this estimate it was assumed that the percentage change in profits and nonlabor costs per unit of output from 1919 to 1925 was the same for all regions); (b) Leven's 1919 estimate, relative wage rates, and relative physical volume of construction. In the final estimate (a) was weighted two and (b) one. Wages were estimated for other years by interpolating on the basis of dollar volume of construction in each region. The dollar volume and physical volume estimates for five regions throughout, and for two other regions (East and West South Central) for part of the period, were based on figures furnished by the F. W. Dodge Corporation. Other dollar volume figures (especially for the Mountain and Pacific states) were based on urban building permits and physical volume figures on num-ber of permits, on building sand and gravel sold and on cement shipments (Bureau of Mines).

Item (10), bank salaries, was apportioned to regions on the basis of estimated salaries for those regions for fiscal years ended June 30, 1920, 1922, 1924, and 1926. These estimates were based on national bank salaries, and total assets of national and all banks for each region. The percentage distribution for each calendar year was determined by interpolation. The estimates for item (11), salaries of teachers and executives in public, elementary, and secondary schools, were based on data for total salaries by states and average salaries for the United States for fiscal years ended June 30, 1918, 1920, 1922, 1924, and 1925 from the Bureau of Education. Totals for calendar years and the percentage distributions were estimated by inter-polation. Item (12) was prorated on income figures from the Bureau of Internal Revenue for wages and salaries, and item (13) on figures for income from business partnerships, rents and royalties, interest, dividends, and fiduciary income.

The apportioned items (6) to (13) were then totaled, and King's estimates for nonagricultural realized income were apportioned on these totals. The apportioned totals of agricultural and nonagricultural income were added to make the indexes of total realized income. The percentage distribution of nonagricultural income may be compared with Leven's distribution of nonagricultural current income. It appears that the three regions in the northeastern part of the United States have consistently larger percentages according to this crude apportionment than they do according to Leven's more accurate apportionment, presumably because they have a larger proportion of the higher money incomes which are reported in the income

CHART 3.—REALIZED INCOME OF
THE NEW ENGLAND REGION,
1919–1926. (1919–1925
AVERAGE = 100
PER CENT)

CHART 4.—PER CAPITA REALIZED
INCOME AND COST OF LIVING;
NEW ENGLAND REGION, 1919–
1926. (1919–1925 AVERAGE =
100 PER CENT)

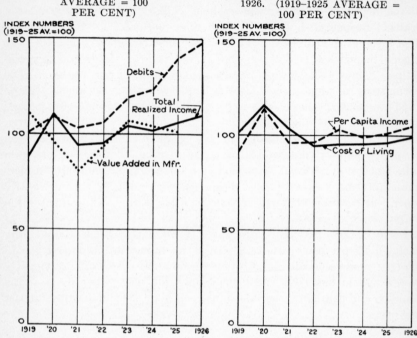

New England.

New England.—New England is like the more prosperous parts of
the country in receiving a large proportion of its income from manufacturing, in having a dense population, and a high per capita income in

tax returns, a discrepancy which probably does not invalidate the year-to-year comparisons, which are the chief point of present interest. The following table shows
the per cent distribution of total realized income, 1919–1921:

	1919		1920		1921	
	Leven's estimate	Present estimate	Leven's estimate	Present estimate	Leven's estimate	Present estimate
New England	8	9	9	10	9	10
Middle Atlantic	27	27	28	29	30	31
East North Central	22	23	23	23	21	22
West North Central	11	11	10	9	9	8
South Atlantic	10	9	9	9	9	8
East South Central	5	4	4	4	4	4
West South Central	7	7	7	6	7	6
Mountain	3	3	3	3	3	3
Pacific	7	7	7	7	8	8
Total United States	100	100	100	100	100	100

1919. Less than 5 per cent of the income comes from agriculture. But New England's income in the last few years has not grown as rapidly as the income of the country as a whole. Chart 3 compares the index of realized income with debits to individual accounts in eleven centers. The income peak in 1920 is higher than that of debits, but after 1923 income increases only slightly, while debits rise with the growth of speculation. Chart 4 shows a per capita income index, and an index of urban living costs for wage earners (Boston and Portland). Between 1919 and 1923 there is an apparent gain in per capita income, corrected for changes in prices in this predominantly urban community. But thereafter, when price changes are allowed for, per capita income has probably been about constant. Value added in manufacturing, that is, revenue from sales less cost of materials, is a rough index of accrued income produced by manufacturing. According to the census, this actually declined nearly 6 per cent between 1923 and 1925 in New England. Value added in the manufacture of boots and shoes (other than rubber) declined about 13 per cent in these two years, and this item for cotton goods manufacture declined 25 per cent. In 1923, these two industries accounted for 13 per cent of all value added in manufacturing in New England. Evidently New England has been losing in competition with other parts of the country, and can hardly be said to have been prosperous during the past few years.

TABLE 28.—INCOME INDEXES AND RELATED DATA, NEW ENGLAND REGION, 1919 TO 1926

(1919 = 100 for all items except as noted)

	1919	1920	1921	1922	1923	1924	1925	1926
Index of total realized income....	100	126	107	108	118	116	120	a125
Debits to individual accounts in eleven centers (relative to 1919 as 100).....................	100	109	102	105	117	121	137	146
Total population July 1 (thousands).....................	7,355	7,450	7,568	7,668	7,777	7,894	7,986	8,092
Farm population Jan. 1 (thousands).....................	.....	626	.....	.....	.....	.....	658	.....
Index of per capita income.......	100	124	104	104	112	108	110	a114
Index of urban cost of living (Boston and Portland).............	100	114	101	92	93	93	94	97
	Millions of dollars		*Millions of dollars*		*Millions of dollars*		*Millions of dollars*	
Value added to all manufactures..	3,231	.....	2,376	.....	3,125	.....	2,936	.....
Value added to boots and shoes (except rubbers)...............	.....	.....	.....	.....	188	.....	164	.....
Value added to cotton goods.....	.....	.....	.....	.....	332	.....	251	.....

a Preliminary estimate.

The Middle Atlantic States.—The three Middle Atlantic states, New York, New Jersey, and Pennsylvania, with about one-fifth of the

CHART 5.—REALIZED INCOME OF THE MIDDLE ATLANTIC RE- GION, 1919–1926. (1919–1925 AVERAGE = 100 PER CENT)

CHART 6.—PER CAPITA REALIZED INCOME AND COST OF LIVING; MIDDLE ATLANTIC REGION, 1919–1926. (1919–1925 AVER- AGE = 100 PER CENT)

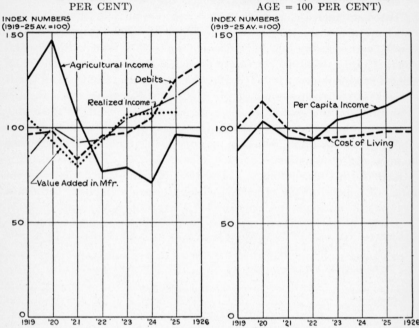

total population in 1920, received one-quarter of the national income in 1919, and probably as much as 30 per cent of the total in 1926. Chart 5 shows the growth of realized income, and of debits to individual accounts in 20 centers. In spite of the rapid rise of the latter since 1923, the total percentage increase of income since 1919 is greater than that

TABLE 29.—INCOME INDEXES AND RELATED DATA, MIDDLE ATLANTIC REGION, 1919 TO 1926

(1919 = 100 for all items except as noted)

	1919	1920	1921	1922	1923	1924	1925	1926
Index of total income realized from agriculture..........................	100	116	84	61	62	56	76	75
Index of all other realized income.......	100	119	111	113	127	134	141	152
Index of total realized income...........	100	118	109	110	124	131	138	148
Debits to individual accounts in twenty centers (relative to 1919 as 100)	100	101	86	99	100	109	129	138
Total population July 1 (thousands)......	22,101	22,417	22,815	23,131	23,496	23,897	24,238	24,597
Farm population January 1 (thousands)..	......	1,893	......	......	......	......	1,818	......
Index of per capita income.............	100	116	106	105	117	121	126	133
Index of urban cost of living (Buffalo, New York, Philadelphia, Pittsburg, Scranton)	100	114	100	94	95	96	98	98
Value added to all manufactures (millions of dollars)...........................	8,431	......	6,443	......	8,596	......	8,727	......

of debits. The per capita income index and an index of the cost of living for wage earners in five cities (urban income represents over 95 per cent of all income) are compared in Chart 6. The spread between the two lines increases each year, and we may fairly conclude that per capita income, corrected for price changes, has shown a pretty steady growth, with scarcely a setback even in depression years. Clearly this growth has not been due to agriculture, which has shown a decline of realized income in every region during the eight-year period. And Chart 5 seems to show almost as clearly that manufacturing has not been responsible for the growth of income that has occurred. Presumably the explanation is to be found in the other industry groups (except mining), transportation, banking, construction, trade, government, and the unclassified industries.

East North Central Region.—The East North Central region, or the states of Ohio, Indiana, Illinois, Michigan, and Wisconsin, is both a

CHART 7.—TOTAL AND AGRICULTURAL INCOME; EAST NORTH CENTRAL REGION, 1919–1926. (1919–1925 AVERAGE = 100 PER CENT)

CHART 8.—NONAGRICULTURAL INCOME, DEBITS AND VALUE ADDED IN MANUFACTURE; EAST NORTH CENTRAL REGION, 1919–1926. (1919–1925 AVERAGE = 100 PER CENT)

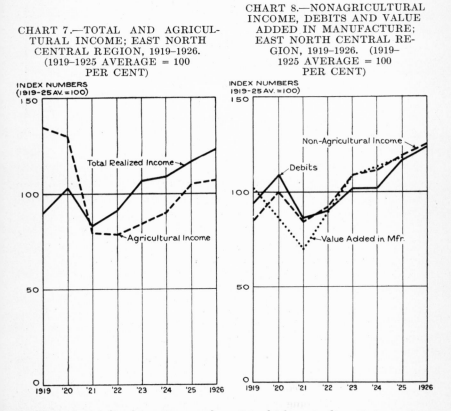

highly industrialized territory and one in which agriculture is important. Its per capita income was not so high as the older portion of the North in 1919, but it received about 22 per cent of the country's income.

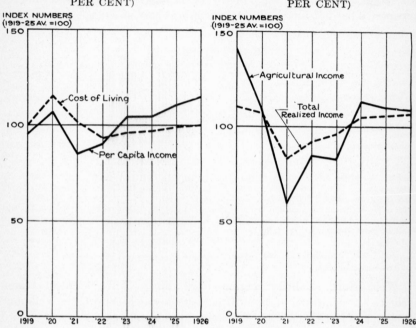

CHART 9.—PER CAPITA REALIZED INCOME AND COST OF LIVING; EAST NORTH CENTRAL REGION, 1919–1926. (1919–1925 AVERAGE = 100 PER CENT)

CHART 10.—TOTAL AND AGRICULTURAL REALIZED INCOME; WEST NORTH CENTRAL REGION, 1919–1926. (1919–1925 AVERAGE = 100 PER CENT)

Chart 7 compares the index of total realized income and that for income realized from agriculture. Total income has apparently grown steadily since 1921, though not so rapidly as in the Middle Atlantic region. Since 1923 it has been above the 1920 peak. Agricultural income remains at about 60 per cent of the 1919 figure from 1921 to 1924, and then rises to about 80 per cent of the 1919 income in 1925 and 1926. Nonagricultural income and debits to individual accounts in 24 centers are compared in Chart 8. The fluctuations of the two curves are fairly similar, except for the last two years when debits rise steeply toward the income curve, reflecting the growth of speculative activity. Prior to 1925, debits have a much more gentle upward trend than the nonagricultural income index. Manufacturing appears more nearly to have kept pace with the growth of nonagricultural income than in the Middle Atlantic states, but here, too, other lines (mining not included) must be looked to to account for the growth of income.

The per capita income index is compared with an index of the cost of living in five cities in Chart 9. While this cost index is far from satisfactory as a measure of price changes for all classes of income recipients, it suggests a very considerable gain since 1922. Farm population declined between 1920 and 1925, but agricultural income declined still more, so that per capita agricultural income fell 14 per cent in these five years, while nonagricultural income per capita of nonfarm population rose 4 per cent. The East North Central region has prospered, but the prosperity has not included the agricultural part of the community.

TABLE 30.—INCOME INDEXES AND RELATED DATA, EAST NORTH CENTRAL REGION, 1919 TO 1926

(1919 = 100 for all items except as noted)

	1919	1920	1921	1922	1923	1924	1925	1926
Index of total income realized from agriculture.................................	100	97	59	58	63	67	78	ª80
Index of all other realized income........	100	118	99	108	129	132	140	ª147
Index of total realized income............	100	115	93	101	119	122	131	ª137
Debits to individual accounts in 24 centers relative to 1919 as 100.................	100	116	91	96	109	109	124	132
Total population July 1 (thousands)......	21,301	21,637	22,130	22,459	22,889	23,386	23,789	24,208
Farm population January 1 (thousands)..	......	4,914	......	......	......	......	4,511	
Index of per capita income..............	100	113	90	95	111	111	117	ª121
Index of urban cost of living (five cities)..	100	116	102	93	96	97	99	100
Value added to all manufactures (millions of dollars).............................	7,116	......	4,913	......	7,639	......	8,262	......

ª Preliminary estimate.

West North Central Region.—The West North Central region includes the following states: Minnesota, Iowa, Missouri, the Dakotas, Kansas, and Nebraska. In 1919, agriculture accounted for over one-third of its total realized income. It is not surprising, therefore, that the income of the region is slightly less in 1926 than in 1919, although there has been a steady increase since 1921. Chart 10 shows indexes of total realized income and of agricultural income. The latter slumped even more in 1921 than total income, and in 1926 was less than 80 per cent of the 1919 figure. There is a rough agreement in the movement of debits in 20 centers and nonagricultural income (Chart 11).

The per capita income index is shown in Chart 12. While urban living costs in three cities are an unsatisfactory basis for judging the extent to which price changes have been responsible for the decline after 1920, they suggest a gain in per capita deflated income in 1920–1923, followed by a somewhat smaller decline. If we consider agricultural and nonagricultural income separately, it appears that the former, per capita of farm population, actually increased by 5 per cent from 1920 to 1925, owing to the exodus from the farms, while nonagricultural income, per capita of nonfarm population, declined about 10 per cent. On the whole, it is clear that this region, which had in 1919 a lower per capita income than any other, excepting the three southern regions with large negro population, has not shared to any considerable extent in the general improvement shown by the United States considered as a unit.

CHART   11.—NONAGRICULTURAL
REALIZED INCOME AND DEBITS;
WEST NORTH CENTRAL RE-
GION, 1919–1926.   (1919–1925
AVERAGE = 100
PER CENT)

CHART 12.—PER CAPITA AND COST
OF LIVING REALIZED INCOME;
WEST NORTH CENTRAL RE-
GION, 1919–1926.   (1919–1925
AVERAGE = 100
PER CENT)

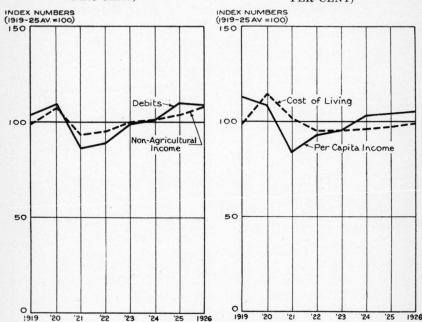

TABLE 31.—INCOME INDEXES AND RELATED DATA, WEST NORTH CENTRAL REGION,
1919 TO 1926

(1919 = 100 for all items except as noted)

	1919	1920	1921	1922	1923	1924	1925	1926
Index of total income realized from agriculture	100	78	43	61	59	81	79	a78
Index of all other realized income	100	108	94	96	101	102	105	a109
Index of total income	100	97	75	83	86	95	96	a97
Debits to individual accounts in 20 centers relative to 1919 as 100	100	105	83	85	95	97	106	105
Total population July 1 (thousands)	12,495	12,581	12,680	12,750	12,842	12,941	13,021	13,108
Farm population January 1 (thousands)		5,172					4,924	
Index of per capita income	100	97	74	82	84	91	92	a93
Index of urban cost of living (three cities)	100	116	103	96	96	97	98	100

a Preliminary estimate.

The South Atlantic Region.—Delaware, Maryland, the District of
Columbia, the Virginias, the Carolinas, Georgia, and Florida, make up
the South Atlantic region.   The per capita income of this region in
1919 was $445.   This was lower than that of the West North Central

CHART 13.—TOTAL AND AGRICUL-
TURAL REALIZED INCOME;
SOUTH ATLANTIC REGION,
1919–1926. (1919–1925
AVERAGE = 100
PER CENT)

CHART 14.—NONAGRICULTURAL
REALIZED INCOME, DEBITS, AND
VALUE ADDED IN MANUFAC-
TURE; SOUTH ATLANTIC RE-
GION, 1919–1926. (1919–1925
AVERAGE = 100
PER CENT)

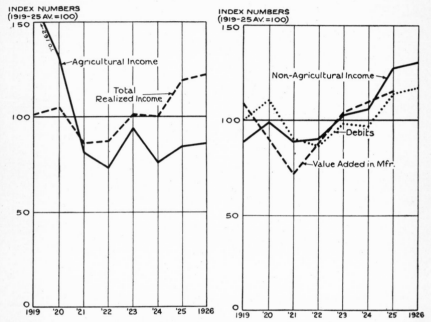

states, but the region drew a smaller percentage of its income from agriculture and a larger percentage from manufacturing. It received about one-tenth of the national income for this year.

The indexes of total realized income and income realized from agriculture are shown in Chart 13. Total income in 1923 and 1924 was about the same as in 1919, and nearly 20 per cent higher in 1925 and 1926. Agricultural income has been about one-half the 1919 figure since 1921, rising slightly above 50 per cent in 1923 and in 1925–26. Debits in 16 centers and the nonagricultural income index move similarly from year to year, except that income has a steeper trend (Chart 14). Much has been said of the growth of manufacturing in this region, but value added by manufacture has hardly kept pace with the growth of nonagricultural income. The manufacture of cotton goods has not fared as badly as in New England, but value added by the industry was 9 per cent less in 1923 than in 1919, and 17 per cent less in 1925. This industry represented about one-sixth of all value added in 1919. Lumber and timber products manufactures, which represented about one-twelfth of the total, have similarly declined; while tobacco (cigars and cigarettes), with about one-tenth of total value added in 1919, shows an increase of value added of nearly 60 per cent between 1919 and 1925. The sharp rise of nonagricultural income in 1925 is probably in part owing to the Florida boom, which increased the volume of property and salary incomes received in that state.

A per capita income index and an index of the cost of living for wage earners in seven cities are shown in Chart 15. If other living costs have moved at all closely with these, income per capita corrected for price changes was probably below the 1919 level until 1925. The rise in 1925 and slight decline in 1926 suggest the rise and fall of the activity in Florida. Agricultural income per capita of farm population fell 28 per cent from 1920 to 1925, and nonagricultural income per capita rose 2 per cent.

TABLE 32.—INCOME INDEXES AND RELATED DATA, SOUTH ATLANTIC REGION, 1919 TO 1926

(1919 = 100 for all items except as noted)

	1919	1920	1921	1922	1923	1924	1925	1926
Index of total income realized from agriculture	100	81	50	45	58	47	52	ª53
Index of all other realized income	100	113	100	103	117	121	145	ª148
Index of total realized income	100	104	85	86	100	99	117	ª120
Debits to individual accounts in 16 centers relative to 1919 as 100	100	111	90	87	98	97	114	117
Total population July 1 (thousands)	13,892	14,098	14,397	14,616	14,884	15,185	15,418	15,676
Farm population January 1 (thousands)		6,417					5,661	
Index of per capita income	100	102	82	82	93	91	106	ª106
Index of urban cost of living (seven cities)	100	112	100	90	91	91	93	94
	Millions of dollars		Millions of dollars		Millions of dollars		Millions of dollars	
Value added to all manufactures	1,859	......	1,242	......	1,796	......	1,983	....
Value added to cotton goods	314	......	......	......	287	......	260	....
Value added to lumber and timber products	156	......	......	......	132	......	126	....
Value added to tobacco (cigars and cigarettes)	177	......	......	......	229	......	280	....

ª Preliminary estimate.

East South Central Region.—The East South Central states, Kentucky, Tennessee, Alabama, and Mississippi are probably a little better off to-day than they were in 1919, when the per capita realized income was only $345. Agriculture is the predominant industry, but other lines

CHART 15.—PER CAPITA INCOME AND COST OF LIVING; SOUTH ATLANTIC REGION, 1919–1926. (1919–1925 AVERAGE = 100 PER CENT)

CHART 16.—TOTAL AND AGRICULTURAL REALIZED INCOME; EAST SOUTH CENTRAL REGION, 1919–1926. (1919–1925 AVERAGE = 100 PER CENT)

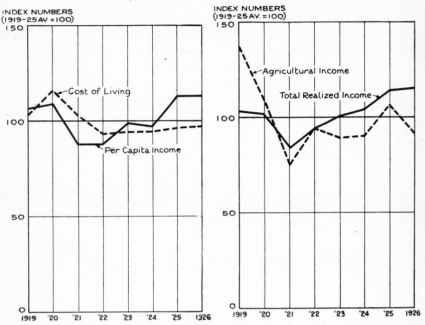

have grown considerably in the last few years, and total realized income was about 12 per cent higher in 1926 than in 1919 or 1920 (Chart 16). Agricultural income, however, was lower in 1922 than in 1919 by about 32 per cent, and has continued at about that level except for 1925. Nonagricultural income and debits in 10 centers are compared in Chart 17; the yearly fluctuations of debits are greater for the most part, but the general upward trends of the two curves since 1921 are very similar.

Per capita income and an index of living costs in three cities are shown in Chart 18. If other living costs for the district have varied approximately as those in this index, per capita income corrected for price changes was low in 1920 and 1921, and in 1925–26 was above the 1919 level. The farm population declined about 10 per cent between 1920 and 1925, so that agricultural income per capita of farm population rose by 6 per cent. As in the grain-raising region of the North Central West, nonagricultural income per capita moved downward, though in this case by only 3 per cent. All this suggests that, while urban income has grown rapidly with the expansion of industry, that expansion has been insufficient to absorb the influx of population from the farms and maintain the earlier income standard.

CHART 17.—NONAGRICULTURAL
INCOME AND DEBITS· EAST
SOUTH CENTRAL REGION,
1919-1926. (1919-1925
AVERAGE = 100
PER CENT)

CHART 18.—PER CAPITA INCOME
AND COST OF LIVING; EAST
SOUTH CENTRAL REGION,
1919-1926. (1919-1925
AVERAGE = 100
PER CENT)

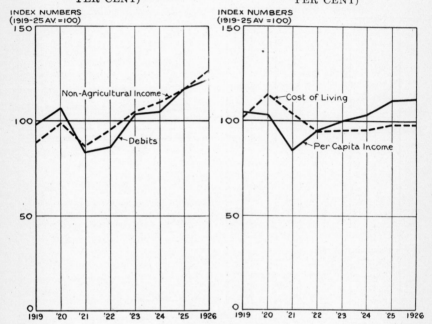

TABLE 33.—INCOME INDEXES AND RELATED DATA, EAST SOUTH CENTRAL REGION,
1919 TO 1926

(1919 = 100 for all items except as noted)

	1919	1920	1921	1922	1923	1924	1925	1926
Index of total income realized from agriculture	100	80	55	69	65	66	78	ᵃ67
Index of all other realized income	100	112	98	107	119	124	132	ᵃ141
Index of total realized income	100	99	81	92	98	101	111	ᵃ112
Debits to individual accounts in ten centers (relative to 1919 as 100)	100	109	85	88	106	107	120	125
Total population July 1 (thousands)	8,867	8,919	8,993	9,043	9,108	9,184	9,246	9,309
Farm population January 1 (thousands)		5,183					4,632	
Index of per capita income	100	98	80	90	95	98	106	ᵃ107
Index of urban cost of living (three cities)	100	112	101	92	93	93	96	96

ᵃ Preliminary estimate.

West South Central Region.—The West South Central region, which consists of Arkansas, Louisiana, Oklahoma, and Texas, is like the West North Central and East South Central regions in drawing more than one-third of its income from agriculture in 1919. And the story is similar. Total realized income was only 7.5 per cent higher in 1926

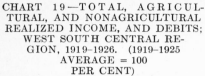

CHART 19—TOTAL, AGRICUL-
TURAL, AND NONAGRICULTURAL
REALIZED INCOME, AND DEBITS;
WEST SOUTH CENTRAL RE-
GION, 1919–1926. (1919–1925
AVERAGE = 100
PER CENT)

CHART 20.—PER CAPITA INCOME
AND COST OF LIVING; WEST
SOUTH CENTRAL REGION,
1919–1926. (1919–1925
AVERAGE = 100
PER CENT)

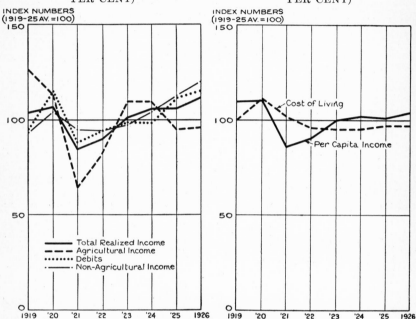

than in 1919. Agricultural income was about 15 per cent lower in 1923 than in 1919, and has since declined (Chart 19). Nonagricultural income apparently fell less in 1921 than it had risen in the preceding year and in 1926 was about 15 per cent above the 1920 peak. Debits in 15 centers and nonagricultural income agree approximately as to trend, but debits fluctuate more widely. Per capita income declined more in 1921 than urban living costs (Houston and New Orleans—Chart 20), and the rise since has apparently not been sufficient to bring per capita income back to the 1919 level, price changes being allowed for. And in 1919 the per capita income was lower than in any other region except the East South Central. In part, this poor showing is owing to a rapid growth of population, 13 per cent in the seven years as against 11 per cent for the country as a whole, a growth which is suggestive of immigration from across the border. In contrast to the East South Central and West North Central regions, agricultural income per capita of farm population declined about 10 per cent between 1920 and 1925. Nonagricultural income per capita declined still more, 14 per cent. Clearly the West South Central states have not been particularly well off during the last few years.

TABLE 34.—INCOME INDEXES AND RELATED DATA, WEST SOUTH CENTRAL REGION,
1919 TO 1926

(1919 = 100 for all items except as noted)

	1919	1920	1921	1922	1923	1924	1925	1926
Index of total income realized from agriculture	100	90	51	65	87	87	75	ª76
Index of all other realized income	100	112	102	101	105	112	122	ª129
Index of total realized income	100	103	81	86	97	102	102	ª107
Debits to individual accounts in 15 centers (relative to 1919 as 100)	100	121	93	99	104	104	118	122
Total population July 1 (thousands)	10,163	10,316	10,538	10,687	10,882	11,105	11,287	11,479
Farm population January 1 (thousands)		5,228					4,736	
Index of per capita income	100	101	78	82	91	93	92	ª95
Index of cost of living (two cities)	100	112	102	96	95	95	97	97

ª Preliminary estimate.

CHART 21.—TOTAL AND AGRICULTURAL REALIZED INCOME; MOUNTAIN REGION, 1919–1926. (1919–1925 AVERAGE = 100 PER CENT)

CHART 22.—NONAGRICULTURAL REALIZED INCOME AND DEBITS; MOUNTAIN REGION, 1919–1926. (1919–1925 AVERAGE = 100 PER CENT)

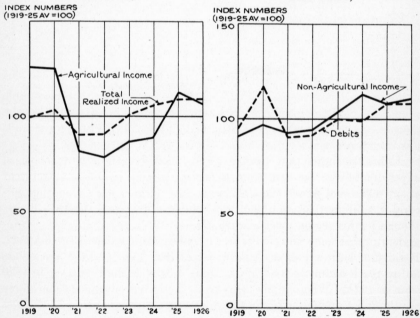

The Mountain Region.—Montana, Idaho, Wyoming, Utah, Colorado, New Mexico, Arizona and Nevada comprise the Mountain region, a large and sparsely populated area, with less than four persons to the square mile in 1920. While the per capita income, at $634, was higher than for the South and the Central West in 1919, only 3.2 per cent of the

CHART 23.—PER CAPITA REALIZED
INCOME AND COST OF LIVING;
MOUNTAIN REGION,
1919–1926. (1919–1925
AVERAGE = 100
PER CENT)

CHART 24.—TOTAL AND AGRICUL-
TURAL REALIZED INCOME;
PACIFIC REGION, 1919–1926.
(1919–1925 AVERAGE = 100
PER CENT)

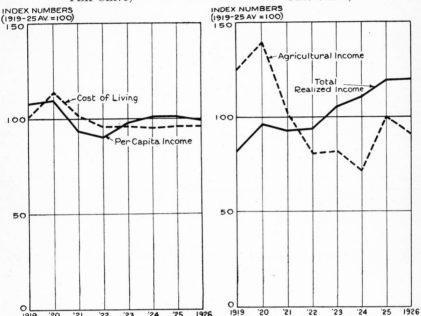

national total was received in this region. Agriculture, a considerable
proportion of which is animal husbandry, accounted for 30 per cent of the
income of the Mountain region in 1919, and manufacturing pay rolls
less than 9 per cent.

Chart 21 shows that total realized income of the region increased
approximately 23 per cent from 1921 to 1926 and was in the latter year
about 6 per cent above the 1920 peak. As in the other regions, agricultural income in 1925 and 1926 was considerably below the 1919 figure,
though in this region it was higher than in the years 1921–1924. Nonagricultural income and debits in 11 centers are compared in Chart 22.
Both show a growth of about 20 per cent from 1921 to 1926, but debits
fail to reach again the 1920 peak, while income is slightly lower in 1926
than in 1924. Whether this 1924 peak in nonagricultural income shows
anything but an inaccuracy in the index may be questioned. An analysis
of the index shows it to be owing to the salary and property income
items assigned to regions on the basis of income tax data, which suggests
a possible shift in the residence of the property income receiving classes.

The per capita income index drops to 85 per cent of the 1919 figure in
1921–22, rises to 94.5 per cent in 1924–25, and then declines slightly to
92 in 1926, while the cost of living for wage earners in Denver in 1926 is

95 per cent of the 1919 figure (Chart 23). As in several other regions, the per capita agricultural income rose from 1920 to 1925, while non-agricultural income per capita of nonfarm population declined, the former being 105 per cent on the 1920 base in 1925, and the latter 88 per cent.

TABLE 35.—INCOME INDEXES AND RELATED DATA, MOUNTAIN REGION, 1919 TO 1926

(1919 = 100 for all items except as noted)

	1919	1920	1921	1922	1923	1924	1925	1926
Index of total income realized from agriculture	100	99	65	62	69	70	89	ᵃ85
Index of all other realized income	100	107	102	104	115	124	119	ᵃ122
Index of total realized income	100	104	91	91	101	107	110	ᵃ110
Debits to individual accounts in eleven centers (relative to 1919 as 100)	100	124	95	97	106	105	114	114
Total population July 1 (thousands)	3,298	3,371	3,478	3,551	3,646	3,754	3,842	3,936
Farm population January 1 (thousands)	......	1,168	......	......	......	......	1,012	......
Index of per capita income	100	102	86	84	91	94	94	ᵃ92
Index of cost of living (Denver)	100	113	101	95	95	94	95	95

ᵃ Preliminary estimate.

Pacific States.—The Pacific states, California, Oregon, and Washington receive a considerably smaller proportion of their income from agriculture than any other region west of the Mississippi and south of Mason and Dixon's line, and a slightly larger proportion in the form of manufacturing pay roll. Less than 7 per cent of the total national income is received in this region, but the per capita income of $793 was higher than for any other region in 1919.

Chart 24 shows the indexes of total and agricultural realized income. The former shows nearly as rapid a growth since 1921 as in the Middle Atlantic states, while agricultural income declines steadily from 1920 to 1924, and rises distinctly in 1925 only to fall slightly again in 1926. Debits in 14 centers and the nonagricultural income index are shown in Chart 25. The latter shows a slight gain even in 1921, while in 1925 and 1926 it rises less rapidly than debits, presumably because speculative activity has considerably influenced the rise of debits. Evidently manufacturing has had little to do with the rapid growth of income in this region. The increase shown by the income index is largely the result of growth in the property and higher salary incomes, and may well be due in part to a shift in the residence of persons receiving these classes of income.

The per capita income index rises distinctly above the index of cost of living for urban wage earners in four centers after 1921. Agricultural income per capita of farm population apparently fell about 29 per cent between 1920 and 1925, while nonagricultural income per capita of nonfarm population rose about 12 per cent. The urban population has clearly been prosperous during the past few years.

CHART 25.—NONAGRICULTURAL REALIZED INCOME, DEBITS, AND VALUE ADDED IN MANUFACTURE; PACIFIC REGION, 1919–1926. (1919–1925 AVERAGE = 100 PER CENT)

CHART 26.—PER CAPITA REALIZED INCOME AND COST OF LIVING; PACIFIC REGION, 1919–1926. (1919–1925 AVERAGE = 100 PER CENT)

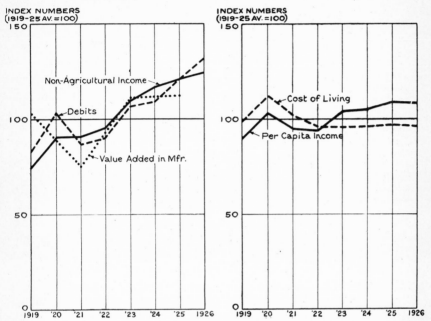

TABLE 36.—INCOME INDEXES AND RELATED DATA, PACIFIC REGION, 1919 TO 1926

(1919 = 100 for all items except as noted)

	1919	1920	1921	1922	1923	1924	1925	1926
Index of total income realized from agriculture...........................	100	112	82	65	66	57	80	[a]73
Index of all other realized income........	100	120	121	126	146	155	161	[a]164
Index of total realized income...........	100	118	113	114	130	136	145	[a]146
Debits to individual accounts in 14 centers (relative to 1919 as 100)..............	100	124	105	108	128	131	145	159
Total population July 1 (thousands)......	5,492	5,635	5,846	5,986	6,170	6,382	6,553	6,731
Farm population January 1 (thousands)..	......	1,014	......	......	......	......	1,030	.....
Index of per capita income..............	100	115	106	104	116	117	121	[a]120
Index of urban cost of living (five cities)...	100	113	103	97	97	97	98	97
Value added to all manufactures (millions of dollars)...........................	1,289	......	944	......	1,397	......	1,414	.....

[a] Preliminary estimate.

V. THE INCOMES OF THE HIGHER AND LOWER INCOME CLASSES

How have the different income strata of population fared? There is no satisfactory method of answering this question fully from available income data. But it is possible to separate from the rest of the national income that portion which is reported to the Bureau of Internal Revenue, and to estimate the number of persons who are dependent upon that income. This will not throw much light on the distribution of income among the lower and middle income classes. But it will enable us to determine the average per capita income of the bulk of the population. Moreover, it will throw some light on the question as to whether the distribution of income has been getting less or more nearly equal. Since we can estimate the proportion of total population dependent on the income reported for income tax purposes for each year, we have a basis for comparing the income distribution of different years.

The income tax data include certain items which are not properly regarded as a part of realized income (capital gains from sale of assets and profits from sale of real estate and securities). These items, moreover, fluctuate erratically from year to year. Table 37, column (1) shows total reported income with these items omitted. And in column (2) are given the estimated number of persons claimed in the returns as depending on "realized" money income.[37] Because the tax returns include

[37] Estimates of the number of persons claimed as dependent upon income reported in the Federal individual income tax returns were first made by the Federal Trade Commission for 1917–1923. The method here employed for this purpose consists in calculating: (1) number of head-of-family tax returns; (2) number of single returns; (3) total personal exemption; (4) total dependents claimed; (5) total number of persons claimed as dependent on reported income. (1) equals number of joint returns of husbands and wives, and returns of husbands whose wives file separately, plus number of single heads of families, male and female, plus one-half the number of community property returns. (2) equals "all other" returns, male and female. (3) equals (1) multiplied by personal exemption for head of a family plus (2) multiplied by single person's personal exemption. (4) equals total personal exemption and credit for dependents minus (3) divided by credit allowed for each dependent. (5) equals (4) plus (2) multiplied by the number of joint returns of husbands and wives and returns of husbands whose wives file separately, plus number of all other returns except returns of wives filing separately.

With regard to the accuracy of this method of estimate, the following points should be noted: (a) No incomes under $5,000 are classed as community property incomes. Hence, beginning with 1920, a part of the "wives filing separate returns" may represent community property returns under $5,000. This would tend to an underestimate of (1) and an overestimate of (4) and (5). (b) Estates filing returns are treated as living persons, which would tend to an overestimate of (5). (c) Some personal exemptions, owing to change of status or death, are for less than one year. Hence (3) tends to be overestimated, and (4) and (5) underestimated. (d) In the higher income groups, the deduction for personal exemption and credit for dependents may be omitted, thus tending to an underestimate of (5). On the whole, the tendency is toward too small an estimate, perhaps by as much as 1 per cent, but this error is not likely to affect greatly the accuracy of the analysis based on these estimates. Indeed an error in this direction presumably acts as a partial offset to whatever under-reporting of income there may be. A further possible source of error lies in the fact that the income tax statistics for net incomes of less than $5,000 are based on samples, and are not exhaustive statistics. Lorenz curve

little of the nonmoney income included in King's income estimates, total national income disbursed in money appears to be the best conception of the national income to employ for purposes of comparison. This is shown in column (3) and total population in column (4).

TABLE 37.—MONEY INCOME AND POPULATION OF THE UNITED STATES AND OF THE CLASS SUBJECT TO THE FEDERAL INCOME TAX, 1918–1926

	(1)	(2)	(3)	(4)	(5)	(6)
	Reported income[a] (billions of dollars)	Dependent population (millions)	Total money income (billions of dollars)	Total population (millions)	(1) ÷ (3)	(2) ÷ (4)
					Per cent	
1918...................	17.5	10.8	51.9	104.3	33.6	10.4
1919...................	21.4	12.3	57.2	105.0	37.5	11.7
1920...................	25.7	17.3	65.5	106.4	39.2	16.3
1921...................	22.9	14.8	55.8	108.3	41.0	13.7
1922...................	23.9	15.5	59.0	109.7	40.5	14.1
1923...................	28.1	17.9	67.1	111.4	42.0	16.1
1924...................	28.1	16.8	69.6	113.4	40.3	14.8
1925...................	22.3	9.3	74.3	115.0	30.1	8.1
1926...................	23.1	9.3	77.9	116.4	29.6	8.0
1924 over $3,000..........	17.8	7.3	69.6	113.4	25.5	6.4
1924 over $5,000..........	10.3	2.0	69.6	113.4	14.7	1.8
1925 over $5,000..........	12.2	2.3	74.3	115.0	16.4	2.0
1926 over $5,000..........	13.2	2.6	77.9	116.4	17.0	2.2

[a] Income reported to the Bureau of Internal Revenue, excepting capital net gains and profits from the sale of real estate and securities.

The table also shows the percentage ratios for reported to total money income, and for number of persons dependent on reported income to total population (last two columns).

It is difficult to compare one year with another when the data are in this form. But it is possible in 1924, knowing what proportion of the national income the richest 1.7 per cent of the population receive, what proportion the richest 6.4 per cent receive, and what proportion the richest 14.8 per cent receive, to estimate mathematically what proportion of the income is received by the richest 10 per cent. And on the basis of the analysis of this year, we can also estimate the proportion of income going to the richest 10 per cent in other years. These estimates are shown in Chart 27.

If the distribution of income in any year were equal, any 10 per cent of the population would receive just 10 per cent of the income. Hence,

points were plotted, using both column (2) and estimated total number of persons other than dependents, and the rating of the several years as to deviation from equality was not very different in the two cases.

CHART 27.—APPROXIMATE PERCENTAGE OF MONEY INCOME OF THE
UNITED STATES RECEIVED BY THE WEALTHIEST TEN PER CENT
OF THE POPULATION, 1918–1926

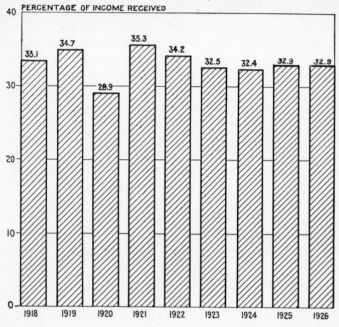

the excess of the proportion of income over 10 per cent received by the
richest tenth of the population in any year measures the inequality of
distribution in that year.   It is possible that the errors in these estimates
are so great as to make one year appear to have a more nearly equal
distribution than another, when actually it has a less nearly equal
distribution.[38]   But the available evidence certainly does not tend to
confirm the theory some have advanced that the distribution of income
was more nearly equal during the war, and has since tended in the direction
of increasing inequality.   Roughly, it would seem that 1920 had the most
nearly equal distribution, and 1921 the least.   The years 1923 and 1924 are
of more nearly equal distribution than most of the others, while 1919 to
1922, excepting 1921, are at the other extreme.   The years 1918, 1925,
and 1926 fall between these extremes.   The year-to-year variations in
approach to equality are more prominent than any trend.

In the section on the distribution of income among the different
industry groups we considered the per capita income received by persons
living on farms.   Only a small proportion of the total income of the farm

---

[38] The data refer only to the deviations from equality of distribution for the
richer portion of the country.   It is possible, of course, for the deviation from equality
to be greater for the richer portion of the country, say in 1921 as compared to 1920,
and for the reverse to be the case with the poorer portion.

population is reported in the income tax returns, and by making allowance for this overlap of farm income and the income statistics of the Bureau of Internal Revenue[39] it is possible to estimate the income of the bulk of the nonfarm population, *i.e.*, all the nonfarm population whose income fell below the legal reporting limits. Both because of price changes and because of changes in the income-tax reporting limits, the figures for different years are not comparable. In 1920, the average per capita income, received in money by that part of the nonfarm population which was not dependent on income, reported to the Bureau of Internal Revenue was about $596. There were radical price changes and minor changes in the tax law between 1920 and 1921. The average money income for the bulk of the nonfarm population was about $470 in 1921, $478 in 1922, and $528 in 1923. There was no change in the requirements for filing returns in these three years, but prices declined some between 1921 and 1922, and rose slightly between 1922 and 1923. Apparently, therefore, there was a considerable gain in money income, corrected for price changes, between 1921 and 1923. In 1924, which is not comparable with either the preceding or the following years because of changes in the law, average per capita money income of the bulk of the nonfarm population was approximately $541. The fact that the deflated per capita income for the entire population rose in 1924, in spite of the mild recession of business, makes it seem probable that the increase from $528 to $541 was not entirely owing to changes in the law. The same law applied to 1925 and to 1926. Average money income for the bulk of the nonfarm population was about $603 in 1925 and $625 in 1926. On the whole, these figures are consistent with the view that this part of the population has enjoyed an increasing income since 1921. But in interpreting these figures it must be remembered that they refer to total money income, not to consumed income, and that the upper income limit is too high to throw much light upon the condition of the lower income classes. We cannot say with certainty whether a smaller proportion of the population in 1926 than in 1920 falls below any given minimum standard of living.

[39] The estimated overlap equals agricultural money income other than wages, multiplied by reported profits in agriculture, divided by money profits in agriculture, that is, total estimated profit less value of agricultural products consumed by farm population.

Midyear farm population estimates (made by linear interpolation between census data for 1920 and 1925) and population dependent on reported incomes were deducted from total population and an estimate of overlap was added. Estimated overlap equals farm population multiplied by number of reporting enterprisers in agriculture, divided by estimated number of enterprisers in agriculture. If these methods of estimating overlap are at all accurate, the overlap of income is less than 2 per cent of the money income of the bulk of the nonfarm population, and the population overlap is less than 1.5 per cent of the bulk of the nonfarm population.

VI. SUMMARY

Judged by growth of national income, the last few years have been an era of great prosperity for the country as a whole, with slight recessions of business in 1924 and 1927. During this period the per capita realized income has considerably exceeded all previous records, even when price changes are allowed for. In this respect the condition of the United States stands in marked contrast to that of England.

But when the various regions of the country are considered separately, it appears that only a part of the United States has enjoyed this prosperity—the Middle Atlantic, the East North Central, and the Pacific states, an area which includes less than one-half the population and receives somewhat more than one-half the national income. The rest of the country can hardly be said to have prospered during these years. New England's manufactures have waned, and the South, the Middle West, and the Mountain states have suffered with the depression of agriculture.

There is little satisfactory information on the question as to distribution of national income among the different income classes. The evidence we have examined shows nothing that would indicate that the upper income classes have enjoyed either more or less than their accustomed share of the national income in recent years. The per capita income of the bulk of the urban population has apparently increased considerably, and the decline of farm population since 1920 has probably resulted in a commensurate increase in per capita income for the agricultural community, price changes allowed for. Average annual labor income of salaried employees, measured in dollars of constant purchasing power, has risen steadily since the war, and the growth in deflated annual wages per employee has grown still more rapidly. The rise of salaries has apparently been most marked in banking, and of wages in the construction industry.[40] The share of stockholders and of individual enterprisers in total realized income in the past few years has fully held its own, and there is little reason to believe that prosperity has been profitless. Neither does it appear that the share of employees in the national dividend has been declining in recent years.

The growth of national income has been in spite of the depression in agriculture. And while the increase in the income realized from the mineral extractive industries has kept pace with the increase in total income, an important part of this industry group, coal mining, does not appear to have been particularly profitable. The manufacturing and public utility industries have prospered, but have been accounting for a declining proportion of total income. The growth of national income

---

[40] In this connection, attention is again called to the possibility of error in both of these estimates because of the inadequacy of the basic data.

by industries is conveniently summarized in Table 38. The income disbursed by governments is naturally a smaller proportion of the total income to-day than during the war. A considerable and increasing

TABLE 38.—PER CENT DISTRIBUTION OF TOTAL REALIZED INCOME AMONG THE SEVERAL INDUSTRY GROUPS, UNITED STATES, 1913–14 AND 1918–1926

	1913	1914	1918	1919	1920	1921	1922	1923	1924	1925	1926	1927	1928
Agriculture[a]	14	14	19	19	15	11	11	11	11	11	11	10	10
Mining, etc	3	3	3	3	3	3	3	3	3	3	3	..	..
Manufacturing	21	19	24	24	26	21	21	23	21	21	21	..	..
Construction	4	4	2	3	3	3	3	3	4	4	4	..	..
Transportation, etc	9	9	9	9	10	10	9	9	8	8	8	..	..
Banking	1	1	1	1	1	1	1	1	1	1	1	..	..
Merchandising	13	13	11	12	12	13	13	14	14	15	15	14	15
Governments	6	6	10	9	7	9	9	8	8	7	8	..	..
Unclassified industries	20	21	12	11	13	18	19	18	20	20	20	..	..
Miscellaneous income	9	10	9	9	10	11	11	10	10	10	9	..	..
Total income	100	100	100	100	100	100	100	100	100	100	100	..	..

[a] Includes rental value of farmers' homes owned.

proportion of our national income comes from foreign investments. Merchandising and the large group of unclassified industries and occupations have contributed more than proportionately to the recent growth of national income, as have the smaller groups, banking and construction.

Several significant facts regarding the nature and functioning of our economic system are brought out by the analysis of income: The two great impersonal forms of economic organization, corporations and governments, now disburse nearly one-half of our national money income, and during the war the proportion was even higher. There has been an appreciable increase in the proportion of total money income which may be called "fixed incomes"—salaries, interest, and rents—a change making for the increased stability of business conditions. The financial policy of corporations has come to be of such a character that cash dividends approximate the nature of fixed incomes to a marked degree, and fluctuate scarcely more on the whole with business conditions than nonagricultural wage payments. The responsiveness of output and of the employment of labor and capital assets to price changes, notably in agriculture, is not very prompt. Improved technique and efficiency of operation have apparently been associated with a more rapid growth of output of goods and services than of income (measured in dollars of constant purchasing power to the income recipients) in several industry groups—mining, electric power, and, for a part of the time, railroads and manufacturing. Changes in technique and probably in bargaining power must be reckoned as important factors in determining the distribution of income among the different industries.

A REVIEW

By Wesley C. Mitchell

I. THE MAZE OF ECONOMIC CHANGES AND A CLUE

The preceding chapters form a moving picture of the economic changes now going on in the United States. They show scenes from real life registered from various angles by a group of skilled observers. Starting with a survey of the kinds and quantities of goods American families are consuming, the scene shifts to the work people are doing in factories and mines, on construction jobs, railways, ships and farms. Another shift focuses attention upon the activities of labor organizations and of management. Then come the impersonal records of price fluctuations, capital accumulations, banking and international dealings. The close links into the beginning—it shows the inflow of incomes which enable American families to sustain their varied consumption.

This record presents striking contrasts. Consumption as a whole has increased, but the consumption of certain great staples has shrunk. While trade at large has flourished, certain branches have languished— notably ship building, the railway equipment industry, and agriculture; in less measure the textile, coal and shoe trades. Pay-roll disbursements of factories have expanded, but manufacturing employment has diminished. Business profits have been large, but so also have been the number of bankruptcies. Great quantities of gold have flowed into the country, but wholesale prices have sagged much of the time. Income as a whole has grown larger, but important sections of the country have made little gain, and important occupations have suffered loss.

Impressionistic writers often disregard such diversities of fortune. One can paint a glowing picture of American prosperity which emphasizes the triumphs of mass production in automatic factories, the success of large-scale farming with power machinery, the rapid spread of chain stores, the co-operation of labor unions in enlarging output, the economy of high wages, our new position in international finance. Or one can paint a picture of average and subaverage performance by ordinary men struggling with difficult circumstances and ending in discouragement or failure. Both pictures may be true to life, so far as they go. Both are easy to make—one has only to select from the abundant materials those which harmonize with the chosen theme. Both are easy to understand because they show no incompatible elements. But neither picture satisfies an observer who uses his eyes.

A just picture is neither easy to make nor easy to understand after it has been made. Trustworthy general impressions must be based upon study of what is happening in different geographical sections, in different industries, business enterprises, labor organizations, markets, professional societies, trade associations, and Government bureaus. No individual is equipped to gather and to analyze all of the evidence which should be canvassed. For that there is needed the critical skill of engineers, business executives, public officials, bankers, economists, statisticians, labor specialists and agricultural experts. Even in his own department, each of these men finds diverse developments. Often there is a striking contrast between average current performance and exceptional achievements which are important more for what they promise in the future than for what they represent in the present. At times, national totals or averages can be drawn up to summarize the general situation as seen from some angle; but the very estimators who present such figures emphasize the differences hidden in the general results. And when the contributions of numerous specialists have been assembled in one volume, there still remains the task of assimilating all the elements—of understanding the picture as a whole.[1]

The best clue to the maze of recent economic changes is supplied by economic history. What has been happening in the United States is the latest phase of cumulative processes which have dominated western life since the Industrial Revolution got under way. Powerful as these processes are, they were appreciably influenced by the sudden outbreak of the war and by the sudden return of peace. By changing the conditions amidst which the old influences worked, these world shocks contributed to strange results.

II. THE CONTINUING FORCES—SCIENCE AND ECONOMIC CHANGE

The nineteenth century brought an unprecedented increase in the number of Europeans, an unprecedented spread of Europeans over the

---

[1] Not that all factors which have affected the economic fortunes of the United States in recent years are adequately presented in the survey. We have had to shape our inquiries according to our means. Little is said about the enormous advantages which this country, in sharp contrast to Europe, enjoys from the absence of internal tariff barriers, or about the mixed effects of the tariff upon imports. The influence of Federal, state and local taxation is mentioned here and there; but it is not systematically discussed. Previous inquiries had shown how difficult it would be to get conclusive data concerning the economic reactions of the Eighteenth Amendment; with the limited time and money at our disposal it seemed futile to scratch the skin of that controverted issue. Immigration restriction is dealt with incidentally; it merits far closer analysis than we have been able to provide. But even with these omissions and others of less moment, we have a rather bewildering array of factors to set in order.

earth, and marked changes in their relation to other peoples.[2]   These multiplying numbers, moreover, gradually attained a higher level of material comfort than the mass of their progenitors had ever enjoyed.

These great changes in the fortunes of mankind were made possible by the application of science to the work of producing, transporting, manufacturing, and distributing goods.   Increasingly wide and exact knowledge of natural processes underlay the invention of the steam engine, the locomotive, the steamship; the smelting of iron with coal; the improvements in mining and metallurgy; the development of the telegraph, ocean cable, telephone, dynamo, transmission line, radio; the industrial applications of chemistry and biology, the increasing precision of work, the system of interchangeable parts, the progress toward automatic mechanisms, the linking of machines into continuous processes for mass production; the rise of the oil and rubber industries; the perfecting of the internal combustion engine, the automobile and the airplane.

In the course of the century, a technique of material progress was developed.   Science spread from its ancient stronghold of mathematics into a systematic study of the most varied phenomena, including the phenomena of living processes and consciousness.   The industrial application of scientific discoveries was secured by the rise and differentiation of the engineering professions.   From the parent stock of military engineers there developed in turn civil engineers, mechanical, mining, marine, sanitary, gas, chemical, electrical, efficiency and production engineers—each group trained in the fundamental sciences and experienced in industrial practice.   Business men were prompt to see the profit which could be drawn from the use of the new methods.   Indeed, the Industrial Revolution had been preceded by a Commercial Revolution.

[2] Prof. Walter F. Willcox has kindly supplied the following estimates of the population of the world in millions of persons.   He thinks that his figure for the number of Europeans outside of Europe in 1900 is probably too low.

	1800	1850	1900	1925
Population of European origin:				
In Europe..	187	266	401	475
Outside of Europe...............................	16	50	100	164
Total...	203	316	501	639
Population of non-European origin..................	609	777	994	1,107
Total world population............................	813	1,093	1,495	1,746

Rates of increase from 1800 to 1925:	
Population of European origin.....................	215 per cent
Population of non-European origin................	82 per cent
Total world population.........................	115 per cent

Encouraged by the gradual expansion of demand, business leaders had been reorganizing methods of producing, transporting and distributing goods to secure greater efficiency. But this quiet process was enormously stimulated by the "great inventions" and the numberless inventions which followed. For these technical improvements not only increased efficiency more than mere reorganization of old processes could do; they also widened the markets at surprising speed and thus created ever larger opportunities for the business organizer to seize.

Not only did the new technique enable men to produce more from their known resources, it also brought distant resources within reach and discovered new treasures which were turned to human use. Vast new granaries were developed in the Mississippi Valley, Argentina and Canada; vast new ranges for cattle and sheep stretched from Texas to Montana and over much of Argentina and Australia. The textile mills of England were fed cotton from the South Atlantic and Gulf states, Egypt and India; silk from China and Japan; wool from Argentina and Australia; coarser fibers from Mexico and the Philippines. European soils were replenished from Chilean nitrates. Iron ranges of great extent were found in North America; copper came from Michigan, Montana, Arizona, Utah, Chile and Peru; gold flowed from Brazil, California, Australia, Alaska and South Africa; petroleum pools were found dotted over the globe. Most important of all for the new technique, coal deposits, surpassing those of England in extent, were developed in Europe and America. Science enabled the generations which applied it to tap energy from the sun, accumulated through millions of years. As research, engineering and business enterprise were developed, so also was prospecting. The world was combed over as never before by men with piercing eyes and long plans.

By no means all the increase in efficiency took the form of a net gain in current livelihood. To use the technique founded on science, men had to build machines, factories, railways, roads, warehouses and sewers. In developing new resources, they had to dig mines; to break the prairies and fence in farms; to make homes in strange habitats. And this work of re-equipping themselves for making consumers' goods was never done. Every discovery put to use on a commercial scale meant a new equipment job, often of great extent. But after all this work on the means of production was done, there remained an ever larger flow of the things men eat and wear, house and amuse themselves with.

The net gain in ability to provide for their desires brought men the possibility of raising their standard of consumption, of reducing their hours of work, of giving their children more education, of increasing their numbers. They took a slice of each of these goods, rather than all of one. They worked somewhat less hard as the decades went by; they raised their standards of consumption appreciably; they established compulsory education and reduced illiteracy; they added to the population. Any one of these changes might have been made on a larger scale had not men taken their gains in various forms.

The pace at which the sciences grow, and the pace at which their discoveries are applied to the work of the world, keep changing. In any given field of scientific discovery or commercial application, a period of revolutionary changes is followed by rapid expansion as the new discovery is fitted into the existing body of knowledge or the existing structure of industry; then expansion tends to slow down. One after another, many of our leading industries have gone through this cycle of changes since 1800. In any given decade in any given country, some parts of its economic mechanism were being made over, some parts were growing steadily, some parts were changing little. Hence the growth of industry as a whole has been less unsteady than the growth of its component parts. The pace has not been uniform, however; even from the national viewpoint there have been periods of more rapid and less rapid advance.

Population growth also has its changes of pace. The nations which lead in science and industry have been increasing their numbers more slowly of late than in the earlier part of the nineteenth century. This change is explained by experts as so many modern changes are explained—it is attributed in large part to the practical application of scientific knowledge. From a critical study of European evidence, Sir William Beveridge concludes: "The practice of birth control, that is to say, the deliberate prevention of fertilization, suddenly increased about 1880, not because there was then any change of economic conditions making restriction of families suddenly more desirable than before, but because the means of birth control were perfected and the knowledge of them was spread, both by those interested in their sale and by disinterested propagandists."[3] That may not be all of the story, but, whatever its causes, the reduction of the birth rate meant that as men acquired more knowledge they absorbed a smaller share of the gains from applied science in propagating their kind, and thereby increased the possibility of shortening hours and of raising the standard of living.

The whole process of gaining new knowledge and putting it to use has had to make headway against other human interests—particularly man's interest in getting the better of his fellowmen. Business friction, class struggles, and national wars check science and the peaceful arts; they impoverish the participants and usually injure the bystanders as well.

[3] "The Fall of Fertility among European Races," *Economica*, March, 1925, No. 13, p. 20.

III. THE WAR AND ECONOMIC CHANGES

Of the checks which economic progress has suffered since the Industrial Revolution began, the gravest was inflicted by the war of 1914–1918. For all the great nations which lead in science and industry were directly involved in this desperate struggle, and all the lesser nations on the same cultural plane were either belligerents or harassed neighbors of the belligerents. Never had warring powers mobilized their brains and brawn, their industrial equipment, and their financial resources so skillfully to harm the persons and property of their enemies. Of the damages inflicted and suffered, we need here note only such items as help to account for the postwar changes in American conditions and practices.

The elaborate equipment for attack and defense demanded by up-to-date standards of military efficiency meant that every soldier at the front had to be served by several workers behind the lines. In desperate haste, each belligerent organized its industry and trade to produce a maximum output of military supplies and the indispensable minimum of goods for civilians. A large part of the most efficient workers had to be withdrawn from production and others hurriedly trained to take their places. Old factories had to be remodeled for war uses and new plants built that would serve no peace-time purpose. Governments had to intervene on a grand scale in operations where private initiative had been deemed more effective. Long-run advantages and deliberate planning had to be sacrificed to immediate needs. Despite prodigies of energy on the part of many leaders and devotion on the part of the masses, the industrial changes of the war were attended by enormous wastes, in addition to the wastes which the reorganization was intended to effect.

In finance the war brought even wilder confusion than in industry. Monetary and banking policies were dictated, not by the economic interests of peoples, but by the pressure of circumstances. Specie payments were suspended in several countries almost immediately. Wholesale prices, wages, and costs of living, in terms of the irredeemable paper currencies, underwent fantastic fluctuations, and made necessary awkward schemes of government control. Millions of people had much of their property quietly confiscated through no fault of their own, and thousands grew suddenly rich not by virtue of service. Taxes mounted to heights which seemed unbearable, but public debts swelled faster still. No rule of rational finance could be followed when it ran counter to the plea of necessity.

The latest estimates indicate that "the war carried off in round numbers thirteen million mobilized men." The war is charged further with a large share of responsibility for the ten million deaths during the influenza epidemic of 1918, and the scarcely less destructive epidemics which followed in Eastern Europe. Census figures show that the total population of Europe declined more than ten millions between 1910 and 1920. The loss from 1917 to 1920 must have been considerably greater.[4]

Thus the war left Europe with fewer people; these people were less well-nourished, less able-bodied, less self-reliant; their industrial equipment was in poor physical condition and in good part useless for peacetime production; their soils were depleted from the lack of fertilizers; they had sacrificed a large part of their farm animals; they had laid waste considerable stretches of land and ruined many towns. When peace returned, they faced the task of demobilizing their soldiers and war workers, releasing their government controls, reorganizing their industrial forces, and restoring their capital equipment while prices were still fluctuating violently, and while political prospects, domestic and international, were most uncertain. Economic welfare in Europe had received a setback indeed.

The economic position of the United States improved greatly in comparison with Europe's during the war. But that was more because European losses were staggering than because American gains were spectacular.

Business in this country recovered from depression in the second half of 1915 with remarkable rapidity, thanks largely to war orders. Then we had a year of intense business prosperity in 1916, followed in 1917–18 by the hectic economic activity which prevailed among all the belligerents. If taxes were heavy, current profits were very large. Nor were the gains confined to the profit-making classes. Wage rates may not have kept even pace with the cost of living, but employment was full and there was a widespread reduction in standard working time between 1914 and 1920, which Dr. Leo Wolman estimates at five hours a week.

Listing the deductions is a more complicated matter. There was an uncommonly large share of haste and waste, as well as of profits, in war-contract work during 1915 and 1916. Though we were not forced to suspend specie payments, our whole system of prices suffered convulsions almost matching those of the Civil War. In 1917 we sought to mobilize all our economic resources in a hurry for military ends, and had to demobilize the war workers, as well as the army, in 1919. Our railways declined in efficiency. We poured millions into war plants and ships that had to be scrapped after the armistice. We took about 5,000,000 of our best producers out of civilian life. We lost 116,000 soldiers and sailors, and shared in the influenza epidemic of 1918. These costs were real, and must be considered in any accounting of the economic effects

---

[4] Walter F. Willcox, "Military Losses in the World War," *Journal of the American Statistical Association*, September, 1928, Vol. XXIII, pp. 304–5; and "Population and the World War," *ibid.*, June, 1923, Vol. XVIII, pp. 699–712.

of the war just as much as the profits which the war brought to American business enterprises.

Even if items which cannot be expressed adequately in dollars were set aside, it would be exceedingly difficult to strike a balance between the war gains and the war losses. That task is not attempted here. But it is proper to note the fluctuations in the country's "real" income during the war, that is, income in dollars of constant purchasing power. These figures, given in Chapter XII, are estimates based on the critical study of a vast mass of materials; they have been made and revised with scrupulous care; they are probably the most reliable, as well as the most inclusive, index of changes in the economic position of the average family. In the last full year before the war, a year which began with brisk trade but ended in dullness, the per capita income of Americans, taken at the retail prices of 1925, was $621. (See Chapter XII, Table 1, column 6.) Starting with this figure as 100, per capita income shrank to 97 in 1914, rose to 99 in 1915, to 106 in 1916, remained constant at that level in 1917, and then declined to 105 in 1918. On this showing, we were far from impoverished during the war; but our economic progress was not remarkably rapid.[5]

Nor can we close the reckoning of the war's influence upon real income with 1918, either in the United States or in other countries. The readjustment of economic activities to peace is one of the costs of war. And that readjustment is more than a matter of beating swords into ploughshares. In proportion as the belligerent nations had succeeded in mobilizing all their economic resources for war, not only their governments, but also their business enterprises and individual citizens had to reorganize their plans after the armistice. The business mistakes made during this period of confusion are largely chargeable to the confusion itself. Other countries found the process of readjusting even more

[5] The showing is less favorable if we take the everyday conception of income as including only sums received in money. On this basis, the per capita figures, expressed in dollars of 1925 purchasing power, run as follows:

	Per capita income	Relative income
1913	$551	100
1914	530	96
1915	543	99
1916	582	106
1917	573	104
1918	551	100

The chief items omitted in these figures and included in those underlying the text discussion are farm products used by the families which produce them, the rental value of houses owned by their occupiers, and interest on the value of semidurable consumers' commodities in the possession of families.

difficult than did the United States. All our allies made matters worse, as did we, by committing economic blunders in 1919 for which they paid in 1921. What happened is sketched briefly in the next section. But here we should note that income in the United States sank in the early years of peace. Indeed, average real income per capita in the United States during the eight years of war and postwar readjustments, 1914 to 1921, was less than the per capita income of 1913. That is not a record of prosperity.

IV. PEACE AND THE ECONOMIC CONVULSIONS OF 1919–1921

Readily as they had accepted the economic regulations and restrictions imposed during the war, the American people threw off the yoke eagerly after the armistice. The "dollar-a-year" men returned to their offices; the munitions plants closed and their workers dispersed; the soldiers in training camps and in France were sent back to their homes as rapidly as might be. Government price-fixing ended, and everyone was at liberty to charge what he could get for his goods. The rationing of raw materials, the granting of transportation "priorities," the conservation program, the Federal regulation of imports and exports, and the Government control over shipping stopped at various dates. When the Transportation Act of February, 1920, provided for returning the railroads to private control, practically nothing was left of the war-time mobilization.

It was not "business as usual," however, to which Americans returned in 1919, but business as dominated by postwar conditions. Early in the year there was grave uncertainty regarding the trend of affairs. Wholesale prices declined from December to February or March; there was much loose talk about the necessity of "liquidating labor;" the prevailing business attitude was one of "watchful waiting." But, early in the spring, signs of eager demand for consumers' goods began to appear. In April, Federal Reserve agents reported that "the business community has given up the thought that it may profitably await a further considerable reduction in prices . . ."[6] In July, the Bureau of Labor Statistics wholesale price index (as then constituted) jumped from 207 to 219, and business boomed.

The extraordinary demand for goods, which produced this sudden transition from hesitation to feverish activity, came partly from foreign countries. The underfed European populations bid eagerly for our foodstuffs; also they were short of raw materials for their mills. Aided by American credits, governmental and private, they could pay for what they needed. So the physical volume of exports and their prices rose together. The value of shipments to Europe reached nearly $5,200,000,-000 in 1919, 25 per cent higher than the preceding record, and double the

[6] *Federal Reserve Bulletin*, May, 1919.

money value in any year since then. The removal of restrictions upon foreign trade enabled our other customers also to buy in proportion to their respective needs. The increase in the value of total exports over 1918 reached $1,771,000,000.

Domestic demands were scarcely less keen. Economies in consumption, partly voluntary and partly forced, had been practiced widely in 1917–18. Hence there was need for buying more than the customary quantities of clothing, household furnishings and other semidurable comforts. Ordinary building had been discouraged during the war as a nonessential industry, and there was pressing call for more houses. Crops in 1918 had been but moderately good; stocks had been kept low; numerous branches of civilian production had been purposely restricted. High prices were asked, for the current supply of finished commodities soon proved inadequate. But for a time customers were willing to pay almost any price for prompt deliveries. Employment had been full for three years, soldiers commonly had substantial sums due them when mustered out, new jobs were readily had at high money wages, everyone seemed tired of economizing.

Under these circumstances, 1919 developed into a great trading year. Interest rates remained fairly low until late autumn; the Treasury was floating its great Victory loans that summer and wanted easy money to facilitate subscriptions. Orders for goods from merchants, contractors and manufacturers promised a continuation of good times. A run-away market developed on the New York Stock Exchange for industrials. Paper profits, present and prospective, seemed very high.

But 1919 was a poor year from the point of view of production. The harvests, indeed, turned out well; there was a large yield of wheat and there were fair crops of corn and cotton. It was in mining and industry that the record was bad. The following collection of indexes of production, in Table 1, made on unlike plans by different investigators, all agree in showing that output in physical terms was decidedly less in 1919 than in the preceding years. By strenuous effort we had kept production at a high level in 1917 and 1918, despite the withdrawal of more than a million men from our mines and factories. In the first year of peace, when many of these men got back to work, efficiency declined. These indexes of physical production confirm and are confirmed by the estimates of per capita income in dollars of constant purchasing power. The figure for 1918 had been $651. For 1919 it was $611.

More insight into the nature of the industrial inefficiency of 1919 is provided by the indexes from the censuses of manufactures presented in Chapter II. The most significant figures for the present purpose relate to productivity per wage earner. Of course one expects average productivity per worker to rise gradually in a country which keeps abreast of technical progress. Such an advance we find from 1899 to 1909—the index of productivity per worker in this period runs 100 in 1899, 104 in 1904, and 110 in 1909. We may explain the relapse to 108 in 1914 by the business depression of that year. But the further decline to 104 in the boom year 1919 must mean that both management and labor were deplorably lax. Probably it means also that, during the war, we had neglected our industrial equipment for civilian production and made but few improvements in method.

TABLE 1.—INDEXES OF PHYSICAL PRODUCTION IN THE UNITED STATES BY YEARS: 1913–1919

Year	Index of Production in Basic Industries, Federal Reserve Board revised,[a] 1919 = 100	Index of Industrial Production, Standard Statistical Company,[b] "Normal" = 100	Harvard Indexes of Physical Volume of Production "Normal" = 100[c]		
			Mining	Manufacture	Agriculture
1913.................	96	106	102	102	94
1914.................	86	92	95	91	106
1915.................	96	100	99	98	110
1916.................	114	116	108	112	96
1917.................	116	114	112	109	101
1918.................	110	105	110	104	100
1919.................	100	95	95	98	101

[a] Includes 4 types of metal production, 2 types of textiles, 3 types of fuel, 4 types of animal and 2 of vegetable foods, lumber, cement, leather, newsprint and 3 types of tobacco products—22 series in all. See *Federal Reserve Bulletin*, May, 1924, p. 422.

[b] Includes 39 series of production or consumption data—a somewhat more inclusive list than the Federal Reserve Board's "basic industries." "Secular trend is eliminated and correction made for normal seasonal variation." See *Statistical Bulletin* of the Standard Statistical Company, April 21, 1924, p. 28.

[c] The indexes, originally made by E. E. Day, in their latest form. See W. Floyd Maxwell, "The Physical Volume of Production in the United States," *Review of Economic Statistics*, July, 1927, p. 143.

The business boom of 1919 developed with extraordinary quickness, and in rather extreme form, the internal stresses characteristic of such episodes. A rapid expansion of commercial loans reduced the reserve ratios of the Federal Reserve banks below 50 per cent in October. On November 3, the New York bank raised its rediscount rate. Stock prices tumbled promptly. But as usually happens in booms, commercial activity continued to expand for some months after the stock-market collapse. The further expansion of commitments added to the accumulating tension. Though the other Reserve banks followed the example of New York in raising their rediscount rates, the Reserve ratio continued to sag. By February, 1920, the figure was below 43 per cent, and there it remained for several months of growing uneasiness. Meanwhile, prices at wholesale climbed unsteadily to 247 in May—an advance of 54 points on the prewar base since the dizzy rise had started in March of the preceding year. Then came the turn. Slowly at first, soon rapidly, prices gave way. In half the time it had taken prices to rise 54 points, they dropped 68 points.[7]

At the close of the Civil War, wholesale prices had fallen from 216 in January, 1865, to 158 in July—a drop of over 25 per cent in six months. That fall produced no grave crisis. The business community had expected the greenback dollar to appreciate in gold when the Confederacy collapsed. Grant's successes against Lee and Sherman's march to the sea gave timely warning of what was coming, both at the front and behind the lines. Because business men prepared for the worst, keeping commitments and inventories at a minimum, the country passed through this sudden fall of prices with extraordinary success.

The corresponding drop of prices in 1920–21 caught the business community in a different frame of mind and in a different technical position. Perhaps if the fall had come soon after the armistice, when many expected it and almost everyone was cautious, it would have passed off much as in 1865. But prices had risen in 1919, the volume of trade had expanded, profits had been high, the preliminary warnings of the Federal Reserve banks had been ineffectual, and, when the turn came, many business enterprises were caught with heavy inventories and heavy future commitments. So the fall of prices, which started gently enough, was accentuated by the efforts of embarrassed houses to turn commodities into cash. Every price decline made the financial position of overexpanded enterprises worse, reinforced the fears of insolvency and the pressure for liquidating indebtedness, thus increased the pressure to realize upon stocks of goods, and so forced prices lower still.

Three favorable factors prevented this crisis from degenerating into a panic. Though European demand for our goods declined somewhat from the high level of 1919, the demand from other countries scored a more than compensating increase. The total value of our exports exceeded $8,228,000,000 in 1920—which still stands as the record figure. Second, retail demand from domestic consumers remained active to the end of the year. The Federal Trade Commission estimates total retail sales as nearly 35 billion dollars in 1919 and over 38 billions in 1920.[9] Third, and probably most important, the Federal Reserve System, with its organization of banking reserves, enabled our banks to meet the

[7] Here the latest form of the Bureau of Labor Statistics index on the 1913 base is used. See *Index Numbers of Wholesale Prices on Prewar Base*, U. S. Department of Labor, 1928, pp. 7, 8.

[8] See Wesley C. Mitchell, *Gold Prices and Wages under the Greenback Standard*, Berkeley, Calif., 1908, p. 23. The index used is the unweighted median of the relative prices of 92 commodities.

[9] See *National Wealth and Income*, Senate Doc., No. 126, 69th Cong., 1st Sess,. Washington, 1926, pp. 306–313.

emergency needs of business far more effectively than in previous crises. There was no such suspension of payments by banks, no such refusal of credit to solvent enterprises, as in 1893 and 1907.

The net resultant of the complex of forces was a drastic financial liquidation, which presently produced, and was then aggravated by, a severe industrial depression. Business enterprises, fearing for their solvency, canceled orders freely; enterprises in a less precarious condition bought hand-to-mouth on the falling markets; concerns which had been making up stocks of raw materials reduced their working forces instead of buying new stocks. Discharges mounted month by month, until the number of unemployed in 1921 alarmed the nation.[10] In consequence, retail buying fell off—by 7.6 billion dollars, according to the Federal Trade Commission. Thus one of the timbers which had shored up business in 1920 gave way under the prolongation of the strain. A second support failed; other countries were suffering misfortunes like our own, so that our exports dropped 3.7 billion dollars, 45 per cent, below the preceding year.

Amidst these unfavorable circumstances, business losses swelled to prodigious figures. The rise of prices from the middle of 1915 to May, 1920, had rendered money-making overeasy. Speculation in commodities had been encouraged; the penalties for inefficient operation and risky financing had been relaxed. The numbers and the liabilities of bankruptcies had declined to half their prewar levels. Thus, when prices began their precipitous fall, the American business community contained a dangerously large proportion of weak enterprises. Despite the extraordinary efforts of bankers, supported by the Federal Reserve System, to prevent avoidable failures, business mortalities trebled between 1919

---

[10] President Harding called a Conference on Unemployment, of which Mr. Hoover was chairman. For a committee of the conference, the National Bureau of Economic Research made a fact-finding study, published in 1923 under the title *Business Cycles and Unemployment*. In this report, the best estimates we could make of the extent of unemployment in 1921 were summarized thus:

"There seems good ground for believing that, in actual diminution of employment, the depression of 1921 was almost twice as acute as that of 1908 and at least twice as acute as that of 1914–15." William A. Berridge (p. 59).

"The figures show that the depression brought about a reduction in the number employed in every industry except the hand trades, and the trivial increase in that one field is scarcely sufficient to keep pace with the growth of population. The reduction in all industries amounted to about 4,000,000 workers, or nearly one-seventh of all persons employed at the crest of the 1920 boom." Willford I. King (p. 86).

The new estimate, given in the chapter on labor in the present report, states the "average minimum volume of unemployment" at 4,225,000 in 1921 as compared with 1,305,000 in 1920. These figures are not inconsistent with the earlier ones; for they give averages for years on a minimum basis, whereas King used quarterly data and attempted to reach a maximum figure.

and 1921. Liabilities increased more than fivefold.[11] What happened to the bulk of enterprises is perhaps best indicated by the reports of corporations to the Internal Revenue Office, though even these official returns must be accepted with reservations. As the following table shows, more than half of the corporations reported that they lost money

TABLE 2.—CORPORATE INCOME TAX RETURNS[a]

Year	Thousands of corporations reporting	Percentage reporting		Total net income of corporations reporting net incomes (millions of dollars)	Total deficit of corporations reporting no net income (millions of dollars)	Net income of all reporting corporations (millions of dollars)
		Net income	No net income			
	(1)	(2)	(3)	(4)	(5)	(6)
1916	341	61	39	8,766	657	8,109
1917	351	66	34	10,730	630	10,100
1918	318	64	36	8,362	690	7,672
1919	320	65	35	9,411	996	8,415
1920	346	59	41	7,903	2,029	5,874
1921	356	48	52	4,336	3,878	458
1922	383	56	44	6,964	2,194	4,770
1923	399	58	42	8,322	2,014	6,308
1924	417	57	43	7,587	2,224	5,363
1925	430	59	41	9,584	1,963	7,621
1926	455	57	43	9,673	2,169	7,504
1927[b]	453	55	45	8,068	2,311	5,757

[a] From *Statistical Abstract of the United States*, 1926, pp. 190, 191, and *Statistics of Income*, Treasury Department, 1925–1927.

[b] Preliminary report, based on returns filed to August 31, 1928.

in 1921. If we subtract the deficits of the losers from the net incomes of the concerns which admitted making money, we find that the balance of profits falls from eight billions of dollars in 1919 to less than half a billion in 1921. Probably that statement exaggerates the drop in net corporate income. But it is safe to say that, in the course of the drastic readjustment, a considerable fraction of the accumulated war-time profits was swallowed up.[12]

[11] Dun's figures, as given by the *Statistical Abstract*, are as follows:

	Number of commercial failures	Aggregate liabilities in millions of dollars	Average liabilities
1919	6,451	113	$17,561
1920	8,881	295	33,230
1921	19,652	627	31,926

[12] Mr. George O. May, one of the directors of the National Bureau who has intimate knowledge of such matters, points out some of the uncertainties which becloud these figures.

During the period of the excess-profits tax, profits were affected by several unusual factors. For example, war contracts were let in many cases on highly profitable terms, with the thought in mind that a major fraction of the profits would be recouped

TABLE 3.—A CONSPECTUS OF BUSINESS CONDITIONS IN 17 COUNTRIES, 1919–1921

Country	1919	1920	1921
United States	Revival, prosperity.	Prosperity, recession, depression.	Depression.
European allies:			
England	Revival, prosperity.	Prosperity, recession, depression.	Deep depression.
France	Depression, revival, boom.	Prosperity, recession, depression.	Depression, revival.
Italy	Mild depression, revival.	Recession, depression	Depression, panic.
British colonies:			
Canada	Revival, prosperity.	Prosperity, recession.	Depression.
South Africa	Revival, prosperity.	Prosperity, recession, depression.	Deep depression.
Australia	Prosperity.	Prosperity, recession.	Depression.
India	Revival, prosperity.	Prosperity, recession, depression.	Depression.
European neutrals:			
Sweden	Depression, revival.	Boom, recession, depression.	Depression.
Netherlands	Revival, prosperity.	Prosperity, recession, depression.	Depression.
South American powers:			
Argentina	Prosperity.	Prosperity, recession.	Depression.
Brazil	Prosperity.	Prosperity, recession, depression.	Severe depression.
Oriental powers:			
Japan	Depression, revival, prosperity.	Prosperity, recession, depression.	Depression.
China	Prosperity.	Prosperity, recession, depression.	Depression.
Central powers and Russia:			
Germany	Depression.	Depression.	Revival, Spring.
Austria	Depression.	Slow revival.	Revival.
Russia	Depression.	Depression.	Depression.

Rearranged from Willard L. Thorp, *Business Annals*, National Bureau of Economic Research, 1926, p. 86.

through the tax. On the other hand, large sums were spent for advertising or other plans for future expansion and charged as current expenses.

One of the chief reasons why the profits reported in 1917 were so much larger than in 1918 is that in the former year the tax was retroactive. Hence there was less opportunity in 1917 than in 1918 to enter into transactions which would reduce taxable income. In comparing 1917 with later years, it should be noted also that the law has been made more liberal to the taxpayer in important respects; for instance, by allowing discovery depletion and by increasing depletion allowances at large.

Finally, there is little duplication of income in the returns, but much duplication of losses. That is, the net-income figures exclude dividends received from other corporations; but if one corporation loses money and fails, it will report its loss directly, and other corporations which are its creditors or stockholders will also report what they have lost by its failure. Hence the figures in the last column of the table overstate the fluctuations in net corporate income, while the figures in column 4 understate them.

Though the boom of 1919, the crisis of 1920, and the depression of 1921 followed the pattern of earlier cycles, we have seen how much this cycle was influenced by economic conditions resulting from the war and its sudden ending.   These influences were world-wide.   If American business men were betrayed by postwar demands into unwise courses, so were business men in all countries similarly situated.   Table 3, based upon a critical study of business conditions by Dr. Willard L. Thorp, gives a conspectus of conditions in seventeen countries, classified according to their relation to the war.   It shows that the course of business affairs in the United States from 1919 to 1921 was almost exactly paralleled by the course of affairs in the leading European allies, in four great British dependencies on four continents, in the two European neutrals studied, in two South American nations, in Japan and in China. Each of these thirteen countries had its ordinary supplies for civilian uses gravely restricted during the war; to each peace brought a hectic season of activity (mildest in Italy); each suffered a recession in 1920 and a depression in 1921.   In only three countries does the record differ widely from that of the United States, and these are countries where the fortunes of war and peace had an opposite cast.   Russia's internal troubles kept her economic life in disorder.   Germany and Austria suffered depression in 1919–1920 while their victorious opponents enjoyed prosperity, and emerged into revivals in 1920–1921 while their opponents were liquidating postwar booms.   Not until this liquidation was finished did economic life resume its independent way.   Even then, factors arising from the war continued to exercise an important influence.

V. FACTORS AFFECTING AMERICAN FORTUNES IN 1922–1927

Among the factors which have shaped economic developments in the United States since the first postwar cycle ended its wild career, we may note first certain unfavorable conditions which business has had to surmount.

Conditions in Other Countries.—Prosperity in other countries to which it sells its products tends to beget prosperity in the producing nation.   Similarly, depression in foreign markets reacts unfavorably upon domestic business.   These international influences gain in scope and energy as nations are drawn closer together by improvements in transportation and communications.   Hence the business annals of the nineteenth century show a secular trend toward increasing similarity of economic fortunes among trading nations.   Though capable of meeting most of its own needs and separated from the other leaders in commerce by broad oceans, the United States feels the reflex influence of business conditions in every country with which it deals on an appreciable scale.

Prosperity here is heightened by active foreign demand for our products, and depression abroad is an unfavorable factor in our home affairs.[13]

Such prosperity as the United States has enjoyed since 1922 owes less than usual to foreign stimulation and support. Table 4, a continuation of Table 3, shows that few countries have fared so well as we in the last six years. Compared with most of the nations represented, if not judged by the standard we like to set for American prosperity, the United States has been well off.

Department of Commerce figures support this inference from business annals. After an extraordinary fall from 1920 to 1921 or 1922, the value of American exports and imports began to increase again. But imports increased at the more rapid rate. In 1919–1921, the value of our imports made only 56 per cent of the value of our exports. In 1922–1927, this percentage rose to 86. That figure is decidedly higher than the prewar average of 78 per cent in 1910–1914. When 1913 records are taken as 100, the averages for 1922–1927 show the following changes:[14]

The physical volume of imports has increased 66 per cent.
The physical volume of exports has increased 33 per cent.

The prices of imports have increased 31 per cent.
The prices of exports have increased 38 per cent.

The dollar values of imports have increased 117 per cent.
The dollar values of exports have increased 81 per cent.

If we grant that the real goal of economic effort is to secure goods for meeting human wants, it follows that a country's gains from international trade consist of its imports. Exports represent costs—prices paid for the goods desired. In this sense, the fact that our imports have grown faster than our exports means that the outside world had increased its contribution to our economic welfare more rapidly than we have increased our contribution to the economic welfare of other countries. But from the business point of view, the preceding figures mean that by enlarging our purchases more than our sales we have stimulated trade in other countries more than other countries have stimulated trade here.[15]

---

[13] See Willard L. Thorp, *Business Annals*, National Bureau of Economic Research, 1926, pp. 73–100.

[14] See *Commerce Yearbook*, 1928, Vol. 1, pp. 86 and 91.

[15] The percentage changes in our imports and exports have varied widely from one class of commodities to another and from country to country. It is solely to the broadest features of our foreign commerce as a whole that the statements in the text refer. It should be noted also that the discussion is confined to the merchandise factor in international dealings. A fuller discussion covering "invisible" as well as visible items may be found in Chap. XI, Foreign Markets and Credits.

TABLE 4.—CONSPECTUS OF BUSINESS FLUCTUATIONS IN 17 COUNTRIES 1922–1927

Country	1922	1923	1924
United States	Revival, prosperity.	Prosperity, recession.	Mild depression, revival.
European allies:			
England	Depression.	Depression.	Depression (lessening).
France	Revival.	Prosperity.	Prosperity.
Italy	Depression.	Depression, revival.	Prosperity (moderate).
British colonies:			
Canada	Depression, revival.	Prosperity (moderate).	Recession.
South Africa	Depression.	Revival.	Prosperity (mild).
Australia	Revival (slow).	Revival.	Recession (mild).
India	Depression.	Revival (slow).	Revival.
European neutrals:			
Sweden	Depression, revival.	Revival.	Prosperity (mild).
Netherlands	Depression.	Depression.	Revival.
South American powers:			
Argentina	Depression.	Depression (lessening).	Revival.
Brazil	Depression (lessening).	Revival.	Recession.
Oriental powers:			
Japan	Depression.	Depression.	Depression.
China	Depression.	Depression.	Depression.
Central powers and Russia:			
Germany	Revival, recession.	Depression.	Revival, check.
Austria	Recession (uneven).	Depression.	Depression (financial).
Russia	Depression, revival.	Revival, recession.	Depression, revival.

	1925	1926	1927
United States	Prosperity.	Prosperity, slight recession at close.	Mild contraction.
European allies:			
England	Depression.	Depression.	Revival.
France	Prosperity.	Prosperity, recession.	Depression, revival.
Italy	Prosperity.	Recession.	Depression.
British colonies:			
Canada	Revival, prosperity.	Prosperity.	Prosperity.
South Africa	Prosperity.	Prosperity (mild).	Uneven prosperity.
Australia	Revival, prosperity.	Prosperity.	Prosperity.
India	Prosperity (mild).	Depression.	Revival.
European neutrals:			
Sweden	Prosperity (mild).	Prosperity (uneven).	Prosperity.
Netherlands	Prosperity (mild).	Prosperity (mild).	Prosperity.
South American powers:			
Argentina	Prosperity.	Recession.	Revival.
Brazil	Depression.	Depression.	Depression.
Oriental powers:			
Japan	Depression, revival.	Depression.	Depression.
China	Depression.	Depression.	Depression.
Central powers and Russia:			
Germany	Revival, recession.	Depression, revival.	Revival.
Austria	Depression.	Depression, revival.	Revival continued.
Russia	Prosperity, recession.	Prosperity.	Prosperity.

Further, unless the most inclusive of statistical indexes are grievously in error, our domestic business as a whole has grown faster than our foreign business. Comparisons like those just given, which credit exports with an 81 per cent increase, show that on the basis of 1913 records as 100:

> The dollar volume of the average national income per year in 1922–1926 increased 121 per cent.
>
> The dollar volume of average yearly bank clearings outside of New York in 1922–1927 increased 175 per cent.

So, too, the Department of Commerce finds that the value of manufactured goods produced in the United States has grown much faster since 1919 than the value of manufactured exports. Indeed, the fraction of these products exported in 1925 was smaller than the prewar average.[16]

In particular, American prosperity has been marred by agricultural depression, and agricultural depression has been due in part to foreign conditions.

The war brought an increased export demand for American breadstuffs and meat. When the United States entered the struggle, and millions of tons of shipping were required for transporting our army to France, there was further reason for avoiding the long hauls of food from Argentina, Australia and India. There was danger also that enlistments would reduce our harvests. One of the first war measures of the Government was the creation of a Food Administration. In other industries, price-fixing meant setting of maximum prices; Congress itself set a minimum price of $2 a bushel on wheat, and authorized the President to raise the minimum higher if need be.

Farmers responded to these war demands as fully as they could. According to the census returns, they had increased the area harvested by 28 million acres between 1899 and 1909; between 1909 and 1919 they added 37 million acres. Yields are always at the mercy of the weather; but the Harvard index of physical production in agriculture shows an

[16] Exports of manufactured goods in relation to domestic production, in millions of dollars, are shown in the following table.[a] The value of materials entering factories is necessarily approximate, and hence is expressed as a maximum or minimum.

Year	Materials excluding duplication,	Value added by manufacture	Total value	Export	
				Value	Per cent
1919	12,500–14,500	24,800	38,300–40,300	5,449	13.5–14.2
1921	8,000– 9,400	18,330	26,300–27,700	2,722	9.8–10.3
1923	11,500–13,200	25,850	37,300–39,100	2,625	6.7– 7.0
1925	12,000–13,500	26,800	38,500–40,000	3,079	7.6– 8.0

[a] From *Commerce Yearbook*, 1928, Vol. I, p. 93.

acceleration in the rate of growth when averages are taken for several years. This index rose 5 points on the 1899 basis between 1904–1908 and 1909–1913, 12 points between 1909–1913 and 1914–1918, and 2 points more between the war period and 1919–1921—though the last year was one of poor crops.

Thus the war left American agriculture with expanded facilities for production. And the good times had lasted long enough to let even this occupation, which must wait upon nature, base its finances on the unstable prospect of continued high prices and high profits. In the corn belt, the regions where wheat growing was expanding, and in certain tobacco-planting sections, farm lands had risen to prices unheard of before, and thousands of enterprising men had bought all the land they could acquire by stretching their credit to the utmost.

The imperious needs of underfed Europeans had swelled our agricultural exports in 1919 to more than 4 billion dollars—much more than the war-year figures. Even in 1920, agricultural exports were valued at nearly 3.5 billions. But then came a sudden fall in the foreign demand. The total value of agricultural exports shrank in 1921 by 1.3 billion dollars, and in 1922–1927 it fluctuated about an average lower than that of 1921—1.9 billions as compared with 2.1.

For this shrinkage in exports it is easy to account. Price reductions are a large part, but not all, of the story. After demobilization, European farmers could get all the labor they required; gradually they restored their depleted stocks of farm animals and their accustomed use of fertilizers. Also there were fewer European mouths to feed in 1920 than there had been in 1917, or even in 1910. Thus Europe became less dependent on foreign countries for food than it had been during the war. Second, shipping became superabundant, freights fell to very low levels, and the world's commerce slipped back toward its old channels. The United States lost most of its war-time advantage from a short haul. Third, our competitors in food production—especially Argentina, Canada and Australia—were expanding their output of meat and cereals vigorously. With cheaper lands, they could make things most uncomfortable in world markets for farmers in the United States. Finally, cotton crops were small in these years, mainly because of the boll weevil, and the high level of prices made it difficult for the impoverished countries of Europe to buy the quantity needed to furnish employment in their factories and cotton fabrics to their people.

Reckoned in physical units, our agricultural exports remained above the prewar levels in 1922–1927. But they fell below the levels to which American farmers had adjusted their output in 1917–1920. To sell even these reduced quantities, they have had to accept prices which in most cases were low in comparison with the prices of other commodities.

TABLE 5.—DOMESTIC EXPORTS OF AGRICULTURAL PRODUCTS FROM THE UNITED
STATES, BY AVERAGES OF PERIODS OF YEARS

Calendar years	Total value of agricultural exports (domestic)	Values of exports of		Physical quantities of exports of	
		Five grains	Cotton	Five grains	Cotton
	Millions of dollars	*Millions of dollars*	*Millions of dollars*	*Millions of bushels*	*Millions of bales*
1909–1913...............	966.5	88.1	541.7	112.9	8.5
1914–1918...............	1,842.8	386.8	511.1	315.2	6.1
1919–1921...............	3,221.1	638.4	936.0	358.9	6.4
1922–1927...............	1,942.1	288.6	855.3	191.6	7.8

Sources: *Commerce Yearbooks.*
Monthly Summary of Foreign Commerce.
Foreign Commerce and Navigation of the United States.

Table 5 shows the basic facts concerning exports. Table 6, comparing production and exports, is even more illuminating. More than in average prewar years, American farmers, with their increased output, had to depend on the domestic markets. They fared ill, and their hard times created more difficulties for other American industries than the prevalence of depression in foreign countries.

TABLE 6.—PRODUCTION OF AGRICULTURAL PRODUCTS IN THE UNITED STATES AND
PROPORTION EXPORTED, BY CENSUS YEARS

(In millions of dollars)

Year	Agricultural products excluding duplication and seeds	Domestic exports of agricultural products	Per cent exported	Value of manufactured foodstuffs[a]	Export of manufactured foodstuffs	Per cent exported[a]
1899...............	3,450	[b]818.7	23.7	1,700– 1,900	312	16.4–18.4
1904...............	4,600	[b]843.0	18.3	2,250– 2,550	296	11.6–13.2
1909...............	6,100	903.2	14.8	2,950– 3,450	281	8. 2–9.5
1914...............	7,500	1,114.0	14.9	3,750– 4,350	374	8.6–10.0
1919...............	15,700	4,096.0	26.1	9,500–10,900	1,963	18.0–20.7
1921...............	9,200	2,114.9	23.0	6,250– 6,950	685	9.9–11.0
1923...............	11,300	1,820.5	16.1	7,200– 8,000	583	7.3– 8.1
1925...............	12,400	2,136.2	17.2	8,000– 9,000	574	6.4– 7.2

Sources: *Commerce Yearbooks* and *Agricultural Yearbooks.*
[a] Maximum and minimum figures are used because the value of materials entering factories must be estimated from imperfect data.
[b] Values for calendar years estimated by averaging the values for the two adjacent fiscal years ending June 30.

The Prime Factor Making for Prosperity.—Past experience has taught us that a period of depression will presently be followed by a business revival. But when this revival will come, and whether it will develop into full-blown prosperity, are matters which the past does not tell. Each cycle has its own special features which require special explanations. How the United States managed to attain a higher per capita income in 1922–1927 than ever before, though conditions in most other countries were not favorable, and though its basic industry, agriculture, was depressed, is the outstanding problem of the cycles of 1921–1924, 1924–1927 and 1927 to date.

The preceding chapters give many partial answers to this question. All these answers may be condensed into one: Since 1921, Americans have applied intelligence to the day's work more effectively than ever before. Thus the prime factor in producing the extraordinary changes in the economic fortunes of the European peoples during the nineteenth century is the prime factor in producing the prosperity of the United States in recent years. The old process of putting science into industry has been followed more intensively than before; it has been supplemented by tentative efforts to put science into business management, trade-union policy, and Government administration.

Concrete instances of technical improvements in many mining, metallurgical, and fabricating processes are given in the chapters on industry. The remarkable results achieved are demonstrated statistically from census data showing output per worker. Similar, though less striking, instances appear in the chapter on construction. Without help from any extraordinary invention, the railroads also have attained a higher level of operating efficiency.[17] In farming there is an intriguing report of new machines and new methods coming into use. Here too, the record of average output per worker shows considerable gains.

All this means that since 1921 Americans have found ways of producing more physical goods per hour of labor than before. They have received larger average incomes because they have produced more commodities and services.[18] That is true in the aggregate, although not all

---

[17] Dr. Julius H. Parmelee, director of the Bureau of Railway Economics, has kindly furnished a backward extension of the "index of railway operating efficiency," mentioned by Professor Cunningham in a preceding chapter. The yearly averages, on a 1920–1924 base, run as follows: 1920, 99.7; 1921, 95.3; 1922, 96.5; 1923, 103.5; 1924, 104.8; 1925, 109.4; 1926, 113.5; 1927, 115.2; 1928, Jan.–Nov., 118.1.

[18] Increased productivity per man at work does not necessarily mean larger real income per head of the population. In some industries the output per worker rises in periods of business depression when total output falls; because the less efficient hands have been laid off; because the men kept on the pay roll are afraid of discharge when new jobs are scarce and so work harder than usual; because only the best-equipped or best-managed plants can keep running at all, or for other reasons. As will presently be shown more at length, the number of men at work in two of our greatest branches of industry—farming and manufacturing—has been reduced. But the reductions in numbers at work have not offset the increases in output per remaining worker, even in these branches. There remains a net gain in real income per capita for the whole country.

who have contributed to the increase in physical production have shared in the increase of real income. The important exceptions to the general rule will be discussed presently.

The reality of the gains made by improving the technique of farming, railroading, manufacturing, and building seems to be established beyond question. There is room for doubt only concerning the pace of recent progress in comparison with earlier spurts of technical improvement. Comparisons between output per worker in later years and in 1919 often show sensational gains. But that is largely because 1919 made a wretched record of physical inefficiency. According to Chapter II, Industry, the census of manufactures places this year below 1914, and still further below 1909, in output per worker. The above-cited estimates of national income per capita in dollars of constant purchasing power confirm this showing, and so do index numbers of physical production in Table 1. Nor does 1921, a year of severe depression, afford a satisfactory basis of comparison. Thus it is difficult to measure the technical progress of 1922–1927, with the data now available. It is still more difficult to make reliable measurements for earlier years, when censuses were taken at longer intervals and fewer supplementary figures were published. But doubts whether the rate of improvement in the past six years is unprecedented are not of great moment. It remains clear that the Industrial Revolution is not a closed episode; we are living in the midst of it, and the economic problems of to-day are largely problems of its making.

While the details of the latest technical advances always possess thrilling interest, perhaps there is more of promise for the future in the chapters on recent changes in economic policy. The efforts to apply scientific methods to such matters are in an early stage of development. The sciences which underlie these efforts—psychology, sociology, economics—are far less advanced than physics and chemistry. The experts who are making the applications—personnel managers, advertising specialists, sales directors, business economists and statisticians—are less rigorously trained than engineers. It is even harder to measure the results they achieve than to determine what difference a new machine makes in unit costs. Nor are business executives so generally convinced of the practical value of the rather intangible services which the new professions can render as they are of the indispensability of engineering advice. Yet it is conceivable that applications of the social sciences, now in their tentative stage, will grow into contributions of great moment to economic welfare. Certainly the chapters in this report on marketing, management and labor show that many enterprising business concerns and some enterprising trade unions are trying new policies, and often getting results which they deem good.

Perhaps none of the changes reported here will prove more important in the long run than the change in the economic theories on which the

American Federation of Labor and certain outside unions are acting. That organizations of wage earners should grasp the relations between productivity and wages, and that they should take the initiative in pressing constructive plans for increasing efficiency upon employers, is not wholly without precedent; but the spread of such ideas and the vigor with which they are acted on by large organizations must startle those who have believed that trade unions are brakes upon economic progress.

Scarcely less significant is the report from the employing side. Our investigators believe that the art of business management turned a corner in 1921, cultivating since then more skillful understanding of the whole situation and nicer adjustment of means to the immediate environment. Numerous corporations and some trade associations are maintaining research bureaus of their own. Among the managerial devices experimented with, are co-ordinated staffs in place of one "big boss," bonus payments to executives and "incentive wages" for the rank and file, operating budgets, forecasts of business conditions, close inventory control, personnel management and employee representation. Most of these devices are attempts to understand and to utilize the psychological forces which control human behavior, or the economic forces which control business activity. "There is today not only more production per man, more wages per man and more horse power per man; there is also more management per man."[19] Marketing—traditionally the part of business in which native shrewdness, experience and "personal magnetism" have been held all-important—even marketing is being permeated by applied psychology. Costly investigations of "consumer appeal," of advertising "pull," of "sales resistance"—the very terms

[19] On this passage Colonel M. C. Rorty comments as follows:

One of the most significant results arising from improvements in the science of management has been an increasing ability to secure from large units or "chains" the type of individual efficiency that a few years ago could be secured only in the small organization working under the direct supervision of a competent employer-owner. Under the older type of organization there was a gain in efficiency with size, up to the point where the reductions in costs, through ability to specialize and functionalize the work of a larger group of workers and the increases in process, purchasing and selling efficiency under larger scale operation, began to be more than offset by a reduced general efficiency due to the inability of the employer-owner to maintain close contacts with the members of the enlarged organization. Recent developments in management methods, and in accounting and statistical control, have apparently broken down these former economic limitations on the size of the individual organization or "chain," with the result that practically all types of business and industry are now open to efficient large-scale corporate control. If this tendency persists, it may represent a fundamental economic change having very far-reaching consequences. The field of operations for the independent owner-manager will be steadily restricted, and the young man of capacity and intelligence will have to look forward more than ever before to a career in which, except by some rare combination of good fortune and adaptability to circumstances, he will continue throughout to be a subordinate worker in a large corporation organization.

would have been unintelligible to our fathers—show that sales managers are trying to base their planning upon factual studies of human behavior. And the rapid spread of chain stores and of installment selling show that marketing methods are no more standing still than is industrial technique.

By the side of these rather definite changes in trade-union and in business policy, we may set the influence of certain general ideas which have gained wide currency in the last few years.

First, there is the spirit of caution, manifested in minimizing future commitments, in hand-to-mouth buying by merchants, in efforts to keep down inventories or to pass the need for keeping large stocks on to the concern from which one buys. This lesson is taught afresh by every great crisis. The staggering financial losses of 1920–21 enforced the old moral emphatically; the sagging course of commodity prices has kept it in mind, and the increased operating efficiency of producers and railroads has made possible close scheduling of merchandise transactions. The Florida land boom and the stock-market adventure of 1928 indicate the course American business might have taken in the absence of all restraint.

Associated with the prudence which has tempered enterprise is a more systematic effort to learn from experience. Here there seems to be a new emphasis, if not a new practice. Most can be learned from experience when it is exactly known, and seen in relation to its environment. The most exact records of economic experience are statistical in form. Since the war, an increasing number of officials, publicists and business men have fostered the keeping of better statistical records, and have analyzed past experience as a guide to future planning. Every reader must realize that, without the aid of the new statistics which this widespread effort has provided, the present survey of recent economic changes would be more imperfect than it is. What is of use in providing a factual basis for determining economic trends at large is not less useful in determining the factors which affect the success of private enterprises.

More publicity concerning business operations and closer co-operation among business enterprises should also be noted as characteristic of the day. These are features of American practice which impress all our foreign visitors; the older rules of secretiveness and rivalry seem to have maintained themselves more rigidly in other countries. Perhaps the growth of trade associations and the expansion of their programs is the clearest evidence of the new attitude. No doubt every industry has its recalcitrants who, for one reason or another, refuse to play on the team; but certainly there is a marked increase of readiness to join co-operative programs of research and publicity, to interchange trade information, to standardize products where standardization is good business, to consult about methods and practices—in short, to treat the industry for many purposes as a unit in whose prosperity all members have a common interest, and to inspire good will in the public by open dealings.

Fourth, belief in the economy of high wages has become prevalent among the abler business executives, much as belief in increasing productivity has become prevalent among the abler trade-union leaders.[20] To find a market for the wares turned out by mass production and urged on consumers by national advertising, it is patently necessary to have corresponding purchasing power in the hands of consumers. Since studies of the national income have demonstrated that wages constitute by far the largest stream of personal income, it follows that wages per man—or rather, wages per family—must be increased as production is expanded. Perhaps most people would have accepted this argument in the abstract at any time in the last hundred years. But many employers in the past would have retorted with the assertion that high wages undermine the moral stamina of the masses. To-day such talk is far less common in the United States. Not only do many business executives admit the general principle that paying high wages is good policy; they are ready to assume what they consider their share of the responsibility for putting the principle into practice.

The share of Government in recent economic changes has not been made the subject of a separate chapter. But the service of one public agency, the Federal Reserve System, is treated in the chapter on banking, and the services of the Departments of Commerce, Agriculture, and Labor in collecting and diffusing knowledge are mentioned in several places. If the prime factor making for prosperity has been the application of intelligence to the day's work, then Government agencies must be credited with an indispensable, though indirect, part in what has been accomplished.

Further, our Federal Government has of late years manifested a more intelligent attitude toward problems of economic organization than it has manifested in the past. To treat business enterprises as agencies for performing social services, to facilitate their operations, and to hold them to this conception of their function, is a policy exceedingly difficult to carry out. It requires a delicate combination of constructive intervention at some points and of clearing away obstacles at other points. No one can say that this policy has become characteristic of Government in all of its dealings with business, any more than one can say that the doctrine of high wages is accepted by all employers, or the theory that increased productivity benefits labor is accepted by all trade-unionists. Yet no one who has watched Federal policy, as practiced by the numerous agencies which have to deal with economic issues, will question that a change has occurred. Efforts to check extortion have not ceased; but more regularly than in the past they are accompanied by active efforts

[20] The rise of this idea is sketched in Section VII, p. 885.

to heighten the efficiency of what are judged to be legitimate enterprises. Farmers and exporters are not the only beneficiaries.

To repeat: all of the changes making for prosperity which have been recalled in this section, together with many others noted in preceding chapters, can be summed up under a single head—applying fresh intelligence to the day's work. From the use of abstruse researches in pure science to the use of broad economic conceptions and the use of common sense, the method of American progress in 1922–1928 has been the old method of taking thought. Peace let us turn our thoughts to common matters, the hard times of 1921 spurred our efforts, and the complicated consequences our efforts produced have kept us thinking.

VI. HARDSHIPS CAUSED BY INCREASING EFFICIENCY

Among the consequences which improvements in industrial technique or in business methods produce in an individualistic state, are hardships of various kinds. The victims are partly business competitors who are a bit slow in adopting new methods; partly industries or geographic regions affected indirectly; partly individuals who find their services no longer needed. To follow all the complicated difficulties produced by recent economic advances in the United States is out of the question; but a few chains of cause and effect may be traced link by link. For the queer mixture of prosperity and depression noted at the outset of this chapter is due largely to the pressure which some group's growing efficiency puts upon other groups.

Reductions in Unit-costs, Prices, and Profits.—The technical advances of recent years in the United States have been largely advances in the direction of more economical production. A greater volume of goods has been turned out at lower costs per unit. Now larger supplies sent to market tend to depress prices.

In most periods of prosperity this tendency has been more than offset by an increase in demand. The cases have been few indeed when the index numbers of wholesale prices have failed to rise in the prosperous phase of a cycle. And there are clear marks of the standard reaction in our period. The Bureau of Labor Statistics index number advanced from 91.4 in January, 1922, to 104.5 in March, 1923. On the mild recession of that year it reversed its course and declined to 94.9 in June, 1924. When business picked up again, the index began to climb once more, reaching 104.8 in March, 1925. From that point it receded unsteadily to 93.7 in April and May, 1927. Judged by prewar standards, these fluctuations have about the average amplitude.[21] The remarkable fact is that prices sagged through the prosperous year 1926. Taking the

---

[21] Here I am using the enlarged Bureau of Labor Statistics index on the 1926 base. See *Monthly Labor Review*, July, 1928. For a comparison of the amplitudes of prewar and postwar cycles in wholesale prices, see Table 11, p. 893.

whole period from 1922 to 1927, the trend has been a gently declining one. Prices at wholesale have fallen at the rate of 0.1 per cent per annum.[22]

Monetary factors, which are often held responsible for changes in wholesale price levels, can scarcely be held responsible in this case. In 1922–1927 international gold movements added $760,000,000 net to our stock, and "earmarking" operations took less than $200,000,000 of this sum out of monetary use. The banks suffered no stringency; indeed they increased their other investments, because commercial borrowers asked less credit than the banks would have been glad to lend. So far as domestic conditions are concerned, business activity and the easy money market might have combined to produce a vigorous advance of prices.

But, though the fact is commonly overlooked, the course of prices cannot be explained in any commercial nation of these days by domestic conditions alone. Commodities subject to international trade on a considerable scale cannot long maintain prices higher in one country than in another by margins which exceed costs of carriage and handling, plus import duties. Price fluctuations in different countries are tied even closer to each other, as a rule, than actual prices; for though import duties may establish a considerable spread between market prices in two countries, these duties are not subject to very frequent change. Shipping charges have been particularly low in the period under review, so that this factor has interfered less than usual with market uniformity. Even countries with inconvertible currencies are bound to the world system of prices, and to its fluctuations, through the rate of exchange.

It is true that a large proportion of the articles dealt in on wholesale markets, in such a country as the United States, are not exported or imported on an appreciable scale. But economists have long since shown that the prices of different goods prevailing in any country at any time are closely related to each other through the channels of supply and demand. Domestic prices thus constitute a system, in the sense that a change in the price of any commodity affects, and is in turn affected by, changes in the prices of a host of other goods. The statistical aspect of these interrelations is briefly developed in the preceding chapter on price movements. Since all domestic prices are thus related to each other, and since a considerable fraction of these prices are related to foreign prices, changes in the general level of wholesale prices in any one country must be related to the changes taking place in the wholesale price levels of other countries.

The validity of this conclusion has been statistically demonstrated. For example, comparisons covering the 20 years 1890–1910, based on American, English, French and German wholesale indexes of unlike

[22] See Chap. IX, Price Movements.

construction show strict conformity in the major movements and prevailing conformity in the minor movements also.[23] Even during the
war, when commerce was so greatly hampered, American prices in gold
followed the gyrations of European paper prices reduced to a gold
basis.[24] Again in the first postwar cycle, the conformity discussed above
in general business conditions in a long list of countries was matched by
conformity in the course of wholesale prices, so far as index numbers
are available to show what happened.

That a similar conformity of wholesale price fluctuations in various
important countries marked the period 1922–1927 appears from the following charts, which show index numbers for 15 countries on a prewar base,
with the paper-money entries reduced to their gold equivalents. It will
be noted that the curves, which spread unusually far apart during the
war, have approached each other again. This tendency is most marked
in the countries where prices had diverged most widely from the average
course. Also it will be noted that prices in the United States pursue a
middle path. They run on a lower level compared with the prewar base
than prices in some countries, and on a higher relative level than in other

CHART 1.—INDEX NUMBERS OF WHOLESALE PRICES IN UNITED STATES,
GREAT BRITAIN AND FRANCE, 1922–1928.

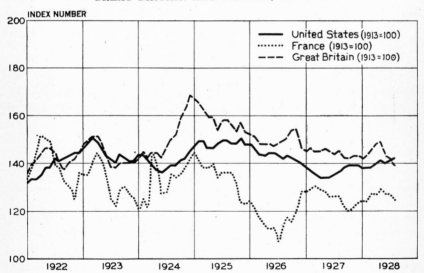

[23] See Chart 8 in the writer's *Business Cycles,* Berkeley, California, 1913, p. 121.
Index numbers including substantially identical lists of commodities in the United
States and England, the United States and France, and the United States and
Germany, show scarcely closer agreement than the standard series made from diver-
gent list.

[24] See "International Price Comparisons. History of Prices during the War."
War Industries Board, *Price Bulletin* No. 2, Washington, 1919.

CHART 2.—INDEX NUMBERS OF WHOLESALE PRICES IN UNITED STATES, NETHERLANDS, SWEDEN AND GERMANY, 1922–1928.

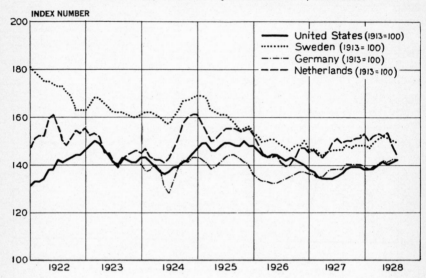

CHART 3.—INDEX NUMBERS OF WHOLESALE PRICES IN UNITED STATES, BELGIUM AND ITALY, 1922–1928.

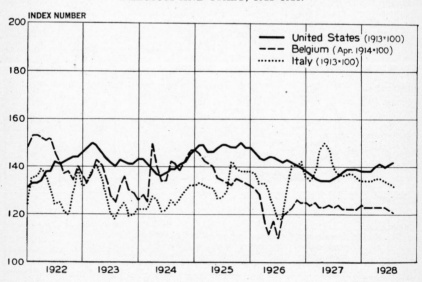

CHART 4.—INDEX NUMBERS OF WHOLESALE PRICES IN UNITED STATES, AUSTRIA AND SWITZERLAND, 1922–1928.

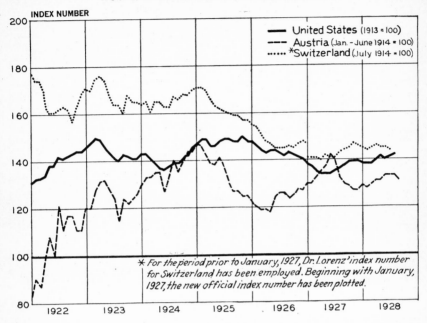

CHART 5.—INDEX NUMBERS OF WHOLESALE PRICES IN UNITED STATES, CANADA, INDIA AND SOUTH AFRICA, 1922–1928.

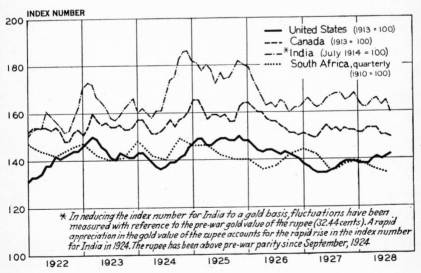

countries.   Of course, market fluctuations in this country have influenced
quotations in every other nation; but they have also been influenced by
the latter quotations.   It seems a fair inference from these charts, with
their convincing evidence of a common bond among the changes in price
levels of different nations, that prices in this country could not have
risen rapidly in 1922–1927 unless the forces behind the local advance
had been powerful enough to pull world markets up.[25]

CHART 6.—INDEX NUMBERS OF WHOLESALE PRICES IN UNITED STATES,
JAPAN AND AUSTRALIA, 1922–1928.

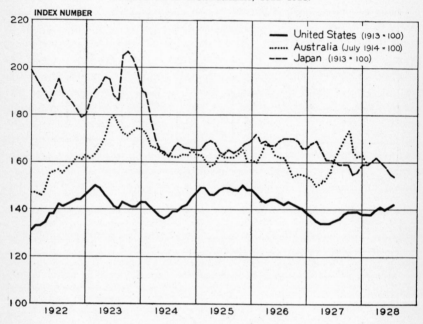

[25] The index numbers used in the charts are as follows:

United States—United States Bureau of Labor Statistics.   Revised index shifted to
1913 equal 100.

Great Britain—"Statist" index number, 1913 equal 100.   From January, 1922, to
April, 1925, original value of the index was deflated by the exchange rate, New
York on London.

France—Index number from the *Bulletin de la Statistique Générale de la France*, deflated
by gold parity value, New York on Paris, 1913 equal 100.   Values for June, July,
and August, 1928—new currency values now published in the *Monthly Bulletin
of Statistics* of the League of Nations.

Netherlands—Official index compiled by the Central Bureau of Statistics.   The
index was originally computed on the base 1901–1910, and has been shifted to
the 1913 base in the *Monthly Bulletin of Statistics* of the League of Nations.
From January, 1922, to April, 1925, the original value of the index was deflated
by exchange rates, New York on Amsterdam.

Sweden—Compiled by Kommerskollegium, 1913 equal 100.

Thus the reduction in unit costs, and the increase in the supply of wares turned out by improved methods, combined with international forces to keep the American price level from rising buoyantly in the active years of our period, as it has done in most periods of prosperity. Presumably, the international factors have been more potent than the domestic factors in producing the results. Yet we may count the reductions in cost by industrial leaders and the increases in output among the manifestations of efficiency which have contributed to the difficulties of making money in this period.

Sagging prices make it harder to conduct business with profit because many of the expenses of an enterprise are fixed by long contracts or by understandings hard to alter, and cannot be cut to offset a reduction in selling rates. Above, we noticed how the rapidly rising prices of the war and of 1919 swelled paper profits and reduced bankruptcies. Also we noted how the sudden fall of prices in 1920–21 turned profits into losses and swelled bankruptcies. In 1922–1927, we find an intermediate result. Concerns in the van of technical progress have done handsomely. But the prices at which they could market their large outputs with profit to themselves have meant loss and even failure to less aggressive rivals. Dun's statistics of commercial failures yield the annual averages shown in Table 7. The average number of failures in 1922–1927 has

---

Germany—1924 through 1928, new index number, 1913 equal 100. Source: *Wirtschaft und Statistik.*

Belgium—1922 through 1926, April, 1914 equal 100, gold basis. Series compiled by Ministry of Industry and Labor Statistics. Deflated by gold parity value— New York on Brussels. Values for 1927 and 1928 published on the new currency base.

Italy—1922 through 1927, gold basis. Gold parity value, New York on Rome, used to deflate series compiled by Chamber of Commerce and Industry of Milan, 1913 equal 100. 1928 values quoted on new currency base.

Austria—For 1922 kronen prices were deflated by gold parity values. 1923–1927, gold basis, January-June 1914 equal 100, as published in the *Statistische Nachrichten.* New series begins in 1928. The value for January, 1928, is identical with the value of the former series.

Switzerland—For 1922 through 1926, Dr. Lorenz index number, July 1914 equal 100. From January, 1927, new official index number used. From January, 1922, to October, 1924, the original value of the index was deflated by the exchange rate, New York on Berne.

Canada—Dominion Bureau of Statistics—1913 equal 100.

Japan—Bank of Japan, 1913 equal 100. From January, 1922, to August, 1928, the original value of the index was deflated by exchange rate, New York on Yokohama.

South Africa—Official index number compiled by Census Office, 1910 equal 100.

Australia—Commonwealth Bureau of Census and Statistics, July, 1914 equal 100.

India—Official index number of wholesale prices at Calcutta, compiled by the Department of Statistics, July, 1914 equal 100.

actually exceeded the number in 1921, but the total and the average liabilities have grown smaller.

TABLE 7.—COMMERCIAL FAILURES

	Annual averages		
	Thousands of failures	Millions of dollars of liabilities	Average liabilities in thousands of dollars
1919–20...................	7.7	204	27
1921.......................	19.7	627	32
1922–1927.................	21.5	513	24

Source: *Commerce Yearbook*, 1928, Vol. I, p. 51.

"Profitless prosperity," like so many popular paradoxes, combines an element of truth with an element of falsehood. One expects a period of unusually rapid increase in efficiency to be a period of more than usual inequality of profits. This expectation has been borne out by the experience of 1922–1927. As a whole, corporate incomes reported to the Internal Revenue Bureau and summarized in Table 2, have been large in the latest years for which we have data; but they have not equaled the records of 1916–1919.

Whether the enterprises which have lagged behind in cost reductions and in earnings are mainly smaller enterprises, as has been contended, is less sure. Of course this contention tends to become true with the lapse of time, for the simple reason that the exceptionally profitable enterprises grow exceptionally fast. The profitable enterprises of to-day tend to become the large enterprises of tomorrow. But Dr. Thorp's section of the chapter on industry shows that there is no close relationship between large size and low unit-cost, or between large size and high rates of profit. It seems to be middle-sized enterprises, rather than small ones, which have felt the severest pressure. But the facts, as the census shows them, are complicated and cannot be adequately presented in a brief statement.

The Competition of New Products and New Tastes.—Scarcely less characteristic of our period than unit-cost reductions is the rapid expansion in the production and sale of products little used or wholly unknown a generation or even a decade ago. Among consumers' goods, the conspicuous instances are automobiles, radios and rayon. But the list includes also oil-burning furnaces, gas stoves, household electrical appliances in great variety, automobile accessories, antifreezing mixtures, cigarette lighters, propeller pencils, wrist watches, airplanes, and what not. Among producers' goods we have the truck and the tractor competing with the horse and the mule, reinforced concrete competing with brick and lumber, the high-tension line competing with the steam engine, fuel oil competing with coal, not to mention excavating machines, belt conveyors, paint sprayers, and "automatics" of many sorts competing with manual labor.

Changes in taste are in large part merely the consumers' response to the solicitation of novel products, effectively presented by advertising. But that is not all of the story; the consumer is free to choose what he likes among the vociferous offerings, and sometimes reveals traces of initiative. In what other terms can one explain the changes in diet pointed out in the first chapter? Americans are consuming fewer calories per capita; they are eating less wheat and corn but more dairy products, vegetable oils, sugar, fresh vegetables and fruit. More families than ever before are sending their sons and daughters to college—surely that is not a triumph of "high-powered" salesmanship. Young children, girls and women, are wearing lighter and fewer clothes. The short skirt, the low shoe, the silk or rayon stocking, "athletic" underwear, the soft collar, sporting suits and sporting goods, have an appeal which makers of rival articles have not been able to overcome. And, in a sense, every consumers' good, from college to candy, is a rival of every other consumers' good, besides being a rival of the savings bank.

"When the makers of one product get a larger slice of the consumer's dollar, the slices left for the makers of other products get smaller." This way of accounting for the hardships met by certain long-established industries in 1922–1927, such, for example, as the leather and woolen trades, is popular and sound, so far as it goes. But it does not take account of the fact that desire for new goods, or the pressure of installment purchases once made, may lead people to work harder or more steadily, and so get more dollars to spend. Presumably the enticements of automobiles and radios, of wrist watches and electric refrigerators, of correspondence courses and college, have steadied many youths, set many girls hunting for jobs and kept many fathers of families to the mark. Also a considerable part of the country's former bill for intoxicants has been available to spend in other ways. How much allowance we should make for these factors nobody knows. All one can say with assurance is that consumption per capita has increased in volume to match the increased per capita output of consumers' goods taken altogether. Yet the increase in consumption has not been rapid enough to prevent shifts in the kind of goods bought from pressing hard upon the makers of articles waning in popular favor.

So too in the realm of producers' goods. Despite the active building campaign, the lumber industry has had hard sledding. Coal mining has not prospered, and can attribute part of its difficulties to other fuels, water power, and more economical ways of burning coal itself. Breeders of draft animals have found their markets cut into by motor vehicles.

Railways have lost traffic to trucks and omnibusses—though the loss in freight tonnage is held by Professor Cunningham to be less than the public supposes. Steam-engine builders have had to change their products or reduce their output. It is not necessary to multiply examples; most technical improvements reduce the demand for some other good, and so create difficulties for those who supply the latter.

Geographical Shifts in Industry and Trade.—Just as definite a gain may be made in productivity by shifting factories to better locations, or by reorganizing channels of supply, as by installing automatic machines. Besides the drift of cotton manufacturing to the South, of which everyone thinks, and the more recent drift of shoe manufacturing to the West, the chapter on industry shows a prevailing tendency toward geographical decentralizing of production. The proportion of the output of many goods coming from the old headquarters is on the decline. The chapter on agriculture indicates a parallel development in farming. The cotton belt is stretching west, the wheat belt west and northwest; the dairying and the market-garden areas are moving in various directions. Finally, the chapter on marketing shows a concentration of trade in cities and towns at the expense of villages.

Doubtless these changes are to the advantage of those who make them. If they proved unprofitable, they would be abandoned. But it is equally clear that we have here another feature of increasing efficiency which brings losses as well as gains. New England may not lose as much as North Carolina and St. Louis gain from the shifts in the cotton and shoe trades—that is a question of the totals. And New England may devise new ways of using its labor, its capital, its manufacturing sites, and its ingenuity, more profitable than the old—necessity is often the mother of invention. If these efforts succeed, they may create fresh difficulties felt elsewhere. Similar truisms might be recited concerning the other cases in point. But whatever happens in the future, we must not let the dazzle of the high lights blind us to the sectional shadows.

"Technological Unemployment."—Among all the hardships imposed by increasing efficiency, most publicity has been given to the decline in the number of wage earners employed by factories. That is a matter of the gravest concern in view of the millions of families affected or threatened by the change, and in view of their slender resources. To it special attention has been paid in this investigation.

The new phrase coined to describe what is happening, "technological unemployment," designates nothing new in the facts, though the numbers affected may be large beyond precedent. Ever since Ricardo shocked his rigid disciples by admitting that the introduction of "labor-saving" machinery may cause a temporary diminution of employment, economists have discussed this problem. Granting Ricardo's admission, they have nevertheless held that, in the long run, changes in method which heighten efficiency tend to benefit wage earners. English experience since Ricardo's day seems to bear out this contention. The power looms, which put an end to hand-loom weaving after tragic struggles, have not reduced the number of British workers employed in weaving, or cut their average earnings. The railways, which displaced the old mail coaches and carters, have not reduced the number of transport workers or made them poorer. And the new trades of building and caring for the elaborate modern equipment must not be forgotten. There doubtless are cases in which improvements in methods have caused what promises to be a permanent reduction in the number of persons employed in an industry. By defining industry narrowly, these cases can be made numerous. But the broad result plainly has been that the industrial triumphs of the nineteenth century increased the demand for labor and increased its rewards. "Labor-saving" machinery has turned out to be job-making machinery.

To recall these familiar facts should not diminish by one jot our rating of the hardships suffered by men who are thrown out of jobs. They and their families often undergo severe privation before new employment can be found; the new jobs may pay less than the old or be less suitable; too often the displaced man never finds a new opening. Technical progress is continually made at cost to individuals who have committed no fault and committed no avoidable error of judgment. No organized plan has been evolved for preventing such hardships, aside from the schemes devised by some trade unions for tiding their members over mechanical revolutions in their crafts. The nations have left the remedy to "natural forces;" they have trusted that the expansion of production, which improvements bring about, will presently open new places for the displaced workers.

The problem of what happened in the short period 1922–1927, then, is to find how many wage earners were displaced in that time, how many of the displaced found new jobs promptly, and what these new jobs were. To answer these questions accurately would require far better data than are to be had. There are few branches of statistics in which the United States lags further behind the leaders than in statistics of employment. What we have been able to learn comes to this:

Starting with the 1920 census of occupations and reckoning forward, it is estimated that by 1927 there had been an increase of about 5,100,000 employees 16 years of age and over, who looked to nonagricultural occupations for a living. The figure allows for the fact that some 860,000 persons had left the farms to seek livelihoods elsewhere, and the more than offsetting fact that the number of pupils over 15, enrolled in schools and colleges, had risen by 1,430,000 between 1920 and 1927.

Of the 5,100,000 net additions to nonagricultural job seekers, a few turned to mining and allied occupations; 100,000 entered public services, over 600,000 engaged in construction work of some sort, nearly a million attached themselves to "transportation and communication," 1,400,000 became mercantile employees, and more than two and a half millions took to miscellaneous occupations in hotels, restaurants, garages, repair shops, moving-picture places, barber shops, hospitals, insurance work, professional offices, and the like. Manufacturing is the only large occupational group, aside from farming, to show a decline. There the number of employees fell from about 11,200,000 in 1920 to about 10,600,000 in 1927—a drop of 600,000. (See Chap. VI, Labor, Section IV.)

All these data are estimates of the net changes in numbers of persons "attached to" the occupations in question. They show that American wage earners met "technological unemployment" in manufacturing mainly by turning to other ways of making a living. The decline from 1920 to 1927 in the number of persons actually at work in manufacturing enterprises is put at 825,000, but the number of *unemployed* among the people who depended on factory work for a living increased only 240,000 between 1920 and 1927, according to the best figures available. If these estimates are approximately correct, then some 585,000 of the workers laid off by factories had taken up other occupations. That is, 71 per cent of the workers displaced had attached themselves to new trades by 1927.

Adopting a new occupation, however, does not guarantee getting a new job. The surplus workers from our farms and factories who hunted for fresh openings increased unemployment in other fields. The expansion of business, particularly the expansion of miscellaneous and mercantile occupations, made places for perhaps four and a half million new wage earners. But the supply of new jobs has not been equal to the number of new workers plus the old workers displaced. Hence there has been a net increase of unemployment, between 1920 and 1927, which exceeds 650,000 people.

The number of the unemployed has varied from year to year with cyclical changes in business activity. It surpassed all previous records in the depression of 1921; it declined rather slowly in the revival of 1922; even in the busy year 1923 it remained higher than in 1920; it rose in the mild recession of 1924, declined on the return of activity in 1925–26, and then mounted again in 1927. The final estimates presented in the chapter on labor may be summarized as follows:

TABLE 8.—ESTIMATED AVERAGE MINIMUM VOLUME OF UNEMPLOYMENT IN THE
UNITED STATES, 1920–1927

Year	Nonagricultural wage and salary earners	Average minimum number unemployed	Percentage unemployed
1920.	27,558,000	1,401,000	5.1
1921.	27,989,000	4,270,000	15.3
1922.	28,505,000	3,441,000	12.1
1923.	29,293,000	1,532,000	5.2
1924.	30,234,000	2,315,000	7.7
1925.	30,941,000	1,775,000	5.7
1926.	31,808,000	1,669,000	5.2
1927.	32,695,000	2,055,000	6.3

It must be emphasized that these figures are merely the best estimates which it is possible to make from the scattered and imperfect materials available. They are subject to considerable margins of error. They minimize the seriousness of unemployment. Finally, even as minimum figures, these estimates do not profess to show the high points reached by unemployment in bad seasons—they give only yearly averages.

One may wonder at the versatility, initiative and mobility of Americans, as evidenced afresh by their prompt shifting of occupations on so great a scale in recent years. One may wonder also at the rapid expansion of the trades which have absorbed some five million employees in seven years without reducing wage rates. But one must not forget that these shiftings have been compulsory in large measure; men have been forced out of farming and forced out of factories as well as pulled into automobile services, shops and restaurants. And the employment balance is on the unfavorable side. While our economic progress has meant larger per capita earnings for all workers taken together, it has imposed severe suffering upon hundreds of thousands of individuals.

The Domestic Difficulties of Agriculture.—It was noted above that American farming owes part of its difficulties in 1922–1927 to reductions in foreign demand and increases in foreign supply. It must now be added that fresh difficulties have been created for farmers by changes in domestic demand, and by the successful efforts of farmers to increase their own efficiency as producers.

Chapter I shows that, all in all, the standard of living has been rising in the United States of late. But Americans have been eating less food per capita than once they did. The greater diversification of diet has been advantageous to dairymen, market gardeners and fruit growers; but the bulk of farmers have lost more than they have gained from the changes. Americans have also been wearing less clothing than formerly, and that hurts the market for cotton planters and wool growers. Moreover, there has been a shift from cotton and woolen fabrics toward silk and rayon. Finally, the goods on which American families have spent freely—automobiles and their accessories, gasoline, household furnishings and equipment, radios, travel, amusements and sports—are goods in which little agricultural produce is used.

To make matters harder, the firmness of wage rates in the flourishing industries has forced farmers to pay relatively high wages for such hired labor as they have needed. Taxes on farm property have risen in every year covered by the record. While the prices farmers had to pay for operating supplies and equipment, as well as for consumers' goods, dropped sharply in 1921, they did not drop nearly so much as the prices which farmers received for their products. Fluctuations in the two sets of prices since 1921 have redressed the inequality only in part.[26]

It is a grave error to think of American farmers as the passive but complaining victims of calamity. Chapter VIII shows that they have exhibited as vigorous a capacity for self-help as any other large section of the community. The qualities which enabled their forerunners to subdue the wilderness reappear in the efforts of the present generation to work a way out of the postwar tangle.

But agriculture is a business of very slow turnover. Agriculture is also an extrahazardous business, which depends for results on averages over a series of harvests. The dislocations it faces at present are partly the result of continuing secular trends, rather than cyclical fluctuations which reverse themselves every few years. And agriculture is a business in which millions of producers are working each on his own account. A concerted policy is exceedingly difficult to organize. What one farmer does to help himself often makes matters harder for other farmers. That is the aspect of the farm problem which requires attention here.

The individual farmer, hard pressed by low prices and high fixed costs, has tried several ways to better his fortunes. One way alleviates the lot of other farmers, whether it turns out well for himself or not. It is to give up farming. Dr. C. J. Galpin estimates that there was a net decrease of farm population amounting to 460,000 persons in 1922, perhaps a larger number in 1923, 182,000 in 1924 when city jobs were harder to get, and 479,000 in 1926. We have already noticed Dr. M. B. Givens' estimate that in 1920–1927 upwards of a million migrants from the farm sought other occupations. So far as reduction in number of workers goes, there is a close parallel between the record of farming and of manufacturing.[27]

---

[26] See the latest Department of Agriculture indexes in Chapter VIII, p. 548.

[27] Commenting upon this passage, Dr. E. G. Nourse suggests that this shrinkage in the number of farm workers seems likely to continue. Agriculture bids fair definitely and permanently to lose numbers as a result of changes in technique. The new branches of farming which are growing up take many less hands than are displaced in the old staple lines. Thus the industry as a whole is giving up workers to other callings.

This considerable shift in population has been accompanied by a much slighter decline in the area of land cultivated. The abandonment of poor farms has unquestionably been accelerated by hard times, though we lack comprehensive data to show on what scale. On the other hand, wide tracts of former waste lands have been reclaimed and wider tracts of former cattle ranges have been brought under the plow. The net outcome of these contrary movements is perhaps best shown by the Department of Agriculture's report of the acreage in 19 principal crops. From 351 million acres in 1919, the area declined unsteadily to 342 millions in 1924, rose above 350 millions in 1926, and then shrank by three-quarters of a million acres in 1927.

But the smaller numbers of workers left on farms, cultivating slightly less land, have increased their output—again paralleling developments in manufacturing. The Department of Agriculture's index showing "mass of crop production" mounted from 100 in 1919—a year of fair harvests—to 102 in 1922, 104 in 1925, and 106 in 1927. If these figures were reduced to a per capita basis, the rate of increase would be decidedly greater. Of course, every farmer who has enlarged his output has contributed his mite toward keeping down prices. Agricultural depression had forced the individual farmer to meet his narrow margins above cost by raising more units to sell, and selling more units has tended to make these margins narrower still.

Increased productivity per worker in agriculture has been achieved in the same way as increased productivity per worker in manufacturing— by putting more intelligence into the work. For decades, agricultural experiment stations, colleges, state bureaus, farm papers, and the Department of Agriculture in Washington have been actively seeking to learn and to teach better methods of farming. From drainage to the choice of crops, the breeding of stock and the building of fireplaces, scarcely any feature of farming as a technical process, as a business enterprise, or as a way of making a home but has been studied intensively and written up extensively. Slowly the lessons have been learned by an increasing number of farmers and farmers' wives. The pressure of hard times speeded up the application of knowledge to practice, despite the fact that hard times cut down the farmers' ability to accumulate the capital which many of the changes require.

One of the conspicuous changes in methods of farming has reacted most unfavorably upon the demand for farm products. The number of tractors in use on farms is estimated to have increased from 80,000 in January, 1918, to 380,000 in 1922, and 770,000 in January, 1928. This change has been accompanied by a decrease in the number of horses and mules on farms from about 26,400,000 in 1918 and 1919 to 20,100,000 in 1928. An even greater decline was occurring at the same time in the number of horses and mules in cities. A not inconsiderable branch of animal husbandry thus lost much of its market. What was worse, at least 15 to 18 million acres of hay and grain land lost its market also.

To get a just impression of the versatility farmers have shown in coping with their difficulties, one must turn back to the chapter on agriculture, or even to the books there cited. That with all their courage and ability they have not yet succeeded in regaining their former measure of prosperity, must be ascribed partly to the slowness of agricultural processes themselves, partly to the halting recuperation of Europe and its reactions on other countries, and partly to the fact that increasing efficiency has added to the supply of farm products or cut down the demand.

Agricultural depression has not been confined to the United States. In many other countries, the tillers of the soil have been engaged in a similar struggle with unfavorable conditions of supply and demand. Their efforts to make up for the relatively low prices received for their products by marketing larger quantities, and their compulsory retrenchments of expenditure, have reacted unfavorably upon the fortunes of American farmers, just as the similar actions of American farmers have made conditions harder for them. Round a good part of the globe, the productivity of agriculture has been rising, while in most of the leading industrial nations other branches of production have grown slowly if at all. The effect upon prices in the great world markets has been striking. The demand for agricultural products as a whole is inelastic compared with the demand for many industrial products. That is, a relatively small increase in the current supply of foodstuffs, the great agricultural staple, brings a relatively large decline in market prices. Hence the change in the international balance of agricultural and non-agricultural output has created a difficult situation for farmers, even in the few countries, like the United States, where production in other lines has increased rapidly.

What has been the net effect of all the factors, domestic and foreign, influencing the economic fortunes of American farmers, is hard to ascertain. The preceding chapters on agriculture and on national income present the facts from various angles. That is desirable; for no simple summary of so complicated a situation can be adequate. But perhaps the following figures, which purport to show the changing relations between the average per capita incomes of farmers and of the whole population, are as significant as any which might be chosen.

Though the estimates from which these percentages are drawn (columns 10 and 11 of Table 12 in Chap. XII) are the best results our investigators have been able to get from the available data, they are subject to an uncertain margin of error. That the figures differ in certain respects from what most people, including our investigators themselves, would expect to find is not seriously disturbing; for expectations in such matters are notoriously biased by cases which have impressed our minds because of their striking character.

TABLE 9.—ESTIMATED PER CAPITA INCOMES OF AMERICAN FARMERS AS PERCENTAGES OF ESTIMATED PER CAPITA INCOMES OF THE TOTAL POPULATION, IN VARIOUS YEARS

Prewar years		Postwar years	
1913.................	39 per cent	1919.................	57 per cent
1914.................	39 per cent	1920.................	46 per cent
		1921.................	34 per cent
		1922.................	35 per cent
		1923.................	36 per cent
		1924.................	37 per cent
		1925.................	39 per cent

On the face of these returns, American farmers gained greatly in relative economic status between the beginning and the end of the war, though, even at their peak, agricultural incomes per capita remained far below the national average. The catastrophic drop from 1919 to 1921 wiped out all of this gain and considerably more. If our estimates are reliable, by 1925 farmers had won back to their prewar position in comparison with average per capita incomes in other occupations, but they were by no means so well off as in 1919–20. Unfortunately, the data for similar computations in years since 1925 are not yet available.

Even if these results be accepted as probably more reliable than general impressions, they do not represent adequately the farmer's relative position in the national economy. In particular, they show nothing of the financial entanglements into which many of the most enterprising American farmers were drawn in the flush years. A man may make as good a current income now as before the war and still be far worse off, if he is carrying a greatly increased load of debts. And quite apart from that, the not unfavorable income comparison which 1925 makes with prewar years is due to the use of shrinking per capita figures for farmers and swelling per capita figures for the total population. An industry which keeps up its per capita quota of the national income because thousands of workers withdraw from it cannot be regarded as flourishing.

VII. THE INTERRELATIONS AMONG ECONOMIC CHANGES

The Factors Already Discussed.—So far, the contrasts noted at the outset of this chapter between the economic fortunes of different income groups, different industries, and different sections of the United States in 1922–1927, have been traced to three factors—or rather to three great complexes of factors. (1) Foreign conditions on the whole have been none too favorable to American business, and they have been eminently unfavorable to American agriculture. Important branches of industry have enjoyed a large increase in foreign sales; but had Europe been prosperous, American prosperity would have been less "spotty" and more intense.[28] (2) Such prosperity as we have enjoyed has been earned by many-sided and strenuous efforts, in which millions of people have shared, to improve our technical methods, our business management, our trade-union policy, and our Government administration. (3) While increasing efficiency has added to real income, it has put pressure, often rising to severe hardship, upon competitors, direct and indirect. The factory hand competing with the "automatic" machine, the horse farmer competing with the tractor farmer, the lumber industry competing with the cement industry, the New England cotton mill competing with the North Carolina cotton mill, the independent retailer competing with the chain store, the clothing trade competing with the makers of automobiles and radios for slices of the consumers' dollars, have had a hard time.

This analysis is not simple, but it is still too schematic. There is no hope of learning and telling the whole story in realistic detail. Yet one further factor of great moment and two sets of "economic reactions" must be introduced before a summing up is attempted.

Retardation in the Growth of Population and Its Effects.—The additional factor to be taken into account concerns population growth. In sketching the main lines of nineteenth century experience, it was noted that the fruits of the tree of applied knowledge can be consumed in several ways. One way is to increase population as fast as the tree increases its yield. If that course is pushed to the limit, there can be no reduction of working hours and no advance in the standard of living. The latter gains are contingent upon keeping the growth of population slower than the gain in productive efficiency. And before the close of the century the European stock had sensibly reduced its birth rate.

This reduction of birth rates has been going on during our period in most of the states of the Union. The decline seems to be more rapid than the decline in death rates. Moreover, first the war and then legislation restricted immigration. The chapter on labor sums up the results in the following way:

[28] Once more the reader is reminded that this summary deals only with broad features. Important details, passed by in silence here, are brought out in the preceding chapters.

	Net immigration into the United States	Average per year
Prewar period July 1, 1907–June, 30, 1914............	4,645,590	663,656
War and early postwar period July 1, 1914–June 30, 1921............	1,253,652	179,093
Quota-restriction period July 1, 1921–June 30, 1927............	1,873,311	312,219

Combined, the birth-rate and death-rate changes and the changes in migration reduced the average annual increase of population from 1,800,000 in 1920–1925 to 1,545,000 in 1925–1928.

The retardation in population growth has affected the whole social situation profoundly in ways which concern the student of sociology and politics quite as deeply as they concern the economist. It will be long before the full effects upon national life become clear. But certain prompt economic consequences must be noted.

At the close of the war, when a fall in the price level like that of 1865 was expected by many, business executives frequently said that the first task of reorganization was to "liquidate labor." The great buying campaign of 1919 and the accompanying uprush of prices caused a postponement of this program. For a time it was hard to get men enough, even at rising rates. When prices fell precipitously in 1920–21 and unemployment was rife, the moment to insist on wage reductions seemed to have come. But the trade unions offered strenuous resistance, despite the number of the temporarily idle. Their resistance was more effective than it could have been had not the growth of population been retarded for some years. The prices of labor were cut, to be sure, but not cut as much as the prices of consumers' goods. Hence, when employment became tolerably full again toward the close of 1922, wage earners found themselves in possession of relatively large purchasing power. Then the economic advantages of a broad consumers' market began to appear. Employers discovered that their inability to "liquidate labor" had been fortunate for themselves, as well as for their employees. The doctrine of high wages found conspicuous champions among the business leaders, and their formulations favored its spread. Discoveries in science, as well as in practical life, have often been made thus by observing the consequences of a thwarted effort.

In most periods of prosperity, wage rates lag somewhat behind living costs on the rise. The indications are that these paradoxical "prosperity losses" to wage earners have not cut much figure during 1922–1927. Wholesale prices have sagged slightly, and living costs have advanced but little. Though the percentage of unemployment has risen since 1923, wage rates have been firmly maintained on the whole, if not increased somewhat.

This result also must be ascribed in part to the relatively slow increase in the number of job hunters. Had there been no legal check on immigration in 1922–1927, unemployment would have attained large proportions, and the difficulty of maintaining wage rates would have been greater.

Moreover, it seems sound to ascribe a part of the gains in technical efficiency, which have been so characteristic of recent years, to the high price of labor. An employee to whom one pays high wages may represent low labor cost. But if he is to be so efficient as to be cheap, he must be provided with good equipment and aided by good management. More horse power per man and better management per man, to twist Mr. Dennison's flexible phrase, are needed to secure more production per man; and more production must be had per man when more wages are paid per man.

All this discussion on a per capita basis is proper; to make clear how proper, consider the effect of retardation in population growth upon aggregate production and wealth. Had there been no reduction in birth rates and no restriction of immigration, the United States would contain several millions more people than it does. As large or a larger fraction of the greater population would be "engaged in gainful occupations," and, despite more unemployment and a less advanced stage of industrial technique, the workers would probably be producing a greater volume of goods. Thus, the national income would be rising faster than it is; but per capita income would be growing slower than it is. Since birth-rate restriction seems to be voluntary, and since immigration restriction certainly is, we must conclude that Americans are preferring to raise the economic level of average life rather than to maximize national wealth.

Mutually Moderating and Mutually Intensifying Reactions.—The two sets of economic reactions still to be noted may be thought of as the mutually moderating effects of factors opposing each other, and as the mutually intensifying effects of factors working in the same direction.

Like the set of economic reactions already discussed—the pressure exerted on competitors by those who increase their own efficiency—these moderating and intensifying effects arise from the basic feature of economic organization. Though modern society accepts the principle of individual responsibility, each individual gets his money income wholly by serving others, and gets his real income mainly by consuming goods other people have made. Thus everyone depends both on the buying power of other consumers and on the efficiency of other producers. And what is true of every individual is true, *mutatis mutandis*, of every business enterprise. These intricate relations of interdependence tangle the skein of economic causes and effects beyond the present power of man to unravel. Every development is the net resultant of numerous causes and also the cause of numerous effects. But though we can not disentangle all the crisscrossing influences of the factors which have shaped American fortunes in 1922–1927, we can follow certain of their salient reactions upon each other.

To take first the moderating effects of opposing factors: American prosperity in 1922–1927, in nonagricultural lines, would have been decidedly greater had the six million American farmers been flourishing. Every man thrown out of work has subtracted an iota from the national dividend and an iota from the demand for goods. Every business that has failed has made a tiny difference in our ability to provide for our wants and to market our products. The United States as a whole would have been better off if all foreign countries had enjoyed fortunes equal to its own.

On the other hand, the farmers would have been in far worse plight if the majority of Americans had not been receiving relatively large incomes, and if American factories and railways had not been highly efficient as servants of agriculture. So too, the unemployed would have been more numerous, and their difficulties in getting new jobs greater, had the country suffered from industrial depression. Finally, other countries would have been worse off, had we not been in position to import freely, and to make large loans.

There can be no doubt about the reality or the importance of these reactions of hardship in diminishing prosperity, and of prosperity in diminishing hardship. But there seems to be no way of measuring such complicated influences with the data available.

Clearer still are the effects of one favorable development in reinforcing other favorable developments, and the corresponding intensification of misfortune by misfortune. In this period and in our country, the former set of cumulations has been more in evidence than the latter. And it is necessary to bring these reactions of favorable developments upon each other into the foreground of our final picture. For we cannot understand any single factor in the situation, such as increasing technological efficiency, the rising standard of living, the relatively stable price level, the large volume of construction, the abundance of capital and credit, or large income disbursements, without noting how other factors favored its development.

Take, for example, keener intelligence applied to the day's work, which increased the physical output of goods. That has meant the possibility of larger average real incomes per capita. To distribute these goods, market experts cultivated the desires of the people for a freer and more varied consumption; they developed plans by which the eager could satisfy wants before they could pay. A sound monetary and banking system provided the requisite currency and credit to run this whole process of producing and distributing a swelling river of goods. Price fluctuations were held within narrow limits by a combination of prudence among business men, unit-cost reductions by technical experts, skill on the part of bankers, and the course of foreign markets. This relative stability of prices reinforced the pressure upon all parties to exercise caution, calculate closely, and watch costs; it also helped to keep world prices relatively stable. Since prices were not buoyant, business enterprises had to maintain a high level of efficiency in order to make profits, and that fact intensified the application of intelligence with which this paragraph started. By the aid of the reinforced efficiency, it has been possible to pay high wages and salaries, meet interest and rental charges, distribute liberal dividends, and still retain large surpluses for protecting or expanding business ventures. The large income disbursements provided the purchasing power to which the market experts appealed for the purchase of the increased physical output of goods. Meanwhile, the considerable profits reaped by the large number of efficient enterprises made them eager to grow. At the same time, prosperous families wanted better housing; prosperous communities wanted larger schools; prosperous states wanted hard-surfaced roads. So the routine business of providing current income was supplemented by an exceptional volume of new construction to provide industrial equipment of all kinds, office buildings, single dwellings, apartments, hotels, theaters, schools and highways. That required capital running into billions of dollars. The demand was met without strain from the surpluses of business enterprises and the savings of individuals whose higher standards of living had not absorbed all of their money incomes. And of course the construction work, as it proceeded, enlarged the market for a vast variety of goods, and enlarged the disbursements of income.

So one might go on indefinitely, tracing the fashion in which each of the prosperity-producing factors in the situation has increased the activity out of which it grew, and thus promoted conditions which heightened its own efficiency. The broad facts, however, are patent. And no·elaboration would lead to a convincing evaluation of what credit belongs to any single factor taken by itself. Drop out any of the developments recalled in the preceding paragraph, and the process as a whole would be altered. It is just as impossible to say what high wages, large construction, skillful marketing, railroad efficiency, or abundant credit contributed to prosperity, as it is to say how much agricultural depression, technological unemployment, or the lingering troubles of Europe have diminished the prosperity which might have been attained but for these drawbacks.

Net Effects upon Average Per Capita Income.—Reasons were given above for accepting the estimate of per capita income, expressed in dollars of constant purchasing power, as the most inclusive, and probably the most reliable, summary of the net results flowing from all the myriad changes which affect the economic welfare of the country's people. Accordingly, we return to these figures as the best general conclusion of the whole investigation. Two series of figures are given. The first shows income received in money; the second "disbursed income"—that is, money receipts plus the value of income yielded by homes occupied by their owners and by household goods, the value of farm produce consumed by the producers and minor items of similar nature. The first series corresponds closely to the common conception of income, but the other is a better index of economic welfare. The following comments refer to the second series.*

TABLE 10.—PER CAPITA INCOME IN THE UNITED STATES EXPRESSED IN 1925 DOLLARS

	Income received in money	Disbursed income
1913...................	$554	$621
1917...................	579	656
1919...................	510	611
1920...................	520	600
1921...................	500	576
1922...................	557	625
1923...................	616	679
1924...................	628	697
1925...................	647	714
1926...................	659[a]	733[a]

[a] Preliminary.

From the trough in which the war and the war-dominated cycle of 1919–1921 left the country, Americans raised their average fortunes to the prewar level in a single year of reviving activity. A second year of great gains left the old records far behind. Since 1923, progress has been steady, but less rapid.

Unless these figures are very far in error, not only absolutely but also relatively, the final verdict upon the years 1922–1926, and presumably upon 1927 and 1928, for which the income record is yet incomplete,

* The difference between income received in money and disbursed income appears to be decreasing rapidly in relation to total income, with some indications of an absolute decrease as well. Presumably this change is explained, in part, by the increasing percentage of the population that lives in rented quarters.—Note by M. C. Rorty, Director.

must be that they brought good times to the majority of our people—
though by no means to all.

VIII. BUSINESS CYCLES IN 1921–1927

The Question whether Business Cycles Have Been "Ironed Out."—
A final characteristic of the last few years in the United States is the
relative stability of business. It is not by oversight that little is said
about business cycles in the preceding chapters. In statistical parlance,
the conspicuous feature of recent economic changes is the rising trend in
output per worker and average income, rather than cyclical fluctuations.
The United States has not had a genuine "boom" in business at large
since 1919; it has not had a "commercial crisis" since 1920, or a severe
depression since 1921. Violent contrasts of economic fortune are
found; but they run side by side in different industries. Violent changes
in certain activities have occurred from year to year; but they have been
localized industrially or geographically, like the rise and collapse of the
Florida land speculation. Even the "bull market" on the New York.
Stock Exchange, which has reached such heights in 1928–29, seems not
to have infected business in commodities. For the country as a whole,
both current opinions and statistical indexes indicate that production,
transportation and distribution have been maintained for the last few
years on a high, but not exceedingly high, level, with brief periods of
contraction, to which the term "depression" seems scarcely applicable.

This relative stability has encouraged optimists to say that "the
business cycle" has been "ironed out" in the United States; that our
last cycle ended in 1921, and that we need not fear a serious reaction in
the future. The forecast in this statement we may leave for the future
to test, reserving our attention to what has already happened.

The validity of the optimistic view depends on the meaning attached
to the term "business cycles." If no fluctuation in economic activity
be counted a cycle unless it includes a boom, crisis, and severe depression—
as these vague terms are commonly understood—then it is true that the
United States has had no business cycle since 1919–1921. But on that
interpretation, "the business cycle" was "ironed out" in the United
States before the war. From 1909 to 1913 the oscillations in general
business activity were notably moderate. Nor was that the first stretch
of rather uneventful business years either in this country or elsewhere, as
Dr. Willard L. Thorp's collection of *Business Annals* shows. However, a
discussion of recent changes in business cycles is of little use when conducted in such vague terms. Not unless the amplitudes of successive
cycles can be measured and compared, is it possible to reach definite
conclusions.

How This Question Can Be Answered.—For some time the National
Bureau has been engaged in making such measurements. Though

designed for a larger purpose, they can be applied to the present problem. All the statistical series representing changes in economic activities by months or quarters, for as many years as possible, are being collected for several countries and analyzed on a uniform plan, to find how they behave during business cycles. From these materials we may select the leading American series which cover several prewar cycles, add a few especially significant series covering a briefer period, and arrange the measurements to answer the question in hand.

The first step, in measuring the amplitudes of cyclical fluctuations in statistical series, is to fix a set of "reference dates" marking the beginning, peak, and ending of the general business cycles in each country dealt with. These dates show the year and month of successive cyclical revivals and recessions. They are determined roughly by a study of business annals and made more precise by a study of what statistical data are available from case to case. (2) Each series is then broken into "reference-cycle segments" on the basis of the reference dates. (3) The average value of a series during each reference-cycle segment is computed, and the original data are turned into percentages of these averages as 100. This use of percentages, or relatives, makes it possible to compare the fluctuations of the same series in different cycles and of different series in the same cycle. It eliminates the greater part of the secular trends of the series, but retains what may be called the "intra-cycle trends." (4) The relatives are examined to see whether they show appreciable seasonal variations. If so, the seasonals are determined and eliminated by methods which need not be described. After this step has been taken, a series is in shape to have its cyclical behavior measured in various ways.

The measurements of present concern relate to the amplitude of the rise from the early trough in a cycle to the peak, and of the fall from the peak to the subsequent trough. Such figures are given in Table 12. Though the basic chronology is furnished by the list of reference dates, the low, high, low turning points given in the table are those found in the several series. Most series lead or lag behind the revivals and recessions in general business. To diminish the influence of random fluctuations, we use three-months averages centered, instead of actual standings in the single months when a series touches its peak or trough.

The Duration of Prewar and Postwar Cycles in General Business.— Before examining this table in detail, it is well to see how recent business cycles in the United States compare with their predecessors in respect to duration. Table 11, giving the reference dates used in marking off cycles in general business activity over a period of 73 years, provides the necessary data.

Of course, there is an element of the arbitrary in fixing the beginning and end of these cycles so definitely as the table pretends to do. In dealing with a single series, one commonly, though not invariably, finds clearly marked cyclical turning points. But in a collection of different series these points never all fall in the same month. Yet some month within the period when most series touch bottom and turn up, or reach the peak and turn down, must be selected as a marker, even though its claim to represent the turn of the general tide may be no better than that of several neighboring months. The uncertainty which month to select is greatest when business continues active or dull on much the same level for a considerable time before it declines or rises. One of the most difficult problems presented by the whole list of reference dates in Table 11 is when to date the recession in the latest cycle covered. November 1926, was finally fixed upon, though almost equally good cases can be made out for several other months ranging from April, 1925, when wholesale prices began receding from their peak, to March, 1927, when the operating revenues of railroads began to decline. Our practice in such cases is to choose a date as near the end of the nearly level stretch as the data justify.

TABLE 11.—STANDARD REFERENCE DATES FOR BUSINESS CYCLES, UNITED STATES

Expansion		Contraction		Duration in months		
Revival	High	Recession	Low	Expansion	Contraction	Full cycle
January 1855 to June 1857		July 1857 to December 1858		30	18	48
January 1859 to October 1860		November 1860 to June 1861		22	8	30
July 1861 to April 1865		May 1865 to December 1867		46	32	78
January 1868 to June 1869		July 1869 to December 1870		18	18	36
January 1871 to October 1873		November 1873 to March 1879		34	65	99
April 1879 to March 1882		April 1882 to May 1885		36	38	74
June 1885 to March 1887		April 1887 to April 1888		22	13	35
May 1888 to July 1890		August 1890 to May 1891		27	10	37
June 1891 to January 1893		February 1893 to June 1894		20	17	37
July 1894 to December 1895		January 1896 to June 1897		18	18	36
July 1897 to June 1899		July 1899 to December 1900		24	18	42
January 1901 to September 1902		October 1902 to August 1904		21	23	44
September 1904 to May 1907		June 1907 to June 1908		33	13	46
July 1908 to January 1910		February 1910 to January 1912		19	24	43
February 1912 to January 1913		February 1913 to December 1914		12	23	35
January 1915 to August 1918		September 1918 to April 1919		44	8	52
May 1919 to January 1920		February 1920 to September 1921		9	20	29
October 1921 to May 1923		June 1923 to July 1924		20	14	34
August 1924 to October 1926		November 1926 to December 1927		27	14	41
Average duration						
19 cycles, 1855 to 1927, ...				25.4	20.7	46.1
13 cycles, 1885 to 1927, ...				22.8	16.5	39.3

Accepting these decisions, we find certain peculiarities in the duration of recent cycles. (1) The World-War cycle brought a period of activity exceeded in length only by the expansion phase of the Civil-War cycle. The subsequent contraction lasted only eight months, and is matched in brevity only by the contraction which preceded the Civil War. These two segments produce the longest full cycle the country has experienced in a generation, though it falls far short of three earlier cycles covered by the table. (2) The first postwar cycle was correspondingly brief—29 months as against 52. Its period of expansion was the shortest in the record, less than a third of the full cycle. On the average, the phase of expansion lasts appreciably longer than the phase of contraction. (3) The cycle of 1921–1924 represented a return toward the average duration and the average relations of the two phases. But it still fell five months short of the average for full cycles since 1885—a more representative figure for current experience than the average which includes the Civil War and the prolonged depression of the 1870's. (4) A still closer return to the average appears in the last cycle. The reference dates make it 41 months long, or 1.7 months longer than the preferred average. The prosperous phase is an unusually large fraction of the whole; but, as said above, the date for recession in this case is hard to fix.

So far as durations go, then, business cycles have reverted to type after the aberrations of the war. Of course that historical fact does not justify anyone in counting upon 40-month cycles in the near future, for the table shows that cycle lengths are "subject to change without notice."

Conformity of Different Activities to the Standard Cyclical Pattern.—If business cycles are in process of being "ironed out," as time passes we shall find an increasing number of series which do not undergo cyclical contractions. Twenty series are included in Table 12. How many of them show all the recessions in recent years which Table 11 shows for general business? And what series depart from this standard pattern? The answers may be given in schedule form.

Ten series conform to the standard cyclical pattern throughout the period since 1914.

One series (interest rates on commercial paper) passed through two cycles during the war, but has conformed closely since 1919.

Two series (bank clearings outside of New York City and liabilities of bankrupt concerns) skipped the mild recession at the end of the war, but have conformed closely since 1921.

One series (exports of merchandise) has only three cycles since 1914, instead of the standard number four. But this series did not conform with regularity before the war, presumably because the volume of merchandise which the United States can sell abroad depends more upon business conditions in foreign countries than upon business conditions at home.

Three series (the index number of farm prices of crops, cattle and hog receipts at Chicago) have the standard number of cycles, but the dates of their turning points are erratic. Such is the usual case with agricultural series, for the weather changes which exert such an influence upon farm prices, fodder crops and the marketing of stock, seldom run a course parallel to general business activity for several years in succession.

Three series skipped the cyclical decline of 1926–27—anthracite coal production, dividend disbursements by industrial corporations, and number of shares sold on the New York Stock Exchange. Hog receipts had turned downward in 1923 and cattle receipts in December, 1924. All the other series in our sample, 15 out of 20, suffered a fall beginning in some month between April, 1925 and March, 1927.

The test here applied to determine whether the behavior of a given series conforms to the standard cyclical pattern is rather exacting. Unless a series rises within the period labeled expansion in Table 11, and falls within the period labeled contraction, it is set down as failing in conformity. A change in this practice will be called for if the effort to smooth out business cycles succeeds gradually. For in smoothing out these cycles the stage should come when alternating phases of expansion and contraction will be reduced to alternating accelerations and retardations of a rising secular trend. A cycle will remain; but it will be so attenuated that the statistician will have to measure it in varying rates of increase, not in plus and minus items. Even now such measurements are useful. They prove that general business conditions exercise some influence upon processes which skip cyclical declines. If the measurements in Table 12 were made into average rates of change per month, they would show a higher degree of conformity to the standard cyclical pattern than is credited here. But so long as fundamental business factors, like employment, bank clearings, wholesale prices, physical production, new construction, and railroad revenues continue to exhibit actual declines, we have not attained the acceleration-retardation stage. What progress toward that stage can we claim?

The Amplitudes of Prewar, War and Postwar Business Cycles.— A sharp picture of each of the last five cycles in the United States, against a background of prewar experience, can be drawn from the amplitude entries in Table 12. Thirteen of the twenty series cover seven or more prewar cycles, and conform passably in timing to most or to all of the standard reference cycles since 1914.

(1) In the last prewar cycle, February 1912 to December 1914, the amplitude of the rise was relatively slight. Imports and immigration are the only series among the thirteen which rose more than the prewar average.

The contraction promised for a time to have the same gentle character; but it was aggravated by the outbreak of the war in July 1914. Even so, the amplitude of the fall failed to reach the prewar average in seven of the thirteen series. Of course male immigration from the belligerent countries was severely checked by the call to the colors; that is the only series in which the decline was much greater than usual.

All in all, the cycle was exceptionally mild.

(2) In the war cycle, January, 1915 to April, 1919, the rise exceeded the prewar average, except in anthracite coal shipments, immigration,

TABLE 12.—AMPLITUDE OF THE CYCLICAL FLUCTUATIONS IN LEADING AMERICAN TIME SERIES DURING PREWAR, WAR AND POSTWAR BUSINESS CYCLES
The amplitudes are expressed in percentages of the average value of a series during each business cycle. Seasonal variations are eliminated.

	Dates of cyclical turning points			Standing at cyclical turning points			Amplitudes of cyclical fluctuations		
	First low	High	Last low	First low	High	Last low	Rise	Fall	Rise and fall
Index of General Business. American Telephone and Telegraph Company.									
Prewar cycles. Average of 10..	....	....	....	88.5	110.6	87.2	22.1	23.4	45.5
Last prewar cycle..............	May '11	Jan. '13	Dec. '14	96	109	81	13	28	41
War cycle....................	Jan. '15	Nov. '16	Mar. '19	76	110	86	34	24	58
Postwar cycles................	Apr. '19	Mar. '20	July '21	98	117	77	19	40	59
	Aug. '21	June '23	July '24	75	117	87	42	30	72
	Aug. '24	Oct. '26	Dec. '27	82	105	92	23	13	36
Index of Industrial Employment. Jerome and Bureau of Labor Statistics.									
Prewar cycles. Average of 7...	....	....	....	89.4	106.3	96.3	16.9	10.0	26.9
Last prewar cycle..............	Jan. '12	Feb. '13	Jan. '15	97	103	95	6	8	14
War cycle....................	Feb. '15	Feb. '17	Feb. '19	84	108	95	24	13	37
Postwar cycles................	Mar. '19	June '20	Jan. '21	101	116	76	15	40	55
	Feb. '21	June '23	July '24	82	109	91	27	18	45
	Aug. '24	Mar. '26	Jan. '28	94	104	93	10	11	21
Immigration, male.									
Prewar cycles. Average of 14...	....	....	....	56.7	159.8	62.9	103.1	96.9	200.0
Last prewar cycle..............	Aug. '11	July '13	Feb. '15	64	208	18	144	190	334
War cycle....................	Mar. '15	Sept. '16	Nov. '17	77	168	21	91	147	238
Postwar cycles................	Dec. '17	Jan. '21	Mar. '22	105	179	26	74	153	227
	Apr. '22	July '23	Aug. '25	28	248	46	220	202	422
	Sept. '25	May '26	June '28	76	121	77	45	44	89
Index of Industrial Production, revised. Includes Mining. Standard Statistics Corporation.									
Prewar cycle..................	Jan. '11	May '13	Nov. '14	74	114	74	40	40	80
War cycle....................	Dec. '14	Oct. '16	May '19	59	113	87	54	26	80
Postwar cycles................	June '19	Mar. '20	Apr. '21	95	119	78	24	41	65
	May '21	May '23	June '24	66	119	91	53	28	81
	July '24	Sept. '26	Dec. '27	79	108	96	29	12	41
Pig iron production. Daily average.									
Prewar cycles. Average of 9...	....	....	....	59.9	127.4	72.4	67.6	55.0	122.6
Last prewar cycle..............	Aug. '11	Feb. '13	Dec. '14	76	125	63	49	62	111
War cycle....................	Jan. '15	July '18	May '19	48	116	68	68	48	116
Postwar cycles................	June '19	Mar. '20	July '21	89	140	39	51	101	152
	Aug. '21	June '23	July '24	34	143	69	109	74	183
	Aug. '24	Sept. '26	Dec. '27	63	117	86	54	31	85
Anthracite coal shipments.									
Prewar cycles. Average of 8....	....	....	....	72.1	126.1	82.5	54.0	43.6	97.6
Last prewar cycle..............	Aug. '09	Aug. '12	Feb. '14	78	124	84	46	40	86
War cycle....................	Mar. '14	July '18	Mar. '19	78	127	67	49	60	109
Postwar cycles................	Apr. '19	July '20	July '21	98	116	92	48	24	72
	Dec. '21	Dec. '22	Mar. '25	99	139	94	40	45	85

No cyclical decline since 1925.

TABLE 12.—AMPLITUDE OF THE CYCLICAL FLUCTUATIONS IN LEADING AMERICAN TIME SERIES DURING PREWAR, WAR AND POSTWAR BUSINESS CYCLES (*Continued*)

	Dates of cyclical turning points			Standing at cyclical turning points			Amplitudes of cyclical fluctuations		
	First low	High	Last low	First low	High	Last low	Rise	Fall	Rise and fall
Cattle receipts at Chicago.									
Prewar cycles. Average of 15..	....	....	....	65.1	140.5	78.7	75.4	61.8	137.2
Last prewar cycle	July '12	Apr. '13	Nov. '14	95	116	52	21	64	85
War cycle	Jan. '15	Sept. '18	Mar. '19	42	148	100	106	48	154
Postwar cycles	Apr. '19	Dec. '19	July '21	96	126	75	30	51	81
	Aug. '21	Apr. '23	Nov. '23	76	120	81	44	39	83
	Dec. '23	Dec. '24	Nov. '25	81	115	86	34	27	61
Live hog receipts at Chicago.									
Prewar cycles. Average of 12..	....	....	....	55.8	144.6	67.4	88.8	77.2	166.0
Last prewar cycle	Jan. '13	Sept. '13	Nov. '14	87	141	71	54	70	124
War cycle	Dec. '14	Oct. '16	Sept. '17	61	140	59	79	81	160
Postwar cycles	Oct. '17	Mar. '18	Apr. '20	57	138	63	81	75	156
	May '20	Aug. '21	Feb. '22	67	124	88	57	36	93
	Mar. '22	July '23	Feb. '27	80	148	69	68	79	147
Wholesale prices. Bureau of Labor Statistics index number for all commodities.									
Prewar cycles. Average of 7...	....	....	....	94.7	106.4	98.6	11.7	7.8	19.5
Last prewar cycle	June '11	Sept. '13	Dec. '14	95	103	98	8	5	13
War cycle	Jan. '15	Sept. '18	Feb. '19	63	133	126	70	7	77
Postwar cycles	Mar. '19	May '20	Jan. '22	97	124	70	27	54	81
	Feb. '22	Apr. '23	June '24	92	106	96	14	10	24
	July '24	Mar. '25	May '27	96	105	94	9	11	20
Farm price of crops index. Department of Agriculture.									
Prewar cycles. Average of 2...	....	....	....	89.0	115.5	85.0	26.5	30.5	57.0
Last prewar cycle	June '11	June '12	July '13	86	120	83	34	37	71
War cycles	Aug. '13	Mar. '15	Sept. '15	82	110	92	28	18	46
	Oct. '15	Mar. '18	July '18	59	143	116	84	27	111
Postwar cycles	Aug. '18	June '20	July '21	98	145	47	47	98	145
	Aug. '21	Aug. '25	May '27	83	115	95	32	20	52
Operating revenues of Class I railroads.									
Prewar cycles. Average of 2...	....	....	....	79	109	94	30	15	45
Last prewar cycle	Feb. '12	May '13	Nov. '14	88	109	87	21	22	43
War cycle	Dec. '14	Aug. '18	Mar. '19	66	142	118	76	24	100
Postwar cycles	Apr. '19	Sept. '20	Jan. '22	81	119	89	38	30	68
	Feb. '22	May '23	Aug. '24	87	116	96	29	20	49
	Sept. '24	Feb. '27	Dec. '27	90	107	90	17	17	34
Bank clearings outside of New York. Daily average.									
Prewar cycles. Average of 10..	....	....	....	76.8	115.5	94.8	38.7	20.7	59.4
Last prewar cycle	May '11	Jan. '13	Nov. '14	88	110	90	22	20	42
War cycle	Dec. '14	Sept. '20	May '21	47	157	100	110	58	167
Postwar cycles	June '21	May '23	June '24	77	113	105	36	8	44
	July '24	Dec. '25	Jan. '27	81	105	97	24	7	32

TABLE 12.—AMPLITUDE OF THE CYCLICAL FLUCTUATIONS IN LEADING AMERICAN
TIME SERIES DURING PREWAR, WAR AND POSTWAR BUSINESS CYCLES
(*Continued*)

	Dates of cyclical turning points			Standing at cyclical turning points			Amplitudes of cyclical fluctuations		
	First low	High	Last low	First low	High	Last low	Rise	Fall	Rise and fall
Bank clearings in New York City. Daily average.									
Prewar cycles. Average of 16..	....	....	....	67.2	137.6	76.1	70.4	61.6	132.0
Last prewar cycle.............	May '11	Oct. '12	Sept. '14	86	121	64	35	57	92
War cycle...................	Oct. '14	Dec. '16	Mar. '18	37	123	94	86	29	115
Postwar cycles..............	Apr. '18	Mar. '20	Oct. '21	66	120	78	54	42	96
	Nov. '21	Mar. '23	Sept. '23	80	110	86	30	24	54
	Oct. '23	Mar. '26	Nov. '26	83	118	89	35	29	64
Building permits issued, total values. Bradstreet's.									
Prewar cycles. Average of 2...	....	....	....	62	123	75	61	48	109
Last prewar cycle.............	Mar. '11	June '12	Dec. '14	80	124	65	44	59	103
War cycle...................	Jan. '15	July '16	Dec. '18	76	175	34	101	144	245
Postwar cycles..............	Jan. '19	Jan. '20	Dec. '20	17	141	64	125	77	202
	Jan. '21	Feb. '24	July '24	34	157	90	123	67	190
	Aug. '24	Oct. '26	July' 27	72	124	79	52	45	97
Total exports of merchandise.									
Prewar cycles. Average of 10..	....	....	....	71.7	129.9	86.6	58.2	43.3	101.5
Last prewar cycle.............	Sept. '08	Nov. '12	Aug. '14	66	139	66	73	73	146
War cycle...................	Sept. '14	June '17	Nov. '17	28	168	106	142	62	204
Postwar cycles..............	Dec. '17	June '19	Dec. '21	75	193	45	118	148	266
	Jan. '22	Mar. '25	Dec. '27	67	120	96	53	24	77
Total imports of merchandise.									
Prewar cycles. Average of 12..	....	....	....	78.3	125.1	84.5	46.7	40.6	87.3
Last prewar cycle.............	May '11	Dec. '13	Jan. '15	78	131	78	53	53	106
War cycle...................	Feb. '15	May '18	June '19	55	144	136	89	8	97
Postwar cycles..............	July '19	July '20	July '21	84	160	53	76	107	183
	Aug. '21	Mar. '23	Aug. '24	74	128	94	54	34	88
	Sept. '24	Jan. '26	Dec. '27	76	115	94	39	16	55
Interest rates on commercial paper. New York City.									
Prewar cycles. Average of 17..	....	....	....	71.7	145.6	71.5	73.9	74.0	147.9
Last prewar cycle.............	Dec. '11	June '13	Mar. '14	71	135	76	64	59	123
War cycles..................	Apr. '14	Sept. '14	Apr. '16	97	155	75	58	80	138
	May '16	Sept. '18	Feb. '19	92	138	114	46	24	70
Postwar cycles..............	Mar. '19	Aug. '20	Aug. '22	75	123	60	48	63	111
	Sept. '22	Nov. '23	Oct. '24	86	111	68	25	43	68
	Nov. '24	Oct. '26	Nov. '27	80	111	97	31	14	45
Dividend payments by industrial corporations.									
Prewar cycles. Average of 3...	....	....	....	54.0	131.0	68.7	77.0	62.3	139.3
Last prewar cycle.............	Jan. '11	Apr. '13	Dec. '14	40	119	71	79	48	127
War cycle...................	Jan. '15	June '17	Aug. '19	52	157	97	105	60	165
Postwar cycles..............	Sept. '19	May '20	June '22	99	112	87	13	25	38
	No cyclical decline since 1922.								

TABLE 12.—AMPLITUDE OF THE CYCLICAL FLUCTUATIONS IN LEADING AMERICAN TIME SERIES DURING PREWAR, WAR AND POSTWAR BUSINESS CYCLES (*Continued*)

	Dates of cyclical turning points			Standing at cyclical turning points			Amplitudes of cyclical fluctuations		
	First low	High	Last low	First low	High	Last low	Rise	Fall	Rise and fall
Number of shares sold on the New York Stock Exchange.									
Prewar cycles. Average of 8...	....	....	....	49.8	172.9	44.5	123.1	128.4	251.5
Last prewar cycle.............	May '11	Sept. '11	Dec. '14	69	120	26	51	94	145
War cycle....................	Jan. '15	Nov. '16	Aug. '18	12	211	51	199	160	359
Postwar cycles..............	Sept. '18	July '19	Oct. '21	39	237	53	198	184	382
	Nov. '21	Apr. '22	May '24	65	139	61	74	78	152
	No cyclical decline since 1924.								

	First high	Low	Last high	First high	Low	Last high	Fall	Rise	Fall and rise
Liabilities of business failures. Bradstreet's.									
Prewar cycles. Average of 8...	....	....	....	250.9	49.5	268.0	201.4	218.5	419.9
Last prewar cycle.............	Feb. '11	July '11	June '14	105	64	289	41	225	266
War cycle....................	July '14	Jan. '20	Sept. '20	391	37	595	354	558	912
Postwar cycles..............	Oct. '20	May '23	Jan. '24	147	59	146	88	107	195
	Feb. '24	Mar. '25	Mar. '27	175	65	174	110	109	219

which was held at a low level by European restrictions, and commercial-paper rates, which were affected by the establishment of the Federal Reserve System and the huge imports of gold. The index of factory employment scored an exceptional gain. Otherwise the spectacular advances appear in prices and "dollar series." The increases in physical production, while above the average, were less striking.

The decline of 1918–19 exceeded the prewar average in five series, which include the American Telephone and Telegraph Company's *Index of General Business*, factory employment, anthracite shipments, immigration (which does not fit the reference dates well in this cycle), and number of shares sold. In the remaining eight series, the decline was less than usual. As noted above, outside clearings and liabilities of failures show no cyclical contraction at all in 1918–19.

Thus the war cycle was characterized by a prolonged advance to very high levels, particularly marked in prices and dollar values, followed by a brief and moderate reaction.

(3) The first postwar cycle, May, 1919 to September, 1921, started from a relatively high point, because the preceding contraction had been so moderate. When a fresh expansion began in May, 1919, it was not possible to make large percentage gains in many lines. But wholesale

prices, imports, and number of shares sold (the one series which had fallen heavily in 1918–19) surpassed their average prewar rises.

The contraction was violent. Not merely wholesale prices, but also most of the "dollar series," employment, pig iron output, and shares sold fell much more than they had fallen in the average prewar cycle. Less than average declines occurred only in anthracite coal, cattle receipts, commercial-paper rates, and New York clearings. Each of these exceptional cases has a special explanation.

In summary, this cycle presents a subaverage advance from a level left high by the preceding contraction, followed by a crash of values. On the basis of prewar experience, a bank suspension was on the cards. The Federal Reserve System proved its strength by averting that catastrophe.

(4) In the second postwar cycle, October, 1921 to July, 1924, recovery from the low points touched in 1921 constituted a fair cyclical advance without the attainment of high levels. And not a few industries did have a brief season of exceptional activity in the early months of 1923. In our sample of thirteen series, six rose more than their prewar averages and seven rose less.

The contraction presents a similar picture. Six series fell more than the prewar average, seven fell less. With two exceptions, the series which rose little were the series which fell little and *vice versa*. Anthracite coal had a less than average rise and a more than average fall, while imports had a more than average fall and a less than average rise.

In amplitude as well as in duration, then, the cycle, of 1921–1924 marks a return to the familiar type. Before the war it would have ranked as an average case, save that the recession from the peak was attended by less than the usual banking strain.

(5) The latest completed cycle in American business, August, 1924 to December, 1927, is quite different in character. On the rise, only one series in our list (the American Telephone and Telegraph Company's *Index of General Business*) exceeds its prewar average, and that excess is confined to the decimal column. All the other series which permit the comparison show a subaverage advance.

On the decline two series, industrial employment and wholesale prices, exceed their prewar averages. All the others shrink less than usual or not at all.

Adding together the cyclical rise and the cyclical fall, we find that wholesale prices is the only series with a total swing exceeding its prewar average. That average is 19.5 points. The corresponding figure in 1924–1927 is 20 points.

Compared with prewar averages, then, the cycle which ended in 1927 was a mild affair. It still looks mild, if tried by severer standards. We found the last prewar cycle to have been notably moderate. Yet only one series in our list (wholesale prices again) had a larger rise and fall in 1924–1927 than in 1912–1914. All the other series in Table 12, which permit the comparison, make the latest cycle even milder than the last cycle before the war.

To find prewar precedents for cyclical fluctuations so slight as those of 1924–1927, we must resort to the cycle-by-cycle record of each series. For more than half of the list, we can find one or more prewar cases when the cyclical decline was smaller than in 1926–27. But Table 13, which presents this comparison, shows that these individual cases are scattered through eight different cycles. For three of the thirteen series, prewar experience, as recorded in statistics, contains no match in mildness for the latest decline. And two more series show no cyclical decline in the last few years.

TABLE 13.—CYCLICAL DECLINES IN THE BUSINESS CYCLE OF 1924–1927 COMPARED WITH THE SMALLEST CYCLICAL DECLINES FOUND IN ANY PREWAR CYCLE COVERED BY THE AVAILABLE STATISTICS

13 American series covering 7 or more prewar cycles, arranged in order of their cyclical declines in 1924–1927.

The amplitudes are stated in percentages of the average value of the series during the cycle referred to.

Title of the series	Number of prewar cycles covered	Amplitude of cyclical decline in 1924-1927	Smallest cyclical decline found in a prewar cycle	
			Amplitude of the decline	Dates
Liability of business failures, Bradstreet's.	8	109	101	1st quarter '90–4th quarter '90
Immigration, male..................	14	44	38	1st quarter '88–2nd quarter '89
Pig iron production.................	9	31	26	Oct. '87–Feb. '88
Bank clearings in New York City......	16	29	24	July '95–Sept. '96
Exports............................	10	24	21	Dec. '03–Jan. '05
Imports...........................	12	16*a*	21	Aug. '87–Apr. '88
Interest rates on commercial paper....	17	14*a*	29	Oct. '67–Jun '68
Index of General Business. American Telephone & Telegraph Company...	10	13	8	March '99–Dec. '00
Index of Industrial Employment. Jerome and Bureau of Labor Statistics.	7	11	3	Dec. '00–Apr. '01 and Feb. '10–Dec. '11
Index number of wholesale prices, Bureau of Labor Statistics.	7	11	4	March '00–June '01, Feb. '03–Oct. '04 and Mar. '10–May '11
Bank clearings outside New York City.	10	8*a*	9	Nov. '99–Sept. '00
Anthracite coal production or shipments............................	8	none	31	March '87–Oct. '87
Number of shares sold on the New York Stock Exchange..............	8	none	68	June '89–March '91

a The cyclical decline in the business cycle of 1924–1927 is less than the smallest cyclical decline in any prewar cycle covered by the record.

The figures presented in Table 12 express most accurately the difference in amplitude between the latest cycle and its predecessors; but a graphic presentation may be added. The charts which follow cover only the most significant series in our sample. They differ from Table 12 in two ways. (1) The cyclical turning dates used in making the charts are those given in Table 11 for cycles in general business, whereas the turning points used in making the tables are those found in each series. One purpose of this shift is to show that the cyclical pattern is not rubbed out of business changes by stretching all the different series analyzed upon a common time scale, regardless of the dates at which they reached their several peaks and troughs. Of course, the apparent amplitudes of the swings are reduced by this method of presentation, for the lowest and highest points in no series coincide precisely with our reference dates for revival and recession. But, though flattened somewhat in every case, the cyclical pattern remains clear. (2) Instead of presenting only the lowest and highest points of a cycle, the charts show also the progress of expansion from the trough to the peak, and of contraction from the peak to the trough. The interval between a revival and the next recession is divided into three parts as nearly equal as may be, and an average of the relatives is made for each third. The interval between the recession and the next revival is subdivided in the same way. Thus the cyclical behavior of a series is represented in each cycle by eight observations—its average standing in the three months centering on the revival date, its average standing in successive thirds of the phase of expansion, its average standing in the three months centering on the recession date, and its average standing in successive thirds of the phase of contraction. A ninth observation, the average standing in the three months centering on the next revival, is added to show how cycles link into their successors.

These charts confirm pictorially the mildness of the latest cycle in comparison with prewar averages. In some cases, however, rather close scrutiny is necessary to establish the difference. Of course the tables offer more precise comparisons, and when one is interested in the movements of any single series, the use of its own highest and lowest points is the proper procedure. But the charts make plainer than the tables the prevalence of a cyclical pattern in business changes, as well as the difference in this pattern from one type of transactions to another. For example, the contrast between the conforming cycles of imports and the nonconforming cycles of exports stands out clearly. So also does the relation between the pattern for number of shares sold on the Stock Exchange and the pattern for New York clearings. But charts speak well enough for themselves.

While the evidence which has been presented in this rather technical section is not exhaustive, it covers such a variety of economic factors, and such important ones, as to justify a conclusion. Business cycles

AVERAGE BEHAVIOR OF VARIOUS ECONOMIC SERIES DURING PREWAR BUSINESS
CYCLES AND THEIR BEHAVIOR DURING THE CYCLE OF 1924–1927

The curves connect averages of relatives (based upon the average value of the series charted in each cycle) during nine stages of the cycles in general business marked off by the standard set of reference dates shown in Table 11. These stages are as follows: 3 months centered on the reference date for revival; successive thirds of the period of expansion; 3 months centered on the reference dates for recession; successive thirds of the period of contraction, and 3 months centered on the reference date for the next revival. The upper time scales show the average intervals from the center of one of these stages to the next during prewar cycles. The lower time scale shows the corresponding intervals in the cycle of 1924–1927.

CHART 7.—INDEX OF GENERAL BUSINESS ACTIVITY, AMERICAN TELE-
PHONE AND TELEGRAPH COMPANY.

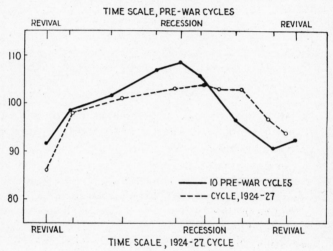

CHART 8.—INDEX OF FACTORY EMPLOYMENT, JEROME AND BUREAU
OF LABOR STATISTICS.

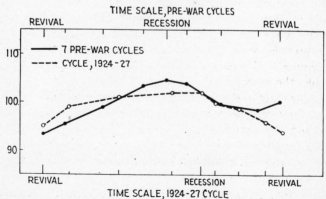

CHART 9.—PIG IRON PRODUCTION.

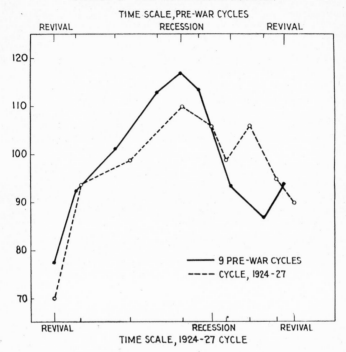

CHART 10.—WHOLESALE PRICES, ALL COMMODITIES, UNITED STATES
BUREAU OF LABOR STATISTICS.

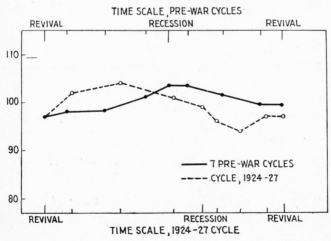

CHART 11.—BANK CLEARINGS OUTSIDE OF NEW YORK CITY.

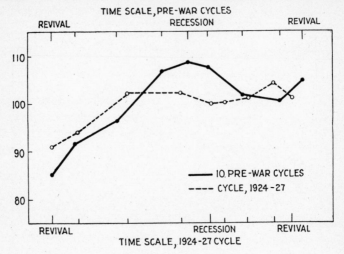

CHART 12.—BANK CLEARINGS IN NEW YORK CITY.

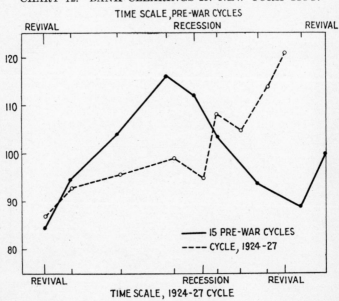

CHART 13.—TOTAL EXPORTS.

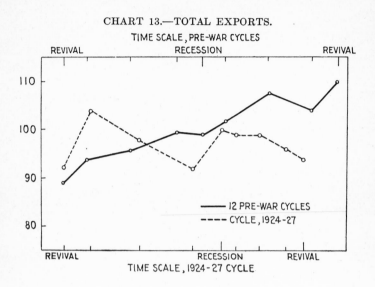

TIME SCALE, PRE-WAR CYCLES

REVIVAL   RECESSION   REVIVAL

———— 12 PRE-WAR CYCLES

－－－－ CYCLE, 1924-27

REVIVAL   RECESSION   REVIVAL

TIME SCALE, 1924-27 CYCLE

CHART 14.—TOTAL IMPORTS.

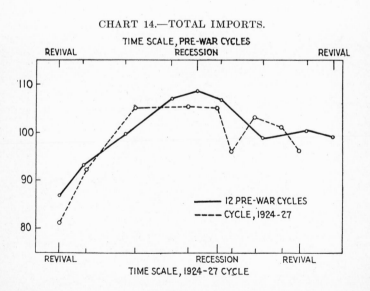

TIME SCALE, PRE-WAR CYCLES

REVIVAL   RECESSION   REVIVAL

———— 12 PRE-WAR CYCLES

－－－－ CYCLE, 1924-27

REVIVAL   RECESSION   REVIVAL

TIME SCALE, 1924-27 CYCLE

CHART 15.—IMMIGRATION, MALES.

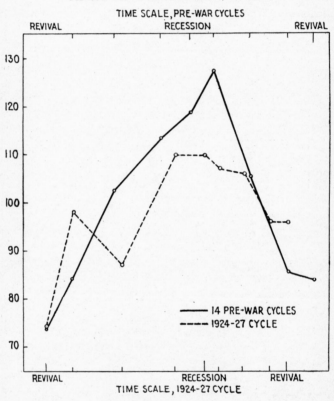

CHART 16.—COMMERCIAL PAPER RATES, NEW YORK CITY.

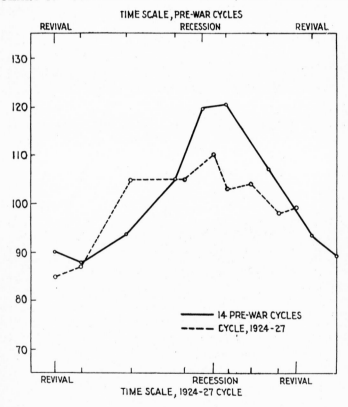

CHART 17.—NUMBER OF SHARES SOLD, NEW YORK STOCK EXCHANGE.

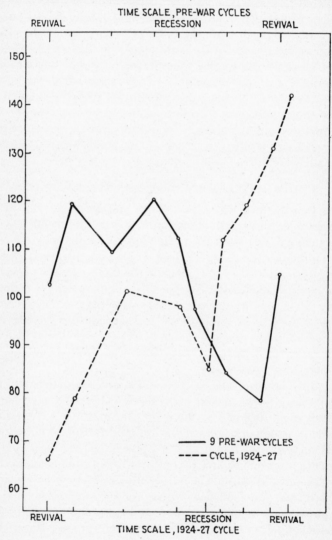

TIME SCALE, PRE-WAR CYCLES

REVIVAL   RECESSION   REVIVAL

9 PRE-WAR CYCLES
CYCLE, 1924-27

REVIVAL   RECESSION   REVIVAL

TIME SCALE, 1924-27 CYCLE

have not been "ironed out" in the United States. But to the recent economic changes described in the preceding chapters we may add another accomplishment: the amplitude of cyclical fluctuations has been reduced. This reduction dates only from 1924, but it extends beyond 1927. With the significant exception of stock-market dealings and closely related processes, the latest statistics indicate that the expansion which began in January, 1928, was proceeding at a temperate pace when this report went to press in March, 1929. Of course, that is no proof that moderation will characterize the later stages of the current cycle or its successors. For we can ascribe the mildness of recent fluctuations only in part to intelligent management. Every factor which has restrained prosperity has had its share in preventing the development of an unhealthy boom, and so in guarding against a violent relapse. If and when Europe regains its prewar level of prosperity, world prices rise, and American agriculture works out of its troubles, then our skill in controlling business cycles will be put to a severer test.

IX. HOW MATTERS STAND IN THE SPRING OF 1929

Forecasting the future is no part of the present task. But we should not close the record without noting that recent developments may appear less satisfactory in retrospect than they appear at present.

Even on the face of affairs, all is not well. Americans have seen more uniformly fortunate times: for example, in 1906, when the Secretary of the Treasury was praying that the country might be delivered from more prosperity. The condition of agriculture, the volume of unemployment, the textile trades, coal mining, the leather industries, present grave problems not only to the people immediately concerned, but also to their fellow citizens. How rapidly these conditions will mend, we do not know. Some may grow worse.

Nor can we be sure that the industries now prosperous will prolong indefinitely their recent record of stability. That we have not had a serious crisis since 1920 or a severe depression since 1921 is no guarantee that we shall be equally prudent, skillful and fortunate in the years to come. If we are to maintain business prosperity, we must continue to earn it month after month and year after year by intelligent effort. The incomes disbursed to consumers, and to wage earners in particular, must be increased on a scale sufficient to pay for the swelling volume of consumers' goods sent to market. The credit structure must be kept in due adjustment to the earnings of business enterprises. Security prices must not outrun prospective profits capitalized at the going rate of interest. Commodity stocks must be held in line with current sales. Overcommitments of all sorts must be avoided. The building of new industrial equipment must not be overrapid. These and the similar matters which might be mentioned present delicate problems of management which will find their practical solutions in the daily decisions of business executives. Perhaps errors are being kept within the limits of tolerance. Perhaps no serious setback will occur for years to come. But we are leaving 1921 well behind us, and there are signs that the caution inspired by that disastrous year is wearing thin.

Whether the recent rate of progress in the arts of industry and business can be maintained is another uncertainty. Past experience, as summed up in the introductory chapter, suggests that the pace will slacken presently, and that years may pass before we see such another well-maintained advance. But that is a matter in which experience is not a trustworthy guide. Scientific research, industrial invention and business pioneering all lead into the unknown. They are fascinating ventures which energetic minds will ever be trying, whether the tangible rewards prove great or small. All that is certain is that whatever progress in efficiency we continue to make must be won by the same type of bold and intelligent work that has earned our recent successes.

APPENDIX A

FIELD INTERVIEW SCHEDULE USED IN MANAGEMENT SURVEY

The field investigators were given standard instructions for using the Interview Schedule. The instructions included three items which the reader will find it helpful to keep in mind when considering the various questions:

Regard the words "recent" and "recently" as meaning during the past 10 years, with particular emphasis on the period since 1921.

Wherever the word TREND appears, give the years in which practice changed or new developments occurred and attempt to indicate the nature and direction of very recent changes in policy or practice, including changes which the person interviewed anticipates in the near future.

Words printed in *italics* directly after a question should be used, wherever applicable, as the answer, by encircling the particular words which constitute a correct answer. But expand the answer wherever necessary for clearness.

RECENT ECONOMIC CHANGES MANAGEMENT SURVEY FIELD INTERVIEW SCHEDULE	Company.................... Location.................... Interviewer.......Date.......
Persons Interviewed Names	Titles	Number of years with this company

IDENTIFYING DATA

A. Character of enterprise: *Manufacturing, Wholesale, Mail Order, Public Utility, Other* (describe). (Note changes during recent years, giving years).

B. Products:
  1. Lines of products made or sold. (Note recent changes).
  2. Per cent (of total dollar volume) sold for use by "ultimate consumers"?.....
  3. Per cent sold for use by "producers" (*i.e.*, for capital or material accounts)?..
  4. Price range or sector: *Top? Middle? Low?* (If this question is inapplicable, explain why).
  5. Per cent of manufacturing cost spent for materials?......direct labor?.....
     indirect labor?......burden?......

C. History:
    1. Year business was established?...
    2. First and subsequent locations of major plant and general office, with reasons for and years of moves.
D. Corporate relations and control:
    1. Recent corporate changes. (Note subsidiaries, mergers, or any other special forms recently developed, giving years).
    2. Present ownership: *Closely controlled? Widely diffused?*
    3. Per cent of capital stock held by employees?.............................'.
    4. Per cent of employees owning stock?..................................
    5. Further comments regarding control.
E. Expansion: List all manufacturing, sales, and other branch plants, offices, stores, etc.

Location	Date established	Date acquired	Date abandoned or disposed of	Functions (*e.g.*, manufacturing, sales, general office, etc)	Approximate number of employees in 1919 (or when established, if since then)	Approximate number of employees (now and when discontinued)

GENERAL OBSERVATIONS OF FIELD INTERVIEWER (TO BE RECORDED AFTER COMPLETING SURVEY)

Note your observations, citing evidence where possible, regarding such things as:
A. Tendencies toward centralization or decentralization of authority and responsibility.
B. Apparent changes in character of managerial personnel, *e.g.*, scientist type replacing opportunist.
C. Notions of obligation or responsibility to consumers, investors, employers, competitors, public at large, Government.
D. Influence of banks and other financial houses on business control.
E. Opinions regarding the value of various types of business associations, *e.g.*, trade associations, chambers of commerce, employers' associations, etc.
F. Opinions regarding the value of various types of business publications, *e.g.*, general business periodicals, trade journals, books, and other similar channels of information.
G. Opinions of executives regarding training for business, and relation of business and educational institutions.
H. Does the management aim for improved results more from perfection of facilities and methods or from increased employee skill and morale?

RELATIVE IMPORTANCE OF MANAGERIAL PROBLEMS

In the judgment of the ranking person interviewed, what was (or is), in each of the years shown, the relative importance to the business of—

	1919	1924	1928
Organizing ability..................................			
Supervision of subordinate executives.............			
Labor management................................			
Management of plant, equipment, processes.........			
Purchasing......................................			
Creation of product demand......................			
Supplying market with product...................			
New product development.........................			
Finance...			
Other (specify):			
....			

I. ORGANIZATION

A. Functionalization:

1. What instances have there been of positions or departments recently established to perform staff or functional duties—rather than to exercise executive or "lines" control—affecting either the entire concern or certain divisions only, *e.g.*, manufacturing., sales, accounting., etc.? (Describe briefly the nature of functions in each case, give year established or discontinued.)

2. What instances have there been of staff positions or departments recently established to investigate problems or carry on research, submitting findings, but purely advisory? (Indicate scope and place in organization and give examples of more important researches. Give year established or discontinued).

3. Who else (position, not name) in the organization in recent years has carried on research, and in relation to what subjects?

4. What outside research agencies have been utilized, when, and how?

5. What use has been made of the results of your own and of outside researches?

B. Co-ordination:

1. Upon what means (or combination of means) do you chiefly rely for co-ordination? (*e.g.*, one-man control; systematic interchange of information; occasional conferences; staff positions; established committees; executive committee replacing chief executive for control and co-ordination; organization chart; standard practice instructions; others—describe).

2. Which of the foregoing have been used and discontinued recently, when and why?

3. If committees are used, what are the functions of the more important ones, when were they established and what departments are represented in each case?

4. Indicate for organization charts and/or standard practice instructions, if used—
    (a) By whose authority are they issued?
    (b) How and by whom are they kept current?
    (c) Whether they define job duties and relations?
    (d) Whether they are published to the organization—how?......
        to whom?......

C. Executive technique:

1. What changes have occurred in recent years in personnel of major executive positions? (Give positions and years, but *not* names).

2. How many persons have been promoted within past (give years) to important executive, supervisory, or staff positions?...........................

3. How many persons have been hired from outside within past five years for important executive, supervisory, or staff positions?..................

4. What special means are used to prepare or qualify employees for positions of responsibility? (Briefly describe and give history).

5. What outside sources for executive and expert talent have been found most satisfactory? (Note especially recent experience and TREND).

    (a) For immediate assignment (*e.g., other companies; same or other business; college faculties; etc.*).

    (b) Potential (*e.g., college, business or technical graduates; others*).

6. What methods of evaluating executive ability and performance have been tried, and with what success or results? (*e.g., tests, ratings*).

7. What special methods of remuneration for executives have been tried, when, and with what success or results? (Recent changes).

D. Preplanning and budgeting:

1. How, by whom, and when are major or "*master*" plans of the company determined? (Note especially use of internal and external statistics).

2. Are you finding it possible (or advisable) to *plan further in advance* than formerly? or are business conditions enforcing (or counselling) a shorter planning interval?

3. (If systematic budgets are prepared): In what year was budgeting begun?...

4. Are preliminary estimates made by department heads?....................

    If so, are department heads furnished data to guide them?

    (a) Relating to future company policies......how?

    (b) Relating to the business trend......how?

5. Are there budget conferences?.......................................

6. Is the final budget determined *in conference?* or by the *budget officer?* or by the *chief executive?* or *otherwise?* (specify).

7. Are departmental budgets divided into controllable and uncontrollable expenses?...

8. For what period is the budget prepared?...............................

9. How are revisions effected?

10. Is the budget used as basis for loans from banks?

11. Do the banks require it?

12. What essential changes in your budget practice have been made in recent years, when, and why?

E. Forecasting:

1. To what statistical or forecasting services does the company subscribe?

2. Who (positions, not names) receive the publications of these services, and how are they used?

3. Are the amounts of material purchased, or the amounts of inventory carried, influenced in any regular way by the predictions published by such services?

4. Has such influence in the past been generally helpful?

5. (If new buildings have been built since 1920) was decision to enlarge based solely on evident growth of the business, or were you seriously influenced as to the time of expansion by predictions of such services?

6. Did experience later show that it had been wise to rely on such statistical or forecasting assistance?

II. MANUFACTURING

A. Purchasing:
1. Who (position, not name) buys major materials?
2. Who buys minor materials?
3. What purchasing records are maintained and how used?
4. Which is your more usual practice: To seek *competitive bids?* To continue purchases from *tested vendors?* (TREND).
5. Which is your more usual practice: To *split orders* among several vendors? To place orders with exclusive vendors? (TREND).
6. What methods have you adopted to help reduce sales expenses of your vendors? (*e.g., appointments with salesmen; increased use of annual contracts; repeat orders placed by correspondence or by telephone; other*—specify).

B. Inventory control:
1. What departments or executives are responsible respectively for the inventory investment in—
   (a) Raw materials?..
   (b) Goods in process?..
   (c) Finished goods?................... ....
2. Do you have established maxima and minima?
   How long have you used them?
   How are they kept up to date?

C. Production management:
Planning—
1. Is planning functionalized?......When first?......
2. Does it include *routing, scheduling, despatching?*
3. What important changes have there been in recent years in the functions or organization of the planning department or in its relation to other departments?

Recording and costing—
1. (If "standard costs" are used): How are standard costs established for—
   (a) Direct labor?...
   (b) Indirect labor?...
   (c) Material?...
   (d) Overhead?...
2. Are standard costs modified from time to time in the light of changing business conditions?......How often?..........................
3. How are standard costs used? (*e.g., fixing selling prices; prompt determination of profit and loss; standard for department heads to work to; other*—specify).
4. Are actual (not standard) costs used as check against performance of separate portions of the organization?............................
5. Are costs (*actual or standard?*) used to determine cost of idleness, thus influencing contracting for extra work?

Material standards—
1. Are you—
   (a) Increasing the precision of your material specifications?........
   (b) Making greater use of generally accepted trade standards?
       If so, are they mainly standards approved by the United States Bureau of Standards?
   (c) Doing both (a) and (b) with respect to different materials?......
2. What new methods of testing materials have you adopted in recent years, and what did they supplant?

Processing standards—

1. What methods are now used in establishing quality standards?
2. What recent changes in such methods have been made?
3. In what cases (if any) have the possibilities of poor product been practically eliminated through improvements in method or equipment?
4. What means are used to maintain quality standards? (*e.g., executive pressure; standard job instructions; financial incentives—what sort? nonfinancial incentives—what sort? inspectors; automatic inspection. TREND*).
5. In what ways have you enlisted the co-operation of employees in waste elimination?

Maintenance—

1. How old is the major portion of the plant?......Recent addition?......
2. Do you check operating conditions of buildings, power, machinery, lighting, and other equipment periodically, against standards?..... How long has this practice been followed?.....................
3. Do you schedule (a) replacements?......(b) maintenance?......How?

Quantity standards—

1. What methods are now used in establishing quantity standards? (*e.g., analysis of past records; time study—over all? or elemental? ascertainment of machine speeds; motion study; other*—specify).
2. Is it customary, before establishing a quantity standard, to standardize methods and/or equipment to reduce likelihood of delays or errors?
3. What recent changes in methods of establishing quantity standards have been made?
4. What means are used to maintain quantity standards? (*e.g., executive pressure; standard job instructions; financial incentives—what sort? nonfinancial incentives—what sort? mechanical handling equipment; other*—specify. *TREND*).

D. Output:

1. To what extent has your product per employee-hour (or on other suitable basis) increased or decreased in recent years?
2. What have been the major causes of this change in efficiency? (*e.g., mechanization; process changes; layout; simplification; production control; employees' attitude; training; labor turnover; other*—specify).

E. Technical changes (in manufacturing methods or equipment):

1. What have been the major reasons for recent technical changes? (*e.g., to offset high labor costs? to meet price competition? to meet quality competition? other*—specify).
2. Which of the recent technical improvements resulted from continuous research or experimentation to improve methods?
3. Are further improvements already developed awaiting expedient time for use?
4. Do you anticipate that future advances (*i.e.*, in next decade or two) will be *more rapid?* or *equally rapid?* or *less rapid?*
5. Do you anticipate that future increases in efficiency will result principally from technical improvements and/or from better handling of "human element," or other causes? (specify).

F. Extent and fullness of operation:

1. Use of facilities—
   (a) Has there been in recent years marked over-expansion of this company's facilities?......When?......For what purpose?
   (b) Has there been in recent years marked over-expansion of the industry through new or enlarged plants?......When?......Due to what situation?

(c) What increase in output would be possible for this company without added facilities?

(d) To what extent are present idle facilities obsolescent? (Note whether written off, if mentioned).

(e) When (approximately) were present idle facilities purchased?

(f) What are present normal working schedules (hours and shifts), and in what respects have they changed materially in recent years?

(g) How would working two or three shifts affect costs?

2. As a result of recent technical changes, approximately how many employees were (and in what years)—

(a) Transferred to other work?.......................................

(b) Trained for new operations on same work?.........................

(c) Released from company?...

3. What classes of workers, as regards types of skill, were affected in each of the ways indicated in the previous question?

4. How are those who were released from company now employed (if known)? *e.g.*, other industries in district, especially new concerns, retail or other concerns, etc.

5. What effects have recent technical changes had upon the type or period of initial training required?

6. Has there been in recent years a marked increase in the proportion of jobs so specialized as to involve practically no carry-over of skill? (Note examples).

G. Personnel practice:

1. Organization—Through what changes, as regards organization, function, and relation to other departments, has the personnel department passed in recent years, and what is its present status?

2. Employment technique—

(a) Who (position, not name) is responsible for selection of new employees? (TREND).

(b) When and how have you altered recently your personnel standards? (regarding, *e.g.*, sex, age, race, nationality, citizenship, religion, physique, education, marital status, union membership, other— specify).

(c) Which of the following aids to selection have you found practicable, and which have you tried and abandoned? (TREND).

Interview (who does?)..

Tests (what sort?)..

Medical examination?..

Job specifications?...

Other (specify)..

(d) Are labor turnover figures tabulated?...........................

How often?...

How refined is the analysis?...................................

How used?..

Are data submitted to any outside agency for comparison with other companies?......What? (TREND).

3. Vocational adjustment—

(a) In following up the progress of new employees, which of these are used: *performance records; attendance records; ratings; tests* (what sort?); *medical examination; other?* (specify). (TREND).

(b) What is the practice regarding transferring from job to job or from department to department? (TREND).

(c) What systematic practice for making promotions has been developed, when put into effect? (Describe briefly).

(d) Are employees leaving interviewed, by whom, and for what purposes? What exceptions, if any? (TREND).

4. Training and education—
   (a) What are the organization and facilities, including relations with outside agencies, for training or advancing the educational interests of employees? (TREND).
   (b) Which of the following training means do you use: *Preliminary job training; apprentice course* (what trades or subjects?); *classes— company subjects; classes—general or cultural; foremen's conferences; executive training courses; "flying squadron;" special training of college men; alien education; library; company publications; other?* (specify).
   (c) Which of the foregoing have been tried and discontinued?...... When?......Why?......

5. Incentives—
   (a) How are job or trade differentials (for wage rates and salaries) determined? (*e.g., market; union scale; job classification based on job study; job evaluation by some special method*—describe).
   (b) What are the prevailing types of rates? (*e.g., time; piece, bonus or premium; etc.*) (TREND).
   (c) Is an extra wage paid employees upon dismissal? (TREND). Under what conditions?
   (d) What special bonuses are paid? (*e.g., annual; length-of-service; group; etc.*)
   (e) What is the practice, and how altered in recent years, regarding payment for—
   Overtime?
   Absences?
   Holidays?
   Vacations?
   Transportation?
   Lunches?
   (f) What financial rewards are offered for employees' suggestions, and with what results? (TREND).

6. Separations—
   (a) Age of retirement.

7. Wages.

8. Provisions for workers' security—
   (a) What has been done toward regularizing employment, when and how? ......What are the outstanding obstacles to regularization?
   (b) What has been done along the lines of accident prevention?
   (c) What studies have been made of fatigue and monotony?
   (d) What company provisions are there for insurance? (Include mention of mutual benefit associations, insurance provisions of unions, and indicate company's part in their support).
   Pensions? formal? contributory? funded? actuarially sound? reinsured?
   Savings plan?
   Stock (or bond) purchase plan?
   Others?

9. Services for employees—Which of the following have been provided and when —social, athletic, recreational activities; employee magazine; store, or

special buying privileges; loan fund; credit unions?   Which discontinued
—when?......why?

10. Joint relations—
    (a) Are relations between the management and employees based upon—
        Supervisory contact only with individuals?
        Occasional special committees (how composed and selected)?
        Employee representation plan?
           When established?   (Note any comments as to its effectiveness).
        Union agreement?   (Note comments).
    (b) In what respects have joint relations altered in recent years?

11. Personnel research—What special research has been conducted, when, and
    how utilized?   (*e.g.*, *tests for selection and placement; application blank data
    correlated with performance; rating procedure; fatigue; health; accidents;
    compensation methods; labor turnover*).

III. MARKETING

A. Selling:
  1. Organization—
    (a) What is the structure of your selling organization?   (Brief description,
        showing relationships within sales department and to other depart-
        ments).
    (b) What structural changes have occurred in recent years?
    (c) What auxiliary or functional sales activities have been performed in
        recent years by special divisions of the sales organization or desig-
        nated individuals?   (Note when each was established and when any
        were discontinued, *e.g.*, sales promotion, sales engineering, sales
        counsel [outside], etc.)
    (d) To what extent, and when, in recent years, have you increased or
        decreased the number of missionary salesmen as compared with
        regular salesmen?
    (e) In what respects and when have there been changes in policy respecting
        employing sales engineers for designing and engineering service,
        demonstration, or installation?
  2. Personnel—What are your practices, and in what respects and when during
    recent years have they changed respecting methods of—
    (a) Selecting salesmen?
    (b) Training salesmen?
    (c) Remunerating salesmen?
  3. Sales control—
    (a) In what respects, and when in recent years, have methods of routing
        salesmen been changed?   (*e.g.*, respecting permitting salesmen to
        choose own routes; length of trips; other—specify).
    (b) In what respects, and when recently, have the sizes of sales territories
        been altered?
    (c) When was the use of sales quotas instituted?......When abandoned?
      ......When were (or are) quotas used as a basis for remuneration?
      ......
    (d) When recently, and to what extent, have changes been made in the
        frequency of calls?......in frequency of sales reports?......
  4. Sales costs—
    (a) What methods of analyzing costs of distribution have been adopted
        recently, and with what results?   (*e.g.*, by *classes of product;* by

classes of customers; by *types of salesmen;* by *territories; others—* specify).

   (b) What per cent of total sales represented direct selling expense in 1919? in 1924? in 1928?

5. Advertising—

   (a) In what respects, and when recently, have advertising methods been changed with respect to media used, area (*e.g.,* local, sectional, national, international), type (*e.g.,* institutional or product), etc.?

   (b) What per cent of total sales represented advertising expense in 1919? in 1924? in 1928?

B. Merchandising:

1. In what respects, and when recently, have methods of co-ordinating sales with production been changed? (*e.g.,* appointment of *merchandise manager; merchandise committee*—how composed? *other*—specify; briefly describe present process).

2. Where is responsibility now placed for—

   (a) Selection of products?......Where previously?......When changed? ......

   (b) Design of products?......Where previously?......When changed? ......

   (c) Pricing of products?......Where previously?......When changed? ......

   (d) Scheduling production in relation to sales?......Where previously? ......When changed?......

3. (If market analyses are (or were) made)—

   (a) When begun?......When discontinued?......

   (b) What objectives? (*e.g., setting quotas; allocation of sales territories; evaluation of competition; determination of proper sales channels; other*—specify).

4. (If distribution analyses are (or were) made)—

   (a) When begun?......When discontinued?......

   (b) What objectives? (*e.g., discovery of new uses; reaction of market to product; other*—specify.)

5. Market—

   (a) What per cent of your market is local?......Sectional?......National? ......International?......

   (b) What changes in policy respecting market areas have occurred in recent years? When?

   (c) What per cent of sales are through brokers?......Through sales agents? ......To manufacturers and other industrial users?......To wholesalers?......To chain store companies......To individual retailers? ......To individual consumers?......(through your own stores or by canvassers). Other? (specify).

   (d) What changes in policy respecting trade channels have occurred in recent years? When?

   (e) Do you face competition from concerns producing *similar products?* from industries making *substitute products?*

   (f) On what basis is a share of total business sought? (*e.g., territorial advantages; product advantages; varying price sector; other*—specify).

   (g) What special means are used to protect from competition? (*e.g., patents; trade marks; brands; secret processes; other*—specify).

6. Trade channels—
   Wholesalers.

Small retailers.
Department stores.
Chain stores.

IV. OFFICE MANAGEMENT

A. Functionalization: (If there is an "office manager"): What are the major functions and scope of authority of the office manager? (TREND).
B. Control: What has been done in recent years along such lines as layout? Routing of work? Job study? Salary classification? Standardization and simplification of forms? Standard instructions? etc. (TREND).
C. Mechanization: What types of office equipment have been—
  1. Recently installed.
  2. Recently abandoned.

Supplement	1919	1924	1928
Number of employees in production (direct labor)			
Number of employees in sales			
Annual sales (index number)			
Product—physical volume (state unit)			

APPENDIX B

ECONOMIC MOVEMENTS IN THE UNITED STATES

Table 1.—Indexes of Prices, 1922–1927

Index	Average annual rate of change (per cent)
Wholesale commodity prices:	
Index of United States Bureau of Labor Statistics[a]	− 0.1
Foods	+ 2.3
Farm products	+ 1.2
Hides and leather products	+ 0.2
Chemicals and drugs	− 0.5
Building materials	− 1.3
Textile products	− 1.5
House furnishing goods	− 1.5
Fuel and lighting	− 2.7
Metals and metal products[b]	− 1.5
Clothing[b]	− 1.8
Raw materials (1923–1927)	− 0.2
Finished products (1923–1927)	− 0.7
Semimanufactured articles (1923–1927)	− 4.8
Indexes for minor groups, United States Bureau of Labor Statistics:[a]	
Foods—	
Meats	+ 5.1
Butter, cheese, and milk	+ 1.9
Other foods	+ 0.3
Farm products—	
Livestock and poultry	+ 5.5
Grains	+ 3.5
Other farm products	− 1.2
Hides and leather products—	
Boots and shoes	+ 0.8
Leather	+ 0.4
Hides and skins	− 1.5
Chemicals and drugs—	
Chemicals	+ 0.6
Drugs and pharmaceuticals	+ 0.4
Fertilizer materials	− 1.0
Wholesale chemical prices (index of the *Oil and Paint Reporter*)—	
Drugs and pharmaceuticals (40 drugs)	+ 4.6
Essential oils (20 oils)	+ 2.7
Crude drugs (35 drugs)	+ 1.2
Building materials—	
Brick	− 1.1
Structural steel	− 1.4
Portland cement	− 1.7
Lumber	− 1.9
Composite lumber prices (indexes of the *Lumber Manufacturer and Dealer*)—	
Hardwood	− 0.9
Softwood	− 1.7
Textile products—	
Textile products, other than cotton, silk and wool	+ 6.0
Woolen and worsted goods	0.0
Cotton goods	− 1.8
Silk and rayon	− 5.8
House furnishing goods—	
Furnishings	+ 0.1
Furniture	− 3.7

TABLE 1.—INDEXES OF PRICES, 1922–1927 (*Continued*)

Index	Average annual rate of change (per cent)
Fuel and lighting—	
Anthracite coal..	− 0.2
Petroleum products..	− 1.8
Bituminous coal...	− 4.5
Coke...	− 5.6
Miscellaneous—	
Rubber, crude...	+16.8
Cattle feed...	+ 0.1
Paper and pulp..	− 0.5
Metals and metal products—	
Nonferrous metals...	+ 1.9
Iron and steel..	− 1.9
Agricultural products, at wholesale[c,d].......................	+ 0.7
Nonagricultural products, at wholesale[c,d]....................	− 1.8
Index numbers of the prices of raw materials and of manufactured goods made from these materials (United States Bureau of Labor Statistics):[b]	
Raw materials (27 price series)................................	+ 1.1
Manufactured goods (70 price series)..........................	+ 1.8
Group index numbers, wholesale prices, of the National Bureau of Economic Research:[e]	
Index numbers for major groups—	
Agricultural products.......................................	+ 1.0
Nonagricultural products....................................	− 1.1
Foreign products...	+ 3.4
Domestic products..	− 0.4
Products of American farms..................................	+ 0.7
All other commodities.......................................	− 0.5
All agricultural products, excluding rubber, processed textiles, leather, and shoes..	+ 1.8
All other commodities (*i.e.*, industrial goods)...............	− 0.9
Raw materials..	+ 1.4
Processed materials..	− 0.4
Consumers' goods...	+ 0.3
Producers' goods...	0.0
Foods...	+ 2.0
Nonfoods..	− 0.9
Animal products..	+ 1.2
Cultivated vegetable products...............................	+ 0.5
Mineral products...	− 0.9
Forest products..	− 1.6
Index numbers for minor groups—	
Agricultural products—	
Producers' goods..	+ 1.3
Consumers' goods..	+ 0.7
Raw materials...	+ 2.1
Processed materials.....................................	+ 0.4
Producers' goods, raw...................................	+ 1.9
Producers' goods, processed.............................	+ 0.6
Consumers' goods, raw...................................	+ 2.8
Consumers' goods, processed.............................	+ 0.4
Foreign[f]...	+ 3.0
Domestic[f]..	+ 0.8
Nonagricultural products—	
Consumers' goods..	− 0.5
Producers' goods..	− 0.9
Raw materials...	0.0

TABLE 1.—INDEXES OF PRICES, 1922–1927 (*Continued*)

Index	Average annual rate of change (per cent)
Processed materials..	− 1.3
Producers' goods, raw.....................................	+ 0.1
Producers' goods, processed.............................	− 1.2
Consumers' goods, raw....................................	+ 0.8
Consumers' goods, processed.............................	− 0.8
Foreign..	+ 6.0
Domestic..	− 1.5
Products of American farms—*a*	
Raw materials..	+ 1.2
Processed materials......................................	+ 0.4
Commodities not products of American farms—	
Raw materials..	+ 1.7
Processed materials......................................	− 1.1
Agricultural products, excluding rubber, processed textiles, leather, and shoes—	
Raw materials..	+ 1.9
Processed materials......................................	+ 1.7
All other commodities (industrial goods)—	
Raw materials..	+ 0.5
Processed materials......................................	− 1.2
Raw materials—	
Agricultural products....................................	+ 2.1
Nonagricultural products.................................	0.0
Commodities not products of American farms..............	+ 1.7
Products of American farms...............................	+ 1.2
Agricultural products, excluding rubber, processed textiles, leather, and shoes...................................	+ 1.9
All other commodities (industrial goods).................	+ 0.5
Consumers' goods...	+ 2.3
Producers' goods...	+ 1.3
Foods...	+ 3.0
Nonfoods..	− 0.1
Forest products..	+ 9.6
Cultivated vegetable products............................	+ 3.1
Animal products..	+ 0.3
Mineral products...	− 0.3
Processed materials—	
Agricultural products....................................	+ 0.4
Nonagricultural products.................................	− 1.3
Products of American farms...............................	+ 0.4
Commodities not products of American farms..............	− 1.1
Agricultural products, excluding rubber, processed textiles, leather, and shoes...................................	+ 1.7
All other commodities (industrial goods).................	− 1.2
Consumers' goods...	0.0
Producers' goods...	− 0.7
Foods...	+ 1.4
Nonfoods..	− 1.0
Animal products..	+ 1.6
Cultivated vegetable products............................	− 0.6
Mineral products...	− 1.0
Forest products..	− 1.9
Consumers' goods—	
Raw materials..	+ 2.3
Processed materials......................................	0.0
Agricultural products....................................	+ 0.7

TABLE 1.—INDEXES OF PRICES, 1922–1927 (*Continued*)

Index	Average annual rate of change (per cent)
Nonagricultural products	− 0.5
Foods	+ 1.7
Nonfoods	− 1.0
Producers' goods—	
Raw materials	+ 1.3
Processed materials	− 0.7
Agricultural products	+ 1.3
Nonagricultural products	− 0.9
Foods	+ 2.6
Nonfoods	− 0.6
Foods—	
Raw materials	+ 3.0
Processed materials	+ 1.4
Producers' goods	+ 2.6
Consumers' goods	+ 1.7
Producers' goods, raw	+ 3.0
Producers' goods, processed	+ 1.1
Consumers' goods, raw	+ 2.8
Consumers' goods, processed	+ 1.4
Nonfoods—	
Raw materials	− 0.1
Processed materials	− 1.0
Producers' goods	− 0.6
Consumers' goods	− 1.0
Producers' goods, raw	0.0
Producers' goods, processed	− 0.8
Consumers' goods, raw	+ 0.8
Consumers' goods, processed	− 1.1
Animal products—	
Processed materials	+ 1.6
Raw materials	+ 0.3
Cultivated vegetable products—	
Raw materials	+ 3.1
Processed materials	− 0.6
Mineral products—	
Raw materials	− 0.3
Processed materials	− 1.0
Forest products—	
Raw materials	+ 9.6
Processed materials	− 1.9
Prices of commodities at the farm:	
Index of United States Bureau of Agricultural Economics	+ 1.1
Meat animals	+ 6.6
Grain	+ 4.3
Fruits and vegetables	+ 4.0
Dairy and poultry	+ 0.2
Unclassified commodities	− 3.7
Cotton	− 7.5
Retail food prices:	
Index of the U. S. Bureau of Labor Statistics	+ 2.4
Meats	+ 3.2
Cereals	+ 2.2
Dairy products	+ 1.2
Retail sugar prices, index, 51 cities	− 4.0
Retail coal prices, index, 51 cities	− 0.1

TABLE 1.—INDEXES OF PRICES, 1922–1927 (*Continued*)

Index	Average annual rate of change (per cent)
Cost of living:	
Index of the United States Bureau of Labor Statistics..............	+ 0.7
Food..	+ 2.6
Miscellaneous..	+ 0.4
Fuel and light...	+ 0.3
Housing...	0.0
Furniture and furnishings..................................	− 0.6
Clothing..	− 1.2
General price level:	
Index of the Federal Reserve Bank of New York...................	+ 1.5
Security prices...	+ 9.1
Wages...	+ 2.8
Food prices, retail...	+ 2.4
Equipment and machinery...................................	+ 1.3
Prices at the farm...	+ 1.1
Automobile prices..	+ 0.9
Hardware prices, wholesale.................................	+ 0.3
Rents...	0.0
Realty values..	− 0.1
Cost of living items other than food and rents.................	− 0.3
Transportation costs.......................................	− 1.5
Industrial commodity prices, at wholesale.....................	− 1.8
Building costs:	
Building material prices (Bureau of Standards)—	
Frame buildings...	− 0.2
Brick buildings..	− 0.5
Construction costs—	
Index of construction costs, *Engineering News Record*...........	+ 1.8
Index of construction costs, Associated General Contractors of America...	+ 0.9
Factory building costs, Aberthaw Construction Co..............	+ 1.4
Indexes of costs, by building types—	
Indexes of the American Appraisal Co.—	
Brick building, wood frame...........................	+ 0.9
Frame building......................................	+ 0.8
Reinforced concrete building.........................	+ 0.4
Brick building, steel frame...........................	+ 0.2

FOOTNOTES FOR TABLE 1.

ᵃ Unless otherwise noted, the index numbers of the United States Bureau of Labor Statistics which have been employed in the present calculations are the revised measures, on the 1926 base. For the purpose of the present computations, the revised sub-group index numbers have been carried back one year to include 1922.

ᵇ Computed from unrevised (1913 base) index numbers of the United States Bureau of Labor Statistics.

ᶜ Index numbers computed by the Bureau of Agricultural Economics and the Bureau of Labor Statistics.

ᵈ These index numbers are those begun by the Federal Reserve Board, employing the data of the Bureau of Labor Statistics, and carried through 1927 by the Bureau of Labor Statistics. The classifications are those of the Federal Reserve Board. The classifications are arbitrary, as pointed out by the Bureau of Labor Statistics, "Index Numbers of Wholesale Prices on Prewar Base." They do not agree with the classifications employed in constructing the index numbers from which the measures in the next section have been computed.

ᵉ The measures included in this section are based upon unpublished index numbers prepared by the National Bureau of Economic Research. The data employed are the price quotations compiled by the United States Bureau of Labor Statistics. The index numbers are unweighted geometric means of relatives on the 1913 base. In certain cases the classifications of commodities upon which these index numbers are based differ from the classifications employed in the construction of currently published index numbers in which the same group names are used. This is true of the classifications of agricultural and nonagricultural products, producers' goods and consumers' goods, raw materials and processed materials. A complete account of the present classifications will be published by the National Bureau of Economic Research.

ᶠ The goods upon which these index numbers are based are of purely domestic origin and of purely foreign origin (or practically so), in so far as consumption in the United States is concerned. Goods coming from both domestic and foreign sources have been omitted.

ᵍ Among products of American farms are included goods of which part of the American supply may come from foreign sources. There is, thus, an important difference between this group and the group of ' agricultural products, domestic" which is listed on p. 923.

TABLE 2.—COMMODITY PRICES, 1922–1927

Commodity	Average annual rate of change in—	
	Farm price (per cent)	Wholesale price (per cent)
Agricultural products, raw:		
Grains—		
Wheat	+ 5.8	[a]+ 5.2
Wheat	......	[b]+ 3.2
Rye	+ 4.6	+ 5.0
Barley	+ 3.8	+ 4.2
Corn	+ 2.7	+ 4.0
Oats	+ 2.2	+ 2.7
Fruits and vegetables—		
Potatoes, white	+13.6	+13.1
Sweet potatoes	+ 4.5	+ 3.4
Grapefruit	+ 3.0	
Beans	− 1.1	− 5.8
Oranges	− 2.2	+ 0.2
Apples	− 4.3	− 6.6
Meat animals—		
Hogs	+ 7.8	+ 6.9
Calves	+ 6.1	
Cattle	+ 5.9	+ 4.5
Sheep	+ 3.9	+ 1.5
Lambs	+ 3.5	+ 1.0
Dairy and poultry products—		
Butter	+ 2.7	+ 1.8
Chickens	+ 2.4	+ 2.4
Eggs	+ 0.5	+ 0.8
Milk	− 1.6	+ 2.6
Cotton and cottonseed—		
Cottonseed	− 7.3	− 7.3
Cotton	− 7.5	− 7.0
Unclassified commodities—		
Hay	+ 0.7	− 2.7
Wool	− 0.2	− 4.4
Horses	− 1.3	......
Flaxseed	− 1.5	− 2.7
Other agricultural products, raw—		
Rubber, plantation	......	+16.4
Hides	......	+ 0.1
Sugar, raw	......	− 5.0
Tobacco, leaf	......	− 7.1
Silk, raw	......	− 7.3
Agricultural products, processed:		
Meats—		
Pork, mess	......	+ 7.5
Pork, fresh	......	+ 6.4
Beef	......	+ 3.6
Lamb	......	+ 0.9
Other products, processed—		
Flour, wheat	......	+ 3.3
Leather, side chrome	......	+ 3.2
Tobacco, plug	......	− 0.2
Leather, glazed kid	......	− 0.7
Leather, sole union backs	......	− 0.9
Silk, spun	......	− 1.5

TABLE 2.—COMMODITY PRICES, 1922–1927 (*Continued*)

Commodity	Average annual rate of change in—	
	Farm price (per cent)	Wholesale price (per cent)
Tobacco, smoking..................................	......	− 4.1
Sugar, granulated, index 51 cities....................	......	− 4.2
Sugar, granulated, New York......................	......	− 5.0
Nonagricultural products, raw:		
Tin..	......	+13.9
Lead...	......	+ 3.3
Zinc...	......	+ 2.5
Wood pulp.......................................	......	+ 0.1
Anthracite coalᶜ.................................	......	− 0.2
Copper...	......	− 0.7
Crude petroleum..................................	......	− 1.8
Silver..	......	− 2.7
Bituminous coalᶜ.................................	......	− 4.5
Iron ore...	......	− 5.4
Pig iron..	......	− 7.3
Nonagricultural products, processed:		
Zinc, sheet.......................................	......	+ 5.2
Lead pipe..	......	+ 3.5
Wrapping paper..................................	......	+ 2.3
Lubricating oil, paraffin..........................	......	+ 2.1
Fuel oil, Pennsylvania............................	......	+ 1.9
Kerosene...	......	+ 0.6
Copper wire......................................	......	− 0.9
Brickᶜ..	......	− 1.1
Structural steelᶜ.................................	......	− 1.4
Portland cementᶜ.................................	......	− 1.7
Lumberᶜ..	......	− 1.9
Steel billets......................................	......	− 2.0
Newsprint..	......	− 2.8
Gasoline..	......	− 4.6
Cokeᶜ..	......	− 5.6

ᵃ Hard winter, Kansas City.

ᵇ Northern spring, Minneapolis.

ᶜ The rates of price change for this commodity have been computed from indexes secured by combining price quotations from a number of markets or for a number of grades.

TABLE 3.—PRODUCTION, 1922–1927[a]

Series	Average annual rate of change (per cent)
Raw materials:	
Minerals—	
Zinc	+ 8.6
Copper, mine production	+ 8.4
Lead	+ 7.7
Crude petroleum	+ 7.4
Iron ore	+ 3.6
Bituminous coal	+ 3.5
Anthracite coal	+ 3.3
Silver	+ 0.1
Crops, production—	
Flaxseed	+11.3
Cotton	+ 9.2
Barley	+ 5.9
Rice	+ 1.5
Hay, tame	+ 1.0
Wheat, total	− 0.4
Spring wheat	+ 1.3
Winter wheat	− 1.0
Oats	− 0.5
Corn	− 1.1
Tobacco	− 1.2
Potatoes	− 3.9
Apples	− 3.9
Rye	−13.3
Crops, total value[b]	− 3.0
Animal products, marketings:[c].	
Fish	+ 9.4
Milk, New Yrok	+ 3.9
Poultry	+ 2.9
Wool	+ 2.5
Sheep	+ 1.7
Cattle and calves	0.0
Eggs	− 0.5
Hogs	− 4.1
Forest products—	
Gum (rosin and turpentine)	+ 5.3
Distilled wood	+ 0.7
Lumber	+ 0.4
Pulp wood	+ 0.1
Manufactured goods:[d]	
Chemicals, oils, etc.—	
Petroleum refining—	
Gasoline	+17.3
Fuel oil	+ 8.6
Lubricating oil	+ 6.7
Kerosene	+ 1.2
Vegetable oils, total	+12.1
Cottonseed oil—	
Crude	+16.3
Refined	+15.0
Cocoanut oil—	
Refined	+12.3
Crude	+ 7.5
Stone and clay products—	
Cement	+ 7.5
Face brick	+ 4.1
Tobacco—	
Cigarettes	+12.1
Manufactured tobacco and snuff	− 0.9
Cigars	− 1.7
Metals, excepting iron and steel—	
Blister-copper	+ 8.5
Tin, deliveries from port warehouses	+ 4.9
Iron and steel—	
Machine tools, new orders	+10.7
Steel sheets, production	+ 8.2
Foundry equipment, new orders	+ 5.0
Steel ingots, production	+ 4.3
Pig iron, production	+ 4.1
Iron ore, consumption	+ 3.3
Steel castings, new orders	− 1.7
Lumber products—Flooring, maple and oak	+ 7.2
Foodstuffs—	
Slaughtering and meat packing—	
Calves slaughtered	+ 3.7
Sheep slaughtered	+ 3.3

TABLE 3.—PRODUCTION, 1922–1927ᵃ (*Continued*)

Series	Average annual rate of change (per cent)
Cattle slaughtered	+ 2.5
Hogs slaughtered	− 2.7
Meats	− 0.3
Lamb	+ 3.7
Beef	+ 1.9
Pork	− 2.0
Animal fats	− 1.4
Butter	+ 5.9
Sugar meltings (raw cane sugar)	+ 1.4
Wheat flour	− 0.3
Milk, condensed and evaporated	+ 3.8
Paper and printing—	
Wood pulp—	
Chemical	+ 5.4
Mechanical	+ 2.1
Paper, total	+ 4.2
Newsprint—	
Canada	+14.1
United States	+ 1.6
Other paper—	
Paper board	+ 6.2
Book paper	+ 5.6
Fine paper	+ 5.6
Wrapping paper	+ 4.2
Newsprint consumption	+ 8.1
Textiles—	
Cotton goods—	
Cotton consumption	+ 3.8
Fine cotton goods, production, New Bedford	+ 2.9
Total spindle hours	+ 2.0
Cotton cloth, exports	− 0.2
Active spindles	− 0.7
Finished cotton goods, billings	− 2.9
Woolens—	
Wool machinery activity	− 3.7
Consumption of raw wool	− 4.3
Carpet and rug loom activity	− 4.4
Wool receipts at Boston, total	− 5.1
Knit underwear, production	− 0.8
Silks—	
Silk deliveries	+10.1
Silk loom activity	+ 7.1
Leather and leather products—	
Sole leather	− 0.2
Upper leather—	
Goat and kid	+ 1.3
Calf and kip	− 1.5
Cattle	− 4.5
Boots and shoes	+ 0.2
Coke production, total	+ 4.5
By-product	+ 8.1
Beehive	− 6.6
Vehicles for land transportation—	
Automobiles	+ 4.2
Trucks	+10.9
Passenger cars	+ 3.8
Locomotives completed	−10.8
Shipbuilding	− 0.1
Miscellaneous—	
Tires, pneumatic	+10.0
Inner tubes	+ 7.3
Crude rubber consumption, total	+ 6.3
Crude rubber consumption for tires	+ 7.4
Electric power production	+10.5

ᵃ Monthly and annual values of most of the series from which the following rates were computed are published currently in the *Survey of Current Business* or in the *Federal Reserve Bulletin*. Full descriptions of the several series, with statements concerning the sources, will be found in these publications.

ᵇ Dollar value series.

ᶜ Certain of the series listed in the table dealing with distribution are here employed as indexes of production.

ᵈ The general grouping follows that employed by the Department of Commerce, but the constituent items are not the same in all cases as those entering into the Department indexes.

TABLE 4.—THE DISTRIBUTION OF GOODS; SUPPLEMENTARY SERIES MEASURING
MARKETING MOVEMENTS, 1922–1927

Series	Average annual rate of change (per cent)
Animal products, marketings (Indexes of Department of Commerce)ᵃ......	+ 1.1
Fish...	+ 9.4
Milk, New York..................................	+ 3.9
Poultry...	+ 2.9
Wool..	+ 2.5
Sheep...	+ 1.7
Cattle and calves...............................	0.0
Eggs..	− 0.5
Hogs..	− 4.1
Crop marketings:	
Cotton products.................................	+ 9.2
Fruits..	+ 2.8
Vegetables......................................	+ 1.5
Grains..	− 2.6
Other shipments and receipts:ᵇ	
Silk deliveries..................................	+10.1
Steel sheets, shipments..........................	+ 7.6
Iron ore shipments..............................	+ 2.9
Finished cotton goods, shipments.................	+ 0.1
Finished cotton goods, billings..................	− 2.9
Total wool receipts at Boston....................	− 5.1
Domestic...................................	+ 2.4
Foreign....................................	−12.0
Livestock movements—	
Sheep and lambs...........................	+ 1.7
Cattle and calves..........................	0.0
Hogs......................................	− 4.5
Imports, individual commodities:	
Hides and skins.................................	− 6.4
Goat skins.................................	+ 1.3
Sheep skins................................	− 3.1
Calf skins.................................	− 5.1
Cattle hides...............................	−10.7
Cotton cloth....................................	−19.4
Exports, individual commodities: Cotton cloth.......	+ 0.2

ᵃ Fish: Fish landings in Boston, Seattle, Portland, Me., and Gloucester.   Milk: Receipts in Greater New York.   Poultry: Receipts of dressed poultry in New York, Chicago, Philadelphia, Boston, and San Francisco.   Wool: Receipts of domestic wool at Boston.   Cattle and calves, hogs, sheep: Receipts in 67 markets.   Eggs: Receipts in New York, Chicago, Philadelphia, Boston and San Francisco.

ᵇ Deliveries of raw silk from principal warehouses in New York City, indicating approximate consumption by mills.   Compiled by the Silk Association of America.   Published currently in the *Survey of Current Business*.   Iron ore shipments through Upper Great Lakes ports.   The data from which the measures for steel sheets, cotton goods and wool have been computed are published, and the sources are described, in the *Survey of Current Business*.   The data on livestock movements relate to receipts at 60 or 70 markets.   They are compiled by the Bureau of Agricultural Economics.

TABLE 5.—COMMODITY STOCKS, 1922–1927[a]

Series	Average annual rate of change (per cent)
Raw materials:	
Nonfood materials, for manufacture—	
Textiles—	
Cotton—	
Total world visible	+10.0
Total domestic	+ 7.0
Silk	+ 7.4
Wool	− 7.8
Minerals—	
Crude petroleum	− 0.1
Iron ore	− 1.1
Zinc	− 1.7
Tin	− 4.1
Copper—	
Blister	+ 5.6
Refined	−15.0
Other commodities—	
Unmanufactured tobacco (including imported types)	+ 3.6
Wood pulp—	
Mechanical	+10.8
Chemical	− 7.9
Crude rubber, domestic stocks	− 2.9
Raw foodstuffs—	
Cottonseed	+15.2
Corn, visible supply	+14.1
Barley, visible supply	+13.0
Raw cane sugar	+12.7
Rice, domestic at mills and dealers	+ 6.5
Wheat, visible supply	+ 4.1
Oats, visible supply	+ 0.6
Rye, visible supply	− 4.8
Manufactured goods:	
Manufactured commodities, nonfoods—	
Portland cement	+18.3
Steel sheets	+ 8.0
Gasoline, stocks at refineries	+13.4
Lubricating oil, stocks at refineries	+ 8.0
Kerosene, stocks at refineries	+ 4.1
Gas and fuel oils, stocks at refineries	− 5.5
Total paper	+ 6.6
Newsprint paper, stocks in United States and Canadian mills	+ 6.1
Newsprint paper, stocks at publishers, United States	+ 2.0
Leather, upper, finished	− 9.6
Leather, sole and belting, finished	−17.4
Manufactured foodstuffs:	
Vegetable oils, refined	+21.0
Cottonseed oil, refined	+19.3
Animal fats	+ 2.1
Sugar, refined	+16.3
Butter, cold storage holdings	+ 7.2
Condensed and evaporated milk	+ 3.4
Wheat, flour	− 1.2
Pork products, cold storage holdings	− 0.2
Beef, cold storage holdings	− 3.2
Lamb, cold storage holdings	− 7.5

[a] The series from which the present figures have been compiled appear in the *Survey of Current Business*. Details concerning the individual series will be found in that publication. The groupings employed by the Bureau of the Census in the construction of indexes of commodity stocks have been used in classifying the individual series, but it is not to be assumed that the indexes of the Census Bureau are constructed from the series listed.

Table 6.—Employment, Pay Roll, and Per Capita Earnings in Manufacturing Industries, 1922–1927[a]

Industry	Average annual rate of change in		
	Employment (per cent)	Pay rolls (per cent)	Per capita earnings (per cent)
Lumber and its products:			
Lumber, sawmills	−4.1	−0.7	+3.5
Furniture	+0.4	+2.9	+2.5
Lumber, millwork	−1.3	+0.6	+1.9
Stone, clay, and glass products:			
Glass	−0.4	+3.1	+3.5
Pottery	+1.5	+4.6	+3.0
Brick, tile, terra cotta	−0.4	+2.4	+2.8
Cement[b]	−3.3	−2.2	+1.1
Iron and steel and their products:			
Hardware	−2.6	+1.6	+4.3
Machine tools[c]	+0.8	+3.8	+3.0
Iron and steel	+0.2	+3.0	+2.7
Foundry and machine shop	−1.3	+0.9	+2.2
Structural iron work[c]	−0.4	+1.7	+2.1
Stoves	−4.8	−3.5	+1.5
Steam fittings, and steam and hot water heating apparatus[c]	−2.1	−0.8	+1.3
Cast iron pipe	−0.8	−0.8	0.0
Miscellaneous industries:			
Agricultural implements	−1.1	+6.1	+5.0
Rubber boots and shoes	−1.0	+2.5	+3.5
Electrical machinery, apparatus, and supplies	+1.1	+3.7	+2.6
Shipbuilding, steel	+0.7	+3.2	+2.5
Pianos and organs	−0.9	+1.5	+2.4
Automobile tires	+1.3	+3.4	+2.0
Paper and printing:			
Printing, book and job	+1.4	+4.1	+2.6
Paper boxes	+1.0	+3.4	+2.4
Paper and pulp	−0.4	+1.9	+2.3
Printing, newspapers	+3.6	+5.6	+1.9
Food and kindred products:			
Confectionery[b]	−4.1	−1.8	+2.4
Ice cream[b]	−2.0	+0.2	+2.3
Baking[d]	+1.3	+2.9	+1.6
Slaughtering and meat packing	−3.6	−2.5	+1.2
Flour	−3.8	−2.8	+1.0
Sugar refining, cane[b]	−2.0	−1.7	+0.3
Chemical and allied products:			
Chemicals	+0.3	+3.8	+3.5
Fertilizers	−0.2	+2.7	+2.9
Petroleum refining	+0.6	−0.3	−0.9
Vehicles for land transportation:			
Car building and repairing, steam railroads	−3.8	−1.7	+2.2
Carriages and wagons	−4.3	−3.1	+1.2
Car building and repairing, electric railroads	−2.3	−1.5	+0.8
Automobiles	+3.1	+3.8	+0.7
Textiles and their products:			
Hosiery and knit goods	−0.2	+4.4	+4.6
Silk goods	+1.0	+4.0	+2.9
Shirts and collars	−4.4	−2.7	+1.8
Dyeing and finishing textiles	+0.6	+2.5	+1.8
Millinery and lace goods	−7.1	−5.6	+1.6
Cotton goods	−2.7	−1.0	+1.7
Woolen and worsted goods	−3.1	−2.3	+0.8
Clothing, women's	−4.6	−4.3	+0.3
Carpets and rugs	−0.4	−0.6	−0.2
Clothing, men's	−4.2	−5.5	−1.3
Tobacco products:			
Chewing and smoking tobacco and snuff	−2.6	−0.4	+2.2
Cigars and cigarettes	−4.9	−5.0	−0.1
Metal and metal products, other than iron and steel:			
Brass, bronze, and copper products[e]	−0.9	−0.7	+0.2
Stamped and enameled ware	−1.0	−1.9	−0.9
Leather and its products:			
Leather	−2.3	−0.4	+1.9
Boots and shoes	−2.4	−3.5	−1.1

[a] The data from which these rates have been computed were compiled by the United States Bureau of Labor Statistics. The rates of change in employment and pay rolls were derived from the data as compiled; the rates of change in per capita earnings were computed from the employment and pay roll figures. Except where otherwise noted, the rates were computed from data for the period July 1922–December 1927.

[b] Series begins April, 1923.

[c] Series begins May, 1923.

[d] Series begins Sept., 1922.

[e] Series is for 1923–1927.

INDEX

Page references to Vol. II are in **boldfaced** type.

/